A WORLD CHECKLIST OF BIRDS

A WORLD CHECKLIST OF BIRDS

Burt L. Monroe, Jr.

Charles G. Sibley

Yale University Press

New Haven and London

Printed in the United States of America by Edwards Brothers, Inc., Ann Arbor, Michigan.

ISBN 0-300-05547-1
Library of Congress catalog number: 93-60341

A catalogue record for this book is available from the British Library.

The paper in this book meets the guidelines for permanence and durability of the Committee on Production Guidelines for Book Longevity of the Council on Library Resources.

10   9   8   7   6   5   4   3   2   1

CONTENTS

Introduction	xv
Abbreviations	xvii
Class AVES	1
Order STRUTHIONIFORMES	1
Family Struthionidae (Ostrich)	1
Family Rheidae (Rheas)	1
Family Casuariidae	1
Tribe Casuariini (Cassowaries)	1
Tribe Dromaiini (Emu)	1
Family Apterygidae (Kiwis)	1
Order TINAMIFORMES	1
Family Tinamidae (Tinamous)	1
Order CRACIFORMES	3
Family Cracidae (Chachalacas, Guans, etc.)	3
Family Megapodiidae (Megapodes)	5
Order GALLIFORMES	5
Family Phasianidae (Grouse, Turkeys, Pheasants, Partridges, etc.)	5
Family Numididae (Guineafowls)	11
Family Odontophoridae (New World Quails)	12
Order ANSERIFORMES	13
Family Anhimidae (Screamers)	13
Family Anseranatidae (Magpie Goose)	13

Family Dendrocygnidae (Whistling-Ducks)   13
Family Anatidae   13
   Subfamily Oxyurinae (Stiff-tailed Ducks)   13
   Subfamily Stictonettinae (*Stictonetta*)   14
   Subfamily Cygninae (Swans)   14
   Subfamily Anatinae   14
      Tribe Anserini (Geese)   14
      Tribe Anatini (Typical Ducks)   16

Order TURNICIFORMES   19
   Family Turnicidae (Buttonquails)   19

Order PICIFORMES   19
   Family Indicatoridae (Honeyguides)   19
   Family Picidae (Woodpeckers, Wrynecks)   20
   Family Megalaimidae (Asian Barbets)   27
   Family Lybiidae (African Barbets)   28
   Family Ramphastidae   30
      Subfamily Capitoninae (New World Barbets)   30
      Subfamily Ramphastinae (Toucans)   30

Order GALBULIFORMES   32
   Family Galbulidae (Jacamars)   32
   Family Bucconidae (Puffbirds)   32

Order BUCEROTIFORMES   33
   Family Bucerotidae (Typical Hornbills)   33
   Family Bucorvidae (Ground-Hornbills)   35

Order UPUPIFORMES   35
   Family Upupidae (Hoopoes)   35
   Family Phoeniculidae (Woodhoopoes)   35
   Family Rhinopomastidae (Scimitarbills)   36

Order TROGONIFORMES   36
   Family Trogonidae (Trogons)   36
      Subfamily Apalodermatinae (African Trogons)   36
      Subfamily Trogoninae   36
         Tribe Trogonini (New World Trogons)   36
         Tribe Harpactini (Asian Trogons)   37

Order CORACIIFORMES   37
   Family Coraciidae (Typical Rollers)   37
   Family Brachypteraciidae (Ground-Rollers)   38
   Family Leptosomidae (Cuckoo-Rollers)   38

Family Momotidae (Motmots)   38
Family Todidae (Todies)   39
Family Alcedinidae (Alcedinid Kingfishers)   39
Family Halcyonidae (Halcyonid Kingfishers)   40
Family Cerylidae (Cerylid Kingfishers)   42
Family Meropidae (Bee-eaters)   42

Order COLIIFORMES   43
Family Coliidae   43
Subfamily Coliinae (Typical Mousebirds)   43
Subfamily Urocoliinae (Long-tailed Mousebirds)   43

Order CUCULIFORMES   43
Family Cuculidae (Old World Cuckoos)   43
Family Centropodidae (Coucals)   46
Family Coccyzidae (American Cuckoos)   47
Family Opisthocomidae (Hoatzin)   48
Family Crotophagidae   48
Tribe Crotophagini (Anis)   48
Tribe Guirini (Guira Cuckoo)   48
Family Neomorphidae (Roadrunners, Ground-Cuckoos)   48

Order PSITTACIFORMES   48
Family Psittacidae (Parrots and Allies)   48

Order APODIFORMES   60
Family Apodidae (Typical Swifts)   60
Family Hemiprocnidae (Crested-Swifts)   63

Order TROCHILIFORMES   63
Family Trochilidae   63
Subfamily Phaethornithinae (Hermits)   63
Subfamily Trochilinae (Typical Hummingbirds)   64

Order MUSOPHAGIFORMES   74
Family Musophagidae   74
Subfamily Musophaginae (Turacos)   74
Subfamily Criniferinae (Plantain-eaters)   75

Order STRIGIFORMES   75
Family Tytonidae (Barn and Grass Owls)   75
Family Strigidae (Typical Owls)   76
Family Aegothelidae (Owlet-Nightjars)   81
Family Podargidae (Australian Frogmouths)   82
Family Batrachostomidae (Asian Frogmouths)   82

Family Steatornithidae (Oilbird)   82
Family Nyctibiidae (Potoos)   82
Family Eurostopodidae (Eared-Nightjars)   83
Family Caprimulgidae   83
  Subfamily Chordeilinae (Nighthawks)   83
  Subfamily Caprimulginae (Nightjars)   83

Order COLUMBIFORMES   86
Family Raphidae (Dodos, Solitaires)   86
Family Columbidae (Pigeons, Doves)   86

Order GRUIFORMES   96
Family Eurypygidae (Sunbittern)   96
Family Otididae (Bustards)   96
Family Gruidae   97
  Subfamily Balearicinae (Crowned-Cranes)   97
  Subfamily Gruinae (Typical Cranes)   97
Family Heliornithidae   98
  Tribe Aramini (Limpkin)   98
  Tribe Heliornithini (Sungrebes)   98
Family Psophiidae (Trumpeters)   98
Family Cariamidae (Seriemas)   98
Family Rhynochetidae (Kagu)   98
Family Rallidae (Rails, Gallinules, Coots)   98
Family Mesitornithidae (Mesites)   103

Order CICONIIFORMES   103
Suborder CHARADRII   103
Family Pteroclidae (Sandgrouse)   103
Family Thinocoridae (Seedsnipe)   103
Family Pedionomidae (Plains-wanderer)   103
Family Scolopacidae   104
  Subfamily Scolopacinae (Woodcock, Snipe)   104
  Subfamily Tringinae (Sandpipers, Curlews, Phalaropes)   104
Family Rostratulidae (Paintedsnipe)   106
Family Jacanidae (Jacanas)   106
Family Chionidae (Sheathbills)   107
Family Pluvianellidae (Magellanic Plover)   107
Family Burhinidae (Thick-knees)   107
Family Charadriidae   107
  Subfamily Recurvirostrinae   107
    Tribe Haematopodini (Oystercatchers)   107
    Tribe Recurvirostrini (Avocets, Stilts)   108

Subfamily Charadriinae (Plovers, Lapwings)   108
Family Glareolidae   110
Subfamily Dromadinae (Crab-plover)   110
Subfamily Glareolinae (Pratincoles, Coursers)   110
Family Laridae   111
Subfamily Larinae   111
Tribe Stercorariini (Skuas, Jaegers)   111
Tribe Rynchopini (Skimmers)   111
Tribe Larini (Gulls)   111
Tribe Sternini (Terns)   113
Subfamily Alcinae (Auks, Murres, Puffins)   115
Suborder CICONII   115
Infraorder FALCONIDES   115
Family Accipitridae   115
Subfamily Pandioninae (Osprey)   115
Subfamily Accipitrinae (Hawks, Eagles)   115
Family Sagittariidae (Secretarybird)   124
Family Falconidae (Caracaras, Falcons)   124
Infraorder CICONIIDES   126
Parvorder PODICIPEDIDA   126
Family Podicipedidae (Grebes)   126
Parvorder PHAETHONTIDA   126
Family Phaethontidae (Tropicbirds)   126
Parvorder SULIDA   127
Superfamily SULOIDEA   127
Family Sulidae (Boobies, Gannets)   127
Family Anhingidae (Anhingas)   127
Superfamily PHALACROCORACOIDEA   127
Family Phalacrocoracidae (Cormorants)   127
Parvorder CICONIIDA   128
Superfamily ARDEOIDEA   128
Family Ardeidae (Herons, Bitterns, Egrets)   128
Superfamily SCOPOIDEA   131
Family Scopidae (Hammerhead)   131
Superfamily PHOENICOPTEROIDEA   131
Family Phoenicopteridae (Flamingos)   131
Superfamily THRESKIORNITHOIDEA   131
Family Threskiornithidae (Ibises, Spoonbills)   131
Superfamily PELECANOIDEA   132
Family Pelecanidae   132
Subfamily Balaenicipitinae (Shoebill)   132
Subfamily Pelecaninae (Pelicans)   132

Superfamily CICONIOIDEA 133
Family Ciconiidae 133
Subfamily Cathartinae (New World Vultures) 133
Subfamily Ciconiinae (Storks) 133
Superfamily PROCELLARIOIDEA 133
Family Fregatidae (Frigatebirds) 133
Family Spheniscidae (Penguins) 134
Family Gaviidae (Loons) 134
Family Procellariidae 135
Subfamily Procellariinae (Petrels, Shearwaters, Diving-
Petrels) 135
Subfamily Diomedeinae (Albatrosses) 137
Subfamily Hydrobatinae (Storm-Petrels) 138

Order PASSERIFORMES 138
Suborder TYRANNI 138
Family Acanthisittidae (New Zealand Wrens) 138
Family Pittidae (Pittas) 139
Family Eurylaimidae (Broadbills) 140
Family Philepittidae (Asities) 140
Family *Incertae sedis** (*Sapayoa*) 140
Family Tyrannidae 140
Subfamily Pipromorphinae (Mionectine Flycatchers,
Corythopis) 140
Subfamily Tyranninae (Tyrant Flycatchers) 142
Subfamily Tityrinae 154
Tribe Schiffornithini (*Schiffornis*) 154
Tribe Tityrini (Becards, Tityras) 154
Subfamily Cotinginae (Cotingas, Plantcutters, Sharpbill) 154
Subfamily Piprinae (Manakins) 157
Family Thamnophilidae (Typical Antbirds) 158
Family Furnariidae 165
Subfamily Furnariinae (Ovenbirds) 165
Subfamily Dendrocolaptinae (Woodcreepers) 172
Family Formicariidae (Ground Antbirds) 174
Family Conopophagidae (Gnateaters) 176
Family Rhinocryptidae (Tapaculos) 177
Suborder PASSERI 178
Parvorder CORVIDA 178
Superfamily MENUROIDEA 178
Family Climacteridae (Australo-Papuan Treecreepers) 178
Family Menuridae 178

Subfamily Menurinae (Lyrebirds) 178
Subfamily Atrichornithinae (Scrub-birds) 179
Family Ptilonorhynchidae (Bowerbirds) 179
Superfamily MELIPHAGOIDEA 179
Family Maluridae 179
Subfamily Malurinae 179
Tribe Malurini (Fairywrens) 179
Tribe Stipiturini (Emuwrens) 180
Subfamily Amytornithinae (Grasswrens) 180
Family Meliphagidae (Honeyeaters, *Ephthianura*,
Ashbyia) 181
Family Pardalotidae 186
Subfamily Pardalotinae (Pardalotes) 186
Subfamily Dasyornithinae (Bristlebirds) 187
Subfamily Acanthizinae 187
Tribe Sericornithini (Scrubwrens) 187
Tribe Acanthizini (Thornbills, Whitefaces, etc.) 188
Superfamily CORVOIDEA 189
Family Petroicidae (Australo-Papuan Robins, *Drymodes*) 189
Family Irenidae (Fairy-bluebirds, Leafbirds) 191
Family Orthonychidae (Logrunners, Chowchillas) 191
Family Pomatostomidae (Australo-Papuan Babblers) 191
Family Laniidae (True Shrikes = *Lanius, Corvinella,
Eurocephalus*) 191
Family Vireonidae (Vireos, Peppershrikes, etc.) 193
Family Corvidae 195
Subfamily Cinclosomatinae (Quail-thrushes, Whipbirds) 195
Subfamily Corcoracinae (Australian Chough,
Apostlebird) 195
Subfamily Pachycephalinae 195
Tribe Neosittini (Sittellas) 195
Tribe Mohouini (*Mohoua*) 196
Tribe Falcunculini (Shrike-tits, *Oreoica, Rhagologus*) 196
Tribe Pachycephalini (Whistlers, Shrike-thrushes) 196
Subfamily Corvinae 198
Tribe Corvini (Crows, Magpies, Jays, Nutcrackers) 198
Tribe Paradisaeini (Birds-of-paradise, *Melampitta*) 202
Tribe Artamini (Currawongs, Woodswallows, *Pityriasis,
Peltops*) 203
Tribe Oriolini (Orioles, Cuckooshrikes) 204
Subfamily Dicrurinae 208
Tribe Rhipidurini (Fantails) 208

Tribe Dicrurini (Drongos) 209
Tribe Monarchini (Monarchs, Magpie-larks) 210
Subfamily Aegithininae (Ioras) 213
Subfamily Malaconotinae 213
Tribe Malaconotini (Bushshrikes) 213
Tribe Vangini (Helmetshrikes, Vangas, *Batis,*
Platysteira) 215
Family Callaeatidae (New Zealand Wattlebirds) 217
Parvorder *Incertae sedis*/Family Picathartidae (*Chaetops,*
Picathartes) 217
Parvorder PASSERIDA 217
Superfamily MUSCICAPOIDEA 217
Family Bombycillidae 217
Tribe Dulini (Palmchat) 217
Tribe Ptilogonatini (Silky-flycatchers) 217
Tribe Bombycillini (Waxwings) 218
Family Cinclidae (Dippers) 218
Family Muscicapidae 218
Subfamily Turdinae (True Thrushes, *Chlamydochaera,*
Brachypteryx, Alethe) 218
Subfamily Muscicapinae 225
Tribe Muscicapini (Old World Flycatchers) 225
Tribe Saxicolini (Chats) 228
Family Sturnidae 233
Tribe Sturnini (Starlings, Mynas) 233
Tribe Mimini (Mockingbirds, Thrashers, Catbirds) 237
Superfamily SYLVIOIDEA 238
Family Sittidae 238
Subfamily Sittinae (Nuthatches) 238
Subfamily Tichodrominae (Wallcreeper) 239
Family Certhiidae 239
Subfamily Certhiinae 239
Tribe Certhiini (Northern Creepers) 239
Tribe Salpornithini (African Creeper) 239
Subfamily Troglodytinae (Wrens) 239
Subfamily Polioptilinae (Verdin, Gnatwrens,
Gnatcatchers) 242
Family Paridae 243
Subfamily Remizinae (Penduline-Tits) 243
Subfamily Parinae (Titmice, Chickadees) 243
Family Aegithalidae (Long-tailed Tits, Bushtits) 245

Family Hirundinidae   246

  Subfamily Pseudochelidoninae (River-Martins)   246

  Subfamily Hirundininae (Swallows)   246

Family Regulidae (Kinglets)   249

Family Pycnonotidae (Bulbuls)   249

Family Hypocoliidae (*Hypocolius*)   253

Family Cisticolidae (African Warblers)   254

Family Zosteropidae (White-eyes)   258

Family Sylviidae   261

  Subfamily Acrocephalinae (Leaf-Warblers)   261

  Subfamily Megalurinae (Grass-Warblers)   268

  Subfamily Garrulacinae (Laughingthrushes)   269

  Subfamily Sylviinae   271

   Tribe Timaliini (Babblers, *Rhabdornis*)   271

   Tribe Chamaeini (Wrentit)   278

   Tribe Sylviini (*Sylvia*)   278

Superfamily PASSEROIDEA   279

Family Alaudidae (Larks)   279

Family Nectariniidae   282

  Subfamily Promeropinae (Sugarbirds)   282

  Subfamily Nectariniinae   282

   Tribe Dicaeini (Flowerpeckers)   282

   Tribe Nectariniini (Sunbirds, Spiderhunters)   283

Family Melanocharitidae   288

   Tribe Melanocharitini (*Melanocharis*)   288

   Tribe Toxorhamphini (*Toxorhamphus*, *Oedistoma*)   288

Family Paramythiidae (*Paramythia*, *Oreocharis*)   288

Family Passeridae   288

  Subfamily Passerinae (Sparrows, Rock-Sparrows, etc.)   288

  Subfamily Motacillinae (Wagtails, Pipits)   289

  Subfamily Prunellinae (Accentors, Dunnock)   292

  Subfamily Ploceinae (Weavers)   292

  Subfamily Estrildinae   296

   Tribe Estrildini (Estrildine Finches)   296

   Tribe Viduini (Whydahs)   301

Family Fringillidae   302

  Subfamily Peucedraminae (*Peucedramus*)   302

  Subfamily Fringillinae   302

   Tribe Fringillini (Chaffinches, Brambling)   302

   Tribe Carduelini (Goldfinches, Crossbills, etc.)   302

   Tribe Drepanidini (Hawaiian Honeycreepers)   306

Subfamily Emberizinae 307

  Tribe Emberizini (Buntings, Longspurs, Towhees) 307

  Tribe Parulini (Wood Warblers, *Zeledonia*) 313

  Tribe Thraupini (Tanagers, Swallow Tanager,
      Neotropical Honeycreepers, Plushcap, Tanager
      Finch, Seedeaters, Flower-piercers, etc.) 317

  Tribe Cardinalini (Cardinals) 331

  Tribe Icterini (Troupials, Meadowlarks, New World
      Blackbirds, etc.) 333

Index of Genera 337

Index of English Names 349

INTRODUCTION

A World Checklist of Birds is based on Sibley and Monroe, *Distribution and Taxonomy of Birds of the World* (Yale University Press, 1990), as updated by a *Supplement* (Yale University Press, 1993); this supplement includes changes and corrections of the original text that were brought to our attention through 30 September 1992. Thus, *A World Checklist of Birds* corresponds in classification, sequence, and treatment of scientific and English names to the updated version of Sibley and Monroe. The classification in the original text was based on Sibley and Ahlquist, *Phylogeny and Classification of Birds* (Yale University Press, 1990); reasons for subsequent changes are given in the *Supplement*.

How to use *A World Checklist*. The book is intended for anyone interested in birds. It presents the Latin and English names of the 9,702 species in Sibley and Monroe (1990) as updated by the *Supplement*. It provides an abbreviated description of geographic distribution to indicate the regions where each species occurs (see list of abbreviations and symbols on pages xvii–xix). Well-marked subspecies that have been considered to be species in the recent past, or may be so recognized in the future, are also listed. A box for checking off species observed in the field and space for brief notes are provided, except for those species long extinct. *A World Checklist* will be a useful desk reference for anyone needing to refer to the latest scientific and English names of birds of the world, such as museum workers, wildlife biologists, and nature writers. It will be of special interest to the thousands of birders who will use it to record the species (and subspecific groups) they have observed and to check on geographic distributions and correct names.

A World Checklist is a taxonomic listing in the Sibley-Ahlquist-Monroe (SAM) classification. Those unfamiliar with SAM may find it difficult to locate a particular group or species. The sequence of higher categories is given in the Contents, which includes major groupings as well as English names for most categories (as in Sibley and

Monroe 1990). Numbers of genera and species included in each higher category are given in square brackets following the text entry of the higher category, in the following format: [{NUMBER OF GENERA}/{number of species}]. There are two indexes, one of genera and one of English names. A complete index of species names (more than 33,000 entries) is available in Sibley and Monroe (1990), as made current by the *Supplement.*

In *A World Checklist,* species entries are in boldface italics and justified to the left margin of the columns. Names of taxa not recognized by us as species but treated as species by others or displaying characteristics that suggest possible species status (that is, "groups," as defined in Sibley and Monroe 1990), are printed in italics, indented under the appropriate species, and preceded by an asterisk (*). A convenient line for checking off these taxa precedes each asterisk.

Acknowledgments. We thank the following persons for their suggestions and corrections for the *Supplement* and for *A World Checklist:* Per Alström, Richard C. Banks, Mark Beaman, Bruce M. Beehler, M. Ralph Browning, P. A. Clancey, William S. Clark, James F. Clements, Paul R. Clyne, Normand David, Paul DeBenedictis, Edward C. Dickinson, R. J. Dowsett, C. Craig Farquhar, Gary M. Fellers, L. D. C. Fishpool, Asbjørn Folvik, James Hancock, Graham Higman, Steve N. G. Howell, Tim Inskipp, Mort Isler, Phyllis Isler, Alan C. Kemp, Ben King, Lars Larsson, Ian Lewis, S. M. Lister, Richard Liversidge, Ian McAllan, Linda R. Macaulay, Glenn R. Mahler, Joe T. Marshall, Krister Mild, Urban Olsson, Kenneth C. Parkes, Robert B. Payne, William S. Peckover, Alan P. Peterson, Missy Peterson, H. Douglas Pratt, Robert S. Ridgely, J. T. R. Sharrock, Hadoram Shirihai, Fred C. Sibley, Alfred E. Smalley, Phoebe Snetsinger, James R. Stewart, J. Denis Summers-Smith, Y. Swaab, and Don A. Turner.

Burt L. Monroe, Jr.
Charles G. Sibley

ABBREVIATIONS

Afgh (Afghanistan)
Afr (Africa)
Alas (Alaska)
Ald (Aldabra Islands)
Aleut (Aleutian Islands)
Amaz (Amazonia)
Amer (Americas)
Ams (Amsterdam Island)
And (Andaman Islands)
Ang (Angola)
Ann (Annobón)
Ant (Antarctica)
Argen (Argentina)
Ariz (Arizona)
Aru (Aru Islands)
Atl (Atlantic)
Auck (Auckland Islands)
Aust (Australia)
Aust reg (Australian region)
Bah (Bahamas)
Baja (Baja California)
Berm (Bermuda)
Bism (Bismarck Archipelago)
Bol (Bolivia)
Born (Borneo)
Braz (Brazil)

BC (British Columbia)
Brit (British Isles)
Calif (California)
Camer (Cameroon)
Can Is (Canary Islands)
C Verde (Cape Verde Islands)
Carib (Caribbean Sea)
Carol (Caroline Islands)
Cay (Cayman Islands)
CA (Central America)
Chia (Chiapas)
Chris (Christmas Island, Indian Ocean)
Colom (Colombia)
Comm (Commander Islands)
Com (Comoro Islands)
Cors (Corsica)
cosm (cosmopolitan)
CR (Costa Rica)
Coz (Cozumel Island)
Djib (Djibouti)
e Atl (eastern Atlantic islands)
Ecua (Ecuador)
Eth (Ethiopia)
Eura (Eurasia)
Euro (Europe)
Falk (Falkland Islands)

FdeN (Fernando de Noronha)
Fla (Florida)
Galap (Galapagos Islands)
Gd Caym (Grand Cayman)
G Ant (Greater Antilles)
G Sunda (Greater Sunda Islands)
Green (Greenland)
Guade (Guadeloupe)
Guat (Guatemala)
Guia (Guianas)
Haw Is (Hawaiian Islands)
Hend (Henderson Island)
Himal (Himalayas)
Hisp (Hispaniola)
Hol (Holarctic)
Hond (Honduras)
Ice (Iceland)
Indoc (Indochina)
Indon (Indonesia)
int (interior)
is (islands)
Jam (Jamaica)
JF (Juan Fernández Islands)
Kerg (Kerguelen Islands)
L Ant (Lesser Antilles)
L Sunda (Lesser Sunda Islands)
L Howe (Lord Howe Island)
Loy (Loyalty Islands)
Mad (Madagascar)
Malay (Malay peninsula)
Mari (Marianas Islands)
Marq (Marquesas)
Marsh (Marshall Islands)
Masc (Mascarene Islands)
Maur (Mauritius)
Medit (Mediterranean region)
Melan (Melanesia)
Mex (Mexico)
Micro (Micronesia)
MA (Middle America)
M East (Middle East)

Moluc (Moluccas)
Mong (Mongolia)
Mor (Morocco)
mts (mountains)
Moz (Mozambique)
Nearc (Nearctic)
N Cal (New Caledonia)
NG (New Guinea)
NZ (New Zealand)
Nica (Nicaragua)
Nico (Nicobar Islands)
NA (North America)
NS (Nova Scotia)
Oax (Oaxaca)
O (Ocean)
OW (Old World)
Pac (Pacific)
Palaw (Palawan)
Palea (Palearctic)
Pan (Panama)
Pant (Pantepui)
pen (peninsular)
Phil (Philippines)
Polyn (Polynesia)
Prin (Príncipe)
PR (Puerto Rico)
Que (Quebec)
reg (region)
Réun (Réunion)
Revil (Revillagigedo Islands)
Rodr (Rodrigues)
Ryu (Ryukyu Islands)
ST (São Tomé)
Sard (Sardinia)
Seyc (Seychelles)
Sib (Siberia)
SL (Sierra Leone)
Soc (Society Islands)
Solom (Solomon Islands)
Som (Somalia)
SA (South America)

S Afr (South Africa)
S Aust (South Australia)
S Georgia (South Georgia)
S Hem (Southern Hemisphere)
sp (generally range of species, except
    other groups)
subant is (subantarctic islands)
subsah (subsaharan)
Sulaw (Sulawesi)
Sulu (Sulu Archipelago)
Sum (Sumatra)
Sunda (Greater and Lesser Sunda
    islands)
Tanim (Tanimbar Islands)
Tanz (Tanzania)
Tas (Tasmania)
Tex (Texas)
Thai (Thailand)
Tob (Tobago)
Trin (Trinidad)
TdaC (Tristan da Cunha)

trop (tropics)
Tuam (Tuamotu)
Ugan (Uganda)
US (United States)
Vanu (Vanuatu)
Ven (Venezuela)
Ver (Veracruz)
Viet (Vietnam)
Wall (Wallacea)
W Indies (West Indies)
W Aust (Western Australia)
w Pap (western Papuan islands)
Yuc (Yucatán peninsula)
Zamb (Zambia)

† (Extinct)
♦ (Introduced)
◇ (Winters in)
◇ - (Winters to)
- (to)

Class **AVES**
Subclass NEORNITHES [2063/9702]
Infraclass EOAVES [14/57]
Parvclass RATITAE [14/57]
Order **STRUTHIONIFORMES** [5/10]
Suborder STRUTHIONI [2/3]
Infraorder STRUTHIONIDES [1/1]
Family **Struthionidae** [1/1]

❑ *Struthio camelus*. OSTRICH. (Afr)............................ _____
___*S. *(c.) camelus*. AFRICAN OSTRICH. (Afr)
___*S. *(c.) molybdophanes*. SOMALI OSTRICH. (ne Afr)

Infraorder RHEIDES [1/2]
Family **Rheidae** [1/2]

❑ *Rhea americana*. GREATER RHEA. (sc SA).................... _____

❑ *Rhea pennata*. LESSER RHEA. (w,s SA)....................... _____
___*R. *(p.) tarapacensis*. PUNA RHEA. (Andes w SA)
___*R. *(p.) pennata*. DARWIN'S RHEA. (s SA)

Suborder CASUARII [3/7]
Family **Casuariidae** [2/4]
Tribe Casuariini [1/3]

❑ *Casuarius casuarius*. SOUTHERN CASSOWARY. (Aust, NG)........ _____

❑ *Casuarius bennetti*. DWARF CASSOWARY. (NG)................. _____

❑ *Casuarius unappendiculatus*. NORTHERN CASSOWARY. (NG)....... _____

Tribe Dromaiini [1/1]

❑ *Dromaius novaehollandiae*. EMU. (Aust).................... _____

Family **Apterygidae** [1/3]

❑ *Apteryx australis*. BROWN KIWI. (NZ)...................... _____

❑ *Apteryx owenii*. LITTLE SPOTTED KIWI. (s NZ)............... _____

❑ *Apteryx haastii*. GREAT SPOTTED KIWI. (s NZ)............... _____

Order **TINAMIFORMES** [9/47]
Family **Tinamidae** [9/47]

❑ *Tinamus tao*. GREY TINAMOU. (Amaz)....................... _____

❑ *Tinamus solitarius*. SOLITARY TINAMOU. (se SA).............. _____

❑ *Tinamus osgoodi*. BLACK TINAMOU. (w SA)................... _____

❑ *Tinamus major*. GREAT TINAMOU. (MA, SA) .... _____

❑ *Tinamus guttatus*. WHITE-THROATED TINAMOU. (Amaz).......... _____

❑ *Nothocercus bonapartei*. HIGHLAND TINAMOU. (mts s CA, w SA)... _____

❑ *Nothocercus julius.* TAWNY-BREASTED TINAMOU. (Andes w SA) . . . . _____

❑ *Nothocercus nigrocapillus.* HOODED TINAMOU. (Andes Peru, Bol). . . _____

❑ *Crypturellus berlepschi.* BERLEPSCH'S TINAMOU. (nw SA). . . . . _____

❑ *Crypturellus cinereus.* CINEREOUS TINAMOU. (Amaz). . . . . _____

❑ *Crypturellus soui.* LITTLE TINAMOU. (MA, w SA, Amaz). . . . . _____

❑ *Crypturellus ptaritepui.* TEPUI TINAMOU. (Pant n SA). . . . . _____

❑ *Crypturellus obsoletus.* BROWN TINAMOU. (SA). . . . . _____
   ___*C. (o.) obsoletus.* BROWN TINAMOU. (sp)
   ___*C. (o.) traylori.* TRAYLOR'S TINAMOU. (e Peru)

❑ *Crypturellus cinnamomeus.* THICKET TINAMOU. (MA). . . . . _____

❑ *Crypturellus undulatus.* UNDULATED TINAMOU. (SA). . . . . _____

❑ *Crypturellus transfasciatus.* PALE-BROWED TINAMOU. (cw SA). . . . . _____

❑ *Crypturellus strigulosus.* BRAZILIAN TINAMOU. (Amaz, e Braz). . . . . _____

❑ *Crypturellus boucardi.* SLATY-BREASTED TINAMOU. (c MA). . . . . _____

❑ *Crypturellus kerriae.* CHOCO TINAMOU. (e Pan, nw Colom). . . . . _____

❑ *Crypturellus erythropus.* RED-LEGGED TINAMOU. (nw SA, n Amaz) . _____
   ___*C. (e.) columbianus.* COLOMBIAN TINAMOU. (nw Colom)
   ___*C. (e.) idoneus.* SANTA MARTA TINAMOU. (nw SA)
   ___*C. (e.) saltuarius.* MAGDALENA TINAMOU. (nc Colom)
   ___*C. (e.) erythropus.* RED-LEGGED TINAMOU. (n Amaz)

❑ *Crypturellus duidae.* GREY-LEGGED TINAMOU. (nw Amaz). . . . . _____

❑ *Crypturellus noctivagus.* YELLOW-LEGGED TINAMOU. (e Braz). . . . . . _____

❑ *Crypturellus atrocapillus.* BLACK-CAPPED TINAMOU. (Peru, Bol). . . . _____
   ___*C. (a.) atrocapillus.* BLACK-CAPPED TINAMOU. (Peru)
   ___*C. (a.) garleppi.* GARLEPP'S TINAMOU. (n Bol)

❑ *Crypturellus variegatus.* VARIEGATED TINAMOU. (Amaz, e Braz). . . . _____

❑ *Crypturellus brevirostris.* RUSTY TINAMOU. (w,n Amaz). . . . . _____

❑ *Crypturellus bartletti.* BARTLETT'S TINAMOU. (w Amaz). . . . . _____

❑ *Crypturellus parvirostris.* SMALL-BILLED TINAMOU. (c,sc SA). . . . . . _____

❑ *Crypturellus casiquiare.* BARRED TINAMOU. (nw Amaz). . . . . _____

❑ *Crypturellus tataupa.* TATAUPA TINAMOU. (c,sc SA). . . . . _____

❑ *Rhynchotus rufescens.* RED-WINGED TINAMOU. (c,sc SA). . . . . _____

❑ *Nothoprocta taczanowskii.* TACZANOWSKI'S TINAMOU. (Andes Peru) _____

❑ *Nothoprocta kalinowskii.* KALINOWSKI'S TINAMOU. (Andes Peru). . . . _____

❑ *Nothoprocta ornata.* ORNATE TINAMOU. (Andes sw SA). . . . . _____

❑ *Nothoprocta pentlandii.* ANDEAN TINAMOU. (Andes w SA). . . . . _____

❑ *Nothoprocta cinerascens.* BRUSHLAND TINAMOU. (sc SA). . . . . _____

❑ *Nothoprocta perdicaria.* CHILEAN TINAMOU. (Andes Chile). . . . ./ _____

❑ *Nothoprocta curvirostris.* CURVE-BILLED TINAMOU. (Andes w SA) . _____

❑ *Nothura darwinii.* DARWIN'S NOTHURA. (mts sw,sc SA). . . . . _____

❑ *Nothura chacoensis.* CHACO NOTHURA. (sc SA). . . . . _____

❑ *Nothura maculosa.* SPOTTED NOTHURA. (e,se SA). . . . . _____

❑ *Nothura minor.* LESSER NOTHURA. (se Braz). . . . . _____

❑ *Nothura boraquira.* WHITE-BELLIED NOTHURA. (se SA). . . . . _____

❑ *Taoniscus nanus.* DWARF TINAMOU. (se Braz). . . . . _____

❑ *Eudromia elegans.* ELEGANT CRESTED-TINAMOU. (sw SA). . . . . _____

❑ *Eudromia formosa.* QUEBRACHO CRESTED-TINAMOU. (sc SA). . . . . . . _____

❑ *Tinamotis pentlandii.* PUNA TINAMOU. (Andes sw SA). . . . . _____

❑ *Tinamotis ingoufi.* PATAGONIAN TINAMOU. (Andes s SA). . . . . _____

Infraclass NEOAVES [2049/9645]
Parvclass GALLOANSERAE [122/443]
Superorder GALLOMORPHAE [74/282]
Order **CRACIFORMES** [17/69]
Suborder CRACI [11/50]
Family **Cracidae** [11/50]

❑ *Ortalis vetula.* PLAIN CHACHALACA. (s Tex, n MA). . . . . _____

❑ *Ortalis cinereiceps.* GREY-HEADED CHACHALACA. (CA, nw SA). . . . . _____

❑ *Ortalis garrula.* CHESTNUT-WINGED CHACHALACA. (n Colom). . . . . . _____

❑ *Ortalis ruficauda.* RUFOUS-VENTED CHACHALACA. (Tob, nw SA). . . . _____
   ___*O. (r.) ruficrissa.* RUFOUS-VENTED CHACHALACA. (nw SA)
   ___*O. (r.) ruficauda.* RUFOUS-TIPPED CHACHALACA. (Tob, Ven)

❑ *Ortalis erythroptera.* RUFOUS-HEADED CHACHALACA. (cw SA). . . . . . _____

❑ *Ortalis wagleri.* RUFOUS-BELLIED CHACHALACA. (nw Mex). . . . . _____

❑ *Ortalis poliocephala.* WEST MEXICAN CHACHALACA. (w Mex). . . . . . _____

❑ *Ortalis canicollis.* CHACO CHACHALACA. (sc SA). . . . . _____

❑ *Ortalis leucogastra.* WHITE-BELLIED CHACHALACA. (Pac MA). . . . . . _____

❑ *Ortalis guttata.* SPECKLED CHACHALACA. (SA). . . . . _____
   ___*O. (g.) columbiana.* COLOMBIAN CHACHALACA. (Colom)
   ___*O. (g.) guttata.* SPECKLED CHACHALACA. (Amaz)
   ___*O. (g.) araucuan.* BRAZILIAN CHACHALACA. (e Braz)
   ___*O. (g.) squamata.* SCALED CHACHALACA. (se Braz)

❑ *Ortalis motmot.* LITTLE CHACHALACA. (n Amaz). . . . . _____

❑ *Ortalis superciliaris.* BUFF-BROWED CHACHALACA. (ne Braz). . . . . . _____

❑ *Penelope argyrotis.* BAND-TAILED GUAN. (nw SA). . . . . _____

❑ *Penelope barbata.* BEARDED GUAN. (sw Ecua, nw Peru). . . . . _____

❑ *Penelope ortoni.* BAUDO GUAN. (w Colom, w Ecua). . . . . _____

❑ *Penelope montagnii.* ANDEAN GUAN. (mts w SA). . . . . _____

❑ *Penelope marail.* MARAIL GUAN. (n SA). . . . . _____

❑ *Penelope superciliaris.* RUSTY-MARGINED GUAN. (c,e SA). . . . . _____

❑ *Penelope dabbenei.* RED-FACED GUAN. (se Bol, nw Argen). . . . . _____

❑ *Penelope purpurascens.* CRESTED GUAN. (MA, nw SA). . . . . _____

❑ *Penelope perspicax.* CAUCA GUAN. (sw Colom). . . . . _____

❑ *Penelope albipennis.* WHITE-WINGED GUAN. (nw Peru). . . . . _____

❑ *Penelope jacquacu.* SPIX'S GUAN. (Amaz). _____
    ___*P. (j.) jacquacu.* SPIX'S GUAN. (w Amaz)
    ___*P. (j.) granti.* GREEN-BACKED GUAN. (n Amaz)

❑ *Penelope obscura.* DUSKY-LEGGED GUAN. (c,e SA). . . . . _____

❑ *Penelope pileata.* WHITE-CRESTED GUAN. (c Braz). . . . . _____

❑ *Penelope ochrogaster.* CHESTNUT-BELLIED GUAN. (e,sc Braz). . . . . . . _____

❑ *Penelope jacucaca.* WHITE-BROWED GUAN. (int ne Braz). . . . . _____

❑ *Pipile pipile.* TRINIDAD PIPING-GUAN. (Trin). . . . . _____

❑ *Pipile cumanensis.* BLUE-THROATED PIPING-GUAN. (Amaz). . . . . _____
    ___*P. (c.) cumanensis.* WHITE-HEADED PIPING-GUAN. (Amaz)
    ___*P. (c.) grayi.* GRAY'S PIPING-GUAN. (sw Amaz)

❑ *Pipile cujubi.* RED-THROATED PIPING-GUAN. (s Amaz). . . . . _____
    ___*P. (c.) cujubi.* STRIPE-CROWNED PIPING-GUAN. (n,wc Braz)
    ___*P. (c.) nattereri.* NATTERER'S PIPING-GUAN. (s Amaz)

❑ *Pipile jacutinga.* BLACK-FRONTED PIPING-GUAN. (se SA). . . . . _____

❑ *Aburria aburri.* WATTLED GUAN. (mts w SA). . . . . _____

❑ *Chamaepetes unicolor.* BLACK GUAN. (mts CR, w Pan). . . . . _____

❑ *Chamaepetes goudotii.* SICKLE-WINGED GUAN. (mts w SA). . . . . _____

❑ *Penelopina nigra.* HIGHLAND GUAN. (mts c MA). . . . . _____

❑ *Oreophasis derbianus.* HORNED GUAN. (mts Chia, Guat). . . . . _____

❑ *Nothocrax urumutum.* NOCTURNAL CURASSOW. (w Amaz). . . . . _____

❑ *Mitu tomentosa.* CRESTLESS CURASSOW. (n Amaz). . . . . _____

❑ *Mitu salvini.* SALVIN'S CURASSOW. (w Amaz). . . . . _____

❑ *Mitu tuberosa.* RAZOR-BILLED CURASSOW. (Amaz). . . . . _____

❑ *Mitu mitu.* ALAGOAS CURASSOW. (e Braz). . . . . _____

❑ *Pauxi pauxi.* HELMETED CURASSOW. (mts nw SA). . . . . _____

❑ *Pauxi unicornis.* HORNED CURASSOW. (Andes c Peru, c Bol). . . . . . . _____

❑ *Crax rubra.* GREAT CURASSOW. (MA, nw SA). . . . . _____

❑ *Crax alberti.* BLUE-KNOBBED CURASSOW. (n Colom). . . . . _____

❑ *Crax daubentoni.* YELLOW-KNOBBED CURASSOW. (n SA)......... _____

❑ *Crax alector.* BLACK CURASSOW. (n Amaz).................... _____

❑ *Crax globulosa.* WATTLED CURASSOW. (w Amaz).............. _____

❑ *Crax fasciolata.* BARE-FACED CURASSOW. (c SA).............. _____
___*C. (f.) pinima.* NATTERER'S CURASSOW. (nc Braz)
___*C. (f.) fasciolata.* FASCIATED CURASSOW. (c SA)

❑ *Crax blumenbachii.* RED-BILLED CURASSOW. (se Braz)........... _____

Suborder MEGAPODII [6/19]
Family **Megapodiidae** [6/19]

❑ *Alectura lathami.* AUSTRALIAN BRUSH-TURKEY. (ne Aust)........ _____

❑ *Aepypodius arfakianus.* WATTLED BRUSH-TURKEY. (w Pap, NG).... _____

❑ *Aepypodius bruijnii.* BRUIJN'S BRUSH-TURKEY. (w Pap)........... _____

❑ *Talegalla cuvieri.* RED-BILLED BRUSH-TURKEY. (w Pap, nw NG).... _____

❑ *Talegalla fuscirostris.* BLACK-BILLED BRUSH-TURKEY. (Aru, s NG) . _____

❑ *Talegalla jobiensis.* BROWN-COLLARED BRUSH-TURKEY. (NG)...... _____

❑ *Macrocephalon maleo.* MALEO. (Sulaw)...................... _____

❑ *Megapodius nicobariensis.* NICOBAR SCRUBFOWL. (Nico)........ _____

❑ *Megapodius cumingii.* TABON SCRUBFOWL. (Born, Sulaw, Phil)..... _____

❑ *Megapodius bernsteinii.* SULA SCRUBFOWL. (is E of Sulaw)....... _____

❑ *Megapodius reinwardt.* ORANGE-FOOTED SCRUBFOWL. (Aust reg)... _____
___*M. (f.) reinwardt.* ORANGE-FOOTED SCRUBFOWL. (Aust reg)
___*M. (f.) tenimberensis.* TANIMBAR SCRUBFOWL. (Tanim)

❑ *Megapodius freycinet.* DUSKY SCRUBFOWL. (e Wall, nw NG)....... _____

❑ *Megapodius affinis.* NEW GUINEA SCRUBFOWL. (n NG)........... _____

❑ *Megapodius eremita.* MELANESIAN SCRUBFOWL. (Bism, Solom)..... _____

❑ *Megapodius layardi.* VANUATU SCRUBFOWL. (Vanuatu).......... _____

❑ *Megapodius laperouse.* MICRONESIAN SCRUBFOWL. (Mari, Palau)... _____
___*M. (l.) senex.* PALAU SCRUBFOWL. (Mari)
___*M. (l.) laperouse.* MARIANA SCRUBFOWL. (Palau)

❑ *Megapodius pritchardii.* NIAUFOOU SCRUBFOWL. (n Tonga)....... _____

❑ *Megapodius wallacei.* MOLUCCAN SCRUBFOWL. (Moluc, w Pap)..... _____

❑ *Leipoa ocellata.* MALLEEFOWL. (sw,s Aust).................... _____

Order **GALLIFORMES** [57/213]
Parvorder PHASIANIDA [48/182]
Superfamily PHASIANOIDEA [44/176]
Family **Phasianidae** [44/176]

❏ *Lerwa lerwa.* SNOW PARTRIDGE. (Himal). . . . . _____

❏ *Ammoperdix griseogularis.* SEE-SEE PARTRIDGE. (sw Asia). . . . . _____

❏ *Ammoperdix heyi.* SAND PARTRIDGE. (cs Palea). . . . . _____

❏ *Tetraogallus caucasicus.* CAUCASIAN SNOWCOCK. (mts s Russia). . . . _____

❏ *Tetraogallus caspius.* CASPIAN SNOWCOCK. (mts sw Asia). . . . . _____

❏ *Tetraogallus tibetanus.* TIBETAN SNOWCOCK. (Himal). . . . . _____

❏ *Tetraogallus altaicus.* ALTAI SNOWCOCK. (mts sw Sib, w Mong). . . . _____

❏ *Tetraogallus himalayensis.* HIMALAYAN SNOWCOCK. (Himal). . . . . . _____

❏ *Tetraophasis obscurus.* CHESTNUT-THROATED PARTRIDGE. (w China) _____

❏ *Tetraophasis szechenyii.* BUFF-THROATED PARTRIDGE. (Himal). . . . . _____

❏ *Alectoris graeca.* ROCK PARTRIDGE. (mts c,se Euro). . . . . _____

❏ *Alectoris chukar.* CHUKAR. (s Euras; ◆ w NA). . . . . _____

❏ *Alectoris philbyi.* PHILBY'S PARTRIDGE. (sw Arabia). . . . . _____

❏ *Alectoris magna.* RUSTY-NECKLACED PARTRIDGE. (mts ne China). . . . _____

❏ *Alectoris barbara.* BARBARY PARTRIDGE. (Can Is, n Afr). . . . . _____

❏ *Alectoris rufa.* RED-LEGGED PARTRIDGE. (sw Euro). . . . . _____

❏ *Alectoris melanocephala.* ARABIAN PARTRIDGE. (Arabia). . . . . _____

❏ *Francolinus francolinus.* BLACK FRANCOLIN. (s Asia; ◆ Haw Is). . . . _____

❏ *Francolinus pictus.* PAINTED FRANCOLIN. (s India). . . . . _____

❏ *Francolinus pintadeanus.* CHINESE FRANCOLIN. (se Asia). . . . . _____

❏ *Francolinus pondicerianus.* GREY FRANCOLIN. (s Asia; ◆ Haw Is) . _____

❏ *Francolinus gularis.* SWAMP FRANCOLIN. (n India). . . . . _____

❏ *Francolinus coqui.* COQUI FRANCOLIN. (Afr). . . . . _____

❏ *Francolinus albogularis.* WHITE-THROATED FRANCOLIN. (w Afr). . . . _____

❏ *Francolinus schlegelii.* SCHLEGEL'S FRANCOLIN. (subsah Afr). . . . . . _____

❏ *Francolinus lathami.* FOREST FRANCOLIN. (w,c Afr). . . . . _____

❏ *Francolinus sephaena.* CRESTED FRANCOLIN. (e,s Afr). . . . . _____
   ___*F. (s.) sephaena.* CRESTED FRANCOLIN. (e,s Afr)
   ___*F. (s.) rovuma.* KIRK'S FRANCOLIN. (e Afr)

❏ *Francolinus streptophorus.* RING-NECKED FRANCOLIN. (mts c Afr) . _____

❏ *Francolinus finschi.* FINSCH'S FRANCOLIN. (wc Afr). . . . . _____

❏ *Francolinus africanus.* GREY-WINGED FRANCOLIN. (s Afr). . . . . _____

❏ *Francolinus levaillantii.* RED-WINGED FRANCOLIN. (c,e,s Afr). . . . . . _____

❏ *Francolinus psilolaemus.* MOORLAND FRANCOLIN. (ne Afr). . . . . . . _____

❏ *Francolinus shelleyi.* SHELLEY'S FRANCOLIN. (e Afr)............ _____
  ___*F. (s.) shelleyi.* SHELLEY'S FRANCOLIN. (e Afr)
  ___*F. (s.) elgonensis.* ELGON FRANCOLIN. (mts ec Afr)

❏ *Francolinus levaillantoides.* ORANGE RIVER FRANCOLIN. (ne,s Afr) _____
  ___*F. (l.) gutturalis.* ACACIA FRANCOLIN. (ne Afr)
  ___*F. (l.) levaillantoides.* ORANGE RIVER FRANCOLIN. (s Afr)

❏ *Francolinus nahani.* NAHAN'S FRANCOLIN. (ec Afr)............. _____

❏ *Francolinus hartlaubi.* HARTLAUB'S FRANCOLIN. (sw Afr)........ _____

❏ *Francolinus bicalcaratus.* DOUBLE-SPURRED FRANCOLIN. (w Afr)... _____

❏ *Francolinus clappertoni.* CLAPPERTON'S FRANCOLIN. (subsah Afr)... _____

❏ *Francolinus icterorhynchus.* HEUGLIN'S FRANCOLIN. (ec Afr)..... _____

❏ *Francolinus harwoodi.* HARWOOD'S FRANCOLIN. (c Eth).......... _____

❏ *Francolinus adspersus.* RED-BILLED FRANCOLIN. (sc Afr)........ _____

❏ *Francolinus capensis.* CAPE FRANCOLIN. (sw Afr)............. _____

❏ *Francolinus hildebrandti.* HILDEBRANDT'S FRANCOLIN. (e Afr)..... _____

❏ *Francolinus natalensis.* NATAL FRANCOLIN. (se Afr)............ _____

❏ *Francolinus ahantensis.* AHANTA FRANCOLIN. (w Afr)........... _____

❏ *Francolinus squamatus.* SCALY FRANCOLIN. (c Afr)............ _____

❏ *Francolinus griseostriatus.* GREY-STRIPED FRANCOLIN. (w Ang).... _____

❏ *Francolinus leucoscepus.* YELLOW-NECKED SPURFOWL. (ne Afr).... _____

❏ *Francolinus rufopictus.* GREY-BREASTED SPURFOWL. (nw Tanz).... _____

❏ *Francolinus afer.* RED-NECKED SPURFOWL. (c,e,s Afr)........... _____
  ___*F. (a.) cranchii.* CRANCH'S SPURFOWL. (c,e Afr)
  ___*F. (a.) afer.* BARE-THROATED SPURFOWL. (s Afr)

❏ *Francolinus swainsonii.* SWAINSON'S SPURFOWL. (sc,s Afr)....... _____

❏ *Francolinus erckelii.* ERCKEL'S FRANCOLIN. (ne Afr)............ _____

❏ *Francolinus ochropectus.* OCHRE-BREASTED FRANCOLIN. (mts Djib) _____

❏ *Francolinus castaneicollis.* CHESTNUT-NAPED FRANCOLIN. (ne Afr) _____
  ___*F. (c.) castaneicollis.* CHESTNUT-NAPED FRANCOLIN. (ne Afr)
  ___*F. (c.) atrifrons.* ETHIOPIAN FRANCOLIN. (s Eth)

❏ *Francolinus nobilis.* HANDSOME FRANCOLIN. (mts ec Afr)........ _____

❏ *Francolinus jacksoni.* JACKSON'S FRANCOLIN. (mts e Ugan, w Ken) _____

❏ *Francolinus camerunensis.* CAMEROON FRANCOLIN. (mts s Camer) _____

❏ *Francolinus swierstrai.* SWIERSTRA'S FRANCOLIN. (mts Ang)....... _____

❏ *Perdix perdix.* GREY PARTRIDGE. (Eura; ◆ NA)................. _____

❏ *Perdix dauurica.* DAURIAN PARTRIDGE. (c Asia).............. _____

❏ *Perdix hodgsoniae.* TIBETAN PARTRIDGE. (Himal)............... _____

❑ *Rhizothera longirostris.* LONG-BILLED PARTRIDGE. (se Asia). . . . . . . _____

❑ *Margaroperdix madagascarensis.* MADAGASCAR PARTRIDGE. (Mad) _____

❑ *Melanoperdix nigra.* BLACK PARTRIDGE. (se Asia). . . . . _____

❑ *Coturnix coturnix.* COMMON QUAIL. (Palea, Afr). . . . . _____
   ___*C. (c.) coturnix.* EURASIAN QUAIL. (Palea; ◊ Afr)
   ___*C. (c.) africana.* AFRICAN QUAIL. (Afr)

❑ *Coturnix japonica.* JAPANESE QUAIL. (e Asia; ◆ Haw Is). . . . . _____

❑ *Coturnix pectoralis.* STUBBLE QUAIL. (Aust). . . . . _____

❑ *Coturnix novaezelandiae.* NEW ZEALAND QUAIL. (†NZ). . . . . _____

❑ *Coturnix coromandelica.* RAIN QUAIL. (s Asia). . . . . _____

❑ *Coturnix delegorguei.* HARLEQUIN QUAIL. (Afr, Mad). . . . . _____

❑ *Coturnix ypsilophora.* BROWN QUAIL. (Aust reg). . . . . _____
   ___*C. (y.) australis.* BROWN QUAIL. (L Sunda, Aust, NG)
   ___*C. (y.) ypsilophora.* SWAMP QUAIL. (Tas)

❑ *Coturnix adansonii.* BLUE QUAIL. (Afr). _____

❑ *Coturnix chinensis.* BLUE-BREASTED QUAIL. (s Asia, Aust reg). . . . . _____

❑ *Anurophasis monorthonyx.* SNOW MOUNTAIN QUAIL. (mts c NG). . . _____

❑ *Perdicula asiatica.* JUNGLE BUSH-QUAIL. (India). . . . . _____

❑ *Perdicula argoondah.* ROCK BUSH-QUAIL. (India). . . . . _____

❑ *Perdicula erythrorhyncha.* PAINTED BUSH-QUAIL. (pen India). . . . . . _____

❑ *Perdicula manipurensis.* MANIPUR BUSH-QUAIL. (ne India). . . . . _____

❑ *Arborophila torqueola.* HILL PARTRIDGE. (s,se Asia). . . . . _____

❑ *Arborophila rufogularis.* RUFOUS-THROATED PARTRIDGE. (Himal). . . _____

❑ *Arborophila atrogularis.* WHITE-CHEEKED PARTRIDGE. (se Asia). . . . _____

❑ *Arborophila crudigularis.* FORMOSAN PARTRIDGE. (Taiwan). . . . . . . _____

❑ *Arborophila mandellii.* CHESTNUT-BREASTED PARTRIDGE. (Himal) . _____

❑ *Arborophila brunneopectus.* BAR-BACKED PARTRIDGE. (sc,se Asia) . _____

❑ *Arborophila rufipectus.* SICHUAN PARTRIDGE. (sw China). . . . . _____

❑ *Arborophila orientalis.* GREY-BREASTED PARTRIDGE. (se Asia). . . . . _____
   ___*A. (o.) campbelli.* CAMPBELL'S PARTRIDGE. (Malaya)
   ___*A. (o.) orientalis.* GREY-BREASTED PARTRIDGE. (G Sunda)

❑ *Arborophila javanica.* CHESTNUT-BELLIED PARTRIDGE. (Java). . . . . _____

❑ *Arborophila hyperythra.* RED-BREASTED PARTRIDGE. (mts. Born). . . _____
   ___*A. (h.) hyperythra.* RED-BREASTED PARTRIDGE. (ne Born)
   ___*A. (h.) erythrophrys.* KINABALU PARTRIDGE. (ne Born)

❑ *Arborophila gingica.* WHITE-NECKLACED PARTRIDGE. (se China). . . . _____

❑ *Arborophila davidi.* ORANGE-NECKED PARTRIDGE. (s Viet). . . . . _____

❏ *Arborophila cambodiana.* CHESTNUT-HEADED PARTRIDGE. (se Asia). _____

❏ *Arborophila rubrirostris.* RED-BILLED PARTRIDGE. (Sum). . . . . _____

❏ *Arborophila ardens.* HAINAN PARTRIDGE. (mts. Hainan). . . . . _____

❏ *Arborophila chloropus.* SCALY-BREASTED PARTRIDGE. (se Asia). . . . _____

❏ *Arborophila merlini.* ANNAM PARTRIDGE. (c Viet). . . . . _____

❏ *Arborophila charltonii.* CHESTNUT-NECKLACED PARTRIDGE. (se Asia) _____

❏ *Caloperdix oculea.* FERRUGINOUS PARTRIDGE. (se Asia). . . . . _____

❏ *Haematortyx sanguiniceps.* CRIMSON-HEADED PARTRIDGE. (Born). . _____

❏ *Rollulus rouloul.* CRESTED PARTRIDGE. (se Asia). . . . . _____

❏ *Ptilopachus petrosus.* STONE PARTRIDGE. (subsah Afr). . . . . _____

❏ *Bambusicola fytchii.* MOUNTAIN BAMBOO-PARTRIDGE. (s,se Asia). . . _____

❏ *Bambusicola thoracica.* CHINESE BAMBOO-PARTRIDGE. (s China). . . _____

❏ *Galloperdix spadicea.* RED SPURFOWL. (India). . . . . _____

❏ *Galloperdix lunulata.* PAINTED SPURFOWL. (c,pen India). . . . . _____

❏ *Galloperdix bicalcarata.* CEYLON SPURFOWL. (Ceylon). . . . . _____

   Ophrysia superciliosa. HIMALAYAN QUAIL. (†w Himal). . . . . _____

❏ *Ithaginis cruentus.* BLOOD PHEASANT. (Himal). . . . . _____

❏ *Tragopan melanocephalus.* WESTERN TRAGOPAN. (w Himal). . . . . . . _____

❏ *Tragopan satyra.* SATYR TRAGOPAN. (Himal). . . . . _____

❏ *Tragopan blythii.* BLYTH'S TRAGOPAN. (Himal). . . . . _____

❏ *Tragopan temminckii.* TEMMINCK'S TRAGOPAN. (mts s,se Asia). . . . . _____

❏ *Tragopan caboti.* CABOT'S TRAGOPAN. (mts se China). . . . . _____

❏ *Pucrasia macrolopha.* KOKLASS PHEASANT. (mts s Asia). . . . . _____

❏ *Lophophorus impejanus.* HIMALAYAN MONAL. (w,c Himal). . . . . _____

❏ *Lophophorus sclateri.* SCLATER'S MONAL. (e Himal). . . . . _____

❏ *Lophophorus lhuysii.* CHINESE MONAL. (mts c China). . . . . _____

❏ *Gallus gallus.* RED JUNGLEFOWL. (s,se Asia; ◆ cosm). . . . . _____

❏ *Gallus sonneratii.* GREY JUNGLEFOWL. (pen India). . . . . _____

❏ *Gallus lafayetii.* CEYLON JUNGLEFOWL. (Ceylon). . . . . _____

❏ *Gallus varius.* GREEN JUNGLEFOWL. (Java, L Sunda). . . . . _____

❏ *Lophura leucomelanos.* KALIJ PHEASANT. (mts s,se Asia). . . . . _____
   ___*L. (l.) leucomelanos.* KALIJ PHEASANT. (w,c Himal)
   ___*L. (l.) lathami.* HORSFIELD'S PHEASANT. (e Himal)
   ___*L. (l.) lineata.* LINEATED PHEASANT. (mts se Asia)

❏ *Lophura nycthemera.* SILVER PHEASANT. (mts s,se Asia). . . . . _____

❏ *Lophura imperialis.* IMPERIAL PHEASANT. (mts Laos, c Viet). . . . . . . _____

❑ *Lophura edwardsi.* EDWARDS'S PHEASANT. (c Viet). . . . . _____

❑ *Lophura hatinhensis.* VIETNAMESE PHEASANT. (nc Viet). . . . . _____

❑ *Lophura swinhoii.* SWINHOE'S PHEASANT. (mts Taiwan). . . . . _____

❑ *Lophura hoogerwerfi.* SUMATRAN PHEASANT. (mts n Sum). . . . . _____

❑ *Lophura inornata.* SALVADORI'S PHEASANT. (mts c,s Sum). . . . . . . _____

❑ *Lophura erythrophthalma.* CRESTLESS FIREBACK. (se Asia). . . . . . . _____

❑ *Lophura ignita.* CRESTED FIREBACK. (se Asia). . . . . _____
   ___*L. (i.) rufa.* MALAYSIAN FIREBACK. (Malay, n,c Sum)
   ___*L. (i.) ignita.* VIEILLOT'S FIREBACK. (s Sum, Born)

❑ *Lophura diardi.* SIAMESE FIREBACK. (se Asia). . . . . _____

❑ *Lophura bulweri.* BULWER'S PHEASANT. (Born). . . . . _____

❑ *Crossoptilon harmani.* TIBETAN EARED-PHEASANT. (ec Himal). . . . . _____

❑ *Crossoptilon crossoptilon.* WHITE EARED-PHEASANT. (mts sc China) _____

❑ *Crossoptilon mantchuricum.* BROWN EARED-PHEASANT. (ne China) _____

❑ *Crossoptilon auritum.* BLUE EARED-PHEASANT. (mts nc China). . . . . _____

❑ *Catreus wallichi.* CHEER PHEASANT. (Himal). . . . . _____

❑ *Syrmaticus ellioti.* ELLIOT'S PHEASANT. (mts e China). . . . . _____

❑ *Syrmaticus humiae.* HUME'S PHEASANT. (mts s,se Asia). . . . . _____

❑ *Syrmaticus mikado.* MIKADO PHEASANT. (mts Taiwan). . . . . _____

❑ *Syrmaticus soemmerringii.* COPPER PHEASANT. (Japan). . . . . _____

❑ *Syrmaticus reevesii.* REEVES'S PHEASANT. (mts c China). . . . . _____

❑ *Phasianus colchicus.* COMMON PHEASANT. (Eura; ◆ cosm). . . . . . . _____
   ___*P. (c.) colchicus.* COMMON PHEASANT. (sc Eura)
   ___*P. (c.) torquatus.* RING-NECKED PHEASANT. (e,s,se Asia)
   ___*P. (c.) versicolor.* GREEN PHEASANT. (Japan; ◆ Haw Is)

❑ *Chrysolophus pictus.* GOLDEN PHEASANT. (mts c,s China; ◆ Brit). . . _____

❑ *Chrysolophus amherstiae.* LADY AMHERST'S PHEASANT. (mts s Asia) _____

❑ *Polyplectron chalcurum.* BRONZE-TAILED PEACOCK-PHEASANT. (Sum) _____

❑ *Polyplectron inopinatum.* MOUNTAIN PEACOCK-PHEASANT. (Malay). _____

❑ *Polyplectron germaini.* GERMAIN'S PEACOCK-PHEASANT. (s Viet). . . . _____

❑ *Polyplectron bicalcaratum.* GREY PEACOCK-PHEASANT. (s,se Asia) . _____

❑ *Polyplectron malacense.* MALAYAN PEACOCK-PHEASANT. (Malay) . . _____

❑ *Polyplectron schleiermacheri.* BORNEAN PEACOCK-PHEASANT. (Born)_____

❑ *Polyplectron emphanum.* PALAWAN PEACOCK-PHEASANT. (Palaw) . _____

❑ *Rheinardia ocellata.* CRESTED ARGUS. (se Asia). . . . . _____
   ___*R. (o.) ocellata.* OCELLATED ARGUS. (Indoc)
   ___*R. (o.) nigrescens.* CRESTED ARGUS. (Malaya)

❑ *Argusianus argus.* GREAT ARGUS. (se Asia). . . . . _____

❑ *Afropavo congensis.* CONGO PEAFOWL. (c,ce Zaire). . . . . _____

❑ *Pavo cristatus.* INDIAN PEAFOWL. (India; ◆ cosm). . . . . _____

❑ *Pavo muticus.* GREEN PEAFOWL. (s,se Asia). . . . . _____

❑ *Dendragapus falcipennis.* SIBERIAN GROUSE. (mts e Sib). . . . . _____

❑ *Dendragapus canadensis.* SPRUCE GROUSE. (n,cw NA). . . . . _____
   ___*D. (c.) canadensis.* SPRUCE GROUSE. (n NA)
   ___*D. (c.) franklinii.* FRANKLIN'S GROUSE. (cw NA)

❑ *Dendragapus obscurus.* BLUE GROUSE. (mts w Na). . . . . _____
   ___*D. (o.) fuliginosus.* SOOTY GROUSE. (nw NA)
   ___*D. (o.) obscurus.* DUSKY GROUSE. (wc Na)

❑ *Lagopus lagopus.* WILLOW PTARMIGAN. (n Hol). . . . . _____
   ___*L. (l.) lagopus.* WILLOW PTARMIGAN. (n Hol)
   ___*L. (l.) scoticus.* RED GROUSE. (Brit)

❑ *Lagopus mutus.* ROCK PTARMIGAN. (n Hol). . . . . _____

❑ *Lagopus leucurus.* WHITE-TAILED PTARMIGAN. (mts nw,wc NA). . . . _____

❑ *Tetrao tetrix.* BLACK GROUSE. (n Eura). _____

❑ *Tetrao mlokosiewiczi.* CAUCASIAN GROUSE. (mts sw Eura). . . . . _____

❑ *Tetrao urogallus.* WESTERN CAPERCAILLIE. (n,nc Eura). . . . . _____

❑ *Tetrao parvirostris.* BLACK-BILLED CAPERCAILLIE. (e Asia). . . . . . . _____

❑ *Bonasa bonasia.* HAZEL GROUSE. (n Eura). . . . . _____

❑ *Bonasa sewerzowi.* CHINESE GROUSE. (mts c China). . . . . _____

❑ *Bonasa umbellus.* RUFFED GROUSE. (n,c NA). . . . . _____

❑ *Centrocercus urophasianus.* SAGE GROUSE. (w NA). . . . . _____

❑ *Tympanuchus phasianellus.* SHARP-TAILED GROUSE. (w NA). . . . . . _____

❑ *Tympanuchus cupido.* GREATER PRAIRIE-CHICKEN. (c NA). . . . . _____

❑ *Tympanuchus pallidicinctus.* LESSER PRAIRIE-CHICKEN. (sc US). . . . _____

❑ *Meleagris gallopavo.* WILD TURKEY. (c,s NA, n,c Mex). . . . . _____

❑ *Agriocharis ocellata.* OCELLATED TURKEY. (nc MA). . . . . _____

Superfamily NUMIDOIDEA [4/6]
Family **Numididae** [4/6]

❑ *Agelastes meleagrides.* WHITE-BREASTED GUINEAFOWL. (w Afr). . . . _____

❑ *Agelastes niger.* BLACK GUINEAFOWL. (wc Afr). . . . . _____

❑ *Numida meleagris.* HELMETED GUINEAFOWL. (Afr; ◆ cosm). . . . . . . _____
   ___*N. (m.) galeata.* WEST AFRICAN GUINEAFOWL. (w Afr; ◆ cosm)
   ___*N. (m.) meleagris.* HELMETED GUINEAFOWL. (ne Afr)
   ___*N. (m.) mitrata.* TUFTED GUINEAFOWL. (s Afr)

❏ *Guttera plumifera.* PLUMED GUINEAFOWL. (wc Afr)............. _____

❏ *Guttera pucherani.* CRESTED GUINEAFOWL. (Afr)............... _____
　　___*G. (p.) edouardi.* CRESTED GUINEAFOWL. (w,c,se Afr)
　　___*G. (p.) pucherani.* KENYA GUINEAFOWL. (ne Afr)

❏ *Acryllium vulturinum.* VULTURINE GUINEAFOWL. (ne Afr)........ _____

Parvorder ODONTOPHORIDA [9/31]
Family **Odontophoridae** [9/31]

❏ *Dendrortyx barbatus.* BEARDED WOOD-PARTRIDGE. (mts ne Mex)... _____

❏ *Dendrortyx macroura.* LONG-TAILED WOOD-PARTRIDGE. (c Mex)... _____

❏ *Dendrortyx leucophrys.* BUFFY-CROWNED WOOD-PARTRIDGE. (c MA) _____

❏ *Oreortyx pictus.* MOUNTAIN QUAIL. (mts w NA)................ _____

❏ *Callipepla squamata.* SCALED QUAIL. (sw US, n,c Mex).......... _____

❏ *Callipepla douglasii.* ELEGANT QUAIL. (w Mex)................ _____

❏ *Callipepla californica.* CALIFORNIA QUAIL. (w NA; ◆ Aust, Haw Is). _____

❏ *Callipepla gambelii.* GAMBEL'S QUAIL. (sw NA, nw Mex; ◆ Haw Is). _____

❏ *Philortyx fasciatus.* BANDED QUAIL. (c Mex)................. _____

❏ *Colinus virginianus.* NORTHERN BOBWHITE. (Nearc; ◆ NZ)........ _____

❏ *Colinus nigrogularis.* BLACK-THROATED BOBWHITE. (c MA)....... _____

❏ *Colinus cristatus.* CRESTED BOBWHITE. (CA, n SA)............. _____
　　___*C. (c.) leucopogon.* SPOT-BELLIED BOBWHITE. (Pac c CA)
　　___*C. (c.) cristatus.* CRESTED BOBWHITE. (s CA, n SA)

❏ *Odontophorus gujanensis.* MARBLED WOOD-QUAIL. (s CA, n,c SA). _____

❏ *Odontophorus capueira.* SPOT-WINGED WOOD-QUAIL. (e,se SA).... _____

❏ *Odontophorus melanotis.* BLACK-EARED WOOD-QUAIL. (CA)...... _____

❏ *Odontophorus erythrops.* RUFOUS-FRONTED WOOD-QUAIL. (nw SA) _____

❏ *Odontophorus atrifrons.* BLACK-FRONTED WOOD-QUAIL. (nw SA). . _____

❏ *Odontophorus hyperythrus.* CHESTNUT WOOD-QUAIL. (Colom)..... _____

❏ *Odontophorus melanonotus.* DARK-BACKED WOOD-QUAIL. (nw SA) _____

❏ *Odontophorus speciosus.* RUFOUS-BREASTED WOOD-QUAIL. (wc SA) _____

❏ *Odontophorus dialeucos.* TACARCUNA WOOD-QUAIL. (Pan, nw SA) _____

❏ *Odontophorus strophium.* GORGETED WOOD-QUAIL. (c Colom)..... _____

❏ *Odontophorus columbianus.* VENEZUELAN WOOD-QUAIL. (w,n Ven) _____

❏ *Odontophorus leucolaemus.* BLACK-BREASTED WOOD-QUAIL. (s CA) _____

❏ *Odontophorus balliviani.* STRIPE-FACED WOOD-QUAIL. (sw SA).... _____

❏ *Odontophorus stellatus.* STARRED WOOD-QUAIL. (wc SA)........ _____

❏ *Odontophorus guttatus.* SPOTTED WOOD-QUAIL. (MA).......... _____

❑ *Dactylortyx thoracicus.* SINGING QUAIL. (MA). . . . . _____

❑ *Cyrtonyx montezumae.* MONTEZUMA QUAIL. (sw US, Mex). . . . . . . _____
   ___*C. (m.) montezumae.* MONTEZUMA QUAIL. (sw US, n,c Mex)
   ___*C. (m.) sallei.* SALLE'S QUAIL. (cw Mex)

❑ *Cyrtonyx ocellatus.* OCELLATED QUAIL. (mts c MA). . . . . _____

❑ *Rhynchortyx cinctus.* TAWNY-FACED QUAIL. (CA, nw SA). . . . . _____

Superorder ANSERIMORPHAE [48/161]
Order **ANSERIFORMES** [48/161]
Infraorder ANHIMIDES [3/4]
Superfamily ANHIMOIDEA [2/3]
Family **Anhimidae** [2/3]

❑ *Anhima cornuta.* HORNED SCREAMER. (n,c SA). . . . . _____

❑ *Chauna chavaria.* NORTHERN SCREAMER. (nw SA). . . . . _____

❑ *Chauna torquata.* SOUTHERN SCREAMER. (s SA). . . . . _____

Superfamily ANSERANATOIDEA [1/1]
Family **Anseranatidae** [1/1]

❑ *Anseranas semipalmata.* MAGPIE GOOSE. (Aust, s NG). . . . . _____

Infraorder ANSERIDES [45/157]
Family **Dendrocygnidae** [3/9]

❑ *Dendrocygna guttata.* SPOTTED WHISTLING-DUCK. (Sulaw-Bism). . . _____

❑ *Dendrocygna eytoni.* PLUMED WHISTLING-DUCK. (n,e Aust). . . . . . . _____

❑ *Dendrocygna bicolor.* FULVOUS WHISTLING-DUCK. (trop cosm). . . . . _____

❑ *Dendrocygna arcuata.* WANDERING WHISTLING-DUCK. (Indon-Aust) _____

❑ *Dendrocygna javanica.* LESSER WHISTLING-DUCK. (s Asia-w Indon) _____

❑ *Dendrocygna viduata.* WHITE-FACED WHISTLING-DUCK. (trop cosm) _____

❑ *Dendrocygna arborea.* WEST INDIAN WHISTLING-DUCK. (W Indies) _____

❑ *Dendrocygna autumnalis.* BLACK-BELLIED WHISTLING-D. (s US-SA) _____

❑ *Thalassornis leuconotus.* WHITE-BACKED DUCK. (Afr, Mad). . . . . . . _____

Family **Anatidae** [43/148]
Subfamily Oxyurinae [3/9]

❑ *Oxyura dominica.* MASKED DUCK. (sw US-SA, G Ant). . . . . _____

❑ *Oxyura jamaicensis.* RUDDY DUCK. (NA, n CA, W Indies; ◊-Mex) . _____

❑ *Oxyura ferruginea.* ANDEAN DUCK. (Andes SA). . . . . _____

❑ *Oxyura leucocephala.* WHITE-HEADED DUCK. (s Palea; ◊-n Afr). . . . _____

❑ *Oxyura maccoa.* MACCOA DUCK. (mts e,s Afr). . . . . _____

❑ *Oxyura vittata.* LAKE DUCK. (s SA)......................... _____

❑ *Oxyura australis.* BLUE-BILLED DUCK. (s Aust)................. _____

❑ *Biziura lobata.* MUSK DUCK. (Aust)....................... _____

❑ *Heteronetta atricapilla.* BLACK-HEADED DUCK. (sc,s SA)......... _____

Subfamily Stictonettinae [1/1]

❑ *Stictonetta naevosa.* FRECKLED DUCK. (s,e Aust)............... _____

Subfamily Cygninae [2/7]

❑ *Cygnus olor.* MUTE SWAN. (n,c Eura; ◆ c NA, s Afr)............ _____

❑ *Cygnus atratus.* BLACK SWAN. (Aust)...................... _____

❑ *Cygnus melanocorypha.* BLACK-NECKED SWAN. (s SA).......... _____

❑ *Cygnus cygnus.* WHOOPER SWAN. (n,c Palea; ◊-n Afr, c Asia)...... _____

❑ *Cygnus buccinator.* TRUMPETER SWAN. (w NA)................ _____

❑ *Cygnus columbianus.* TUNDRA SWAN. (n Hol; ◊-n Eura, US)...... _____
    ___*C. (c.) bewickii.* BEWICK'S SWAN. (n Palea; ◊-n Eura)
    ___*C. (c.) columbianus.* WHISTLING SWAN. (n NA; ◊-US)

❑ *Coscoroba coscoroba.* COSCOROBA SWAN. (s SA)............... _____

Subfamily Anatinae [37/131]
Tribe Anserini [14/43]

❑ *Anser cygnoides.* SWAN GOOSE. (e Eura)..................... _____

❑ *Anser brachyrhynchus.* PINK-FOOTED GOOSE. (nw Palea)......... _____

❑ *Anser fabalis.* BEAN GOOSE. (n,c Eura; ◊-n Afr, China)........... _____
    ___*A. (f.) fabalis.* FOREST BEAN-GOOSE. (sp)
    ___*A (f.) serrirostris.* TUNDRA BEAN-GOOSE. (n Rus-n Sib)

❑ *Anser albifrons.* GREATER WHITE-FRONTED GOOSE. (n Hol; ◊-c Hol) _____
    ___*A. (a.) albifrons.* GREATER WHITE-FRONTED GOOSE. (sp)
    ___*A. (a.) elgasi.* TULE GOOSE. (s Alas; ◊ c Calif)

❑ *Anser erythropus.* LESSER WHITE-FRONTED GOOSE. (n Eura; ◊-n Afr) _____

❑ *Anser anser.* GREYLAG GOOSE. (n,c Eura; ◊-n Afr, s Asia)......... _____

❑ *Anser indicus.* BAR-HEADED GOOSE. (mts s Asia; ◊-s,se Asia)...... _____

❑ *Anser caerulescens.* SNOW GOOSE. (ne Sib, n NA; ◊-n Mex, s US)... _____
    ___*A. (c.) caerulescens.* BLUE GOOSE. (nc Can; ◊-ne Mex, se US)
    ___*A. (c.) hyperboreus.* SNOW GOOSE. (sp)

❑ *Anser rossii.* ROSS'S GOOSE. (n NA; ◊-sw US)................. _____

❑ *Anser canagica.* EMPEROR GOOSE. (ne Sib, w Alaska; ◊-Calif)...... _____

❑ *Branta sandvicensis.* NENE. (Haw Is)....................... _____

❏ *Branta canadensis.* CANADA GOOSE. (NA; ◆ Euro, NZ). . . . . _____
   ___*B. (c.) minima.* CACKLING GOOSE. (w,n Alaska; ◊-Calif)
   ___*B. (c.) canadensis.* CANADA GOOSE. (NA; ◊ c Mex)
   ___*B. (c.) leucopareia.* TUNDRA GOOSE. (Aleut; ◊-Japan, Calif)
   ___*B. (c.) hutchinsii.* HUTCHINS'S GOOSE. (nc NA; ◊-ne Mex)

❏ *Branta leucopsis.* BARNACLE GOOSE. (n Palea; ◊-n Afr). . . . . _____

❏ *Branta bernicla.* BRENT GOOSE. (Hol; ◊-n Afr, nw Mex, US). . . . . . _____
   ___*B. (b.) bernicla.* WHITE-BELLIED BRANT. (nw Palea, n NA; ◊-n Afr, US)
   ___*B. (b.) nigricans.* BLACK BRANT. (ne Sib, nw NA; ◊-China, nw Mex)

❏ *Branta ruficollis.* RED-BREASTED GOOSE. (w Sib; ◊-w Euro, n Afr) . _____

❏ *Cereopsis novaehollandiae.* CAPE BARREN GOOSE. (s Aust). . . . . . . _____

❏ *Cyanochen cyanopterus.* BLUE-WINGED GOOSE. (Eth). . . . . _____

❏ *Chloephaga melanoptera.* ANDEAN GOOSE. (Andes s SA). . . . . _____

❏ *Chloephaga picta.* UPLAND GOOSE. (mts s SA). . . . . _____

❏ *Chloephaga hybrida.* KELP GOOSE. (s SA). . . . . _____

❏ *Chloephaga poliocephala.* ASHY-HEADED GOOSE. (s SA). . . . . _____

❏ *Chloephaga rubidiceps.* RUDDY-HEADED GOOSE. (s SA). . . . . _____

❏ *Neochen jubata.* ORINOCO GOOSE. (Amaz). . . . . _____

❏ *Alopochen aegyptiacus.* EGYPTIAN GOOSE. (Afr; ◆ Euro). . . . . _____

❏ *Tadorna ferruginea.* RUDDY SHELDUCK. (s Palea; ◊-n Afr). . . . . _____

❏ *Tadorna cana.* SOUTH AFRICAN SHELDUCK. (s Afr). . . . . _____

❏ *Tadorna tadornoides.* AUSTRALIAN SHELDUCK. (s Aust). . . . . _____

❏ *Tadorna variegata.* PARADISE SHELDUCK. (NZ). . . . . _____

   Tadorna cristata. CRESTED SHELDUCK. (†e Asia). . . . . _____

❏ *Tadorna tadorna.* COMMON SHELDUCK. (Palea; ◊-n Afr, s,se Asia) . _____

❏ *Tadorna radjah.* RADJAH SHELDUCK. (e Indon, Aust, NG). . . . . _____

❏ *Tachyeres pteneres.* FLIGHTLESS STEAMERDUCK. (s SA). . . . . _____

❏ *Tachyeres leucocephalus.* CHUBUT STEAMERDUCK. (s Argen). . . . . . _____

❏ *Tachyeres brachypterus.* FALKLAND STEAMERDUCK. (Falk). . . . . _____

❏ *Tachyeres patachonicus.* FLYING STEAMERDUCK. (s SA). . . . . _____

❏ *Plectropterus gambensis.* SPUR-WINGED GOOSE. (Afr). . . . . _____

❏ *Cairina moschata.* MUSCOVY DUCK. (MA, SA). . . . . _____

❏ *Cairina scutulata.* WHITE-WINGED DUCK. (se Asia). . . . . _____

❏ *Pteronetta hartlaubii.* HARTLAUB'S DUCK. (w,c Afr). . . . . _____

❏ *Sarkidiornis melanotos.* COMB DUCK. (trop cosm). . . . . _____
   ___*S. (m.) melanotos.* AFRICAN COMB-DUCK. (Afr, Mad, s,se Asia)
   ___*S. (m.) sylvicola.* AMERICAN COMB-DUCK. (s CA, SA)

❑ *Nettapus pulchellus.* Green Pygmy-goose. (e Indon, Aust, NG). . . . _____

❑ *Nettapus coromandelianus.* Cotton Pygmy-goose. (s Asia-Aust) . _____

❑ *Nettapus auritus.* African Pygmy-goose. (Afr, Mad). . . . . _____

Tribe Anatini [23/88]

❑ *Callonetta leucophrys.* Ringed Teal. (s SA). . . . . _____

❑ *Aix sponsa.* Wood Duck. (NA; ◊-c Mex, Bah). . . . . _____

❑ *Aix galericulata.* Mandarin Duck. (e Asia; ◆ Brit). . . . . _____

❑ *Chenonetta jubata.* Maned Duck. (Aust). _____

❑ *Amazonetta brasiliensis.* Brazilian Teal. (SA). . . . . _____

❑ *Merganetta armata.* Torrent Duck. (mts w,s SA). . . . . _____
 ___*M. (a.) colombiana.* Colombian Torrent-Duck. (nw SA)
 ___*M. (a.) leucogenis.* Peruvian Torrent-Duck. (wc SA)
 ___*M. (a.) armata.* Chilean Torrent-Duck. (s SA)

❑ *Hymenolaimus malacorhynchus.* Blue Duck. (mts NZ). . . . . _____

❑ *Salvadorina waigiuensis.* Salvadori's Teal. (mts NG. . . . . _____

❑ *Anas specularioides.* Crested Duck. (Andes sw,s SA). . . . . _____

❑ *Anas specularis.* Spectacled Duck. (Andes s SA). . . . . _____

❑ *Anas capensis.* Cape Teal. (Afr). . . . . _____

❑ *Anas strepera.* Gadwall. (Palea, n NA; ◊-n Afr, s Asia, Mex). . . . . _____
 ___*A. (s.) strepera.* Common Gadwall. (sp)
  A. (s.) couesi. Coues's Gadwall. (†n Line Is)

❑ *Anas falcata.* Falcated Duck. (e Asia; ◊-se Asia). . . . . _____

❑ *Anas penelope.* Eurasian Wigeon. (n,c Eura; ◊-n Afr, Indon, NA) . _____

❑ *Anas americana.* American Wigeon. (n,c NA; ◊-n SA). . . . . _____

❑ *Anas sibilatrix.* Chiloe Wigeon. (s SA). . . . . _____

❑ *Anas sparsa.* African Black Duck. (Afr). _____

❑ *Anas rubripes.* American Black Duck. (e NA). . . . . _____

❑ *Anas fulvigula.* Mottled Duck. (sc,se NA). . . . . _____

❑ *Anas platyrhynchos.* Mallard. (Palea, NA; ◊-n Afr, s Asia, n MA). _____
 ___*A. (p.) platyrhynchos.* Common Mallard. (sp)
 ___*A. (p.) diazi.* Mexican Mallard. (sw US, Mex)

❑ *Anas wyvilliana.* Hawaiian Duck. (Haw Is). . . . . _____

❑ *Anas laysanensis.* Laysan Duck. (Laysan). . . . . _____

❑ *Anas poecilorhyncha.* Spot-billed Duck. (e,s,se Asia; ◊-se Asia). . . _____
 ___*A. (p.) zonorhyncha.* Eastern Spot-billed Duck. (e Asia; ◊-se Asia)
 ___*A. (p.) poecilorhyncha.* Indian Spot-billed Duck. (s,se Asia)

❑ *Anas luzonica.* Philippine Duck. (Phil). . . . . _____

❑ *Anas superciliosa*. PACIFIC BLACK DUCK. (Indon-Oceania, Aust). . . . _____

❑ *Anas undulata*. YELLOW-BILLED DUCK. (Afr). . . . . _____

❑ *Anas melleri*. MELLER'S DUCK. (Mad). _____

❑ *Anas discors*. BLUE-WINGED TEAL. (NA; ◊-SA). . . . . _____

❑ *Anas cyanoptera*. CINNAMON TEAL. (w NA, w,s SA). . . . . _____

❑ *Anas smithii*. CAPE SHOVELER. (s Afr). . . . . _____

❑ *Anas platalea*. RED SHOVELER. (s SA). . . . . _____

❑ *Anas rhynchotis*. AUSTRALIAN SHOVELER. (Aust, NZ). . . . . _____

❑ *Anas clypeata*. NORTHERN SHOVELER. (Hol; ◊-s Afr, Indon, n SA). . . _____

❑ *Anas bernieri*. BERNIER'S TEAL. (Mad). . . . . _____

❑ *Anas gibberifrons*. SUNDA TEAL. (And, Indon). . . . . _____
  ___*A. (g.) albogularis*. ANDAMAN TEAL. (And)
  ___*A. (g.) gibberifrons*. SUNDA TEAL. (Indon)

❑ *Anas gracilis*. GREY TEAL. (e Indon-Solom, Aust, NZ). . . . . _____

❑ *Anas castanea*. CHESTNUT TEAL. (Aust). . . . . _____

❑ *Anas aucklandica*. BROWN TEAL. (NZ, subant is). . . . . _____
  ___*A. (a.) chlorotis*. BROWN TEAL. (NZ)
  ___*A. (a.) aucklandica*. FLIGHTLESS TEAL. (subant is)

❑ *Anas bahamensis*. WHITE-CHEEKED PINTAIL. (W Indies, SA, Galap) _____
  ___*A. (b.) bahamensis*. WHITE-CHEEKED PINTAIL. (W Indies, SA)
  ___*A. (b.) galapagensis*. GALAPAGOS PINTAIL. (Galap)

❑ *Anas erythrorhyncha*. RED-BILLED DUCK. (Afr, Mad). . . . . _____

❑ *Anas flavirostris*. SPECKLED TEAL. (w,s SA). . . . . _____
  ___*A. (f.) andinum*. ANDEAN TEAL. (Andes nw SA)
  ___*A. (f.) flavirostris*. YELLOW-BILLED TEAL. (w,s SA)

❑ *Anas acuta*. NORTHERN PINTAIL. (Palea, NA; ◊-s Afr, Indon, n SA) . _____

❑ *Anas eatoni*. EATON'S PINTAIL. (Crozet, Kerg). . . . . _____
  ___*A. (e.) drygalskii*. CROZET PINTAIL. (Crozet)
  ___*A. (e.) eatoni*. KERGUELEN PINTAIL. (Kerg)

❑ *Anas georgica*. YELLOW-BILLED PINTAIL. (Andes SA). . . . . _____
  ___*A. (g.) niceforoi*. NICEFORO'S PINTAIL. (†Colom)
  ___*A. (g.) spinicauda*. YELLOW-BILLED PINTAIL. (w,s SA)
  ___*A. (g.) georgica*. SOUTH GEORGIA PINTAIL. (S Georgia)

❑ *Anas querquedula*. GARGANEY. (Eura; ◊-s Afr, Aust). . . . . _____

❑ *Anas formosa*. BAIKAL TEAL. (n,c Sib; ◊-s Asia). . . . . _____

❑ *Anas crecca*. COMMON TEAL. (n Hol; ◊-trop). . . . . _____
  ___*A. (c.) crecca*. COMMON TEAL. (n Palea; ◊-OW trop)
  ___*A. (c.) carolinensis*. GREEN-WINGED TEAL. (n NA; ◊-Amer trop)

❑ *Anas puna*. PUNA TEAL. (Andes sw SA). . . . . _____

❑ *Anas versicolor*. SILVER TEAL. (s SA). _____

❑ *Anas hottentota.* HOTTENTOT TEAL. (Afr, Mad). . . . . _____

❑ *Malacorhynchus membranaceus.* PINK-EARED DUCK. (Aust). . . . . . . _____

❑ *Marmaronetta angustirostris.* MARBLED TEAL. (s Palea). . . . . _____

Rhodonessa caryophyllacea. PINK-HEADED DUCK. (†India). . . . . _____

❑ *Netta rufina.* RED-CRESTED POCHARD. (Palea; ◊-n Afr, s Asia). . . . . . _____

❑ *Netta peposaca.* ROSY-BILLED POCHARD. (s SA). . . . . _____

❑ *Netta erythrophthalma.* SOUTHERN POCHARD. (SA, Afr). . . . . _____

❑ *Aythya ferina.* COMMON POCHARD. (Palea; ◊-c Afr, s,se Asia). . . . . . _____

❑ *Aythya valisineria.* CANVASBACK. (n NA; ◊-Mex, s US). . . . . _____

❑ *Aythya americana.* REDHEAD. (n NA; ◊-nCA, n W Indies). . . . . _____

❑ *Aythya collaris.* RING-NECKED DUCK. (NA; ◊-CA, W Indies). . . . . . _____

❑ *Aythya nyroca.* FERRUGINOUS POCHARD. (Palea; ◊-n Afr, s,se Asia) . _____

❑ *Aythya innotata.* MADAGASCAR POCHARD. (e Mad). . . . . _____

❑ *Aythya baeri.* BAER'S POCHARD. (e Eura; ◊-s,se Asia). . . . . _____

❑ *Aythya australis.* HARDHEAD. (Aust reg, sw Oceania). . . . . _____

❑ *Aythya fuligula.* TUFTED DUCK. (Eura; ◊-n Afr, s,se Asia). . . . . _____

❑ *Aythya novaeseelandiae.* NEW ZEALAND SCAUP. (NZ). . . . . _____

❑ *Aythya marila.* GREATER SCAUP. (n Hol; ◊-s Palea, s US). . . . . _____

❑ *Aythya affinis.* LESSER SCAUP. (n NA; ◊-n SA). . . . . _____

❑ *Somateria mollissima.* COMMON EIDER. (n Hol; ◊-s Euro, n US). . . . _____
    ___*S. (m.) mollissima.* COMMON EIDER. (n Hol; ◊-s Euro, n US)
    ___*S. (m.) v-nigrum.* PACIFIC EIDER. (nw NA; ◊-nw US)

❑ *Somateria spectabilis.* KING EIDER. (n Hol; ◊-n Eura, US). . . . . _____

❑ *Somateria fischeri.* SPECTACLED EIDER. (n Sib, Alas; ◊-nw NA). . . . . _____

❑ *Polysticta stelleri.* STELLER'S EIDER. (n Eura, Alas; ◊-nw NA). . . . . . _____

Camptorhynchus labradorius. LABRADOR DUCK. (†ne NA). . . . . _____

❑ *Histrionicus histrionicus.* HARLEQUIN DUCK. (n Hol; ◊-c Euro, US). _____

❑ *Clangula hyemalis.* LONG-TAILED DUCK. (n Hol; ◊-s Palea, s US). . . _____

❑ *Melanitta nigra.* BLACK SCOTER. (n Hol; ◊-s Palea, s US). . . . . _____
    ___*M. (n.) nigra.* BLACK SCOTER. (n Eura; ◊-s Palea)
    ___*M. (n.) americana.* AMERICAN SCOTER. (n NA; ◊-s US)

❑ *Melanitta perspicillata.* SURF SCOTER. (n NA; ◊-n Mex, s US). . . . . . _____

❑ *Melanitta fusca.* WHITE-WINGED SCOTER. (n Hol; ◊-s Palea, s US). . . _____
    ___*M. (f.) fusca.* VELVET SCOTER. (n Eura; ◊-s Palea)
    ___*M. (f.) stejnegeri.* ASIATIC SCOTER. (n Sib; ◊-e Asia)
    ___*M. (f.) deglandi.* WHITE-WINGED SCOTER. (n NA; ◊-s US)

❑ *Bucephala clangula.* COMMON GOLDENEYE. (n Hol; ◊-s Palea, Mex)_____

❏ *Bucephala islandica.* BARROW'S GOLDENEYE. (n Hol; ◊-c US)...... _____

❏ *Bucephala albeola.* BUFFLEHEAD. (n NA, Ice; ◊-Mex, G Ant)...... _____

❏ *Mergellus albellus.* SMEW. (n Eura; ◊-n Afr, s Asia)............. _____

❏ *Lophodytes cucullatus.* HOODED MERGANSER. (NA; ◊-Mex)....... _____

❏ *Mergus octosetaceus.* BRAZILIAN MERGANSER. (e,sc SA)......... _____

❏ *Mergus serrator.* RED-BREASTED MERGANSER. (n Hol; ◊-Medit, Mex)_____

❏ *Mergus squamatus.* SCALY-SIDED MERGANSER. (ce Asia; ◊-China) . _____

❏ *Mergus merganser.* COMMON MERGANSER. (n Hol; ◊-s Palea, c Mex). _____

❏ *Mergus australis.* AUCKLAND ISLANDS MERGANSER. (Auck)....... _____

Parvclass TURNICAE [2/17]
Order **TURNICIFORMES** [2/17]
Family **Turnicidae** [2/17]

❏ *Turnix sylvatica.* SMALL BUTTONQUAIL. (w Palea, Afr, s Asia-Phil) _____

❏ *Turnix maculosa.* RED-BACKED BUTTONQUAIL. (Indon-Phil, Aust) . _____

❏ *Turnix nana.* BLACK-RUMPED BUTTONQUAIL. (Afr).............. _____

❏ *Turnix hottentotta.* HOTTENTOT BUTTONQUAIL. (S Afr)........... _____

❏ *Turnix tanki.* YELLOW-LEGGED BUTTONQUAIL. (s,se Asia)........ _____

❏ *Turnix ocellata.* SPOTTED BUTTONQUAIL. (n Phil).............. _____

❏ *Turnix suscitator.* BARRED BUTTONQUAIL. (s,se Asia, Indon, Phil). . . _____
___*T. (s.) suscitator.* BARRED BUTTONQUAIL. (sp)
___*T. (s.) powelli.* SUNDA BUTTONQUAIL. (L Sunda)

❏ *Turnix nigricollis.* MADAGASCAR BUTTONQUAIL. (Mad).......... _____

❏ *Turnix melanogaster.* BLACK-BREASTED BUTTONQUAIL. (ce Aust). . . _____

❏ *Turnix castanota.* CHESTNUT-BACKED BUTTONQUAIL. (n Aust)...... _____

❏ *Turnix olivii.* BUFF-BREASTED BUTTONQUAIL. (ne Aust).......... _____

❏ *Turnix varia.* PAINTED BUTTONQUAIL. (s,e Aust, N Cal).......... _____
___*T. (v.) varia.* PAINTED BUTTONQUAIL. (s,e Aust)
___*T. (v.) novaecaledoniae.* NEW CALEDONIAN BUTTONQUAIL. (N Cal)

❏ *Turnix worcesteri.* WORCESTER'S BUTTONQUAIL. (n Phil)......... _____

❏ *Turnix everetti.* SUMBA BUTTONQUAIL. (Sumba)............... _____

❏ *Turnix pyrrhothorax.* RED-CHESTED BUTTONQUAIL. (e Aust)....... _____

❏ *Turnix velox.* LITTLE BUTTONQUAIL. (Aust)................... _____

❏ *Ortyxelos meiffrenii.* LARK BUTTONQUAIL. (subsah Afr).......... _____

Parvclass PICAE [51/356]
Order **PICIFORMES** [51/356]
Infraorder PICIDES [32/356]
Family **Indicatoridae** [4/17]

❑ *Indicator maculatus.* SPOTTED HONEYGUIDE. (w,c Afr)........... _____

❑ *Indicator variegatus.* SCALY-THROATED HONEYGUIDE. (s,e Afr)..... _____

❑ *Indicator indicator.* GREATER HONEYGUIDE. (Afr).............. _____

❑ *Indicator archipelagicus.* MALAYSIAN HONEYGUIDE. (se Asia)...... _____

❑ *Indicator minor.* LESSER HONEYGUIDE. (Afr)................. _____

❑ *Indicator conirostris.* THICK-BILLED HONEYGUIDE. (w,c Afr)...... _____

❑ *Indicator willcocksi.* WILLCOCKS'S HONEYGUIDE. (w,c Afr)....... _____

❑ *Indicator exilis.* LEAST HONEYGUIDE. (w,c Afr)............... _____

❑ *Indicator pumilio.* DWARF HONEYGUIDE. (mts ec Afr)........... _____

❑ *Indicator meliphilus.* PALLID HONEYGUIDE. (e,c Afr)........... _____

❑ *Indicator xanthonotus.* YELLOW-RUMPED HONEYGUIDE. (Himal).... _____

❑ *Melichneutes robustus.* LYRE-TAILED HONEYGUIDE. (w,c Afr)..... _____

❑ *Melignomon eisentrauti.* YELLOW-FOOTED HONEYGUIDE. (w Afr)... _____

❑ *Melignomon zenkeri.* ZENKER'S HONEYGUIDE. (w Afr)........... _____

❑ *Prodotiscus insignis.* CASSIN'S HONEYGUIDE. (w,c Afr).......... _____

❑ *Prodotiscus zambesiae.* GREEN-BACKED HONEYGUIDE. (e,c Afr)..... _____

❑ *Prodotiscus regulus.* WAHLBERG'S HONEYGUIDE. (Afr)........... _____

Family **Picidae** [28/216]

❑ *Jynx torquilla.* EURASIAN WRYNECK. (Palea; ◊-c Afr, s,se Asia)..... _____

❑ *Jynx ruficollis.* RUFOUS-NECKED WRYNECK. (Afr)............... _____

❑ *Picumnus innominatus.* SPECKLED PICULET. (s,se Asia).......... _____

❑ *Picumnus aurifrons.* BAR-BREASTED PICULET. (Amaz)........... _____
    ___*P. (a.) borbae.* BAR-BREASTED PICULET. (w Amaz)
    ___*P. (a.) aurifrons.* GOLDEN-FRONTED PICULET. (n,c Amaz)

❑ *Picumnus pumilus.* ORINOCO PICULET. (nw Amaz)............. _____

❑ *Picumnus lafresnayi.* LAFRESNAYE'S PICULET. (w Amaz)......... _____

❑ *Picumnus exilis.* GOLDEN-SPANGLED PICULET. (nc,e SA)......... _____

❑ *Picumnus fuscus.* RUSTY-NECKED PICULET. (sc SA)............. _____

❑ *Picumnus sclateri.* ECUADORIAN PICULET. (cw SA)............. _____

❑ *Picumnus squamulatus.* SCALED PICULET. (n SA).............. _____

❑ *Picumnus spilogaster.* WHITE-BELLIED PICULET. (n SA).......... _____
    ___*P. (s.) spilogaster.* WHITE-BELLIED PICULET. (sp)
    ___*P. (s.) pallidus.* PARA PICULET. (nc Braz)

❑ *Picumnus minutissimus.* GUIANAN PICULET. (Guia)............. _____

❑ *Picumnus pygmaeus.* SPOTTED PICULET. (e Braz).............. _____

❑ *Picumnus steindachneri.* SPECKLE-CHESTED PICULET. (ne Peru).... _____

❑ *Picumnus varzeae.* VARZEA PICULET. (Amaz Braz). . . . . _____

❑ *Picumnus cirratus.* WHITE-BARRED PICULET. (ne,sc SA). . . . . _____
   ___*P. (c.) cirratus.* WHITE-BARRED PICULET. (ne SA)
   ___*P. (c.) pilcomayensis.* PILCOMAYO PICULET. (sc SA)

❑ *Picumnus dorbygnianus.* OCELLATED PICULET. (sw SA). . . . . _____

❑ *Picumnus temminckii.* OCHRE-COLLARED PICULET. (se Braz). . . . . . _____

❑ *Picumnus albosquamatus.* WHITE-WEDGED PICULET. (sc,e SA). . . . . _____
   ___*P. (a.) albosquamatus.* WHITE-WEDGED PICULET. (sc SA)
   ___*P. (a.) guttifer.* GUTTATE PICULET. (c,e Braz)

❑ *Picumnus rufiventris.* RUFOUS-BREASTED PICULET. (wc SA). . . . . . _____

❑ *Picumnus fulvescens.* TAWNY PICULET. (ne Braz). . . . . _____

❑ *Picumnus limae.* OCHRACEOUS PICULET. (e Braz). . . . . _____

❑ *Picumnus nebulosus.* MOTTLED PICULET. (se SA). . . . . _____

❑ *Picumnus castelnau.* PLAIN-BREASTED PICULET. (wc SA). . . . . _____

❑ *Picumnus subtilis.* FINE-BARRED PICULET. (Peru). . . . . _____

❑ *Picumnus olivaceus.* OLIVACEOUS PICULET. (CA, nw SA). . . . . _____

❑ *Picumnus granadensis.* GREYISH PICULET. (Colom). . . . . _____

❑ *Picumnus cinnamomeus.* CHESTNUT PICULET. (nw SA). . . . . _____

❑ *Sasia africana.* AFRICAN PICULET. (c Afr). . . . . _____

❑ *Sasia abnormis.* RUFOUS PICULET. (se Asia). . . . . _____

❑ *Sasia ochracea.* WHITE-BROWED PICULET. (s,se Asia). . . . . _____

❑ *Nesoctites micromegas.* ANTILLEAN PICULET. (Hisp). . . . . _____

❑ *Melanerpes candidus.* WHITE WOODPECKER. (e SA). . . . . _____

❑ *Melanerpes lewis.* LEWIS'S WOODPECKER. (w Can, w US; ◊-n Mex) . _____

❑ *Melanerpes herminieri.* GUADELOUPE WOODPECKER. (Guade). . . . . _____

❑ *Melanerpes portoricensis.* PUERTO RICAN WOODPECKER. (PR). . . . . _____

❑ *Melanerpes erythrocephalus.* RED-HEADED WOODPECKER. (e NA) . _____

❑ *Melanerpes formicivorus.* ACORN WOODPECKER. (w NA-nw SA). . . _____

❑ *Melanerpes pucherani.* BLACK-CHEEKED WOODPECKER. (MA-nw SA) _____

❑ *Melanerpes chrysauchen.* GOLDEN-NAPED WOODPECKER. (CR-Colom)_____
   ___*M. (c.) chrysauchen.* GOLDEN-NAPED WOODPECKER. (sw CR, Pan)
   ___*M. (c.) pulcher.* BEAUTIFUL WOODPECKER. (c Colom)

❑ *Melanerpes cruentatus.* YELLOW-TUFTED WOODPECKER. (Amaz). . . _____

❑ *Melanerpes flavifrons.* YELLOW-FRONTED WOODPECKER. (se SA). . . _____

❑ *Melanerpes cactorum.* WHITE-FRONTED WOODPECKER. (sc SA). . . . _____

❑ *Melanerpes striatus.* HISPANIOLAN WOODPECKER. (Hisp). . . . . _____

❑ *Melanerpes radiolatus.* JAMAICAN WOODPECKER. (Jam). . . . . _____

❑ *Melanerpes chrysogenys.* GOLDEN-CHEEKED WOODPECKER. (w Mex) _____

❑ *Melanerpes hypopolius.* GREY-BREASTED WOODPECKER. (Mex). . . . _____

❑ *Melanerpes pygmaeus.* YUCATAN WOODPECKER. (Yuc-Hond). . . . . . _____

❑ *Melanerpes rubricapillus.* RED-CROWNED WOODPECKER. (s CA-n SA) _____

❑ *Melanerpes uropygialis.* GILA WOODPECKER. (sw US, n Mex). . . . . . _____

❑ *Melanerpes carolinus.* RED-BELLIED WOODPECKER. (e NA). . . . . . . _____

❑ *Melanerpes superciliaris.* WEST INDIAN WOODPECKER. (n W Indies). _____
   ___*M. (s.) superciliaris.* WEST INDIAN WOODPECKER. (n Bah, Cuba)
   ___*M. (s.) caymanensis.* CAYMAN WOODPECKER. (Gd Caym)

❑ *Melanerpes aurifrons.* GOLDEN-FRONTED WOODPECKER. (cs US, MA) _____

❑ *Melanerpes hoffmannii.* HOFFMANN'S WOODPECKER. (s Hond-c CR) _____

❑ *Sphyrapicus varius.* YELLOW-BELLIED SAPSUCKER. (NA; ◊-n SA). . . _____

❑ *Sphyrapicus nuchalis.* RED-NAPED SAPSUCKER. (w NA; ◊-c Mex). . . _____

❑ *Sphyrapicus ruber.* RED-BREASTED SAPSUCKER. (w NA). . . . . _____

❑ *Sphyrapicus thyroideus.* WILLIAMSON'S SAPSUCKER. (mts w NA). . . . _____

❑ *Xiphidiopicus percussus.* CUBAN GREEN WOODPECKER. (Cuba). . . . . _____

❑ *Campethera punctuligera.* FINE-SPOTTED WOODPECKER. (w,nc Afr). _____

❑ *Campethera nubica.* NUBIAN WOODPECKER. (e Afr). . . . . _____

❑ *Campethera bennettii.* BENNETT'S WOODPECKER. (w,s Afr). . . . . _____

❑ *Campethera scriptoricauda.* REICHENOW'S WOODPECKER. (e Afr). . . _____

❑ *Campethera abingoni.* GOLDEN-TAILED WOODPECKER. (Afr). . . . . . . _____

❑ *Campethera mombassica.* MOMBASA WOODPECKER. (e Afr). . . . . . . _____

❑ *Campethera notata.* KNYSNA WOODPECKER. (S Afr). . . . . _____

❑ *Campethera maculosa.* LITTLE GREEN WOODPECKER. (w Afr). . . . . . _____

❑ *Campethera cailliautii.* GREEN-BACKED WOODPECKER. (w,c,e Afr) . _____
   ___*C. (c.) permista.* GREEN-BACKED WOODPECKER. (w,c Afr)
   ___*C. (c.) cailliautii.* LITTLE SPOTTED WOODPECKER. (c,e Afr)

❑ *Campethera tullbergi.* TULLBERG'S WOODPECKER. (mts c Afr). . . . . . _____
   ___*C. (t.) tullbergi.* TULLBERG'S WOODPECKER. (wc Afr)
   ___*C. (t.) taeniolaema.* FINE-BANDED WOODPECKER. (ec Afr)

❑ *Campethera nivosa.* BUFF-SPOTTED WOODPECKER. (w,c Afr). . . . . . . _____

❑ *Campethera caroli.* BROWN-EARED WOODPECKER. (w,c Afr). . . . . . . _____

❑ *Geocolaptes olivaceus.* GROUND WOODPECKER. (S Afr). . . . . _____

❑ *Dendropicos elachus.* LITTLE GREY WOODPECKER. (subsah Afr). . . . _____

❑ *Dendropicos poecilolaemus.* SPECKLE-BREASTED WOODP. (c Afr). . . _____

❑ *Dendropicos abyssinicus.* ABYSSINIAN WOODPECKER. (mts Eth). . . . . _____

❑ *Dendropicos fuscescens.* CARDINAL WOODPECKER. (Afr). . . . . _____

❏ *Dendropicos lugubris.* MELANCHOLY WOODPECKER. (w Afr). . . . . . . _____

❏ *Dendropicos gabonensis.* GABON WOODPECKER. (c Afr). . . . . _____

❏ *Dendropicos stierlingi.* STIERLING'S WOODPECKER. (e Afr). . . . . _____

❏ *Dendropicos namaquus.* BEARDED WOODPECKER. (c,s,e Afr). . . . . . . _____

❏ *Dendropicos pyrrhogaster.* FIRE-BELLIED WOODPECKER. (w Afr). . . . _____

❏ *Dendropicos xantholophus.* GOLDEN-CROWNED WOODPECKER. (c Afr) _____

❏ *Dendropicos elliotii.* ELLIOT'S WOODPECKER. (c Afr). . . . . _____
    ___*D. (e.) johnstoni.* JOHNSTON'S WOODPECKER. (mts wc Afr)
    ___*D. (e.) elliotii.* ELLIOT'S WOODPECKER. (sc,ec Afr)

❏ *Dendropicos goertae.* GREY WOODPECKER. (w,c,ne Afr). . . . . _____

❏ *Dendropicos spodocephalus.* GREY-HEADED WOODPECKER. (e Afr) . _____

❏ *Dendropicos griseocephalus.* OLIVE WOODPECKER. (mts s,ec Afr). . . _____

❏ *Dendropicos obsoletus.* BROWN-BACKED WOODPECKER. (nc, e Afr) . _____

❏ *Dendrocopos temminckii.* SULAWESI WOODPECKER. (Sulaw). . . . . . . _____

❏ *Dendrocopos maculatus.* PHILIPPINE WOODPECKER. (Phil). . . . . _____
    ___*D. (m.) maculatus.* PHILIPPINE WOODPECKER. (sp)
    ___*D. (m.) ramsayi.* RAMSAY'S WOODPECKER. (Sulu)

❏ *Dendrocopos nanus.* BROWN-CAPPED WOODPECKER. (s Asia). . . . . . _____

❏ *Dendrocopos moluccensis.* SUNDA WOODPECKER. (se Asia). . . . . . . _____

❏ *Dendrocopos canicapillus.* GREY-CAPPED WOODPECKER. (s,e Asia) . _____

❏ *Dendrocopos kizuki.* PYGMY WOODPECKER. (e Asia). . . . . _____

❏ *Dendrocopos minor.* LESSER SPOTTED WOODPECKER. (Palea). . . . . . _____

❏ *Dendrocopos auriceps.* BROWN-FRONTED WOODPECKER. (sc Asia). . . _____

❏ *Dendrocopos macei.* FULVOUS-BREASTED WOODPECKER. (s,se Asia). _____

❏ *Dendrocopos atratus.* STRIPE-BREASTED WOODPECKER. (se Asia). . . . _____

❏ *Dendrocopos mahrattensis.* YELLOW-CROWNED WOODPECKER. (s Asia)_____

❏ *Dendrocopos dorae.* ARABIAN WOODPECKER. (Arabia). . . . . _____

❏ *Dendrocopos hyperythrus.* RUFOUS-BELLIED WOODPECKER. (s,se Asia)_____

❏ *Dendrocopos cathpharius.* CRIMSON-BREASTED WOODPECKER. (s Asia)_____

❏ *Dendrocopos darjellensis.* DARJEELING WOODPECKER. (mts s Asia) . _____

❏ *Dendrocopos medius.* MIDDLE SPOTTED WOODPECKER. (w Eura). . . . _____

❏ *Dendrocopos leucotos.* WHITE-BACKED WOODPECKER. (Eura). . . . . . _____
    ___*D. (l.) leucotos.* WHITE-BACKED WOODPECKER. (n Eura)
    ___*D. (l.) lilfordi.* LILFORD'S WOODPECKER. (s Euro)

❏ *Dendrocopos major.* GREAT SPOTTED WOODPECKER. (Palea). . . . . . . _____

❏ *Dendrocopos syriacus.* SYRIAN WOODPECKER. (wc Eura). . . . . _____

❏ *Dendrocopos leucopterus.* WHITE-WINGED WOODPECKER. (sc Asia) . _____

❑ *Dendrocopos assimilis.* SIND WOODPECKER. (se Iran, Pak)........ _____

❑ *Dendrocopos himalayensis.* HIMALAYAN WOODPECKER. (Himal).... _____

❑ *Picoides lignarius.* STRIPED WOODPECKER. (mts s SA)........... _____

❑ *Picoides mixtus.* CHECKERED WOODPECKER. (se SA)............. _____

❑ *Picoides nuttallii.* NUTTALL'S WOODPECKER. (Calif, nw Baja)....... _____

❑ *Picoides scalaris.* LADDER-BACKED WOODPECKER. (sw,cs US, MA) . _____

❑ *Picoides pubescens.* DOWNY WOODPECKER. (NA).............. _____

❑ *Picoides borealis.* RED-COCKADED WOODPECKER. (se US)........ _____

❑ *Picoides stricklandi.* STRICKLAND'S WOODPECKER. (sw US-n,c Mex) _____
   ___*P. (s.) arizonae.* ARIZONA WOODPECKER. (sw US, w,n Mex)
   ___*P. (s.) stricklandi.* STRICKLAND'S WOODPECKER. (c Mex)

❑ *Picoides villosus.* HAIRY WOODPECKER. (NA, MA)............. _____

❑ *Picoides albolarvatus.* WHITE-HEADED WOODPECKER. (mts w NA) .. _____

❑ *Picoides tridactylus.* THREE-TOED WOODPECKER. (n Hol)......... _____

❑ *Picoides arcticus.* BLACK-BACKED WOODPECKER. (n NA)......... _____

❑ *Veniliornis callonotus.* SCARLET-BACKED WOODPECKER. (cw SA)... _____

❑ *Veniliornis dignus.* YELLOW-VENTED WOODPECKER. (Andes w SA) . _____

❑ *Veniliornis nigriceps.* BAR-BELLIED WOODPECKER. (Andes w SA)... _____

❑ *Veniliornis fumigatus.* SMOKY-BROWN WOODPECKER. (MA, w SA) . _____

❑ *Veniliornis passerinus.* LITTLE WOODPECKER. (nw,sc SA)........ _____

❑ *Veniliornis frontalis.* DOT-FRONTED WOODPECKER. (Andes sw SA) . _____

❑ *Veniliornis spilogaster.* WHITE-SPOTTED WOODPECKER. (se SA)..... _____

❑ *Veniliornis sanguineus.* BLOOD-COLORED WOODPECKER. (Guia).... _____

❑ *Veniliornis kirkii.* RED-RUMPED WOODPECKER. (s CA, nw SA)...... _____

❑ *Veniliornis chocoensis.* CHOCO WOODPECKER. (w Colom)........ _____

❑ *Veniliornis cassini.* GOLDEN-COLLARED WOODPECKER. (n SA)...... _____

❑ *Veniliornis affinis.* RED-STAINED WOODPECKER. (n,c SA)......... _____

❑ *Veniliornis maculifrons.* YELLOW-EARED WOODPECKER. (se Braz) . _____

❑ *Piculus simplex.* RUFOUS-WINGED WOODPECKER. (c,s CA)........ _____

❑ *Piculus callopterus.* STRIPE-CHEEKED WOODPECKER. (Pan)........ _____

❑ *Piculus litae.* LITA WOODPECKER. (nw SA).................... _____

❑ *Piculus leucolaemus.* WHITE-THROATED WOODPECKER. (w SA)..... _____

❑ *Piculus flavigula.* YELLOW-THROATED WOODPECKER. (Amaz)...... _____

❑ *Piculus chrysochloros.* GOLDEN-GREEN WOODPECKER. (e Pan, SA) . _____

❑ *Piculus aurulentus.* YELLOW-BROWED WOODPECKER. (se SA)...... _____

❑ *Piculus auricularis.* GREY-CROWNED WOODPECKER. (w Mex)...... _____

❑ *Piculus rubiginosus.* GOLDEN-OLIVE WOODPECKER. (MA, w,n SA) . _____
  ___*P. (r.) aeruginosus.* BRONZE-WINGED WOODPECKER. (ne Mex)
  ___*P. (r.) rubiginosus.* GOLDEN-OLIVE WOODPECKER. (sp)

❑ *Piculus rivolii.* CRIMSON-MANTLED WOODPECKER. (mts w SA). . . . . . _____

❑ *Colaptes atricollis.* BLACK-NECKED WOODPECKER. (Andes Peru). . . . _____

❑ *Colaptes punctigula.* SPOT-BREASTED WOODPECKER. (e Pan-n,c SA). _____

❑ *Colaptes melanochloros.* GREEN-BARRED WOODPECKER. (sc,se SA) _____
  ___*C. (m.) melanolaimus.* GOLDEN-BREASTED WOODPECKER. (sc SA)
  ___*C. (m.) melanochloros.* GREEN-BARRED WOODPECKER. (se SA)

❑ *Colaptes auratus.* NORTHERN FLICKER. (NA, MA, w W Indies). . . . . _____
  ___*C. (a.) auratus.* YELLOW-SHAFTED FLICKER. (n,e NA)
  ___*C. (a.) chrysocaulosus.* CUBAN FLICKER. (Cuba, Gd Caym)
  ___*C. (a.) cafer.* RED-SHAFTED FLICKER. (w NA, Mex)
  ___*C. (a.) mexicanoides.* GUATEMALAN FLICKER. (mts c MA)

❑ *Colaptes chrysoides.* GILDED FLICKER. (sw US, nw Mex). . . . . _____

❑ *Colaptes fernandinae.* FERNANDINA'S FLICKER. (Cuba). . . . . _____

❑ *Colaptes pitius.* CHILEAN FLICKER. (mts s SA). . . . . _____

❑ *Colaptes rupicola.* ANDEAN FLICKER. (Andes sw SA). . . . . _____

❑ *Colaptes campestris.* CAMPO FLICKER. (nc,c,e,se SA). . . . . _____
  ___*C. (c.) campestris.* CAMPO FLICKER. (Amaz)
  ___*C. (c.) campestroides.* FIELD FLICKER. (se SA)

❑ *Celeus brachyurus.* RUFOUS WOODPECKER. (s,se Asia). . . . . _____

❑ *Celeus loricatus.* CINNAMON WOODPECKER. (CA, nw SA). . . . . _____

❑ *Celeus grammicus.* SCALY-BREASTED WOODPECKER. (w Amaz). . . . . _____

❑ *Celeus undatus.* WAVED WOODPECKER. (ne SA). . . . . _____

❑ *Celeus castaneus.* CHESTNUT-COLORED WOODPECKER. (MA). . . . . . . _____

❑ *Celeus elegans.* CHESTNUT WOODPECKER. (n SA). . . . . _____
  ___*C. (e.) jumana.* CHESTNUT-CRESTED WOODPECKER. (nc SA)
  ___*C. (e.) elegans.* RUSSET-CRESTED WOODPECKER. (ne SA)

❑ *Celeus lugubris.* PALE-CRESTED WOODPECKER. (sc SA). . . . . _____

❑ *Celeus flavescens.* BLOND-CRESTED WOODPECKER. (e SA). . . . . _____

❑ *Celeus flavus.* CREAM-COLORED WOODPECKER. (Amaz). . . . . _____

❑ *Celeus spectabilis.* RUFOUS-HEADED WOODPECKER. (sw,ec SA). . . . . _____

❑ *Celeus torquatus.* RINGED WOODPECKER. (n Amaz). . . . . _____

❑ *Dryocopus galeatus.* HELMETED WOODPECKER. (se SA). . . . . _____

❑ *Dryocopus pileatus.* PILEATED WOODPECKER. (NA). . . . . _____

❑ *Dryocopus lineatus.* LINEATED WOODPECKER. (MA, SA). . . . . _____

❑ *Dryocopus schulzi.* BLACK-BODIED WOODPECKER. (sc SA). . . . . _____

❑ *Dryocopus javensis.* WHITE-BELLIED WOODPECKER. (s,se Asia-Phil). _____

❑ *Dryocopus hodgei.* ANDAMAN WOODPECKER. (And). . . . . _____

❑ *Dryocopus martius.* BLACK WOODPECKER. (Eura). . . . . _____

❑ *Campephilus pollens.* POWERFUL WOODPECKER. (Andes nw SA). . . . _____

❑ *Campephilus haematogaster.* CRIMSON-BELLIED WOODP. (CA-SA). . _____
   ___*C. (h.) splendens.* SPLENDID WOODPECKER. (s CA, nw SA)
   ___*C. (h.) haematogaster.* CRIMSON-BELLIED WOODPECKER. (w SA)

❑ *Campephilus rubricollis.* RED-NECKED WOODPECKER. (Amaz). . . . . . _____

❑ *Campephilus robustus.* ROBUST WOODPECKER. (se SA). . . . . _____

❑ *Campephilus guatemalensis.* PALE-BILLED WOODPECKER. (MA). . . . _____

❑ *Campephilus melanoleucos.* CRIMSON-CRESTED WOODP. (CA-SA) . _____

❑ *Campephilus gayaquilensis.* GUAYAQUIL WOODPECKER. (nw SA). . . _____

❑ *Campephilus leucopogon.* CREAM-BACKED WOODPECKER. (sc SA) . _____

❑ *Campephilus magellanicus.* MAGELLANIC WOODPECKER. (s SA). . . . _____

❑ *Campephilus imperialis.* IMPERIAL WOODPECKER. (mts n Mex). . . . . _____

❑ *Campephilus principalis.* IVORY-BILLED WOODPECKER. (se US, Cuba) _____
   ___*C. (p.) principalis.* NORTHERN IVORY-BILLED WOODPECKER. (†se US)
   ___*C. (p.) bairdii.* CUBAN IVORY-BILLED WOODPECKER. (Cuba)

❑ *Picus mineaceus.* BANDED WOODPECKER. (se Asia). . . . . _____

❑ *Picus chlorolophus.* LESSER YELLOWNAPE. (s,se Asia). . . . . _____

❑ *Picus puniceus.* CRIMSON-WINGED WOODPECKER. (se Asia). . . . . . . _____

❑ *Picus flavinucha.* GREATER YELLOWNAPE. (s,se Asia). . . . . _____

❑ *Picus mentalis.* CHECKER-THROATED WOODPECKER. (se Asia). . . . . . _____

❑ *Picus viridanus.* STREAK-BREASTED WOODPECKER. (se Asia). . . . . . . _____

❑ *Picus vittatus.* LACED WOODPECKER. (se Asia). . . . . _____

❑ *Picus xanthopygaeus.* STREAK-THROATED WOODPECKER. (s,se Asia). _____

❑ *Picus squamatus.* SCALY-BELLIED WOODPECKER. (mts s Asia). . . . . . _____

❑ *Picus awokera.* JAPANESE WOODPECKER. (mts Japan). . . . . _____

❑ *Picus [viridis] vviridis.* EURASIAN GREEN WOODPECKER. (w Eura). . . _____
   ___*P. (v.) viridis.* EURASIAN GREEN WOODPECKER. (sp)
   ___*P. (v.) sharpei.* IBERIAN WOODPECKER. (sw Euro)

❑ *Picus vaillantii.* LEVAILLANT'S WOODPECKER. (mts nw Afr). . . . . . . _____

❑ *Picus rabieri.* RED-COLLARED WOODPECKER. (Indoc). . . . . _____

❑ *Picus erythropygius.* BLACK-HEADED WOODPECKER. (se Asia). . . . . . _____

❑ *Picus canus.* GREY-FACED WOODPECKER. (mts Eura). . . . . _____

❑ *Dinopium rafflesii.* OLIVE-BACKED WOODPECKER. (se Asia). . . . . . . _____

❑ *Dinopium shorii.* HIMALAYAN FLAMEBACK. (s Asia). . . . . _____

❑ *Dinopium javanense.* COMMON FLAMEBACK. (s,se Asia). . . . . _____

❑ *Dinopium benghalense.* BLACK-RUMPED FLAMEBACK. (s Asia). . . . . _____

❑ *Chrysocolaptes lucidus.* GREATER FLAMEBACK. (s Asia-Phil). . . . . . _____

❑ *Chrysocolaptes festivus.* WHITE-NAPED WOODPECKER. (pen India). . . _____

❑ *Gecinulus grantia.* PALE-HEADED WOODPECKER. (s,se Asia). . . . . . . _____

❑ *Gecinulus viridis.* BAMBOO WOODPECKER. (se Asia). . . . . _____

❑ *Sapheopipo noguchii.* OKINAWA WOODPECKER. (Okinawa). . . . . _____

❑ *Blythipicus rubiginosus.* MAROON WOODPECKER. (se Asia). . . . . . . _____

❑ *Blythipicus pyrrhotis.* BAY WOODPECKER. (mts s,se Asia). . . . . _____

❑ *Reinwardtipicus validus.* ORANGE-BACKED WOODPECKER. (se Asia) _____

❑ *Meiglyptes tristis.* BUFF-RUMPED WOODPECKER. (se Asia). . . . . _____

❑ *Meiglyptes jugularis.* BLACK-AND-BUFF WOODPECKER. (se Asia). . . . _____

❑ *Meiglyptes tukki.* BUFF-NECKED WOODPECKER. (se Asia). . . . . _____

❑ *Hemicircus concretus.* GREY-AND-BUFF WOODPECKER. (se Asia). . . . _____

❑ *Hemicircus canente.* HEART-SPOTTED WOODPECKER. (s,se Asia). . . . _____

❑ *Mulleripicus fulvus.* ASHY WOODPECKER. (Sulaw). . . . . _____

❑ *Mulleripicus funebris.* SOOTY WOODPECKER. (Phil). . . . . _____
 ___*M. (f.) funebris.* SOOTY WOODPECKER. (n Phil)
 ___*M. (f.) fuliginosus.* TWEEDDALE'S WOODPECKER. (se Phil)

❑ *Mulleripicus pulverulentus.* GREAT SLATY WOODPECKER. (s,se Asia) _____

Infraorder RAMPHASTIDES [19/123]
Superfamily MEGALAIMOIDEA [3/26]
Family **Megalaimidae** [3/26]

❑ *Psilopogon pyrolophus.* FIRE-TUFTED BARBET. (se Asia). . . . . _____

❑ *Megalaima virens.* GREAT BARBET. (mts s Asia). . . . . _____

❑ *Megalaima lagrandieri.* RED-VENTED BARBET. (Indoc). . . . . _____

❑ *Megalaima zeylanica.* BROWN-HEADED BARBET. (India). . . . . _____

❑ *Megalaima lineata.* LINEATED BARBET. (s,se Asia). . . . . _____

❑ *Megalaima viridis.* WHITE-CHEEKED BARBET. (sw India). . . . . _____

❑ *Megalaima faiostricta.* GREEN-EARED BARBET. (se Asia). . . . . _____

❑ *Megalaima corvina.* BROWN-THROATED BARBET. (Java). . . . . _____

❑ *Megalaima chrysopogon.* GOLD-WHISKERED BARBET. (se Asia). . . . . _____

❑ *Megalaima rafflesii.* RED-CROWNED BARBET. (se Asia). . . . . _____

❑ *Megalaima mystacophanos.* RED-THROATED BARBET. (se Asia). . . . . _____

❑ *Megalaima javensis.* BLACK-BANDED BARBET. (Java). . . . . _____

❑ *Megalaima flavifrons.* YELLOW-FRONTED BARBET. (Ceylon)....... _____

❑ *Megalaima franklinii.* GOLDEN-THROATED BARBET. (mts se Asia)... _____

❑ *Megalaima oorti.* BLACK-BROWED BARBET. (mts se Asia)......... _____
   ___*M. (o.) oorti.* BLACK-BROWED BARBET. (sp)
   ___*M. (o.) faber.* HAINAN BARBET. (Hainan)
   ___*M. (o.) nuchalis.* TAIWAN BARBET. (Taiwan)

❑ *Megalaima asiatica.* BLUE-THROATED BARBET. (s,se Asia)........ _____

❑ *Megalaima monticola.* MOUNTAIN BARBET. (mts n Borneo)....... _____

❑ *Megalaima incognita.* MOUSTACHED BARBET. (se Asia).......... _____

❑ *Megalaima henricii.* YELLOW-CROWNED BARBET. (se Asia)....... _____

❑ *Megalaima armillaris.* FLAME-FRONTED BARBET. (Java, Bali)...... _____

❑ *Megalaima pulcherrima.* GOLDEN-NAPED BARBET. (mts n Borneo) . _____

❑ *Megalaima australis.* BLUE-EARED BARBET. (s,se Asia).......... _____

❑ *Megalaima eximia.* BORNEAN BARBET. (mts Borneo)............ _____

❑ *Megalaima rubricapilla.* CRIMSON-FRONTED BARBET. (s India)..... _____
   ___*M. (r.) malabarica.* CRIMSON-THROATED BARBET. (sw India)
   ___*M. (r.) rubricapilla.* CRIMSON-FRONTED BARBET. (Ceylon)

❑ *Megalaima haemacephala.* COPPERSMITH BARBET. (s Asia-Phil).... _____

❑ *Calorhamphus fuliginosus.* BROWN BARBET. (se Asia).......... _____

Superfamily LYBIOIDEA [7/42]
Family **Lybiidae** [7/42]

❑ *Gymnobucco calvus.* NAKED-FACED BARBET. (w,wc Afr)......... _____

❑ *Gymnobucco peli.* BRISTLE-NOSED BARBET. (w Afr)............. _____

❑ *Gymnobucco sladeni.* SLADEN'S BARBET. (c Afr).............. _____

❑ *Gymnobucco bonapartei.* GREY-THROATED BARBET. (c Afr)....... _____

❑ *Stactolaema leucotis.* WHITE-EARED BARBET. (e,se Afr).......... _____

❑ *Stactolaema anchietae.* ANCHIETA'S BARBET. (wc Afr).......... _____

❑ *Stactolaema whytii.* WHYTE'S BARBET. (ec,se Afr)............. _____
   ___*S. (w.) whytii.* WHYTE'S BARBET. (ec Afr)
   ___*S. (w.) sowerbyi.* SOWERBY'S BARBET. (se Afr)

❑ *Stactolaema olivacea.* GREEN BARBET. (ce,s Afr)............. _____
   ___*S. (o.) olivacea.* GREEN BARBET. (ce Afr)
   ___*S. (o.) woodwardi.* WOODWARD'S BARBET. (c S Afr)

❑ *Pogoniulus scolopaceus.* SPECKLED TINKERBIRD. (w,c Afr)....... _____

❑ *Pogoniulus coryphaeus.* WESTERN TINKERBIRD. (mts c Afr)....... _____

❑ *Pogoniulus leucomystax.* MOUSTACHED TINKERBIRD. (mts e Afr)... _____

❑ *Pogoniulus simplex.* GREEN TINKERBIRD. (se Afr).............. _____

❑ *Pogoniulus atroflavus.* RED-RUMPED TINKERBIRD. (w,c Afr)...... _____

❑ *Pogoniulus subsulphureus..*YELLOW-THROATED TINKERBIRD. (w,c Afr)_____

❑ *Pogoniulus bilineatus.* YELLOW-RUMPED TINKERBIRD. (Afr)........ _____
   ___*P. (b.) leucolaima.* LEMON-RUMPED TINKERBIRD. (w,c Afr)
   ___*P. (b.) bilineatus.* GOLDEN-RUMPED TINKERBIRD. (e,se Afr)

❑ *Pogoniulus chrysoconus.* YELLOW-FRONTED TINKERBIRD. (Afr)..... _____

❑ *Pogoniulus pusillus.* RED-FRONTED TINKERBIRD. (ne,se Afr)...... _____

❑ *Buccanodon duchaillui.* YELLOW-SPOTTED BARBET. (w,c Afr)..... _____

❑ *Tricholaema hirsuta.* HAIRY-BREASTED BARBET. (w,c Afr)........ _____
   ___*T. (h.) hirsuta.* HAIRY-BREASTED BARBET. (w,nc Afr)
   ___*T. (h.) flavipunctata.* SPOT-HEADED BARBET. (wc Afr)

❑ *Tricholaema diademata.* RED-FRONTED BARBET. (ne Afr)........ _____

❑ *Tricholaema frontata.* MIOMBO BARBET. (sc Afr)............... _____

❑ *Tricholaema leucomelas.* PIED BARBET. (s Afr)................. _____

❑ *Tricholaema lacrymosa.* SPOT-FLANKED BARBET. (e Afr)........ _____

❑ *Tricholaema melanocephala.* BLACK-THROATED BARBET. (ne Afr) . _____
   ___*T. (m.) melanocephala.* BLACK-THROATED BARBET. (sp)
   ___*T. (m.) flavibuccalis.* YELLOW-CHEEKED BARBET. (nc Tanz)

❑ *Lybius undatus.* BANDED BARBET. (Eth).................... _____

❑ *Lybius vieilloti.* VIEILLOT'S BARBET. (nc Afr)............... _____

❑ *Lybius leucocephalus.* WHITE-HEADED BARBET. (c Afr).......... _____
   ___*L. (l.) leucocephalus.* WHITE-HEADED BARBET. (nc Afr)
   ___*L. (l.) senex.* WHITE BARBET. (nc Afr)
   ___*L. (l.) albicauda.* WHITE-TAILED BARBET. (sc Kenya)
   ___*L. (l.) leucogaster.* WHITE-BELLIED BARBET. (cw Ang)

❑ *Lybius chaplini.* CHAPLIN'S BARBET. (sc Zamb)............... _____

❑ *Lybius rubrifacies.* RED-FACED BARBET. (ec Afr)............... _____

❑ *Lybius guifsobalito.* BLACK-BILLED BARBET. (ne Afr)............ _____

❑ *Lybius torquatus.* BLACK-COLLARED BARBET. (c,s Afr).......... _____

❑ *Lybius melanopterus.* BROWN-BREASTED BARBET. (e Afr)........ _____

❑ *Lybius minor.* BLACK-BACKED BARBET. (c Afr)................ _____
   ___*L. (m.) minor.* BLACK-BACKED BARBET. (wc Afr)
   ___*L. (m.) macclounii.* MACCLOUNIE'S BARBET. (c Afr)

❑ *Lybius bidentatus.* DOUBLE-TOOTHED BARBET. (w,c Afr)......... _____

❑ *Lybius dubius.* BEARDED BARBET. (w,wc Afr)................. _____

❑ *Lybius rolleti.* BLACK-BREASTED BARBET. (nc Afr)............. _____

❑ *Trachyphonus purpuratus.* YELLOW-BILLED BARBET. (w,c Afr)..... _____

❑ *Trachyphonus vaillantii.* CRESTED BARBET. (sc,s Afr)........... _____

❑ *Trachyphonus margaritatus.* YELLOW-BREASTED BARBET. (nc Afr) . _____

❑ *Trachyphonus erythrocephalus.* RED-AND-YELLOW BARBET. (ne Afr) _____

❑ *Trachyphonus darnaudii.* D'ARNAUD'S BARBET. (ne Afr). . . . . _____

❑ *Trachyphonus usambiro.* USAMBIRO BARBET. (sw Kenya, nw Tanz). _____

Superfamily RAMPHASTOIDEA [9/55]
Family **Ramphastidae** [9/55]
Subfamily Capitoninae [3/14]

❑ *Capito aurovirens.* SCARLET-CROWNED BARBET. (w Amaz). . . . . _____

❑ *Capito maculicoronatus.* SPOT-CROWNED BARBET. (Pan, nw SA). . . . _____

❑ *Capito squamatus.* ORANGE-FRONTED BARBET. (nw SA). . . . . _____

❑ *Capito hypoleucus.* WHITE-MANTLED BARBET. (c Colom). . . . . _____

❑ *Capito dayi.* BLACK-GIRDLED BARBET. (sw Amaz). . . . . _____

❑ *Capito quinticolor.* FIVE-COLORED BARBET. (e Colom). . . . . _____

❑ *Capito niger.* BLACK-SPOTTED BARBET. (c SA). . . . . _____
   ___*C. (n.) niger.* BLACK-SPOTTED BARBET. (nc SA)
   ___*C. (n.) auratus.* GILDED BARBET. (Amaz)

❑ *Capito brunneipectus.* BROWN-CHESTED BARBET. (nc Braz). . . . . . . _____

❑ *Eubucco richardsoni.* LEMON-THROATED BARBET. (w Amaz). . . . . . . _____

❑ *Eubucco bourcierii.* RED-HEADED BARBET. (s CA, nw SA). . . . . _____

❑ *Eubucco tucinkae.* SCARLET-HOODED BARBET. (Andes e Peru). . . . . . _____

❑ *Eubucco versicolor.* VERSICOLORED BARBET. (Andes sw SA). . . . . . . _____

❑ *Semnornis frantzii.* PRONG-BILLED BARBET. (mts CR, w Pan). . . . . . _____

❑ *Semnornis ramphastinus.* TOUCAN BARBET. (Andes nw SA). . . . . . . _____

Subfamily Ramphastinae [6/41]

❑ *Aulacorhynchus prasinus.* EMERALD TOUCANET. (mts MA, w SA) . _____
   ___*A. (p.) prasinus.* EMERALD TOUCANET. (sp)
   ___*A. (p.) caeruleogularis.* BLUE-THROATED TOUCANET. (CR, Pan)

❑ *Aulacorhynchus sulcatus.* GROOVE-BILLED TOUCANET. (mts n SA) _____
   ___*A. (s.) calorhynchus.* YELLOW-BILLED TOUCANET. (nw SA)
   ___*A. (s.) sulcatus.* GROOVE-BILLED TOUCANET. (n Ven)

❑ *Aulacorhynchus derbianus.* CHESTNUT-TIPPED TOUCANET. (w SA) . _____

❑ *Aulacorhynchus haematopygus.* CRIMSON-RUMPED T. (nw SA). . . . . _____

❑ *Aulacorhynchus huallagae.* YELLOW-BROWED TOUCANET. (n Peru) _____

❑ *Aulacorhynchus coeruleicinctis.* BLUE-BANDED TOUCANET. (sw SA) _____

❑ *Pteroglossus inscriptus.* LETTERED ARACARI. (wc SA). . . . . _____

❑ *Pteroglossus viridis.* GREEN ARACARI. (n SA). . . . . _____

❑ *Pteroglossus bitorquatus.* RED-NECKED ARACARI. (c Amaz). . . . . . . _____

❑ *Pteroglossus azara.* IVORY-BILLED ARACARI. (w,n Amaz)......... _____
   ___*P. (a.) flavirostris.* IVORY-BILLED ARACARI. (n Amaz)
   ___*P. (a.) azara.* AZARA ARACARI. (w Amaz)

❑ *Pteroglossus mariae.* BROWN-MANDIBLED ARACARI. (Amaz)...... _____

❑ *Pteroglossus castanotis.* CHESTNUT-EARED ARACARI. (c SA)...... _____

❑ *Pteroglossus aracari.* BLACK-NECKED ARACARI. (e SA)........... _____

❑ *Pteroglossus torquatus.* COLLARED ARACARI. (MA, nw SA)....... _____

❑ *Pteroglossus frantzii.* FIERY-BILLED ARACARI. (CR, w Pan)....... _____

❑ *Pteroglossus sanguineus.* STRIPE-BILLED ARACARI. (e Pan, nw SA) . _____

❑ *Pteroglossus erythropygius.* PALE-MANDIBLED ARACARI. (e Ecua)... _____

❑ *Pteroglossus pluricinctus.* MANY-BANDED ARACARI. (w Amaz)..... _____

❑ *Pteroglossus beauharnaesii.* CURL-CRESTED ARACARI. (w Amaz)... _____

❑ *Baillonius bailloni.* SAFFRON TOUCANET. (e,se Braz)............ _____

❑ *Andigena laminirostris.* PLATE-BILLED MOUNTAIN-TOUCAN. (nw SA) _____

❑ *Andigena hypoglauca.* GREY-BREASTED MOUNTAIN-TOUCAN. (w SA)_____

❑ *Andigena cucullata.* HOODED MOUNTAIN-TOUCAN. (Andes wc SA) . _____

❑ *Andigena nigrirostris.* BLACK-BILLED MOUNTAIN-TOUCAN. (nw SA). _____

❑ *Selenidera spectabilis.* YELLOW-EARED TOUCANET. (s CA, Colom) . _____

❑ *Selenidera reinwardtii.* GOLDEN-COLLARED TOUCANET. (w Amaz) . _____
   ___*S. (r.) reinwardtii.* GOLDEN-COLLARED TOUCANET. (cw Amaz)
   ___*S. (r.) langsdorffii.* LANGSDORFF'S TOUCANET. (sp)

❑ *Selenidera nattereri.* TAWNY-TUFTED TOUCANET. (n Amaz)........ _____

❑ *Selenidera culik.* GUIANAN TOUCANET. (n Amaz)............... _____

❑ *Selenidera maculirostris.* SPOT-BILLED TOUCANET. (c,se SA)...... _____

❑ *Selenidera gouldii.* GOULD'S TOUCANET. (ne Bol, ne Braz)........ _____

❑ *Ramphastos sulfuratus.* KEEL-BILLED TOUCAN. (MA, nw SA)...... _____

❑ *Ramphastos brevis.* CHOCO TOUCAN. (nw SA)................. _____

❑ *Ramphastos citreolaemus.* CITRON-THROATED TOUCAN. (nw SA)... _____

❑ *Ramphastos culminatus.* YELLOW-RIDGED TOUCAN. (Amaz)...... _____

❑ *Ramphastos vitellinus.* CHANNEL-BILLED TOUCAN. (n,e SA)....... _____
   ___*R. (v.) vitellinus.* CHANNEL-BILLED TOUCAN. (n SA)
   ___*R. (v.) ariel.* ARIEL TOUCAN. (e,se Braz)

❑ *Ramphastos dicolorus.* RED-BREASTED TOUCAN. (se SA)......... _____

❑ *Ramphastos swainsonii.* CHESTNUT-MANDIBLED TOUCAN.(CA, nw SA)_____

❑ *Ramphastos ambiguus.* BLACK-MANDIBLED TOUCAN. (nw SA)..... _____

❑ *Ramphastos tucanus.* RED-BILLED TOUCAN. (Amaz)............. _____

❑ *Ramphastos cuvieri.* CUVIER'S TOUCAN. (n Amaz)............... _____

❏ *Ramphastos toco*. TOCO TOUCAN. (c,se SA)................. _____

Parvclass CORACIAE [67/309]
Superorder GALBULIMORPHAE [15/51]
Order **GABULIFORMES** [15/51]
Infraorder GALBULIDES [5/18]
Family **Galbulidae** [5/18]

❏ *Galbalcyrhynchus leucotis*. WHITE-EARED JACAMAR. (w Amaz)..... _____

❏ *Galbalcyrhynchus purusianus*. CHESTNUT JACAMAR. (sw,c Amaz) . _____

❏ *Brachygalba salmoni*. DUSKY-BACKED JACAMAR. (e Pan-nw Colom). _____

❏ *Brachygalba goeringi*. PALE-HEADED JACAMAR. (n SA).......... _____

❏ *Brachygalba lugubris*. BROWN JACAMAR. (Amaz)............... _____

❏ *Brachygalba albogularis*. WHITE-THROATED JACAMAR. (w Amaz)... _____

❏ *Jacamaralcyon tridactyla*. THREE-TOED JACAMAR. (se Braz)....... _____

❏ *Galbula albirostris*. YELLOW-BILLED JACAMAR. (n Amaz)......... _____

❏ *Galbula cyanicollis*. BLUE-NECKED JACAMAR. (c Amaz).......... _____

❏ *Galbula ruficauda*. RUFOUS-TAILED JACAMAR. (MA, SA)......... _____
___*G. (r.) melanogenia*. BLACK-CHINNED JACAMAR. (MA, w Colom)
___*G. (r.) ruficauda*. RUFOUS-TAILED JACAMAR. (e Pan, n SA)
___*G. (r.) rufoviridis*. RUFOUS-AND-GREEN JACAMAR. (se SA)

❏ *Galbula galbula*. GREEN-TAILED JACAMAR. (n Amaz)............ _____

❏ *Galbula pastazae*. COPPERY-CHESTED JACAMAR. (se Colom, e Ecua). _____

❏ *Galbula tombacea*. WHITE-CHINNED JACAMAR. (w Amaz)......... _____

❏ *Galbula cyanescens*. BLUISH-FRONTED JACAMAR. (w Amaz)....... _____

❏ *Galbula chalcothorax*. PURPLISH JACAMAR. (w Amaz)........... _____

❏ *Galbula leucogastra*. BRONZY JACAMAR. (w Amaz)............. _____

❏ *Galbula dea*. PARADISE JACAMAR. (Amaz).................... _____

❏ *Jacamerops aureus*. GREAT JACAMAR. (s CA, n,c SA)........... _____

Infraorder BUCCONIDES [10/33]
Family **Bucconidae** [10/33]

❏ *Notharchus macrorhynchos*. WHITE-NECKED PUFFBIRD. (MA, SA) . _____
___*N. (m.) macrorhynchos*. WHITE-NECKED PUFFBIRD. (MA, n,c SA)
___*N. (m.) swainsoni*. BUFF-BELLIED PUFFBIRD. (se SA)

❏ *Notharchus pectoralis*. BLACK-BREASTED PUFFBIRD. (Pan, nw SA) . _____

❏ *Notharchus ordii*. BROWN-BANDED PUFFBIRD. (wc Amaz)........ _____

❏ *Notharchus tectus*. PIED PUFFBIRD. (s CA, n,c SA)............. _____

❏ *Bucco macrodactylus*. CHESTNUT-CAPPED PUFFBIRD. (w Amaz)..... _____

❏ *Bucco tamatia*. SPOTTED PUFFBIRD. (Amaz).................... _____

❑ *Bucco noanamae.* SOOTY-CAPPED PUFFBIRD. (nw Colom)......... _____

❑ *Bucco capensis.* COLLARED PUFFBIRD. (Amaz)................ _____

❑ *Nystalus radiatus.* BARRED PUFFBIRD. (Pan, nw SA)............. _____

❑ *Nystalus chacuru.* WHITE-EARED PUFFBIRD. (c,sc SA)............ _____

❑ *Nystalus striolatus.* STRIOLATED PUFFBIRD. (w Amaz)............ _____

❑ *Nystalus maculatus.* SPOT-BACKED PUFFBIRD. (c,e SA)........... _____

❑ *Hypnelus ruficollis.* RUSSET-THROATED PUFFBIRD. (n,nc SA)....... _____
   ___*H. (r.) ruficollis.* RUSSET-THROATED PUFFBIRD. (n SA)
   ___*H. (r.) bicinctus.* TWO-BANDED PUFFBIRD. (n Amaz)

❑ *Malacoptila fusca.* WHITE-CHESTED PUFFBIRD. (w Amaz)......... _____

❑ *Malacoptila semicincta.* SEMICOLLARED PUFFBIRD. (sw Amaz)..... _____

❑ *Malacoptila striata.* CRESCENT-CHESTED PUFFBIRD. (e Braz)....... _____

❑ *Malacoptila fulvogularis.* BLACK-STREAKED PUFFBIRD. (w SA)..... _____

❑ *Malacoptila rufa.* RUFOUS-NECKED PUFFBIRD. (c Amaz).......... _____

❑ *Malacoptila panamensis.* WHITE-WHISKERED PUFFB. (MA-nw SA) . _____

❑ *Malacoptila mystacalis.* MOUSTACHED PUFFBIRD. (mts nw SA)..... _____

❑ *Micromonacha lanceolata.* LANCEOLATED MONKLET. (s CA-nw SA). _____

❑ *Nonnula rubecula.* RUSTY-BREASTED NUNLET. (c,se SA)......... _____

❑ *Nonnula sclateri.* FULVOUS-CHINNED NUNLET. (sw Amaz)........ _____

❑ *Nonnula brunnea.* BROWN NUNLET. (cw Amaz)............... _____

❑ *Nonnula frontalis.* GREY-CHEEKED NUNLET. (Pan, nw Colom)...... _____

❑ *Nonnula ruficapilla.* RUFOUS-CAPPED NUNLET. (Amaz).......... _____

❑ *Nonnula amaurocephala.* CHESTNUT-HEADED NUNLET. (w Amaz)... _____

❑ *Hapaloptila castanea.* WHITE-FACED NUNBIRD. (Andes nw SA)..... _____

❑ *Monasa atra.* BLACK NUNBIRD. (n Amaz)................... _____

❑ *Monasa nigrifrons.* BLACK-FRONTED NUNBIRD. (Amaz).......... _____

❑ *Monasa morphoeus.* WHITE-FRONTED NUNBIRD. (CA, SA)........ _____
   ___*M. (m.) grandior.* COSTA RICAN NUNBIRD. (Hond-w Pan)
   ___*M. (m.) pallescens.* PALE-WINGED NUNBIRD. (e Pan, Colom)
   ___*M. (m.) morphoeus.* WHITE-FRONTED NUNBIRD. (c,e SA)

❑ *Monasa flavirostris.* YELLOW-BILLED NUNBIRD. (w Amaz)........ _____

❑ *Chelidoptera tenebrosa.* SWALLOW-WING. (Amaz)............. _____

Superorder BUCEROTIMORPHAE [12/66]
Order **BUCEROTIFORMES** [9/56]
Family **Bucerotidae** [8/54]

❑ *Tockus albocristatus.* WHITE-CRESTED HORNBILL. (w,c Afr)........ _____

❑ *Tockus hartlaubi.* BLACK DWARF HORNBILL. (w,c Afr)........... _____

❑ *Tockus camurus.* RED-BILLED DWARF HORNBILL. (w,c Afr)....... _____

❑ *Tockus monteiri.* MONTEIRO'S HORNBILL. (sw Afr)............. _____

❑ *Tockus erythrorhynchus.* RED-BILLED HORNBILL. (Afr).......... _____

❑ *Tockus flavirostris.* EASTERN YELLOW-BILLED HORNBILL. (ne Afr)... _____

❑ *Tockus leucomelas.* SOUTHERN YELLOW-BILLED HORNBILL. (s Afr) . _____

❑ *Tockus jacksoni.* JACKSON'S HORNBILL. (ne Afr)............... _____

❑ *Tockus deckeni.* VON DER DECKEN'S HORNBILL. (e Afr).......... _____

❑ *Tockus alboterminatus.* CROWNED HORNBILL. (e,s Afr).......... _____

❑ *Tockus bradfieldi.* BRADFIELD'S HORNBILL. (sw Afr)............ _____

❑ *Tockus fasciatus.* AFRICAN PIED HORNBILL. (w,wc Afr).......... _____
　　___*T. (f.) semifasciatus.* ALLIED HORNBILL. (w Afr)
　　___*T. (f.) fasciatus.* AFRICAN PIED HORNBILL. (wc Afr)

❑ *Tockus hemprichii.* HEMPRICH'S HORNBILL. (mts ne Afr)......... _____

❑ *Tockus nasutus.* AFRICAN GREY HORNBILL. (Afr reg)............ _____

❑ *Tockus pallidirostris.* PALE-BILLED HORNBILL. (sc Afr).......... _____

❑ *Ocyceros griseus.* MALABAR GREY-HORNBILL. (sw India)......... _____

❑ *Ocyceros gingalensis.* CEYLON GREY-HORNBILL. (Ceylon)........ _____

❑ *Ocyceros birostris.* INDIAN GREY-HORNBILL. (s Asia)............ _____

❑ *Anthracoceros coronatus.* MALABAR PIED-HORNBILL. (s,se India)... _____

❑ *Anthracoceros albirostris.* ORIENTAL PIED-HORNBILL. (s,se Asia)... _____
　　___*A. (a.) albirostris.* NORTHERN PIED-HORNBILL. (s,se Asia)
　　___*A. (a.) convexus.* MALAYSIAN PIED-HORNBILL. (G Sunda)

❑ *Anthracoceros malayanus.* BLACK HORNBILL. (se Asia).......... _____

❑ *Anthracoceros marchei.* PALAWAN HORNBILL. (sw Phil)......... _____

❑ *Anthracoceros montani.* SULU HORNBILL. (Sulu)............... _____

❑ *Buceros rhinoceros.* RHINOCEROS HORNBILL. (se Asia).......... _____

❑ *Buceros bicornis.* GREAT HORNBILL. (s,se Asia)............... _____

❑ *Buceros hydrocorax.* RUFOUS HORNBILL. (Phil)............... _____

❑ *Buceros vigil.* HELMETED HORNBILL. (se Asia)............... _____

❑ *Anorrhinus tickelli.* BROWN HORNBILL. (s,se Asia)............ _____
　　___*A. (t.) austeni.* ASSAM HORNBILL. (ne India)
　　___*A. (t.) tickelli.* BROWN HORNBILL. (se Asia)

❑ *Anorrhinus galeritus.* BUSHY-CRESTED HORNBILL. (se Asia)....... _____

❑ *Penelopides manillae.* LUZON HORNBILL. (n Phil)............... _____

❑ *Penelopides mindorensis.* MINDORO HORNBILL. (wc Phil)......... _____

❑ *Penelopides panini.* TARICTIC HORNBILL. (c Phil)............... _____

❑ *Penelopides samarensis.* SAMAR HORNBILL. (ec Phil). . . . . _____

❑ *Penelopides affinis.* MINDANAO HORNBILL. (s Phil). . . . . _____

❑ *Penelopides exarhatus.* SULAWESI HORNBILL. (Sulaw). . . . . _____

❑ *Aceros comatus.* WHITE-CROWNED HORNBILL. (se Asia). . . . . _____

❑ *Aceros nipalensis.* RUFOUS-NECKED HORNBILL. (s Asia). . . . . _____

❑ *Aceros corrugatus.* WRINKLED HORNBILL. (se Asia). . . . . _____

❑ *Aceros waldeni.* WRITHED-BILLED HORNBILL. (c Phil). . . . . _____

❑ *Aceros leucocephalus.* WRITHED HORNBILL. (se Phil). . . . . _____

❑ *Aceros cassidix.* KNOBBED HORNBILL. (Sulaw). . . . . _____

❑ *Aceros undulatus.* WREATHED HORNBILL. (s,se Asia). . . . . _____

❑ *Aceros narcondami.* NARCONDAM HORNBILL. (And). . . . . _____

❑ *Aceros everetti.* SUMBA HORNBILL. (Sumba). . . . . _____

❑ *Aceros subruficollis.* PLAIN-POUCHED HORNBILL. (se Asia). . . . . _____

❑ *Aceros plicatus.* BLYTH'S HORNBILL. (Moluc-NG reg). . . . . _____

❑ *Ceratogymna bucinator.* TRUMPETER HORNBILL. (sc,se Afr). . . . . . . _____

❑ *Ceratogymna fistulator.* PIPING HORNBILL. (w,c Afr). . . . . _____

❑ *Ceratogymna brevis.* SILVERY-CHEEKED HORNBILL. (c Afr). . . . . _____

❑ *Ceratogymna subcylindricus.* BLACK-AND-WHITE-CASQUED H. (Afr) . _____

❑ *Ceratogymna cylindricus.* BROWN-CHEEKED HORNBILL. (w Afr). . . . _____

❑ *Ceratogymna albotibialis.* WHITE-THIGHED HORNBILL. (c Afr). . . . . _____

❑ *Ceratogymna atrata.* BLACK-CASQUED HORNBILL. (w,c Afr). . . . . . . _____

❑ *Ceratogymna elata.* YELLOW-CASQUED HORNBILL. (w Afr). . . . . _____

Family **Bucorvidae** [1/2]

❑ *Bucorvus abyssinicus.* ABYSSINIAN GROUND-HORNBILL. (subsah Afr) _____

❑ *Bucorvus leadbeateri.* SOUTHERN GROUND-HORNBILL. (s,e Afr). . . . . _____

Order **UPUPIFORMES** [3/10]
Infraorder UPUPIDES [1/2]
Family **Upupidae** [1/2]

❑ *Upupa epops.* EURASIAN HOOPOE. (Eura-c Afr; ◊-s Asia). . . . . _____

❑ *Upupa africana.* AFRICAN HOOPOE. (sc,s Afr, Mad). . . . . _____
    ___*U. (a.) africana.* AFRICAN HOOPOE. (sc,s Afr)
    ___*U. (a.) marginata.* MADAGASCAR HOOPOE. (Mad)

Infraorder PHOENICULIDES [2/8]
Family **Phoeniculidae** [1/5]

❑ *Phoeniculus purpureus.* GREEN WOODHOOPOE. (Afr). . . . . _____

❑ *Phoeniculus damarensis.* VIOLET WOODHOOPOE. (sw,ne Afr)...... _____
   ___*P. (d.) damarensis.* VIOLET WOODHOOPOE. (sw Afr)
   ___*P. (d.) granti.* GRANT'S WOODHOOPOE. (ne Afr)

❑ *Phoeniculus somaliensis.* BLACK-BILLED WOODHOOPOE. (ne Afr)... _____

❑ *Phoeniculus bollei.* WHITE-HEADED WOODHOOPOE. (w,c,ec Afr).... _____

❑ *Phoeniculus castaneiceps.* FOREST WOODHOOPOE. (w,c Afr)....... _____

Family **Rhinopomastidae** [1/3]

❑ *Rhinopomastus aterrimus.* BLACK SCIMITAR-BILL. (w,c Afr)....... _____

❑ *Rhinopomastus cyanomelas.* COMMON SCIMITAR-BILL. (s,e Afr).... _____

❑ *Rhinopomastus minor.* ABYSSINIAN SCIMITAR-BILL. (ne Afr)....... _____

Superorder CORACIIMORPHAE [40/192]
Order **TROGONIFORMES** [6/39]
Family **Trogonidae** [6/39]
Subfamily Apalodermatinae [1/3]

❑ *Apaloderma narina.* NARINA TROGON. (Afr)................... _____

❑ *Apaloderma aequatoriale.* BARE-CHEEKED TROGON. (wc Afr)...... _____

❑ *Apaloderma vittatum.* BAR-TAILED TROGON. (mts c,ce Afr)....... _____

Subfamily Trogoninae [5/36]
Tribe Trogonini [4/25]

❑ *Pharomachrus mocinno.* RESPLENDENT QUETZAL. (mts MA)....... _____

❑ *Pharomachrus antisianus.* CRESTED QUETZAL. (mts w SA)........ _____

❑ *Pharomachrus fulgidus.* WHITE-TIPPED QUETZAL. (mts nw SA)..... _____

❑ *Pharomachrus auriceps.* GOLDEN-HEADED QUETZAL. (Pan, w SA) . _____

❑ *Pharomachrus pavoninus.* PAVONINE QUETZAL. (Amaz)......... _____

❑ *Euptilotis neoxenus.* EARED TROGON. (mts s Ariz, n,c Mex)....... _____

❑ *Priotelus temnurus.* CUBAN TROGON. (mts Cuba)............... _____

❑ *Priotelus roseigaster.* HISPANIOLAN TROGON. (Hisp)............. _____

❑ *Trogon massena.* SLATY-TAILED TROGON. (MA, nw SA).......... _____
   ___*T. (m.) massena.* SLATY-TAILED TROGON. (MA)
   ___*T. (m.) australis.* CHAPMAN'S TROGON. (nw SA)

❑ *Trogon melanurus.* BLACK-TAILED TROGON. (Pan, w,c SA)........ _____
   ___*T. (m.) macroura.* LARGE-TAILED TROGON. (Pan, nw SA)
   ___*T. (m.) melanurus.* BLACK-TAILED TROGON. (cw,wc SA)

❑ *Trogon clathratus.* LATTICE-TAILED TROGON. (CR, w Pan)........ _____

❑ *Trogon comptus.* WHITE-EYED TROGON. (nw SA).............. _____

❑ *Trogon bairdii.* BAIRD'S TROGON. (sw CR, w Pan).............. _____

❑ *Trogon viridis.* White-tailed Trogon. (Pan, SA). . . . . _____

❑ *Trogon citreolus.* Citreoline Trogon. (w Mex). . . . . _____

❑ *Trogon melanocephalus.* Black-headed Trogon. (MA). . . . . _____

❑ *Trogon mexicanus.* Mountain Trogon. (mts n MA). . . . . _____

❑ *Trogon elegans.* Elegant Trogon. (sw US, MA). . . . . _____
  ___*T. (e.) ambiguus.* Coppery-tailed Trogon. (sw US, n,c Mex)
  ___*T. (e.) elegans.* Elegant Trogon. (s Mex, CA)

❑ *Trogon collaris.* Collared Trogon. (MA, SA). . . . . _____
  ___*T. (c.) puella.* Jalapa Trogon. (MA)
  ___*T. (c.) collaris.* Collared Trogon. (Pan, SA)

❑ *Trogon aurantiiventris.* Orange-bellied Trogon. (CR, w Pan). . . . _____

❑ *Trogon personatus.* Masked Trogon. (mts SA). . . . . _____
  ___*T. (p.) personatus.* Masked Trogon. (sp)
  ___*T. (p.) temperatus.* Highland Trogon. (Andes nw SA)

❑ *Trogon rufus.* Black-throated Trogon. (CA, SA). . . . . _____

❑ *Trogon surrucura.* Surucua Trogon. (e,se SA). . . . . _____
  ___*T. (s.) surrucura.* Surucua Trogon. (se SA)
  ___*T. (s.) aurantius.* Brazilian Trogon. (e Braz)

❑ *Trogon curucui.* Blue-crowned Trogon. (c SA). . . . . _____

❑ *Trogon violaceus.* Violaceous Trogon. (MA, SA). . . . . _____
  ___*T. (v.) caligatus.* Gartered Trogon. (MA, nw SA)
  ___*T. (v.) violaceus.* Violaceous Trogon. (nc SA)
  ___*T. (v.) ramonianus.* Amazonian Trogon. (Amaz)

Tribe Harpactini [1/11]

❑ *Harpactes reinwardtii.* Blue-tailed Trogon. (Sum, Java). . . . . _____

❑ *Harpactes fasciatus.* Malabar Trogon. (s India). . . . . _____

❑ *Harpactes kasumba.* Red-naped Trogon. (se Asia). . . . . _____

❑ *Harpactes diardii.* Diard's Trogon. (se Asia). . . . . _____

❑ *Harpactes ardens.* Philippine Trogon. (Phil). . . . . _____

❑ *Harpactes whiteheadi.* Whitehead's Trogon. (mts n Born). . . . . . . _____

❑ *Harpactes orrhophaeus.* Cinnamon-rumped Trogon. (se Asia). . . . _____

❑ *Harpactes duvaucelii.* Scarlet-rumped Trogon. (se Asia). . . . . _____

❑ *Harpactes oreskios.* Orange-breasted Trogon. (se Asia). . . . . _____

❑ *Harpactes erythrocephalus.* Red-headed Trogon. (mts s,se Asia) . _____

❑ *Harpactes wardi.* Ward's Trogon. (mts se Asia). . . . . _____

Order **CORACIIFORMES** [34/153]
Suborder CORACII [6/18]
Superfamily CORACIOIDEA [5/17]
Family **Coraciidae** [2/12]

❏ *Coracias garrulus.* EUROPEAN ROLLER. (Palea; ◊-s Afr)........... _____

❏ *Coracias abyssinica.* ABYSSINIAN ROLLER. (nc Afr reg).......... _____

❏ *Coracias caudata.* LILAC-BREASTED ROLLER. (e,s Afr)........... _____
   ___*C. (c.) lorti.* BLUE-BREASTED ROLLER. (ne Afr)
   ___*C. (c.) caudata.* LILAC-BREASTED ROLLER. (s,ce Afr)

❏ *Coracias spatulata.* RACKET-TAILED ROLLER. (s Afr)............ _____
   ___*C. (s.) spatulata.* RACKET-TAILED ROLLER. (sc,s Afr)
   ___*C. (s.) weigalli.* WEIGALL'S ROLLER. (se Afr)

❏ *Coracias noevia.* RUFOUS-CROWNED ROLLER. (Afr)............. _____

❏ *Coracias benghalensis.* INDIAN ROLLER. (s,se Asia)............. _____
   ___*C. (b.) benghalensis.* NORTHERN ROLLER. (s Asia)
   ___*C. (b.) indica.* SOUTHERN ROLLER. (pen India)
   ___*C. (b.) affinis.* BURMESE ROLLER. (se Asia)

❏ *Coracias temminckii.* PURPLE-WINGED ROLLER. (Sulaw).......... _____

❏ *Coracias cyanogaster.* BLUE-BELLIED ROLLER. (subsah Afr)........ _____

❏ *Eurystomus glaucurus.* BROAD-BILLED ROLLER. (Afr, Mad)........ _____

❏ *Eurystomus gularis.* BLUE-THROATED ROLLER. (w,c Afr).......... _____

❏ *Eurystomus orientalis.* DOLLARBIRD. (s,e Asia-Aust, NG)........ _____

❏ *Eurystomus azureus.* PURPLE ROLLER. (Moluc)................ _____

Family **Brachypteraciidae** [3/5]

❏ *Brachypteracias leptosomus.* SHORT-LEGGED GROUND-R. (Mad).... _____

❏ *Brachypteracias squamigera.* SCALY GROUND-ROLLER. (ne,ce Mad). _____

❏ *Atelornis pittoides.* PITTA-LIKE GROUND-ROLLER. (nw,e Mad)...... _____

❏ *Atelornis crossleyi.* RUFOUS-HEADED GROUND-ROLLER. (e Mad).... _____

❏ *Uratelornis chimaera.* LONG-TAILED GROUND-ROLLER. (sw Mad)... _____

Superfamily LEPTOSOMOIDEA [1/1]
Family **Leptosomidae** [1/1]

❏ *Leptosomus discolor.* CUCKOO ROLLER. (Mad, Com)............. _____

Suborder ALCEDINI [28/135]
Infraorder ALCEDINIDES [25/109]
Parvorder MOMOTIDA [6/9]
Family **Momotidae** [6/9]

❏ *Hylomanes momotula.* TODY MOTMOT. (MA, nw Colom)........ _____

❏ *Aspatha gularis.* BLUE-THROATED MOTMOT. (mts c MA)......... _____

❏ *Electron platyrhynchum.* BROAD-BILLED MOTMOT. (CA, nw,c SA) . _____
   ___*E. (p.) platyrhynchum.* BROAD-BILLED MOTMOT. (CA, nw SA)
   ___*E. (p.) pyrrholaemum.* PLAIN-TAILED MOTMOT. (Amaz)

❑ *Electron carinatum.* KEEL-BILLED MOTMOT. (c MA). . . . . _____

❑ *Eumomota superciliosa.* TURQUOISE-BROWED MOTMOT. (c MA). . . . _____

❑ *Baryphthengus martii.* RUFOUS MOTMOT. (CA, w,wc SA). . . . . _____

❑ *Baryphthengus ruficapillus.* RUFOUS-CAPPED MOTMOT. (se SA). . . . _____

❑ *Momotus mexicanus.* RUSSET-CROWNED MOTMOT. (Mex, Guat). . . . _____

❑ *Momotus momota.* BLUE-CROWNED MOTMOT. (MA, SA). . . . . _____
     ___*M. (m.) coeruliceps.* BLUE-CROWNED MOTMOT. (ne Mex)
     ___*M. (m.) lessonii.* LESSON'S MOTMOT. (s Mex, CA)
     ___*M. (m.) subrufescens.* TAWNY-BELLIED MOTMOT. (e Pan, nw SA)
     ___*M. (m.) momota.* BLUE-DIADEMED MOTMOT. (SA)
     ___*M. (m.) aequatorialis.* HIGHLAND MOTMOT. (w SA)

Parvorder TODIDA [1/5]
Family **Todidae** [1/5]

❑ *Todus multicolor.* CUBAN TODY. (Cuba). _____

❑ *Todus angustirostris.* NARROW-BILLED TODY. (Hisp). . . . . _____

❑ *Todus mexicanus.* PUERTO RICAN TODY. (PR). . . . . _____

❑ *Todus todus.* JAMAICAN TODY. (Jam). . . . . _____

❑ *Todus subulatus.* BROAD-BILLED TODY. (Hisp). . . . . _____

Parvorder ALCEDINIDA [3/25]
Family **Alcedinidae** [3/25]

❑ *Alcedo hercules.* BLYTH'S KINGFISHER. (s Asia). . . . . _____

❑ *Alcedo atthis.* COMMON KINGFISHER. (Palea-Indon, NG reg). . . . . . . _____

❑ *Alcedo semitorquata.* HALF-COLLARED KINGFISHER. (ne,sc,s Afr). . . . _____

❑ *Alcedo quadribrachys.* SHINING-BLUE KINGFISHER. (w,c Afr). . . . . . . _____

❑ *Alcedo meninting.* BLUE-EARED KINGFISHER. (s Asia-Phil). . . . . _____

❑ *Alcedo azurea.* AZURE KINGFISHER. (Moluc, Aust, NG reg). . . . . _____

❑ *Alcedo websteri.* BISMARCK KINGFISHER. (Bism). . . . . _____

❑ *Alcedo euryzona.* BLUE-BANDED KINGFISHER. (se Asia). . . . . _____

❑ *Alcedo cyanopecta.* INDIGO-BANDED KINGFISHER. (Phil). . . . . _____

❑ *Alcedo argentata.* SILVERY KINGFISHER. (se,s Phil). . . . . _____

❑ *Alcedo cristata.* MALACHITE KINGFISHER. (Afr). . . . . _____

❑ *Alcedo vintsioides.* MADAGASCAR KINGFISHER. (Mad, Com). . . . . . . _____

❑ *Alcedo thomensis.* SAO TOME KINGFISHER. (ST). . . . . _____

❑ *Alcedo nais.* PRINCIPE KINGFISHER. (Prín). . . . . _____

❑ *Alcedo leucogaster.* WHITE-BELLIED KINGFISHER. (w,c Afr). . . . . . . _____

❑ *Alcedo coerulescens.* SMALL BLUE KINGFISHER. (w Indon). . . . . _____

❑ *Alcedo pusilla.* LITTLE KINGFISHER. (Moluc-Aust, NG reg)......... _____

❑ *Ceyx lepidus.* VARIABLE KINGFISHER. (Phil, Moluc-NG reg)........ _____

❑ *Ceyx erithacus.* BLACK-BACKED KINGFISHER. (s Asia-Phil)......... _____

❑ *Ceyx rufidorsa.* RUFOUS-BACKED KINGFISHER. (se Asia, Phil)....... _____

❑ *Ceyx melanurus.* PHILIPPINE KINGFISHER. (Phil)................ _____

❑ *Ceyx fallax.* SULAWESI KINGFISHER. (Sulaw).................. _____

❑ *Ispidina madagascariensis.* MADAGASCAR PYGMY-KINGFISHER. (Mad)_____

❑ *Ispidina picta.* AFRICAN PYGMY-KINGFISHER. (Afr).............. _____

❑ *Ispidina lecontei.* DWARF KINGFISHER. (w,c Afr).............. _____

Parvorder CERYLIDA [15/70]
Superfamily HALCYONOIDEA [12/61]
Family **Halcyonidae** [12/61]

❑ *Lacedo pulchella.* BANDED KINGFISHER. (se Asia)............... _____

❑ *Dacelo novaeguineae.* LAUGHING KOOKABURRA. (e,se Aust)....... _____

❑ *Dacelo leachii.* BLUE-WINGED KOOKABURRA. (n,e Aust, s NG)..... _____

❑ *Dacelo tyro.* SPANGLED KOOKABURRA. (Aru, NG).............. _____

❑ *Dacelo gaudichaud.* RUFOUS-BELLIED KOOKABURRA. (NG reg)..... _____

❑ *Clytoceyx rex.* SHOVEL-BILLED KOOKABURRA. (NG)............. _____

❑ *Cittura cyanotis.* LILAC-CHEEKED KINGFISHER. (Sulaw).......... _____

❑ *Pelargopsis amauropterus.* BROWN-WINGED KINGFISHER. (s,se Asia). _____

❑ *Pelargopsis capensis.* STORK-BILLED KINGFISHER. (s Asia-Phil)..... _____

❑ *Pelargopsis melanorhyncha.* BLACK-BILLED KINGFISHER. (Sulaw)... _____

❑ *Halcyon coromanda.* RUDDY KINGFISHER. (e,s Asia-Phil)......... _____

❑ *Halcyon badia.* CHOCOLATE-BACKED KINGFISHER. (w,c Afr)....... _____

❑ *Halcyon smyrnensis.* WHITE-THROATED KINGFISHER. (s Asia-Phil) . _____

❑ *Halcyon pileata.* BLACK-CAPPED KINGFISHER. (s,se Asia; ◊-Phil).... _____

❑ *Halcyon cyanoventris.* JAVAN KINGFISHER. (Java, Bali).......... _____

❑ *Halcyon leucocephala.* GREY-HEADED KINGFISHER. (Afr reg)....... _____

❑ *Halcyon senegalensis.* WOODLAND KINGFISHER. (Afr)........... _____
　　___*H. (s.) senegalensis.* WOODLAND KINGFISHER. (w,c Afr)
　　___*H. (s.) cyanoleuca.* ANGOLA KINGFISHER. (sc,s Afr)

❑ *Halcyon senegaloides.* MANGROVE KINGFISHER. (e,se Afr)........ _____

❑ *Halcyon malimbica.* BLUE-BREASTED KINGFISHER. (w,c Afr)....... _____

❑ *Halcyon albiventris.* BROWN-HOODED KINGFISHER. (c,s Afr)....... _____

❑ *Halcyon chelicuti.* STRIPED KINGFISHER. (Afr)................ _____

❑ *Todirhamphus nigrocyaneus.* BLUE-BLACK KINGFISHER. (NG reg)... _____

❑ *Todirhamphus winchelli.* RUFOUS-LORED KINGFISHER. (c,s Phil).... _____

❑ *Todirhamphus diops.* BLUE-AND-WHITE KINGFISHER. (n Moluc)..... _____

❑ *Todirhamphus lazuli.* LAZULI KINGFISHER. (s Moluc)............ _____

❑ *Todirhamphus macleayii.* FOREST KINGFISHER. (Aust-NG reg)..... _____

❑ *Todirhamphus albonotatus.* NEW BRITAIN KINGFISHER. (s Bism).... _____

❑ *Todirhamphus leucopygius.* ULTRAMARINE KINGFISHER. (Solom)... _____

❑ *Todirhamphus farquhari.* CHESTNUT-BELLIED KINGFISHER. (Vanu). _____

❑ *Todirhamphus pyrrhopygia.* RED-BACKED KINGFISHER. (Aust)...... _____

❑ *Todirhamphus recurvirostris.* FLAT-BILLED KINGFISHER. (Samoa)... _____

❑ *Todirhamphus cinnamominus.* MICRONESIAN KINGFISHER. (w Pac) _____
   ___*T. (c.) miyakoensis.* RYUKYU KINGFISHER. (Ryu)
   ___*T. (c.) cinnamominus.* GUAM KINGFISHER. (Guam)
   ___*T. (c.) reaichenbachll.* CAROLINE ISLANDS KINGFISHER. (Carol)

❑ *Todirhamphus funebris.* SOMBRE KINGFISHER. (n Moluc)......... _____

❑ *Todirhamphus chloris.* COLLARED KINGFISHER. (ne Afr-Aust, s Pac) _____

❑ *Todirhamphus enlgma.* TALAUD KINGFISHER. (Talaud).......... _____

❑ *Todirhamphus saurophaga.* BEACH KINGFISHER. (NG reg),....... _____

❑ *Todirhamphus australasia.* CINNAMON-BANDED KINGFISHER. (Wall) _____

❑ *Todirhamphus sanctus.* SACRED KINGFISHER. (Aust reg-s Pac)...... _____

❑ *Todirhamphus veneratus.* TAHITI KINGFISHER. (e Soc)........... _____

❑ *Todirhamphus ruficollaris.* MANGAIA KINGFISHER. (s Cook)....... _____

❑ *Todirhamphus tuta.* CHATTERING KINGFISHER. (sc Polyn)......... _____

❑ *Todirhamphus godeffroyi.* MARQUESAN KINGFISHER. (s Marq)..... _____

❑ *Todirhamphus gambieri.* TUAMOTU KINGFISHER. (nw Tuam)...... _____

❑ *Caridonax fulgidus.* WHITE-RUMPED KINGFISHER. (L Sunda)....... _____

❑ *Melidora macrorrhina.* HOOK-BILLED KINGFISHER. (NG reg)....... _____

❑ *Actenoides bougainvillei.* MOUSTACHED KINGFISHER. (Sol)....... _____

❑ *Actenoides concretus.* RUFOUS-COLLARED KINGFISHER. (se Asia).... _____

❑ *Actenoides lindsayi.* SPOTTED KINGFISHER. (n,c Phil)............ _____

❑ *Actenoides hombroni.* BLUE-CAPPED KINGFISHER. (s Phil)........ _____

❑ *Actenoides monachus.* GREEN-BACKED KINGFISHER. (Sulaw)...... _____

❑ *Actenoides princeps.* SCALY KINGFISHER. (mts Sulaw)........... _____

❑ *Syma torotoro.* YELLOW-BILLED KINGFISHER. (Aust, NG reg)...... _____

❑ *Syma megarhyncha.* MOUNTAIN KINGFISHER. (mts NG).......... _____

❑ *Tanysiptera hydrocharis.* LITTLE PARADISE-KINGFISHER. (Aru, NG) _____

❏ *Tanysiptera galatea.* COMMON PARADISE-KINGFISHER. (Moluc-NG) _____

❏ *Tanysiptera ellioti.* KOFIAU PARADISE-KINGFISHER. (w Pap)........ _____

❏ *Tanysiptera riedelii.* BIAK PARADISE-KINGFISHER. (w NG)......... _____

❏ *Tanysiptera carolinae.* NUMFOR PARADISE-KINGFISHER. (w NG).... _____

❏ *Tanysiptera nympha.* RED-BREASTED PARADISE-KINGFISHER. (NG) . _____

❏ *Tanysiptera danae.* BROWN-HEADED PARADISE-KINGFISHER. (se NG) _____

❏ *Tanysiptera sylvia.* BUFF-BREASTED PARADISE-KINGFISHER. (Aust reg) _____
    ___*T. (s.) sylvia.* BUFF-BREASTED PARADISE-KINGFISHER. (ne Aust)
    ___*T. (s.) nigriceps.* BLACK-HEADED PARADISE-KINGFISHER. (NG reg)

Superfamily CERYLOIDEA [3/9]
Family **Cerylidae** [3/9]

❏ *Megaceryle maxima.* GIANT KINGFISHER. (Afr)................ _____

❏ *Megaceryle lugubris.* CRESTED KINGFISHER. (s,e Asia)........... _____

❏ *Megaceryle alcyon.* BELTED KINGFISHER. (NA; ◊-n SA).......... _____

❏ *Megaceryle torquata.* RINGED KINGFISHER. (s Tex-SA)........... _____

❏ *Ceryle rudis.* PIED KINGFISHER. (Afr)......................... _____

❏ *Chloroceryle amazona.* AMAZON KINGFISHER. (MA, SA)......... _____

❏ *Chloroceryle americana.* GREEN KINGFISHER. (c Tex-SA)........ _____

❏ *Chloroceryle inda.* GREEN-AND-RUFOUS KINGFISHER. (CA, SA)..... _____

❏ *Chloroceryle aenea.* AMERICAN PYGMY KINGFISHER. (CA, SA)..... _____

Infraorder MEROPIDES [3/26]
Family **Meropidae** [3/26]

❏ *Nyctyornis amictus.* RED-BEARDED BEE-EATER. (se Asia)......... _____

❏ *Nyctyornis athertoni.* BLUE-BEARDED BEE-EATER. (s,se Asia)....... _____

❏ *Meropogon forsteni.* PURPLE-BEARDED BEE-EATER. (Sulaw)........ _____

❏ *Merops gularis.* BLACK BEE-EATER. (w,c Afr)................. _____

❏ *Merops muelleri.* BLUE-HEADED BEE-EATER. (w,c Afr)........... _____

❏ *Merops bulocki.* RED-THROATED BEE-EATER. (subsah Afr)........ _____

❏ *Merops bullockoides.* WHITE-FRONTED BEE-EATER. (c,s Afr)....... _____

❏ *Merops pusillus.* LITTLE BEE-EATER. (Afr).................... _____

❏ *Merops variegatus.* BLUE-BREASTED BEE-EATER. (ne,c Afr)........ _____
    ___*M. (v.) lafresnayii.* ETHIOPIAN BEE-EATER. (mts ne Afr)
    ___*M. (v.) variegatus.* BLUE-BREASTED BEE-EATER. (c Afr)

❏ *Merops oreobates.* CINNAMON-CHESTED BEE-EATER. (mts e Afr).... _____

❏ *Merops hirundineus.* SWALLOW-TAILED BEE-EATER. (Afr)........ _____

❑ *Merops breweri.* BLACK-HEADED BEE-EATER. (wc Afr)............ _____

❑ *Merops revoilii.* SOMALI BEE-EATER. (ne Afr)................. _____

❑ *Merops albicollis.* WHITE-THROATED BEE-EATER. (n,c Afr reg)...... _____

❑ *Merops orientalis.* LITTLE GREEN BEE-EATER. (subsah Afr-s,se Asia). _____

❑ *Merops boehmi.* BOEHM'S BEE-EATER. (se Afr)................. _____

❑ *Merops viridis.* BLUE-THROATED BEE-EATER. (se Asia-Phil)....... _____

❑ *Merops persicus.* BLUE-CHEEKED BEE-EATER. (n Afr, s Asia; ◊-s Afr) _____

❑ *Merops superciliosus.* MADAGASCAR BEE-EATER. (s,e Afr, Mad).... _____

❑ *Merops philippinus.* BLUE-TAILED BEE-EATER. (s Asia-Phil, NG reg) _____

❑ *Merops ornatus.* RAINBOW BEE-EATER. (Aust, NG; ◊-Wall)....... _____

❑ *Merops apiaster.* EUROPEAN BEE-EATER. (s Palea, S Afr; ◊ Afr, India) _____

❑ *Merops leschenaulti.* CHESTNUT-HEADED BEE-EATER. (s,se Asia).... _____

❑ *Merops malimbicus.* ROSY BEE-EATER. (w,c Afr)............... _____

❑ *Merops nubicus.* NORTHERN CARMINE BEE-EATER. (subsah Afr).... _____

❑ *Merops nubicoides.* SOUTHERN CARMINE BEE-EATER. (c,s Afr)...... _____

Parvclass COLIAE [2/6]
Order **COLIIFORMES** [2/6]
Family **Coliidae** [2/6]
Subfamily Coliinae [1/4]

❑ *Colius striatus.* SPECKLED MOUSEBIRD. (c,s Afr)............... _____

❑ *Colius leucocephalus.* WHITE-HEADED MOUSEBIRD. (e Afr)....... _____

❑ *Colius castanotus.* RED-BACKED MOUSEBIRD. (wc Afr).......... _____

❑ *Colius colius.* WHITE-BACKED MOUSEBIRD. (s Afr).............. _____

Subfamily Urocoliinae [1/2]

❑ *Urocolius macrourus.* BLUE-NAPED MOUSEBIRD. (subsah Afr)...... _____

❑ *Urocolius indicus.* RED-FACED MOUSEBIRD. (s Afr)............. _____

Parvclass PASSERAE [1805/8514]
Superorder CUCULIMORPHAE [30/143]
Order **CUCULIFORMES** [30/143]
Infraorder CUCULIDES [22/127]
Parvorder CUCULIDA [18/109]
Superfamily CUCULOIDEA [17/79]
Family **Cuculidae** [17/79]

❑ *Oxylophus jacobinus.* PIED CUCKOO. (Afr, s Asia).............. _____
　　___*O. (j.) pica.* BLACK-AND-WHITE CUCKOO. (Afr)
　　___*O. (j.) jacobinus.* PIED CUCKOO. (s Asia; ◊-e Afr)

❑ *Oxylophus levaillantii.* LEVAILLANT'S CUCKOO. (Afr)........... . _____

❑ *Clamator coromandus.* CHESTNUT-WINGED CUCKOO. (s,se Asia).... _____

❑ *Clamator glandarius.* GREAT SPOTTED CUCKOO. (sw Palea, Afr).... _____

❑ *Pachycoccyx audeberti.* THICK-BILLED CUCKOO. (Afr)........... _____

❑ *Cuculus crassirostris.* SULAWESI HAWK-CUCKOO. (Sulaw)........ _____

❑ *Cuculus sparverioides.* LARGE HAWK-CUCKOO. (mts s,se Asia)..... _____

❑ *Cuculus varius.* COMMON HAWK-CUCKOO. (s Asia)............. _____

❑ *Cuculus vagans.* MOUSTACHED HAWK-CUCKOO. (se Asia)........ _____

❑ *Cuculus fugax.* HODGSON'S HAWK-CUCKOO. (e,se Asia-Phil)...... _____
   ___*C. (f.) hyperythrus.* NORTHERN HAWK-CUCKOO. (e Asia; ◊-s Asia)
   ___*C. (f.) fugax.* HODGSON'S HAWK-CUCKOO. (s,se Asia)
   ___*C. (f.) pectoralis.* PHILIPPINE HAWK-CUCKOO. (Phil)

❑ *Cuculus solitarius.* RED-CHESTED CUCKOO. (Afr).............. _____

❑ *Cuculus clamosus.* BLACK CUCKOO. (Afr).................... _____

❑ *Cuculus micropterus.* INDIAN CUCKOO. (s,se Asia; ◊-Phil)........ _____

❑ *Cuculus canorus.* COMMON CUCKOO. (Palea; ◊-Afr, Phil)......... _____

❑ *Cuculus gularis.* AFRICAN CUCKOO. (Afr)..................... _____

❑ *Cuculus saturatus.* ORIENTAL CUCKOO. (e,se Eura; ◊-Aust reg).... _____
   ___*C. (s.) saturatus.* ORIENTAL CUCKOO. (e Eura; ◊-Aust reg)
   ___*C. (s.) lepidus.* SUNDA CUCKOO. (se Asia)

❑ *Cuculus poliocephalus.* LESSER CUCKOO. (s,e Asia)............. _____

❑ *Cuculus rochii.* MADAGASCAR CUCKOO. (Mad; ◊-s,e Afr)......... _____

❑ *Cuculus pallidus.* PALLID CUCKOO. (Aust; ◊-L Sunda, NG)........ _____

❑ *Cercococcyx mechowi.* DUSKY LONG-TAILED CUCKOO. (w,c Afr).... _____

❑ *Cercococcyx olivinus.* OLIVE LONG-TAILED CUCKOO. (w,c Afr)..... _____

❑ *Cercococcyx montanus.* BARRED LONG-TAILED C. (mts e Afr)...... _____

❑ *Cacomantis sonneratii.* BANDED BAY CUCKOO. (s Asia-sw Phil).... _____

❑ *Cacomantis passerinus.* GREY-BELLIED CUCKOO. (s Asia)......... _____

❑ *Cacomantis merulinus.* PLAINTIVE CUCKOO. (s Asia-Phil)........ _____

❑ *Cacomantis sepulcralis.* RUSTY-BREASTED CUCKOO. (se Asia-Phil) . _____

❑ *Cacomantis variolosus.* BRUSH CUCKOO. (e Indon-n,e Aust, NG reg) _____

❑ *Cacomantis castaneiventris.* CHESTNUT-BREASTED CUCKOO. (Aust reg)_____

❑ *Cacomantis heinrichi.* MOLUCCAN CUCKOO. (n Moluc).......... _____

❑ *Cacomantis flabelliformis.* FAN-TAILED CUCKOO. (Aust-NG reg).... _____

❑ *Rhamphomantis megarhynchus.* LONG-BILLED CUCKOO. (NG reg) . _____

❑ *Chrysococcyx minutillus.* LITTLE BRONZE-CUCKOO. (se Asia-Aust) . _____

❏ *Chrysococcyx russatus.* GOULD'S BRONZE-CUCKOO. (Born-Aust reg). _____

❏ *Chrysococcyx rufomerus.* GREEN-CHEEKED BRONZE-CUCKOO. (Wall). _____

❏ *Chrysococcyx crassirostris.* PIED BRONZE-CUCKOO. (e Indon-w NG). _____

❏ *Chrysococcyx lucidus.* SHINING BRONZE-CUCKOO. (Aust-s Pac)..... _____
   ___*C. (l.) plagosus.* GOLDEN BRONZE-CUCKOO. (Aust; ◊Indon, NG)
   ___*C. (l.) lucidus.* SHINING BRONZE-CUCKOO. (NZ-s Pac; ◊-NG reg)

❏ *Chrysococcyx basalis.* HORSFIELD'S BRONZE-CUCKOO. (Aust; ◊-Indon)_____

❏ *Chrysococcyx ruficollis.* RUFOUS-THROATED BRONZE-CUCKOO. (NG). _____

❏ *Chrysococcyx meyeri.* WHITE-EARED BRONZE-CUCKOO. (w Pap, NG). _____

❏ *Chrysococcyx maculatus.* ASIAN EMERALD CUCKOO. (s Asia)..... _____

❏ *Chrysococcyx xanthorhynchus.* VIOLET CUCKOO. (s Asia-Phil)..... _____

❏ *Chrysococcyx osculans.* BLACK-EARED CUCKOO. (Aust; ◊-Indon)... _____

❏ *Chrysococcyx flavigularis.* YELLOW-THROATED CUCKOO. (w,c Afr).. _____

❏ *Chrysococcyx klaas.* KLAAS'S CUCKOO. (Afr)................. _____

❏ *Chrysococcyx cupreus.* AFRICAN EMERALD CUCKOO. (Afr)........ _____

❏ *Chrysococcyx caprius.* DIDERIC CUCKOO. (Afr reg)............. _____

❏ *Caliechthrus leucolophus.* WHITE-CROWNED KOEL. (w Pap, NG).... _____

❏ *Surniculus lugubris.* DRONGO CUCKOO. (s Asia-Phil, n Moluc)..... _____

❏ *Microdynamis parva.* DWARF KOEL. (NG)..................... _____

❏ *Eudynamys scolopacea.* ASIAN KOEL. (se Asia-Phil, NG)......... _____

❏ *Eudynamys melanorhyncha.* BLACK-BILLED KOEL. (Sulaw)....... _____

❏ *Eudynamys cyanocephala.* AUSTRALIAN K. (Aust, s NG; ◊-Indon)... _____

❏ *Eudynamys taitensis.* LONG-TAILED KOEL. (NZ; ◊-s Pac)......... _____

❏ *Scythrops novaehollandiae.* CHANNEL-BILLED CUCKOO. (Indon-Aust)_____

❏ *Ceuthmochares aereus.* YELLOWBILL. (Afr)................... _____

❏ *Phaenicophaeus diardi.* BLACK-BELLIED MALKOHA. (se Asia)...... _____

❏ *Phaenicophaeus sumatranus.* CHESTNUT-BELLIED MALKOHA. (se Asia)_____

❏ *Phaenicophaeus tristis.* GREEN-BILLED MALKOHA. (s,se Asia)...... _____

❏ *Phaenicophaeus viridirostris.* BLUE-FACED MALKOHA. (s India)..... _____

❏ *Phaenicophaeus leschenaultii.* SIRKEER MALKOHA. (s Asia)....... _____

❏ *Phaenicophaeus chlorophaeus.* RAFFLES'S MALKOHA. (se Asia).... _____

❏ *Phaenicophaeus javanicus.* RED-BILLED MALKOHA. (se Asia)...... _____

❏ *Phaenicophaeus calyorhynchus.* YELLOW-BILLED MALKOHA. (Sulaw)_____

❏ *Phaenicophaeus curvirostris.* CHESTNUT-BREASTED MALK. (se Asia). _____

❏ *Phaenicophaeus pyrrhocephalus.* RED-FACED MALKOHA. (Ceylon). _____

❏ *Phaenicophaeus superciliosus.* RED-CRESTED MALKOHA. (n Phil)... _____

❏ *Phaenicophaeus cumingi.* SCALE-FEATHERED MALKOHA. (n Phil)... _____

❏ *Carpococcyx radiceus.* SUNDA GROUND-CUCKOO. (Sum, Born)..... _____

❏ *Carpococcyx renauldi.* CORAL-BILLED GROUND-CUCKOO. (se Asia) . _____

  Coua delalandei. SNAIL-EATING COUA. (†ne Mad)............... _____

❏ *Coua gigas.* GIANT COUA. (w,s Mad)......................... _____

❏ *Coua coquereli.* COQUEREL'S COUA. (w Mad)................. _____

❏ *Coua serriana.* RED-BREASTED COUA. (ne Mad)............... _____

❏ *Coua reynaudii.* RED-FRONTED COUA. (nw,e Mad)............. _____

❏ *Coua cursor.* RUNNING COUA. (sw Mad)..................... _____

❏ *Coua ruficeps.* RED-CAPPED COUA. (w Mad)................. _____

❏ *Coua cristata.* CRESTED COUA. (Mad)....................... _____

❏ *Coua verreauxi.* VERREAUX'S COUA. (sw Mad)............... _____

❏ *Coua caerulea.* BLUE COUA. (nw,e Mad)..................... _____

Superfamily CENTROPODOIDEA [1/30]
Family **Centropodidae** [1/30]

❏ *Centropus milo.* BUFF-HEADED COUCAL. (Solom)............... _____

❏ *Centropus goliath.* GOLIATH COUCAL. (n Moluc)............... _____

❏ *Centropus violaceus.* VIOLACEOUS COUCAL. (Bism)............ _____

❏ *Centropus menbeki.* GREATER BLACK COUCAL. (NG reg)......... _____

❏ *Centropus ateralbus.* PIED COUCAL. (Bism)................... _____

❏ *Centropus phasianinus.* PHEASANT COUCAL. (Timor-NG, Aust)..... _____
   ___*C. (p.) mui.* TIMOR COUCAL. (Timor)
   ___*C. (p.) phasianinus.* PHEASANT COUCAL. (NG, Aust)

❏ *Centropus spilopterus.* KAI COUCAL. (Kai).................... _____

❏ *Centropus bernsteini.* LESSER BLACK COUCAL. (w,c NG)......... _____

❏ *Centropus chalybeus.* BIAK COUCAL. (w NG)................. _____

❏ *Centropus rectunguis.* SHORT-TOED COUCAL. (se Asia).......... _____

❏ *Centropus steerii.* BLACK-HOODED COUCAL. (c Phil)............. _____

❏ *Centropus sinensis.* GREATER COUCAL. (s Asia-sw Phil).......... _____

❏ *Centropus andamanensis.* BROWN COUCAL. (And)............. _____

❏ *Centropus nigrorufus.* SUNDA COUCAL. (Java)................. _____

❏ *Centropus viridis.* PHILIPPINE COUCAL. (Phil)................. _____

❏ *Centropus toulou.* MADAGASCAR COUCAL. (Mad, Seyc).......... _____

❏ *Centropus grillii.* BLACK COUCAL. (Afr)...................... _____

❑ *Centropus bengalensis.* LESSER COUCAL. (s Asia-Phil, Moluc). . . . . . _____

❑ *Centropus chlororhynchus.* GREEN-BILLED COUCAL. (Ceylon). . . . . . _____

❑ *Centropus leucogaster.* BLACK-THROATED COUCAL. (w Afr). . . . . _____

❑ *Centropus neumanni.* NEUMANN'S COUCAL. (wc Afr). . . . . _____

❑ *Centropus anselli.* GABON COUCAL. (wc Afr). . . . . _____

❑ *Centropus monachus.* BLUE-HEADED COUCAL. (w,c Afr). . . . . _____

❑ *Centropus cupreicaudus.* COPPERY-TAILED COUCAL. (sc Afr). . . . . . . _____

❑ *Centropus senegalensis.* SENEGAL COUCAL. (w,c Afr). . . . . _____

❑ *Centropus superciliosus.* WHITE-BROWED COUCAL. (c,e Afr reg). . . . _____

❑ *Centropus burchelli.* BURCHELL'S COUCAL. (se Afr). . . . . _____

❑ *Centropus melanops.* BLACK-FACED COUCAL. (c,s Phil). . . . . _____

❑ *Centropus celebensis.* BAY COUCAL. (Sulaw). . . . . _____

❑ *Centropus unirufus.* RUFOUS COUCAL. (n Phil). . . . . _____

Parvorder COCCYZIDA [4/18]
Family **Coccyzidae** [4/18]

❑ *Coccyzus pumilus.* DWARF CUCKOO. (n SA). . . . . _____

❑ *Coccyzus cinereus.* ASH-COLORED CUCKOO. (sc SA). . . . . _____

❑ *Coccyzus erythropthalmus.* BLACK-BILLED CUCKOO. (e NA; ◊ SA) . _____

❑ *Coccyzus americanus.* YELLOW-BILLED CUCKOO. (c,s NA, n Mex). . . _____

❑ *Coccyzus euleri.* PEARLY-BREASTED CUCKOO. (sc SA; ◊-n SA). . . . . _____

❑ *Coccyzus minor.* MANGROVE CUCKOO. (MA, s Fla, WIndies, n SA) . _____

❑ *Coccyzus ferrugineus.* COCOS CUCKOO. (Cocos). . . . . _____

❑ *Coccyzus melacoryphus.* DARK-BILLED CUCKOO. (SA, Galap). . . . . . _____

❑ *Coccyzus lansbergi.* GREY-CAPPED CUCKOO. (n SA; ◊-sw SA). . . . . . _____

❑ *Hyetornis pluvialis.* CHESTNUT-BELLIED CUCKOO. (Jam). . . . . _____

❑ *Hyetornis rufigularis.* BAY-BREASTED CUCKOO. (Hisp). . . . . _____

❑ *Piaya cayana.* SQUIRREL CUCKOO. (MA, SA). . . . . _____

❑ *Piaya melanogaster.* BLACK-BELLIED CUCKOO. (wc SA). . . . . _____

❑ *Piaya minuta.* LITTLE CUCKOO. (e Pan, SA). . . . . _____

❑ *Saurothera merlini.* GREAT LIZARD-CUCKOO. (Bah, Cuba). . . . . _____

❑ *Saurothera vetula.* JAMAICAN LIZARD-CUCKOO. (Jam). . . . . _____

❑ *Saurothera longirostris.* HISPANIOLAN LIZARD-CUCKOO. (Hisp). . . . . _____

❑ *Saurothera vieilloti.* PUERTO RICAN LIZARD-CUCKOO. (PR). . . . . _____

Infraorder CROTOPHAGIDES [8/16]
Parvorder OPISTHOCOMIDA [1/1]
Family **Opisthocomidae** [1/1]

❑ *Opisthocomus hoazin.* HOATZIN. (Amaz)...................... _____

Parvorder CROTOPHAGIDA [2/4]
Family **Crotophagidae** [2/4]
Tribe Crotophagini [1/3]

❑ *Crotophaga major.* GREATER ANI. (e Pan, SA)............... _____

❑ *Crotophaga ani.* SMOOTH-BILLED ANI. (s Fla, W Indies, s CA, SA) . _____

❑ *Crotophaga sulcirostris.* GROOVE-BILLED ANI. (s Tex, MA, SA).... _____

Tribe Guirini [1/1]

❑ *Guira guira.* GUIRA CUCKOO. (se SA)...................... _____

Parvorder NEOMORPHIDA [5/11]
Family **Neomorphidae** [5/11]

❑ *Tapera naevia.* STRIPED CUCKOO. (MA, SA)................. _____

❑ *Morococcyx erythropygus.* LESSER GROUND-CUCKOO. (Pac MA).... _____

❑ *Dromococcyx phasianellus.* PHEASANT CUCKOO. (MA, SA)....... _____

❑ *Dromococcyx pavoninus.* PAVONINE CUCKOO. (SA)............. _____

❑ *Geococcyx californianus.* GREATER ROADRUNNER. (sw,sc US, Mex). _____

❑ *Geococcyx velox.* LESSER ROADRUNNER. (MA)................ _____

❑ *Neomorphus geoffroyi.* RUFOUS-VENTED GROUND-CUCKOO. (CA-SA)_____

❑ *Neomorphus squamiger.* SCALED GROUND-CUCKOO. (c Amaz Braz). _____

❑ *Neomorphus radiolosus.* BANDED GROUND-CUCKOO. (nw SA)...... _____

❑ *Neomorphus rufipennis.* RUFOUS-WINGED GROUND-CUCKOO. (n SA) _____

❑ *Neomorphus pucheranii.* RED-BILLED GROUND-CUCKOO. (w Amaz). _____

Superorder PSITTACIMORPHAE [80/360]
Order **PSITTACIFORMES** [80/360]
Family **Psittacidae** [80/360]

❑ *Chalcopsitta atra.* BLACK LORY. (NG reg)................... _____
  ___*C. (a.) atra.* BLACK LORY. (w Pap, w NG)
  ___*C. (a.) insignis.* RAJAH LORY. (nw NG)

❑ *Chalcopsitta duivenbodei.* BROWN LORY. (n NG)............... _____

❑ *Chalcopsitta sintillata.* YELLOW-STREAKED LORY. (Aru, s NG)..... _____

❑ *Chalcopsitta cardinalis.* CARDINAL LORY. (Bism, Solom)......... _____

❑ *Eos histrio.* RED-AND-BLUE LORY. (n Wall)................... _____

❑ *Eos squamata.* VIOLET-NECKED LORY. (n Moluc, w Pap)......... _____

❑ *Eos bornea.* RED LORY. (s Moluc)............................. _____

❑ *Eos reticulata.* BLUE-STREAKED LORY. (Tanim)................. _____

❑ *Eos cyanogenia.* BLACK-WINGED LORY. (nw NG)............... _____

❑ *Eos semilarvata.* BLUE-EARED LORY. (s Moluc)................ _____

❑ *Pseudeos fuscata.* DUSKY LORY. (w Pap, NG)................. _____

❑ *Trichoglossus ornatus.* ORNATE LORIKEET. (Sulaw)............. _____

❑ *Trichoglossus haematodus.* RAINBOW LORIKEET. (Wall-Vanu, Aust). _____

❑ *Trichoglossus rubritorquis.* RED-COLLARED LORIKEET. (n Aust)..... _____

❑ *Trichoglossus euteles.* OLIVE-HEADED LORIKEET. (e L Sunda)...... _____

❑ *Trichoglossus flavoviridis.* YELLOW-AND-GREEN LORIKEET. (Sulaw). _____

❑ *Trichoglossus johnstoniae.* MINDANAO LORIKEET. (mts s Phil)...... _____

❑ *Trichoglossus rubiginosus.* POHNPEI LORIKEET. (e Carol)......... _____

❑ *Trichoglossus chlorolepidotus.* SCALY-BREASTED LORIKEET. (e Aust) _____

❑ *Psitteuteles versicolor.* VARIED LORIKEET. (n Aust)............. _____

❑ *Psitteuteles iris.* IRIS LORIKEET. (c L Sunda)................... _____

❑ *Psitteuteles goldiei.* GOLDIE'S LORIKEET. (mts NG)............. _____

❑ *Lorius garrulus.* CHATTERING LORY. (n Moluc)................ _____

❑ *Lorius domicella.* PURPLE-NAPED LORY. (s Moluc)............. _____

❑ *Lorius lory.* BLACK-CAPPED LORY. (w Pap, NG)................ _____

❑ *Lorius hypoinochrous.* PURPLE-BELLIED LORY. (e NG, Bism)....... _____

❑ *Lorius albidinuchus.* WHITE-NAPED LORY. (mts c Bism).......... _____

❑ *Lorius chlorocercus.* YELLOW-BIBBED LORY. (e Solom).......... _____

❑ *Phigys solitarius.* COLLARED LORY. (Fiji).................... _____

❑ *Vini australis.* BLUE-CROWNED LORIKEET. (sc Polyn)............ _____

❑ *Vini kuhlii.* KUHL'S LORIKEET. (e Tubuai).................... _____

❑ *Vini stepheni.* STEPHEN'S LORIKEET. (Henderson). .... _____

❑ *Vini peruviana.* BLUE LORIKEET. (w Tuam).................... _____

❑ *Vini ultramarina.* ULTRAMARINE LORIKEET. (cw Marq).......... _____

❑ *Glossopsitta concinna.* MUSK LORIKEET. (se Aust).............. _____

❑ *Glossopsitta pusilla.* LITTLE LORIKEET. (se Aust)............... _____

❑ *Glossopsitta porphyrocephala.* PURPLE-CROWNED LORIKEET. (s Aust) _____

❑ *Charmosyna palmarum.* PALM LORIKEET. (sw Polyn)............ _____

❑ *Charmosyna rubrigularis.* RED-CHINNED LORIKEET. (NG, Bism).... _____

❑ *Charmosyna meeki.* MEEK'S LORIKEET. (mts Solom)............. _____

❑ *Charmosyna toxopei.* BLUE-FRONTED LORIKEET. (mts s Moluc)..... _____

❑ *Charmosyna multistriata.* STRIATED LORIKEET. (mts w NG)........ _____

❑ *Charmosyna wilhelminae.* PYGMY LORIKEET. (mts NG).......... _____

❑ *Charmosyna rubronotata.* RED-FRONTED LORIKEET. (w Pap, NG)... _____

❑ *Charmosyna placentis.* RED-FLANKED LORIKEET. (Moluc-Solom)... _____

   Charmosyna diadema. NEW CALEDONIAN LORIKEET. (†N Cal)...... _____

❑ *Charmosyna amabilis.* RED-THROATED LORIKEET. (mts Fiji)........ _____

❑ *Charmosyna margarethae.* DUCHESS LORIKEET. (Solom)......... _____

❑ *Charmosyna pulchella.* FAIRY LORIKEET. (mts NG)............. _____

❑ *Charmosyna josefinae.* JOSEPHINE'S LORIKEET. (mts w,c NG)...... _____

❑ *Charmosyna papou.* PAPUAN LORIKEET. (mts NG)............. _____

❑ *Oreopsittacus arfaki.* PLUM-FACED LORIKEET. (mts NG).......... _____

❑ *Neopsittacus musschenbroekii.* YELLOW-BILLED LORIKEET. (NG)... _____

❑ *Neopsittacus pullicauda.* ORANGE-BILLED LORIKEET. (mts c,e NG) . _____

❑ *Probosciger aterrimus.* PALM COCKATOO. (Aru-NG, n Queens)..... _____

❑ *Calyptorhynchus baudinii.* WHITE-TAILED BLACK-C. (sw Aust)..... _____

❑ *Calyptorhynchus latirostris.* SLENDER-BILLED BLACK-C. (sw Aust) . _____

❑ *Calyptorhynchus funereus.* YELLOW-TAILED BLACK-C. (e,se Aust) . _____
   ___*C. (f.) funereus.* YELLOW-TAILED BLACK-COCKATOO. (e Aust)
   ___*C. (f.) xanthanotus.* YELLOW-TINTED BLACK-COCKATOO. (se Aust)

❑ *Calyptorhynchus banksii.* RED-TAILED BLACK-COCKATOO. (Aust)... _____

❑ *Calyptorhynchus lathami.* GLOSSY BLACK-COCKATOO. (e Aust).... _____

❑ *Callocephalon fimbriatum.* GANG-GANG COCKATOO. (se Aust)..... _____

❑ *Eolophus roseicapillus.* GALAH. (Aust)....................... _____

❑ *Cacatua leadbeateri.* PINK COCKATOO. (int,s Aust).............. _____

❑ *Cacatua sulphurea.* YELLOW-CRESTED COCKATOO. (Wall)........ _____

❑ *Cacatua galerita.* SULPHUR-CRESTED C. (e Wall, NG, n,e Aust)..... _____

❑ *Cacatua ophthalmica.* BLUE-EYED COCKATOO. (Bism)........... _____

❑ *Cacatua moluccensis.* SALMON-CRESTED COCKATOO. (s Moluc)..... _____

❑ *Cacatua alba.* WHITE COCKATOO. (c,n Moluc)................. _____

❑ *Cacatua haematuropygia.* PHILIPPINE COCKATOO. (Phil)......... _____

❑ *Cacatua goffini.* TANIMBAR COCKATOO. (Tanim).............. _____

❑ *Cacatua sanguinea.* LITTLE COCKATOO. (Aust; ◊-s NG).......... _____

❑ *Cacatua pastinator.* WESTERN CORELLA. (sw Aust)............. _____

❑ *Cacatua tenuirostris.* LONG-BILLED CORELLA. (se Aust).......... _____

❑ *Cacatua ducorpsii.* DUCORPS'S COCKATOO. (e Solom)............ _____

❑ *Nymphicus hollandicus.* COCKATIEL. (Aust)................... _____

❑ *Nestor notabilis.* KEA. (s NZ)............................. _____

    Nestor productus. NORFOLK ISLAND KAKA. (†Norfolk).......... _____

❑ *Nestor meridionalis.* NEW ZEALAND KAKA. (NZ)............... _____

❑ *Micropsitta keiensis.* YELLOW-CAPPED PYGMY-PARROT. (Kai-w Pap). _____

❑ *Micropsitta geelvinkiana.* GEELVINK PYGMY-PARROT. (w NG)...... _____

❑ *Micropsitta pusio.* BUFF-FACED PYGMY-PARROT. (NG, Bism)....... _____

❑ *Micropsitta meeki.* MEEK'S PYGMY-PARROT. (Bism)............. _____

❑ *Micropsitta finschii.* FINSCH'S PYGMY-PARROT. (Bism, Solom)...... _____

❑ *Micropsitta bruijnii.* RED-BREASTED PYGMY-PARROT. (s Moluc-Solom)_____

❑ *Cyclopsitta gulielmitertii.* ORANGE-BREASTED FIG-PARROT. (Aru-NG)_____

❑ *Cyclopsitta diophthalma.* DOUBLE-EYED FIG-PARROT. (Aru-NG, Aust) _____
   ___*C. (d.) diophthalma.* DOUBLE-EYED FIG-PARROT. (Aru-ne Aust)
   ___*C. (d.) coxeni.* COXEN'S FIG-PARROT. (ce Aust)

❑ *Psittaculirostris desmarestii.* LARGE FIG-PARROT. (w Pap, w,s NG) . _____

❑ *Psittaculirostris edwardsii.* EDWARDS'S FIG-PARROT. (ne NG)...... _____

❑ *Psittaculirostris salvadorii.* SALVADORI'S FIG-PARROT. (n NG)...... _____

❑ *Bolbopsittacus lunulatus.* GUAIABERO. (Phil)................. _____

❑ *Psittinus cyanurus.* BLUE-RUMPED PARROT. (se Asia)........... _____

❑ *Psittacella brehmii.* BREHM'S TIGER-PARROT. (mts NG).......... _____

❑ *Psittacella picta.* PAINTED TIGER-PARROT. (mts c,e NG).......... _____

❑ *Psittacella modesta.* MODEST TIGER-PARROT. (mts w,c NG)....... _____

❑ *Psittacella madaraszi.* MADARASZ'S TIGER-PARROT. (mts c,e NG)... _____

❑ *Geoffroyus geoffroyi.* RED-CHEEKED PARROT. (Indon-ne Aust)...... _____

❑ *Geoffroyus simplex.* BLUE-COLLARED PARROT. (mts NG)......... _____

❑ *Geoffroyus heteroclitus.* SINGING PARROT. (Bism, Solom)........ _____

❑ *Prioniturus montanus.* MONTANE RACQUET-TAIL. (mts n Phil)..... _____

❑ *Prioniturus waterstradti.* MINDANAO RACQUET-TAIL. (mts s Phil)... _____

❑ *Prioniturus platenae.* BLUE-HEADED RACQUET-TAIL. (cw Phil)...... _____

❑ *Prioniturus luconensis.* GREEN RACQUET-TAIL. (n Phil).......... _____

❑ *Prioniturus discurus.* BLUE-CROWNED RACQUET-TAIL. (Phil)...... _____

❑ *Prioniturus verticalis.* BLUE-WINGED RACQUET-TAIL. (sw Phil)..... _____

❑ *Prioniturus flavicans.* YELLOW-BREASTED RACQUET-TAIL. (Sulaw) . _____

❑ *Prioniturus platurus.* GOLDEN-MANTLED RACQUET-TAIL. (Wall).... _____

❏ *Prioniturus mada.* BURU RACQUET-TAIL. (s Moluc)..............

❏ *Tanygnathus megalorynchos.* GREAT-BILLED PARROT. (Wall-w NG).

❏ *Tanygnathus lucionensis.* BLUE-NAPED PARROT. (n Born, Phil).....

❏ *Tanygnathus sumatranus.* BLUE-BACKED PARROT. (Sulaw, n Phil) .

❏ *Tanygnathus gramineus.* BLACK-LORED PARROT. (s Moluc).......

❏ *Eclectus roratus.* ECLECTUS PARROT. (L Sunda-Solom, ne Aust)....

❏ *Psittrichas fulgidus.* PESQUET'S PARROT. (mts NG)..............

❏ *Prosopeia splendens.* CRIMSON SHINING-PARROT. (Fiji)..........

❏ *Prosopeia personata.* MASKED SHINING-PARROT. (Fiji)............

❏ *Prosopeia tabuensis.* RED SHINING-PARROT. (Fiji)...............

❏ *Alisterus scapularis.* AUSTRALIAN KING-PARROT. (e Aust)........

❏ *Alisterus amboinensis.* MOLUCCAN KING-PARROT. (Wall-w NG)....

❏ *Alisterus chloropterus.* PAPUAN KING-PARROT. (NG).............

❏ *Aprosmictus jonquillaceus.* OLIVE-SHOULDERED PARROT. (L Sunda).

❏ *Aprosmictus erythropterus.* RED-WINGED PARROT. (s NG, n,e Aust) .

❏ *Polytelis swainsonii.* SUPERB PARROT. (se Aust)................

❏ *Polytelis anthopeplus.* REGENT PARROT. (sw,se Aust)............

❏ *Polytelis alexandrae.* ALEXANDRA'S PARROT. (w,c Aust)..........

❏ *Purpureicephalus spurius.* RED-CAPPED PARROT. (sw Aust).......

❏ *Platycercus zonarius.* PORT LINCOLN RINGNECK. (w,c Aust).......

❏ *Platycercus barnardi.* MALLEE RINGNECK. (e,se Aust)...........
   ___*P. (b.) macgillivrayi.* CLONCURRY RINGNECK. (e Aust)
   ___*P. (b.) barnardi.* MALLEE RINGNECK. (se Aust)

❏ *Platycercus caledonicus.* GREEN ROSELLA. (Tas)................

❏ *Platycercus elegans.* CRIMSON ROSELLA. (e,se Aust).............

❏ *Platycercus flaveolus.* YELLOW ROSELLA. (se Aust).............

❏ *Platycercus venustus.* NORTHERN ROSELLA. (n Aust).............

❏ *Platycercus adscitus.* PALE-HEADED ROSELLA. (ne,e Aust)........

❏ *Platycercus eximius.* EASTERN ROSELLA. (se Aust)..............

❏ *Platycercus icterotis.* WESTERN ROSELLA. (sw Aust).............

❏ *Northiella haematogaster.* BLUEBONNET. (s Aust)...............
   ___*N. (h.) naretha.* LITTLE BLUEBONNET. (sw Aust)
   ___*N. (h.) haematogaster.* COMMON BLUEBONNET. (sc,se Aust)

❏ *Psephotus haematonotus.* RED-RUMPED PARROT. (se Aust)........

❏ *Psephotus varius.* MULGA PARROT. (int s Aust)................

❏ *Psephotus dissimilis.* HOODED PARROT. (nc Aust)...............

❑ *Psephotus chrysopterygius.* GOLDEN-SHOULDERED PARROT. (ne Aust) _____

❑ *Psephotus pulcherrimus.* PARADISE PARROT. (†ec Aust). . . . . _____

❑ *Cyanoramphus unicolor.* ANTIPODES PARAKEET. (Antipodes). . . . . . _____

❑ *Cyanoramphus cookii.* NORFOLK ISLAND PARAKEET. (Norfolk). . . . . _____

❑ *Cyanoramphus novaezelandiae.* RED-FRONTED PARAKEET. (NZ reg). _____
   ___*C. (n.) saisseti.* NEW CALEDONIAN PARAKEET. (N Cal)
   C. (n.) subflavescens. LORD HOWE ISLAND PARAKEET. (†L Howe)
   ___*C. (n.) novaezelandiae.* RED-FRONTED PARAKEET. (NZ reg)

❑ *Cyanoramphus auriceps.* YELLOW-FRONTED PARAKEET. (NZ reg). . . _____

  Cyanoramphus zealandicus. BLACK-FRONTED PARAKEET. (†se Soc) . _____

❑ *Cyanoramphus ulietanus.* RAIATEA PARAKEET. (ec Soc). . . . . _____

❑ *Eunymphicus cornutus.* HORNED PARAKEET. (N Cal, nw Loy). . . . . . _____
   ___*E. (c.) cornutus.* HORNED PARAKEET. (N Cal)
   ___*E. (c.) uvaeensis.* OUVEA PARAKEET. (nw Loy)

❑ *Neopsephotus bourkii.* BOURKE'S PARROT. (int Aust). . . . . _____

❑ *Neophema chrysostoma.* BLUE-WINGED PARROT. (se Aust). . . . . _____

❑ *Neophema elegans.* ELEGANT PARROT. (sw,se Aust). . . . . _____

❑ *Neophema petrophila.* ROCK PARROT. (sw,sc Aust). . . . . _____

❑ *Neophema chrysogaster.* ORANGE-BELLIED PARROT. (sw Tas). . . . . . _____

❑ *Neophema pulchella.* TURQUOISE PARROT. (se Aust). . . . . _____

❑ *Neophema splendida.* SCARLET-CHESTED PARROT. (int sw,sc Aust) . _____

❑ *Lathamus discolor.* SWIFT PARROT. (Tasm; ◊-se Aust). . . . . _____

❑ *Melopsittacus undulatus.* BUDGERIGAR. (Aust; ◆ se US). . . . . _____

❑ *Pezoporus wallicus.* GROUND PARROT. (sw,se Aust). . . . . _____

❑ *Geopsittacus occidentalis.* NIGHT PARROT. (int Aust). . . . . _____

❑ *Strigops habroptilus.* KAKAPO. (NZ). . . . . _____

  Mascarinus mascarinus. MASCARENE PARROT. (†Réun). . . . . _____

❑ *Coracopsis vasa.* VASA PARROT. (Com, Mad). . . . . _____

❑ *Coracopsis nigra.* BLACK PARROT. (Com, Mad, n Seyc). . . . . _____

❑ *Psittacus erithacus.* GREY PARROT. (w,c Afr). . . . . _____

❑ *Poicephalus robustus.* BROWN-NECKED PARROT. (w,c,s Afr). . . . . . . _____
   ___*P. (r.) suahelicus.* BROWN-NECKED PARROT. (sp)
   ___*P. (r.) robustus.* CAPE PARROT. (e S Afr)

❑ *Poicephalus gulielmi.* RED-FRONTED PARROT. (w,c Afr). . . . . _____

❑ *Poicephalus senegalus.* SENEGAL PARROT. (w Afr). . . . . _____

❑ *Poicephalus crassus.* NIAM-NIAM PARROT. (c Afr). . . . . _____

❑ *Poicephalus meyeri.* MEYER'S PARROT. (c,e,s Afr). . . . . _____

❑ *Poicephalus flavifrons.* YELLOW-FRONTED PARROT. (mts Eth)...... _____

❑ *Poicephalus rufiventris.* RED-BELLIED PARROT. (e,se Afr).......... _____

❑ *Poicephalus cryptoxanthus.* BROWN-HEADED PARROT. (se Afr)..... _____

❑ *Poicephalus rueppellii.* RUEPPELL'S PARROT. (sw Afr)........... _____

❑ *Agapornis canus.* GREY-HEADED LOVEBIRD. (Mad).............. _____

❑ *Agapornis pullarius.* RED-HEADED LOVEBIRD. (w,c Afr).......... _____

❑ *Agapornis taranta.* BLACK-WINGED LOVEBIRD. (mts Eth)......... _____

❑ *Agapornis swindernianus.* BLACK-COLLARED LOVEBIRD. (w,c Afr) . _____

❑ *Agapornis roseicollis.* ROSY-FACED LOVEBIRD. (sw Afr).......... _____

❑ *Agapornis fischeri.* FISCHER'S LOVEBIRD. (mts ec Afr)........... _____

❑ *Agapornis personatus.* YELLOW-COLLARED LOVEBIRD. (mts ec Afr) . _____

❑ *Agapornis lilianae.* LILIAN'S LOVEBIRD. (se Afr)............... _____

❑ *Agapornis nigrigenis.* BLACK-CHEEKED LOVEBIRD. (sc Afr)....... _____

❑ *Loriculus vernalis.* VERNAL HANGING-PARROT. (s,se Asia)....... _____

❑ *Loriculus beryllinus.* CEYLON HANGING-PARROT. (Ceylon)....... _____

❑ *Loriculus philippensis.* COLASISI. (Phil)..................... _____
   ___*L. (p.) philippensis.* COLASISI. (sp)
   ___*L. (p.) bonapartei.* BLACK-BILLED HANGING-PARROT. (Sulu)

❑ *Loriculus galgulus.* BLUE-CROWNED HANGING-PARROT. (se Asia)... _____

❑ *Loriculus stigmatus.* SULAWESI HANGING-PARROT. (Sulaw)....... _____

❑ *Loriculus amabilis.* MOLUCCAN HANGING-PARROT. (Wall)........ _____

❑ *Loriculus catamene.* SANGIHE HANGING-PARROT. (Sangihe)....... _____

❑ *Loriculus aurantiifrons.* ORANGE-FRONTED HANGING-PARROT. (NG). _____

❑ *Loriculus tener.* GREEN-FRONTED HANGING-PARROT. (Bism)...... _____

❑ *Loriculus exilis.* RED-BILLED HANGING-PARROT. (Sulaw)......... _____

❑ *Loriculus pusillus.* YELLOW-THROATED HANGING-PARROT. (Java, Bali)_____

 Loriculus flosculus. WALLACE'S HANGING-PARROT. (†Flores)....... _____

❑ *Psittacula eupatria.* ALEXANDRINE PARAKEET. (s,se Asia)......... _____

 Psittacula wardi. SEYCHELLES PARAKEET. (†Seyc).............. _____

❑ *Psittacula krameri.* ROSE-RINGED PARAKEET. (nc Afr-s Asia; ◆ cosm) _____

❑ *Psittacula echo.* MAURITIUS PARAKEET. (Maur)............... _____

 Psittacula exsul. NEWTON'S PARAKEET. (†Rodr)............... _____

❑ *Psittacula himalayana.* SLATY-HEADED PARAKEET. (Himal)....... _____

❑ *Psittacula finschii.* GREY-HEADED PARAKEET. (mts se Asia)....... _____

❑ *Psittacula intermedia.* INTERMEDIATE PARAKEET. (Himal n India)... _____

❑ *Psittacula cyanocephala.* PLUM-HEADED PARAKEET. (ne Pak, India) . _____

❑ *Psittacula roseata.* BLOSSOM-HEADED PARAKEET. (se Asia)........ _____

❑ *Psittacula columboides.* MALABAR PARAKEET. (sw India)......... _____

❑ *Psittacula calthropae.* LAYARD'S PARAKEET. (Ceylon)........... _____

❑ *Psittacula derbiana.* DERBYAN PARAKEET. (Himal sw China)....... _____

❑ *Psittacula alexandri.* RED-BREASTED PARAKEET. (s,se Asia)....... _____

❑ *Psittacula caniceps.* NICOBAR PARAKEET. (Nico)............... _____

❑ *Psittacula longicauda.* LONG-TAILED PARAKEET. (se Asia)........ _____

❑ *Anodorhynchus hyacinthinus.* HYACINTH MACAW. (e SA)......... _____

❑ *Anodorhynchus leari.* INDIGO MACAW. (mts ne Braz)............ _____

   Anodorhynchus glaucus. GLAUCOUS MACAW. (†se SA).......... _____

❑ *Cyanopsitta spixii.* LITTLE BLUE MACAW. (e Braz)............. _____

❑ *Ara ararauna.* BLUE-AND-YELLOW MACAW. (e Pan, SA).......... _____

❑ *Ara glaucogularis.* BLUE-THROATED MACAW. (sc SA)........... _____

❑ *Ara militaris.* MILITARY MACAW. (MA, w SA)................ _____

❑ *Ara ambigua.* GREAT GREEN MACAW. (CA, nw SA)............. _____

❑ *Ara macao.* SCARLET MACAW. (MA, Amaz SA)............... _____

❑ *Ara chloropterus.* RED-AND-GREEN MACAW. (e Pan, SA)........ _____

   Ara cubensis. CUBAN MACAW. (†Cuba)...................... _____

   Ara tricolor. HISPANIOLAN MACAW. (†Hisp)................. _____

❑ *Ara rubrogenys.* RED-FRONTED MACAW. (Andes c Bol).......... _____

❑ *Ara severa.* CHESTNUT-FRONTED MACAW. (Pan, n,c SA).......... _____

❑ *Ara manilata.* RED-BELLIED MACAW. (Amaz).................. _____

❑ *Ara couloni.* BLUE-HEADED MACAW. (w Amaz)................ _____

❑ *Ara maracana.* BLUE-WINGED MACAW. (e SA)................ _____

❑ *Ara auricollis.* YELLOW-COLLARED MACAW. (sc SA)............. _____

❑ *Ara nobilis.* RED-SHOULDERED MACAW. (e SA)................ _____

❑ *Aratinga acuticaudata.* BLUE-CROWNED PARAKEET. (SA)......... _____

❑ *Aratinga guarouba.* GOLDEN PARAKEET. (ne Braz)............. _____

❑ *Aratinga holochlora.* GREEN PARAKEET. (MA)................ _____
   ___*A. (h.) holochlora.* GREEN PARAKEET. (Mex)
   ___*A. (h.) brevipes.* SOCORRO PARAKEET. (Revil)
   ___*A. (h.) rubritorquis.* RED-THROATED PARAKEET. (mts n CA)

❑ *Aratinga strenua.* PACIFIC PARAKEET. (Pac c MA)............. _____

❑ *Aratinga wagleri.* SCARLET-FRONTED PARAKEET. (mts w SA)....... _____
   ___*A. (w.) wagleri.* SCARLET-FRONTED PARAKEET. (nw SA)
   ___*A. (w.) frontata.* CORDILLERAN PARAKEET. (wc SA)

❑ *Aratinga mitrata.* MITRED PARAKEET. (Andes w SA). . . . . _____
   ___*A. (m.) alticola.* CHAPMAN'S PARAKEET. (sp)
   ___*A. (m.) mitrata.* MITRED PARAKEET. (c Peru)

❑ *Aratinga erythrogenys.* RED-MASKED PARAKEET. (cw SA). . . . . _____

❑ *Aratinga finschi.* CRIMSON-FRONTED PARAKEET. (s CA). . . . . _____

❑ *Aratinga leucophthalmus.* WHITE-EYED PARAKEET. (SA). . . . . _____

❑ *Aratinga euops.* CUBAN PARAKEET. (Cuba). . . . . _____

❑ *Aratinga chloroptera.* HISPANIOLAN PARAKEET. (Hisp). . . . . _____

❑ *Aratinga solstitialis.* SUN PARAKEET. (n Amaz). . . . . _____

❑ *Aratinga jandaya.* JANDAYA PARAKEET. (ne Braz). . . . . _____

❑ *Aratinga auricapilla.* GOLDEN-CAPPED PARAKEET. (e Braz). . . . . . . _____

❑ *Aratinga weddellii.* DUSKY-HEADED PARAKEET. (n SA). . . . . _____

❑ *Aratinga nana.* OLIVE-THROATED PARAKEET. (MA, Jam). . . . . _____
   ___*A. (n.) astec.* AZTEC PARAKEET. (MA)
   ___*A. (n.) nana.* JAMAICAN PARAKEET. (Jam)

❑ *Aratinga canicularis.* ORANGE-FRONTED PARAKEET. (Pac MA). . . . . _____

❑ *Aratinga aurea.* PEACH-FRONTED PARAKEET. (s Amaz). . . . . _____

❑ *Aratinga pertinax.* BROWN-THROATED PARAKEET. (w Pan, n SA). . . . _____
   ___*A. (p.) ocularis.* VERAGUAS PARAKEET. (w Pan)
   ___*A. (p.) pertinax.* BROWN-THROATED PARAKEET. (n SA; ◆ e G Ant)

❑ *Aratinga cactorum.* CAATINGA PARAKEET. (e Braz). . . . . _____

❑ *Nandayus nenday.* NANDAY PARAKEET. (sc SA). . . . . _____

❑ *Leptosittaca branickii.* GOLDEN-PLUMED PARAKEET. (Andes w SA) . _____

❑ *Ognorhynchus icterotis.* YELLOW-EARED PARROT. (Andes nw SA) . _____

❑ *Rhynchopsitta pachyrhyncha.* THICK-BILLED PARROT. (nw Mex). . . . _____

❑ *Rhynchopsitta terrisi.* MAROON-FRONTED PARROT. (mts n Mex). . . . . _____

  Conuropsis carolinensis. CAROLINA PARAKEET. (†se US). . . . . _____

❑ *Cyanoliseus patagonus.* BURROWING PARAKEET. (s SA). . . . . _____

❑ *Pyrrhura cruentata.* BLUE-THROATED PARAKEET. (e Braz). . . . . _____

❑ *Pyrrhura devillei.* BLAZE-WINGED PARAKEET. (sc SA). . . . . _____

❑ *Pyrrhura frontalis.* MAROON-BELLIED PARAKEET. (se SA). . . . . _____

❑ *Pyrrhura perlata.* PEARLY PARAKEET. (e Amaz Braz). . . . . _____

❑ *Pyrrhura rhodogaster.* CRIMSON-BELLIED PARAKEET. (c Amaz). . . . . _____

❑ *Pyrrhura molinae.* GREEN-CHEEKED PARAKEET. (sc SA). . . . . _____

❑ *Pyrrhura picta.* PAINTED PARAKEET. (wc Pan, Amaz). . . . . _____

❑ *Pyrrhura leucotis.* WHITE-EARED PARAKEET. (n Ven, e Braz). . . . . . . _____

❑ *Pyrrhura viridicata.* SANTA MARTA PARAKEET. (mts ne Colom). . . . . _____

❑ *Pyrrhura egregia.* FIERY-SHOULDERED PARAKEET. (Pant n SA)...... _____

❑ *Pyrrhura melanura.* MAROON-TAILED PARAKEET. (Amaz Braz)..... _____
   ___*P. (m.) chapmani.* MAGDALENA PARAKEET. (c Colom)
   ___*P. (m.) melanura.* MAROON-TAILED PARAKEET. (sp)
   ___*P. (m.) berlepschi.* BERLEPSCH'S PARAKEET. (e Peru)

❑ *Pyrrhura orcesi.* EL ORO PARAKEET. (Andes w Ecua)............ _____

❑ *Pyrrhura rupicola.* BLACK-CAPPED PARAKEET. (wc SA).......... _____

❑ *Pyrrhura albipectus.* WHITE-NECKED PARAKEET. (e Ecua)........ _____

❑ *Pyrrhura calliptera.* BROWN-BREASTED PARAKEET. (ec Colom)..... _____

❑ *Pyrrhura hoematotis.* RED-EARED PARAKEET. (mts n Ven)........ _____

❑ *Pyrrhura rhodocephala.* ROSE-HEADED PARAKEET. (mts w Ven).... _____

❑ *Pyrrhura hoffmanni.* SULPHUR-WINGED PARAKEET. (mts CR, w Pan). _____

❑ *Enicognathus ferrugineus.* AUSTRAL PARAKEET. (s SA).......... _____

❑ *Enicognathus leptorhynchus.* SLENDER-BILLED PARAKEET. (c Chile) . _____

❑ *Myiopsitta monachus.* MONK PARAKEET. (sc SA; ◆e US, W Indies). _____

❑ *Bolborhynchus aymara.* GREY-HOODED PARAKEET. (Andes sc SA) . _____

❑ *Bolborhynchus aurifrons.* MOUNTAIN PARAKEET. (w,w SA)....... _____

❑ *Bolborhynchus lineola.* BARRED PARAKEET. (mts MA, w SA)..... _____

❑ *Bolborhynchus orbygnesius.* ANDEAN PARAKEET. (Andes sw SA)... _____

❑ *Bolborhynchus ferrugineifrons.* RUFOUS-FRONTED PARAKEET. (Colom)_____

❑ *Forpus cyanopygius.* MEXICAN PARROTLET. (w Mex)............ _____

❑ *Forpus passerinus.* GREEN-RUMPED PARROTLET. (n,nc SA)....... _____

❑ *Forpus xanthopterygius.* BLUE-WINGED PARROTLET. (SA)........ _____

❑ *Forpus conspicillatus.* SPECTACLED PARROTLET. (e Pan, nw SA).... _____

❑ *Forpus sclateri.* DUSKY-BILLED PARROTLET. (n,w Amaz)......... _____

❑ *Forpus coelestis.* PACIFIC PARROTLET. (Pac wc SA)............. _____

❑ *Forpus xanthops.* YELLOW-FACED PARROTLET. (Andes n Peru)..... _____

❑ *Brotogeris tirica.* PLAIN PARAKEET. (e,se Braz)................ _____

❑ *Brotogeris versicolurus.* CANARY-WINGED PARAKEET. (ne SA)...... _____

❑ *Brotogeris chiriri.* YELLOW-CHEVRONED PARAKEET. (sc,se SA)..... _____

❑ *Brotogeris pyrrhopterus.* GREY-CHEEKED PARAKEET. (cw SA)...... _____

❑ *Brotogeris jugularis.* ORANGE-CHINNED PARAKEET. (MA, nw SA)... _____

❑ *Brotogeris cyanoptera.* COBALT-WINGED PARAKEET. (w Amaz)..... _____
   ___*B. (c.) cyanoptera.* COBALT-WINGED PARAKEET. (sp)
   ___*B. (c.) gustavi.* BLUE-MARGINED PARAKEET. (n Peru)

❑ *Brotogeris chrysopterus.* GOLDEN-WINGED PARAKEET. (n,c Amaz)... _____

❏ *Brotogeris sanctithomae.* TUI PARAKEET. (w Amaz). . . . . _____

❏ *Nannopsittaca panychlora.* TEPUI PARROTLET. (Pant n SA). . . . . _____

❏ *Nannopsittaca dachilleae.* AMAZONIAN PARROTLET. (sw Amaz). . . . _____

❏ *Touit batavica.* LILAC-TAILED PARROTLET. (n SA). . . . . _____

❏ *Touit huetii.* SCARLET-SHOULDERED PARROTLET. (Amaz). . . . . _____

❏ *Touit costaricensis.* RED-FRONTED PARROTLET. (CR, w Pan). . . . . . . _____

❏ *Touit dilectissima.* BLUE-FRONTED PARROTLET. (e Pan, nw SA). . . . . _____

❏ *Touit purpurata.* SAPPHIRE-RUMPED PARROTLET. (n Amaz). . . . . _____

❏ *Touit melanonotus.* BROWN-BACKED PARROTLET. (e Braz). . . . . _____

❏ *Touit surda.* GOLDEN-TAILED PARROTLET. (e Braz). . . . . _____

❏ *Touit stictoptera.* SPOT-WINGED PARROTLET. (mts nw SA). . . . . _____

❏ *Pionites melanocephala.* BLACK-HEADED PARROT. (n Amaz). . . . . . . _____

❏ *Pionites leucogaster.* WHITE-BELLIED PARROT. (Amaz). . . . . _____

❏ *Pionopsitta pileata.* PILEATED PARROT. (se SA). . . . . _____

❏ *Pionopsitta haematotis.* BROWN-HOODED PARROT. (MA, nw SA). . . . _____

❏ *Pionopsitta pulchra.* ROSE-FACED PARROT. (nw SA). . . . . _____

❏ *Pionopsitta barrabandi.* ORANGE-CHEEKED PARROT. (w Amaz). . . . . _____

❏ *Pionopsitta pyrilia.* SAFFRON-HEADED PARROT. (e Pan, nw SA). . . . . _____

❏ *Pionopsitta caica.* CAICA PARROT. (ne SA). _____

❏ *Gypopsitta vulturina.* VULTURINE PARROT. (nc Braz). . . . . _____

❏ *Hapalopsittaca melanotis.* BLACK-WINGED PARROT. (Andes wc SA). _____

❏ *Hapalopsittaca amazonina.* RUSTY-FACED PARROT. (Andes nw SA). _____

❏ *Hapalopsittaca fuertesi.* INDIGO-WINGED PARROT. (mts wc Colom) . _____

❏ *Hapalopsittaca pyrrhops.* RED-FACED PARROT. (Andes wc SA). . . . . _____

❏ *Graydidascalus brachyurus.* SHORT-TAILED PARROT. (Amaz). . . . . . . _____

❏ *Pionus menstruus.* BLUE-HEADED PARROT. (s CA, n,c SA). . . . . _____

❏ *Pionus sordidus.* RED-BILLED PARROT. (mts w,n SA). . . . . _____

❏ *Pionus maximiliani.* SCALY-HEADED PARROT. (sc,se SA). . . . . _____

❏ *Pionus tumultuosus.* SPECKLE-FACED PARROT. (Andes w SA). . . . . . _____
   ___*P. (t.) seniloides.* WHITE-CAPPED PARROT. (nw SA)
   ___*P. (t.) tumultuosus.* PLUM-CROWNED PARROT. (wc SA)

❏ *Pionus senilis.* WHITE-CROWNED PARROT. (MA). . . . . _____

❏ *Pionus chalcopterus.* BRONZE-WINGED PARROT. (mts nw SA). . . . . . _____

❏ *Pionus fuscus.* DUSKY PARROT. (n,c Amaz). . . . . _____

❏ *Amazona leucocephala.* CUBAN PARROT. (n W Indies). . . . . _____

❑ *Amazona collaria.* YELLOW-BILLED PARROT. (Jam). . . . . _____

❑ *Amazona ventralis.* HISPANIOLAN PARROT. (Hisp). . . . . _____

❑ *Amazona albifrons.* WHITE-FRONTED PARROT. (n MA). . . . . _____

❑ *Amazona xantholora.* YELLOW-LORED PARROT. (nc MA). . . . . _____

❑ *Amazona agilis.* BLACK-BILLED PARROT. (mts w Jam). . . . . _____

❑ *Amazona vittata.* PUERTO RICAN PARROT. (PR). . . . . _____

❑ *Amazona tucumana.* TUCUMAN PARROT. (mts s SA). . . . . _____

❑ *Amazona pretrei.* RED-SPECTACLED PARROT. (se SA). . . . . _____

❑ *Amazona viridigenalis.* RED-CROWNED PARROT. (ne Mex; ◆ US). . . _____

❑ *Amazona finschi.* LILAC-CROWNED PARROT. (w Mex). . . . . _____

❑ *Amazona autumnalis.* RED-LORED PARROT. (MA, nw SA). . . . . _____
   ___*A. (a.) autumnalis.* RED-LORED PARROT. (n Ma)
   ___*A. (a.) salvini.* SALVIN'S PARROT. (s CA, nw SA)
   ___*A. (a.) diadema.* DIADEMED PARROT. (nw Amaz Braz)

❑ *Amazona dufresniana.* BLUE-CHEEKED PARROT. (mts n SA). . . . . . . _____

❑ *Amazona rhodocorytha.* RED-BROWED PARROT. (e Braz). . . . . _____

❑ *Amazona brasiliensis.* RED-TAILED PARROT. (se Braz). . . . . _____

❑ *Amazona festiva.* FESTIVE PARROT. (w Amaz). . . . . _____

❑ *Amazona xanthops.* YELLOW-FACED PARROT. (sc SA). . . . . _____

❑ *Amazona barbadensis.* YELLOW-SHOULDERED PARROT. (n Ven). . . . . _____

❑ *Amazona aestiva.* BLUE-FRONTED PARROT. (sc,se SA). . . . . _____

❑ *Amazona oratrix.* YELLOW-HEADED PARROT. (n MA). . . . . _____

❑ *Amazona auropalliata.* YELLOW-NAPED PARROT. (c MA). . . . . _____

❑ *Amazona ochrocephala.* YELLOW-CROWNED PARROT. (CA, Amaz) . _____

❑ *Amazona amazonica.* ORANGE-WINGED PARROT. (SA). . . . . _____

❑ *Amazona mercenaria.* SCALY-NAPED PARROT. (mts w SA). . . . . _____

❑ *Amazona farinosa.* MEALY PARROT. (MA, SA). . . . . _____

❑ *Amazona kawalli.* KAWALL'S PARROT. (c Amaz Braz). . . . . _____

❑ *Amazona vinacea.* VINACEOUS PARROT. (se SA). . . . . _____

❑ *Amazona versicolor.* ST. LUCIA PARROT. (mts St. Lucia). . . . . _____

❑ *Amazona arausiaca.* RED-NECKED PARROT. (mts Dominica). . . . . . . _____

❑ *Amazona guildingii.* ST. VINCENT PARROT. (mts St. Vincent). . . . . . _____

❑ *Amazona imperialis.* IMPERIAL PARROT. (mts Dominica). . . . . _____

❑ *Deroptyus accipitrinus.* RED-FAN PARROT. (Amaz). . . . . _____

❑ *Triclaria malachitacea.* BLUE-BELLIED PARROT. (se Braz). . . . . _____

Superorder APODIMORPHAE [127/425]
Order **APODIFORMES** [19/103]
Family **Apodidae** [18/99]

❏ *Cypseloides rutilus.* CHESTNUT-COLLARED SWIFT. (MA, w,n SA). . . . _____

❏ *Cypseloides phelpsi.* TEPUI SWIFT. (Pant n SA). . . . . _____

❏ *Cypseloides niger.* BLACK SWIFT. (mts w NA, MA, W Indies). . . . . . _____

❏ *Cypseloides lemosi.* WHITE-CHESTED SWIFT. (Andes sw Colom). . . . . _____

❏ *Cypseloides rothschildi.* ROTHSCHILD'S SWIFT. (Andes sw SA). . . . . . _____

❏ *Cypseloides fumigatus.* SOOTY SWIFT. (e Bol, se Braz). . . . . _____

❏ *Cypseloides cherriei.* SPOT-FRONTED SWIFT. (mts CR, cn SA). . . . . . _____

❏ *Cypseloides storeri.* WHITE-FRONTED SWIFT. (mts wc Mex). . . . . _____

❏ *Cypseloides cryptus.* WHITE-CHINNED SWIFT. (mts w,n SA; ◊-CA). . . _____

❏ *Cypseloides senex.* GREAT DUSKY SWIFT. (se SA). . . . . _____

❏ *Streptoprocne zonaris.* WHITE-COLLARED SWIFT. (MA, G Ant, SA) . _____

❏ *Streptoprocne biscutata.* BISCUTATE SWIFT. (e Braz). . . . . _____

❏ *Streptoprocne semicollaris.* WHITE-NAPED SWIFT. (w,c Mex). . . . . . . _____

❏ *Hydrochrous gigas.* WATERFALL SWIFT. (mts se Asia). . . . . _____

❏ *Collocalia esculenta.* GLOSSY SWIFTLET. (se Asia-Phil, sw Polyn). . . _____
    ___*C. (e.) affinis.* WHITE-BELLIED SWIFTLET. (se Asia)
    ___*C. (e.) marginata.* GREY-RUMPED SWIFTLET. (Phil)
    ___*C. (e.) esculenta.* GLOSSY SWIFTLET. (L Sunda-sw Polyn)

❏ *Collocalia linchi.* CAVE SWIFTLET. (se Asia). . . . . _____

❏ *Collocalia troglodytes.* PYGMY SWIFTLET. (Phil). . . . . _____

❏ *Collocalia elaphra.* SEYCHELLES SWIFTLET. (Seyc). . . . . _____

❏ *Collocalia francica.* MASCARENE SWIFTLET. (Maur, Réun). . . . . _____

❏ *Collocalia unicolor.* INDIAN SWIFTLET. (sw pen India). . . . . _____

❏ *Collocalia mearnsi.* PHILIPPINE SWIFTLET. (Phil). . . . . _____

❏ *Collocalia infuscata.* MOLUCCAN SWIFTLET. (Wall). . . . . _____

❏ *Collocalia hirundinacea.* MOUNTAIN SWIFTLET. (NG). . . . . _____

❏ *Collocalia spodiopygius.* WHITE-RUMPED SWIFTLET. (Bism-Samoa) . _____

❏ *Collocalia terraereginae.* AUSTRALIAN SWIFTLET. (ne Aust). . . . . _____

❏ *Collocalia brevirostris.* HIMALAYAN SWIFTLET. (s Asia; ◊-se Asia). . . _____
    ___*C. (b.) brevirostris.* HIMALAYAN SWIFTLET. (sp)
    ___*C. (b.) innominata.* CHINESE SWIFTLET. (s China)

❏ *Collocalia vulcanorum.* VOLCANO SWIFTLET. (Java). . . . . _____

❏ *Collocalia rogersi.* INDOCHINESE SWIFTLET. (se Asia). . . . . _____

❏ *Collocalia whiteheadi.* WHITEHEAD'S SWIFTLET. (mts n,s Phil). . . . . . _____

❑ *Collocalia nuditarsus.* BARE-LEGGED SWIFTLET. (mts c,e NG)..... _____

❑ *Collocalia orientalis.* MAYR'S SWIFTLET. (Bism, Solom).......... _____

❑ *Collocalia salangana.* MOSSY-NEST SWIFTLET. (G Sunda, Phil)..... _____

❑ *Collocalia palawanensis.* PALAWAN SWIFTLET. (cw Phil).......... _____

❑ *Collocalia amelis.* GREY SWIFTLET. (e Born, Phil).............. _____

❑ *Collocalia vanikorensis.* UNIFORM SWIFTLET. (Moluc-Solom)...... _____

❑ *Collocalia pelewensis.* PALAU SWIFTLET. (Palau)............... _____

❑ *Collocalia inquieta.* MICRONESIAN SWIFTLET. (Micro)........... _____
 ___*C. (v.) bartschi.* MARIANA SWIFTLET. (Guam)
 ___*C. (v.) inquieta.* CAROLINE ISLANDS SWIFTLET. (Carol)

❑ *Collocalia sawtelli.* ATIU SWIFTLET. (s Cook Is)............... _____

❑ *Collocalia leucophaeus.* TAHITI SWIFTLET. (e Soc)............. _____

❑ *Collocalia ocista.* MARQUESAN SWIFTLET. (Marq).............. _____

❑ *Collocalia maxima.* BLACK-NEST SWIFTLET. (s Asia-w Phil)....... _____

❑ *Collocalia fuciphaga.* EDIBLE-NEST SWIFTLET. (se Asia-Wall)...... _____
 ___*C. (f.) inexpectata.* EDIBLE-NEST SWIFTLET. (And, Nico)
 ___*C. (f.) vestita.* BROWN-RUMPED SWIFTLET. (se Asia)
 ___*C. (f.) fuciphaga.* THUNBERG'S SWIFTLET. (Java, L Sunda)

❑ *Collocalia germani.* GERMAN'S SWIFTLET. (se Asia-Phil)......... _____

❑ *Collocalia papuensis.* PAPUAN SWIFTLET. (n NG).............. _____

❑ *Schoutedenapus myoptilus.* SCARCE SWIFT. (Bioko, e,se Afr)....... _____

❑ *Schoutedenapus schoutedeni.* SCHOUTEDEN'S SWIFT. (e Zaire)...... _____

❑ *Mearnsia picina.* PHILIPPINE NEEDLETAIL. (se Phil)............. _____

❑ *Mearnsia novaeguineae.* PAPUAN NEEDLETAIL. (NG)............. _____

❑ *Zoonavena grandidieri.* MALAGASY SPINETAIL. (Com, Mad)....... _____

❑ *Zoonavena thomensis.* SAO TOME SPINETAIL. (Prín, ST)......... _____

❑ *Zoonavena sylvatica.* WHITE-RUMPED SPINETAIL. (s Asia)........ _____

❑ *Telacanthura ussheri.* MOTTLED SPINETAIL. (Afr).............. _____

❑ *Telacanthura melanopygia.* BLACK SPINETAIL. (w,c Afr)......... _____

❑ *Rhaphidura leucopygialis.* SILVER-RUMPED SPINETAIL. (se Asia).... _____

❑ *Rhaphidura sabini.* SABINE'S SPINETAIL. (w,c Afr).............. _____

❑ *Neafrapus cassini.* CASSIN'S SPINETAIL. (w,c Afr).............. _____

❑ *Neafrapus boehmi.* BAT-LIKE SPINETAIL. (e,s Afr).............. _____

❑ *Hirundapus caudacutus.* WHITE-THROATED NEEDLETAIL. (e,s Asia). _____

❑ *Hirundapus cochinchinensis.* SILVER-BACKED NEEDLETAIL. (se Asia)_____
 ___*H. (c.) rupchandi.* RUPCHAND'S NEEDLETAIL. (c Nepal)
 ___*H. (c.) cochinchinensis.* SILVER-BACKED NEEDLETAIL. (sp)

❏ *Hirundapus giganteus.* BROWN-BACKED NEEDLETAIL. (s,se Asia)... _____

❏ *Hirundapus celebensis.* PURPLE NEEDLETAIL. (n Sulaw, Phil)....... _____

❏ *Chaetura spinicauda.* BAND-RUMPED SWIFT. (s CA, n,nc SA)....... _____

❏ *Chaetura martinica.* LESSER ANTILLEAN SWIFT. (c L Ant)........ _____

❏ *Chaetura cinereiventris.* GREY-RUMPED SWIFT. (CA, s L Ant, SA)... _____
   ___*C. (c.) sclateri.* ASH-RUMPED SWIFT. (sp)
   ___*C. (c.) cinereiventris.* GREY-RUMPED SWIFT. (se SA)

❏ *Chaetura egregia.* PALE-RUMPED SWIFT. (wc SA)............... _____

❏ *Chaetura pelagica.* CHIMNEY SWIFT. (e NA; ◊ SA)............... _____

❏ *Chaetura vauxi.* VAUX'S SWIFT. (w NA-nw SA)............... _____
   ___*C. (v.) vauxi.* VAUX'S SWIFT. (w NA-ne Mex; ◊ n,c MA)
   ___*C. (v.) richmondi.* DUSKY-BACKED SWIFT. (MA, n Ven)
   ___*C. (v.) gaumeri.* YUCATAN SWIFT. (se Mex)

❏ *Chaetura chapmani.* CHAPMAN'S SWIFT. (n,c SA)............... _____

❏ *Chaetura brachyura.* SHORT-TAILED SWIFT. (s CA, s L Ant, SA).... _____

❏ *Chaetura andrei.* ASHY-TAILED SWIFT. (SA)................... _____

❏ *Aeronautes saxatalis.* WHITE-THROATED SWIFT. (w NA, MA)...... _____

❏ *Aeronautes montivagus.* WHITE-TIPPED SWIFT. (mts n,wc SA)...... _____

❏ *Aeronautes andecolus.* ANDEAN SWIFT. (Andes sw SA).......... _____

❏ *Tachornis phoenicobia.* ANTILLEAN PALM-SWIFT. (G Ant)........ _____

❏ *Tachornis furcata.* PYGMY SWIFT. (nw SA)................... _____

❏ *Tachornis squamata.* FORK-TAILED PALM-SWIFT. (SA)........... _____

❏ *Panyptila sanctihieronymi.* GREAT SWALLOW-TAILED SWIFT. (MA) . _____

❏ *Panyptila cayennensis.* LESSER SWALLOW-TAILED SWIFT. (MA, SA). _____

❏ *Cypsiurus parvus.* AFRICAN PALM-SWIFT. (Afr reg, Mad)......... _____
   ___*C. (p.) parvus.* AFRICAN PALM-SWIFT. (Afr reg)
   ___*C. (p.) gracilis.* MADAGASCAR PALM-SWIFT. (Mad)

❏ *Cypsiurus balasiensis.* ASIAN PALM-SWIFT. (s Asia-Phil)......... _____

❏ *Tachymarptis melba.* ALPINE SWIFT. (mts Palea, Afr, Mad, s Asia) . _____

❏ *Tachymarptis aequatorialis.* MOTTLED SWIFT. (mts Afr).......... _____

❏ *Apus alexandri.* ALEXANDER'S SWIFT. (C Verde)............... _____

❏ *Apus apus.* COMMON SWIFT. (Eura; ◊ Afr)................... _____

❏ *Apus unicolor.* PLAIN SWIFT. (e Atl)....................... _____

❏ *Apus niansae.* NYANZA SWIFT. (ne Afr).................... _____

❏ *Apus pallidus.* PALLID SWIFT. (sw,sc Palea; ◊-s Afr, sc Asia)....... _____

❏ *Apus barbatus.* AFRICAN SWIFT. (wc,e,s Afr)................ _____
   ___*A. (b.) sladeniae.* FERNANDO PO SWIFT. (wc Afr)
   ___*A. (b.) barbatus.* AFRICAN SWIFT. (e,s Afr)

❑ *Apus berliozi.* FORBES-WATSON'S SWIFT. (ne Afr). . . . . _____

❑ *Apus bradfieldi.* BRADFIELD'S SWIFT. (sw S Afr). . . . . _____

❑ *Apus balstoni.* MADAGASCAR SWIFT. (Mad). . . . . _____

❑ *Apus pacificus.* FORK-TAILED SWIFT. (e Eura; ◊ Indon-NG, Aust). . . . _____

❑ *Apus acuticauda.* DARK-RUMPED SWIFT. (Himal e India). . . . . _____

❑ *Apus affinis.* LITTLE SWIFT. (Afr reg, s Eura). . . . . _____

❑ *Apus nipalensis.* HOUSE SWIFT. (s Asia-n Phil). . . . . _____

❑ *Apus horus.* HORUS SWIFT. (c,s,ne Afr). . . . . _____

❑ *Apus toulsoni.* LOANDA SWIFT. (cw Afr). _____

❑ *Apus caffer.* WHITE-RUMPED SWIFT. (w Medit, Afr). . . . . _____

❑ *Apus batesi.* BATES'S SWIFT. (w,c Afr). . . . . _____

Family **Hemiprocnidae** [1/4]

❑ *Hemiprocne coronata.* CRESTED TREESWIFT. (s,se Asia). . . . . _____

❑ *Hemiprocne longipennis.* GREY-RUMPED TREESWIFT. (se Asia). . . . . _____

❑ *Hemiprocne mystacea.* MOUSTACHED TREESWIFT. (Moluc-Solom). . . _____

❑ *Hemiprocne comata.* WHISKERED TREESWIFT. (se Asia-Phil). . . . . . . _____

Order **TROCHILIFORMES** [108/322]
Family **Trochilidae** [108/322]
Subfamily Phaethornithinae [4/29]

❑ *Glaucis aenea.* BRONZY HERMIT. (s CA, nw SA). . . . . _____

❑ *Glaucis hirsuta.* RUFOUS-BREASTED HERMIT. (s L Ant, c,e Pan, SA) . _____

❑ *Threnetes niger.* SOOTY BARBTHROAT. (ne SA). . . . . _____

❑ *Threnetes ruckeri.* BAND-TAILED BARBTHROAT. (CA, nw SA). . . . . . _____

❑ *Threnetes leucurus.* PALE-TAILED BARBTHROAT. (Amaz). . . . . _____
   ___*T. (l.) leucurus.* PALE-TAILED BARBTHROAT. (sp)
   ___*T. (l.) loehkeni.* BRONZE-TAILED BARBTHROAT. (ne Braz)

❑ *Phaethornis yaruqui.* WHITE-WHISKERED HERMIT. (nw SA). . . . . . . _____

❑ *Phaethornis guy.* GREEN HERMIT. (s CA, w,n SA). . . . . _____

❑ *Phaethornis syrmatophorus.* TAWNY-BELLIED HERMIT. (nw SA). . . . _____

❑ *Phaethornis superciliosus.* LONG-TAILED HERMIT. (MA, SA). . . . . . . _____
   ___*P. (s.) griseoventer.* JALISCO HERMIT. (nw Mex)
   ___*P. (s.) mexicanus.* HARTERT'S HERMIT. (wc Mex)
   ___*P. (s.) longirostris.* LONG-TAILED HERMIT. (MA, nw SA)
   ___*P. (s.) superciliosus.* RUSTY-BREASTED HERMIT. (n,c SA)

❑ *Phaethornis malaris.* GREAT-BILLED HERMIT. (cn,e SA). . . . . _____
   ___*P. (m.) malaris.* GREAT-BILLED HERMIT. (cn SA)
   ___*P. (m.) margarettae.* MARGARETTA'S HERMIT. (e Braz)

❑ *Phaethornis eurynome.* SCALE-THROATED HERMIT. (se SA). . . . . . . _____

❑ *Phaethornis hispidus.* WHITE-BEARDED HERMIT. (Amaz). . . . . _____

❑ *Phaethornis anthophilus.* PALE-BELLIED HERMIT. (s CA, nw SA). . . _____

❑ *Phaethornis bourcieri.* STRAIGHT-BILLED HERMIT. (Amaz). . . . . _____

❑ *Phaethornis koepckeae.* KOEPCKE'S HERMIT. (mts e Peru). . . . . _____

❑ *Phaethornis philippii.* NEEDLE-BILLED HERMIT. (wc SA). . . . . _____

❑ *Phaethornis squalidus.* DUSKY-THROATED HERMIT. (wc,c,se SA). . . . _____
   ___*P. (s.) rupurumii.* STREAK-THROATED HERMIT. (Amaz)
   ___*P. (s.) squalidus.* SOOTY-THROATED HERMIT. (se Braz)

❑ *Phaethornis augusti.* SOOTY-CAPPED HERMIT. (n SA). . . . . _____

❑ *Phaethornis pretrei.* PLANALTO HERMIT. (sc SA). . . . . _____

❑ *Phaethornis subochraceus.* BUFF-BELLIED HERMIT. (sw SA). . . . . . . _____

❑ *Phaethornis nattereri.* CINNAMON-THROATED HERMIT. (s Amaz). . . . _____

❑ *Phaethornis gounellei.* BROAD-TIPPED HERMIT. (e Braz). . . . . _____

❑ *Phaethornis ruber.* REDDISH HERMIT. (wc,c SA). . . . . _____

❑ *Phaethornis stuarti.* WHITE-BROWED HERMIT. (sw Amaz). . . . . _____

❑ *Phaethornis griseogularis.* GREY-CHINNED HERMIT. (nw,n SA). . . . . _____
   ___*P. (g.) griseogularis.* GREY-CHINNED HERMIT. (nw SA)
   ___*P. (g.) porcullae.* PORCULLA HERMIT. (nw Peru)

❑ *Phaethornis longuemareus.* LITTLE HERMIT. (MA, n,c SA). . . . . _____
   ___*P. (l.) adolphi.* BOUCARD'S HERMIT. (MA, nw SA)
   ___*P. (l.) longirostris.* STRIPE-THROATED HERMIT. (n,c Colom)
   ___*P. (l.) longuemareus.* RUSTY-BREASTED HERMIT. (w Amaz)

❑ *Phaethornis idaliae.* MINUTE HERMIT. (se Braz). . . . . _____

❑ *Eutoxeres aquila.* WHITE-TIPPED SICKLEBILL. (s CA, w SA). . . . . . . _____

❑ *Eutoxeres condamini.* BUFF-TAILED SICKLEBILL. (wc SA). . . . . _____

Subfamily Trochilinae [104/293]

❑ *Androdon aequatorialis.* TOOTH-BILLED HUMMINGBIRD. (Pan-nw SA)_____

❑ *Ramphodon naevius.* SAW-BILLED HERMIT. (se Braz). . . . . _____

❑ *Ramphodon dohrnii.* HOOK-BILLED HERMIT. (se Braz). . . . . _____

❑ *Doryfera johannae.* BLUE-FRONTED LANCEBILL. (w Amaz). . . . . _____

❑ *Doryfera ludovicae.* GREEN-FRONTED LANCEBILL. (mts s CA, w SA). _____

❑ *Phaeochroa cuvierii.* SCALY-BREASTED HUMMINGBIRD. (MA-nw SA)_____
   ___*P. (c.) roberti.* ROBERT'S HUMMINGBIRD. (c MA)
   ___*P. (c.) cuvierii.* CUVIER'S HUMMINGBIRD. (s CA, nw SA)

❑ *Campylopterus curvipennis.* WEDGE-TAILED SABREWING. (n,c MA) . _____
   ___*C. (c.) curvipennis.* CURVE-WINGED SABREWING. (e,s Mex)
   ___*C. (c.) pampa.* WEDGE-TAILED SABREWING. (c MA)

❑ *Campylopterus excellens.* LONG-TAILED SABREWING. (ec Mex)..... _____

❑ *Campylopterus largipennis.* GREY-BREASTED SABREWING. (Amaz) . _____

❑ *Campylopterus rufus.* RUFOUS SABREWING. (mts c MA).......... _____

❑ *Campylopterus hyperythrus.* RUFOUS-BREASTED SABREWING. (Pant). _____

❑ *Campylopterus duidae.* BUFF-BREASTED SABREWING. (Pant nc SA) . _____

❑ *Campylopterus hemileucurus.* VIOLET SABREWING. (mts MA)...... _____

❑ *Campylopterus ensipennis.* WHITE-TAILED SABREWING. (n Ven, Tob) _____

❑ *Campylopterus falcatus.* LAZULINE SABREWING. (mts nw SA)...... _____

❑ *Campylopterus phainopeplus.* SANTA MARTA SABREWING. (n Colom)_____

❑ *Campylopterus villaviscensio.* NAPO SABREWING. (Andes wc SA)... _____

❑ *Eupetomena macroura.* SWALLOW-TAILED HUMMINGBIRD. (n,c SA). _____

❑ *Florisuga mellivora.* WHITE-NECKED JACOBIN. (MA, n,c SA)...... _____

❑ *Melanotrochilus fuscus.* BLACK JACOBIN. (se SA).............. _____

❑ *Colibri delphinae.* BROWN VIOLET-EAR. (MA, SA).............. _____

❑ *Colibri thalassinus.* GREEN VIOLET-EAR. (MA, w SA)........... _____
   ___*C. (t.) thalassinus.* GREEN VIOLET-EAR. (mts n,c MA)
   ___*C. (t.) cyanotus.* MOUNTAIN VIOLET-EAR. (mts s CA, w SA)

❑ *Colibri coruscans.* SPARKLING VIOLET-EAR. (mts w,n SA)........ _____

❑ *Colibri serrirostris.* WHITE-VENTED VIOLET-EAR. (se SA)......... _____

❑ *Anthracothorax viridigula.* GREEN-THROATED MANGO. (n,e SA).... _____

❑ *Anthracothorax prevostii.* GREEN-BREASTED MANGO. (MA, w,n SA). _____
   ___*A. (p.) prevostii.* PREVOST'S MANGO. (MA, cn SA)
   ___*A. (p.) veraguensis.* VERAGUAS MANGO. (w Pan)
   ___*A. (p.) iridescens.* ECUADORIAN MANGO. (cw SA)

❑ *Anthracothorax nigricollis.* BLACK-THROATED MANGO. (Pan, SA) . _____

❑ *Anthracothorax mango.* JAMAICAN MANGO. (Jam).............. _____

❑ *Anthracothorax dominicus.* ANTILLEAN MANGO. (e G Ant)....... _____

❑ *Anthracothorax viridis.* GREEN MANGO. (PR)................. _____

❑ *Avocettula recurvirostris.* FIERY-TAILED AWLBILL. (Amaz)........ _____

❑ *Eulampis jugularis.* PURPLE-THROATED CARIB. (mts L Ant)....... _____

❑ *Eulampis holosericeus.* GREEN-THROATED CARIB. (PR-L Ant)...... _____

❑ *Chrysolampis mosquitus.* RUBY-TOPAZ HUMMINGBIRD. (SA)....... _____

❑ *Orthorhyncus cristatus.* ANTILLEAN CRESTED HUMMINGB. (W Indies)_____

❑ *Klais guimeti.* VIOLET-HEADED HUMMINGBIRD. (CA, w Amaz)...... _____

❑ *Abeillia abeillei.* EMERALD-CHINNED HUMMINGBIRD. (mts c MA).... _____

❑ *Stephanoxis lalandi.* PLOVERCREST. (se SA)................... _____
   ___*S. (l.) lalandi.* BLACK-BREASTED PLOVERCREST. (mts se SA)
   ___*S. (l.) loddigesii.* VIOLET-CRESTED PLOVERCREST. (se Braz)

❏ *Lophornis ornatus.* TUFTED COQUETTE. (n SA)................ _____

❏ *Lophornis gouldii.* DOT-EARED COQUETTE. (c Amaz)........... _____

❏ *Lophornis magnificus.* FRILLED COQUETTE. (c,e Braz).......... _____

❏ *Lophornis brachylopha* SHORT-CRESTED COQUETTE. (sw Mex)..... _____

❏ *Lophornis delattrei* RUFOUS-CRESTED COQUETTE. (s CA, w Amaz) . _____

❏ *Lophornis stictolophus.* SPANGLED COQUETTE. (nw,w SA)........ _____

❏ *Lophornis chalybeus.* FESTIVE COQUETTE. (c,se SA)............. _____
    ___*L. (c.) verreauxi.* BUTTERFLY COQUETTE. (Amaz)
    ___*L. (c.c) chalybeus.* FESTIVE COQUETTE. (se Braz)

❏ *Lophornis pavoninus.* PEACOCK COQUETTE. (Pant nc SA)........ _____

❏ *Lophornis helenae.* BLACK-CRESTED COQUETTE. (MA)........... _____

❏ *Lophornis adorabilis.* WHITE-CRESTED COQUETTE. (s CA)........ _____

❏ *Popelairia popelairii.* WIRE-CRESTED THORNTAIL. (w Amaz)....... _____

❏ *Popelairia langsdorffi.* BLACK-BELLIED THORNTAIL. (wc,c,e SA).... _____

❏ *Popelairia letitiae.* COPPERY THORNTAIL. (Bol)................ _____

❏ *Popelairia conversii.* GREEN THORNTAIL. (s CA, nw SA)......... _____

❏ *Discosura longicauda.* RACKET-TAILED COQUETTE. (nc,e SA)...... _____

❏ *Chlorestes notatus.* BLUE-CHINNED SAPPHIRE. (n,c,se SA)......... _____

❏ *Chlorostilbon canivetii.* FORK-TAILED EMERALD. (MA)........... _____
    ___*C. (cc.) auriceps.* GOLDEN-CROWNED EMERALD. (w Mex)
    ___*C. (c.) forficatus.* COZUMEL EMERALD. (Coz)
    ___*C. (c.) canivetii.* CANIVET'S EMERALD. (n,e MA)
    ___*C. (c.) salvini.* SALVIN'S EMERALD. (c MA)

❏ *Chlorostilbon assimilis.* GARDEN EMERALD. (sw CR, Pan)........ _____

❏ *Chlorostilbon mellisugus.* BLUE-TAILED EMERALD. (n,c SA)....... _____

❏ *Chlorostilbon aureoventris.* GLITTERING-BELLIED EMERALD. (s SA) . _____
    ___*C. (a.) aureoventris.* GLITTERING-BELLIED EMERALD. (sc SA)
    ___*C. (a.) pucherani.* PUCHERAN'S EMERALD. (se Braz)

❏ *Chlorostilbon ricordii.* CUBAN EMERALD. (Cuba, Bah)........... _____

❏ *Chlorostilbon bracei.* BRACE'S EMERALD. (†n Bah)............. _____

❏ *Chlorostilbon swainsonii.* HISPANIOLAN EMERALD. (Hisp)........ _____

❏ *Chlorostilbon maugaeus.* PUERTO RICAN EMERALD. (PR)......... _____

❏ *Chlorostilbon gibsoni.* RED-BILLED EMERALD. (n SA)............ _____

❏ *Chlorostilbon russatus.* COPPERY EMERALD. (mts n SA).......... _____

❏ *Chlorostilbon stenura.* NARROW-TAILED EMERALD. (Andes nw SA) . _____

❏ *Chlorostilbon alice.* GREEN-TAILED EMERALD. (mts n Ven)........ _____

❏ *Chlorostilbon poortmani.* SHORT-TAILED EMERALD. (mts nw SA)... _____
    ___*C. (p.) euchloris.* SANTANDER EMERALD. (c Colom)
    ___*C. (p.) poortmani.* SHORT-TAILED EMERALD. (sp)

❏ *Cynanthus sordidus.* DUSKY HUMMINGBIRD. (mts c Mex). . . . . _____

❏ *Cynanthus latirostris.* BROAD-BILLED HUMMINGBIRD. (sw US-Mex). _____
   ___*C. (l.) latirostris.* BROAD-BILLED HUMMINGBIRD. (sw US, n,c Mex)
   ___*C. (l.) doubledayi.* DOUBLEDAY'S HUMMINGBIRD. (sw Mex)

❏ *Cyanophaia bicolor.* BLUE-HEADED HUMMINGBIRD. (mts c L Ant). . . _____

❏ *Thalurania ridgwayi.* MEXICAN WOODNYMPH. (w Mex). . . . . _____

❏ *Thalurania colombica.* BLUE-CROWNED WOODNYMPH. (CA, n SA) . _____
   ___*T. (c.) townsendi.* BLUE-CROWNED WOODNYMPH. (CA)
   ___*T. (c.) colombica.* COLOMBIAN WOODNYMPH. (n SA)

❏ *Thalurania fannyi.* GREEN-CROWNED WOODNYMPH. (Pan, nw SA) . _____
   ___*T. (f.) fannyi.* GREEN-CROWNED WOODNYMPH. (Pan, nw Colom)
   ___*T. (f.) hypochlora.* EMERALD-BELLIED WOODNYMPH. (nw SA)

❏ *Thalurania furcata.* FORK-TAILED WOODNYMPH. (SA). . . . . _____

❏ *Thalurania watertonii.* LONG-TAILED WOODNYMPH. (e Braz). . . . . . . _____

❏ *Thalurania glaucopis.* VIOLET-CAPPED WOODNYMPH. (se SA). . . . . . _____

❏ *Panterpe insignis.* FIERY-THROATED HUMMINGBIRD. (mts CR-w Pan). _____

❏ *Damophila julie.* VIOLET-BELLIED HUMMINGBIRD. (Pan, nw SA). . . . _____

❏ *Lepidopyga coeruleogularis.* SAPPHIRE-THROATED H. (Pan-n Colom). _____

❏ *Lepidopyga lilliae.* SAPPHIRE-BELLIED HUMMINGBIRD. (cn Colom). . . _____

❏ *Lepidopyga goudoti.* SHINING-GREEN HUMMINGBIRD. (nw SA). . . . . . _____
   ___*L. (g.) luminosa.* LUMINOUS HUMMINGBIRD. (n Colom)
   ___*L. (g.) goudoti.* SHINING-GREEN HUMMINGBIRD. (e Colom, nw Ven)

❏ *Hylocharis xantusii.* XANTUS'S HUMMINGBIRD. (s Baja). . . . . _____

❏ *Hylocharis leucotis.* WHITE-EARED HUMMINGBIRD. (sw US-c MA) . _____

❏ *Hylocharis eliciae.* BLUE-THROATED GOLDENTAIL. (MA-nw Colom). _____

❏ *Hylocharis sapphirina.* RUFOUS-THROATED SAPPHIRE. (SA). . . . . . . _____

❏ *Hylocharis cyanus.* WHITE-CHINNED SAPPHIRE. (n,c SA). . . . . _____

❏ *Hylocharis pyropygia.* FLAME-RUMPED SAPPHIRE. (e Braz). . . . . . . _____

❏ *Hylocharis chrysura.* GILDED HUMMINGBIRD. (sc,se SA). . . . . _____

❏ *Hylocharis grayi.* BLUE-HEADED SAPPHIRE. (e Pan, nw SA). . . . . . . _____

❏ *Chrysuronia oenone.* GOLDEN-TAILED SAPPHIRE. (w Amaz). . . . . . . _____

❏ *Goldmania violiceps.* VIOLET-CAPPED H. (mts e Pan, nw Colom). . . . _____

❏ *Goethalsia bella.* RUFOUS-CHEEKED HUMMINGBIRD. (e Pan, nw Colom)_____

❏ *Trochilus polytmus.* STREAMERTAIL. (Jam). . . . . _____
   ___*T. (p.) polytmus.* RED-BILLED STREAMERTAIL. (w,c Jam)
   ___*T. (p.) scitulus.* BLACK-BILLED STREAMERTAIL. (e Jam)

❏ *Leucochloris albicollis.* WHITE-THROATED HUMMINGBIRD. (se SA) . _____

❏ *Polytmus guainumbi.* WHITE-TAILED GOLDENTHROAT. (SA). . . . . . . _____

❑ *Polytmus milleri.* TEPUI GOLDENTHROAT. (mts s Ven). . . . . _____

❑ *Polytmus theresiae.* GREEN-TAILED GOLDENTHROAT. (Amaz). . . . . . . _____

❑ *Leucippus fallax.* BUFFY HUMMINGBIRD. (cn SA). . . . . _____

❑ *Leucippus baeri.* TUMBES HUMMINGBIRD. (w Peru). . . . . _____

❑ *Leucippus taczanowskii.* SPOT-THROATED HUMMINGBIRD. (n Peru) . _____

❑ *Leucippus chlorocercus.* OLIVE-SPOTTED HUMMINGBIRD. (w Amaz). _____

❑ *Taphrospilus hypostictus.* MANY-SPOTTED HUMMINGB. (w Amaz). . . _____

❑ *Amazilia viridicauda.* GREEN-AND-WHITE HUMMINGBIRD. (c,s Peru) . _____

❑ *Amazilia chionogaster.* WHITE-BELLIED HUMMINGBIRD. (wc SA). . . . _____

❑ *Amazilia candida.* WHITE-BELLIED EMERALD. (MA). . . . . _____

❑ *Amazilia chionopectus.* WHITE-CHESTED EMERALD. (n SA). . . . . _____

❑ *Amazilia versicolor.* VERSICOLORED EMERALD. (nc,c SA). . . . . _____
   ___*A. (v.) versicolor.* VERSICOLORED EMERALD. (sp)
   ___*A. (v.) hollandi.* CUYUNI EMERALD. (s Ven)

❑ *Amazilia luciae.* HONDURAN EMERALD. (Hond). . . . . _____

❑ *Amazilia fimbriata.* GLITTERING-THROATED EMERALD. (SA). . . . . . . _____

❑ *Amazilia distans.* TACHIRA EMERALD. (sw Ven). . . . . _____

❑ *Amazilia lactea.* SAPPHIRE-SPANGLED EMERALD. (nw,sw,c SA). . . . . _____
   ___*A. (l.) zimmeri.* TEPUI EMERALD. (s Ven)
   ___*A. (l.) bartletti.* BARTLETT'S EMERALD. (sw SA)
   ___*A. (l.) lactea.* SAPPHIRE-SPANGLED EMERALD. (e Braz)

❑ *Amazilia amabilis.* BLUE-CHESTED HUMMINGBIRD. (s CA, nw SA). . . _____

❑ *Amazilia decora.* CHARMING HUMMINGBIRD. (sw CR, w Pan). . . . . . _____

❑ *Amazilia rosenbergi.* PURPLE-CHESTED HUMMINGBIRD. (nw SA). . . . _____

❑ *Amazilia boucardi.* MANGROVE HUMMINGBIRD. (Pac CR). . . . . _____

❑ *Amazilia franciae.* ANDEAN EMERALD. (Andes nw SA). . . . . _____

❑ *Amazilia leucogaster.* PLAIN-BELLIED EMERALD. (nw,e SA). . . . . _____

❑ *Amazilia cyanocephala.* AZURE-CROWNED HUMMINGBIRD. (MA). . . . _____
   ___*A. (c.) cyanocephala.* AZURE-CROWNED HUMMINGBIRD. (sp)
   ___*A. (c.) chlorostephana.* MOSQUITIA HUMMINGBIRD. (e Hond, ne Nica)

❑ *Amazilia cyanifrons.* INDIGO-CAPPED HUMMINGBIRD. (CR, n Colom). _____

❑ *Amazilia beryllina.* BERYLLINE HUMMINGBIRD. (n,c MA). . . . . _____

❑ *Amazilia cyanura.* BLUE-TAILED HUMMINGBIRD. (c MA). . . . . _____

❑ *Amazilia saucerrottei.* STEELY-VENTED HUMMINGBIRD. (c CA-nw SA) _____

❑ *Amazilia tobaci.* COPPER-RUMPED HUMMINGBIRD. (n SA). . . . . _____

❑ *Amazilia viridigaster.* GREEN-BELLIED HUMMINGBIRD. (n Amaz). . . . _____

❑ *Amazilia edward.* SNOWY-BREASTED HUMMINGBIRD. (s CA). . . . . . . _____
   ___*A. (e.) niveoventer.* SNOWY-BELLIED HUMMINGBIRD. (sw CR, w Pan)
   ___*A. (e.) edward.* EDWARDS'S HUMMINGBIRD. (c,e Pan)

❑ *Amazilia rutila.* CINNAMON HUMMINGBIRD. (MA). . . . . _____

❑ *Amazilia yucatanensis.* BUFF-BELLIED HUMMINGBIRD. (s Tex-n Guat) _____

❑ *Amazilia tzacatl.* RUFOUS-TAILED HUMMINGBIRD. (MA, nw SA). . . . . _____
   ___*A. (t.) tzacatl.* RUFOUS-TAILED HUMMINGBIRD. (sp)
   ___*A. (t.) handleyi.* ESCUDO HUMMINGBIRD. (nw Pan)

❑ *Amazilia castaneiventris.* CHESTNUT-BELLIED H. (nc Colom). . . . . . _____

❑ *Amazilia amazilia.* AMAZILIA HUMMINGBIRD. (w SA). . . . . _____

❑ *Amazilia viridifrons.* GREEN-FRONTED HUMMINGBIRD. (s Mex). . . . . _____
   ___*A. (v.) viridifrons.* GREEN-FRONTED HUMMINGBIRD. (sp)
   ___*A. (v.) wagneri.* CINNAMON-SIDED HUMMINGBIRD. (s Oax)

❑ *Amazilia violiceps.* VIOLET-CROWNED HUMMINGBIRD. (sw US, Mex). _____

❑ *Eupherusa poliocerca.* WHITE-TAILED HUMMINGBIRD. (mts wc Mex). _____

❑ *Eupherusa eximia.* STRIPE-TAILED HUMMINGBIRD. (MA). . . . . _____

❑ *Eupherusa cyanophrys.* BLUE-CAPPED HUMMINGBIRD. (mts sc Oax). _____

❑ *Eupherusa nigriventris.* BLACK-BELLIED HUMMINGBIRD. (mts s CA). _____

❑ *Elvira chionura.* WHITE-TAILED EMERALD. (mts CA). . . . . _____

❑ *Elvira cupreiceps.* COPPERY-HEADED EMERALD. (mts CR). . . . . _____

❑ *Microchera albocoronata.* SNOWCAP. (s CA). . . . . _____

❑ *Chalybura buffonii.* WHITE-VENTED PLUMELETEER. (s CA, nw SA) . _____
   ___*C. (b.) buffonii.* WHITE-VENTED PLUMELETEER. (sp)
   ___*C. (b.) caeruleogaster.* BLUE-BELLIED PLUMELETEER. (mts.se Colom)
   ___*C. (b.) intermedia.* ECUADORIAN PLUMELETEER. (mts w Ecua, n Peru)

❑ *Chalybura urochrysia.* BRONZE-TAILED PLUMELETEER. (s CA-nw SA) _____
   ___*C. (u.) melanorrhoa.* BLACK-VENTED PLUMELETEER. (Hond-CR)
   ___*C. (u.) urochrysia.* BRONZE-TAILED PLUMELETEER. (Pan, nw SA)

❑ *Aphantochroa cirrochloris.* SOMBRE HUMMINGBIRD. (e,c Braz). . . . . _____

❑ *Lampornis clemenciae.* BLUE-THROATED HUMMINGBIRD. (sw US, Mex)_____

❑ *Lampornis amethystinus.* AMETHYST-THROATED H. (mts n,c MA). . . _____

❑ *Lampornis viridipallens.* GREEN-THROATED MOUNTAIN-GEM. (c MA) _____

❑ *Lampornis sybillae.* GREEN-BREASTED MOUNTAIN-GEM. (Hond-Nic). _____

❑ *Lampornis hemileucus.* WHITE-BELLIED MOUNTAIN-GEM. (mts s CA) _____

❑ *Lampornis castaneoventris.* VARIABLE MOUNTAIN-GEM. (mts s CA). _____
   ___*L. (c.) calolaema.* PURPLE-THROATED MOUNTAIN-GEM. (Nic-w Pan)
   ___*L. (c.) cinereicauda.* GREY-TAILED MOUNTAIN-GEM. (sw CR)
   ___*L. (c.) castaneoventris.* WHITE-THROATED MOUNTAIN-GEM. (w Pan)

❑ *Lamprolaima rhami.* GARNET-THROATED HUMMINGBIRD. (c MA). . . _____

❑ *Adelomyia melanogenys.* SPECKLED HUMMINGBIRD. (mts w,n SA)... _____

❑ *Anthocephala floriceps.* BLOSSOMCROWN. (mts c,ne Colom)....... _____

❑ *Phlogophilus hemileucurus.* ECUADORIAN PIEDTAIL. (Andes wc SA). _____

❑ *Phlogophilus harterti.* PERUVIAN PIEDTAIL. (Andes c,se Peru)..... _____

❑ *Clytolaema rubricauda.* BRAZILIAN RUBY. (se Braz).............. _____

❑ *Heliodoxa imperatrix.* EMPRESS BRILLIANT. (Andes nw SA)....... _____

❑ *Heliodoxa xanthogonys.* VELVET-BROWED BRILLIANT. (mts n SA)... _____

❑ *Heliodoxa gularis.* PINK-THROATED BRILLIANT. (nw Amaz)....... _____

❑ *Heliodoxa branickii.* RUFOUS-WEBBED BRILLIANT. (Andes e Peru)... _____

❑ *Heliodoxa schreibersii.* BLACK-THROATED BRILLIANT. (w Amaz).... _____

❑ *Heliodoxa aurescens.* GOULD'S JEWELFRONT. (w Amaz).......... _____

❑ *Heliodoxa rubinoides.* FAWN-BREASTED BRILLIANT. (Andes nw SA). _____

❑ *Heliodoxa jacula.* GREEN-CROWNED BRILLIANT. (s CA, nw SA)..... _____

❑ *Heliodoxa leadbeateri.* VIOLET-FRONTED BRILLIANT. (mts w,n SA) . _____

❑ *Eugenes fulgens.* MAGNIFICENT HUMMINGBIRD. (mts sw US, MA)... _____
   ___*E. (f.) fulgens.* MAGNIFICENT HUMMINGBIRD. (sw US-Nic)
   ___*E. (f.) spectabilis.* ADMIRABLE HUMMINGBIRD. (CR, w Pan)

❑ *Hylonympha macrocerca.* SCISSOR-TAILED HUMMINGBIRD. (ne Ven). _____

❑ *Sternoclyta cyanopectus.* VIOLET-CHESTED HUMMINGB. (w,n Ven)... _____

❑ *Topaza pyra.* FIERY TOPAZ. (w Amaz)...................... _____

❑ *Topaza pella.* CRIMSON TOPAZ. (nw Amaz).................. _____

❑ *Oreotrochilus chimborazo.* ECUADORIAN HILLSTAR. (nc Ecua)..... _____

❑ *Oreotrochilus estella.* ANDEAN HILLSTAR. (Andes sw SA)........ _____
   ___*O. (e.) stolzmanni.* GREEN-HEADED HILLSTAR. (n Peru)
   ___*O. (e.) estella.* STRIPE-BELLIED HILLSTAR. (sp)
   ___*O. (e.) bolivianus.* BOLIVIAN HILLSTAR. (c Bol)

❑ *Oreotrochilus leucopleurus.* WHITE-SIDED HILLSTAR. (Andes sw SA)_____

❑ *Oreotrochilus melanogaster.* BLACK-BREASTED HILLSTAR. (c Peru) . _____

❑ *Oreotrochilus adela.* WEDGE-TAILED HILLSTAR. (Andes c,s Bol).... _____

❑ *Urochroa bougueri.* WHITE-TAILED HILLSTAR. (Andes w SA)...... _____

❑ *Patagona gigas.* GIANT HUMMINGBIRD. (Andes w,s SA).......... _____

❑ *Aglaeactis cupripennis.* SHINING SUNBEAM. (Andes w SA)........ _____

❑ *Aglaeactis castelnaudii.* WHITE-TUFTED SUNBEAM. (Andes c Peru) . _____

❑ *Aglaeactis aliciae.* PURPLE-BACKED SUNBEAM. (Andes n Peru)..... _____

❑ *Aglaeactis pamela.* BLACK-HOODED SUNBEAM. (Andes wc Bol)..... _____

❑ *Lafresnaya lafresnayi.* MOUNTAIN VELVETBREAST. (mts w SA)..... _____

❑ *Pterophanes cyanopterus.* GREAT SAPPHIREWING. (Andes w SA). . . . _____

❑ *Coeligena coeligena.* BRONZY INCA. (Andes w,n SA). . . . . _____

❑ *Coeligena wilsoni.* BROWN INCA. (Andes nw SA). . . . . _____

❑ *Coeligena prunellei.* BLACK INCA. (Andes e Colom). . . . . _____

❑ *Coeligena torquata.* COLLARED INCA. (Andes w,se SA). . . . . _____
   ___*C. (t.) torquata.* COLLARED INCA. (w SA)
   ___*C. (t.) inca.* GOULD'S INCA. (sw SA)

❑ *Coeligena phalerata.* WHITE-TAILED STARFRONTLET. (ne Colom). . . . _____

❑ *Coeligena orina.* DUSKY STARFRONTLET. (Andes nw Colom). . . . . . . _____

❑ *Coeligena bonapartei.* GOLDEN-BELLIED STARFRONTLET. (nw SA). . . _____
   ___*C. (b.) bonapartei.* GOLDEN-BELLIED STARFRONTLET. (sp)
   ___*C. (b.) eos.* GOLDEN STARFRONTLET. (w Ven)

❑ *Coeligena helianthea.* BLUE-THROATED STARFRONTLET. (mts nw SA) _____

❑ *Coeligena lutetiae.* BUFF-WINGED STARFRONTLET. (Andes nw SA). . . _____

❑ *Coeligena violifer.* VIOLET-THROATED STARFRONTLET. (sw SA). . . . . _____

❑ *Coeligena iris.* RAINBOW STARFRONTLET. (Andes wc SA). . . . . _____

❑ *Ensifera ensifera.* SWORD-BILLED HUMMINGBIRD. (Andes w SA). . . . _____

❑ *Sephanoides sephaniodes.* GREEN-BACKED FIRECROWN. (s SA, JF) . _____

❑ *Sephanoides fernandensis.* JUAN FERNANDEZ FIRECROWN. (JF). . . . . _____

❑ *Boissonneaua flavescens.* BUFF-TAILED CORONET. (Andes nw SA) . _____

❑ *Boissonneaua matthewsii.* CHESTNUT-BREASTED CORONET. (wc SA). _____

❑ *Boissonneaua jardini.* VELVET-PURPLE CORONET. (nw SA). . . . . _____

❑ *Heliangelus mavors.* ORANGE-THROATED SUNANGEL. (Andes nw SA) _____

❑ *Heliangelus spencei.* MERIDA SUNANGEL. (Andes w Ven). . . . . _____

❑ *Heliangelus amethysticollis.* AMETHYST-THROATED SUNANGEL. (w SA) _____
   ___*H. (a.) clarissae.* LONGUEMARE'S SUNANGEL. (nw SA)
   ___*H. (a.) amethysticollis.* AMETHYST-THROATED SUNANGEL. (wc SA)

❑ *Heliangelus strophianus.* GORGETED SUNANGEL. (mts nw SA). . . . . . _____

❑ *Heliangelus exortis.* TOURMALINE SUNANGEL. (Andes w SA). . . . . . . _____
   ___*H. (e.) exortis.* TOURMALINE SUNANGEL. (nw SA)
   ___*H. (e.) micraster.* LITTLE SUNANGEL. (wc SA)

❑ *Heliangelus viola.* PURPLE-THROATED SUNANGEL. (Andes wc SA). . . _____

❑ *Heliangelus regalis.* ROYAL SUNANGEL. (Andes n Peru). . . . . _____

❑ *Eriocnemis nigrivestis.* BLACK-BREASTED PUFFLEG. (Andes n Ecua). _____

❑ *Eriocnemis vestitus.* GLOWING PUFFLEG. (Andes nw SA). . . . . _____

❑ *Eriocnemis godini.* TURQUOISE-THROATED PUFFLEG. (Andes nw SA). _____

❑ *Eriocnemis luciani.* SAPPHIRE-VENTED PUFFLEG. (Andes w SA). . . . . _____

❑ *Eriocnemis cupreoventris.* COPPERY-BELLIED PUFFLEG. (nw SA). . . . _____

❑ *Eriocnemis mosquera.* GOLDEN-BREASTED PUFFLEG. (Andes nw SA). _____

❑ *Eriocnemis glaucopoides.* BLUE-CAPPED PUFFLEG. (Andes sw SA). . . _____

❑ *Eriocnemis mirabilis.* COLORFUL PUFFLEG. (Andes sw Colom). . . . . . _____

❑ *Eriocnemis alinae.* EMERALD-BELLIED PUFFLEG. (Andes w SA). . . . . _____

❑ *Eriocnemis derbyi.* BLACK-THIGHED PUFFLEG. (Andes nw SA). . . . . . _____

❑ *Haplophaedia aureliae.* GREENISH PUFFLEG. (mts e Pan, w SA). . . . . _____

❑ *Haplophaedia lugens.* HOARY PUFFLEG. (Andes nw SA). . . . . _____

❑ *Urosticte benjamini.* PURPLE-BIBBED WHITETIP. (Andes nw SA). . . . . _____

❑ *Urosticte ruficrissa.* RUFOUS-VENTED WHITETIP. (Andes nw SA). . . . _____

❑ *Ocreatus underwoodii.* BOOTED RACKET-TAIL. (mts w,n SA). . . . . . . _____

❑ *Lesbia victoriae.* BLACK-TAILED TRAINBEARER. (Andes w SA). . . . . . _____

❑ *Lesbia nuna.* GREEN-TAILED TRAINBEARER. (Andes w SA). . . . . _____

❑ *Sappho sparganura.* RED-TAILED COMET. (Andes sw SA). . . . . _____

❑ *Polyonymus caroli.* BRONZE-TAILED COMET. (Andes Peru). . . . . _____

❑ *Ramphomicron microrhynchum.* PURPLE-BACKED THORNBILL. (w SA)_____

❑ *Ramphomicron dorsale.* BLACK-BACKED THORNBILL. (ne Colom). . . _____

❑ *Metallura williami.* VIRIDIAN METALTAIL. (Andes nw SA). . . . . _____
    ___*M. (w.) recisa.* COLOMBIAN METALTAIL. (nw Colom)
    ___*M. (w.) williami.* VIRIDIAN METALTAIL. (c Colom)
    ___*M. (w.) primolinus.* ECUADORIAN METALTAIL. (s Colom, n Ecua)
    ___*M. (w.) atrigularis.* BLACK-THROATED METALTAIL. (c,s Ecua)

❑ *Metallura baroni.* VIOLET-THROATED METALTAIL. (Andes sw Ecua). _____

❑ *Metallura odomae.* NEBLINA METALTAIL. (Andes n Peru). . . . . _____

❑ *Metallura theresiae.* COPPERY METALTAIL. (Andes n Peru). . . . . _____

❑ *Metallura eupogon.* FIRE-THROATED METALTAIL. (Andes c,sw Peru). _____

❑ *Metallura aeneocauda.* SCALED METALTAIL. (Andes sw SA). . . . . . . _____
    ___*M. (a.) aeneocauda.* BRASSY METALTAIL. (sp)
    ___*M. (a.) malagae.* REDDISH METALTAIL. (c Bol)

❑ *Metallura phoebe.* BLACK METALTAIL. (Andes Peru). . . . . _____

❑ *Metallura tyrianthina.* TYRIAN METALTAIL. (mts w,n SA). . . . . _____

❑ *Metallura iracunda.* PERIJA METALTAIL. (mts nw SA). . . . . _____

❑ *Chalcostigma ruficeps.* RUFOUS-CAPPED THORNBILL. (Andes w SA). _____

❑ *Chalcostigma olivaceum.* OLIVACEOUS THORNBILL. (Andes sw SA) . _____

❑ *Chalcostigma stanleyi.* BLUE-MANTLED THORNBILL. (Andes wc SA). _____

❑ *Chalcostigma heteropogon.* BRONZE-TAILED THORNBILL. (nw SA). . . _____

❑ *Chalcostigma herrani.* RAINBOW-BEARDED THORNBILL. (nw SA). . . . _____

❏ *Oxypogon guerinii.* BEARDED HELMETCREST. (mts nw SA)........ _____

❏ *Opisthoprora euryptera.* MOUNTAIN AVOCETBILL. (Andes nw SA)... _____

❏ *Taphrolesbia griseiventris.* GREY-BELLIED COMET. (Andes n Peru) . _____

❏ *Aglaiocercus kingi.* LONG-TAILED SYLPH. (mts w SA)............ _____
   ___*A. (k.) kingi.* BLUE-THROATED SYLPH. (sp)
   ___*A. (k.) emmae.* GREEN-TAILED SYLPH. (Colom, w Ven)
   ___*A. (k.) berlepschi.* VENEZUELAN SYLPH. (ne Ven)

❏ *Aglaiocercus coelestis.* VIOLET-TAILED SYLPH. (Andes nw SA)..... _____

❏ *Oreonympha nobilis.* BEARDED MOUNTAINEER. (Andes sc Peru).... _____

❏ *Augastes lumachellus.* HOODED VISORBEARER. (mts e Braz)....... _____

❏ *Augastes scutatus.* HYACINTH VISORBEARER. (mts e Braz)........ _____

❏ *Augastes geoffroyi.* WEDGE-BILLED HUMMINGBIRD. (mts w,n SA)... _____

❏ *Heliothryx barroti.* PURPLE-CROWNED FAIRY. (MA, nw SA)....... _____

❏ *Heliothryx aurita.* BLACK-EARED FAIRY. (Amaz)................ _____

❏ *Heliactin cornuta.* HORNED SUNGEM. (ne,c,se SA).............. _____

❏ *Loddigesia mirabilis.* MARVELOUS SPATULETAIL. (Andes n Peru).... _____

❏ *Heliomaster constantii.* PLAIN-CAPPED STARTHROAT. (Pac MA)..... _____

❏ *Heliomaster longirostris.* LONG-BILLED STARTHROAT. (MA, SA).... _____

❏ *Heliomaster squamosus.* STRIPE-BREASTED STARTHROAT. (e Braz)... _____

❏ *Heliomaster furcifer.* BLUE-TUFTED STARTHROAT. (sc SA)........ _____

❏ *Rhodopis vesper.* OASIS HUMMINGBIRD. (w Peru, n Chile)........ _____

❏ *Thaumastura cora.* PERUVIAN SHEARTAIL. (w Peru, n Chile)....... _____

❏ *Philodice bryantae.* MAGENTA-THROATED WOODSTAR. (mts s CA)... _____

❏ *Philodice mitchellii.* PURPLE-THROATED WOODSTAR. (e Pan-nw SA). _____

❏ *Doricha enicura.* SLENDER SHEARTAIL. (mts c MA)............. _____

❏ *Doricha eliza.* MEXICAN SHEARTAIL. (se Mex)................. _____

❏ *Tilmatura dupontii.* SPARKLING-TAILED HUMMINGBIRD. (mts MA)... _____

❏ *Microstilbon burmeisteri.* SLENDER-TAILED WOODSTAR. (sc SA).... _____

❏ *Calothorax lucifer.* LUCIFER HUMMINGBIRD. (mts sw US, n Mex)... _____

❏ *Calothorax pulcher.* BEAUTIFUL HUMMINGBIRD. (mts c,s Mex)..... _____

❏ *Archilochus colubris.* RUBY-THROATED HUMMINGBIRD. (e NA; ◊-CA) _____

❏ *Archilochus alexandri.* BLACK-CHINNED HUMMINGBIRD. (w NA-Mex) _____

❏ *Calypte anna.* ANNA'S HUMMINGBIRD. (w NA; ◊-n Mex)......... _____

❏ *Calypte costae.* COSTA'S HUMMINGBIRD. (sw US, nw Mex)........ _____

❏ *Calliphlox evelynae.* BAHAMA WOODSTAR. (Bah).............. _____

❏ *Calliphlox amethystina.* AMETHYST WOODSTAR. (SA)........... _____

❑ *Mellisuga helenae.* BEE HUMMINGBIRD. (Cuba)................. _____

❑ *Mellisuga minima.* VERVAIN HUMMINGBIRD. (Jam, Hisp)......... _____

❑ *Stellula calliope.* CALLIOPE HUMMINGBIRD. (mts w NA; ◊ Mex)..... _____

❑ *Atthis heloisa.* BUMBLEBEE HUMMINGBIRD. (mts Mex)........... _____

❑ *Atthis ellioti.* WINE-THROATED HUMMINGBIRD. (mts c MA)........ _____

❑ *Myrtis fanny.* PURPLE-COLLARED WOODSTAR. (cw SA)........... _____

❑ *Eulidia yarrellii.* CHILEAN WOODSTAR. (s Peru, n Chile).......... _____

❑ *Myrmia micrura.* SHORT-TAILED WOODSTAR. (cw SA)........... _____

❑ *Acestrura mulsant.* WHITE-BELLIED WOODSTAR. (Andes w SA)..... _____

❑ *Acestrura bombus.* LITTLE WOODSTAR. (cw SA)................ _____

❑ *Acestrura heliodor.* GORGETED WOODSTAR. (mts nw SA)......... _____

❑ *Acestrura astreans.* SANTA MARTA WOODSTAR. (mts ne Colom).... _____

❑ *Acestrura berlepschi.* ESMERALDAS WOODSTAR. (w Ecua)........ _____

❑ *Chaetocercus jourdanii.* RUFOUS-SHAFTED WOODSTAR. (mts n SA) . _____

❑ *Selasphorus platycercus.* BROAD-TAILED HUMMINGBIRD. (w NA-MA) _____

❑ *Selasphorus rufus.* RUFOUS HUMMINGBIRD. (mts w NA; ◊-Mex, Fla). _____

❑ *Selasphorus sasin.* ALLEN'S HUMMINGBIRD. (w US; ◊ Mex)....... _____

❑ *Selasphorus flammula.* VOLCANO HUMMINGBIRD. (mts s CA)...... _____
    ___*S. (f.) simoni.* CERISE-THROATED HUMMINGBIRD. (wc CR)
    ___*S. (f.) flammula.* ROSE-THROATED HUMMINGBIRD. (c CR)
    ___*S. (f.) torridus.* HELIOTROPE-THROATED HUMMINGBIRD. (se CR, w Pan)

❑ *Selasphorus scintilla.* SCINTILLANT HUMMINGBIRD. (mts s CA)..... _____

❑ *Selasphorus ardens.* GLOW-THROATED HUMMINGBIRD. (mts w Pan) . _____

Superorder STRIGIMORPHAE [50/312]
Order **MUSOPHAGIFORMES** [5/23]
Family **Musophagidae** [5/23]
Subfamily Musophaginae [2/17]

❑ *Tauraco persa.* GUINEA TURACO. (w Afr).................... _____

❑ *Tauraco schuettii.* BLACK-BILLED TURACO. (c Afr)............. _____

❑ *Tauraco schalowi.* SCHALOW'S TURACO. (sc Afr).............. _____

❑ *Tauraco fischeri.* FISCHER'S TURACO. (e Afr)................. _____

❑ *Tauraco livingstonii.* LIVINGSTONE'S TURACO. (e,s Afr).......... _____

❑ *Tauraco corythaix.* KNYSNA TURACO. (S Afr)................ _____

❑ *Tauraco bannermani.* BANNERMAN'S TURACO. (mts sw Camer)..... _____

❑ *Tauraco erythrolophus.* RED-CRESTED TURACO. (w,c Ang)........ _____

❑ *Tauraco macrorhynchus.* YELLOW-BILLED TURACO. (w Afr)....... _____

❑ *Tauraco leucotis*. WHITE-CHEEKED TURACO. (mts ne Afr)......... _____

❑ *Tauraco ruspolii*. RUSPOLI'S TURACO. (mts sc Eth)............. _____

❑ *Tauraco hartlaubi*. HARTLAUB'S TURACO. (mts e Afr)........... _____

❑ *Tauraco leucolophus*. WHITE-CRESTED TURACO. (c Afr).......... _____

❑ *Musophaga johnstoni*. RUWENZORI TURACO. (mts ec Afr)........ _____

❑ *Musophaga porphyreolopha*. PURPLE-CRESTED TURACO. (e,se Afr) . _____

❑ *Musophaga violacea*. VIOLET TURACO. (w Afr)................. _____

❑ *Musophaga rossae*. ROSS'S TURACO. (c Afr)................... _____

Subfamily Criniferinae [3/6]

❑ *Corythaixoides concolor*. GREY GO-AWAY-BIRD. (sc,s Afr)........ _____

❑ *Corythaixoides personatus*. BARE-FACED GO-AWAY-BIRD. (ec,e Afr). _____

❑ *Corythaixoides leucogaster*. WHITE-BELLIED GO-AWAY-BIRD. (e Afr). _____

❑ *Crinifer piscator*. WESTERN GREY PLANTAIN-EATER. (w,c Afr)...... _____

❑ *Crinifer zonurus*. EASTERN GREY PLANTAIN-EATER. (ne,e Afr)...... _____

❑ *Corythaeola cristata*. GREAT BLUE TURACO. (w,c Afr)........... _____

Order **STRIGIFORMES** [45/289]
Suborder STRIGI [25/173]
Parvorder TYTONIDA [2/17]
Family **Tytonidae** [2/17]

❑ *Tyto tenebricosa*. GREATER SOOTY-OWL. (NG, e,se Aust)......... _____

❑ *Tyto multipunctata*. LESSER SOOTY-OWL. (ne Aust)............. _____

❑ *Tyto inexspectata*. MINAHASSA MASKED-OWL. (mts n Sulaw)....... _____

❑ *Tyto nigrobrunnea*. TALIABU MASKED-OWL. (c Wall)............. _____

❑ *Tyto sororcula*. LESSER MASKED-OWL. (se Wall)................ _____

❑ *Tyto manusi*. MANUS MASKED-OWL. (nc Bism)................. _____

❑ *Tyto aurantia*. BISMARCK MASKED-OWL. (se Bism)............. _____

❑ *Tyto novaehollandiae*. AUSTRALIAN MASKED-OWL. (s NG, Aust).... _____
___*T. (n.) calabyi*. NEW GUINEA MASKED-OWL. (s NG)
___*T. (n.) novaehollandiae*. AUSTRALIAN MASKED-OWL. (Aust)

❑ *Tyto castanops*. TASMANIAN MASKED-OWL. (Tas).............. _____

❑ *Tyto rosenbergii*. SULAWESI OWL. (Sulaw).................... _____

❑ *Tyto soumagnei*. MADAGASCAR RED OWL. (Mad).............. _____

❑ *Tyto alba*. BARN OWL. (cosm)................................ _____

❑ *Tyto glaucops*. ASHY-FACED OWL. (Hisp)..................... _____

❑ *Tyto capensis*. AFRICAN GRASS-OWL. (c,e,s Afr)............... _____

❑ *Tyto longimembris.* EASTERN GRASS-OWL. (s Asia-N Cal, n,e Aust). _____

❑ *Phodilus prigoginei.* CONGO BAY-OWL. (e Zaire). . . . . _____

❑ *Phodilus badius.* ORIENTAL BAY-OWL. (s,se Asia). . . . . _____

Parvorder STRIGIDA [23/156]
Family **Strigidae** [23/156]

❑ *Otus sagittatus.* WHITE-FRONTED SCOPS-OWL. (se Asia). . . . . _____

❑ *Otus rufescens.* REDDISH SCOPS-OWL. (se Asia). . . . . _____

❑ *Otus icterorhynchus.* SANDY SCOPS-OWL. (w,c Afr). . . . . _____

❑ *Otus ireneae.* SOKOKE SCOPS-OWL. (ce Kenya). . . . . _____

❑ *Otus balli.* ANDAMAN SCOPS-OWL. (And). . . . . _____

❑ *Otus spilocephalus.* MOUNTAIN SCOPS-OWL. (mts s,se Asia). . . . . _____
   ___*O. (s.) spilocephalus.* MOUNTAIN SCOPS-OWL. (s,se Asia)
   ___*O. (s.) hambroecki.* FORMOSAN SCOPS-OWL. (Taiwan)
   ___*O. (s.) vandewateri.* VANDEWATER'S SCOPS-OWL. (Sum)
   ___*O. (s.) luciae.* BORNEAN SCOPS-OWL. (Born)

❑ *Otus umbra.* SIMEULUE SCOPS-OWL. (Simeulue). . . . . _____

❑ *Otus angelinae.* JAVAN SCOPS-OWL. (mts Java). . . . . _____

❑ *Otus manadensis.* SULAWESI SCOPS-OWL. (Sulaw). . . . . _____

❑ *Otus longicornis.* LUZON SCOPS-OWL. (mts n Phil). . . . . _____

❑ *Otus mindorensis.* MINDORO SCOPS-OWL. (mts c Phil). . . . . _____

❑ *Otus mirus.* MINDANAO SCOPS-OWL. (mts s Phil). . . . . _____

❑ *Otus hartlaubi.* SAO TOME SCOPS-OWL. (mts ST). . . . . _____

❑ *Otus brucei.* PALLID SCOPS-OWL. (sw,sc Palea). . . . . _____

❑ *Otus flammeolus.* FLAMMULATED OWL. (mts w NA, Mex). . . . . _____

❑ *Otus scops.* COMMON SCOPS-OWL. (Palea-se Asia, Phil, s Afr). . . . . . _____
   ___*O. (s.) scops.* EURASIAN SCOPS-OWL. (Palea; ◊-c Afr)
   ___*O. (s.) sunia.* ORIENTAL SCOPS-OWL. (e Asia-Phil; ◊-s,se Asia)
   ___*O. (s.) senegalensis.* AFRICAN SCOPS-OWL. (Afr reg)

❑ *Otus elegans.* ELEGANT SCOPS-OWL. (s Japan-n Phil). . . . . _____

❑ *Otus mantananensis.* MANTANANI SCOPS-OWL. (n Born, wc,s Phil) . _____
   ___*O. (m.) mantananensis.* MANTANANI SCOPS-OWL. (n Born, wc Phil)
   ___*O. (m.) sibutuensis.* SULU SCOPS-OWL. (Sulu)

❑ *Otus magicus.* MOLUCCAN SCOPS-OWL. (Seyc, Indon-w NG). . . . . . . _____
   ___*O. (m.) insularis.* SEYCHELLES SCOPS-OWL. (Seyc)
   ___*O. (m.) enganensis.* ENGGANO SCOPS-OWL. (Enggano)
   ___*O. (m.) magicus.* MOLUCCAN SCOPS-OWL. (Wall)
   ___*O. (m.) albiventris.* FLORES SCOPS-OWL. (c L Sunda)
   ___*O. (m.) beccarii.* PAPUAN SCOPS-OWL. (nw NG)

❑ *Otus rutilus.* MALAGASY SCOPS-OWL. (Pemba, Com, Mad). . . . . _____
 ___*O. (r.) pembaensis.* PEMBA SCOPS-OWL. (Pemba)
 ___*O. (r.) capnodes.* ANJOUAN SCOPS-OWL. (Com)
 ___*O. (r.) rutilus.* MADAGASCAR SCOPS-OWL. (Mad)

❑ *Otus pauliani.* COMORO SCOPS-OWL. (Com). . . . . _____

❑ *Otus brookii.* RAJAH SCOPS-OWL. (G Sunda). . . . . _____

❑ *Otus bakkamoena.* COLLARED SCOPS-OWL. (s,se,e Asia). . . . . _____
 ___*O. (b.) bakkamoena.* INDIAN SCOPS-OWL. (s Asia)
 ___*O. (b.) lempiji.* COLLARED SCOPS-OWL. (e,se Asia)
 ___*O. (b.) semitorques.* JAPANESE SCOPS-OWL. (Kuril, Japan, Izu)

❑ *Otus mentawi.* MENTAWAI SCOPS-OWL. (is w Sum). . . . . _____

❑ *Otus fuliginosus.* PALAWAN SCOPS-OWL. (sw Phil). . . . . _____

❑ *Otus megalotis.* PHILIPPINE SCOPS-OWL. (Phil). . . . . _____
 ___*O. (m.) megalotis.* PHILIPPINE SCOPS-OWL. (n Phil)
 ___*O. (m.) nigrorum.* NEGROS SCOPS-OWL. (sc Phil)
 ___*O. (m.) everetti.* EVERETT'S SCOPS-OWL. (ce,s Phil)

❑ *Otus silvicola.* WALLACE'S SCOPS-OWL. (c L Sunda). . . . . _____

❑ *Otus leucotis.* WHITE-FACED SCOPS-OWL. (Afr). . . . . _____

❑ *Otus kennicottii.* WESTERN SCREECH-OWL. (w NA, MA). . . . . _____
 ___*O. (k.) kennicottii.* WESTERN SCREECH-OWL. (w NA, Mex)
 ___*O. (k.) vinaceus.* VINACEOUS SCREECH-OWL. (sw US, nw Mex)
 ___*O. (k.) seductus.* BALSAS SCREECH-OWL. (cw Mex)
 ___*O. (k.) lambi.* OAXACA SCREECH-OWL. (w,c Oax)
 ___*O. (k.) cooperi.* PACIFIC SCREECH-OWL. (Pac c MA)

❑ *Otus asio.* EASTERN SCREECH-OWL. (e NA, ne Mex). . . . . _____

❑ *Otus trichopsis.* WHISKERED SCREECH-OWL. (mts sw US, MA). . . . . _____

❑ *Otus choliba.* TROPICAL SCREECH-OWL. (s CA, SA). . . . . _____

❑ *Otus koepckeae.* KOEPCKE'S SCREECH-OWL. (mts wc SA). . . . . _____

❑ *Otus roboratus.* WEST PERUVIAN SCREECH-OWL. (nw Peru). . . . . . . _____
 ___*O. (r.) pacificus.* COASTAL SCREECH-OWL. (sp)
 ___*O. (r.) roboratus.* WEST PERUVIAN SCREECH-OWL. (Andes)

❑ *Otus clarkii.* BARE-SHANKED SCREECH-OWL. (mts s CA, nw Colom). _____

❑ *Otus barbarus.* SANTA BARBARA SCREECH-OWL. (mts Chia, n Guat). _____

❑ *Otus ingens.* RUFESCENT SCREECH-OWL. (mts w SA). . . . . _____
 ___*O. (i.) colombianus.* COLOMBIAN SCREECH-OWL. (w Colom)
 ___*O. (i.) ingens.* RUFESCENT SCREECH-OWL. (sp)

❑ *Otus marshalli.* CLOUD-FOREST SCREECH-OWL. (Andes cw SA). . . . . _____
 ___*O. (m.) petersoni.* CINNAMON SCREECH-OWL. (s Ecua, n Peru)
 ___*O. (m.) marshalli.* CLOUD-FOREST SCREECH-OWL. (e Peru)

❑ *Otus watsonii.* TAWNY-BELLIED SCREECH-OWL. (Amaz). . . . . _____
 ___*O. (w.) watsonii.* TAWNY-BELLIED SCREECH-OWL. (w Amaz)
 ___*O. (w.) usta.* AUSTRAL SCREECH-OWL. (c Amaz)

❑ *Otus atricapillus*. VARIABLE SCREECH-OWL. (MA, SA). . . . . _____
   ___*O. (a.) guatemalae*. VARIABLE SCREECH-OWL. (MA, w,n SA)
   ___*O. (a.) hoyi*. HOY'S SCREECH-OWL. (mts nw Argen)
   ___*O. (a.) atricapillus*. BLACK-CAPPED SCREECH-OWL. (se SA)

❑ *Otus vermiculatus*. VERMICULATED SCREECH-OWL. (s CA-nw SA) . _____

❑ *Otus sanctaecatarinae*. LONG-TUFTED SCREECH-OWL. (se SA). . . . . . _____

❑ *Otus lawrencii*. BARE-LEGGED OWL. (Cuba). . . . . _____

❑ *Otus nudipes*. PUERTO RICAN SCREECH-OWL. (e G Ant). . . . . _____

❑ *Otus podarginus*. PALAU OWL. (Palau). . . . . _____

❑ *Otus albogularis*. WHITE-THROATED SCREECH-OWL. (mts w SA). . . . _____

❑ *Mimizuku gurneyi*. LESSER EAGLE-OWL. (se Phil). . . . . _____

❑ *Bubo virginianus*. GREAT HORNED OWL. (NA, MA, SA). . . . . _____

❑ *Bubo bubo*. EURASIAN EAGLE-OWL. (Palea). . . . . _____

❑ *Bubo bengalensis*. ROCK EAGLE-OWL. (s Asia). . . . . _____

❑ *Bubo ascalaphus*. PHARAOH EAGLE-OWL. (n Afr reg). . . . . _____

❑ *Bubo capensis*. CAPE EAGLE-OWL. (e,s Afr). . . . . _____
   ___*B. (c.) mackinderi*. MACKINDER'S EAGLE-OWL. (mts e Afr)
   ___*B. (c.) capensis*. CAPE EAGLE-OWL. (s Afr)

❑ *Bubo africanus*. SPOTTED EAGLE-OWL. (Afr reg). . . . . _____

❑ *Bubo poensis*. FRASER'S EAGLE-OWL. (w,c Afr). . . . . _____

❑ *Bubo vosseleri*. USAMBARA EAGLE-OWL. (mts ne Tanz). . . . . _____

❑ *Bubo nipalensis*. SPOT-BELLIED EAGLE-OWL. (s,se Asia). . . . . _____

❑ *Bubo sumatranus*. BARRED EAGLE-OWL. (se Asia). . . . . _____

❑ *Bubo shelleyi*. SHELLEY'S EAGLE-OWL. (w,c Afr). . . . . _____

❑ *Bubo lacteus*. VERREAUX'S EAGLE-OWL. (Afr). . . . . _____

❑ *Bubo coromandus*. DUSKY EAGLE-OWL. (s,se Asia). . . . . _____

❑ *Bubo leucostictus*. AKUN EAGLE-OWL. (w,c Afr). . . . . _____

❑ *Bubo philippensis*. PHILIPPINE EAGLE-OWL. (Phil). . . . . _____

❑ *Ketupa blakistoni*. BLAKISTON'S FISH-OWL. (e Asia). . . . . _____

❑ *Ketupa zeylonensis*. BROWN FISH-OWL. (s,se Asia). . . . . _____

❑ *Ketupa flavipes*. TAWNY FISH-OWL. (s,se Asia). . . . . _____

❑ *Ketupa ketupu*. BUFFY FISH-OWL. (se Asia). . . . . _____

❑ *Scotopelia peli*. PEL'S FISHING-OWL. (Afr). . . . . _____

❑ *Scotopelia ussheri*. RUFOUS FISHING-OWL. (w Afr). . . . . _____

❑ *Scotopelia bouvieri*. VERMICULATED FISHING-OWL. (w,c Afr). . . . . . . _____

❑ *Nyctea scandiaca*. SNOWY OWL. (n Hol; ◊-s US, c Eura). . . . . _____

❑ *Strix seloputo.* SPOTTED WOOD-OWL. (se Asia-sw Phil)........... _____

❑ *Strix ocellata.* MOTTLED WOOD-OWL. (n,c India)............... _____

❑ *Strix leptogrammica.* BROWN WOOD-OWL. (s,se Asia)........... _____

❑ *Strix aluco.* TAWNY OWL. (Palea)........................... _____

❑ *Strix butleri.* HUME'S OWL. (sw Eura)....................... _____

❑ *Strix occidentalis.* SPOTTED OWL. (w NA, n,c Mex)............ _____
   ___*S. (o.) occidentalis.* CALIFORNIA SPOTTED-OWL. (w NA)
   ___*S. (o.) lucida.* MOUNTAIN SPOTTED-OWL. (wc NA, n,c Mex)

❑ *Strix varia.* BARRED OWL. (NA, Mex)........................ _____

❑ *Strix fulvescens.* FULVOUS OWL. (mts c MA)................. _____

❑ *Strix hylophila.* RUSTY-BARRED OWL. (se SA)................ _____

❑ *Strix rufipes.* RUFOUS-LEGGED OWL. (s SA)................. _____

❑ *Strix uralensis.* URAL OWL. (Eura)......................... _____

❑ *Strix davidi.* SICHUAN WOOD-OWL. (mts c China)............. _____

❑ *Strix nebulosa.* GREAT GREY OWL. (n Hol; ◊-n US, c Eura)....... _____

❑ *Strix virgata.* MOTTLED OWL. (MA, SA)...................... _____

❑ *Strix nigrolineata.* BLACK-AND-WHITE OWL. (MA, nw SA)........ _____

❑ *Strix huhula.* BLACK-BANDED OWL. (SA)..................... _____

❑ *Strix albitarsus.* RUFOUS-BANDED OWL. (Andes w SA).......... _____

❑ *Strix woodfordii.* AFRICAN WOOD-OWL. (Afr)................. _____

❑ *Jubula lettii.* MANED OWL. (w,c Afr)....................... _____

❑ *Lophostrix cristata.* CRESTED OWL. (MA, w Amaz)............. _____

❑ *Pulsatrix perspicillata.* SPECTACLED OWL. (MA, SA)............ _____

❑ *Pulsatrix melanota.* BAND-BELLIED OWL. (w Amaz)............. _____

❑ *Pulsatrix koeniswaldiana.* TAWNY-BROWED OWL. (se SA)........ _____

❑ *Surnia ulula.* NORTHERN HAWK OWL. (Hol; ◊-s Euro, n US)....... _____

❑ *Glaucidium passerinum.* EURASIAN PYGMY-OWL. (nw,c Eura)...... _____

❑ *Glaucidium brodiei.* COLLARED OWLET. (mts s,se Asia).......... _____

❑ *Glaucidium perlatum.* PEARL-SPOTTED OWLET. (Afr)............ _____

❑ *Glaucidium californicum.* NORTHERN PYGMY-OWL. (w NA-s Baja) . _____

❑ *Glaucidium gnoma.* MOUNTAIN PYGMY-OWL. (mts sw US-c MA)... _____

❑ *Glaucidium jardinii.* ANDEAN PYGMY-OWL. (mts s CA, w SA)..... _____

❑ *Glaucidium bolivianum.* YUNGAS PYGMY-OWL. (Andes wc SA).... _____

❑ *Glaucidium hardyi.* HARDY'S PYGMY-OWL. (Amaz Braz)......... _____

❑ *Glaucidium minutissimum.* LEAST PYGMY-OWL. (MA, SA)........ _____
   ___*G. (m.) griseiceps.* LEAST PYGMY-OWL. (MA, nw SA)
   ___*G. (m.) minutissimum.* AMAZONIAN PYGMY-OWL. (n,c SA)

❑ *Glaucidium brasilianum.* FERRUGINOUS PYGMY-OWL. (s Tex-SA)... _____

❑ *Glaucidium peruanum.* PERUVIAN PYGMY-OWL. (w Ecua, Peru).... _____

❑ *Glaucidium nanum.* AUSTRAL PYGMY-OWL. (s SA)............... _____

❑ *Glaucidium siju.* CUBAN PYGMY-OWL. (Cuba)................. _____

❑ *Glaucidium tephronotum.* RED-CHESTED OWLET. (w,c Afr)....... _____

❑ *Glaucidium sjostedti.* SJOSTEDT'S OWLET. (c Afr)............... _____

❑ *Glaucidium cuculoides.* ASIAN BARRED OWLET. (mts s,se Asia)..... _____

❑ *Glaucidium castanopterum.* JAVAN OWLET. (Java, Bali).......... _____

❑ *Glaucidium radiatum.* JUNGLE OWLET. (s Asia)................ _____

❑ *Glaucidium castanonotum.* CHESTNUT-BACKED OWLET. (Ceylon)... _____

❑ *Glaucidium capense.* AFRICAN BARRED OWLET. (sc,s Afr)........ _____

❑ *Glaucidium castaneum.* CHESTNUT OWLET. (w,c Afr)............ _____

❑ *Glaucidium ngamiense.* NGAMI OWLET. (sc Afr)................ _____

❑ *Glaucidium scheffleri.* SCHEFFLER'S OWLET. (ce Afr)............ _____

❑ *Glaucidium albertinum.* ALBERTINE OWLET. (ec Afr)............ _____

❑ *Xenoglaux loweryi.* LONG-WHISKERED OWLET. (mts cn Peru)....... _____

❑ *Micrathene whitneyi.* ELF OWL. (sw US, n,nc Mex)............. _____

❑ *Athene noctua.* LITTLE OWL. (Palea, n Afr; ◆ NZ)............. _____

❑ *Athene brama.* SPOTTED OWLET. (s,se Asia)................. _____

❑ *Athene blewitti.* FOREST OWLET. (mts c India)................ _____

❑ *Speotyto cunicularia.* BURROWING OWL. (NA-SA, W Indies; ◊-MA). _____

❑ *Aegolius funereus.* BOREAL OWL. (n Hol; ◊-Japan, n US)......... _____

❑ *Aegolius acadicus.* SAW-WHET OWL. (mts n NA-c MA; ◊-s US)..... _____
   ___*A. (a.) acadicus.* NORTHERN SAW-WHET OWL. (sp)
   ___*A. (a.) ridgwayi.* UNSPOTTED SAW-WHET OWL. (c MA)

❑ *Aegolius harrisii.* BUFF-FRONTED OWL. (SA)................. _____

❑ *Ninox rufa.* RUFOUS OWL. (Aru-NG, n,ne Aust)................ _____

❑ *Ninox strenua.* POWERFUL OWL. (e,se Aust)................. _____

❑ *Ninox connivens.* BARKING OWL. (n Moluc-NG, Aust)........... _____

❑ *Ninox rudolfi.* SUMBA BOOBOOK. (c L Sunda)................. _____

❑ *Ninox boobook.* SOUTHERN BOOBOOK. (Aust)................. _____
   ___*N. (b.) ocellata.* NORTHERN BOOBOOK. (sp)
   ___*N. (b.) lurida.* RED BOOBOOK. (ne Aust)
   ___*N. (b.) boobook.* AUSTRALIAN BOOBOOK. (se Aust)
   ___*N. (b.) leucopsis.* SPOTTED BOOBOOK. (Tasm)

❑ *Ninox novaeseelandiae.* MOREPORK. (e L Sunda-NG-NZ)........ _____
   ___*N. (n.) novaeseelandiae.* MOREPORK. (e L Sunda-NG)
   ___*N. (n.) albaria.* LORD HOWE ISLAND BOOBOOK. (L Howe)
   ___*N. (n.) undulata.* NORFOLK ISLAND BOOBOOK. (Norfolk)

❑ *Ninox scutulata.* BROWN HAWK-OWL. (ec,s Asia-Phil)............ _____
  ___*N. (s.) scutulata.* BROWN HAWK-OWL. (sp)
  ___*N. (s.) obscura.* HUME'S HAWK-OWL. (And, Nico)

❑ *Ninox affinis.* ANDAMAN HAWK-OWL. (And, Nic)............... _____

❑ *Ninox superciliaris.* WHITE-BROWED HAWK-OWL. (w,sw Mad)...... _____

❑ *Ninox philippensis.* PHILIPPINE HAWK-OWL (Phil)............... _____
  ___*N. (p.) philippensis.* PHILIPPINE HAWK-OWL. (n,c Phil)
  ___*N. (p.) spilonota.* MINDORO HAWK-OWL. (c Phil)
  ___*N. (p.) spilocephala.* MINDANAO HAWK-OWL. (s Phil)

❑ *Ninox ochracea.* OCHRE-BELLIED HAWK-OWL. (Sulaw).......... _____

❑ *Ninox squamipila.* MOLUCCAN HAWK-OWL. (Chris, Wall)........ _____
  ___*N. (s.) natalis.* CHRISTMAS ISLAND HAWK-OWL. (Chris)
  ___*N. (s.) squamipila.* MOLUCCAN HAWK-OWL. (Moluc, Tanim)

❑ *Ninox theomacha.* JUNGLE HAWK-OWL. (NG)................. _____

❑ *Ninox meeki.* MANUS HAWK-OWL. (n Bism).................. _____

❑ *Ninox punctulata.* SPECKLED HAWK-OWL. (Sulaw)............. _____

❑ *Ninox variegata.* BISMARCK HAWK-OWL. (e Bism)............. _____

❑ *Ninox odiosa.* RUSSET HAWK-OWL. (se Bism)................. _____

❑ *Ninox jacquinoti.* SOLOMON ISLANDS HAWK-OWL. (Solom)....... _____

❑ *Uroglaux dimorpha.* PAPUAN HAWK-OWL. (NG)............... _____

  Sceloglaux albifacies. LAUGHING OWL. (†NZ)................. _____

❑ *Pseudoscops grammicus.* JAMAICAN OWL. (Jam)............... _____

❑ *Asio stygius.* STYGIAN OWL. (MA, SA)..................... _____

❑ *Asio otus.* LONG-EARED OWL. (Hol; ◊-Mex, s US, n Afr, s Asia)..... _____

❑ *Asio abyssinicus.* ABYSSINIAN OWL. (mts ne Afr)............... _____

❑ *Asio madagascariensis.* MADAGASCAR OWL. (Mad)............. _____

❑ *Asio clamator.* STRIPED OWL. (MA, SA)................... _____

❑ *Asio flammeus.* SHORT-EARED OWL. (NA-SA, Eura; ◊-n Afr, Phil)... _____

❑ *Asio capensis.* MARSH OWL. (Afr, Mad)................... _____

❑ *Nesasio solomonensis.* FEARFUL OWL. (Solom)................ _____

Suborder AEGOTHELI [1/8]
Family **Aegothelidae** [1/8]

❑ *Aegotheles crinifrons.* LONG-WHISKERED OWLET-NIGHTJAR. (Moluc) _____

❑ *Aegotheles insignis.* FELINE OWLET-NIGHTJAR. (mts NG)......... _____

❑ *Aegotheles cristatus.* AUSTRALIAN OWLET-NIGHTJAR. (s NG, Aust) . _____

❑ *Aegotheles savesi.* NEW CALEDONIAN OWLET-NIGHTJAR. (s N Cal) . _____

❑ *Aegotheles bennettii.* BARRED OWLET-NIGHTJAR. (Aru, NG)....... _____

❏ *Aegotheles wallacii.* WALLACE'S OWLET-NIGHTJAR. (Aru-NG)...... _____

❏ *Aegotheles archboldi.* ARCHBOLD'S OWLET-NIGHTJAR. (mts c NG)... _____

❏ *Aegotheles albertisi.* MOUNTAIN OWLET-NIGHTJAR. (mts NG)...... _____

Suborder CAPRIMULGI [19/108]
Infraorder PODARGIDES [2/14]
Family **Podargidae** [1/3]

❏ *Podargus strigoides.* TAWNY FROGMOUTH. (Aust)............... _____

❏ *Podargus papuensis.* PAPUAN FROGMOUTH. (Aru-NG, ne Aust)..... _____

❏ *Podargus ocellatus.* MARBLED FROGMOUTH. (Aru-Solom, e Aust)... _____
   ___*P. (o.) ocellatus.* MARBLED FROGMOUTH. (Aru-Solom, ne Aust)
   ___*P. (o.) plumiferus.* PLUMED FROGMOUTH. (ce Aust)

Family **Batrachostomidae** [1/11]

❏ *Batrachostomus auritus.* LARGE FROGMOUTH. (se Asia).......... _____

❏ *Batrachostomus harterti.* DULIT FROGMOUTH. (mts c Born)....... _____

❏ *Batrachostomus septimus.* PHILIPPINE FROGMOUTH. (Phil)........ _____

❏ *Batrachostomus stellatus.* GOULD'S FROGMOUTH. (se Asia)....... _____

❏ *Batrachostomus moniliger.* CEYLON FROGMOUTH. (sw India)...... _____

❏ *Batrachostomus hodgsoni.* HODGSON'S FROGMOUTH. (mts s,se Asia). _____

❏ *Batrachostomus poliolophus.* SHORT-TAILED FROGMOUTH. (Sum)... _____

❏ *Batrachostomus mixtus.* BORNEAN FROGMOUTH. (mts n,c Born).... _____

❏ *Batrachostomus affinis.* BLYTH'S FROGMOUTH. (se Asia)......... _____
   ___*B. (a.) continentalis.* INDOCHINESE FROGMOUTH. (Indoc)
   ___*B. (a.) affinis.* BLYTH'S FROGMOUTH. (Malaya-G Sunda)

❏ *Batrachostomus javensis.* JAVAN FROGMOUTH. (w,c Java)........ _____

❏ *Batrachostomus cornutus.* SUNDA FROGMOUTH. (G Sunda)....... _____

Infraorder CAPRIMULGIDES [17/94]
Parvorder STEATORNITHIDA [2/8]
Superfamily STEATORNITHOIDEA [1/1]
Family **Steatornithidae** [1/1]

❏ *Steatornis caripensis.* OILBIRD. (e Pan, n,w SA)............... _____

Superfamily NYCTIBIOIDEA [1/7]
Family **Nyctibiidae** [1/7]

❏ *Nyctibius grandis.* GREAT POTOO. (CA, n,c,se SA).............. _____

❏ *Nyctibius aethereus.* LONG-TAILED POTOO. (n,wc,se SA)......... _____
   ___*N. (a.) longicaudatus.* LONG-TAILED POTOO. (n,wc SA)
   ___*N. (a.) aethereus.* LARGE-TAILED POTOO. (se SA)

❑ *Nyctibius jamaicensis.* COMMON POTOO. (n,c MA, G Sunda). . . . . . . _____
___*N. (j.) jamaicensis.* COMMON POTOO. (n,c MA, Jam)
___*N. (j.) abbotti.* HISPANIOLAN POTOO. (Hisp)

❑ *Nyctibius griseus.* GREY POTOO. (s CA, SA). . . . . _____
___*N. (g.) griseus.* GREY POTOO. (s CA, n,nc SA)
___*N. (g.) cornutus.* PARAGUAYAN POTOO. (sc SA)

❑ *Nyctibius maculosus.* ANDEAN POTOO. (mts w SA). . . . . _____

❑ *Nyctibius leucopterus.* WHITE-WINGED POTOO. (ce Braz). . . . . _____

❑ *Nyctibius bracteatus.* RUFOUS POTOO. (n,w Amaz). . . . . _____

Parvorder CAPRIMULGIDA [15/86]
Superfamily EUROSTOPOIDEA [1/7]
Family **Eurostopodidae** [1/7]

❑ *Eurostopodus argus.* SPOTTED EARED-NIGHTJAR. (Aust; ◊-Aru). . . . . _____

❑ *Eurostopodus mystacalis.* WHITE-THROATED EARED-N. (Aust-NG) . _____

❑ *Eurostopodus diabolicus.* SATANIC EARED-NIGHTJAR. (n Sulaw). . . . _____

❑ *Eurostopodus papuensis.* PAPUAN EARED-NIGHTJAR. (w Pap, NG). . . _____

❑ *Eurostopodus archboldi.* MOUNTAIN EARED-NIGHTJAR. (c,se NG). . . _____

❑ *Eurostopodus temminckii.* MALAYSIAN EARED-NIGHTJAR. (se Asia). _____

❑ *Eurostopodus macrotis.* GREAT EARED-NIGHTJAR. (s Asia-Phil). . . . . _____

Superfamily CAPRIMULGOIDEA [14/79]
Family **Caprimulgidae** [14/79]
Subfamily Chordeilinae [4/9]

❑ *Lurocalis semitorquatus.* SHORT-TAILED NIGHTHAWK. (MA, SA). . . . _____
___*L. (s.) semitorquatus.* SHORT-TAILED NIGHTHAWK. (MA, nw Amaz)
___*L. (s.) nattereri.* CHESTNUT-BANDED NIGHTHAWK. (n,c SA)

❑ *Lurocalis rufiventris.* RUFOUS-BELLIED NIGHTHAWK. (mts w SA). . . . _____

❑ *Chordeiles pusillus.* LEAST NIGHTHAWK. (nc,c SA). . . . . _____

❑ *Chordeiles rupestris.* SAND-COLORED NIGHTHAWK. (w Amaz). . . . . . _____

❑ *Chordeiles acutipennis.* LESSER NIGHTHAWK. (w US, MA, SA). . . . . _____

❑ *Chordeiles minor.* COMMON NIGHTHAWK. (NA, MA; ◊ SA). . . . . . . _____

❑ *Chordeiles gundlachii.* ANTILLEAN NIGHTHAWK. (s Fla-n W Indies). _____

❑ *Nyctiprogne leucopyga.* BAND-TAILED NIGHTHAWK. (Amaz). . . . . . . _____

❑ *Podager nacunda.* NACUNDA NIGHTHAWK. (SA). . . . . _____

Subfamily Caprimulginae [10/70]

❑ *Nyctidromus albicollis.* PAURAQUE. (s Tex, MA, SA). . . . . _____

❑ *Phalaenoptilus nuttallii.* COMMON POORWILL. (w NA, Mex). . . . . . . _____

❑ *Siphonorhis americanus.* JAMAICAN POORWILL. (†Jam). . . . . _____

❑ *Siphonorhis brewsteri.* LEAST POORWILL. (Hisp). . . . . _____

❑ *Nyctiphrynus mcleodii.* EARED POORWILL. (mts w Mex). . . . . _____

❑ *Nyctiphrynus yucatanicus.* YUCATAN POORWILL. (ce MA). . . . . _____

❑ *Nyctiphrynus ocellatus.* OCELLATED POORWILL. (s CA, SA). . . . . . . _____

❑ *Caprimulgus carolinensis.* CHUCK-WILL'S-WIDOW. (se NA; ◊-n SA). _____

❑ *Caprimulgus rufus.* RUFOUS NIGHTJAR. (s CA, sc L Ant, SA). . . . . . _____
   ___*C. (r.) minimus.* RUDDY NIGHTJAR. (s CA, n SA)
   ___*C. (r.) otiosus.* ST. LUCIA NIGHTJAR. (sc L Ant)
   ___*C. (r.) rufus.* RUFOUS NIGHTJAR. (SA)

❑ *Caprimulgus cubanensis.* GREATER ANTILLEAN NIGHTJAR. (G Ant) . _____
   ___*C. (c.) cubanensis.* CUBAN NIGHTJAR. (Cuba)
   ___*C. (c.) ekmani.* HISPANIOLAN NIGHTJAR. (Hisp)

❑ *Caprimulgus salvini.* TAWNY-COLLARED NIGHTJAR. (e Mex). . . . . . . _____

❑ *Caprimulgus badius.* YUCATAN NIGHTJAR. (ce MA). . . . . _____

❑ *Caprimulgus sericocaudatus.* SILKY-TAILED NIGHTJAR. (c SA). . . . . _____

❑ *Caprimulgus ridgwayi.* BUFF-COLLARED NIGHTJAR. (sw US-c MA) . _____

❑ *Caprimulgus vociferus.* WHIP-POOR-WILL. (NA, MA; ◊ MA). . . . . . . _____
   ___*C. (v.) arizonae.* STEPHENS'S WHIP-POOR-WILL. (w NA, MA)
   ___*C. (v.) vociferus.* EASTERN WHIP-POOR-WILL. (e NA)

❑ *Caprimulgus noctitherus.* PUERTO RICAN NIGHTJAR. (PR). . . . . _____

❑ *Caprimulgus saturatus.* DUSKY NIGHTJAR. (mts CR, w Pan). . . . . . . _____

❑ *Caprimulgus longirostris.* BAND-WINGED NIGHTJAR. (SA). . . . . _____

❑ *Caprimulgus cayennensis.* WHITE-TAILED NIGHTJAR. (s CA-n SA) . _____

❑ *Caprimulgus candicans.* WHITE-WINGED NIGHTJAR. (sc SA). . . . . . . _____

❑ *Caprimulgus maculicaudus.* SPOT-TAILED NIGHTJAR. (MA, SA). . . . _____

❑ *Caprimulgus parvulus.* LITTLE NIGHTJAR. (SA). . . . . _____

❑ *Caprimulgus anthonyi.* SCRUB NIGHTJAR. (cw SA). . . . . _____

❑ *Caprimulgus maculosus.* CAYENNE NIGHTJAR. (Guia). . . . . _____

❑ *Caprimulgus nigrescens.* BLACKISH NIGHTJAR. (Amaz). . . . . _____

❑ *Caprimulgus whitelyi.* RORAIMAN NIGHTJAR. (Pant nc SA). . . . . _____

❑ *Caprimulgus hirundinaceus.* PYGMY NIGHTJAR. (e Braz). . . . . _____

❑ *Caprimulgus binotatus.* BROWN NIGHTJAR. (wc Afr). . . . . _____

❑ *Caprimulgus ruficollis.* RED-NECKED NIGHTJAR. (sw Palea; ◊-w Afr). _____

❑ *Caprimulgus indicus.* GREY NIGHTJAR. (s Asia, Palau; ◊ se Asia-Phil)_____

❑ *Caprimulgus europaeus.* EURASIAN NIGHTJAR. (Palea; ◊ Afr). . . . . . _____

❑ *Caprimulgus fraenatus.* SOMBRE NIGHTJAR. (ne Afr). . . . . _____

❑ *Caprimulgus rufigena.* RUFOUS-CHEEKED NIGHTJAR. (c,s Afr)...... _____

❑ *Caprimulgus aegyptius.* EGYPTIAN NIGHTJAR. (sw,sc Palea)....... _____

❑ *Caprimulgus mahrattensis.* SYKES'S NIGHTJAR. (sc Asia)......... _____

❑ *Caprimulgus centralasicus.* VAURIE'S NIGHTJAR. (w China)....... _____

❑ *Caprimulgus nubicus.* NUBIAN NIGHTJAR. (ne Afr reg)........... _____

❑ *Caprimulgus eximius.* GOLDEN NIGHTJAR. (subsah Afr)......... _____

❑ *Caprimulgus madagascariensis.* MADAGASCAR NIGHTJAR. (Ald-Mad)_____

❑ *Caprimulgus macrurus.* LARGE-TAILED NIGHTJAR. (s Asia-Bism, Aust)_____

❑ *Caprimulgus atripennis.* JERDON'S NIGHTJAR. (pen India)......... _____

❑ *Caprimulgus manillensis.* PHILIPPINE NIGHTJAR. (Phil).......... _____

❑ *Caprimulgus celebensis.* SULAWESI NIGHTJAR. (n Sulaw)......... _____

❑ *Caprimulgus donaldsoni.* DONALDSON-SMITH'S NIGHTJAR. (ne Afr) . _____

❑ *Caprimulgus nigriscapularis.* BLACK-SHOULDERED N. (w,c Afr).... _____

❑ *Caprimulgus pectoralis.* FIERY-NECKED NIGHTJAR. (c,s Afr)....... _____
  ___*C. (p.) fervidus.* FIERY-NECKED NIGHTJAR. (sp)
  ___*C. (p.) pectoralis.* SOUTH AFRICAN NIGHTJAR. (S Afr)

❑ *Caprimulgus prigoginei.* ITOMBWE NIGHTJAR. (ce Zaire)......... _____

❑ *Caprimulgus poliocephalus.* MONTANE NIGHTJAR. (mts c Afr)...... _____
  ___*C. (p.) poliocephalus.* ABYSSINIAN NIGHTJAR. (ce Afr)
  ___*C. (p.) guttifer.* USAMBARA NIGHTJAR. (ec Afr)
  ___*C. (p.) koesteri.* MOCO NIGHTJAR. (wc Afr)

❑ *Caprimulgus ruwenzorii.* RUWENZORI NIGHTJAR. (mts ce Afr)...... _____

❑ *Caprimulgus asiaticus.* INDIAN NIGHTJAR. (s,se Asia)............. _____

❑ *Caprimulgus natalensis.* SWAMP NIGHTJAR. (Afr)............... _____

❑ *Caprimulgus inornatus.* PLAIN NIGHTJAR. (w,c,ne Afr reg)........ _____
  ___*C. (i.) inornatus.* PLAIN NIGHTJAR. (sp)
  ___*C. (i.) ludovicianus.* LUDOVIC'S NIGHTJAR. (sw Eth)

❑ *Caprimulgus stellatus.* STAR-SPOTTED NIGHTJAR. (ne Afr)........ _____

❑ *Caprimulgus affinis.* SAVANNA NIGHTJAR. (s Asia-Phil).......... _____
  ___*C. (a.) monticolus.* FRANKLIN'S NIGHTJAR. (s,se Asia)
  ___*C. (a.) affinis.* SAVANNA NIGHTJAR. (Sunda-Phil)

❑ *Caprimulgus tristigma.* FRECKLED NIGHTJAR. (Afr)............. _____

❑ *Caprimulgus concretus.* BONAPARTE'S NIGHTJAR. (Sum, Born)..... _____

❑ *Caprimulgus pulchellus.* SALVADORI'S NIGHTJAR. (Sum, Java)...... _____

❑ *Caprimulgus enarratus.* COLLARED NIGHTJAR. (nw,e Mad)....... _____

❑ *Caprimulgus batesi.* BATES'S NIGHTJAR. (c Afr)............... _____

❑ *Caprimulgus climacurus.* LONG-TAILED NIGHTJAR. (w,c Afr; ◊-e Afr)_____

❑ *Caprimulgus clarus.* SLENDER-TAILED NIGHTJAR. (ne Afr)........ _____

❏ *Caprimulgus fossii.* SQUARE-TAILED NIGHTJAR. (c,s Afr). . . . . _____

❏ *Macrodipteryx longipennis.* STANDARD-WINGED N. (subsah Afr). . . . _____

❏ *Macrodipteryx vexillarius.* PENNANT-WINGED N. (s Afr; ◊-c,e Afr). . . _____

❏ *Hydropsalis climacocerca.* LADDER-TAILED NIGHTJAR. (Amaz). . . . . _____

❏ *Hydropsalis brasiliana.* SCISSOR-TAILED NIGHTJAR. (c,sc SA). . . . . . _____

❏ *Uropsalis segmentata.* SWALLOW-TAILED NIGHTJAR. (Andes w SA) . _____

❏ *Uropsalis lyra.* LYRE-TAILED NIGHTJAR. (Andes w SA). . . . . _____

❏ *Macropsalis creagra.* LONG-TRAINED NIGHTJAR. (se Braz). . . . . _____

❏ *Eleothreptus anomalus.* SICKLE-WINGED NIGHTJAR. (se SA). . . . . . . _____

Superorder PASSERIMORPHAE [1518/7274]
Order **COLUMBIFORMES** [42/316]
Family **Raphidae** [2/3]

Raphus cucullatus. DODO. (†Maur). . . . . _____

Raphus solitarius. REUNION SOLITAIRE. (†Réun). . . . . _____

Pezophaps solitaria. RODRIGUEZ SOLITAIRE. (†Rodr). . . . . _____

Family **Columbidae** [40/313]

❏ *Columba livia.* ROCK PIGEON. (Eura; ◆ cosm). . . . . _____

❏ *Columba rupestris.* HILL PIGEON. (mts ec,s Asia). . . . . _____

❏ *Columba leuconota.* SNOW PIGEON. (mts s Asia). . . . . _____

❏ *Columba guinea.* SPECKLED PIGEON. (w,nc,e,s Afr). . . . . _____

❏ *Columba albitorques.* WHITE-COLLARED PIGEON. (mts w Eth). . . . . . _____

❏ *Columba oenas.* STOCK PIGEON. (Palea; ◊-n Afr). . . . . _____

❏ *Columba oliviae.* SOMALI PIGEON. (mts n Som). . . . . _____

❏ *Columba eversmanni.* PALE-BACKED PIGEON. (sc Asia). . . . . _____

❏ *Columba palumbus.* COMMON WOOD-PIGEON. (Palea; ◊ n Afr-s Asia)_____

❏ *Columba trocaz.* TROCAZ PIGEON. (Madeira). . . . . _____

❏ *Columba bollii.* BOLLE'S PIGEON. (mts w,c Can Is). . . . . _____

❏ *Columba junoniae.* LAUREL PIGEON. (Can Is). . . . . _____

❏ *Columba unicincta.* AFEP PIGEON. (w,c Afr). . . . . _____

❏ *Columba sjostedti.* CAMEROON OLIVE-PIGEON. (mts wc Afr). . . . . . . _____

❏ *Columba thomensis.* SAO TOME OLIVE-PIGEON. (ST). . . . . _____

❏ *Columba arquatrix.* AFRICAN OLIVE-PIGEON. (e,s Afr). . . . . _____

❏ *Columba pollenii.* COMORO OLIVE-PIGEON. (Com). . . . . _____

❏ *Columba hodgsonii.* SPECKLED WOOD-PIGEON. (mts s Asia). . . . . . . _____

❑ *Columba albinucha.* WHITE-NAPED PIGEON. (wc,e Afr). . . . . _____

❑ *Columba pulchricollis.* ASHY WOOD-PIGEON. (mts s Asia). . . . . _____

❑ *Columba elphinstonii.* NILGIRI WOOD-PIGEON. (sw India). . . . . _____

❑ *Columba torringtoni.* CEYLON WOOD-PIGEON. (mts Ceylon). . . . . . . _____

❑ *Columba punicea.* PALE-CAPPED PIGEON. (s,se Asia). . . . . _____

❑ *Columba argentina.* SILVERY WOOD-PIGEON. (Sum, is n Born). . . . . _____

❑ *Columba palumboides.* ANDAMAN WOOD-PIGEON. (And, Nico). . . . . _____

❑ *Columba janthina.* JAPANESE WOOD-PIGEON. (is w Pac). . . . . _____

❑ *Columba vitiensis.* METALLIC PIGEON. (Wall, Phil-Samoa). . . . . _____

❑ *Columba leucomela.* WHITE-HEADED PIGEON. (e Aust). . . . . _____

❑ *Columba versicolor.* BONIN WOOD-PIGEON. (Bonin). . . . . _____

❑ *Columba jouyi.* RYUKYU PIGEON. (Ryu). . . . . _____

❑ *Columba pallidiceps.* YELLOW-LEGGED PIGEON. (Bism, Solom). . . . . _____

❑ *Columba leucocephala.* WHITE-CROWNED PIGEON. (s Fla, W Indies). _____

❑ *Columba speciosa.* SCALED PIGEON. (MA, SA). . . . . _____

❑ *Columba squamosa.* SCALY-NAPED PIGEON. (W Indies). . . . . _____

❑ *Columba corensis.* BARE-EYED PIGEON. (nw SA),,,,,,,,,,,,,,, _____

❑ *Columba picazuro.* PICAZURO PIGEON. (ce SA). . . . . _____

❑ *Columba maculosa.* SPOT-WINGED PIGEON. (s SA). . . . . _____

❑ *Columba fasciata.* BAND-TAILED PIGEON. (mts w NA, CA, w SA). . . _____
   ___*C. (f.) fasciata.* BAND-TAILED PIGEON. (w NA, CA)
   ___*C. (f.) albilinea.* WHITE-NECKED PIGEON. (s CA, SA)

❑ *Columba araucana.* CHILEAN PIGEON. (s SA). . . . . _____

❑ *Columba caribaea.* RING-TAILED PIGEON. (mts Jam). . . . . _____

❑ *Columba cayennensis.* PALE-VENTED PIGEON. (MA, SA). . . . . _____

❑ *Columba flavirostris.* RED-BILLED PIGEON. (s Tex, MA). . . . . _____

❑ *Columba oenops.* PERUVIAN PIGEON. (Andes n Peru). . . . . _____

❑ *Columba inornata.* PLAIN PIGEON. (G Ant). _____

❑ *Columba plumbea.* PLUMBEOUS PIGEON. (SA). . . . . _____

❑ *Columba subvinacea.* RUDDY PIGEON. (s CA, w,wc,n SA). . . . . _____
   ___*C. (s.) subvinacea.* RUDDY PIGEON. (s CA, Amaz)
   ___*C. (s.) berlepschi.* BERLEPSCH'S PIGEON. (s CA, nw SA)
   ___*C. (s.) purpureotincta.* PURPLE-TINTED PIGEON. (cn SA)

❑ *Columba nigrirostris.* SHORT-BILLED PIGEON. (MA, nw Colom). . . . . _____

❑ *Columba goodsoni.* DUSKY PIGEON. (nw SA). . . . . _____

❑ *Columba iriditorques.* WESTERN BRONZE-NAPED PIGEON. (w,c Afr) . _____

❏ *Columba malherbii.* SAO TOME BRONZE-NAPED PIGEON. (ST-Ann) . _____

❏ *Columba delegorguei.* EASTERN BRONZE-NAPED PIGEON. (e,s Afr). . . _____

❏ *Columba picturata.* MADAGASCAR TURTLE-DOVE. (Mad reg). . . . . . . _____

❏ *Columba larvata.* LEMON DOVE. (wc,e,se Afr). . . . . _____
___*C. (l.) simplex.* WESTERN LEMON-DOVE. (wc Afr)
___*C. (l.) larvata.* EASTERN LEMON-DOVE. (e,se Afr)

❏ *Columba mayeri.* PINK PIGEON. (Maur). . . . . _____

❏ *Streptopelia turtur.* EUROPEAN TURTLE-DOVE. (c,sw Palea; ◊-s Afr). . _____

❏ *Streptopelia hypopyrrha.* ADAMAWA TURTLE-DOVE. (mts cw Afr). . . _____

❏ *Streptopelia lugens.* DUSKY TURTLE-DOVE. (mts ne,e Afr). . . . . _____

❏ *Streptopelia orientalis.* ORIENTAL TURTLE-DOVE. (c,sc Asia). . . . . . _____

❏ *Streptopelia senegalensis.* LAUGHING DOVE. (sc,s Eura, e,se Afr). . . . _____

❏ *Streptopelia chinensis.* SPOTTED DOVE. (s Asia-Phil; ◆ cosm). . . . . . _____

❏ *Streptopelia decipiens.* MOURNING COLLARED-DOVE. (Afr). . . . . . . _____

❏ *Streptopelia vinacea.* VINACEOUS DOVE. (w,nc,ne Afr). . . . . _____

❏ *Streptopelia capicola.* RING-NECKED DOVE. (e,s Afr). . . . . _____

❏ *Streptopelia tranquebarica.* RED COLLARED-DOVE. (s Asia-n Phil) . _____

❏ *Streptopelia semitorquata.* RED-EYED DOVE. (Afr reg). . . . . _____

❏ *Streptopelia decaocto.* EURASIAN COLLARED-DOVE. (w Palea-s Asia). _____

❏ *Streptopelia roseogrisea.* AFRICAN COLLARED-DOVE. (subsah Afr) . _____

❏ *Streptopelia reichenowi.* WHITE-WINGED COLLARED-DOVE. (ne Afr). _____

❏ *Streptopelia bitorquata.* ISLAND COLLARED-DOVE. (Sunda-Phil). . . . . _____

❏ *Macropygia unchall.* BARRED CUCKOO-DOVE. (mts s,se Asia). . . . . . _____
___*M. (u.) tusalia.* BAR-TAILED CUCKOO-DOVE. (s,se Asia)
___*M. (u.) unchall.* BARRED CUCKOO-DOVE. (G Sunda)

❏ *Macropygia rufipennis.* ANDAMAN CUCKOO-DOVE. (And, Nico). . . . _____

❏ *Macropygia tenuirostris.* PHILIPPINE CUCKOO-DOVE. (Taiwan, Phil). _____

❏ *Macropygia emiliana.* RUDDY CUCKOO-DOVE. (Sunda). . . . . _____

❏ *Macropygia amboinensis.* SLENDER-BILLED CUCKOO-D. (Wall-Bism) _____

❏ *Macropygia magna.* DUSKY CUCKOO-DOVE. (Wall). . . . . _____

❏ *Macropygia phasianella.* BROWN CUCKOO-DOVE. (e Aust). . . . . _____

❏ *Macropygia ruficeps.* LITTLE CUCKOO-DOVE. (mts se Asia). . . . . _____

❏ *Macropygia nigrirostris.* BLACK-BILLED CUCKOO-DOVE. (NG, Bism). _____

❏ *Macropygia mackinlayi.* MACKINLAY'S CUCKOO-DOVE. (Bism-Vanu) _____

❏ *Reinwardtoena reinwardtsi.* GREAT CUCKOO-DOVE. (Moluc-NG). . . _____

❏ *Reinwardtoena browni.* PIED CUCKOO-DOVE. (Bism). . . . . _____

❑ *Reinwardtoena crassirostris.* CRESTED CUCKOO-DOVE. (mts Solom). _____

❑ *Turacoena manadensis.* WHITE-FACED CUCKOO-DOVE. (Sulaw). . . . _____

❑ *Turacoena modesta.* BLACK CUCKOO-DOVE. (ec L Sunda). . . . . _____

❑ *Turtur abyssinicus.* BLACK-BILLED WOOD-DOVE. (subsah Afr). . . . . . _____

❑ *Turtur chalcospilos.* EMERALD-SPOTTED WOOD-DOVE. (s,e Afr). . . . . _____

❑ *Turtur afer.* BLUE-SPOTTED WOOD-DOVE. (Afr). . . . . _____

❑ *Turtur tympanistria.* TAMBOURINE DOVE. (Afr). . . . . _____

❑ *Turtur brehmeri.* BLUE-HEADED WOOD-DOVE. (w,c Afr). . . . . _____

❑ *Oena capensis.* NAMAQUA DOVE. (Afr reg, Mad). . . . . _____

❑ *Chalcophaps indica.* EMERALD DOVE. (s Asia-Phil, Aust, sw Polyn). _____
   ___*C. (i.) indica.* INDIAN EMERALD-DOVE. (s Asia-Phil, w Pap)
   ___*C. (i.) chrysochlora.* PACIFIC EMERALD-DOVE. (L Sunda-sw Polyn, n,e Aust)

❑ *Chalcophaps stephani.* STEPHAN'S DOVE. (Sulaw-Solom). . . . . _____

❑ *Henicophaps albifrons.* NEW GUINEA BRONZEWING. (Aru-NG). . . . . _____

❑ *Henicophaps foersteri.* NEW BRITAIN BRONZEWING. (sc Bism). . . . . . _____

❑ *Phaps chalcoptera.* COMMON BRONZEWING. (Aust). . . . . _____

❑ *Phaps elegans.* BRUSH BRONZEWING. (sw,e,se Aust). . . . . _____

❑ *Phaps histrionica.* FLOCK BRONZEWING. (int cn Aust; ◊-s,e Aust). . . . _____

❑ *Geophaps lophotes.* CRESTED PIGEON. (int Aust). . . . . _____

❑ *Geophaps plumifera.* SPINIFEX PIGEON. (int,n Aust). . . . . _____
   ___*G. (p.) plumifera.* SPINIFEX PIGEON. (sp)
   ___*G. (p.) ferruginea.* RED-PLUMED PIGEON. (cw W Aust)

❑ *Geophaps smithii.* PARTRIDGE PIGEON. (cn Aust). . . . . _____

❑ *Geophaps scripta.* SQUATTER PIGEON. (ne,ce Aust). . . . . _____
   ___*G. (s.) peninsulae.* NORTHERN SQUATTER-PIGEON. (ne Aust)
   ___*G. (s,) scripta.* SOUTHERN SQUATTER-PIGEON. (ce Aust)

❑ *Petrophassa albipennis.* WHITE-QUILLED ROCK-PIGEON. (nw Aust) . _____

❑ *Petrophassa rufipennis.* CHESTNUT-QUILLED ROCK-PIGEON. (cn Aust)_____

❑ *Geopelia cuneata.* DIAMOND DOVE. (n,int Aust). . . . . _____

❑ *Geopelia striata.* ZEBRA DOVE. (se Asia; ◆ Phil, is). . . . . _____

❑ *Geopelia maugeus.* BARRED DOVE. (Wall). . . . . _____

❑ *Geopelia placida.* PEACEFUL DOVE. (s NG, Aust). . . . . _____

❑ *Geopelia humeralis.* BAR-SHOULDERED DOVE. (s NG, Aust). . . . . . . _____

❑ *Leucosarcia melanoleuca.* WONGA PIGEON. (se Aust). . . . . _____

   Ectopistes migratorius. PASSENGER PIGEON. (†e NA). . . . . _____

❑ *Zenaida macroura.* MOURNING DOVE. (NA, MA, n W Indies). . . . . . _____

❑ *Zenaida graysoni.* SOCORRO DOVE. (Revil). . . . . _____

❑ *Zenaida auriculata.* EARED DOVE. (s L Ant, SA). . . . . _____

❑ *Zenaida aurita.* ZENAIDA DOVE. (se Mex, W Indies). . . . . _____

❑ *Zenaida asiatica.* WHITE-WINGED DOVE. (sw US-cw SA). . . . . _____
   ___*Z. (a.) asiatica.* WHITE-WINGED DOVE. (sw US, MA, n W Indies)
   ___*Z. (a.) meloda.* PACIFIC DOVE. (cw SA)

❑ *Zenaida galapagoensis.* GALAPAGOS DOVE. (Galap). . . . . _____

❑ *Columbina inca.* INCA DOVE. (sw US, MA). . . . . _____

❑ *Columbina squammata.* SCALED DOVE. (n,e SA). . . . . _____

❑ *Columbina passerina.* COMMON GROUND-DOVE. (s US-c SA). . . . . . _____

❑ *Columbina minuta.* PLAIN-BREASTED GROUND-DOVE. (MA, SA). . . . _____

❑ *Columbina talpacoti.* RUDDY GROUND-DOVE. (MA, SA). . . . . _____

❑ *Columbina buckleyi.* ECUADORIAN GROUND-DOVE. (cw SA). . . . . . _____

❑ *Columbina picui.* PICUI GROUND-DOVE. (sc SA). . . . . _____

❑ *Columbina cruziana.* CROAKING GROUND-DOVE. (cw SA). . . . . _____

❑ *Columbina cyanopis.* BLUE-EYED GROUND-DOVE. (sc Braz). . . . . . . _____

❑ *Claravis pretiosa.* BLUE GROUND-DOVE. (MA, SA). . . . . _____

❑ *Claravis mondetoura.* MAROON-CHESTED GROUND-DOVE. (MA-n SA) _____

❑ *Claravis godefrida.* PURPLE-WINGED GROUND-DOVE. (se SA). . . . . . _____

❑ *Metriopelia ceciliae.* BARE-FACED GROUND-DOVE. (Andes sw SA) . _____

❑ *Metriopelia morenoi.* BARE-EYED GROUND-DOVE. (Andes nw Argen) _____

❑ *Metriopelia melanoptera.* BLACK-WINGED GROUND-DOVE. (w SA) . _____

❑ *Metriopelia aymara.* GOLDEN-SPOTTED GROUND-DOVE. (sw SA). . . . _____

❑ *Uropelia campestris.* LONG-TAILED GROUND-DOVE. (c SA). . . . . . . _____

❑ *Leptotila verreauxi.* WHITE-TIPPED DOVE. (s Tex, MA, SA). . . . . . . _____
   ___*L. (v.) verreauxi.* WHITE-TIPPED DOVE. (s Tex, MA, w,n SA)
   ___*L. (v.) brasiliensis.* BRAZILIAN DOVE. (c,sc SA)

❑ *Leptotila megalura.* WHITE-FACED DOVE. (Andes sw SA). . . . . _____

❑ *Leptotila plumbeiceps.* GREY-HEADED DOVE. (MA, w Colom). . . . . _____

❑ *Leptotila battyi.* BROWN-BACKED DOVE. (Pac w Pan). . . . . _____

❑ *Leptotila wellsi.* GRENADA DOVE. (mts Grenada). . . . . _____

❑ *Leptotila rufaxilla.* GREY-FRONTED DOVE. (SA). . . . . _____

❑ *Leptotila jamaicensis.* CARIBBEAN DOVE. (G Ant, is MA). . . . . _____

❑ *Leptotila pallida.* PALLID DOVE. (Pac nw SA). . . . . _____

❑ *Leptotila cassini.* GREY-CHESTED DOVE. (c,s MA, nw Colom). . . . . _____

❑ *Leptotila ochraceiventris.* OCHRE-BELLIED DOVE. (wc SA). . . . . . . _____

❑ *Leptotila conoveri.* TOLIMA DOVE. (Andes c Colom). . . . . _____

❑ *Geotrygon lawrencii.* PURPLISH-BACKED QUAIL-DOVE. (c,s MA). . . . _____

❑ *Geotrygon costaricensis.* BUFF-FRONTED QUAIL-DOVE. (mts s CA) . _____

❑ *Geotrygon saphirina.* SAPPHIRE QUAIL-DOVE. (nw SA, w Amaz). . . . _____
   ___*G. (s.) purpurata.* PURPLE-CROWNED QUAIL-DOVE. (nw SA)
   ___*G. (s.) saphirina.* SAPPHIRE QUAIL-DOVE. (w Amaz)

❑ *Geotrygon caniceps.* GREY-HEADED QUAIL-DOVE. (Cuba, Hisp). . . . . _____

❑ *Geotrygon versicolor.* CRESTED QUAIL-DOVE. (mts Jam). . . . . _____

❑ *Geotrygon veraguensis.* OLIVE-BACKED QUAIL-DOVE. (s CA-nw SA) _____

❑ *Geotrygon albifacies.* WHITE-FACED QUAIL-DOVE. (mts MA). . . . . . . _____

❑ *Geotrygon chiriquensis.* RUFOUS-BREASTED QUAIL-DOVE. (s CA). . . _____

❑ *Geotrygon goldmani.* RUSSET-CROWNED QUAIL-DOVE. (s CA-nw SA). _____

❑ *Geotrygon linearis.* LINED QUAIL-DOVE. (mts n SA). . . . . _____

❑ *Geotrygon frenata.* WHITE-THROATED QUAIL-DOVE. (Andes w SA) . _____
   ___*G. (f.) bourcieri.* BOURCIER'S QUAIL-DOVE. (nw SA)
   ___*G. (f.) erythropareia.* DARK QUAIL-DOVE. (e Ecua)
   ___*G. (f.) frenata.* PINK-FACED QUAIL-DOVE. (sw SA)

❑ *Geotrygon chrysia.* KEY WEST QUAIL-DOVE. (G Ant, Bah). . . . . _____

❑ *Geotrygon mystacea.* BRIDLED QUAIL-DOVE. (c,se W Indies). . . . . . . _____

❑ *Geotrygon violacea.* VIOLACEOUS QUAIL-DOVE. (s CA, SA). . . . . _____

❑ *Geotrygon montana.* RUDDY QUAIL-DOVE. (W Indies, MA, SA). . . . _____
   ___*G. (m.) montana.* RUDDY QUAIL-DOVE. (G Ant, MA, SA)
   ___*G. (m.) martinica.* MARTINIQUE QUAIL-DOVE. (L Ant)

❑ *Starnoenas cyanocephala.* BLUE-HEADED QUAIL-DOVE. (Cuba). . . . . _____

❑ *Caloenas nicobarica.* NICOBAR PIGEON. (se Asia-Palau, Solom). . . . . _____

❑ *Gallicolumba luzonica.* LUZON BLEEDING-HEART. (n Phil). . . . . _____

❑ *Gallicolumba platenae.* MINDORO BLEEDING-HEART. (c Phil). . . . . . _____

❑ *Gallicolumba keayi.* NEGROS BLEEDING-HEART. (c Phil). . . . . _____

❑ *Gallicolumba criniger.* MINDANAO BLEEDING-HEART. (se Phil). . . . . _____

❑ *Gallicolumba menagei.* SULU BLEEDING-HEART. (Sulu). . . . . _____

❑ *Gallicolumba rufigula.* CINNAMON GROUND-DOVE. (Aru-NG). . . . . . _____

❑ *Gallicolumba tristigmata.* SULAWESI GROUND-DOVE. (Sulaw). . . . . . _____

❑ *Gallicolumba jobiensis.* WHITE-BIBBED GROUND-DOVE. (NG-Solom) _____

❑ *Gallicolumba kubaryi.* CAROLINE ISLANDS GROUND-DOVE. (Carol) . _____

❑ *Gallicolumba erythroptera.* POLYNESIAN GROUND-DOVE. (se Polyn). _____

❑ *Gallicolumba xanthonura.* WHITE-THROATED GROUND-DOVE. (Mari) _____

❑ *Gallicolumba stairi.* FRIENDLY GROUND-DOVE. (cs Polyn). . . . . _____

❑ *Gallicolumba sanctaecrucis.* SANTA CRUZ GROUND-DOVE. (e Melan) _____

❑ *Gallicolumba ferruginea.* TANNA GROUND-DOVE. (s Vanu). . . . . _____

❑ *Gallicolumba salamonis.* THICK-BILLED GROUND-DOVE. (Solom). . . _____

❑ *Gallicolumba rubescens.* MARQUESAN GROUND-DOVE. (Marq). . . . . _____

❑ *Gallicolumba beccarii.* BRONZE GROUND-DOVE. (NG-Solom). . . . . . _____

❑ *Gallicolumba canifrons.* PALAU GROUND-DOVE. (Palaui). . . . . _____

❑ *Gallicolumba hoedtii.* WETAR GROUND-DOVE. (Wetar). . . . . _____

❑ *Trugon terrestris.* THICK-BILLED GROUND-PIGEON. (w Pap, NG). . . . _____

   Microgoura meeki. CHOISEUL PIGEON. (†nw Solom). . . . . _____

❑ *Otidiphaps nobilis.* PHEASANT PIGEON. (Aru-NG). . . . . _____

❑ *Phapitreron leucotis.* WHITE-EARED BROWN-DOVE. (Phil). . . . . _____

❑ *Phapitreron amethystina.* AMETHYST BROWN-DOVE. (mts Phil). . . . . _____

❑ *Phapitreron cinereiceps.* DARK-EARED BROWN-DOVE. (mts s Phil). . . _____

❑ *Treron fulvicollis.* CINNAMON-HEADED GREEN-PIGEON. (se Asia). . . . _____

❑ *Treron olax.* LITTLE GREEN-PIGEON. (se Asia). . . . . _____

❑ *Treron vernans.* PINK-NECKED GREEN-PIGEON. (se Asia-Phil). . . . . . _____

❑ *Treron bicincta.* ORANGE-BREASTED GREEN-PIGEON. (s,se Asia). . . . . _____

❑ *Treron pompadora.* POMPADOUR GREEN-PIGEON. (s Asia-Phil, Wall). _____
   ___*T. (p.) pompadora.* POMPADOUR GREEN-PIGEON. (s,se Asia)
   ___*T. (p.) chloroptera.* ANDAMAN GREEN-PIGEON. (And, Nico)
   ___*T. (p.) axillaris.* PHILIPPINE GREEN-PIGEON. (Phil)
   ___*T. (p.) aromatica.* BURU GREEN-PIGEON. (sc Wall)

❑ *Treron curvirostra.* THICK-BILLED GREEN-PIGEON. (s Asia-w Phil). . . _____

❑ *Treron griseicauda.* GREY-CHEEKED GREEN-PIGEON. (G Sunda). . . . . _____

❑ *Treron floris.* FLORES GREEN-PIGEON. (w,c L Sunda). . . . . _____

❑ *Treron teysmannii.* SUMBA GREEN-PIGEON. (Sumba). . . . . _____

❑ *Treron psittacea.* TIMOR GREEN-PIGEON. (c L Sunda). . . . . _____

❑ *Treron capellei.* LARGE GREEN-PIGEON. (se Asia). . . . . _____

❑ *Treron phoenicoptera.* YELLOW-FOOTED GREEN-PIGEON. (s,se Asia). _____

❑ *Treron waalia.* BRUCE'S GREEN-PIGEON. (subsah Afr reg). . . . . _____

❑ *Treron calva.* AFRICAN GREEN-PIGEON. (Afr). . . . . _____
   ___*T. (c.) calva.* AFRICAN GREEN-PIGEON. (w,c,ne Afr)
   ___*T. (c.) delalandii.* DELALANDE'S GREEN-PIGEON. (se Afr)

❑ *Treron sanctithomae.* SAO TOME GREEN-PIGEON. (ST). . . . . _____

❑ *Treron pembaensis.* PEMBA GREEN-PIGEON. (Pemba). . . . . _____

❑ *Treron australis.* MADAGASCAR GREEN-PIGEON. (Mad reg). . . . . _____

❑ *Treron apicauda.* PIN-TAILED GREEN-PIGEON. (s,se Asia). . . . . _____

❑ *Treron oxyura.* SUMATRAN GREEN-PIGEON. (Sum, w Java). . . . . _____

❑ *Treron seimundi.* YELLOW-VENTED GREEN-PIGEON. (se Asia). . . . . . . _____

❑ *Treron sphenura.* WEDGE-TAILED GREEN-PIGEON. (sAsia-w Indon) . _____
    ___*T. (s.) sphenura.* WEDGE-TAILED GREEN-PIGEON. (s,se Asia)
    ___*T. (s.) korthalsi.* KORTHALS'S GREEN-PIGEON. (G Sunda-Lombok)

❑ *Treron sieboldii.* WHITE-BELLIED GREEN-PIGEON. (s,e Asia). . . . . . . _____

❑ *Treron formosae.* WHISTLING GREEN-PIGEON. (Ryu, Taiwan, n Phil). _____

❑ *Ptilinopus porphyreus.* PINK-HEADED FRUIT-DOVE. (Sum-Bali). . . . . _____

❑ *Ptilinopus cinctus.* BLACK-BACKED FRUIT-DOVE. (L Sunda). . . . . . . _____

❑ *Ptilinopus dohertyi.* RED-NAPED FRUIT-DOVE. (Sumba). . . . . _____

❑ *Ptilinopus alligator.* BLACK-BANDED FRUIT-DOVE. (cn Aust). . . . . . _____

❑ *Ptilinopus marchei.* FLAME-BREASTED FRUIT-DOVE. (mts n Phil). . . . _____

❑ *Ptilinopus merrilli.* CREAM-BELLIED FRUIT-DOVE. (n Phil). . . . . _____

❑ *Ptilinopus occipitalis.* YELLOW-BREASTED FRUIT-DOVE. (Phil). . . . . _____

❑ *Ptilinopus fischeri.* RED-EARED FRUIT-DOVE. (mts Sulaw). . . . . _____

❑ *Ptilinopus jambu.* JAMBU FRUIT-DOVE. (se Asia). . . . . _____

❑ *Ptilinopus leclancheri.* BLACK-CHINNED FRUIT-DOVE. (se China, Phil) _____

❑ *Ptilinopus subgularis.* MAROON-CHINNED FRUIT-DOVE. (Wall). . . . . . _____

❑ *Ptilinopus bernsteinii.* SCARLET-BREASTED FRUIT-DOVE. (n Moluc) . _____

❑ *Ptilinopus magnificus.* WOMPOO FRUIT-DOVE. (w Pap, NG, e Aust). _____

❑ *Ptilinopus perlatus.* PINK-SPOTTED FRUIT-DOVE. (Aru-NG). . . . . . . _____

❑ *Ptilinopus ornatus.* ORNATE FRUIT-DOVE. (NG). . . . . _____

❑ *Ptilinopus tannensis.* TANNA FRUIT-DOVE. (Vanu). . . . . _____

❑ *Ptilinopus aurantiifrons.* ORANGE-FRONTED FRUIT-DOVE. (Aru-NG). _____

❑ *Ptilinopus wallacii.* WALLACE'S FRUIT-DOVE. (e L Sunda-w NG). . . . _____

❑ *Ptilinopus superbus.* SUPERB FRUIT-DOVE. (Wall-Bism, ne Aust). . . _____

❑ *Ptilinopus perousii.* MANY-COLORED FRUIT-DOVE. (s Polyn). . . . . . . _____

❑ *Ptilinopus monacha.* BLUE-CAPPED FRUIT-DOVE. (n Moluc). . . . . _____

❑ *Ptilinopus coronulatus.* CORONETED FRUIT-DOVE. (Aru-NG). . . . . . . _____

❑ *Ptilinopus pulchellus.* BEAUTIFUL FRUIT-DOVE. (w Pap, NG). . . . . . . _____

❑ *Ptilinopus regina.* ROSE-CROWNED FRUIT-DOVE. (s Wall, n,e Aust) . _____

❑ *Ptilinopus roseicapilla.* MARIANA FRUIT-DOVE. (s Mari). . . . . _____

❑ *Ptilinopus greyii.* RED-BELLIED FRUIT-DOVE. (Solom-N Cal). . . . . . . _____

❑ *Ptilinopus richardsii.* SILVER-CAPPED FRUIT-DOVE. (e Solom). . . . . . _____

❑ *Ptilinopus porphyraceus.* CRIMSON-CROWNED FRUIT-DOVE. (sw Pac) _____
    ___*P. (p.) ponapensis.* PURPLE-CAPPED FRUIT-DOVE. (Carol, sw Marsh)
    ___*P. (p.) porphyraceus.* CRIMSON-CROWNED FRUIT-DOVE. (cs Polyn)

❑ *Ptilinopus pelewensis.* PALAU FRUIT-DOVE. (Palau). . . . . _____

❑ *Ptilinopus rarotongensis.* COOK ISLANDS FRUIT-DOVE. (s Cook). . . . _____

❑ *Ptilinopus huttoni.* RAPA FRUIT-DOVE. (se Tubuai). . . . . _____

❑ *Ptilinopus purpuratus.* GREY-GREEN FRUIT-DOVE. (Soc). . . . . _____

❑ *Ptilinopus coralensis.* ATOLL FRUIT-DOVE. (Tuam). . . . . _____

❑ *Ptilinopus chalcurus.* MAKATEA FRUIT-DOVE. (w Tuam). . . . . _____

❑ *Ptilinopus insularis.* HENDERSON ISLAND FRUIT-DOVE. (Hend). . . . . _____

❑ *Ptilinopus mercierii.* RED-MOUSTACHED FRUIT-DOVE. (Marq). . . . . . _____

❑ *Ptilinopus dupetithouarsii.* WHITE-CAPPED FRUIT-DOVE. (Marq). . . . _____

❑ *Ptilinopus rivoli.* WHITE-BIBBED FRUIT-DOVE. (Moluc-Bism). . . . . . . _____

❑ *Ptilinopus solomonensis.* YELLOW-BIBBED FRUIT-DOVE. (NG-Solom)_____

❑ *Ptilinopus viridis.* CLARET-BREASTED FRUIT-DOVE. (s Moluc-NG). . . _____
   ___*P. (v.) viridis.* CLARET-BREASTED FRUIT-DOVE. (s Moluc)
   ___*P. (v.) pectoralis.* PAPUAN FRUIT-DOVE. (w Pap, w NG)
   ___*P. (v.) geelvinkiana.* GEELVINK FRUIT-DOVE. (nw NG)

❑ *Ptilinopus eugeniae.* WHITE-HEADED FRUIT-DOVE. (Solom). . . . . _____

❑ *Ptilinopus hyogastra.* GREY-HEADED FRUIT-DOVE. (n Moluc). . . . . . . _____

❑ *Ptilinopus granulifrons.* CARUNCULATED FRUIT-DOVE. (c Moluc). . . _____

❑ *Ptilinopus iozonus.* ORANGE-BELLIED FRUIT-DOVE. (Aru-NG). . . . . . _____

❑ *Ptilinopus insolitus.* KNOB-BILLED FRUIT-DOVE. (Bism). . . . . _____

❑ *Ptilinopus naina.* DWARF FRUIT-DOVE. (w Pap, NG). . . . . _____

❑ *Ptilinopus melanospila.* BLACK-NAPED FRUIT-DOVE. (Sum-Wall). . . _____

❑ *Ptilinopus arcanus.* NEGROS FRUIT-DOVE. (mts c Phil). . . . . _____

❑ *Ptilinopus victor.* ORANGE DOVE. (cn Fiji). _____

❑ *Ptilinopus luteovirens.* GOLDEN DOVE. (w Fiji). . . . . _____

❑ *Ptilinopus layardi.* WHISTLING DOVE. (sw Fiji). . . . . _____

❑ *Drepanoptila holosericea.* CLOVEN-FEATHERED DOVE. (N Cal). . . . . . _____

❑ *Alectroenas madagascariensis.* MADAGASCAR BLUE-PIGEON. (Mad). _____

❑ *Alectroenas sganzini.* COMORO BLUE-PIGEON. (Ald, Com). . . . . _____

  Alectroenas nitidissima. MAURITIUS BLUE-PIGEON. (†Maur). . . . . _____

❑ *Alectroenas pulcherrima.* SEYCHELLES BLUE-PIGEON. (Seyc). . . . . . . _____

❑ *Ducula poliocephala.* PINK-BELLIED IMPERIAL-PIGEON. (mts Phil). . . _____

❑ *Ducula forsteni.* WHITE-BELLIED IMPERIAL-PIGEON. (mts Sulaw). . . . _____

❑ *Ducula mindorensis.* MINDORO IMPERIAL-PIGEON. (mts c Phil). . . . . _____

❑ *Ducula radiata.* GREY-HEADED IMPERIAL-PIGEON. (mts Sulaw). . . . . _____

❑ *Ducula carola.* SPOTTED IMPERIAL-PIGEON. (Phil). . . . . _____

❏ *Ducula aenea.* GREEN IMPERIAL-PIGEON. (s Asia-Phil)........... _____
   ___*D. (a.) aenea.* GREEN IMPERIAL-PIGEON. (sp)
   ___*D. (a.) oenothorax.* ENGGANO IMPERIAL-PIGEON. (Enggano)

❏ *Ducula perspicillata.* WHITE-EYED IMPERIAL-PIGEON. (Moluc)...... _____

❏ *Ducula concinna.* ELEGANT IMPERIAL-PIGEON. (Wall-is nw NG).... _____

❏ *Ducula pacifica.* PACIFIC IMPERIAL-PIGEON. (sw Oceania)........ _____

❏ *Ducula oceanica.* MICRONESIAN IMPERIAL-PIGEON. (Carol, Marsh) . _____

❏ *Ducula aurorae.* POLYNESIAN IMPERIAL-PIGEON. (Soc, Tuam)...... _____

❏ *Ducula galeata.* MARQUESAN IMPERIAL-PIGEON. (nc Marq)....... _____

❏ *Ducula rubricera.* RED-KNOBBED IMPERIAL-PIGEON. (Bism, Solom) . _____

❏ *Ducula myristicivora.* SPICE IMPERIAL-PIGEON. (is n Moluc-nw NG). _____

❏ *Ducula pistrinaria.* ISLAND IMPERIAL-PIGEON. (is se NG, Bism)..... _____

❏ *Ducula whartoni.* CHRISTMAS ISLAND IMPERIAL-PIGEON. (Chris).... _____

❏ *Ducula rosacea.* PINK-HEADED IMPERIAL-PIGEON. (Wall)......... _____

❏ *Ducula pickeringii.* GREY IMPERIAL-PIGEON. (n Born-s Phil)...... _____

❏ *Ducula basilica.* CINNAMON-BELLIED IMPERIAL-PIGEON. (n Moluc) . _____

❏ *Ducula rufigaster.* PURPLE-TAILED IMPERIAL-PIGEON. (w Pap, NG) . _____

❏ *Ducula finschii.* FINSCH'S IMPERIAL-PIGEON. (Bism)............. _____

❏ *Ducula chalconota.* SHINING IMPERIAL-PIGEON. (mts NG)........ _____

❏ *Ducula latrans.* PEALE'S IMPERIAL-PIGEON. (Fiji)............... _____

❏ *Ducula brenchleyi.* CHESTNUT-BELLIED IMPERIAL-PIGEON. (Solom) . _____

❏ *Ducula bakeri.* BAKER'S IMPERIAL-PIGEON. (mts n Vanu)......... _____

❏ *Ducula goliath.* NEW CALEDONIAN IMPERIAL-PIGEON. (mts N Cal)... _____

❏ *Ducula pinon.* PINON IMPERIAL-PIGEON. (Aru-NG)............. _____

❏ *Ducula melanochroa.* BISMARCK IMPERIAL-PIGEON. (Bism)....... _____

❏ *Ducula mullerii.* COLLARED IMPERIAL-PIGEON. (Aru, NG)........ _____

❏ *Ducula zoeae.* BANDED IMPERIAL-PIGEON. (Aru-NG)............ _____

❏ *Ducula badia.* MOUNTAIN IMPERIAL-PIGEON. (mts s,se Asia)....... _____

❏ *Ducula lacernulata.* DARK-BACKED IMPERIAL-PIGEON. (s Indon).... _____

❏ *Ducula cineracea.* TIMOR IMPERIAL-PIGEON. (mts c L Sunda)...... _____

❏ *Ducula bicolor.* PIED IMPERIAL-PIGEON. (se Asia-Phil, nw NG)..... _____
   ___*D. (b.) bicolor.* NUTMEG IMPERIAL-PIGEON. (sp)
   ___*D. (b.) melanura.* BLACK IMPERIAL-PIGEON. (Moluc)

❏ *Ducula luctuosa.* WHITE IMPERIAL-PIGEON. (Sulaw)............. _____

❏ *Ducula spilorrhoa.* TORRESIAN IMPERIAL-PIGEON. (Aru-NG, Aust) . _____

❏ *Ducula constans.* KIMBERLEY IMPERIAL-PIGEON. (nw Aust)....... _____

❑ *Ducula subflavescens.* YELLOW-TINTED IMPERIAL-PIGEON. (Bism)... _____

❑ *Lopholaimus antarcticus.* TOPKNOT PIGEON. (e Aust)............ _____

❑ *Hemiphaga novaeseelandiae.* NEW ZEALAND PIGEON. (Norfolk, NZ).
      H. (n.) spadicea. NORFOLK ISLAND PIGEON. (†Norfolk)
___*H. (n.) novaeseelandiae.* NEW ZEALAND PIGEON. (NZ)

❑ *Cryptophaps poecilorrhoa.* SOMBRE PIGEON. (mts n,se Sulaw)...... _____

❑ *Gymnophaps albertisii.* PAPUAN MOUNTAIN-PIGEON. (Indon-Bism). _____

❑ *Gymnophaps mada.* LONG-TAILED MOUNTAIN-PIGEON. (s Moluc)... _____

❑ *Gymnophaps solomonensis.* PALE MOUNTAIN-PIGEON. (mts Solom). _____

❑ *Goura cristata.* WESTERN CROWNED-PIGEON. (w Pap, nw NG)...... _____

❑ *Goura victoria.* VICTORIA CROWNED-PIGEON. (n NG)............ _____

❑ *Goura scheepmakeri.* SOUTHERN CROWNED-PIGEON. (s,se NG)..... _____

❑ *Didunculus strigirostris.* TOOTH-BILLED PIGEON. (mts w Samoa).... _____

Order **GRUIFORMES** [53/197]
Suborder GRUI [17/51]
Infraorder EURYPYGIDES [1/1]
Family **Eurypygidae** [1/1]

❑ *Eurypyga helias.* SUNBITTERN. (MA, SA)...................... _____

Infraorder OTIDIDES [6/25]
Family **Otididae** [6/25]

❑ *Tetrax tetrax.* LITTLE BUSTARD. (s Palea; ◊-n Afr, s Asia)......... _____

❑ *Otis tarda.* GREAT BUSTARD. (Palea; ◊-n Afr, s Asia)............. _____

❑ *Neotis denhami.* STANLEY BUSTARD. (Afr)................... _____
___*N. (d.) denhami.* DENHAM'S BUSTARD. (sp)
___*N. (d.) stanleyi.* STANLEY BUSTARD. (S Afr)

❑ *Neotis ludwigii.* LUDWIG'S BUSTARD. (sw S Afr)............... _____

❑ *Neotis nuba.* NUBIAN BUSTARD. (subsah Afr)................. _____

❑ *Neotis heuglinii.* HEUGLIN'S BUSTARD. (ne Afr)............... _____

❑ *Ardeotis arabs.* ARABIAN BUSTARD. (n,nc Afr reg)............. _____

❑ *Ardeotis kori.* KORI BUSTARD. (ne,s Afr).................... _____

❑ *Ardeotis nigriceps.* INDIAN BUSTARD. (s Asia)................ _____

❑ *Ardeotis australis.* AUSTRALIAN BUSTARD. (s NG, Aust).......... _____

❑ *Chlamydotis undulata.* HOUBARA BUSTARD. (s Palea; ◊-s Asia)..... _____

❑ *Eupodotis savilei.* SAVILE'S BUSTARD. (subsah Afr)............. _____

❑ *Eupodotis gindiana.* BUFF-CRESTED BUSTARD. (ne Afr).......... _____

❑ *Eupodotis ruficrista.* RED-CRESTED BUSTARD. (s Afr)............ _____

❑ *Eupodotis afraoides.* WHITE-QUILLED BUSTARD. (s Afr). . . . . _____

❑ *Eupodotis afra.* BLACK BUSTARD. (sw S Afr). . . . . _____

❑ *Eupodotis rueppellii.* RUEPPELL'S BUSTARD. (sw Afr). . . . . _____

❑ *Eupodotis vigorsii.* KAROO BUSTARD. (s Afr). . . . . _____

❑ *Eupodotis humilis.* LITTLE BROWN BUSTARD. (ne Afr). . . . . _____

❑ *Eupodotis senegalensis.* WHITE-BELLIED BUSTARD. (Afr). . . . . _____
   ___*E. (s.) senegalensis.* SENEGAL BUSTARD. (n,e Afr)
   ___*E. (s.) barrowii.* BARROW'S BUSTARD. (wc,s Afr)

❑ *Eupodotis caerulescens.* BLUE BUSTARD. (mts e S Afr). . . . . _____

❑ *Eupodotis melanogaster.* BLACK-BELLIED BUSTARD. (Afr). . . . . _____

❑ *Eupodotis hartlaubii.* HARTLAUB'S BUSTARD. (ne Afr). . . . . _____

❑ *Eupodotis bengalensis.* BENGAL FLORICAN. (Himal s,se Asia). . . . . . _____

❑ *Eupodotis indica.* LESSER FLORICAN. (s Asia). . . . . _____

Infraorder GRUIDES [10/25]
Parvorder GRUIDA [7/22]
Superfamily GRUOIDEA [6/19]
Family **Gruidae** [2/15]
Subfamily Balearicinae [1/2]

❑ *Balearica pavonina.* BLACK CROWNED-CRANE. (subsah Afr). . . . . . . _____

❑ *Balearica regulorum.* GREY CROWNED-CRANE. (e,s Afr). . . . . _____

Subfamily Gruinae [1/13]

❑ *Grus leucogeranus.* SIBERIAN CRANE. (Sib; ◊-s Asia). . . . . _____

❑ *Grus antigone.* SARUS CRANE. (s Asia-n Phil, n Aust). . . . . _____

❑ *Grus rubicunda.* BROLGA. (s NG, Aust). . . . . _____

❑ *Grus vipio.* WHITE-NAPED CRANE. (se Sib, ne China; ◊-s Asia). . . . . . _____

❑ *Grus canadensis.* SANDHILL CRANE. (e Sib, NA, Cuba; ◊-c Mex). . . . _____

❑ *Grus virgo.* DEMOISELLE CRANE. (s,c,e Palea; ◊-ne Afr, s Asia). . . . . _____

❑ *Grus paradisea.* BLUE CRANE. (s Afr). . . . . _____

❑ *Grus carunculatus.* WATTLED CRANE. (ne,s Afr). . . . . _____

❑ *Grus grus.* COMMON CRANE. (Eura; ◊-n Afr, s,se Asia). . . . . _____

❑ *Grus monacha.* HOODED CRANE. (ec Asia; ◊-s Asia). . . . . _____

❑ *Grus americana.* WHOOPING CRANE. (nc NA; ◊-cs US). . . . . _____

❑ *Grus nigricollis.* BLACK-NECKED CRANE. (mts sc Asia; ◊-s Asia). . . . _____

❑ *Grus japonensis.* RED-CROWNED CRANE. (e Eura; ◊-s Asia). . . . . _____

Family **Heliornithidae** [4/4]
Tribe Aramini [1/1]

☐ *Aramus guarauna.* LIMPKIN. (s Fla, G Ant, MA, SA). . . . . _____

Tribe Heliornithini [3/3]

☐ *Podica senegalensis.* AFRICAN FINFOOT. (Afr). . . . . _____

☐ *Heliopais personata.* MASKED FINFOOT. (s,se Asia). . . . . _____

☐ *Heliornis fulica.* SUNGREBE. (MA, SA). . . . . _____

Superfamily PSOPHIOIDEA [1/3]
Family **Psophiidae** [1/3]

☐ *Psophia crepitans.* GREY-WINGED TRUMPETER. (SA). . . . . _____

☐ *Psophia leucoptera.* PALE-WINGED TRUMPETER. (w Amaz). . . . . _____

☐ *Psophia viridis.* DARK-WINGED TRUMPETER. (w Amaz Braz). . . . . . . _____

Parvorder CARIAMIDA [3/3]
Family **Cariamidae** [2/2]

☐ *Cariama cristata.* RED-LEGGED SERIEMA. (se SA). . . . . _____

☐ *Chunga burmeisteri.* BLACK-LEGGED SERIEMA. (sc SA). . . . . _____

Family **Rhynochetidae** [1/1]

☐ *Rhynochetos jubatus.* KAGU. (mts s N Cal). _____

Suborder RALLI [34/143]
Family **Rallidae** [34/143]

☐ *Sarothrura pulchra.* WHITE-SPOTTED FLUFFTAIL. (wc,c Afr). . . . . _____

☐ *Sarothrura elegans.* BUFF-SPOTTED FLUFFTAIL. (c,s Afr). . . . . _____

☐ *Sarothrura rufa.* RED-CHESTED FLUFFTAIL. (Afr). . . . . _____

☐ *Sarothrura lugens.* CHESTNUT-HEADED FLUFFTAIL. (c,sc Afr). . . . . . . _____
   ___*S. (l.) lugens.* CHESTNUT-HEADED FLUFFTAIL. (c Afr)
   ___*S. (l.) lynesi.* LYNES'S FLUFFTAIL. (sc Afr)

☐ *Sarothrura boehmi.* STREAKY-BREASTED FLUFFTAIL. (c Afr). . . . . _____

☐ *Sarothrura affinis.* STRIPED FLUFFTAIL. (mts e,c Afr). . . . . _____

☐ *Sarothrura insularis.* MADAGASCAR FLUFFTAIL. (Mad). . . . . _____

☐ *Sarothrura ayresi.* WHITE-WINGED FLUFFTAIL. (mts ne,s Afr). . . . . . _____

☐ *Sarothrura watersi.* SLENDER-BILLED FLUFFTAIL. (mts e Mad). . . . . . _____

☐ *Himantornis haematopus.* NKULENGU RAIL. (w,c Afr). . . . . _____

☐ *Canirallus oculeus.* GREY-THROATED RAIL. (w,c Afr). . . . . _____

☐ *Canirallus kioloides.* KIOLOIDES RAIL. (nw,e Mad). . . . . _____

❑ *Coturnicops exquisitus.* SWINHOE'S RAIL. (e Asia; ◊-s Asia). . . . . . . _____

❑ *Coturnicops noveboracensis.* YELLOW RAIL. (n,cNA, c Mex). . . . . . . _____

❑ *Coturnicops notatus.* SPECKLED RAIL. (SA). . . . . _____

❑ *Micropygia schomburgkii.* OCELLATED CRAKE. (SA). . . . . _____

❑ *Rallina rubra.* CHESTNUT FOREST-RAIL. (mts w,c NG). . . . . _____

❑ *Rallina leucospila.* WHITE-STRIPED FOREST-RAIL. (mts w NG). . . . . . _____

❑ *Rallina forbesi.* FORBES'S FOREST-RAIL. (mts NG). . . . . _____

❑ *Rallina mayri.* MAYR'S FOREST-RAIL. (mts cn NG). . . . . _____

❑ *Rallina tricolor.* RED-NECKED CRAKE. (L Sunda-Bism, ne Aust). . . . . _____

❑ *Rallina canningi.* ANDAMAN CRAKE. (And). . . . . _____

❑ *Rallina fasciata.* RED-LEGGED CRAKE. (se Asia, Phil; ◊-Wall). . . . . . . _____

❑ *Rallina eurizonoides.* SLATY-LEGGED CRAKE. (s Asia-Phil, Palau). . . _____

❑ *Anurolimnas castaneiceps.* CHESTNUT-HEADED CRAKE. (w Amaz). . . _____

❑ *Anurolimnas viridis.* RUSSET-CROWNED CRAKE. (Amaz). . . . . _____

❑ *Anurolimnas fasciatus.* BLACK-BANDED CRAKE. (w Amaz). . . . . _____

❑ *Laterallus melanophaius.* RUFOUS-SIDED CRAKE. (SA). . . . . _____

❑ *Laterallus levraudi.* RUSTY-FLANKED CRAKE. (n Ven). . . . . _____

❑ *Laterallus ruber.* RUDDY CRAKE. (MA). _____

❑ *Laterallus albigularis.* WHITE-THROATED CRAKE. (CA, nw SA). . . . . _____

❑ *Laterallus exilis.* GREY-BREASTED CRAKE. (CA, SA). . . . . _____

❑ *Laterallus jamaicensis.* BLACK RAIL. (NA, W Indies, n CA, sw SA). . _____

❑ *Laterallus spilonotus.* GALAPAGOS RAIL. (Galap). . . . . _____

❑ *Laterallus leucopyrrhus.* RED-AND-WHITE CRAKE. (se SA). . . . . _____

❑ *Laterallus xenopterus.* RUFOUS-FACED CRAKE. (se SA). . . . . _____

❑ *Nesoclopeus woodfordi.* WOODFORD'S RAIL. (Solom). . . . . _____

❑ *Nesoclopeus poecilopterus.* BAR-WINGED RAIL. (Fiji). . . . . _____

❑ *Gallirallus australis.* WEKA. (NZ). . . . . _____

  Gallirallus lafresnayanus. NEW CALEDONIAN RAIL. (†N Cal). . . . . . . _____

❑ *Gallirallus sylvestris.* LORD HOWE ISLAND RAIL. (L Howe). . . . . _____

❑ *Gallirallus conditicius.* GILBERT RAIL. (sw Marsh). . . . . _____

❑ *Gallirallus okinawae.* OKINAWA RAIL. (s Ryu). . . . . _____

❑ *Gallirallus torquatus.* BARRED RAIL. (Sulaw, Phil, w Pap, nw NG) . _____

❑ *Gallirallus insignis.* NEW BRITAIN RAIL. (cs Bism). . . . . _____

❑ *Gallirallus philippensis.* BUFF-BANDED RAIL. (Indon-s Polyn, Aust). _____

❑ *Gallirallus rovianae.* ROVIANA RAIL. (c Solom). . . . . _____

❏ *Gallirallus owstoni.* GUAM RAIL. (Guam). . . . . _____

  Gallirallus wakensis. WAKE ISLAND RAIL. (†Wake). . . . . _____

  Gallirallus pacificus. TAHITI RAIL. (†Tahiti). . . . . _____

  Gallirallus dieffenbachii. DIEFFENBACH'S RAIL. (†Chatham). . . . . _____

  Gallirallus modestus. CHATHAM ISLANDS RAIL. (†Chatham). . . . . _____

  Gallirallus sharpei. SHARPE'S RAIL. (†Sunda). . . . . _____

❏ *Gallirallus striatus.* SLATY-BREASTED RAIL. (s Asia-Phil). . . . . _____

❏ *Rallus longirostris.* CLAPPER RAIL. (US, n MA, W Indies, n,e SA). . . _____
    ___*R. (l.) obsoletus.* WESTERN RAIL. (w NA, w Mex)
    ___*R. (l.) longirostris.* CLAPPER RAIL. (e NA, ne MA, W Indies, n,e SA)
    ___*R. (l.) tenuirostris.* HIGHLAND RAIL. (int Mex)

❏ *Rallus elegans.* KING RAIL. (e NA, Cuba). . . . . _____

❏ *Rallus wetmorei.* PLAIN-FLANKED RAIL. (nw Ven). . . . . _____

❏ *Rallus limicola.* VIRGINIA RAIL. (NA, c,s Mex, w SA; ◊-n CA). . . . . . _____

❏ *Rallus semiplumbeus.* BOGOTA RAIL. (Andes w SA). . . . . _____
    ___*R. (s.) semiplumbeus.* BOGOTA RAIL. (nc Colom)
    ___*R. (s.) peruvianus.* PERUVIAN RAIL. (Peru)

❏ *Rallus antarcticus.* AUSTRAL RAIL. (Andes w,s SA). . . . . _____

❏ *Rallus aquaticus.* WATER RAIL. (Palea; ◊-n Afr, s,se Asia). . . . . _____

❏ *Rallus caerulescens.* KAFFIR RAIL. (s,e Afr). . . . . _____

❏ *Rallus madagascariensis.* MADAGASCAR RAIL. (e Mad). . . . . _____

❏ *Lewinia mirificus.* BROWN-BANDED RAIL. (n Phil). . . . . _____

❏ *Lewinia pectoralis.* LEWIN'S RAIL. (L Sunda-NG, e,se Aust). . . . . _____

❏ *Lewinia muelleri.* AUCKLAND ISLANDS RAIL. (Auck). . . . . _____

❏ *Dryolimnas cuvieri.* WHITE-THROATED RAIL. (Mad). . . . . _____

❏ *Crecopsis egregia.* AFRICAN CRAKE. (Afr). _____

❏ *Crex crex.* CORN CRAKE. (Eura; ◊-s Afr, Mad). . . . . _____

❏ *Rougetius rougetii.* ROUGET'S RAIL. (mts w,c Eth). . . . . _____

❏ *Aramidopsis plateni.* SNORING RAIL. (mts Sulaw). . . . . _____

❏ *Atlantisia rogersi.* INACCESSIBLE ISLAND RAIL. (TdaC). . . . . _____

❏ *Aramides mangle.* LITTLE WOOD-RAIL. (e Braz). . . . . _____

❏ *Aramides axillaris.* RUFOUS-NECKED WOOD-RAIL. (MA, n SA). . . . . _____

❏ *Aramides cajanea.* GREY-NECKED WOOD-RAIL. (MA, SA). . . . . _____

❏ *Aramides wolfi.* BROWN WOOD-RAIL. (nw SA). . . . . _____

❏ *Aramides ypecaha.* GIANT WOOD-RAIL. (e SA). . . . . _____

❏ *Aramides saracura.* SLATY-BREASTED WOOD-RAIL. (se SA). . . . . _____

❑ *Aramides calopterus.* RED-WINGED WOOD-RAIL. (nw SA)........ _____

❑ *Amaurolimnas concolor.* UNIFORM CRAKE. (MA, SA)........... _____

❑ *Gymnocrex rosenbergii.* BALD-FACED RAIL. (Sulaw)............ _____

❑ *Gymnocrex plumbeiventris.* BARE-EYED RAIL. (n Moluc, Aru-NG) . _____

❑ *Amaurornis akool.* BROWN CRAKE. (s Asia)................... _____

❑ *Amaurornis olivaceus.* BUSH-HEN. (Phil).................... _____

❑ *Amaurornis isabellinus.* ISABELLINE WATERHEN. (Sulaw)........ _____

❑ *Amaurornis moluccanus.* RUFOUS-TAILED WATERHEN. (Wall-Solom) _____

❑ *Amaurornis phoenicurus.* WHITE-BREASTED WATERHEN. (s Asia-Phil) _____

❑ *Amaurornis flavirostra.* BLACK CRAKE. (Afr).................. _____

❑ *Amaurornis olivieri.* SAKALAVA RAIL. (wc Mad)............... _____

❑ *Amaurornis bicolor.* BLACK-TAILED CRAKE. (s,se Asia).......... _____

❑ *Porzana parva.* LITTLE CRAKE. (Eura; ◊-n,e Afr, n India)........ _____

❑ *Porzana pusilla.* BAILLON'S CRAKE. (s,e Palea-e,se Afr, Aust, NZ)... _____

  Porzana palmeri. LAYSAN CRAKE. (†w Haw Is)................ _____

❑ *Porzana porzana.* SPOTTED CRAKE. (w,c Eura; ◊-s Afr, s Asia)...... _____

❑ *Porzana fluminea.* AUSTRALIAN CRAKE. (Aust)................. _____

❑ *Porzana carolina.* SORA. (NA; ◊ s US-SA)................... _____

❑ *Porzana spiloptera.* DOT-WINGED CRAKE. (se SA).............. _____

❑ *Porzana albicollis.* ASH-THROATED CRAKE. (SA).............. _____

  Porzana sandwichensis. HAWAIIAN CRAKE. (†Hawaii)........... _____

❑ *Porzana fusca.* RUDDY-BREASTED CRAKE. (e,s Asia-Phil)......... _____

❑ *Porzana paykullii.* BAND-BELLIED CRAKE. (e Asia; ◊ se Asia)...... _____

❑ *Porzana tabuensis.* SPOTLESS CRAKE. (Phil-s,w Oceania, NZ, Aust) . _____

  Porzana monasa. KOSRAE CRAKE. (†e Carol).................. _____

❑ *Porzana atra.* HENDERSON ISLAND CRAKE. (Henderson).......... _____

❑ *Porzana flaviventer.* YELLOW-BREASTED CRAKE. (MA, G Ant, SA) . _____

❑ *Porzana cinerea.* WHITE-BROWED CRAKE. (se Asia-n Samoa, Aust) . _____

❑ *Aenigomatolimnas marginalis.* STRIPED CRAKE. (Afr, Ald)........ _____

❑ *Cyanolimnas cerverai.* ZAPATA RAIL. (wc Cuba)............... _____

❑ *Neocrex colombianus.* COLOMBIAN CRAKE. (c Pan, nw SA)........ _____

❑ *Neocrex erythrops.* PAINT-BILLED CRAKE. (w Pan, SA, Galap)..... _____

❑ *Pardirallus maculatus.* SPOTTED RAIL. (MA, G Ant, SA)......... _____

❑ *Pardirallus nigricans.* BLACKISH RAIL. (w,sc SA).............. _____

❑ *Pardirallus sanguinolentus.* PLUMBEOUS RAIL. (s SA)........... _____

❑ *Eulabeornis castaneoventris.* CHESTNUT RAIL. (Aru, n Aust)...... _____

❑ *Habroptila wallacii.* INVISIBLE RAIL. (n Moluc)................. _____

❑ *Megacrex inepta.* NEW GUINEA FLIGHTLESS RAIL. (nc,sc NG)...... _____

❑ *Gallicrex cinerea.* WATERCOCK. (s,e Asia-Phil; ◊-L Sunda)....... _____

❑ *Porphyrio porphyrio.* PURPLE SWAMPHEN. (s Palea-Aust, s Oceania). _____
   ___*P. (p.) porphyrio.* PURPLE SWAMPHEN. (sw Palea)
   ___*P. (p.) madagascariensis.* AFRICAN SWAMPHEN. (Afr, Mad)
   ___*P. (p.) poliocephalus.* INDIAN SWAMPHEN. (s,e Asia-s Oceania)
   ___*P. (p.) pulverulentus.* PHILIPPINE SWAMPHEN. (Phil)
   ___*P. (p.) melanotus.* EASTERN SWAMPHEN. (NG, Aust, NZ)
   ___*P. (p.) bellus.* WESTERN SWAMPHEN. (sw Aust)

  Porphyrio albus. LORD HOWE ISLAND SWAMPHEN. (†L Howe)...... _____

❑ *Porphyrio mantelli.* TAKAHE. (mts s NZ)...................... _____

❑ *Porphyrio alleni.* ALLEN'S GALLINULE. (Afr, Mad reg)........... _____

❑ *Porphyrio martinicus.* PURPLE GALLINULE. (s US-SA)........... _____

❑ *Porphyrio flavirostris.* AZURE GALLINULE. (SA)................ _____

  Gallinula pacifica. SAMOAN MOORHEN. (†w Samoa)............. _____

❑ *Gallinula silvestris.* SAN CRISTOBAL MOORHEN. (mts se Solom)..... _____

❑ *Gallinula nesiotis.* TRISTAN MOORHEN. (TdaC, Gough).......... _____
   ___*G. (n.) nesiotis.* TRISTAN MOORHEN. (TdaC)
   ___*G. (n.) comeri.* GOUGH MOORHEN. (Gough)

❑ *Gallinula chloropus.* COMMON MOORHEN. (Hol-s SA, s Afr, Wall) . _____

❑ *Gallinula tenebrosa.* DUSKY MOORHEN. (G Sunda-NG, Aust)...... _____

❑ *Gallinula angulata.* LESSER MOORHEN. (Afr)................. _____

❑ *Gallinula melanops.* SPOT-FLANKED GALLINULE. (SA)........... _____

❑ *Gallinula ventralis.* BLACK-TAILED NATIVE-HEN. (Aust).......... _____

❑ *Gallinula mortierii.* TASMANIAN NATIVE-HEN. (Tas)............. _____

❑ *Fulica cristata.* RED-KNOBBED COOT. (sw Palea, e,s Afr, Mad)...... _____

❑ *Fulica atra.* COMMON COOT. (Palea, s Asia-n Afr; Aust, NG, NZ)... _____

❑ *Fulica alai.* HAWAIIAN COOT. (Haw Is)...................... _____

❑ *Fulica americana.* AMERICAN COOT. (NA-nw SA, n W Indies)..... _____

❑ *Fulica caribaea.* CARIBBEAN COOT. (W Indies, cn SA)........... _____

❑ *Fulica leucoptera.* WHITE-WINGED COOT. (s SA)............... _____

❑ *Fulica ardesiaca.* SLATE-COLORED COOT. (Andes)............... _____

❑ *Fulica armillata.* RED-GARTERED COOT. (s SA)................ _____

❑ *Fulica rufifrons.* RED-FRONTED COOT. (s SA)................ _____

❑ *Fulica gigantea.* GIANT COOT. (Andes sw SA)................. _____

❑ *Fulica cornuta.* HORNED COOT. (Andes sw SA)................ _____

Suborder MESITORNITHI [2/3]
Family **Mesitornithidae** [2/3]

❏ *Mesitornis variegata.* WHITE-BREASTED MESITE. (w,n Mad). . . . . _____

❏ *Mesitornis unicolor.* BROWN MESITE. (e Mad). . . . . _____

❏ *Monias benschi.* SUBDESERT MESITE (sw Mad). . . . . _____

Order **CICONIIFORMES** [255/1022]
Suborder CHARADRII [86/365]
Infraorder PTEROCLIDES [2/16]
Family **Pteroclidae** [2/16]

❏ *Syrrhaptes tibetanus.* TIBETAN SANDGROUSE. (mts c Asia). . . . . _____

❏ *Syrrhaptes paradoxus.* PALLAS'S SANDGROUSE. (mts c Asia-w Euro). _____

❏ *Pterocles alchata.* PIN-TAILED SANDGROUSE. (s Palea; ◊-s Asia). . . . . _____

❏ *Pterocles namaqua.* NAMAQUA SANDGROUSE. (s Afr). . . . . _____

❏ *Pterocles exustus.* CHESTNUT-BELLIED SANDGROUSE. (n Afr-s Asia) . _____

❏ *Pterocles senegallus.* SPOTTED SANDGROUSE. (Afr, sw Asia). . . . . . . _____

❏ *Pterocles gutturalis.* YELLOW-THROATED SANDGROUSE. (e,s Afr). . . . _____

❏ *Pterocles orientalis.* BLACK-BELLIED SANDGROUSE. (s Palea). . . . . . . _____

❏ *Pterocles coronatus.* CROWNED SANDGROUSE. (n Afr, s Asia). . . . . . . _____

❏ *Pterocles personatus.* MADAGASCAR SANDGROUSE. (Mad). . . . . _____

❏ *Pterocles decoratus.* BLACK-FACED SANDGROUSE. (ce Afr). . . . . _____

❏ *Pterocles bicinctus.* DOUBLE-BANDED SANDGROUSE. (s Afr). . . . . . . _____

❏ *Pterocles quadricinctus.* FOUR-BANDED SANDGROUSE. (subsah Afr) . _____

❏ *Pterocles indicus.* PAINTED SANDGROUSE. (cs Asia). . . . . _____

❏ *Pterocles lichtensteinii.* LICHTENSTEIN'S SANDGROUSE. (n Afr-c Asia) _____
   ___*P. (l.) lichtensteinii.* LICHTENSTEIN'S SANDGROUSE. (nc Afr)
   ___*P. (l.) arabicus.* CLOSE-BARRED SANDGROUSE. (sc Asia)

❏ *Pterocles burchelli.* BURCHELL'S SANDGROUSE. (s Afr). . . . . _____

Infraorder CHARADRIIDES [84/349]
Parvorder SCOLOPACIDA [31/103]
Superfamily SCOLOPACOIDEA [24/93]
Family **Thinocoridae** [2/4]

❏ *Attagis gayi.* RUFOUS-BELLIED SEEDSNIPE. (Andes w,sw SA). . . . . . . _____

❏ *Attagis malouinus.* WHITE-BELLIED SEEDSNIPE. (s SA). . . . . _____

❏ *Thinocorus orbignyianus.* GREY-BREASTED SEEDSNIPE. (s SA). . . . . . _____

❏ *Thinocorus rumicivorus.* LEAST SEEDSNIPE. (w,s SA). . . . . _____

Family **Pedionomidae** [1/1]

❏ *Pedionomus torquatus.* PLAINS-WANDERER. (se Aust). . . . . _____

Family **Scolopacidae** [21/88]
Subfamily Scolopacinae [4/25]

❑ *Scolopax rusticola.* EURASIAN WOODCOCK. (Eura; ◊-se Asia, Phil)... _____

❑ *Scolopax mira.* AMAMI WOODCOCK. (n Ryu)................. _____

❑ *Scolopax saturata.* RUFOUS WOODCOCK. (mts Sum, Java, NG)..... _____

❑ *Scolopax celebensis.* SULAWESI WOODCOCK. (n,c Sulaw)......... _____

❑ *Scolopax rochussenii.* MOLUCCAN WOODCOCK. (n Moluc)........ _____

❑ *Scolopax minor.* AMERICAN WOODCOCK. (c,s NA; ◊ se US)....... _____

❑ *Gallinago solitaria.* SOLITARY SNIPE. (mts c,s Asia)............ _____

❑ *Gallinago hardwickii.* LATHAM'S SNIPE. (Japan; ◊ Aust, NZ)...... _____

❑ *Gallinago nemoricola.* WOOD SNIPE. (Himal; ◊s,se Asia)........ _____

❑ *Gallinago stenura.* PINTAIL SNIPE. (c,e Eura; ◊se Asia-Wall, Phil)... _____

❑ *Gallinago megala.* SWINHOE'S SNIPE. (c Asia; ◊ s,se Asia, Phil-Aust). _____

❑ *Gallinago media.* GREAT SNIPE. (nw,nc Eura; ◊e,s Afr).......... _____

❑ *Gallinago gallinago.* COMMON SNIPE. (Hol; ◊-s Afr, Phil, n SA)..... _____
   ___*G. (g.) gallinago.* COMMON SNIPE. (Eura, Aleut; ◊-Afr, Asia, Phil)
   ___*G. (g.) delicata.* WILSON'S SNIPE. (NA; ◊-n SA)

❑ *Gallinago nigripennis.* AFRICAN SNIPE. (e,s Afr)............... _____

❑ *Gallinago macrodactyla.* MADAGASCAR SNIPE. (e Mad)......... _____

❑ *Gallinago paraguaiae.* SOUTH AMERICAN SNIPE. (SA)........... _____
   ___*G. (p.) paraguaiae.* PARAGUAYAN SNIPE. (n,c,sc SA)
   ___*G. (p.) magellanica.* MAGELLANIC SNIPE. (s SA)

❑ *Gallinago andina.* PUNA SNIPE. (Andes sw SA)................ _____

❑ *Gallinago nobilis.* NOBLE SNIPE. (Andes nw SA)............... _____

❑ *Gallinago undulata.* GIANT SNIPE. (nw,se SA)................ _____

❑ *Gallinago jamesoni.* ANDEAN SNIPE. (mts w SA)............... _____

❑ *Gallinago stricklandii.* FUEGIAN SNIPE. (s SA)................ _____

❑ *Gallinago imperialis.* IMPERIAL SNIPE. (Andes w SA)........... _____

❑ *Lymnocryptes minimus.* JACK SNIPE. (n Eura; ◊-trop. Afr, Indon).... _____

❑ *Coenocorypha pusilla.* CHATHAM ISLANDS SNIPE. (Chatham)....... _____

❑ *Coenocorypha aucklandica.* SUBANTARCTIC SNIPE. (s NZ-Snares)... _____

Subfamily Tringinae [17/63]

❑ *Limosa limosa.* BLACK-TAILED GODWIT. (n Eura; ◊-s Afr, Aust)..... _____

❑ *Limosa haemastica.* HUDSONIAN GODWIT. (n NA; ◊ SA)......... _____

❑ *Limosa lapponica.* BAR-TAILED GODWIT. (n Eura-Alas; ◊-Afr, NZ) . _____

❑ *Limosa fedoa.* MARBLED GODWIT. (wc NA; ◊ s US-w,n SA)....... _____

❑ *Numenius minutus.* LITTLE CURLEW. (c Sib; ◊ Indon, Aust, NZ). . . . _____

❑ *Numenius borealis.* ESKIMO CURLEW. (nw NA; ◊ s SA). . . . . _____

❑ *Numenius phaeopus.* WHIMBREL. (n Hol; ◊-Afr, Aust, NZ, SA). . . . . _____
   N. (p.) phaeopus. WHIMBREL. (n Eura; ◊-s Afr, Aust, NZ, s Polyn)
   N. (p.) hudsonicus. HUDSONIAN CURLEW. (n NA; ◊ s US-s SA)

❑ *Numenius tahitiensis.* BRISTLE-THIGHED CURLEW. (w Alas; ◊ s Pac). _____

❑ *Numenius tenuirostris.* SLENDER-BILLED CURLEW. (c Eura; ◊-n Afr). _____

❑ *Numenius arquata.* EURASIAN CURLEW. (n Eura; ◊-s Afr, Indon). . . . _____

❑ *Numenius americanus.* LONG-BILLED CURLEW. (w NA; ◊-n SA). . . . _____

❑ *Numenius madagascariensis.* FAR EASTERN CURLEW. (ne Asia; ◊-NZ)_____

❑ *Bartramia longicauda.* UPLAND SANDPIPER. (NA; ◊ SA). . . . . _____

❑ *Tringa erythropus.* SPOTTED REDSHANK. (n Eura; ◊-c Afr, se Asia) . _____

❑ *Tringa totanus.* COMMON REDSHANK. (Palea; ◊-s Afr, Indon, Phil). . . _____

❑ *Tringa stagnatilis.* MARSH SANDPIPER. (c Eura; ◊-s Afr, Aust). . . . . . _____

❑ *Tringa nebularia.* COMMON GREENSHANK. (n Eura; ◊-s Afr, NZ). . . . _____

❑ *Tringa guttifer.* NORDMANN'S GREENSHANK. (e Sib; ◊-Indon, Phil). . . _____

❑ *Tringa melanoleuca.* GREATER YELLOWLEGS. (n NA; ◊ s US-s SA) . _____

❑ *Tringa flavipes.* LESSER YELLOWLEGS. (n NA; ◊s US-s SA). . . . . _____

❑ *Tringa solitaria.* SOLITARY SANDPIPER. (n NA; ◊s US-s SA). . . . . _____

❑ *Tringa ochropus.* GREEN SANDPIPER. (n Eura; ◊-s Afr, Aust). . . . . . . _____

❑ *Tringa glareola.* WOOD SANDPIPER. (n Eura, Aleut; ◊-s Afr, Aust). . . _____

❑ *Tringa cinerea.* TEREK SANDPIPER. (n Eura; ◊-s Afr, Aust, NZ). . . . . _____

❑ *Tringa hypoleucos.* COMMON SANDPIPER. (Eura, e Afr; ◊-Afr, Aust). _____

❑ *Tringa macularia.* SPOTTED SANDPIPER. (NA; ◊s US-s SA). . . . . _____

❑ *Tringa brevipes.* GREY-TAILED TATTLER. (mts Sib; ◊-Aust, s Polyn) . _____

❑ *Tringa incana.* WANDERING TATTLER. (e Eura, nw NA; ◊-s Pac, SA). _____

❑ *Catoptrophorus semipalmatus.* WILLET. (w,e NA, W Indies; ◊-SA) . _____

❑ *Prosobonia cancellata.* TUAMOTU SANDPIPER. (Tuam). . . . . _____

   Prosobonia leucoptera. TAHITIAN SANDPIPER. (†e Soc). . . . . _____

❑ *Arenaria interpres.* RUDDY TURNSTONE. (Hol; ◊-Afr, NZ, Polyn, SA)_____

❑ *Arenaria melanocephala.* BLACK TURNSTONE. (Alas; ◊-nw Mex). . . . _____

❑ *Limnodromus griseus.* SHORT-BILLED DOWITCHER. (n NA; ◊-c SA) . _____

❑ *Limnodromus scolopaceus.* LONG-BILLED D. (e Sib, nw NA; ◊-MA). _____

❑ *Limnodromus semipalmatus.* ASIAN DOWITCHER. (c Asia; ◊-se Asia). _____

❑ *Aphriza virgata.* SURFBIRD. (mts nw NA; ◊-s SA). . . . . _____

❑ *Calidris tenuirostris.* GREAT KNOT. (mts ne Sib; ◊-Aust)........... _____

❑ *Calidris canutus.* RED KNOT. (n Hol; ◊-s Afr, Aust, NZ, s SA)...... _____

❑ *Calidris alba.* SANDERLING. (n NA; ◊-s Afr, Aust, Polyn, s SA)..... _____

❑ *Calidris pusilla.* SEMIPALMATED SANDPIPER. (e Sib, n NA; ◊-s SA) . _____

❑ *Calidris mauri.* WESTERN SANDPIPER. (ne Sib, nw Alas; ◊-n SA).... _____

❑ *Calidris minuta.* LITTLE STINT. (n Eura; ◊ Afr, s Asia)........... _____

❑ *Calidris ruficollis.* RUFOUS-NECKED STINT. (e Sib-w Alas; ◊-Afr, NZ) _____

❑ *Calidris temminckii.* TEMMINCK'S STINT. (n Eura; ◊-s Afr, Phil)..... _____

❑ *Calidris subminuta.* LONG-TOED STINT. (e Asia; ◊-Aust)........... _____

❑ *Calidris minutilla.* LEAST SANDPIPER. (n NA; ◊ s US-c SA)........ _____

❑ *Calidris fuscicollis.* WHITE-RUMPED SANDPIPER. (n NA; ◊ SA)...... _____

❑ *Calidris bairdii.* BAIRD'S SANDPIPER. (ne Sib, n NA; ◊ wc,s SA)..... _____

❑ *Calidris melanotos.* PECTORAL SANDPIPER. (c,e Sib, n NA; ◊ s SA) . _____

❑ *Calidris acuminata.* SHARP-TAILED SANDPIPER. (ne Sib; ◊ Aust, NZ). _____

❑ *Calidris maritima.* PURPLE SANDPIPER. (Palea, ne NA)........... _____

❑ *Calidris ptilocnemis.* ROCK SANDPIPER. (ne Sib, w Alas; ◊-Calif).... _____

❑ *Calidris alpina.* DUNLIN. (n Hol; ◊-e,s Africa, s Asia, n Mex)....... _____

❑ *Calidris ferruginea.* CURLEW SANDPIPER. (n Sib, n Alas; ◊-Afr, NZ). _____

❑ *Micropalama himantopus.* STILT SANDPIPER. (n NA; ◊ s US-s SA) . _____

❑ *Tryngites subruficollis.* BUFF-BREASTED SANDPIPER. (n NA; ◊ s SA). _____

❑ *Eurynorhynchus pygmeus.* SPOONBILL SANDPIPER. (ne Sib; ◊ se Asia) _____

❑ *Limicola falcinellus.* BROAD-BILLED SANDPIPER. (n Eura; ◊-Afr, NZ). _____

❑ *Philomachus pugnax.* RUFF. (Eura, nw Alas; ◊-s Afr, Aust, n SA)... _____

❑ *Steganopus tricolor.* WILSON'S PHALAROPE. (c NA; ◊ w,s SA)...... _____

❑ *Phalaropus lobatus.* RED-NECKED PHALAROPE. (n Hol; ◊ s oceans) . _____

❑ *Phalaropus fulicaria.* RED PHALAROPE. (n Hol; ◊ s oceans)........ _____

Superfamily JACANOIDEA [7/10]
Family **Rostratulidae** [1/2]

❑ *Rostratula benghalensis.* GREATER PAINTED-S. (Afr-s,e Asia; Aust).. _____

❑ *Rostratula semicollaris.* AMERICAN PAINTED-SNIPE. (s SA)........ _____

Family **Jacanidae** [6/8]

❑ *Actophilornis africanus.* AFRICAN JACANA. (Afr)............... _____

❑ *Actophilornis albinucha.* MADAGASCAR JACANA. (Mad).......... _____

❑ *Microparra capensis.* LESSER JACANA. (Afr).................. _____

❑ *Irediparra gallinacea.* COMB-CRESTED JACANA. (Indon-n,e Aust). . . . _____

❑ *Hydrophasianus chirurgus.* PHEASANT-TAILED JACANA. (s Asia-Phil) _____

❑ *Metopidius indicus.* BRONZE-WINGED JACANA. (s,se Asia). . . . . _____

❑ *Jacana spinosa.* NORTHERN JACANA. (s Tex, MA, G Ant). . . . . _____

❑ *Jacana jacana.* WATTLED JACANA. (Pan, SA). . . . . _____

Parvorder CHARADRIIDA [53/246]
Superfamily CHIONOIDEA [2/3]
Family **Chionidae** [1/2]

❑ *Chionis alba.* SNOWY SHEATHBILL. (subant is, n Ant). . . . . _____

❑ *Chionis minor.* BLACK-FACED SHEATHBILL. (is s Indian O). . . . . _____

Family **Pluvianellidae** [1/1]

❑ *Pluvianellus socialis.* MAGELLANIC PLOVER. (s SA). . . . . _____

Superfamily CHARADRIOIDEA [17/97]
Family **Burhinidae** [1/9]

❑ *Burhinus oedicnemus.* EURASIAN THICK-KNEE. (Eura, se Asia; ◊-Afr) _____

❑ *Burhinus senegalensis.* SENEGAL THICK-KNEE. (subsah Afr). . . . . . . _____

❑ *Burhinus vermiculatus.* WATER THICK-KNEE. (Afr). . . . . _____

❑ *Burhinus capensis.* SPOTTED THICK-KNEE. (Afr reg). . . . . _____

❑ *Burhinus bistriatus.* DOUBLE-STRIPED THICK-KNEE. (Hisp; c MA-n SA)_____

❑ *Burhinus superciliaris.* PERUVIAN THICK-KNEE. (cw SA). . . . . _____

❑ *Burhinus grallarius.* BUSH THICK-KNEE. (Aust; ◊-s NG). . . . . _____

❑ *Burhinus recurvirostris.* GREAT THICK-KNEE. (s,se Asia). . . . . _____

❑ *Burhinus giganteus.* BEACH THICK-KNEE. (se Asia-n Aust, N Cal). . . _____

Family **Charadriidae** [16/88]
Subfamily Recurvirostrinae [5/22]
Tribe Haematopodini [1/11]

❑ *Haematopus ostralegus.* EURASIAN OYSTERCATCHER. (Eura; ◊-Afr). _____

Haematopus meadewaldoi. CANARY ISLANDS O. (†e Can Is). . . . . . . _____

❑ *Haematopus moquini.* AFRICAN OYSTERCATCHER. (s Afr). . . . . _____

❑ *Haematopus finschi.* SOUTH ISLAND OYSTERCATCHER. (mts s NZ). . . _____

❑ *Haematopus bachmani.* BLACK OYSTERCATCHER. (w NA). . . . . _____

❑ *Haematopus palliatus.* AMERICAN OYSTERCATCHER. (s,e US-SA). . . _____

❑ *Haematopus longirostris.* PIED OYSTERCATCHER. (Wall, s NG, Aust). _____

❑ *Haematopus unicolor.* VARIABLE OYSTERCATCHER. (NZ, Chatham). _____
   ___*H. (u.) unicolor.* VARIABLE OYSTERCATCHER. (NZ)
   ___*H. (u.) chathamensis.* CHATHAM ISLANDS OYSTERCATCHER. (Chatham)

❑ *Haematopus fuliginosus.* SOOTY OYSTERCATCHER. (Aust) . . . . _____

❑ *Haematopus ater.* BLACKISH OYSTERCATCHER. (sw,s SA) . . . . _____

❑ *Haematopus leucopodus.* MAGELLANIC OYSTERCATCHER. (s SA) . . . . _____

Tribe Recurvirostrini [4/11]

❑ *Ibidorhyncha struthersii.* IBISBILL. (mts c Asia) . . . . _____

❑ *Himantopus himantopus.* BLACK-WINGED STILT. (c,s Eur, Afr reg) . _____
   ___*H. (h.) himantopus.* BLACK-WINGED STILT. (sp)
   ___*H. (h.) ceylonensis.* CEYLON STILT. (Ceylon)

❑ *Himantopus leucocephalus.* WHITE-HEADED STILT. (Indon-NZ) . . . . . _____

❑ *Himantopus novaezelandiae.* BLACK STILT. (NZ) . . . . _____

❑ *Himantopus mexicanus.* BLACK-NECKED STILT. (Haw Is; NA-SA) . . . _____
   ___*H. (m.) knudseni.* HAWAIIAN STILT. (Haw Is)
   ___*H. (m.) mexicanus.* BLACK-NECKED STILT. (NA-SA)

❑ *Himantopus melanurus.* WHITE-BACKED STILT. (s SA) . . . . _____

❑ *Cladorhynchus leucocephalus.* BANDED STILT. (w,s Aust) . . . . _____

❑ *Recurvirostra avosetta.* PIED AVOCET. (Eura, n Afr; ◊-s Afr, s Asia) . _____

❑ *Recurvirostra americana.* AMERICAN AVOCET. (w NA; ◊ s US-CR) . _____

❑ *Recurvirostra novaehollandiae.* RED-NECKED AVOCET. (Aust; ◊-NZ) _____

❑ *Recurvirostra andina.* ANDEAN AVOCET. (Andes s SA) . . . . _____

Subfamily Charadriinae [11/66]

❑ *Pluvialis apricaria.* EURASIAN GOLDEN-PLOVER. (n Eura; ◊ s Palea) . _____

❑ *Pluvialis fulva.* PACIFIC GOLDEN-PLOVER. (ne Eura-Alas; ◊-Aust, NZ)_____

❑ *Pluvialis dominica.* AMERICAN GOLDEN-PLOVER. (n NA; ◊ s SA) . . . . _____

❑ *Pluvialis squatarola.* GREY PLOVER. (n Hol; ◊-s Afr, Aust, NZ, s SA) _____

❑ *Charadrius obscurus.* RED-BREASTED PLOVER. (NZ) . . . . _____

❑ *Charadrius hiaticula.* COMMON RINGED PLOVER. (n Palea; ◊-Afr, Aust)_____

❑ *Charadrius semipalmatus.* SEMIPALMATED PLOVER. (n NA; ◊-s SA). _____

❑ *Charadrius placidus.* LONG-BILLED PLOVER. (e Asia; ◊-se Asia) . . . . . _____

❑ *Charadrius dubius.* LITTLE RINGED PLOVER. (Palea-Phil; ◊-Afr, Aust) _____

❑ *Charadrius wilsonia.* WILSON'S PLOVER. (s US-n SA; ◊-c SA) . . . . . . _____

❑ *Charadrius vociferus.* KILLDEER. (NA-n W Indies, w SA; ◊-w,n SA). _____

❑ *Charadrius thoracicus.* MADAGASCAR PLOVER. (Mad) . . . . _____

❑ *Charadrius sanctaehelenae.* St. Helena Plover. (St. Helena). . . . . _____

❑ *Charadrius pecuarius.* Kittlitz's Plover. (Afr, Mad). . . . . _____

❑ *Charadrius tricollaris.* Three-banded Plover. (c,e,s Afr, Mad). . . . _____

❑ *Charadrius forbesi.* Forbes's Plover. (w,c Afr). . . . . _____

❑ *Charadrius melodus.* Piping Plover. (c,ne NA; ◊-se US-G Ant). . . . _____

❑ *Charadrius pallidus.* Chestnut-banded Plover. (e,s Afr). . . . . _____

❑ *Charadrius alexandrinus.* Kentish Plover. (Palea-Indon; NA-SA). _____
   ___*C. (a.) alexandrinus.* Kentish Plover. (Palea, G Sunda; ◊-Afr, Phil)
   ___*C. (a.) nivosus.* Snowy Plover. (s US-n SA)
   ___*C. (a.) occidentalis.* Peruvian Plover. (w SA)

❑ *Charadrius marginatus.* White-fronted Plover. (Afr, Mad). . . . . . _____

❑ *Charadrius ruficapillus.* Red-capped Plover. (Aust). . . . . _____

❑ *Charadrius peronii.* Malaysian Plover. (se Asia-Phil). . . . . _____

❑ *Charadrius javanicus.* Javan Plover. (Java). . . . . _____

❑ *Charadrius collaris.* Collared Plover. (MA, SA). . . . . _____

❑ *Charadrius bicinctus.* Double-banded Plover. (NZ; ◊-s Aust, Fiji) _____

❑ *Charadrius alticola.* Puna Plover. (Andes sw SA). . . . . _____

❑ *Charadrius falklandicus.* Two-banded Plover. (s SA). . . . . _____

❑ *Charadrius mongolus.* Mongolian P. (e Asia, w Alas; ◊-Afr, Aust). _____
   ___*C. (m.) mongolus.* Mongolian Plover. (e Sib, w Alas; ◊-Aust, Phil)
   ___*C. (m.) atrifrons.* Tibetan Plover. (Himal sc Asia; ◊-e,s Afr, s Asia)

❑ *Charadrius leschenaultii.* Greater Sand P. (sc Eura; ◊-Afr, NZ). . . _____

❑ *Charadrius asiaticus.* Caspian Plover. (sc Asia; ◊ e,s Afr). . . . . . . _____

❑ *Charadrius veredus.* Oriental Plover. (e Asia; ◊ Indon-Aust). . . . . _____

❑ *Charadrius montanus.* Mountain Plover. (c NA; ◊ sw US-n Mex). . _____

❑ *Charadrius modestus.* Rufous-chested Plover. (s SA). . . . . _____

❑ *Charadrius rubricollis.* Hooded Plover. (s Aust). . . . . _____

❑ *Thinornis novaeseelandiae.* Shore Plover. (Chatham). . . . . _____

❑ *Erythrogonys cinctus.* Red-kneed Dotterel. (int Aust). . . . . _____

❑ *Eudromias morinellus.* Eurasian Dotterel. (n Eura-w,n Alas). . . . _____

❑ *Oreopholus ruficollis.* Tawny-throated Dotterel. (w,s SA). . . . . _____

❑ *Anarhynchus frontalis.* Wrybill. (c NZ). . . . . _____

❑ *Phegornis mitchellii.* Diademed Sandpiper-Plover. (Andes s SA) . _____

❑ *Peltohyas australis.* Inland Dotterel. (int Aust). . . . . _____

❑ *Elseyornis melanops.* Black-fronted Dotterel. (Aust, NZ). . . . . . _____

❑ *Vanellus vanellus.* Northern Lapwing. (Palea; ◊-n Afr, s Asia). . . . _____

❑ *Vanellus crassirostris*. LONG-TOED LAPWING. (c,e,s Afr) . . . . _____

❑ *Vanellus malabaricus*. YELLOW-WATTLED LAPWING. (s Asia) . . . . . . _____

❑ *Vanellus macropterus*. JAVANESE LAPWING. (Java) . . . . _____

❑ *Vanellus tricolor*. BANDED LAPWING. (c,s Aust) . . . . _____

❑ *Vanellus miles*. MASKED LAPWING. (s NG, Aust, NZ; ◊-Wall) . . . . . . _____
___*V. (m.) miles*. MASKED LAPWING. (s NG, n Aust; ◊-Wall)
___*V. (m.) novaehollandiae*. AUSTRALIAN LAPWING. (se Aust, NZ)

❑ *Vanellus armatus*. BLACKSMITH LAPWING. (s,e Afr) . . . . _____

❑ *Vanellus spinosus*. SPUR-WINGED LAPWING. (sc Palea, w,c,ne Afr) . . . _____

❑ *Vanellus duvaucelii*. RIVER LAPWING. (s,se Asia) . . . . _____

❑ *Vanellus tectus*. BLACK-HEADED LAPWING. (subsah Afr) . . . . _____

❑ *Vanellus melanocephalus*. SPOT-BREASTED LAPWING. (mts Eth) . . . . _____

❑ *Vanellus cinereus*. GREY-HEADED LAPWING. (e Asia; ◊-se Asia) . . . . . _____

❑ *Vanellus indicus*. RED-WATTLED LAPWING. (s,se Asia) . . . . _____

❑ *Vanellus albiceps*. WHITE-HEADED LAPWING. (Afr) . . . . _____

❑ *Vanellus senegallus*. WATTLED LAPWING. (Afr) . . . . _____

❑ *Vanellus lugubris*. SENEGAL LAPWING. (w,c,se Afr) . . . . _____

❑ *Vanellus melanopterus*. BLACK-WINGED LAPWING. (mts ne,s Afr) . . . _____

❑ *Vanellus coronatus*. CROWNED LAPWING. (e,s Afr) . . . . _____

❑ *Vanellus superciliosus*. BROWN-CHESTED LAPWING. (w Afr; ◊-e Afr) . . _____

❑ *Vanellus gregarius*. SOCIABLE LAPWING. (Russia; ◊-ne Afr, s Asia) . _____

❑ *Vanellus leucurus*. WHITE-TAILED LAPWING. (sc Asia; ◊-ne Afr) . . . . _____

❑ *Vanellus cayanus*. PIED LAPWING. (SA) . . . . _____

❑ *Vanellus chilensis*. SOUTHERN LAPWING. (SA; ◊-Pan, Trin) . . . . _____
___*V. (c.) cayannensis*. CAYENNE LAPWING. (n,c,sc SA)
___*V. (c.) chilensis*. SOUTHERN LAPWING. (s SA; ◊-Pan, Trin)

❑ *Vanellus resplendens*. ANDEAN LAPWING. (Andes w,s SA) . . . . _____

Superfamily LAROIDEA [34/146]
Family **Glareolidae** [6/18]
Subfamily Dromadinae [1/1]

❑ *Dromas ardeola*. CRAB PLOVER. (ne Afr, s Asia; ◊-Mad, se Asia) . . . . _____

Subfamily Glareolinae [5/17]

❑ *Pluvianus aegyptius*. CROCODILE-BIRD. (nc Afr) . . . . _____

❑ *Rhinoptilus africanus*. DOUBLE-BANDED COURSER. (e,s Afr) . . . . _____

❑ *Rhinoptilus chalcopterus*. BRONZE-WINGED COURSER. (Afr) . . . . _____

❏ *Rhinoptilus cinctus.* THREE-BANDED COURSER. (e,se Afr). . . . . _____

❏ *Rhinoptilus bitorquatus.* JERDON'S COURSER. (se India). . . . . _____

❏ *Cursorius cursor.* CREAM-COLORED COURSER. (n Afr, sc Asia). . . . . . _____

❏ *Cursorius rufus.* BURCHELL'S COURSER. (s Afr). . . . . _____

❏ *Cursorius temminckii.* TEMMINCK'S COURSER. (Afr). . . . . _____

❏ *Cursorius coromandelicus.* INDIAN COURSER. (s Asia). . . . . _____

❏ *Glareola pratincola.* COLLARED PRATINCOLE. (s Palea-Afr; ◊-s Asia). _____

❏ *Glareola maldivarum.* ORIENTAL PRATINCOLE. (e Asia; ◊-n,e Aust) . _____

❏ *Glareola nordmanni.* BLACK-WINGED PRATINCOLE. (s Eura; ◊ Afr) . _____

❏ *Glareola ocularis.* MADAGASCAR PRATINCOLE. (Mad; ◊ e,se Afr). . . . _____

❏ *Glareola nuchalis.* ROCK PRATINCOLE. (w,c,e Afr). . . . . _____
   ___*G. (n.) liberiae.* RUFOUS-COLLARED PRATINCOLE. (w Afr)
   ___*G. (n.) nuchalis.* WHITE-COLLARED PRATINCOLE. (c,e Afr)

❏ *Glareola cinerea.* GREY PRATINCOLE. (w Afr). . . . . _____

❏ *Glareola lactea.* SMALL PRATINCOLE. (s Asia). . . . . _____

❏ *Stiltia isabella.* AUSTRALIAN PRATINCOLE. (Aust; ◊-G Sunda, NG). . . _____

Family **Laridae** [28/128]
Subfamily Larinae [16/105]
Tribe Stercorariini [2/8]

❏ *Catharacta skua.* GREAT SKUA. (nw Eura; ◊ Atl). . . . . _____

❏ *Catharacta antarctica.* SOUTHERN SKUA. (is s Atl; ◊ s oceans). . . . . . _____

❏ *Catharacta lonnbergi.* BROWN SKUA. (is s oceans; ◊-trop oceans). . . _____

❏ *Catharacta chilensis.* CHILEAN SKUA. (s Chile; ◊-trop oceans SA). . . _____

❏ *Catharacta maccormicki.* SOUTH POLAR SKUA. (Ant; ◊-n Pac, n Atl). _____

❏ *Stercorarius pomarinus.* POMARINE JAEGER. (n Hol; ◊ s oceans). . . . _____

❏ *Stercorarius parasiticus.* PARASITIC JAEGER. (n Hol; ◊ s oceans). . . . _____

❏ *Stercorarius longicaudus.* LONG-TAILED JAEGER. (n Hol; ◊-s oceans) _____

Tribe Rynchopini [1/3]

❏ *Rynchops niger.* BLACK SKIMMER. (s US, Mex, SA; ◊ s US-s SA). . . _____

❏ *Rynchops flavirostris.* AFRICAN SKIMMER. (Afr). . . . . _____

❏ *Rynchops albicollis.* INDIAN SKIMMER. (s,se Asia). . . . . _____

Tribe Larini [6/50]

❏ *Larus scoresbii.* DOLPHIN GULL. (s SA). _____

❏ *Larus pacificus.* PACIFIC GULL. (s Aust). _____

❏ *Larus belcheri.* BAND-TAILED GULL. (Pac w,s SA). . . . . _____

❏ *Larus atlanticus.* OLROG'S GULL. (ne Argen; ◊ se SA). . . . . _____

❏ *Larus crassirostris.* BLACK-TAILED GULL. (e Asia). . . . . _____

❏ *Larus modestus.* GREY GULL. (sw SA; ◊-nw SA). . . . . _____

❏ *Larus heermanni.* HEERMANN'S GULL. (sw US-Mex; ◊ sw Can-Guat) _____

❏ *Larus leucophthalmus.* WHITE-EYED GULL. (Red Sea). . . . . _____

❏ *Larus hemprichii.* SOOTY GULL. (ne Afr, se Asia). . . . . _____

❏ *Larus canus.* MEW GULL. (n Hol; ◊-n Afr, e Asia, nw Mex, ne US) . _____
___*L. (c.) canus.* MEW GULL. (sp)
___*L. (c.) kamtschatschensis.* KAMCHATKA GULL. (ne Sib; ◊-e Asia)

❏ *Larus audouinii.* AUDOUIN'S GULL. (is Medit Sea). . . . . _____

❏ *Larus delawarensis.* RING-BILLED GULL. (w,c,ne NA; ◊-s Mex). . . . . _____

❏ *Larus californicus.* CALIFORNIA GULL. (w NA; ◊-w,c Mex). . . . . _____

❏ *Larus marinus.* GREAT BLACK-BACKED GULL. (Palea, ne NA; ◊-se US)_____

❏ *Larus dominicanus.* KELP GULL. (s Afr, s Aust, NZ, s SA-Ant). . . . . _____

❏ *Larus glaucescens.* GLAUCOUS-WINGED GULL. (nw NA; ◊-nw Mex). _____

❏ *Larus occidentalis.* WESTERN GULL. (w NA, ◊-nw Mex). . . . . _____

❏ *Larus livens.* YELLOW-FOOTED GULL. (is Gulf Calif; ◊-s Calif). . . . . . _____

❏ *Larus hyperboreus.* GLAUCOUS GULL. (n Hol; ◊-c Eura, s US). . . . . . _____

❏ *Larus glaucoides.* ICELAND GULL. (Green, ne NA; ◊-US). . . . . _____
___*L. (g.) glaucoides.* ICELAND GULL. (Green; ◊-ne NA)
___*L. (g.) kumlieni.* KUMLIEN'S GULL. (nw Que; ◊-e US)
___*L. (g.) thayeri.* THAYER'S GULL. (nc NA; ◊-US)

❏ *Larus argentatus.* HERRING GULL. (n Hol; ◊-e Afr, s Asia, s CA). . . . _____
___*L. (a.) argentatus.* HERRING GULL. (n Euro, n NA; ◊ sp)
___*L. (a.) heuglini.* HEUGLIN'S GULL. (n Russia, nw Sib; ◊-e Afr, s Asia)
___*L. (a.) vegae.* VEGA GULL. (n Sib; ◊-e Asia, Aleut)

❏ *Larus armenicus.* ARMENIAN GULL. (sc Eura). . . . . _____

❏ *Larus schistisagus.* SLATY-BACKED GULL. (ne Asia; ◊-e Asia). . . . . . _____

❏ *Larus cachinnans.* YELLOW-LEGGED GULL. (s Palea; ◊-ne Afr). . . . . _____
___*L. (c.) atlantis.* ATLANTIC ISLANDS GULL. (e Atl)
___*L. (c.) cachinnans.* YELLOW-LEGGED GULL. (sp)

❏ *Larus fuscus.* LESSER BLACK-BACKED GULL. (n Eura; ◊-Afr, s US) . _____
___*L. (f.) graellsi.* DARK-BACKED GULL. (nw Euro; ◊-w Afr, s US)
___*L. (f.) fuscus.* LESSER BLACK-BACKED GULL. (cn Eura; ◊-e,s Afr)

❏ *Larus ichthyaetus.* GREAT BLACK-HEADED GULL. (sc Eura; ◊-se Asia)_____

❏ *Larus brunnicephalus.* BROWN-HEADED GULL. (sc Asia; ◊-se Asia) . _____

❏ *Larus cirrocephalus.* GREY-HEADED GULL. (Afr, Mad, s SA). . . . . . . _____

❏ *Larus hartlaubii.* KING GULL. (sw Afr). . . . . _____

❏ *Larus novaehollandiae.* SILVER GULL. (Aust, N Cal). . . . . _____

❑ *Larus scopulinus.* RED-BILLED GULL. (NZ)................... _____

❑ *Larus bulleri.* BLACK-BILLED GULL. (NZ)................... _____

❑ *Larus maculipennis.* BROWN-HOODED GULL. (s SA)............. _____

❑ *Larus ridibundus.* COMMON BLACK-HEADED G. (n Palea; ◊-Afr, US). _____

❑ *Larus genei.* SLENDER-BILLED GULL. (s Palea)................. _____

❑ *Larus philadelphia.* BONAPARTE'S GULL. (n NA; ◊-Mex-G Ant)..... _____

❑ *Larus saundersi.* SAUNDERS'S GULL. (mts n China; ◊-e Asia)....... _____

❑ *Larus serranus.* ANDEAN GULL. (Andes wc,sw SA)............. _____

❑ *Larus melanocephalus.* MEDITERRANEAN GULL. (Euro).......... _____

❑ *Larus relictus.* RELICT GULL. (mts c Asia)................. _____

❑ *Larus fuliginosus.* LAVA GULL. (Galap)..................... _____

❑ *Larus atricilla.* LAUGHING GULL. (nw Mex; n,e NA-W Indies; ◊-SA). _____

❑ *Larus pipixcan.* FRANKLIN'S GULL. (wc NA; ◊ SA)............. _____

❑ *Larus minutus.* LITTLE GULL. (n Eura, ne NA; ◊-Medit, n,e US).... _____

❑ *Pagophila eburnea.* IVORY GULL. (n Hol; ◊-n Euro, n,ne NA)...... _____

❑ *Rhodostethia rosea.* ROSS'S GULL. (n Hol; ◊-Arctic waters)....... _____

❑ *Xema sabini.* SABINE'S GULL. (n Hol; ◊ se Pac, s Atl oceans)....... _____

❑ *Creagrus furcatus.* SWALLOW-TAILED GULL. (Galap; ◊-w SA)...... _____

❑ *Rissa tridactyla.* BLACK-LEGGED KITTIWAKE. (n Hol; ◊-n Afr, s US) . _____

❑ *Rissa brevirostris.* RED-LEGGED KITTIWAKE. (w Alas)............. _____

Tribe Sternini [7/44]

❑ *Sterna nilotica.* GULL-BILLED TERN. (Hol, c SA; ◊-Afr, se Asia, SA). _____

❑ *Sterna caspia.* CASPIAN TERN. (Hol-Afr, Aust, NZ; ◊-s Afr, n SA)... _____

❑ *Sterna aurantia.* RIVER TERN. (s,se Asia)..................... _____

❑ *Sterna maxima.* ROYAL TERN. (s,e US-n,s SA, w Afr; ◊-s SA)...... _____

❑ *Sterna elegans.* ELEGANT TERN. (s Calif-w Mex; ◊-sw SA)........ _____

❑ *Sterna bengalensis.* LESSER CRESTED-TERN. (Afr; s Asia-NG, Aust). _____

❑ *Sterna bergii.* GREAT CRESTED-TERN. (s,e Afr; s Asia-Polyn, Aust) . _____

❑ *Sterna bernsteini.* CHINESE CRESTED-TERN. (e China; ◊-Wall)...... _____

❑ *Sterna sandvicensis.* SANDWICH TERN. (Eura, se US-SA; ◊-s Afr)... _____
___*S. (s.) sandvicensis.* SANDWICH TERN. (Eura, se US-MA; ◊ sp)
___*S. (s.) eurygnatha.* CAYENNE TERN. (n,s SA; ◊ e SA)

❑ *Sterna dougallii.* ROSEATE TERN. (local cosm)................. _____

❑ *Sterna striata.* WHITE-FRONTED TERN. (Tasm, NZ-Auck; ◊-e Aust) . _____

❑ *Sterna sumatrana.* BLACK-NAPED TERN. (Seyc-Oceania, Aust)...... _____

❏ *Sterna hirundinacea.* SOUTH AMERICAN TERN. (s SA). . . . . _____

❏ *Sterna hirundo.* COMMON TERN. (Palea, NA-W Indies; ◊-s oceans) . _____

❏ *Sterna paradisaea.* ARCTIC TERN. (n Hol; ◊ subant oceans). . . . . _____

❏ *Sterna vittata.* ANTARCTIC TERN. (is s oceans, Ant pen; ◊-s Afr, s SA)_____

❏ *Sterna virgata.* KERGUELEN TERN. (is s Indian O). . . . . _____

❏ *Sterna forsteri.* FORSTER'S TERN. (NA; ◊ s US-CR, G Ant). . . . . _____

❏ *Sterna trudeaui.* SNOWY-CROWNED TERN. (s SA). . . . . _____

❏ *Sterna albifrons.* LITTLE TERN. (Palea, s,se Asia-Bism, Aust; ◊-s Afr)_____

❏ *Sterna saundersi.* SAUNDERS'S TERN. (ne Afr, s Asia; ◊-se Asia). . . . _____

❏ *Sterna antillarum.* LEAST TERN. (US-CA, W Indies; ◊-e SA). . . . . . . _____

❏ *Sterna superciliaris.* YELLOW-BILLED TERN. (int SA). . . . . _____

❏ *Sterna lorata.* PERUVIAN TERN. (Ecua-n Chile). . . . . _____

❏ *Sterna nereis.* FAIRY TERN. (w,s Aust, NZ, N Cal). . . . . _____

❏ *Sterna balaenarum.* DAMARA TERN. (w,s Afr). . . . . _____

❏ *Sterna repressa.* WHITE-CHEEKED TERN. (n Indian O). . . . . _____

❏ *Sterna acuticauda.* BLACK-BELLIED TERN. (s,se Asia). . . . . _____

❏ *Sterna aleutica.* ALEUTIAN TERN. (e Asia, w,s Alas). . . . . _____

❏ *Sterna lunata.* GREY-BACKED TERN. (Oceania). . . . . _____

❏ *Sterna anaethetus.* BRIDLED TERN. (trop is cosm; ◊ trop oceans). . . . _____

❏ *Sterna fuscata.* SOOTY TERN. (trop is cosm; ◊ trop oceans). . . . . _____

❏ *Chlidonias albostriatus.* BLACK-FRONTED TERN. (NZ). . . . . _____

❏ *Chlidonias hybridus.* WHISKERED TERN. (Old World). . . . . _____

❏ *Chlidonias leucopterus.* WHITE-WINGED T. (Eura-e Afr; ◊-s Afr, NZ). _____

❏ *Chlidonias niger.* BLACK TERN. (Eura, NA; ◊ trop Afr, SA). . . . . . . _____

❏ *Phaetusa simplex.* LARGE-BILLED TERN. (SA). . . . . _____

❏ *Anous stolidus.* BROWN NODDY. (trop is cosm; ◊ trop oceans). . . . . . _____

❏ *Anous minutus.* BLACK NODDY. (is trop Pac, Atl; ◊ trop oceans). . . . _____

❏ *Anous tenuirostris.* LESSER NODDY. (is Indian O). . . . . _____

❏ *Procelsterna cerulea.* BLUE-GREY NODDY. (is trop Pac). . . . . _____
   ___*P. (c.) cerulea.* BLUE NODDY. (sp)
   ___*P. (c.) albivitta.* GREY NODDY. (sw Pac)

❏ *Gygis alba.* COMMON WHITE-TERN. (trop is cosm; ◊ trop oceans). . . . _____
   ___*G. (a.) candida.* COMMON WHITE-TERN. (Seyc, Pac)
   ___*G. (a.) alba.* ATLANTIC WHITE-TERN. (Atl)

❏ *Gygis microrhyncha.* LITTLE WHITE-TERN. (Line-Marq). . . . . _____

❏ *Larosterna inca.* INCA TERN. (sw SA). . . . . _____

Subfamily Alcinae [12/23]

❏ *Alle alle.* Dovekie. (n Hol; ◊-Medit, W Indies). . . . . _____

❏ *Uria aalge.* Common Murre. (n Palea, w,e NA). . . . . _____

❏ *Uria lomvia.* Thick-billed Murre. (n Hol; ◊-e Asia, s US). . . . . _____

❏ *Alca torda.* Razorbill. (nw Palea, ne NA; ◊-Medit, se US). . . . . _____

   Pinguinus impennis. Great Auk. (†n Atl). . . . . _____

❏ *Cepphus grylle.* Black Guillemot. (n Hol; ◊-e US). . . . . _____

❏ *Cepphus columba.* Pigeon Guillemot. (ne Sib-nw NA; ◊-sw US) . _____
   ___*C. (c.) columba.* Pigeon Guillemot. (sp)
   ___*C. (c.) snowi.* Kurile Guillemot. (Kuril)

❏ *Cepphus carbo.* Spectacled Guillemot. (e Eura). . . . . _____

❏ *Brachyramphus marmoratus.* Marbled Murrel. (e Asia-nw NA) . _____

❏ *Brachyramphus brevirostris.* Kittlitz's Murrelet. (Alas). . . . . _____

❏ *Synthliboramphus hypoleucus.* Xantus's Murrelet. (w US, nw Mex)_____
   ___*S. (h.) hypoleucus.* Xantus's Murrelet. (sp)
   ___*S. (h.) scrippsi.* Scripps's Murrelet. (nw Mex)

❏ *Synthliboramphus craveri.* Craveri's Murrelet. (is Gulf Calif). . . _____

❏ *Synthliboramphus antiquus.* Ancient M. (e Asia-nw NA; ◊-nw Mex) _____

❏ *Synthliboramphus wumizusume.* Japanese Murrelet. (is Japan). . . _____

❏ *Ptychoramphus aleuticus.* Cassin's Auklet. (is w NA). . . . . _____

❏ *Cyclorrhynchus psittacula.* Parakeet A. (e Sib-w Alas; ◊-sw US). . _____

❏ *Aethia cristatella.* Crested Auklet. (e Sib, nw NA; ◊-Japan). . . . . . _____

❏ *Aethia pygmaea.* Whiskered Auklet. (e Sib, Aleut; ◊-Japan). . . . . . _____

❏ *Aethia pusilla.* Least Auklet. (e Sib, w Alas; ◊-Japan). . . . . _____

❏ *Cerorhinca monocerata.* Rhinoceros A. (e Asia-w NA; ◊-nw Mex). _____

❏ *Fratercula arctica.* Atlantic Puffin. (ne NA-nw Palea; ◊-n Afr). . . _____

❏ *Fratercula corniculata.* Horned Puffin. (e Sib-nw NA; ◊-sw US) . _____

❏ *Fratercula cirrhata.* Tufted Puffin. (e Asia-nw NA; ◊-sw US). . . . . _____

Suborder CICONII [169/657]
Infraorder FALCONIDES [77/302]
Parvorder ACCIPITRIDA [67/239]
Family **Accipitridae** [66/238]
Subfamily Pandioninae [1/1]

❏ *Pandion haliaetus.* Osprey. (cosm, except SA; ◊-s SA). . . . . _____

Subfamily Accipitrinae [65/237]

❏ *Aviceda cuculoides.* African Baza. (Afr). . . . . _____

❏ *Aviceda madagascariensis.* MADAGASCAR BAZA. (Mad). . . . . _____

❏ *Aviceda jerdoni.* JERDON'S BAZA. (s Asia-Phil). . . . . _____

❏ *Aviceda subcristata.* PACIFIC BAZA. (Wall-Solom, n,e Aust). . . . . _____

❏ *Aviceda leuphotes.* BLACK BAZA. (s,se Asia). . . . . _____

❏ *Leptodon cayanensis.* GREY-HEADED KITE. (MA, SA). . . . . _____

❏ *Leptodon forbesi.* WHITE-COLLARED KITE. (e Braz). . . . . _____

❏ *Chondrohierax uncinatus.* HOOK-BILLED KITE. (MA, SA, e Cuba). . . _____
___*C. (u.) uncinatus.* HOOK-BILLED KITE. (MA, SA)
___*C. (u.) wilsonii.* CUBAN KITE. (e Cuba)

❏ *Henicopernis longicauda.* LONG-TAILED HONEY-BUZZARD. (Aru-NG). _____

❏ *Henicopernis infuscatus.* BLACK HONEY-BUZZARD. (c Bism). . . . . _____

❏ *Pernis apivorus.* EUROPEAN HONEY-BUZZARD. (w,c Eura; ◊-s Afr). . . . _____

❏ *Pernis ptilorhyncus.* ORIENTAL HONEY-BUZZARD. (s,ne Asia-Phil). . . . _____
___*P. (p.) orientalis.* SIBERIAN HONEY-BUZZARD. (ne Asia; ◊-Indon, Phil)
___*P. (p.) ruficollis.* INDIAN HONEY-BUZZARD. (s Asia)
___*P. (p.) torquatus.* MALAYSIAN HONEY-BUZZARD. (se Asia)
___*P. (p.) ptilorhyncus.* JAVAN HONEY-BUZZARD. (Java)
___*P. (p.) palawanensis.* PALAWAN HONEY-BUZZARD. (cw Phil)
___*P. (p.) philippensis.* PHILIPPINE HONEY-BUZZARD. (Phil)

❏ *Pernis celebensis.* BARRED HONEY-BUZZARD. (Sulaw, Phil). . . . . _____

❏ *Lophoictinia isura.* SQUARE-TAILED KITE. (Aust). . . . . _____

❏ *Hamirostra melanosternon.* BLACK-BREASTED BUZZARD. (int Aust) . _____

❏ *Elanoides forficatus.* SWALLOW-TAILED KITE. (se US, MA, SA). . . . . _____

❏ *Macheiramphus alcinus.* BAT HAWK. (Afr, Mad, se Asia, NG). . . . . . _____

❏ *Gampsonyx swainsonii.* PEARL KITE. (w Nica, SA). . . . . _____

❏ *Elanus caeruleus.* BLACK-WINGED KITE. (sw Palea, Afr, s Asia-NG) . _____
___*E. (c.) caeruleus.* BLACK-WINGED KITE. (sw Palea, Afr, s,se Asia)
___*E. (c.) hypoleucos.* INDONESIAN KITE. (Indon, Phil, NG)

❏ *Elanus axillaris.* BLACK-SHOULDERED KITE. (Aust). . . . . _____

❏ *Elanus leucurus.* WHITE-TAILED KITE. (w,s US, MA, SA). . . . . _____

❏ *Elanus scriptus.* LETTER-WINGED KITE. (int Aust). . . . . _____

❏ *Chelictinia riocourii.* SCISSOR-TAILED KITE. (subsah Afr). . . . . _____

❏ *Rostrhamus sociabilis.* SNAIL KITE. (s Fla, Cuba, MA, SA). . . . . _____

❏ *Rostrhamus hamatus.* SLENDER-BILLED KITE. (e Pan, SA). . . . . _____

❏ *Harpagus bidentatus.* DOUBLE-TOOTHED KITE. (MA, SA). . . . . _____

❏ *Harpagus diodon.* RUFOUS-THIGHED KITE. (cn,e,se SA). . . . . _____

❏ *Ictinia mississippiensis.* MISSISSIPPI KITE. (s US; ◊ SA). . . . . _____

❏ *Ictinia plumbea.* PLUMBEOUS KITE. (MA, SA). . . . . _____

❑ *Milvus milvus.* RED KITE. (Palea). . . . . _____
   ___*M. (m.) milvus.* RED KITE. (sp)
   ___*M. (m.) fasciicauda.* CAPE VERDE KITE. (C Verde)

❑ *Milvus migrans.* BLACK KITE. (OW). . . . . _____
   ___*M. (m.) migrans.* BLACK KITE. (sp)
   ___*M. (m.) aegyptius.* YELLOW-BILLED KITE. (Afr reg, Mad)

❑ *Milvus lineatus.* BLACK-EARED KITE. (e Asia; ◊ s,se Asia). . . . . _____

❑ *Haliastur sphenurus.* WHISTLING KITE. (Aust, c,s NG, N Cal). . . . . . . _____

❑ *Haliastur indus.* BRAHMINY KITE. (s Asia-Phil, Solom, n,e Aust). . . . . _____

❑ *Haliaeetus leucogaster.* WHITE-BELLIED FISH-EAGLE. (s Asia-Aust). . . _____

❑ *Haliaeetus sanfordi.* SANFORD'S FISH-EAGLE. (Solom). . . . . _____

❑ *Haliaeetus vocifer.* AFRICAN FISH-EAGLE. (Afr). . . . . _____

❑ *Haliaeetus vociferoides.* MADAGASCAR FISH-EAGLE. (w Mad). . . . . . _____

❑ *Haliaeetus leucoryphus.* PALLAS'S SEA-EAGLE. (c Asia; ◊-s,se Asia) . _____

❑ *Haliaeetus albicilla.* WHITE-TAILED EAGLE. (Palea-sw Alas; ◊-s Eura). _____

❑ *Haliaeetus leucocephalus.* BALD EAGLE. (NA, Comm). . . . . _____

❑ *Haliaeetus pelagicus.* STELLER'S SEA-EAGLE. (e Sib; ◊-e Asia, Aleut). _____

❑ *Ichthyophaga humilis.* LESSER FISH-EAGLE. (s Asia-Sulaw). . . . . _____

❑ *Ichthyophaga ichthyaetus.* GREY-HEADED FISH-EAGLE. (s Asia-Phil) . _____

❑ *Gypohierax angolensis.* PALM-NUT VULTURE. (Afr). . . . . _____

❑ *Gypaetus barbatus.* LAMMERGEIER. (mts s Palea, s Asia, e,s Afr). . . . . _____

❑ *Neophron percnopterus.* EGYPTIAN VULTURE. (s Palea, n,ne Afr). . . . . _____

❑ *Necrosyrtes monachus.* HOODED VULTURE. (Afr). . . . . _____

❑ *Gyps africanus.* WHITE-BACKED VULTURE. (Afr). . . . . _____

❑ *Gyps bengalensis.* WHITE-RUMPED VULTURE. (s,se Asia). . . . . _____

❑ *Gyps indicus.* LONG-BILLED VULTURE. (s,se Asia). . . . . _____
   ___*G. (i.) indicus.* INDIAN VULTURE. (sp)
   ___*G. (i.) tenuirostris.* LONG-BILLED VULTURE. (n India)

❑ *Gyps rueppellii.* RUEPPELL'S GRIFFON. (subsah Afr reg). . . . . _____

❑ *Gyps himalayensis.* HIMALAYAN GRIFFON. (mts sc Asia). . . . . _____

❑ *Gyps fulvus.* EURASIAN GRIFFON. (mts s Palea; ◊-ne Afr, s Asia). . . . . _____

❑ *Gyps coprotheres.* CAPE GRIFFON. (s Afr). . . . . _____

❑ *Aegypius monachus.* CINEREOUS VULTURE. (s Palea; ◊-n Afr). . . . . . . _____

❑ *Torgos tracheliotus.* LAPPET-FACED VULTURE. (Afr reg). . . . . _____

❑ *Trigonoceps occipitalis.* WHITE-HEADED VULTURE. (Afr). . . . . _____

❑ *Sarcogyps calvus.* RED-HEADED VULTURE. (s,se Asia). . . . . _____

❏ *Circaetus gallicus.* SHORT-TOED SNAKE-EAGLE. (Palea-nc Afr, Wall) . _____
  ___*C. (g.) gallicus.* SHORT-TOED SNAKE-EAGLE. (Palea, Wall)
  ___*C. (g.) beaudouini.* BEAUDOUIN'S SNAKE-EAGLE. (subsah Afr)

❏ *Circaetus pectoralis.* BLACK-CHESTED SNAKE-EAGLE. (sc,e,s Afr). . . . _____

❏ *Circaetus cinereus.* BROWN SNAKE-EAGLE. (Afr). . . . . _____

❏ *Circaetus fasciolatus.* FASCIATED SNAKE-EAGLE. (e,se Afr). . . . . _____

❏ *Circaetus cinerascens.* BANDED SNAKE-EAGLE. (Afr). . . . . _____

❏ *Terathopius ecaudatus.* BATELEUR. (Afr reg). . . . . _____

❏ *Spilornis cheela.* CRESTED SERPENT-EAGLE. (s,se,e Asia-Phil). . . . . . . _____
  ___*S. (c.) cheela.* CRESTED SERPENT-EAGLE. (s,se Asia-Phil)
  ___*S. (c.) perplexus.* RYUKYU SERPENT-EAGLE. (sw Ryu)
  ___*S. (c.) abbotti.* SIMEULUE SERPENT-EAGLE. (Simeulue)
  ___*S. (c.) asturinus.* NIAS SERPENT-EAGLE. (Nias)
  ___*S. (c.) sipora.* MENTAWAI SERPENT-EAGLE. (Mentawai)
  ___*S. (c.) natunensis.* NATUNA SERPENT-EAGLE. (n Natuna)

❏ *Spilornis minimus.* NICOBAR SERPENT-EAGLE. (c,s Nico). . . . . _____
  ___*S. (m.) minimus.* SMALL SERPENT-EAGLE. (c Nico)
  ___*S. (m.) klossi.* NICOBAR SERPENT-EAGLE. (s Nico)

❏ *Spilornis kinabaluensis.* MOUNTAIN SERPENT-EAGLE. (mts n Born). . . _____

❏ *Spilornis rufipectus.* SULAWESI SERPENT-EAGLE. (Sulaw). . . . . _____

❏ *Spilornis holospilus.* PHILIPPINE SERPENT-EAGLE. (Phil). . . . . _____

❏ *Spilornis elgini.* ANDAMAN SERPENT-EAGLE. (And). . . . . _____

❏ *Dryotriorchis spectabilis.* CONGO SERPENT-EAGLE. (w,c Afr). . . . . . . _____

❏ *Eutriorchis astur.* MADAGASCAR SERPENT-EAGLE. (ne Mad). . . . . . . _____

❏ *Circus aeruginosus.* WESTERN MARSH-H. (w,c Palea; ◊-Afr, se Asia). _____

❏ *Circus ranivorus.* AFRICAN MARSH-HARRIER. (s,e Afr). . . . . _____

❏ *Circus spilonotus.* EASTERN MARSH-HARRIER. (e Asia, NG; ◊-se Asia). _____
  ___*C. (s.) spilonotus.* SPOTTED MARSH-HARRIER. (e Asia; ◊-sp)
  ___*C. (s.) spilothorax.* SPOT-BACKED MARSH-HARRIER. (c,e NG)

❏ *Circus approximans.* SWAMP HARRIER. (Aust, NZ, NG-s Oceania). . . _____

❏ *Circus maillardi.* MADAGASCAR MARSH-HARRIER. (Mad, Réun). . . . . _____
  ___*C. (m.) maillardi.* MADAGASCAR MARSH-HARRIER. (Mad)
  ___*C. (m.) macrosceles.* REUNION MARSH-HARRIER. (Réun)

❏ *Circus buffoni.* LONG-WINGED HARRIER. (SA). . . . . _____

❏ *Circus assimilis.* SPOTTED HARRIER. (Sulaw, L Sunda, Aust). . . . . . . _____

❏ *Circus maurus.* BLACK HARRIER. (s Afr). _____

❏ *Circus cyaneus.* NORTHERN HARRIER. (Hol; ◊-n Afr, s,se Asia, n SA). _____
  ___*C. (c.) cyaneus.* HEN HARRIER. (Eura; ◊-n Afr, s,se Asia)
  ___*C. (c.) hudsonius.* AMERICAN HARRIER. (NA; ◊-n SA)

❏ *Circus cinereus.* CINEREOUS HARRIER. (w,s SA). . . . . _____

❑ *Circus macrourus.* PALLID HARRIER. (cEura; ◊-s Afr, s Asia). . . . . _____

❑ *Circus melanoleucos.* PIED HARRIER. (e Asia; ◊-se Asia, Phil). . . . . . . _____

❑ *Circus pygargus.* MONTAGU'S HARRIER. (w,c Palea; ◊-s Afr, s Asia) . _____

❑ *Polyboroides typus.* AFRICAN HARRIER-HAWK. (Afr). . . . . _____

❑ *Polyboroides radiatus.* MADAGASCAR HARRIER-HAWK. (Mad). . . . . . . _____

❑ *Kaupifalco monogrammicus.* LIZARD BUZZARD. (Afr). . . . . _____

❑ *Melierax metabates.* DARK CHANTING-GOSHAWK. (Afr reg). . . . . _____

❑ *Melierax poliopterus.* EASTERN CHANTING-GOSHAWK. (e Afr). . . . . . . _____

❑ *Melierax canorus.* PALE CHANTING-GOSHAWK. (s Afr). . . . . _____

❑ *Micronisus gabar.* GABAR GOSHAWK. (Afr reg). . . . . _____

❑ *Accipiter poliogaster.* GREY-BELLIED GOSHAWK. (SA). . . . . _____

❑ *Accipiter trivirgatus.* CRESTED GOSHAWK. (s Asia-Phil). . . . . _____

❑ *Accipiter griseiceps.* SULAWESI GOSHAWK. (Sulaw). . . . . _____

❑ *Accipiter toussenelii.* RED-CHESTED GOSHAWK. (w,c Afr). . . . . _____

❑ *Accipiter tachiro.* AFRICAN GOSHAWK. (e,s Afr). . . . . _____

❑ *Accipiter castanilius.* CHESTNUT-FLANKED SPARROWHAWK. (w,c Afr). _____

❑ *Accipiter badius.* SHIKRA. (Afr, s,se Asia). . . . . _____
___*A. (b.) badius.* NORTHERN SHIKRA. (n,c Afr, s,se Asia)
___*A. (b.) polyzonoides.* SOUTHERN SHIKRA. (s Afr)

❑ *Accipiter butleri.* NICOBAR SPARROWHAWK. (Nico). . . . . _____

❑ *Accipiter brevipes.* LEVANT SPARROWHAWK. (sc Eura; ◊-nc,ne Afr). . . _____

❑ *Accipiter soloensis.* CHINESE GOSHAWK. (e Asia; ◊-se Asia-NG). . . . . _____

❑ *Accipiter francesii.* FRANCES'S GOSHAWK. (Mad, Com). . . . . _____

❑ *Accipiter trinotatus.* SPOT-TAILED GOSHAWK. (Sulaw). . . . . _____

❑ *Accipiter novaehollandiae.* GREY GOSHAWK. (Wall-Solom, n,e Aust). _____
___*A. (n.) hiogaster.* VARIABLE GOSHAWK. (Wall-Bism)
___*A. (n.) pulchellus.* RUFOUS-BREASTED GOSHAWK. (Solom)
___*A. (n.) novaehollandiae.* GREY GOSHAWK. (n,e Aust)

❑ *Accipiter fasciatus.* BROWN GOSHAWK. (Chris-N Cal, Aust). . . . . _____
___*A. (f.) wallacii.* LESSER GOSHAWK. (Chris-N Cal, n Aust)
___*A. (f.) fasciatus.* AUSTRALIAN GOSHAWK. (c,s Aust)

❑ *Accipiter melanochlamys.* BLACK-MANTLED GOSHAWK. (mts NG). . . . _____

❑ *Accipiter albogularis.* PIED GOSHAWK. (Bism, Solom, Santa Cruz). . . . _____

❑ *Accipiter haplochrous.* WHITE-BELLIED GOSHAWK. (N Cal). . . . . _____

❑ *Accipiter rufitorques.* FIJI GOSHAWK. (Fiji). . . . . _____

❑ *Accipiter henicogrammus.* MOLUCCAN GOSHAWK. (n Moluc). . . . . . . _____

❑ *Accipiter luteoschistaceus.* SLATY-MANTLED SPARROWHAWK. (cs Bism)_____

❑ *Accipiter imitator.* IMITATOR SPARROWHAWK. (n,c Solom). . . . . _____

❑ *Accipiter poliocephalus.* GREY-HEADED GOSHAWK. (w Pap, NG). . . . . _____

❑ *Accipiter princeps.* NEW BRITAIN GOSHAWK. (cs Bism). . . . . _____

❑ *Accipiter superciliosus.* TINY HAWK. (s CA, SA). . . . . _____

❑ *Accipiter collaris.* SEMICOLLARED HAWK. (mts nw SA). . . . . _____

❑ *Accipiter erythropus.* RED-THIGHED SPARROWHAWK. (w,c Afr). . . . . . . _____

❑ *Accipiter minullus.* LITTLE SPARROWHAWK. (e,s Afr). . . . . _____

❑ *Accipiter gularis.* JAPANESE SPARROWHAWK. (e Asia; ◊-Indon, Phil) . _____

❑ *Accipiter virgatus.* BESRA. (mts s Asia-Indon, Phil). . . . . _____

❑ *Accipiter nanus.* SMALL SPARROWHAWK. (mts Sulaw). . . . . _____

❑ *Accipiter erythrauchen.* RUFOUS-NECKED SPARROWHAWK. (Moluc). . . _____

❑ *Accipiter cirrocephalus.* COLLARED SPARROWHAWK. (Aru-NG, Aust). _____

❑ *Accipiter brachyurus.* NEW BRITAIN SPARROWHAWK. (cs Bism). . . . . . _____

❑ *Accipiter rhodogaster.* VINOUS-BREASTED SPARROWHAWK. (Sulaw). . . _____

❑ *Accipiter madagascariensis.* MADAGASCAR SPARROWHAWK. (Mad). . . _____

❑ *Accipiter ovampensis.* OVAMPO SPARROWHAWK. (Afr). . . . . _____

❑ *Accipiter nisus.* EURASIAN SPARROWHAWK. (Palea; ◊-n Afr, se Asia) . _____

❑ *Accipiter rufiventris.* RUFOUS-CHESTED SPARROWHAWK. (mts e,s Afr). _____

❑ *Accipiter striatus.* SHARP-SHINNED HAWK. (NA-Mex, G Ant; ◊-s CA). _____

❑ *Accipiter chionogaster.* WHITE-BREASTED HAWK. (mts MA). . . . . _____

❑ *Accipiter ventralis.* PLAIN-BREASTED HAWK. (mts w,n SA). . . . . _____

❑ *Accipiter erythronemius.* RUFOUS-THIGHED HAWK. (sc,se SA). . . . . . . _____

❑ *Accipiter cooperii.* COOPER'S HAWK. (NA, n Mex; ◊-n SA). . . . . _____

❑ *Accipiter gundlachi.* GUNDLACH'S HAWK. (Cuba). . . . . _____

❑ *Accipiter bicolor.* BICOLORED HAWK. (MA, SA). . . . . _____
　　　___*A. (b.) bicolor.* BICOLORED HAWK. (MA, n,c SA)
　　　___*A. (b.) guttifer.* SPOTTED HAWK. (sc SA)
　　　___*A. (b.) chilensis.* CHILEAN HAWK. (s SA)

❑ *Accipiter melanoleucus.* BLACK GOSHAWK. (Afr). . . . . _____

❑ *Accipiter henstii.* HENST'S GOSHAWK. (Mad). . . . . _____

❑ *Accipiter gentilis.* NORTHERN GOSHAWK. (Hol-c Mex; ◊-n Afr, se Asia)_____
　　　___*A. (g.) gentilis.* EURASIAN GOSHAWK. (Palea; ◊-sp)
　　　___*A. (g.) atricapillus.* AMERICAN GOSHAWK. (NA, c Mex)

❑ *Accipiter meyerianus.* MEYER'S GOSHAWK. (Moluc-Solom). . . . . _____

❑ *Erythrotriorchis buergersi.* CHESTNUT-SHOULDERED G. (mts e NG). . . _____

❑ *Erythrotriorchis radiatus.* RED GOSHAWK. (n,e Aust). . . . . _____

❏ *Megatriorchis doriae.* DORIA'S GOSHAWK. (w Pap, NG). . . . . _____

❏ *Urotriorchis macrourus.* LONG-TAILED HAWK. (w,c Afr). . . . . _____

❏ *Butastur rufipennis.* GRASSHOPPER BUZZARD. (subsah,e Afr). . . . . _____

❏ *Butastur teesa.* WHITE-EYED BUZZARD. (s Asia). . . . . _____

❏ *Butastur liventer.* RUFOUS-WINGED BUZZARD. (se Asia). . . . . _____

❏ *Butastur indicus.* GREY-FACED BUZZARD. (e Asia; ◊-Indon, NG). . . . . _____

❏ *Geranospiza caerulescens.* CRANE HAWK. (MA, SA). . . . . _____
　　___*G. (c.) nigra.* BLACKISH CRANE-HAWK. (MA, nw SA)
　　___*G. (c.) caerulescens.* GREY CRANE-HAWK. (Amaz)
　　___*G. (c.) gracilis.* BANDED CRANE-HAWK. (sc,e SA)

❏ *Leucopternis plumbea.* PLUMBEOUS HAWK. (Pan, w SA). . . . . _____

❏ *Leucopternis schistacea.* SLATE-COLORED HAWK. (Amaz). . . . . _____

❏ *Leucopternis princeps.* BARRED HAWK. (s CA, nw SA). . . . . _____

❏ *Leucopternis melanops.* BLACK-FACED HAWK. (Amaz). . . . . _____

❏ *Leucopternis kuhli.* WHITE-BROWED HAWK. (Amaz). . . . . _____

❏ *Leucopternis lacernulata.* WHITE-NECKED HAWK. (se Braz). . . . . _____

❏ *Leucopternis semiplumbea.* SEMIPLUMBEOUS HAWK. (CA, nw SA). . . _____

❏ *Leucopternis albicollis.* WHITE HAWK. (MA, SA). . . . . _____

❏ *Leucopternis occidentalis.* GREY-BACKED HAWK. (mts w Ecua). . . . . . _____

❏ *Leucopternis polionota.* MANTLED HAWK. (se SA). . . . . _____

❏ *Buteogallus aequinoctialis.* RUFOUS CRAB-HAWK. (n,e SA). . . . . _____

❏ *Buteogallus anthracinus.* COMMON BLACK-HAWK. (sw US-n SA). . . . _____
　　___*B. (a.) anthracinus.* COMMON BLACK-HAWK. (sp)
　　___*B. (a.) gundlachii.* CUBAN BLACK-HAWK. (Cuba)

❏ *Buteogallus subtilis.* MANGROVE BLACK-HAWK. (Pac MA, nw SA). . . _____

❏ *Buteogallus urubitinga.* GREAT BLACK-HAWK. (MA, SA). . . . . _____

❏ *Buteogallus meridionalis.* SAVANNA HAWK. (Pan, SA). . . . . _____

❏ *Parabuteo unicinctus.* HARRIS'S HAWK. (MA, SA). . . . . _____

❏ *Busarellus nigricollis.* BLACK-COLLARED HAWK. (MA, SA). . . . . _____

❏ *Geranoaetus melanoleucus.* BLACK-CHESTED BUZZARD-EAGLE. (SA). . _____

❏ *Harpyhaliaetus solitarius.* SOLITARY EAGLE. (MA, w,n SA). . . . . _____

❏ *Harpyhaliaetus coronatus.* CROWNED EAGLE. (sc SA). . . . . _____

❏ *Asturina plagiata.* GREY HAWK. (MA). . . . . _____

❏ *Asturina nitida.* GREY-LINED HAWK. (s CA, SA). . . . . _____

❏ *Buteo magnirostris.* ROADSIDE HAWK. (MA, SA). . . . . _____

❏ *Buteo lineatus.* RED-SHOULDERED HAWK. (US, Mex). . . . . _____

❑ *Buteo ridgwayi.* RIDGWAY'S HAWK. (Hisp). . . . . _____

❑ *Buteo platypterus.* BROAD-WINGED HAWK. (e NA, W Indies; ◊-SA). . . _____

❑ *Buteo leucorrhous.* WHITE-RUMPED HAWK. (SA). . . . . _____

❑ *Buteo brachyurus.* SHORT-TAILED HAWK. (pen Fla, MA, SA). . . . . _____

❑ *Buteo albigula.* WHITE-THROATED HAWK. (mts w SA). . . . . _____

❑ *Buteo swainsoni.* SWAINSON'S HAWK. (w NA, n Mex; ◊ s CA, SA). . . _____

❑ *Buteo albicaudatus.* WHITE-TAILED HAWK. (MA, SA). . . . . _____

❑ *Buteo galapagoensis.* GALAPAGOS HAWK. (Galap). . . . . _____

❑ *Buteo polyosoma.* RED-BACKED HAWK. (mts w,s SA, JF). . . . . _____
   ___*B. (p.) polyosoma.* RED-BACKED HAWK. (w,s SA)
   ___*B. (p.) exsul.* JUAN FERNANDEZ HAWK. (JF)

❑ *Buteo poecilochrous.* PUNA HAWK. (Andes w SA). . . . . _____

❑ *Buteo albonotatus.* ZONE-TAILED HAWK. (sw US, MA, SA). . . . . _____

❑ *Buteo solitarius.* HAWAIIAN HAWK. (e Haw Is). . . . . _____

❑ *Buteo jamaicensis.* RED-TAILED HAWK. (NA, MA, W Indies). . . . . _____
   ___*B. (j.) jamaicensis.* RED-TAILED HAWK. (sp)
   ___*B. (j.) harlani.* HARLAN'S HAWK. (Alas, w Can; ◊-sc US)

❑ *Buteo ventralis.* RUFOUS-TAILED HAWK. (s SA). . . . . _____

❑ *Buteo buteo.* COMMON BUZZARD. (Palea; ◊-s Afr, s,se Asia). . . . . _____
   ___*B. (b.) buteo.* COMMON BUZZARD. (w Palea; ◊-w,nw Afr)
   ___*B. (b.) vulpinus.* WESTERN STEPPE-BUZZARD. (nw,c Eura; ◊-s Afr, n India)
   ___*B. (b.) menetriesi.* EASTERN STEPPE-BUZZARD. (mts sc Eura)
   ___*B. (b.) japonicus.* JAPANESE BUZZARD. (e,ec Asia; ◊-se Asia)

❑ *Buteo oreophilus.* MOUNTAIN BUZZARD. (mts e,s Afr). . . . . _____

❑ *Buteo brachypterus.* MADAGASCAR BUZZARD. (Mad). . . . . _____

❑ *Buteo rufinus.* LONG-LEGGED BUZZARD. (s,sc Palea; ◊-Afr, s Asia). . . _____

❑ *Buteo hemilasius.* UPLAND BUZZARD. (mts e Asia; ◊-s Asia). . . . . . . _____

❑ *Buteo regalis.* FERRUGINOUS HAWK. (w NA; ◊-n Mex). . . . . _____

❑ *Buteo lagopus.* ROUGH-LEGGED HAWK. (n Hol; ◊-s Euro, s US). . . . . . _____

❑ *Buteo auguralis.* RED-NECKED BUZZARD. (n,wc Afr). . . . . _____

❑ *Buteo augur.* AUGUR BUZZARD. (mts e,sc Afr). . . . . _____

❑ *Buteo archeri.* ARCHER'S BUZZARD. (mts n Som). . . . . _____

❑ *Buteo rufofuscus.* JACKAL BUZZARD. (s Afr). . . . . _____

❑ *Morphnus guianensis.* CRESTED EAGLE. (CA, SA). . . . . _____

❑ *Harpia harpyja.* HARPY EAGLE. (MS, SA). . . . . _____

❑ *Harpyopsis novaeguineae.* NEW GUINEA EAGLE. (NG). . . . . _____

❑ *Pithecophaga jefferyi.* GREAT PHILIPPINE EAGLE. (Phil). . . . . _____

❑ *Ictinaetus malayensis.* BLACK EAGLE. (s Asia-Moluc)............ _____

❑ *Aquila pomarina.* LESSER SPOTTED EAGLE. (e Euro-India; ◊-s Afr)... _____

❑ *Aquila clanga.* GREATER SPOTTED EAGLE. (c Eura-s Asia; ◊-n Afr)... _____

❑ *Aquila rapax.* TAWNY EAGLE. (Afr, s Asia).................... _____
   ___*A. (r.) rapax.* AFRICAN TAWNY-EAGLE. (Afr)
   ___*A. (r.) vindhiana.* ASIAN TAWNY-EAGLE. (s Asia)

❑ *Aquila nipalensis.* STEPPE EAGLE. (wc Eura, c Asia; ◊-e Afr, s Asia) . _____
   ___*A. (n.) orientalis.* WESTERN STEPPE-EAGLE. (wc Eura; ◊-e Afr)
   ___*A. (n.) nipalensis.* EASTERN STEPPE-EAGLE. (c Asia; ◊-s Asia)

❑ *Aquila adalberti.* ADALBERT'S EAGLE. (sw Euro)............... _____

❑ *Aquila heliaca.* IMPERIAL EAGLE. (sc Eura; ◊-ne Afr, se Asia)....... _____

❑ *Aquila gurneyi.* GURNEY'S EAGLE. (Moluc-NG)................. _____

❑ *Aquila chrysaetos.* GOLDEN EAGLE. (Hol, n Mex; ◊-n Afr, c Mex).... _____

❑ *Aquila audax.* WEDGE-TAILED EAGLE. (s NG, Aust)............. _____

❑ *Aquila verreauxii.* VERREAUX'S EAGLE. (Afr reg)............... _____

❑ *Aquila wahlbergi.* WAHLBERG'S EAGLE. (Afr)................... _____

❑ *Hieraaetus fasciatus.* BONELLI'S EAGLE. (s Palea, s Asia, L Sunda)... _____

❑ *Hieraaetus spilogaster.* AFRICAN HAWK-EAGLE. (w,e,s Afr)........ _____

❑ *Hieraaetus pennatus.* BOOTED EAGLE. (s,ec Palea; S Afr; ◊-se Asia) . _____

❑ *Hieraaetus morphnoides.* LITTLE EAGLE. (c,e NG, Aust).......... _____

❑ *Hieraaetus ayresii.* AYRES'S HAWK-EAGLE. (Afr)............... _____

❑ *Hieraaetus kienerii.* RUFOUS-BELLIED EAGLE. (s Asia-n,c Phil)...... _____

❑ *Polemaetus bellicosus.* MARTIAL EAGLE. (Afr)................. _____

❑ *Spizastur melanoleucus.* BLACK-AND-WHITE HAWK-EAGLE. (MA, SA) _____

❑ *Lophaetus occipitalis.* LONG-CRESTED EAGLE. (Afr)............. _____

❑ *Spizaetus africanus.* CASSIN'S HAWK-EAGLE. (w,c Afr)........... _____

❑ *Spizaetus cirrhatus.* CHANGEABLE HAWK-EAGLE. (s Asia-Indon)..... _____
   ___*S. (c.) limnaeetus.* CHANGEABLE HAWK-EAGLE. (s Asia-Phil)
   ___*S. (c.) cirrhatus.* CRESTED HAWK-EAGLE. (pen India)
   ___*S. (c.) floris.* SUNDA HAWK-EAGLE. (L Sunda)

❑ *Spizaetus nipalensis.* MOUNTAIN HAWK-EAGLE. (s,e Asia; ◊-se Asia) . _____

❑ *Spizaetus alboniger.* BLYTH'S HAWK-EAGLE. (mts se Asia)......... _____

❑ *Spizaetus bartelsi.* JAVAN HAWK-EAGLE. (Java)................ _____

❑ *Spizaetus lanceolatus.* SULAWESI HAWK-EAGLE. (Sulaw).......... _____

❑ *Spizaetus philippensis.* PHILIPPINE HAWK-EAGLE. (Phil)........... _____

❑ *Spizaetus nanus.* WALLACE'S HAWK-EAGLE. (se Asia)............ _____

❑ *Spizaetus tyrannus.* BLACK HAWK-EAGLE. (MA, SA)............. _____

❑ *Spizaetus ornatus.* ORNATE HAWK-EAGLE. (MA, SA). . . . . _____

❑ *Stephanoaetus coronatus.* CROWNED HAWK-EAGLE. (Afr). . . . . _____

❑ *Oroaetus isidori.* BLACK-AND-CHESTNUT EAGLE. (mts w,n SA). . . . . . . _____

Family **Sagittariidae** [1/1]

❑ *Sagittarius serpentarius.* SECRETARYBIRD. (Afr). . . . . _____

Parvorder FALCONIDA [10/63]
Family **Falconidae** [10/63]

❑ *Daptrius ater.* BLACK CARACARA. (Amaz). . . . . _____

❑ *Daptrius americanus.* RED-THROATED CARACARA. (MA, SA). . . . . _____

❑ *Phalcoboenus carunculatus.* CARUNCULATED CARACARA. (w SA). . . . _____

❑ *Phalcoboenus megalopterus.* MOUNTAIN CARACARA. (Andes sw SA). _____

❑ *Phalcoboenus albogularis.* WHITE-THROATED CARACARA. (s SA). . . . _____

❑ *Phalcoboenus australis.* STRIATED CARACARA. (is s SA). . . . . _____

    Polyborus lutosus. GUADALUPE CARACARA. (†Guadalupe). . . . . _____

❑ *Polyborus plancus.* CRESTED CARACARA. (s US, MA, SA). . . . . _____
   ___*P. (p.) cheriway.* CRESTED CARACARA. (s US, MA, n,nc SA)
   ___*P. (p.) plancus.* SOUTHERN CARACARA. (sc,s SA)

❑ *Milvago chimachima.* YELLOW-HEADED CARACARA. (CR, Pan, SA) . _____

❑ *Milvago chimango.* CHIMANGO CARACARA. (sc,s SA). . . . . _____

❑ *Herpetotheres cachinnans.* LAUGHING FALCON. (MA, SA). . . . . _____

❑ *Micrastur ruficollis.* BARRED FOREST-FALCON. (MA, SA). . . . . _____

❑ *Micrastur plumbeus.* PLUMBEOUS FOREST-FALCON. (Andes nw SA) . _____

❑ *Micrastur gilvicollis.* LINED FOREST-FALCON. (nc,e SA). . . . . _____

❑ *Micrastur mirandollei.* SLATY-BACKED FOREST-FALCON. (s CA-Amaz)_____

❑ *Micrastur semitorquatus.* COLLARED FOREST-FALCON. (MA, SA). . . . _____

❑ *Micrastur buckleyi.* BUCKLEY'S FOREST-FALCON. (w Amaz). . . . . _____

❑ *Spiziapteryx circumcinctus.* SPOT-WINGED FALCONET. (sc SA). . . . . . _____

❑ *Polihierax semitorquatus.* PYGMY FALCON. (ne,s Afr). . . . . _____

❑ *Polihierax insignis.* WHITE-RUMPED FALCON. (se Asia). . . . . _____

❑ *Microhierax caerulescens.* COLLARED FALCONET. (s,se Asia). . . . . . . _____

❑ *Microhierax fringillarius.* BLACK-THIGHED FALCONET. (se Asia). . . . . _____

❑ *Microhierax latifrons.* WHITE-FRONTED FALCONET. (n Born). . . . . . . _____

❑ *Microhierax erythrogenys.* PHILIPPINE FALCONET. (Phil). . . . . _____

❑ *Microhierax melanoleucus.* PIED FALCONET. (s Asia). . . . . _____

❑ *Falco berigora.* BROWN FALCON. (c,e NG, Bism, Aust). . . . . _____

❑ *Falco naumanni.* LESSER KESTREL. (s Palea; ◊-s Afr, s Asia). . . . . _____

❑ *Falco tinnunculus.* COMMON KESTREL. (Eura-Afr; ◊-se Asia, Phil). . . _____

❑ *Falco newtoni.* MADAGASCAR KESTREL. (Mad, Ald). . . . . _____

❑ *Falco punctatus.* MAURITIUS KESTREL. (Maur). . . . . _____

❑ *Falco araea.* SEYCHELLES KESTREL. (Seyc). . . . . _____

❑ *Falco moluccensis.* SPOTTED KESTREL. (Indon). . . . . _____

❑ *Falco cenchroides.* AUSTRALIAN KESTREL. (Chris-c NG, Aust; ◊-NZ). _____

❑ *Falco sparverius.* AMERICAN KESTREL. (NA, MA, W Indies, SA). . . . . _____

❑ *Falco rupicoloides.* GREATER KESTREL. (ne,s Afr). . . . . _____

❑ *Falco alopex.* FOX KESTREL. (subsah Afr). _____

❑ *Falco ardosiaceus.* GREY KESTREL. (Afr). _____

❑ *Falco dickinsoni.* DICKINSON'S KESTREL. (s,ce Afr). . . . . _____

❑ *Falco zoniventris.* BANDED KESTREL. (Mad). . . . . _____

❑ *Falco chicquera.* RED-NECKED FALCON. (Afr, s Asia). . . . . _____

❑ *Falco vespertinus.* RED-FOOTED FALCON. (c Eura; ◊ Afr). . . . . _____

❑ *Falco amurensis.* AMUR FALCON. (e Asia; ◊ e,s Afr, s,se Asia). . . . . . . _____

❑ *Falco eleonorae.* ELEONORA'S FALCON. (sw Palea; ◊-e Afr, Mad). . . . . _____

❑ *Falco concolor.* SOOTY FALCON. (ne Afr reg; ◊ e,s Afr, Mad). . . . . . . _____

❑ *Falco femoralis.* APLOMADO FALCON. (MA, SA). . . . . _____

❑ *Falco columbarius.* MERLIN. (Hol; ◊-nw Afr, Medit, s,se Asia, n SA). _____

❑ *Falco rufigularis.* BAT FALCON. (MA, SA). _____

❑ *Falco subbuteo.* EURASIAN HOBBY. (Palea; ◊-s Afr, Indon). . . . . _____

❑ *Falco cuvierii.* AFRICAN HOBBY. (w,c,e,se Afr). . . . . _____

❑ *Falco severus.* ORIENTAL HOBBY. (s Asia-Phil, Wall, NG, Solom). . . . _____

❑ *Falco longipennis.* AUSTRALIAN HOBBY. (Aust; ◊-Wall, NG, Bism). . . _____

❑ *Falco novaeseelandiae.* NEW ZEALAND FALCON. (NZ, Auck). . . . . _____

❑ *Falco hypoleucos.* GREY FALCON. (int Aust). . . . . _____

❑ *Falco subniger.* BLACK FALCON. (Aust). . . . . _____

❑ *Falco biarmicus.* LANNER FALCON. (w Palea, Afr). . . . . _____

❑ *Falco jugger.* LAGGAR FALCON. (sc Asia). _____

❑ *Falco cherrug.* SAKER FALCON. (c Eura; ◊-ne Afr, n India). . . . . _____

❑ *Falco rusticolus.* GYRFALCON. (n Hol; ◊-w,n Euro, c Asia, n US). . . . . _____

❑ *Falco mexicanus.* PRAIRIE FALCON. (w NA; ◊-c Mex). . . . . _____

❑ *Falco peregrinus.* PEREGRINE FALCON. (cosm). . . . . _____

❑ *Falco pelegrinoides.* BARBARY FALCON. (n Afr, s Palea). . . . . _____

❑ *Falco deiroleucus.* ORANGE-BREASTED FALCON. (MA, SA). . . . . _____

❑ *Falco fasciinucha.* TEITA FALCON. (e,se Afr). . . . . _____

Infraorder CICONIIDES [92/355]
Parvorder PODICIPEDIDA [6/22]
Family **Podicipedidae** [6/22]

❑ *Rollandia rolland.* WHITE-TUFTED GREBE. (s SA, Falk). . . . . _____
___*R. (r.) chilensis.* CHILEAN GREBE. (s SA)
___*R. (r.) rolland.* FALKLAND GREBE. (Falk)

❑ *Rollandia microptera.* SHORT-WINGED GREBE. (Andes sw SA). . . . . . . _____

❑ *Tachybaptus ruficollis.* LITTLE GREBE. (Eura-s Afr, Indon, Solom). . . _____

❑ *Tachybaptus novaehollandiae.* AUSTRALASIAN GREBE. (Aust reg). . . . _____

❑ *Tachybaptus rufolavatus.* ALAOTRA GREBE. (ec Mad). . . . . _____

❑ *Tachybaptus pelzelnii.* MADAGASCAR GREBE. (Mad). . . . . _____

❑ *Tachybaptus dominicus.* LEAST GREBE. (c Tex, MA, n W Indies, SA). . _____

❑ *Podilymbus podiceps.* PIED-BILLED GREBE. (Haw Is; NA-SA). . . . . . . _____

❑ *Podilymbus gigas.* ATITLAN GREBE. (†c Guat). . . . . _____

❑ *Poliocephalus poliocephalus.* HOARY-HEADED GREBE. (Aust, s NZ) . _____

❑ *Poliocephalus rufopectus.* NEW ZEALAND GREBE. (NZ). . . . . _____

❑ *Podiceps major.* GREAT GREBE. (s SA). . . . . _____

❑ *Podiceps grisegena.* RED-NECKED GREBE. (Hol; ◊-s Eura, c US). . . . . _____

❑ *Podiceps cristatus.* GREAT CRESTED GREBE. (Palea-s Afr, Aust, NZ) . _____

❑ *Podiceps auritus.* HORNED GREBE. (n Hol; ◊-s Euro, s Asia, s US). . . . _____

❑ *Podiceps nigricollis.* BLACK-NECKED GREBE. (Hol-Afr; ◊-s Asia, MA). _____

❑ *Podiceps andinus.* COLOMBIAN GREBE. (†Andes ec Colom). . . . . _____

❑ *Podiceps occipitalis.* SILVERY GREBE. (Andes). . . . . _____
___*P. (o.) juninensis.* JUNIN GREBE. (w SA)
___*P. (o.) occipitalis.* SILVERY GREBE. (s SA)

❑ *Podiceps taczanowskii.* PUNA GREBE. (Andes c Peru). . . . . _____

❑ *Podiceps gallardoi.* HOODED GREBE. (s Argen). . . . . _____

❑ *Aechmophorus occidentalis.* WESTERN GREBE. (w NA, n Mex). . . . . . _____

❑ *Aechmophorus clarkii.* CLARK'S GREBE. (w NA). . . . . _____

Parvorder PHAETHONTIDA [1/3]
Family **Phaethontidae** [1/3]

❑ *Phaethon aethereus.* RED-BILLED TROPICBIRD. (trop is). . . . . _____

❑ *Phaethon rubricauda.* RED-TAILED TROPICBIRD. (trop Pac, Indian is) . _____

❑ *Phaethon lepturus.* WHITE-TAILED TROPICBIRD. (trop is). . . . . _____

Parvorder SULIDA [5/50]
Superfamily SULOIDEA[4/13]
Family **Sulidae** [3/9]

❏ *Papasula abbotti.* ABBOTT'S BOOBY. (Chris; ◊ Indian O)............ _____

❏ *Morus bassanus.* NORTHERN GANNET. (n Atl O)................. _____

❏ *Morus capensis.* CAPE GANNET. (is s Afr; ◊-trop Afr oceans)........ _____

❏ *Morus serrator.* AUSTRALIAN GANNET. (se Aust, NZ)............. _____

❏ *Sula nebouxii.* BLUE-FOOTED BOOBY. (Pac MA, SA, Galap)........ _____

❏ *Sula variegata.* PERUVIAN BOOBY. (is Pac SA)................... _____

❏ *Sula dactylatra.* MASKED BOOBY. (trop is; ◊ trop oceans).......... _____

❏ *Sula sula.* RED-FOOTED BOOBY. (trop is; ◊ trop oceans)............ _____

❏ *Sula leucogaster.* BROWN BOOBY. (trop is; ◊ trop oceans).......... _____

Family **Anhingidae** [1/4]

❏ *Anhinga anhinga.* ANHINGA. (se US, MA, Cuba, s L Ant, SA)....... _____

❏ *Anhinga rufa.* AFRICAN DARTER. (Afr, Mad)................... _____

❏ *Anhinga melanogaster.* ORIENTAL DARTER. (s Asia-Phil).......... _____

❏ *Anhinga novaehollandiae.* AUSTRALIAN DARTER. (NG, Aust)....... _____

Superfamily PHALACROCORACOIDEA [1/37]
Family **Phalacrocoracidae** [1/37]

❏ *Phalacrocorax africanus.* LONG-TAILED CORMORANT. (Afr, Mad).... _____

❏ *Phalacrocorax coronatus.* CROWNED CORMORANT. (sw Afr)........ _____

❏ *Phalacrocorax pygmeus.* PYGMY CORMORANT. (sc Eura).......... _____

❏ *Phalacrocorax niger.* LITTLE CORMORANT. (s,se Asia)............. _____

❏ *Phalacrocorax melanoleucos.* LITTLE PIED CORMORANT. (Indon-NZ). _____
     ___*P. (m.) melanoleucos.* LITTLE PIED CORMORANT. (Indon-sw Pac)
     ___*P. (m.) brevirostris.* WHITE-THROATED CORMORANT. (NZ)

  Phalacrocorax perspicillatus. PALLAS'S CORMORANT. (†Comm)...... _____

❏ *Phalacrocorax penicillatus.* BRANDT'S CORMORANT. (Alas-nw Mex) . _____

❏ *Phalacrocorax harrisi.* FLIGHTLESS CORMORANT. (Galap)......... _____

❏ *Phalacrocorax neglectus.* BANK CORMORANT. (sw Afr)........... _____

❏ *Phalacrocorax fuscescens.* BLACK-FACED CORMORANT. (s Aust)..... _____

❏ *Phalacrocorax brasilianus.* NEOTROPIC CORMORANT. (cs US-SA).... _____

❏ *Phalacrocorax auritus.* DOUBLE-CRESTED CORMORANT. (NA-n Mex). _____

❏ *Phalacrocorax fuscicollis.* INDIAN CORMORANT. (s,se Asia)........ _____

❏ *Phalacrocorax varius.* PIED CORMORANT. (Aust, NZ)............. _____

❑ *Phalacrocorax sulcirostris.* LITTLE BLACK CORMORANT. (Aust reg). . . _____

❑ *Phalacrocorax carbo.* GREAT CORMORANT. (ne NA, Eura-Afr, NZ). . . _____
   ___*P. (c.) carbo.* GREAT CORMORANT. (sp)
   ___*P. (c.) lucidus.* WHITE-BREASTED CORMORANT. (Afr)

❑ *Phalacrocorax capillatus.* JAPANESE CORMORANT. (e Asia). . . . . _____

❑ *Phalacrocorax nigrogularis.* SOCOTRA CORMORANT. (is nw Indian O). _____

❑ *Phalacrocorax capensis.* CAPE CORMORANT. (sw Afr). . . . . _____

❑ *Phalacrocorax bougainvillii.* GUANAY CORMORANT. (w,s SA). . . . . . . _____

❑ *Phalacrocorax verrucosus.* KERGUELEN SHAG. (Kerguelen). . . . . _____

❑ *Phalacrocorax atriceps.* IMPERIAL SHAG. (s SA, is s Indian O). . . . . . . _____

❑ *Phalacrocorax bransfieldensis.* ANTARCTIC SHAG. (subant is, Ant). . . _____

❑ *Phalacrocorax georgianus.* SOUTH GEORGIA SHAG. (subant is). . . . . . _____

❑ *Phalacrocorax campbelli.* CAMPBELL ISLAND SHAG. (Campbell). . . . . _____

❑ *Phalacrocorax carunculatus.* ROUGH-FACED SHAG. (is c NZ). . . . . _____

❑ *Phalacrocorax chalconotus.* BRONZE SHAG. (is s NZ). . . . . _____

❑ *Phalacrocorax onslowi.* CHATHAM ISLANDS SHAG. (Chatham). . . . . . . _____

❑ *Phalacrocorax colensoi.* AUCKLAND ISLANDS SHAG. (Auck). . . . . _____

❑ *Phalacrocorax ranfurlyi.* BOUNTY ISLANDS SHAG. (Bounty). . . . . _____

❑ *Phalacrocorax magellanicus.* ROCK SHAG. (s SA). . . . . _____

❑ *Phalacrocorax urile.* RED-FACED CORMORANT. (is n Pac O). . . . . _____

❑ *Phalacrocorax pelagicus.* PELAGIC CORMORANT. (n Pac-nw Mex). . . . _____

❑ *Phalacrocorax aristotelis.* EUROPEAN SHAG. (w Palea). . . . . _____

❑ *Phalacrocorax gaimardi.* RED-LEGGED CORMORANT. (sw,s SA). . . . . . _____

❑ *Phalacrocorax punctatus.* SPOTTED SHAG. (NZ). . . . . _____
   ___*P. (p.) punctatus.* SPOTTED SHAG. (sp)
   ___*P. (p.) oliveri.* BLUE SHAG. (sw NZ)

❑ *Phalacrocorax featherstoni.* PITT ISLAND SHAG. (Chatham). . . . . _____

Parvorder CICONIIDA [80/280]
Superfamily ARDEOIDEA [21/65]
Family **Ardeidae** [21/65]

❑ *Syrigma sibilatrix.* WHISTLING HERON. (ne,sc SA). . . . . _____

❑ *Egretta rufescens.* REDDISH EGRET. (Mex, se US, G Ant; ◊-n SA). . . . _____

❑ *Egretta vinaceigula.* SLATY EGRET. (sc Afr). . . . . _____

❑ *Egretta ardesiaca.* BLACK HERON. (Afr, Mad). . . . . _____

❑ *Egretta tricolor.* TRICOLORED HERON. (s US, MA, SA). . . . . _____

❑ *Egretta novaehollandiae.* WHITE-FACED HERON. (Aust reg-Loy). . . . . _____

❏ *Egretta caerulea.* LITTLE BLUE HERON. (US, MA, W Indies, SA)..... _____

❏ *Egretta garzetta.* LITTLE EGRET. (Old World)................. _____

❏ *Egretta gularis.* WESTERN REEF-EGRET. (w,ne Afr, s Asia)......... _____
___*E. (g.) gularis.* WEST AFRICAN REEF-EGRET. (w Afr)
___*E. (g.) schistacea.* ARABIAN REEF-EGRET. (ne Afr, s Asia)

❏ *Egretta dimorpha.* DIMORPHIC EGRET. (ne Afr, Mad reg).......... _____

❏ *Egretta thula.* SNOWY EGRET. (US, MA, W Indies, SA)........... _____

❏ *Egretta eulophotes.* CHINESE EGRET. (e Asia; ◊-Indon, Phil)........ _____

❏ *Egretta sacra.* PACIFIC REEF-EGRET. (se Asia-Oceania, Aust, NZ).... _____

❏ *Pilherodius pileatus.* CAPPED HERON. (e Pan, SA)............... _____

❏ *Ardea cinerea.* GREY HERON. (Palea-Afr, Mad, se Asia, L Sunda).... _____
___*A. (c.) cinerea.* GREY HERON. (sp)
___*A. (c.) monicae.* MAURITANIAN HERON. (w Afr)

❏ *Ardea herodias.* GREAT BLUE HERON. (NA-Mex, G Ant, Galap, n SA). _____
___*A. (h.) herodias.* GREAT BLUE HERON. (NA-Galap; ◊-n SA)
___*A. (h.) occidentalis.* GREAT WHITE HERON. (s Fla-n SA)

❏ *Ardea cocoi.* COCOI HERON. (e Pan, SA)..................... _____

❏ *Ardea pacifica.* PACIFIC HERON. (Aust; ◊- s NG)................ _____

❏ *Ardea melanocephala.* BLACK-HEADED HERON. (Afr)............. _____

❏ *Ardea humbloti.* HUMBLOT'S HERON. (Mad)................... _____

❏ *Ardea goliath.* GOLIATH HERON. (Afr, sw Asia)................. _____

❏ *Ardea insignis.* WHITE-BELLIED HERON. (Himal)................ _____

❏ *Ardea sumatrana.* GREAT-BILLED HERON. (se Asia-Phil, NG, n Aust). _____

❏ *Ardea purpurea.* PURPLE HERON. (Palea-Afr, Mad, Indon, Phil)...... _____
___*A. (p.) purpurea.* PURPLE HERON. (sp)
___*A. (p.) bournei.* CAPE VERDE HERON. (C Verde)

❏ *Ardea picata.* PIED HERON. (Sulaw, n Aust; ◊-Wall-NG)........... _____

❏ *Casmerodius albus.* GREAT EGRET. (cosm).................... _____
___*C. (a.) albus.* GREAT EGRET. (Old World)
___*C. (a.) egretta.* AMERICAN EGRET. (NA-SA)

❏ *Mesophoyx intermedia.* INTERMEDIATE EGRET. (Afr; s Asia-Aust).... _____
___*M. (i.) brachyrhyncha.* YELLOW-BILLED EGRET. (Afr)
___*M. (i.) intermedia.* LESSER EGRET. (s,se Asia; ◊-Phil)
___*M. (i.) plumifera.* PLUMED EGRET. (Aust)

❏ *Bubulcus ibis.* CATTLE EGRET. (cosm)....................... _____
___*B. (i.) ibis.* COMMON CATTLE-EGRET. (Palea, Afr, NA-SA)
___*B. (i.) coromanda.* EASTERN CATTLE-EGRET. (s,e Asia-Aust, sw Oceania)

❏ *Ardeola ralloides.* SQUACCO HERON. (s Palea, Afr, Mad).......... _____

❏ *Ardeola grayii.* INDIAN POND-HERON. (s Asia)................. _____

❏ *Ardeola bacchus.* CHINESE POND-HERON. (s,se Asia)............. _____

❑ *Ardeola speciosa.* JAVAN POND-HERON. (se Asia-S Phil, L Sunda). . . . _____

❑ *Ardeola idae.* MADAGASCAR POND-HERON. (Mad, Ald; ◊-c,e Afr). . . . _____

❑ *Ardeola rufiventris.* RUFOUS-BELLIED HERON. (e,se Afr). . . . . _____

❑ *Butorides striatus.* STRIATED HERON. (Pan-SA, Old World). . . . . _____

❑ *Butorides virescens.* GREEN HERON. (NA, MA, W Indies; ◊-n SA). . . . _____

❑ *Butorides sundevalli.* GALAPAGOS HERON. (Galap). . . . . _____

❑ *Agamia agami.* AGAMI HERON. (MA, SA). . . . . _____

❑ *Nyctanassa violacea.* YELLOW-CROWNED NIGHT-HERON. (s US-SA) . _____

❑ *Nycticorax nycticorax.* BLACK-CROWNED NIGHT-HERON. (cosm). . . . . _____

❑ *Nycticorax caledonicus.* RUFOUS NIGHT-HERON. (Indon, sw Pac-Aust). _____

❑ *Gorsachius leuconotus.* WHITE-BACKED NIGHT-HERON. (Afr). . . . . . . _____

❑ *Gorsachius magnificus.* WHITE-EARED NIGHT-HERON. (mts se China). . _____

❑ *Gorsachius goisagi.* JAPANESE NIGHT-HERON. (s Japan; ◊-se Asia). . . . _____

❑ *Gorsachius melanolophus.* MALAYAN NIGHT-HERON. (s Asia-Phil). . . _____

❑ *Cochlearius cochlearia.* BOAT-BILLED HERON. (MA, SA). . . . . _____
    ___*C. (c.) zeledoni.* NORTHERN BOAT-BILLED HERON. (n MA)
    ___*C. (c.) cochlearia.* SOUTHERN BOAT-BILLED HERON. (s MA, SA)

❑ *Tigrisoma mexicanum.* BARE-THROATED TIGER-HERON. (MA-nw SA). _____

❑ *Tigrisoma fasciatum.* FASCIATED TIGER-HERON. (s CA, SA). . . . . _____
    ___*T. (f.) salmoni.* SALMON'S TIGER-HERON. (s CA, w,n SA)
    ___*T. (f.) fasciatum.* FASCIATED TIGER-HERON. (se SA)

❑ *Tigrisoma lineatum.* RUFESCENT TIGER-HERON. (CA, SA). . . . . _____
    ___*T. (l.) lineatum.* LINEATED TIGER-HERON. (CA, n,c SA)
    ___*T. (l.) marmoratum.* BANDED TIGER-HERON. (sc,e SA)

❑ *Zonerodius heliosylus.* FOREST BITTERN. (Aru-NG). . . . . _____

❑ *Tigriornis leucolophus.* WHITE-CRESTED BITTERN. (w,c Afr). . . . . . . _____

❑ *Zebrilus undulatus.* ZIGZAG HERON. (n,c SA). . . . . _____

❑ *Ixobrychus involucris.* STRIPE-BACKED BITTERN. (n,sc SA). . . . . _____

❑ *Ixobrychus minutus.* LITTLE BITTERN. (Palea, Afr, Mad; ◊-s Asia). . . . _____

❑ *Ixobrychus sinensis.* YELLOW BITTERN. (s,e Asia-Indon, w Oceania) . _____

❑ *Ixobrychus novaezelandiae.* BLACK-BACKED BITTERN. (Aust; ◊-NZ) . _____

❑ *Ixobrychus exilis.* LEAST BITTERN. (NA, MA, W Indies, SA). . . . . _____

❑ *Ixobrychus eurhythmus.* SCHRENCK'S BITTERN. (e Asia; ◊-se Asia). . . _____

❑ *Ixobrychus cinnamomeus.* CINNAMON BITTERN. (s,e Asia-Phil). . . . . . _____

❑ *Ixobrychus sturmii.* DWARF BITTERN. (Afr). _____

❑ *Dupetor flavicollis.* BLACK BITTERN. (s Asia-Phil, Solom, Aust). . . . . _____

❑ *Botaurus lentiginosus.* AMERICAN BITTERN. (NA-c Mex; ◊-CA). . . . . _____

❏ *Botaurus pinnatus.* PINNATED BITTERN. (MA, SA)............... _____

❏ *Botaurus stellaris.* GREAT BITTERN. (Palea, Afr; ◊-se Asia)......... _____
   ___*B. (s.) stellaris.* EURASIAN BITTERN. (Palea; ◊-se Asia)
   ___*B. (s.) capensis.* AFRICAN BITTERN. (Afr)

❏ *Botaurus poiciloptilus.* AUSTRALASIAN BITTERN. (Aust, NZ, sw Pac) . _____

Superfamily SCOPOIDEA [1/1]
Family **Scopidae** [1/1]

❏ *Scopus umbretta.* HAMERKOP. (Afr, Mad)...................... _____

Superfamily PHOENICOPTEROIDEA [1/5]
Family **Phoenicopteridae** [1/5]

❏ *Phoenicopterus ruber.* GREATER FLAMINGO. (trop OW, Amer)...... _____
   ___*P. (r.) roseus.* GREATER FLAMINGO. (trop OW)
   ___*P. (r.) ruber.* AMERICAN FLAMINGO. (trop Amer)

❏ *Phoenicopterus chilensis.* CHILEAN FLAMINGO. (Andes s SA)...... _____

❏ *Phoenicopterus minor.* LESSER FLAMINGO. (Afr)................ _____

❏ *Phoenicopterus andinus.* ANDEAN FLAMINGO. (Andes sw SA)...... _____

❏ *Phoenicopterus jamesi.* PUNA FLAMINGO. (Andes sw SA).......... _____

Superfamily THRESKIORNITHOIDEA [14/33]
Family **Threskiornithidae** [14/33]

❏ *Eudocimus albus.* WHITE IBIS. (se US, MA, G Ant, n SA)......... _____

❏ *Eudocimus ruber.* SCARLET IBIS. (n,e SA)..................... _____

❏ *Phimosus infuscatus.* WHISPERING IBIS. (n,sc SA).............. _____

❏ *Plegadis falcinellus.* GLOSSY IBIS. (trop OW, Amer)............. _____

❏ *Plegadis chihi.* WHITE-FACED IBIS. (w NA, Mex, sc SA; ◊-CA)...... _____

❏ *Plegadis ridgwayi.* PUNA IBIS. (Andes sw SA)................. _____

❏ *Cercibis oxycerca.* SHARP-TAILED IBIS. (nc SA)................ _____

❏ *Theristicus caerulescens.* PLUMBEOUS IBIS. (sc SA)............. _____

❏ *Theristicus caudatus.* BUFF-NECKED IBIS. (SA)................. _____

❏ *Theristicus branickii.* ANDEAN IBIS. (Andes wc SA)............. _____

❏ *Theristicus melanopis.* BLACK-FACED IBIS. (sw,s SA)............. _____

❏ *Mesembrinibis cayennensis.* GREEN IBIS. (Pan, SA)............. _____

❏ *Bostrychia hagedash.* HADADA IBIS. (Afr)...................... _____

❏ *Bostrychia carunculata.* WATTLED IBIS. (mts Eth)............... _____

❏ *Bostrychia olivacea.* OLIVE IBIS. (trop Afr)................... _____
   ___*B. (o.) olivacea.* OLIVE IBIS. (sp)
   ___*B. (o.) bocagei.* SAO TOME IBIS. (ST)
   ___*B. (o.) rothschildi.* PRINCIPE IBIS. (Prín)

❑ *Bostrychia rara.* SPOT-BREASTED IBIS. (w,c Afr). . . . . _____

❑ *Geronticus eremita.* WALDRAPP. (sw Palea). . . . . _____

❑ *Geronticus calvus.* BALD IBIS. (mts S Afr). . . . . _____

❑ *Lophotibis cristata.* WHITE-WINGED IBIS. (Mad). . . . . _____

❑ *Threskiornis aethiopicus.* SACRED IBIS. (Afr, Iraq, Mad). . . . . _____
   ___**T. (a.) aethiopicus.* SACRED IBIS. (Afr, Iraq)
   ___**T. (a.) bernieri.* MADAGASCAR IBIS. (Mad)

❑ *Threskiornis melanocephalus.* BLACK-HEADED IBIS. (s,se Asia). . . . . . _____

❑ *Threskiornis molucca.* AUSTRALIAN IBIS. (Wall, NG, Aust; ◊-NZ). . . . _____

❑ *Threskiornis spinicollis.* STRAW-NECKED IBIS. (Aust; ◊ s NG, NZ). . . . _____

❑ *Pseudibis papillosa.* RED-NAPED IBIS. (s Asia). . . . . _____

❑ *Pseudibis davisoni.* WHITE-SHOULDERED IBIS. (se Asia). . . . . _____

❑ *Pseudibis gigantea.* GIANT IBIS. (se Asia). . . . . _____

❑ *Nipponia nippon.* CRESTED IBIS. (c China). . . . . _____

❑ *Platalea leucorodia.* EURASIAN SPOONBILL. (Palea, s Asia; ◊-c Afr). . . _____

❑ *Platalea regia.* ROYAL SPOONBILL. (Java, Aust, NZ; ◊-Wall, NG). . . . . _____

❑ *Platalea alba.* AFRICAN SPOONBILL. (Afr, Mad). . . . . _____

❑ *Platalea minor.* BLACK-FACED SPOONBILL. (e Asia; ◊-Phil). . . . . _____

❑ *Platalea flavipes.* YELLOW-BILLED SPOONBILL. (Aust). . . . . _____

❑ *Ajaia ajaja.* ROSEATE SPOONBILL. (se US, MA, W Indies, SA). . . . . . . _____

Superfamily PELECANOIDEA [2/9]
Family **Pelecanidae** [2/9]
Subfamily Balaenicipitinae [1/1]

❑ *Balaeniceps rex.* SHOEBILL. (c Afr). . . . . _____

Subfamily Pelecaninae [1/8]

❑ *Pelecanus onocrotalus.* GREAT WHITE PELICAN. (sc Eura-Afr, se Asia) _____

❑ *Pelecanus rufescens.* PINK-BACKED PELICAN. (Afr, Mad). . . . . _____

❑ *Pelecanus crispus.* DALMATIAN PELICAN. (s Eura; ◊-s Asia). . . . . _____

❑ *Pelecanus philippensis.* SPOT-BILLED PELICAN. (s Asia-Phil). . . . . _____

❑ *Pelecanus conspicillatus.* AUSTRALIAN PELICAN. (Aust; ◊-Indon). . . . . _____

❑ *Pelecanus erythrorhynchos.* AMERICAN WHITE PELICAN. (NA; ◊-CA). . . _____

❑ *Pelecanus occidentalis.* BROWN PELICAN. (NA-Galap, n,e SA). . . . . . . _____

❑ *Pelecanus thagus.* PERUVIAN PELICAN. (Pac sw SA). . . . . _____

Superfamily CICONIOIDEA [11/26]
Family **Ciconiidae** [11/26]
Subfamily Cathartinae [5/7]

☐ *Coragyps atratus*. Black Vulture. (NA, MA, SA)............... _____

☐ *Cathartes aura*. Turkey Vulture. (NA, MA, SA)............... _____

☐ *Cathartes burrovianus*. Lesser Yellow-headed V. (MA-SA)...... _____

☐ *Cathartes melambrotus*. Greater Yellow-headed V. (Amaz)...... _____

☐ *Gymnogyps californianus*. California Condor. (s Calif)......... _____

☐ *Vultur gryphus*. Andean Condor. (mts w,s SA)................ _____

☐ *Sarcoramphus papa*. King Vulture. (MA, SA)................ _____

Subfamily Ciconiinae [6/19]

☐ *Mycteria americana*. Wood Stork. (se US, MA, W Indies, SA)..... _____

☐ *Mycteria cinerea*. Milky Stork. (se Asia-Sulaw)............... _____

☐ *Mycteria ibis*. Yellow-billed Stork. (Afr, Mad)............... _____

☐ *Mycteria leucocephala*. Painted Stork. (s,se Asia)............. _____

☐ *Anastomus oscitans*. Asian Openbill. (s,se Asia)............... _____

☐ *Anastomus lamelligerus*. African Openbill. (Afr, Mad).......... _____

☐ *Ciconia nigra*. Black Stork. (c,s Eura, s Afr; ◊-c Afr, se Asia)...... _____

☐ *Ciconia abdimii*. Abdim's Stork. (subsah Afr reg; ◊-s Afr)........ _____

☐ *Ciconia episcopus*. Woolly-necked Stork. (Afr, s Asia-Phil)...... _____

☐ *Ciconia stormi*. Storm's Stork. (se Asia)..................... _____

☐ *Ciconia maguari*. Maguari Stork. (SA)..................... _____

☐ *Ciconia ciconia*. White Stork. (w,c Palea, s Afr; ◊-s Afr, s Asia).... _____

☐ *Ciconia boyciana*. Oriental Stork. (e Asia; ◊-s Asia)............ _____

☐ *Ephippiorhynchus asiaticus*. Black-necked Stork. (s Asia-Aust)... _____
   ___*E. (a.) asiaticus*. Black-necked Stork. (s,se Asia)
   ___*E. (a.) australis*. Green-necked Stork. (s NG, Aust)

☐ *Ephippiorhynchus senegalensis*. Saddle-billed Stork. (Afr)...... _____

☐ *Jabiru mycteria*. Jabiru. (MA, SA)......................... _____

☐ *Leptoptilos javanicus*. Lesser Adjutant. (s,se Asia)............. _____

☐ *Leptoptilos crumeniferus*. Marabou Stork. (Afr)............... _____

☐ *Leptoptilos dubius*. Greater Adjutant. (s,se Asia)............. _____

Superfamily PROCELLARIOIDEA [30/141]
Family **Fregatidae** [1/5]

☐ *Fregata magnificens*. Magnificent Frigatebird. (trop Pac, Atl).... _____

❑ *Fregata aquila.* ASCENSION FRIGATEBIRD. (Ascension). . . . . _____

❑ *Fregata minor.* GREAT FRIGATEBIRD. (trop oceans). . . . . _____

❑ *Fregata ariel.* LESSER FRIGATEBIRD. (trop oceans). . . . . _____

❑ *Fregata andrewsi.* CHRISTMAS ISLAND FRIGATEBIRD. (Chris). . . . . . . _____

Family **Spheniscidae** [6/17]

❑ *Aptenodytes patagonicus.* KING PENGUIN. (is s oceans). . . . . _____

❑ *Aptenodytes forsteri.* EMPEROR PENGUIN. (Ant). . . . . _____

❑ *Pygoscelis papua.* GENTOO PENGUIN. (is s oceans). . . . . _____

❑ *Pygoscelis adeliae.* ADELIE PENGUIN. (is s oceans, Ant). . . . . _____

❑ *Pygoscelis antarctica.* CHINSTRAP PENGUIN. (is s oceans, Ant pen). . . . _____

❑ *Eudyptes chrysocome.* ROCKHOPPER PENGUIN. (is s oceans). . . . . _____
    ___*E. (c.) chrysocome.* ROCKHOPPER PENGUIN. (sp)
    ___*E. (c.) moseleyi.* MOSELEY'S PENGUIN. (TdaC, s Indian O)

❑ *Eudyptes pachyrhynchus.* FIORDLAND PENGUIN. (s NZ; ◊-Aust). . . . . . _____

❑ *Eudyptes robustus.* SNARES PENGUIN. (Snares; ◊-Aust, NZ). . . . . _____

❑ *Eudyptes sclateri.* ERECT-CRESTED PENGUIN. (is NZ reg; ◊-Aust). . . . . _____

❑ *Eudyptes chrysolophus.* MACARONI PENGUIN. (is s oceans, Ant). . . . . . _____

❑ *Eudyptes schlegeli.* ROYAL PENGUIN. (Macquarie). . . . . _____

❑ *Megadyptes antipodes.* YELLOW-EYED PENGUIN. (NZ reg). . . . . _____

❑ *Eudyptula minor.* LITTLE PENGUIN. (s Aust-NZ). . . . . _____
    ___*E. (m.) minor.* LITTLE PENGUIN. (sp)
    ___*E. (m.) albosignata.* WHITE-FLIPPERED PENGUIN. (s NZ)

❑ *Spheniscus demersus.* JACKASS PENGUIN. (is s Afr). . . . . _____

❑ *Spheniscus humboldti.* HUMBOLDT PENGUIN. (Peru-Chile). . . . . _____

❑ *Spheniscus magellanicus.* MAGELLANIC PENGUIN. (s SA, JF). . . . . _____

❑ *Spheniscus mendiculus.* GALAPAGOS PENGUIN. (Galap). . . . . _____

Family **Gaviidae** [1/5]

❑ *Gavia stellata.* RED-THROATED LOON. (n Hol; ◊-s Eura, nw Mex). . . . . _____

❑ *Gavia arctica.* ARCTIC LOON. (n Palea, w Alas; ◊-Medit, s Asia). . . . . . _____
    ___*G. (a.) arctica.* BLACK-THROATED LOON. (n Palea; ◊-Medit)
    ___*G. (a.) viridigularis.* GREEN-THROATED LOON. (e Asia, w Alas; ◊-s Asia)

❑ *Gavia pacifica.* PACIFIC LOON. (e Sib-n NA; ◊-e Asia, w NA). . . . . _____

❑ *Gavia immer.* COMMON LOON. (w Palea, NA; ◊-s Asia, nw Mex). . . . . _____

❑ *Gavia adamsii.* YELLOW-BILLED LOON. (n Hol; ◊-c Eura, n Mex). . . . . _____

Family **Procellariidae** [22/114]
Subfamily Procellariinae [13/79]

❏ *Macronectes giganteus.* ANTARCTIC GIANT-PETREL. (is s oceans, Ant). _____

❏ *Macronectes halli.* HALL'S GIANT-PETREL. (is s oceans). . . . . _____

❏ *Fulmarus glacialis.* NORTHERN FULMAR. (n Hol; ◊-n oceans). . . . . _____

❏ *Fulmarus glacialoides.* SOUTHERN FULMAR. (subant is, Ant). . . . . _____

❏ *Thalassoica antarctica.* ANTARCTIC PETREL. (Ant; ◊ s oceans). . . . . . . _____

❏ *Daption capense.* CAPE PETREL. (is s oceans). _____

❏ *Pagodroma nivea.* SNOW PETREL. (is s oceans, Ant). . . . . _____
   ___*P. (n.) nivea.* LESSER SNOW-PETREL. (sp)
   ___*P. (n.) confusa.* GREATER SNOW-PETREL. (Balleny, Ant)

❏ *Pterodroma brevirostris.* KERGUELEN PETREL. (is s Alt, Indian oceans) _____

❏ *Pterodroma aterrima.* MASCARENE PETREL. (Réun). . . . . _____

❏ *Pterodroma becki.* BECK'S PETREL. (Bism, Solom). . . . . _____

❏ *Pterodroma rostrata.* TAHITI PETREL. (sw Oceania; ◊-Aust). . . . . _____

❏ *Pterodroma macgillivrayi.* FIJI PETREL. (c Fiji). . . . . _____

❏ *Pterodroma axillaris.* CHATHAM ISLANDS PETREL. (Chatham). . . . . _____

❏ *Pterodroma nigripennis.* BLACK-WINGED PETREL. (is s Pac O). . . . . . . _____

❏ *Pterodroma cervicalis.* WHITE-NECKED PETREL. (Kermadec; ◊ c Pac). . _____

❏ *Pterodroma inexpectata.* MOTTLED PETREL. (is NZ reg; ◊ Pac). . . . . . . _____

❏ *Pterodroma hypoleuca.* BONIN PETREL. (is n Pac O; ◊ c Pac). . . . . _____

❏ *Pterodroma leucoptera.* GOULD'S PETREL. (e Aust-Vanu; ◊ s Pac). . . . _____

❏ *Pterodroma cookii.* COOK'S PETREL. (NZ; ◊ Pac). . . . . _____

❏ *Pterodroma pycrofti.* PYCROFT'S PETREL. (is ne NZ). . . . . _____

❏ *Pterodroma brevipes.* COLLARED PETREL. (Fiji, e Samoa). . . . . _____

❏ *Pterodroma defilippiana.* DEFILIPPE'S PETREL. (se Pac). . . . . _____

❏ *Pterodroma longirostris.* STEJNEGER'S PETREL. (w JF; ◊-e,n Pac). . . . . _____

❏ *Pterodroma alba.* PHOENIX PETREL. (s Oceania). . . . . _____

❏ *Pterodroma arminjoniana.* HERALD PETREL. (is s oceans). . . . . _____
   ___*P. (a.) heraldica.* HERALD PETREL. (s Pac)
   ___*P. (a.) arminjoniana.* TRINDADE PETREL. (s Atl, s Indian O)

❏ *Pterodroma sandwichensis.* HAWAIIAN PETREL. (Haw Is; ◊-s Pac). . . . _____

❏ *Pterodroma phaeopygia.* GALAPAGOS PETREL. (Galap; ◊ e Pac). . . . . . _____

❏ *Pterodroma neglecta.* KERMADEC PETREL. (s Pac). . . . . _____

❏ *Pterodroma externa.* JUAN FERNANDEZ PETREL. (JF; ◊ Pac). . . . . _____

❏ *Pterodroma baraui.* BARAU'S PETREL. (Réun, Rodr). . . . . _____

❏ *Pterodroma ultima.* MURPHY'S PETREL. (s Polyn; ◊ Pac). . . . . _____

❑ *Pterodroma solandri.* PROVIDENCE PETREL. (L Howe; ◊ Pac). . . . . . . _____

❑ *Pterodroma macroptera.* GREAT-WINGED PETREL. (is s oceans). . . . . . _____

❑ *Pterodroma magentae.* MAGENTA PETREL. (Chatham; ◊ s Pac). . . . . . . _____

❑ *Pterodroma lessonii.* WHITE-HEADED PETREL. (is s oceans). . . . . _____

❑ *Pterodroma madeira.* MADEIRA PETREL. (mts Madeira). . . . . _____

❑ *Pterodroma feae.* CAPE VERDE PETREL. (e Atl). . . . . _____

❑ *Pterodroma mollis.* SOFT-PLUMAGED PETREL. (is s Atl, Indian O). . . . . _____

❑ *Pterodroma incerta.* ATLANTIC PETREL. (TdaC; ◊ s Atl). . . . . _____

❑ *Pterodroma cahow.* BERMUDA PETREL. (Berm). . . . . _____

❑ *Pterodroma hasitata.* BLACK-CAPPED PETREL. (W Indies; ◊ Atl). . . . . . _____
   ___*P. (h.) hasitata.* BLACK-CAPPED PETREL. (sp)
   ___*P. (h.) caribbaea.* JAMAICAN PETREL. (†Jam)

❑ *Halobaena caerulea.* BLUE PETREL. (is s oceans, s Chile). . . . . _____

❑ *Pachyptila vittata.* BROAD-BILLED PRION. (NZ reg, TdaC; ◊ s oceans). _____

❑ *Pachyptila salvini.* MEDIUM-BILLED PRION. (is s Indian O). . . . . _____
   ___*P. (s.) salvini.* MEDIUM-BILLED PRION. (sw Indian O)
   ___*P. (s.) macgillivrayi.* MACGILLIVRAY'S PRION. (s Indian O)

❑ *Pachyptila desolata.* ANTARCTIC PRION. (is s oceans, Ant). . . . . _____

❑ *Pachyptila belcheri.* SLENDER-BILLED PRION. (is s oceans, s Chile). . . . _____

❑ *Pachyptila turtur.* FAIRY PRION. (se Aust, NZ, is s oceans). . . . . _____

❑ *Pachyptila crassirostris.* FULMAR PRION. (is s oceans). . . . . _____

❑ *Bulweria bulwerii.* BULWER'S PETREL. (is trop Pac, At). . . . . _____

❑ *Bulweria fallax.* JOUANIN'S PETREL. (s Arabia; ◊ Indian O). . . . . _____

❑ *Procellaria aequinoctialis.* WHITE-CHINNED PETREL. (is s oceans). . . . _____

❑ *Procellaria parkinsoni.* BLACK PETREL. (NZ; ◊ Pac). . . . . _____

❑ *Procellaria westlandica.* WESTLAND PETREL. (mts s NZ). . . . . _____

❑ *Procellaria cinerea.* GREY PETREL. (is s oceans). . . . . _____

❑ *Calonectris diomedea.* CORY'S SHEARWATER. (is e Atl, Medit; ◊ Atl) . _____
   ___*C. (d.) diomedea.* CORY'S SHEARWATER. (sp)
   ___*C. (d.) edwardsii.* CAPE VERDE SHEARWATER. (C Verde)

❑ *Calonectris leucomelas.* STREAKED SHEARWATER. (is e Asia; ◊ Pac) . _____

❑ *Puffinus pacificus.* WEDGE-TAILED SHEARWATER. (is Indian O, Pac) . _____

❑ *Puffinus bulleri.* BULLER'S SHEARWATER. (NZ; ◊ Pac). . . . . _____

❑ *Puffinus carneipes.* FLESH-FOOTED SHEARWATER. (Aust reg; ◊ Pac). . . _____

❑ *Puffinus creatopus.* PINK-FOOTED SHEARWATER. (JF, is Chile; ◊ Pac). _____

❑ *Puffinus gravis.* GREAT SHEARWATER. (is s Atl; ◊- n Atl). . . . . _____

❑ *Puffinus griseus.* SOOTY SHEARWATER. (Aust reg, s SA; ◊ oceans). . . . _____

❑ *Puffinus tenuirostris.* SHORT-TAILED SHEARWATER. (is s Aust; ◊ Pac). _____

❑ *Puffinus nativitatis.* CHRISTMAS ISLAND SHEARWATER. (is Pac)...... _____

❑ *Puffinus puffinus.* MANX SHEARWATER. (is n Atl; ◊ Atl, s oceans).... _____

❑ *Puffinus yelkouan.* MEDITERRANEAN SHEARWATER. (Medit; ◊ e Atl). _____
  ___*P. (y.) mauretanicus.* BALEARIC SHEARWATER. (Balearic)
  ___*P. (y.) yelkouan.* LEVANTINE SHEARWATER. (sp)

❑ *Puffinus auricularis.* TOWNSEND'S SHEARWATER. (Haw Is, Revil).... _____
  ___*P. (a.) newelli.* NEWELL'S SHEARWATER. (Haw Is)
  ___*P. (a.) auricularis.* TOWNSEND'S SHEARWATER. (Revil)

❑ *Puffinus opisthomelas.* BLACK-VENTED SHEARWATER. (is nw Mex)... _____

❑ *Puffinus gavia.* FLUTTERING SHEARWATER. (NZ; ◊ sw Pac)........ _____

❑ *Puffinus huttoni.* HUTTON'S SHEARWATER. (mts s NZ; ◊ sw Pac)..... _____

❑ *Puffinus lherminieri.* AUDUBON'S SHEARWATER. (is trop oceans)..... _____

❑ *Puffinus assimilis.* LITTLE SHEARWATER. (is Atl, Aust reg)......... _____

❑ *Puffinus persicus.* PERSIAN SHEARWATER. (s Persian Gulf)......... _____

❑ *Puffinus bannermani.* BANNERMAN'S SHEARWATER. (is nw Pac)..... _____

❑ *Puffinus heinrothi.* HEINROTH'S SHEARWATER. (c Bism)........... _____

❑ *Pelecanoides garnotii.* PERUVIAN DIVING-PETREL. (is sw SA)....... _____

❑ *Pelecanoides magellani.* MAGELLANIC DIVING-PETREL. (is s SA)..... _____

❑ *Pelecanoides georgicus.* SOUTH GEORGIA DIVING-PETREL. (is s oceans)_____

❑ *Pelecanoides urinatrix.* COMMON DIVING-PETREL. (is s oceans)...... _____
  ___*P. (u.) urinatrix.* COMMON DIVING-PETREL. (Aust reg, s Atl)
  ___*P. (u.) berard.* FALKLAND DIVING-PETREL. (Falk)
  ___*P. (u.) exsul.* KERGUELEN DIVING-PETREL. (sp)

Subfamily Diomedeinae [2/14]

❑ *Diomedea exulans.* WANDERING ALBATROSS. (is s oceans)......... _____

❑ *Diomedea amsterdamensis.* AMSTERDAM ISLAND ALBATROSS. (Ams). _____

❑ *Diomedea epomophora.* ROYAL ALBATROSS. (is s oceans, s NZ)..... _____

❑ *Diomedea irrorata.* WAVED ALBATROSS. (se Galap, is off Ecua)...... _____

❑ *Diomedea albatrus.* SHORT-TAILED ALBATROSS. (Izu; ◊ n Pac)....... _____

❑ *Diomedea nigripes.* BLACK-FOOTED ALBATROSS. (nw,c Pac)........ _____

❑ *Diomedea immutabilis.* LAYSAN ALBATROSS. (c,e Pac)............. _____

❑ *Diomedea melanophris.* BLACK-BROWED ALBATROSS. (is s oceans)... _____

❑ *Diomedea cauta.* SHY ALBATROSS. (is sw Pac; ◊ s oceans)......... _____
  ___*D. (c.) cauta.* SHY ALBATROSS. (is Tas, Auck)
  ___*D. (c.) salvini.* GREY-BACKED ALBATROSS. (Snares, Bounty)
  ___*D. (c.) eremita.* CHATHAM ISLANDS ALBATROSS. (Chatham)

❑ *Diomedea chrysostoma.* GREY-HEADED ALBATROSS. (is s oceans).... _____

❑ *Diomedea chlororhynchos.* YELLOW-NOSED ALBATROSS. (is s oceans). _____

❑ *Diomedea bulleri.* BULLER'S ALBATROSS. (NZ reg; ◊ s Pac). . . . . _____

❑ *Phoebetria fusca.* SOOTY ALBATROSS. (is s Atl, Indian; ◊ s oceans). . . _____

❑ *Phoebetria palpebrata.* LIGHT-MANTLED ALBATROSS. (is s oceans). . . . _____

Subfamily Hydrobatinae [7/21]

❑ *Oceanites oceanicus.* WILSON'S STORM-PETREL. (is s oceans; ◊-n Atl). _____

❑ *Oceanites gracilis.* WHITE-VENTED STORM-PETREL. (Galap, w SA). . . . _____

❑ *Garrodia nereis.* GREY-BACKED STORM-PETREL. (is s oceans). . . . . . . _____

❑ *Pelagodroma marina.* WHITE-FACED STORM-PETREL. (Atl, Aust reg) . _____

❑ *Fregetta tropica.* BLACK-BELLIED STORM-PETREL. (is s oceans). . . . . _____

❑ *Fregetta grallaria.* WHITE-BELLIED STORM-PETREL. (is s oceans). . . . _____

❑ *Nesofregetta fuliginosa.* POLYNESIAN STORM-PETREL. (is s Pac). . . . . _____

❑ *Hydrobates pelagicus.* EUROPEAN STORM-PETREL. (is nw Palea). . . . _____

❑ *Oceanodroma microsoma.* LEAST STORM-PETREL. (is nw Mex). . . . . _____

❑ *Oceanodroma tethys.* WEDGE-RUMPED STORM-PETREL. (Galap, w SA). _____

❑ *Oceanodroma castro.* BAND-RUMPED STORM-PETREL. (n oceans, Galap) _____

❑ *Oceanodroma leucorhoa.* LEACH'S STORM-PETREL. (is n oceans). . . . . _____
   ___*O. (l.) leucorhoa.* LEACH'S STORM-PETREL. (sp)
   ___*O. (l.) socorroensis.* SOCORRO STORM-PETREL. (Guadalupe)

❑ *Oceanodroma monorhis.* SWINHOE'S STORM-PETREL. (is n Pac). . . . . _____

  Oceanodroma macrodactyla. GUADALUPE STORM-PETREL. (†Guadalupe)_____

❑ *Oceanodroma tristrami.* TRISTRAM'S STORM-PETREL. (is n Pac). . . . . _____

❑ *Oceanodroma markhami.* MARKHAM'S STORM-PETREL. (e Pac). . . . . _____

❑ *Oceanodroma matsudairae.* MATSUDAIRA'S STORM-PETREL. (Volcano). _____

❑ *Oceanodroma melania.* BLACK STORM-PETREL. (is s Calif, nw Mex) . _____

❑ *Oceanodroma homochroa.* ASHY STORM-PETREL. (is Calif, nw Mex). _____

❑ *Oceanodroma hornbyi.* RINGED STORM-PETREL. (mts n Chile; ◊ se Pac) _____

❑ *Oceanodroma furcata.* FORK-TAILED STORM-PETREL. (is n Pac). . . . . _____

Order **PASSERIFORMES** [1168/5739]
Suborder TYRANNI [292/1159]
Infraorder ACANTHISITTIDES [2/4]
Family **Acanthisittidae** [2/4]

❑ *Acanthisitta chloris.* RIFLEMAN. (NZ). . . . . _____

❑ *Xenicus longipes.* BUSH WREN. (NZ). . . . . _____

❑ *Xenicus gilviventris.* SOUTH ISLAND WREN. (mts s Nz). . . . . _____

  Xenicus lyalli. STEPHENS ISLAND WREN. (†c NZ). . . . . _____

Infraorder EURYLAIMIDES [11/49]
Superfamily PITTOIDEA [1/31]
Family **Pittidae** [1/31]

❏ *Pitta phayrei.* EARED PITTA. (se Asia)............................ _____

❏ *Pitta nipalensis.* BLUE-NAPED PITTA. (mts s,se Asia)............. _____

❏ *Pitta soror.* BLUE-RUMPED PITTA. (mts se Asia)................... _____

❏ *Pitta oatesi.* RUSTY-NAPED PITTA. (mts se Asia)................. _____

❏ *Pitta schneideri.* SCHNEIDER'S PITTA. (mts n Sum)............... _____

❏ *Pitta caerulea.* GIANT PITTA. (se Asia)......................... _____

❏ *Pitta cyanea.* BLUE PITTA. (s,se Asia).......................... _____

❏ *Pitta guajana.* BANDED PITTA. (se Asia)......................... _____

❏ *Pitta elliotii.* BAR-BELLIED PITTA. (Indoc)..................... _____

❏ *Pitta gurneyi.* GURNEY'S PITTA. (se Asia)....................... _____

❏ *Pitta baudii.* BLUE-HEADED PITTA. (Born)........................ _____

❏ *Pitta sordida.* HOODED PITTA. (s Asia-Phil, Aru-w Bism)......... _____
  ___*P. (s.) sordida.* HOODED PITTA. (se Asia-Phil)
  ___*P. (s.) novaeguineae.* BLACK-HEADED PITTA. (Aru-w Bism)

❏ *Pitta maxima.* IVORY-BREASTED PITTA. (n Moluc)................. _____

❏ *Pitta superba.* SUPERB PITTA. (nw Bism)......................... _____

❏ *Pitta steerii.* AZURE-BREASTED PITTA. (s Phil).................. _____

❏ *Pitta kochi.* WHISKERED PITTA. (mts n Phil)..................... _____

❏ *Pitta erythrogaster.* RED-BELLIED PITTA. (Sulaw-Phil, Bism, n Aust) . _____

❏ *Pitta dohertyi.* SULA PITTA. (e Sulaw).......................... _____

❏ *Pitta arcuata.* BLUE-BANDED PITTA. (mts Born)................... _____

❏ *Pitta granatina.* GARNET PITTA. (se Asia)....................... _____

❏ *Pitta venusta.* BLACK-CROWNED PITTA. (mts Sum, n Born)......... _____

❏ *Pitta angolensis.* AFRICAN PITTA. (Afr)......................... _____

❏ *Pitta reichenowi.* GREEN-BREASTED PITTA. (c Afr)................ _____

❏ *Pitta brachyura.* INDIAN PITTA. (India)......................... _____

❏ *Pitta nympha.* FAIRY PITTA. (e Asia; ◊-se Asia)................. _____

❏ *Pitta moluccensis.* BLUE-WINGED PITTA. (se Asia; ◊-n Aust)...... _____

❏ *Pitta megarhyncha.* MANGROVE PITTA. (se Asia).................. _____

❏ *Pitta elegans.* ELEGANT PITTA. (Wall).......................... _____
  ___*P. (e.) vigorsii.* TWO-STRIPED PITTA. (s Indon is)
  ___*P. (e.) elegans.* ELEGANT PITTA. (L Sunda-Moluc)

❏ *Pitta iris.* RAINBOW PITTA. (cn Aust)........................... _____

❏ *Pitta versicolor.* NOISY PITTA. (e Aust; ◊-s NG)................ _____

❏ *Pitta anerythra.* BLACK-FACED PITTA. (Solom).................... _____

Superfamily EURYLAIMOIDEA [10/18]
Family **Eurylaimidae** [8/14]

❑ *Smithornis capensis.* AFRICAN BROADBILL. (mts w,c,se Afr) . . . . _____

❑ *Smithornis sharpei.* GREY-HEADED BROADBILL. (c Afr) . . . . _____

❑ *Smithornis rufolateralis.* RUFOUS-SIDED BROADBILL. (w,c Afr) . . . . . _____

❑ *Pseudocalyptomena graueri.* GRAUER'S BROADBILL. (mts ec Afr) . . . . _____

❑ *Corydon sumatranus.* DUSKY BROADBILL. (se Asia) . . . . _____

❑ *Cymbirhynchus macrorhynchos.* BLACK-AND-RED BROADBILL. (se Asia)_____

❑ *Eurylaimus javanicus.* BANDED BROADBILL. (se Asia) . . . . _____

❑ *Eurylaimus ochromalus.* BLACK-AND-YELLOW BROADBILL. (se Asia). _____

❑ *Eurylaimus steerii.* WATTLED BROADBILL. (s Phil) . . . . _____

❑ *Serilophus lunatus.* SILVER-BREASTED BROADBILL. (s,se Asia) . . . . . . _____
   ___*S. (l.) rubropygius.* HODGSON'S BROADBILL. (s Asia)
   ___*S. (l.) lunatus.* SILVER-BREASTED BROADBILL. (se Asia)

❑ *Psarisomus dalhousiae.* LONG-TAILED BROADBILL. (s,se Asia) . . . . . . _____

❑ *Calyptomena viridis.* GREEN BROADBILL. (se Asia) . . . . _____

❑ *Calyptomena hosii.* HOSE'S BROADBILL. (mts n Born) . . . . _____

❑ *Calyptomena whiteheadi.* WHITEHEAD'S BROADBILL. (mts n Born) . . . _____

Family **Philepittidae** [2/4]

❑ *Philepitta castanea.* VELVET ASITY. (mts nw,e Mad) . . . . _____

❑ *Philepitta schlegeli.* SCHLEGEL'S ASITY. (w,nw Mad) . . . . _____

❑ *Neodrepanis coruscans.* SUNBIRD ASITY. (nw,e Mad) . . . . _____

❑ *Neodrepanis hypoxantha.* YELLOW-BELLIED ASITY. (ce Mad) . . . . _____

Family *Incertae Sedis* [1/1]

❑ *Sapayoa aenigma.* BROAD-BILLED SAPAYOA. (e Pan, nw SA) . . . . _____

Infraorder TYRANNIDES [278/1105]
Parvorder TYRANNIDA [147/539]
Family **Tyrannidae** [147/539]
Subfamily Pipromorphinae [8/53]

❑ *Mionectes striaticollis.* STREAK-NECKED FLYCATCHER. (Andes w SA). _____

❑ *Mionectes olivaceus.* OLIVE-STRIPED FLYCATCHER. (s CA, w,n SA) . . . _____

❑ *Mionectes oleagineus.* OCHRE-BELLIED FLYCATCHER. (MA, SA) . . . . . _____

❑ *Mionectes macconnelli.* MACCONNELL'S FLYCATCHER. (Amaz) . . . . . . _____

❑ *Mionectes rufiventris.* GREY-HOODED FLYCATCHER. (s,se SA) . . . . _____

❑ *Leptopogon rufipectus.* RUFOUS-BREASTED FLYCATCHER. (w SA) . . . . _____

❑ *Leptopogon taczanowskii.* INCA FLYCATCHER. (Andes Peru). . . . . _____

❑ *Leptopogon amaurocephalus.* SEPIA-CAPPED FLYCATCHER. (MA-SA). _____

❑ *Leptopogon superciliaris.* SLATY-CAPPED FLYCATCHER. (s CA-w,n SA)_____

❑ *Pseudotriccus pelzelni.* BRONZE-OLIVE PYGMY-TYRANT. (s CA-w SA). _____

❑ *Pseudotriccus simplex.* HAZEL-FRONTED PYGMY-TYRANT. (w SA). . . . _____

❑ *Pseudotriccus ruficeps.* RUFOUS-HEADED PYGMY-TYRANT. (w SA). . . _____

❑ *Poecilotriccus ruficeps.* RUFOUS-CROWNED TODY-TYRANT. (w SA). . . _____

❑ *Poecilotriccus capitalis.* BLACK-AND-WHITE TODY-TYRANT. (w Amaz). _____
    ___*P. (c.) capitalis.* BLACK-AND-WHITE TODY-TYRANT. (sp)
    ___*P. (c.) tricolor.* TRICOLORED TODY-TYRANT. (w Braz)

❑ *Poecilotriccus albifacies.* WHITE-CHEEKED TODY-TYRANT. (se Peru) . _____

❑ *Taeniotriccus andrei.* BLACK-CHESTED TYRANT. (n Amaz). . . . . _____

❑ *Hemitriccus minor.* SNETHLAGE'S TODY-TYRANT. (w Amaz). . . . . _____
    ___*H. (m.) minimus.* DWARF TODY-TYRANT. (sp)
    ___*H. (m.) minor.* SNETHLAGE'S TODY-TYRANT. (nc Braz)

❑ *Hemitriccus josephinae.* BOAT-BILLED TODY-TYRANT. (ne SA). . . . . . _____

❑ *Hemitriccus flammulatus.* FLAMMULATED BAMBOO-TYRANT. (w Amaz)_____

❑ *Hemitriccus diops.* DRAB-BREASTED BAMBOO-TYRANT. (se SA). . . . . . _____

❑ *Hemitriccus obsoletus.* BROWN-BREASTED BAMBOO-TYRANT. (se Braz)_____

❑ *Hemitriccus zosterops.* WHITE-EYED TODY-TYRANT. (Amaz). . . . . _____
    ___*H. (z.) zosterops.* WHITE-EYED TODY-TYRANT. (n Amaz)
    ___*H. (z.) griseipectus.* WHITE-BELLIED TODY-TYRANT. (s Amaz)

❑ *Hemitriccus aenigma.* ZIMMER'S TODY-TYRANT. (sc Amaz). . . . . _____

❑ *Hemitriccus orbitatus.* EYE-RINGED TODY-TYRANT. (se Braz). . . . . . . _____

❑ *Hemitriccus iohannis.* JOHANNES'S TODY-TYRANT. (w Amaz). . . . . . . _____

❑ *Hemitriccus striaticollis.* STRIPE-NECKED TODY-TYRANT. (Amaz). . . . _____

❑ *Hemitriccus nidipendulus.* HANGNEST TODY-TYRANT. (se Braz). . . . . _____

❑ *Hemitriccus spodiops.* YUNGAS TODY-TYRANT. (Andes wc Bol). . . . . _____

❑ *Hemitriccus margaritaceiventer.* PEARLY-VENTED TODY-TYRANT. (SA)_____
    ___*H. (m.) impiger.* ACTIVE TODY-TYRANT. (cn SA)
    ___*H. (m.) septentrionalis.* MAGDALENA TODY-TYRANT. (c Colom)
    ___*H. (m.) duidae.* DUIDA TODY-TYRANT. (Pant s Ven)
    ___*H. (m.) margaritaceiventer.* PEARLY-VENTED TODY-TYRANT. (sc SA)

❑ *Hemitriccus inornatus.* PELZELN'S TODY-TYRANT. (nw Amaz Braz) . _____

❑ *Hemitriccus granadensis.* BLACK-THROATED TODY-TYRANT. (w SA) . _____

❑ *Hemitriccus rufigularis.* BUFF-THROATED TODY-TYRANT. (sw SA). . . _____

❑ *Hemitriccus cinnamomeipectus.* CINNAMON-BREASTED TODY-T. (Peru) _____

❑ *Hemitriccus mirandae.* BUFF-BREASTED TODY-TYRANT. (e Braz). . . . . _____

❑ *Hemitriccus kaempferi.* KAEMPFER'S TODY-TYRANT. (se Braz). . . . . . _____

❏ *Hemitriccus furcatus.* FORK-TAILED TODY-TYRANT. (se Braz)...... _____

❏ *Todirostrum senex.* BUFF-CHEEKED TODY-FLYCATCHER. (w Amaz Braz)_____

❏ *Todirostrum russatum.* RUDDY TODY-FLYCATCHER. (Pant nc SA).... _____

❏ *Todirostrum plumbeiceps.* OCHRE-FACED TODY-FLYCATCHER. (sc SA) _____

❏ *Todirostrum latirostre.* RUSTY-FRONTED TODY-FLYCATCHER. (Amaz). _____

❏ *Todirostrum fumifrons.* SMOKY-FRONTED TODY-FLYCATCHER. (n,e SA)_____

❏ *Todirostrum sylvia.* SLATE-HEADED TODY-FLYCATCHER. (MA, n SA). _____

❏ *Todirostrum maculatum.* SPOTTED TODY-FLYCATCHER. (n,c Amaz) . _____

❏ *Todirostrum poliocephalum.* YELLOW-LORED TODY-FLYC. (se Braz).. _____

❏ *Todirostrum cinereum.* COMMON TODY-FLYCATCHER. (MA, SA)..... _____

❏ *Todirostrum viridanum.* MARACAIBO TODY-FLYCATCHER. (ne Ven) . _____

❏ *Todirostrum nigriceps.* BLACK-HEADED TODY-FLYC. (s CA, nw SA).. _____

❏ *Todirostrum pictum.* PAINTED TODY-FLYCATCHER. (n Amaz)....... _____

❏ *Todirostrum chrysocrotaphum.* YELLOW-BROWED TODY-F. (Amaz) . _____

❏ *Todirostrum calopterum.* GOLDEN-WINGED TODY-FLYC. (nw Amaz).. _____

❏ *Todirostrum pulchellum.* BLACK-BACKED TODY-FLYCATCHER. (se Peru)_____

❏ *Corythopis torquata.* RINGED ANTPIPIT. (n,c Amaz).............. _____

❏ *Corythopis delalandi.* SOUTHERN ANTPIPIT. (se SA).............. _____

Subfamily Tyranninae [92/341]

❏ *Phyllomyias fasciatus.* PLANALTO TYRANNULET. (se SA).......... _____

❏ *Phyllomyias zeledoni.* WHITE-FRONTED TYRANNULET. (s CA-w SA) . _____
___*P. (z.) zeledoni.* ZELEDON'S TYRANNULET. (s CA)
___*P. (z.) leucogonys.* WHITE-FRONTED TYRANNULET. (w SA)

❏ *Phyllomyias burmeisteri.* ROUGH-LEGGED TYRANNULET. (sc,se SA)... _____

❏ *Phyllomyias virescens.* GREENISH TYRANNULET. (mts. cn, se SA)..... _____
___*P. (v.) urichi.* URICH'S TYRANNULET. (cn SA)
___*P. (v.) virescens.* GREENISH TYRANNULET. (se SA)

❏ *Phyllomyias reiseri.* REISER'S TYRANNULET. (mts se SA)........... _____

❏ *Phyllomyias sclateri.* SCLATER'S TYRANNULET. (Andes sw SA)...... _____

❏ *Phyllomyias griseocapilla.* GREY-CAPPED TYRANNULET. (se Braz).... _____

❏ *Phyllomyias griseiceps.* SOOTY-HEADED TYRANNULET. (Pan-w,n SA). _____

❏ *Phyllomyias plumbeiceps.* PLUMBEOUS-CROWNED TYRANNULET. (w SA)_____

❏ *Phyllomyias nigrocapillus.* BLACK-CAPPED TYRANNULET. (mts w SA). _____

❏ *Phyllomyias cinereiceps.* ASHY-HEADED TYRANNULET. (nw SA)..... _____

❏ *Phyllomyias uropygialis.* TAWNY-RUMPED TYRANNULET. (w SA)..... _____

❏ *Zimmerius vilissimus.* PALTRY TYRANNULET. (c,s MA, nw Colom). . . _____
___*Z. (v.) vilissimus.* PALTRY TYRANNULET. (nc MA)
___*Z. (v.) parvus.* MISTLETOE TYRANNULET. (CA, nw Colom)

❏ *Zimmerius improbus.* VENEZUELAN TYRANNULET. (mts n SA). . . . . . . _____

❏ *Zimmerius bolivianus.* BOLIVIAN TYRANNULET. (Andes sw SA). . . . . . _____

❏ *Zimmerius cinereicapillus.* RED-BILLED TYRANNULET. (sw Amaz). . . . _____

❏ *Zimmerius gracilipes.* SLENDER-FOOTED TYRANNULET. (Amaz). . . . . . _____
___*Z. (g.) gracilipes.* SLENDER-FOOTED TYRANNULET. (sp)
___*Z. (g.) acer.* GUIANAN TYRANNULET. (n,ne Amaz)

❏ *Zimmerius chrysops.* GOLDEN-FACED TYRANNULET. (mts w,n SA). . . . _____

❏ *Zimmerius viridiflavus.* PERUVIAN TYRANNULET. (Andes c Peru). . . . . _____

❏ *Ornithion inerme.* WHITE-LORED TYRANNULET. (c,e SA). . . . . _____

❏ *Ornithion semiflavum.* YELLOW-BELLIED TYRANNULET. (c MA). . . . . _____

❏ *Ornithion brunneicapillum.* BROWN-CAPPED T. (s CA-nw SA). . . . . . _____

❏ *Camptostoma imberbe.* NORTHERN BEARDLESS-T. (sw US-CR). . . . . . _____

❏ *Camptostoma obsoletum.* SOUTHERN BEARDLESS-T. (s CA, SA). . . . . . _____

❏ *Phaeomyias murina.* MOUSE-COLORED TYRANNULET. (Pan, SA). . . . . _____
___*P. (m.) murina.* MOUSE-COLORED TYRANNULET. (sp)
___*P. (m.) tumbezana.* TUMBES TYRANNULET. (cw SA)

❏ *Nesotriccus ridgwayi.* COCOS FLYCATCHER. (Cocos). . . . . _____

❏ *Capsiempis flaveola.* YELLOW TYRANNULET. (s CA, SA). . . . . _____

❏ *Sublegatus arenarum.* NORTHERN SCRUB-FLYCATCHER. (s CA-Amaz). _____
___*S. (a.) arenarum.* NORTHERN SCRUB-FLYCATCHER. (s CA)
___*S. (a.) glaber.* SMOOTH SCRUB-FLYCATCHER. (Amaz)

❏ *Sublegatus obscurior.* AMAZONIAN SCRUB-FLYCATCHER. (n,c Amaz) . _____

❏ *Sublegatus modestus.* SOUTHERN SCRUB-FLYCATCHER. (sc SA). . . . . . _____

❏ *Suiriri affinis.* CAMPO SUIRIRI. (Amaz). . . . . _____

❏ *Suiriri suiriri.* CHACO SUIRIRI. (sc SA). . . . . _____

❏ *Tyrannulus elatus.* YELLOW-CROWNED TYRANNULET. (s CA, n,c SA). _____

❏ *Myiopagis gaimardii.* FOREST ELAENIA. (Pan, SA). . . . . _____

❏ *Myiopagis caniceps.* GREY ELAENIA. (e Pan, SA). . . . . _____

❏ *Myiopagis subplacens.* PACIFIC ELAENIA. (w Ecua, nw Peru). . . . . . . _____

❏ *Myiopagis flavivertex.* YELLOW-CROWNED ELAENIA. (Amaz). . . . . . . _____

❏ *Myiopagis cotta.* JAMAICAN ELAENIA. (mts Jam). . . . . _____

❏ *Myiopagis viridicata.* GREENISH ELAENIA. (MA, SA). . . . . _____

❏ *Pseudelaenia leucospodia.* GREY-AND-WHITE TYRANNULET. (cs SA) . _____

❏ *Elaenia martinica.* CARIBBEAN ELAENIA. (W Indies, is Carib). . . . . . . _____
___*E. (m.) martinica.* CARIBBEAN ELAENIA. (W Indies, is Yuc)
___*E. (m.) chinchorrensis.* CHINCHORRO ELAENIA. (is w Carib)

❑ *Elaenia flavogaster.* YELLOW-BELLIED ELAENIA. (MA, s L Ant, SA) . _____

❑ *Elaenia spectabilis.* LARGE ELAENIA. (sc,se SA). . . . . _____

❑ *Elaenia ridleyana.* NORONHA ELAENIA. (FdeN). . . . . _____

❑ *Elaenia albiceps.* WHITE-CRESTED ELAENIA. (w,s SA). . . . . _____
   ___*E. (a.) albiceps.* WHITE-CRESTED ELAENIA. (Andes w SA)
   ___*E. (a.) modesta.* PERUVIAN ELAENIA. (Peru, nw Chile)
   ___*E. (a.) chilensis.* CHILEAN ELAENIA. (s SA)

❑ *Elaenia parvirostris.* SMALL-BILLED ELAENIA. (sc SA; ◊-n SA). . . . . . _____

❑ *Elaenia strepera.* SLATY ELAENIA. (sc SA; ◊-n SA). . . . . _____

❑ *Elaenia mesoleuca.* OLIVACEOUS ELAENIA. (se SA). . . . . _____

❑ *Elaenia gigas.* MOTTLE-BACKED ELAENIA. (sw Amaz). . . . . _____

❑ *Elaenia pelzelni.* BROWNISH ELAENIA. (w Amaz). . . . . _____

❑ *Elaenia cristata.* PLAIN-CRESTED ELAENIA. (n,c SA). . . . . _____

❑ *Elaenia ruficeps.* RUFOUS-CROWNED ELAENIA. (n Amaz). . . . . _____

❑ *Elaenia chiriquensis.* LESSER ELAENIA. (s CA, SA). . . . . _____

❑ *Elaenia frantzii.* MOUNTAIN ELAENIA. (mts CA, nw SA). . . . . _____

❑ *Elaenia obscura.* HIGHLAND ELAENIA. (sc,se SA). . . . . _____

❑ *Elaenia dayi.* GREAT ELAENIA. (Pant s Ven). . . . . _____
   ___*E. (d.) tyleri.* DUIDA ELAENIA. (cs Ven)
   ___*E. (d.) dayi.* GREAT ELAENIA. (se Ven)

❑ *Elaenia pallatangae.* SIERRAN ELAENIA. (mts w,n SA). . . . . _____
   ___*E. (p.) pallatangae.* SIERRAN ELAENIA. (Andes w SA)
   ___*E. (p.) olivina.* RORAIMAN ELAENIA. (Pant nc SA)

❑ *Elaenia fallax.* GREATER ANTILLEAN ELAENIA. (mts Jam, Hisp). . . . . . _____

❑ *Mecocerculus leucophrys.* WHITE-THROATED TYRANNULET. (mts SA). _____

❑ *Mecocerculus poecilocercus.* WHITE-TAILED TYRANNULET. (w SA). . . _____

❑ *Mecocerculus hellmayri.* BUFF-BANDED TYRANNULET. (sw SA). . . . . _____

❑ *Mecocerculus calopterus.* RUFOUS-WINGED TYRANNULET. (cw SA). . . _____

❑ *Mecocerculus minor.* SULPHUR-BELLIED TYRANNULET. (w SA). . . . . _____

❑ *Mecocerculus stictopterus.* WHITE-BANDED TYRANNULET. (w SA). . . . _____

❑ *Serpophaga cinerea.* TORRENT TYRANNULET. (mts s CA, w SA). . . . . _____

❑ *Serpophaga nigricans.* SOOTY TYRANNULET. (sc SA). . . . . _____

❑ *Serpophaga hypoleuca.* RIVER TYRANNULET. (Amaz). . . . . _____

❑ *Serpophaga subcristata.* WHITE-CRESTED TYRANNULET. (sc,se SA). . . _____

❑ *Serpophaga munda.* WHITE-BELLIED TYRANNULET. (sc SA). . . . . _____

❑ *Inezia tenuirostris.* SLENDER-BILLED TYRANNULET. (nw SA). . . . . . . _____

❑ *Inezia inornata.* PLAIN TYRANNULET. (sc SA). . . . . _____

❏ *Inezia subflava.* PALE-TIPPED TYRANNULET. (Amaz)............. _____

❏ *Stigmatura napensis.* LESSER WAGTAIL-TYRANT. (c,e SA)......... _____

❏ *Stigmatura budytoides.* GREATER WAGTAIL-TYRANT. (sc,e SA)...... _____

❏ *Uromyias agilis.* AGILE TIT-TYRANT. (Andes nw SA)............. _____

❏ *Uromyias agraphia.* UNSTREAKED TIT-TYRANT. (Andes Peru)....... _____

❏ *Anairetes alpinus.* ASH-BREASTED TIT-TYRANT. (Andes Peru, Bol)... _____

❏ *Anairetes nigrocristatus.* MARANON TIT-TYRANT. (Andes n Peru).... _____

❏ *Anairetes reguloides.* PIED-CRESTED TIT-TYRANT. (cw SA)......... _____

❏ *Anairetes flavirostris.* YELLOW-BILLED TIT-TYRANT. (mts sw,s SA)... _____

❏ *Anairetes fernandezianus.* JUAN FERNANDEZ TIT-TYRANT. (JF)...... _____

❏ *Anairetes parulus.* TUFTED TIT-TYRANT. (Andes w,s SA).......... _____

❏ *Tachuris rubrigastra.* MANY-COLORED RUSH-TYRANT. (cw,s SA).... _____

❏ *Culicivora caudacuta.* SHARP-TAILED GRASS-TYRANT. (sc SA)....... _____

❏ *Polystictus pectoralis.* BEARDED TACHURI. (SA)................. _____

❏ *Polystictus superciliaris.* GREY-BACKED TACHURI. (se Braz)........ _____

❏ *Pseudocolopteryx sclateri.* CRESTED DORADITO. (SA)............. _____

❏ *Pseudocolopteryx acutipennis.* SUBTROPICAL DORADITO. (w SA)..... _____

❏ *Pseudocolopteryx dinellianus.* DINELLI'S DORADITO. (sc SA)........ _____

❏ *Pseudocolopteryx flaviventris.* WARBLING DORADITO. (sc,s SA)..... _____

❏ *Euscarthmus meloryphus.* TAWNY-CROWNED PYGMY-TYRANT. (SA) . _____

❏ *Euscarthmus rufomarginatus.* RUFOUS-SIDED PYGMY-T. (cn,se SA) . _____

❏ *Phylloscartes ophthalmicus.* MARBLE-FACED BRISTLE-TYRANT. (w,n SA)_____

❏ *Phylloscartes venezuelanus.* VENEZUELAN BRISTLE-TYRANT. (n Ven). _____

❏ *Phylloscartes lanyoni.* ANTIOQUIA BRISTLE-TYRANT. (nw Colom).... _____

❏ *Phylloscartes orbitalis.* SPECTACLED BRISTLE-TYRANT. (w SA)...... _____

❏ *Phylloscartes poecilotis.* VARIEGATED BRISTLE-TYRANT. (mts w SA) . _____

❏ *Phylloscartes eximius.* SOUTHERN BRISTLE-TYRANT. (se SA)........ _____

❏ *Phylloscartes nigrifrons.* BLACK-FRONTED TYRANNULET. (Pant s Ven). _____

❏ *Phylloscartes chapmani.* CHAPMAN'S TYRANNULET. (Pant nc SA).... _____

❏ *Phylloscartes gualaquizae.* ECUADORIAN TYRANNULET. (wc SA)..... _____

❏ *Phylloscartes flaviventris.* RUFOUS-LORED TYRANNULET. (Ven, se Peru)_____

❏ *Phylloscartes roquettei.* MINAS GERAIS TYRANNULET. (e Braz)...... _____

❏ *Phylloscartes paulistus.* SAO PAULO TYRANNULET. (se SA)........ _____

❏ *Phylloscartes oustaleti.* OUSTALET'S TYRANNULET. (s Braz)........ _____

❏ *Phylloscartes difficilis.* SERRA DO MAR TYRANNULET. (mts se Braz) . _____

❑ *Phylloscartes ceciliae.* ALAGOAS TYRANNULET. (ne Braz). . . . . _____

❑ *Phylloscartes ventralis.* MOTTLE-CHEEKED TYRANNULET. (sw,sc SA) . _____
   ___*P. (v.) angustirostris.* NARROW-BILLED TYRANNULET. (Andes sw SA)
   ___*P. (v.) ventralis.* MOTTLE-CHEEKED TYRANNULET. (sc SA)

❑ *Phylloscartes flavovirens.* YELLOW-GREEN TYRANNULET. (c,e Pan). . . _____

❑ *Phylloscartes virescens.* OLIVE-GREEN TYRANNULET. (Guia). . . . . _____

❑ *Phylloscartes superciliaris.* RUFOUS-BROWED T. (s CA, nw SA). . . . . . _____

❑ *Phylloscartes sylviolus.* BAY-RINGED TYRANNULET. (se SA). . . . . _____

❑ *Myiornis albiventris.* WHITE-BELLIED PYGMY-TYRANT. (wc SA). . . . . _____

❑ *Myiornis auricularis.* EARED PYGMY-TYRANT. (se SA). . . . . _____

❑ *Myiornis atricapillus.* BLACK-CAPPED PYGMY-TYRANT. (s CA-nw SA) _____

❑ *Myiornis ecaudatus.* SHORT-TAILED PYGMY-TYRANT. (Amaz). . . . . . . _____

❑ *Lophotriccus pileatus.* SCALE-CRESTED PYGMY-TYRANT. (s CA-w,n SA)_____

❑ *Lophotriccus vitiosus.* DOUBLE-BANDED PYGMY-TYRANT. (Amaz). . . . _____
   ___*L. (v.) vitiosus.* DOUBLE-BANDED PYGMY-TYRANT. (sp)
   ___*L. (v.) congener.* GOLDEN-SCALED PYGMY-TYRANT. (w Amaz Braz)

❑ *Lophotriccus eulophotes.* LONG-CRESTED PYGMY-TYRANT. (w Amaz). _____

❑ *Lophotriccus galeatus.* HELMETED PYGMY-TYRANT. (n Amaz). . . . . . . _____

❑ *Atalotriccus pilaris.* PALE-EYED PYGMY-TYRANT. (Pan, nw,n SA). . . . _____

❑ *Oncostoma cinereigulare.* NORTHERN BENTBILL. (MA). . . . . _____

❑ *Oncostoma olivaceum.* SOUTHERN BENTBILL. (e Pan, Amaz). . . . . _____

❑ *Cnipodectes subbrunneus.* BROWNISH FLYCATCHER. (e Pan, n,c SA) . _____

❑ *Rhynchocyclus brevirostris.* EYE-RINGED FLATBILL. (MA, nw SA). . . . _____
   ___*R. (b.) brevirostris.* EYE-RINGED FLATBILL. (MA)
   ___*R. (b.) pacificus.* PACIFIC FLATBILL. (e Pan, nw SA)

❑ *Rhynchocyclus olivaceus.* OLIVACEOUS FLATBILL. (Pan, Amaz). . . . . . _____

❑ *Rhynchocyclus fulvipectus.* FULVOUS-BREASTED FLATBILL. (w SA). . . _____

❑ *Tolmomyias sulphurescens.* YELLOW-OLIVE FLYCATCHER. (MA-SA) . _____

❑ *Tolmomyias assimilis.* YELLOW-MARGINED FLYCATCHER. (s CA-Amaz) _____

❑ *Tolmomyias poliocephalus.* GREY-CROWNED FLYCATCHER. (Amaz). . . _____

❑ *Tolmomyias flaviventris.* YELLOW-BREASTED FLYCATCHER. (SA). . . . . _____

❑ *Platyrinchus saturatus.* CINNAMON-CRESTED SPADEBILL. (Amaz). . . . . _____

❑ *Platyrinchus cancrominus.* STUB-TAILED SPADEBILL. (MA). . . . . _____

❑ *Platyrinchus mystaceus.* WHITE-THROATED SPADEBILL. (s CA-SA). . . _____
   ___*P. (m.) albogularis.* WHITE-THROATED SPADEBILL. (s CA, w,n SA)
   ___*P. (m.) mystaceus.* YELLOW-CRESTED SPADEBILL. (c,se SA)

❑ *Platyrinchus coronatus.* GOLDEN-CROWNED SPADEBILL. (CA, Amaz). _____

❑ *Platyrinchus flavigularis.* YELLOW-THROATED SPADEBILL. (w SA). . . . _____

❑ *Platyrinchus platyrhynchos.* WHITE-CRESTED SPADEBILL. (Amaz). . . . _____

❑ *Platyrinchus leucoryphus.* RUSSET-WINGED SPADEBILL. (se SA). . . . . . _____

❑ *Onychorhynchus coronatus.* ROYAL FLYCATCHER. (MA, SA). . . . . . . _____
___*O. (c.) mexicanus.* NORTHERN ROYAL-FLYCATCHER. (MA, nw SA)
___*O. (c.) occidentalis.* WESTERN ROYAL-FLYCATCHER. (cs SA)
___*O. (c.) coronatus.* AMAZONIAN ROYAL-FLYCATCHER. (Amaz)
___*O. (c.) swainsoni.* SWAINSON'S ROYAL-FLYCATCHER. (se Braz)

❑ *Myiotriccus ornatus.* ORNATE FLYCATCHER. (Andes w SA). . . . . _____

❑ *Myiophobus flavicans.* FLAVESCENT FLYCATCHER. (mts w,n SA). . . . . _____

❑ *Myiophobus phoenicomitra.* ORANGE-CRESTED FLYCATCHER. (nw SA). _____

❑ *Myiophobus inornatus.* UNADORNED FLYCATCHER. (Andes sw SA). . . _____

❑ *Myiophobus roraimae.* RORAIMAN FLYCATCHER. (w,n SA). . . . . _____
___*M. (r.) roraimae.* RORAIMAN FLYCATCHER. (n SA)
___*M. (r.) rufipennis.* PUNO FLYCATCHER. (e Peru)

❑ *Myiophobus pulcher.* HANDSOME FLYCATCHER. (Andes w SA). . . . . . _____

❑ *Myiophobus lintoni.* ORANGE-BANDED FLYCATCHER. (Andes wc SA). . _____

❑ *Myiophobus ochraceiventris.* OCHRACEOUS-BREASTED FLYC. (w SA). _____

❑ *Myiophobus fasciatus.* BRAN-COLORED FLYCATCHER. (s CA, SA). . . . _____
___*M. (f.) fasciatus.* BRAN-COLORED FLYCATCHER. (sp)
___*M. (f.) rufescens.* RUFESCENT FLYCATCHER. (Pac sw SA)

❑ *Myiophobus cryptoxanthus.* OLIVE-CHESTED FLYCATCHER. (wc SA). . _____

❑ *Myiobius erythrurus.* RUDDY-TAILED FLYCATCHER. (CA, Amaz). . . . . _____

❑ *Myiobius villosus.* TAWNY-BREASTED FLYCATCHER. (mts e Pan, w SA)_____

❑ *Myiobius barbatus.* SULPHUR-RUMPED FLYCATCHER. (MA, SA). . . . . _____
___*M. (b.) sulphureipygius.* SULPHUR-RUMPED FLYCATCHER. (MA, nw SA)
___*M. (b.) barbatus.* BEARDED FLYCATCHER. (Amaz)
___*M. (b.) mastacalis.* WHISKERED FLYCATCHER. (se Braz)

❑ *Myiobius atricaudus.* BLACK-TAILED FLYCATCHER. (s CA, SA). . . . . . _____
___*M. (a.) atricaudus.* BLACK-TAILED FLYCATCHER. (sp)
___*M. (a.) ridgwayi.* BUFF-RUMPED FLYCATCHER. (se Braz)

❑ *Pyrrhomyias cinnamomea.* CINNAMON FLYCATCHER. (mts w,n SA). . . _____
___*P. (c.) vieillotioides.* CHESTNUT FLYCATCHER. (n SA)
___*P. (c.) cinnamomea.* CINNAMON FLYCATCHER. (w SA)

❑ *Hirundinea ferruginea.* CLIFF FLYCATCHER. (w SA). . . . . _____

❑ *Hirundinea bellicosa.* SWALLOW FLYCATCHER. (se SA). . . . . _____

❑ *Cnemotriccus fuscatus.* FUSCOUS FLYCATCHER. (SA). . . . . _____

❑ *Lathrotriccus euleri.* EULER'S FLYCATCHER. (s L Ant, SA). . . . . _____
___*L. (e.) lawrencei.* LAWRENCE'S FLYCATCHER. (s L Ant, Amaz)
___*L. (e,) euleri.* EULER'S FLYCATCHER. (s SA)

❑ *Lathrotriccus griseipectus.* GREY-BREASTED FLYCATCHER. (cw SA). . _____

❑ *Aphanotriccus capitalis.* TAWNY-CHESTED FLYCATCHER. (Nic, CR). . . _____

❑ *Aphanotriccus audax.* BLACK-BILLED FLYCATCHER. (e Pan, n Colom). _____

❑ *Xenotriccus callizonus.* BELTED FLYCATCHER. (mts c MA). . . . . _____

❑ *Xenotriccus mexicanus.* PILEATED FLYCATCHER. (mts c Mex). . . . . . . _____

❑ *Mitrephanes phaeocercus.* TUFTED FLYCATCHER. (MA, w SA). . . . . . _____

❑ *Mitrephanes olivaceus.* OLIVE FLYCATCHER. (Andes cw SA). . . . . . . _____

❑ *Contopus borealis.* OLIVE-SIDED FLYCATCHER. (n NA; ◊-SA). . . . . . . _____

❑ *Contopus pertinax.* GREATER PEWEE. (mts Ariz, MA). . . . . _____

❑ *Contopus lugubris.* DARK PEWEE. (mts CR, w Pan). . . . . _____

❑ *Contopus fumigatus.* SMOKE-COLORED PEWEE. (mts w,n SA). . . . . . . _____

❑ *Contopus ochraceus.* OCHRACEOUS PEWEE. (mts CR, w Pan). . . . . . . _____

❑ *Contopus sordidulus.* WESTERN WOOD-PEWEE. (w NA-cMA; ◊ SA). . _____

❑ *Contopus virens.* EASTERN WOOD-PEWEE. (e NA; ◊ SA). . . . . _____

❑ *Contopus cinereus.* TROPICAL PEWEE. (MA, SA). . . . . _____
    ___*C. (c.) brachytarsus.* SHORT-LEGGED PEWEE. (MA)
    ___*C. (c.) cinereus.* TROPICAL PEWEE. (SA)

❑ *Contopus nigrescens.* BLACKISH PEWEE. (w,n,c SA). . . . . _____

❑ *Contopus albogularis.* WHITE-THROATED PEWEE. (n SA). . . . . _____

❑ *Contopus caribaeus.* GREATER ANTILLEAN PEWEE. (Bah, G Ant). . . . . _____

❑ *Contopus latirostris.* LESSER ANTILLEAN PEWEE. (mts PR, n L Ant). . . _____

❑ *Empidonax flaviventris.* YELLOW-BELLIED FLYCATCHER. (n NA; ◊ MA)_____

❑ *Empidonax virescens.* ACADIAN FLYCATCHER. (e NA; ◊-nw SA). . . . . _____

❑ *Empidonax alnorum.* ALDER FLYCATCHER. (NA; ◊ SA). . . . . _____

❑ *Empidonax traillii.* WILLOW FLYCATCHER. (NA; ◊ MA). . . . . _____

❑ *Empidonax albigularis.* WHITE-THROATED FLYCATCHER. (mts MA). . . _____

❑ *Empidonax minimus.* LEAST FLYCATCHER. (NA; ◊ MA). . . . . _____

❑ *Empidonax hammondii.* HAMMOND'S FLYCATCHER. (w NA; ◊ to CA). . _____

❑ *Empidonax wrightii.* GREY FLYCATCHER. (w NA; ◊-s Mex). . . . . _____

❑ *Empidonax oberholseri.* DUSKY FLYCATCHER. (w NA; ◊-Guat). . . . . . _____

❑ *Empidonax affinis.* PINE FLYCATCHER. (mts Mex). . . . . _____

❑ *Empidonax difficilis.* PACIFIC-SLOPE FLYCATCHER. (w NA; ◊-Mex). . . _____
    ___*E. (d.) difficilis.* PACIFIC-SLOPE FLYCATCHER. (sp)
    ___*E. (d.) insulicola.* CHANNEL ISLANDS FLYCATCHER. (Channel Is)

❑ *Empidonax occidentalis.* CORDILLERAN FLYCATCHER. (w NA, Mex). . _____

❑ *Empidonax flavescens.* YELLOWISH FLYCATCHER. (mts MA). . . . . _____

❏ *Empidonax fulvifrons.* BUFF-BREASTED FLYCATCHER. (s Ariz-MA)... _____

❏ *Empidonax atriceps.* BLACK-CAPPED FLYCATCHER. (mts CR, w Pan). _____

❏ *Sayornis phoebe.* EASTERN PHOEBE. (e NA; ◊ se US-e Mex)........ _____

❏ *Sayornis saya.* SAY'S PHOEBE. (w NA, Mex).................... _____

❏ *Sayornis nigricans.* BLACK PHOEBE. (w NA, MA, w,n SA)......... _____
   ___*S. (n.) nigricans.* BLACK PHOEBE. (w NA, MA)
   ___*S. (n.) latirostris.* WHITE-WINGED PHOEBE. (w,n SA)

❏ *Pyrocephalus rubinus.* VERMILION FLYCATCHER. (sw US-SA, Galap). _____
   ___*P. (r.) rubinus.* VERMILION FLYCATCHER. (sp)
   ___*P. (r.) nanus.* GALAPAGOS FLYCATCHER. (Galap)

❏ *Silvicultrix frontalis.* CROWNED CHAT-TYRANT. (Andes w SA)...... _____
   ___*S. (f.) albidiadema.* WHITE-FRONTED CHAT-TYRANT. (Colom)
   ___*S. (f.) frontalis.* CROWNED CHAT-TYRANT. (sp)

❏ *Silvicultrix jelskii.* JELSKI'S CHAT-TYRANT. (Andes sw SA)......... _____

❏ *Silvicultrix diadema.* YELLOW-BELLIED CHAT-TYRANT. (mts w,n SA). _____

❏ *Silvicultrix pulchella.* GOLDEN-BROWED CHAT-TYRANT. (wc SA)..... _____

❏ *Ochthoeca cinnamomeiventris.* SLATY-BACKED CHAT-TYRANT. (w SA)_____
   ___*O. (c.) nigrita.* BLACKISH CHAT-TYRANT. (w Ven)
   ___*O. (c.) cinnamomeiventris.* SLATY-BACKED CHAT-TYRANT. (nw SA)
   ___*O. (c.) thoracica.* CHESTNUT-BELTED CHAT-TYRANT. (wc SA)

❏ *Ochthoeca rufipectoralis.* RUFOUS-BREASTED CHAT-TYRANT. (w SA). _____

❏ *Ochthoeca fumicolor.* BROWN-BACKED CHAT-TYRANT. (Andes w SA). _____
   ___*O. (f.) superciliosa.* RUFOUS-BROWED CHAT-TYRANT. (w Ven)
   ___*O. (f.) fumicolor.* BROWN-BACKED CHAT-TYRANT. (sp)

❏ *Ochthoeca oenanthoides.* D'ORBIGNY'S CHAT-TYRANT. (Andes w SA). _____

❏ *Ochthoeca leucophrys.* WHITE-BROWED CHAT-TYRANT. (Andes w SA) _____

❏ *Ochthoeca piurae.* PIURA CHAT-TYRANT. (Andes nw Peru)........ _____

❏ *Ochthoeca salvini.* TUMBES TYRANT. (Andes w Peru)............ _____

❏ *Colorhamphus parvirostris.* PATAGONIAN TYRANT. (mts s SA)...... _____

❏ *Ochthornis littoralis.* DRAB WATER-TYRANT. (Amaz)............ _____

❏ *Cnemarchus erythropygius.* RED-RUMPED BUSH-TYRANT. (mts w SA). _____

❏ *Myiotheretes striaticollis.* STREAK-THROATED BUSH-TYRANT. (w SA). _____

❏ *Myiotheretes pernix.* SANTA MARTA BUSH-TYRANT. (mts ne Colom). _____

❏ *Myiotheretes fumigatus.* SMOKY BUSH-TYRANT. (mts w SA)....... _____

❏ *Myiotheretes fuscorufus.* RUFOUS-BELLIED BUSH-TYRANT. (sw SA). _____

❏ *Xolmis pyrope.* FIRE-EYED DIUCON. (Andes s SA)................ _____

❏ *Xolmis cinerea.* GREY MONJITA. (SA)........................ _____

❏ *Xolmis coronata.* BLACK-CROWNED MONJITA. (sc SA)............ _____

❑ *Xolmis velata.* WHITE-RUMPED MONJITA. (e,sc SA). . . . . _____

❑ *Xolmis irupero.* WHITE MONJITA. (e,sc SA). . . . . _____

❑ *Xolmis rubetra.* RUSTY-BACKED MONJITA. (w Argen). . . . . _____

❑ *Xolmis salinarum.* SALINAS MONJITA. (nc Argen). . . . . _____

❑ *Heteroxolmis dominicana.* BLACK-AND-WHITE MONJITA. (sc SA). . . . _____

❑ *Neoxolmis rufiventris.* CHOCOLATE-VENTED TYRANT. (s SA). . . . . _____

❑ *Agriornis montana.* BLACK-BILLED SHRIKE-TYRANT. (mts w,s SA). . . _____

❑ *Agriornis andicola.* WHITE-TAILED SHRIKE-TYRANT. (Andes w SA). . . _____

❑ *Agriornis livida.* GREAT SHRIKE-TYRANT. (s SA). . . . . _____

❑ *Agriornis microptera.* GREY-BELLIED SHRIKE-TYRANT. (sc SA). . . . . . _____

❑ *Agriornis murina.* LESSER SHRIKE-TYRANT. (sw SA). . . . . _____

❑ *Polioxolmis rufipennis.* RUFOUS-WEBBED BUSH-TYRANT. (sw SA). . . . _____

❑ *Muscisaxicola maculirostris.* SPOT-BILLED GROUND-TYRANT. (w SA). _____

❑ *Muscisaxicola fluviatilis.* LITTLE GROUND-TYRANT. (wc SA). . . . . . . _____

❑ *Muscisaxicola macloviana.* DARK-FACED GROUND-TYRANT. (s SA). . . _____

❑ *Muscisaxicola capistrata.* CINNAMON-BELLIED GROUND-T. (s Chile). . _____

❑ *Muscisaxicola rufivertex.* RUFOUS-NAPED GROUND-TYRANT. (w,s SA) _____
    ___*M. (r.) occipitalis.* CHESTNUT-NAPED GROUND-TYRANT. (cw SA)
    ___*M. (r.) rufivertex.* RUFOUS-NAPED GROUND-TYRANT. (se,s SA)

❑ *Muscisaxicola juninensis.* PUNA GROUND-TYRANT. (Andes sw SA). . . _____

❑ *Muscisaxicola albilora.* WHITE-BROWED GROUND-TYRANT. (w SA). . . _____

❑ *Muscisaxicola alpina.* PLAIN-CAPPED GROUND-TYRANT. (w SA). . . . . _____
    ___*M. (a.) alpina.* PARAMO GROUND-TYRANT. (nw SA)
    ___*M. (a.) grisea.* PLAIN-CAPPED GROUND-TYRANT. (cw SA)

❑ *Muscisaxicola cinerea.* CINEREOUS GROUND-TYRANT. (Andes sw SA). _____

❑ *Muscisaxicola albifrons.* WHITE-FRONTED GROUND-TYRANT. (sw SA). _____

❑ *Muscisaxicola flavinucha.* OCHRE-NAPED GROUND-TYRANT. (s SA) . _____

❑ *Muscisaxicola frontalis.* BLACK-FRONTED GROUND-TYRANT. (sw SA). _____

❑ *Muscigralla brevicauda.* SHORT-TAILED FIELD-TYRANT. (cw SA). . . . . _____

❑ *Lessonia oreas.* ANDEAN NEGRITO. (Andes sw SA). . . . . _____

❑ *Lessonia rufa.* PATAGONIAN NEGRITO. (s SA; ◊-sc SA). . . . . _____

❑ *Knipolegus striaticeps.* CINEREOUS TYRANT. (sc SA). . . . . _____

❑ *Knipolegus hudsoni.* HUDSON'S BLACK-TYRANT. (c Argen; ◊-sc SA) . _____

❑ *Knipolegus poecilocercus.* AMAZONIAN BLACK-TYRANT. (Amaz). . . . . _____

❑ *Knipolegus signatus.* ANDEAN TYRANT. (Andes sw SA). . . . . _____
    ___*K. (s.) signatus.* BLACK ANDEAN-TYRANT. (n,e Peru)
    ___*K. (s.) cabanisi.* PLUMBEOUS ANDEAN-TYRANT. (sp)

❑ *Knipolegus cyanirostris.* BLUE-BILLED BLACK-TYRANT. (se SA)..... _____

❑ *Knipolegus poecilurus.* RUFOUS-TAILED TYRANT. (mts w,n SA)...... _____

❑ *Knipolegus orenocensis.* RIVERSIDE TYRANT. (Amaz)............. _____
   ___*K. (o.) orenocensis.* ORINOCO RIVER-TYRANT. (n Amaz)
   ___*K. (o.) sclateri.* AMAZON RIVER-TYRANT. (s Amaz)

❑ *Knipolegus aterrimus.* WHITE-WINGED BLACK-TYRANT. (sc SA)..... _____

❑ *Knipolegus nigerrimus.* VELVETY BLACK-TYRANT. (se Braz)........ _____

❑ *Knipolegus lophotes.* CRESTED BLACK -TYRANT. (se SA).......... _____

❑ *Hymenops perspicillatus.* SPECTACLED TYRANT. (sw,sc SA)........ _____

❑ *Fluvicola pica.* PIED WATER-TYRANT. (e Pan, n SA)............. _____

❑ *Fluvicola albiventer.* BLACK-BACKED WATER-TYRANT. (c,sc SA)..... _____

❑ *Fluvicola nengeta.* MASKED WATER-TYRANT. (cw,e SA).......... _____

❑ *Arundinicola leucocephala.* WHITE-HEADED MARSH-TYRANT. (SA) . _____

❑ *Alectrurus tricolor.* COCK-TAILED TYRANT. (sc,se SA)............ _____

❑ *Alectrurus risora.* STRANGE-TAILED TYRANT. (se SA)............. _____

❑ *Gubernetes yetapa.* STREAMER-TAILED TYRANT. (sc SA)........... _____

❑ *Satrapa icterophrys.* YELLOW-BROWED TYRANT. (sc SA; ◊-n SA)..... _____

❑ *Colonia colonus.* LONG-TAILED TYRANT. (CA, SA).............. _____

❑ *Machetornis rixosus.* CATTLE TYRANT. (SA)................... _____

❑ *Muscipipra vetula.* SHEAR-TAILED GREY TYRANT. (se SA)......... _____

❑ *Attila phoenicurus.* RUFOUS-TAILED ATTILA. (sc,se SA; ◊-n SA)..... _____

❑ *Attila cinnamomeus.* CINNAMON ATTILA. (Amaz)................ _____

❑ *Attila torridus.* OCHRACEOUS ATTILA. (nw SA)................. _____

❑ *Attila citriniventris.* CITRON-BELLIED ATTILA. (Andes wc SA)....... _____

❑ *Attila bolivianus.* DULL-CAPPED ATTILA. (Amaz)............... _____

❑ *Attila rufus.* GREY-HOODED ATTILA. (se Braz).................. _____

❑ *Attila spadiceus.* BRIGHT-RUMPED ATTILA. (MA, SA)............. _____

❑ *Casiornis rufa.* RUFOUS CASIORNIS. (sc SA)................... _____

❑ *Casiornis fusca.* ASH-THROATED CASIORNIS. (c,e Braz)............ _____

❑ *Rhytipterna holerythra.* RUFOUS MOURNER. (MA, nw SA)......... _____

❑ *Rhytipterna simplex.* GREYISH MOURNER. (n,c,e SA)............. _____

❑ *Rhytipterna immunda.* PALE-BELLIED MOURNER. (w Amaz)........ _____

❑ *Laniocera rufescens.* SPECKLED MOURNER. (MA, nw SA)......... _____

❑ *Laniocera hypopyrra.* CINEREOUS MOURNER. (n,c,e SA)........... _____

❑ *Sirystes sibilator.* SIRYSTES. (Pan, SA). . . . . _____
   ___*S. (s.) albogriseus.* WHITE-RUMPED SIRYSTES. (Pan, Amaz)
   ___*S. (s.) sibilator.* SIBILANT SIRYSTES. (se SA)

❑ *Myiarchus semirufus.* RUFOUS FLYCATCHER. (nw Peru). . . . . _____

❑ *Myiarchus yucatanensis.* YUCATAN FLYCATCHER. (c MA). . . . . _____

❑ *Myiarchus tuberculifer.* DUSKY-CAPPED FLYCATCHER. (se Ariz-SA) . _____
   ___*M. (t.) tuberculifer.* DUSKY-CAPPED FLYCATCHER. (sp)
   ___*M. (t.) atriceps.* DARK-CAPPED FLYCATCHER. (Andes sw SA)

❑ *Myiarchus barbirostris.* SAD FLYCATCHER. (Jam). . . . . _____

❑ *Myiarchus swainsoni.* SWAINSON'S FLYCATCHER. (SA). . . . . _____
   ___*M. (s.) phaeonotus.* WHITELY'S FLYCATCHER. (nw Amaz)
   ___*M. (s.) pelzelni.* PELZELN'S FLYCATCHER. (c,sc SA)
   ___*M. (s.) swainsoni.* SWAINSON'S FLYCATCHER. (se SA)

❑ *Myiarchus venezuelensis.* VENEZUELAN FLYCATCHER. (Tob, n SA). . . _____

❑ *Myiarchus panamensis.* PANAMA FLYCATCHER. (s CA, nw SA). . . . . . _____

❑ *Myiarchus ferox.* SHORT-CRESTED FLYCATCHER. (SA). . . . . _____

❑ *Myiarchus cephalotes.* PALE-EDGED FLYCATCHER. (mts w,n SA). . . . . _____

❑ *Myiarchus phaeocephalus.* SOOTY-CROWNED FLYCATCHER. (cw SA) . _____

❑ *Myiarchus apicalis.* APICAL FLYCATCHER. (mts c,sw Colom). . . . . . . _____

❑ *Myiarchus cinerascens.* ASH-THROATED FLYCATCHER. (w NA-CA). . . _____

❑ *Myiarchus nuttingi.* NUTTING'S FLYCATCHER. (MA). . . . . _____

❑ *Myiarchus crinitus.* GREAT CRESTED FLYCATCHER. (e NA; ◊-n SA) . _____

❑ *Myiarchus tyrannulus.* BROWN-CRESTED FLYCATCHER. (w NA-SA). . . _____
   ___*M. (t.) magister.* WIED'S CRESTED FLYCATCHER. (w NA, MA)
   ___*M. (t.) brachyurus.* OMETEPE FLYCATCHER. (Pac c CA)
   ___*M. (t.) tyrannulus.* BROWN-CRESTED FLYCATCHER. (SA)

❑ *Myiarchus nugator.* GRENADA FLYCATCHER. (s L Ant). . . . . _____

❑ *Myiarchus magnirostris.* LARGE-BILLED FLYCATCHER. (Galap). . . . . . _____

❑ *Myiarchus validus.* RUFOUS-TAILED FLYCATCHER. (mts Jam). . . . . . . _____

❑ *Myiarchus sagrae.* LA SAGRA'S FLYCATCHER. (n W Indies). . . . . _____

❑ *Myiarchus stolidus.* STOLID FLYCATCHER. (Jam, Hisp). . . . . _____

❑ *Myiarchus antillarum.* PUERTO RICAN FLYCATCHER. (PR, Virgin). . . . _____

❑ *Myiarchus oberi.* LESSER ANTILLEAN FLYCATCHER. (L Ant). . . . . _____

❑ *Deltarhynchus flammulatus.* FLAMMULATED FLYCATCHER. (w Mex) . _____

❑ *Ramphotrigon megacephala.* LARGE-HEADED FLATBILL. (SA). . . . . . . _____

❑ *Ramphotrigon fuscicauda.* DUSKY-TAILED FLATBILL. (w Amaz). . . . . _____

❑ *Ramphotrigon ruficauda.* RUFOUS-TAILED FLATBILL. (Amaz). . . . . . . _____

❑ *Tyrannus niveigularis.* SNOWY-THROATED KINGBIRD. (nw SA). . . . . . _____

❑ *Tyrannus albogularis.* WHITE-THROATED KINGBIRD. (Amaz). . . . . _____

❑ *Tyrannus melancholicus.* TROPICAL KINGBIRD. (sw US, CA, SA). . . . _____

❑ *Tyrannus couchii.* COUCH'S KINGBIRD. (s Tex, n MA). . . . . _____

❑ *Tyrannus vociferans.* CASSIN'S KINGBIRD. (w NA, Mex; ◊-n CA). . . . . _____

❑ *Tyrannus crassirostris.* THICK-BILLED KINGBIRD. (se Ariz, Mex). . . . . _____

❑ *Tyrannus verticalis.* WESTERN KINGBIRD. (w NA; ◊ MA). . . . . _____

❑ *Tyrannus forficata.* SCISSOR-TAILED FLYCATCHER. (sc NA; ◊-CA). . . . _____

❑ *Tyrannus savana.* FORK-TAILED FLYCATCHER. (MA, SA). . . . . _____

❑ *Tyrannus tyrannus.* EASTERN KINGBIRD. (NA; ◊ SA). . . . . _____

❑ *Tyrannus dominicensis.* GREY KINGBIRD. (se US, W Indies, n SA). . . _____

❑ *Tyrannus caudifasciatus.* LOGGERHEAD KINGBIRD. (n W Indies). . . . . _____

❑ *Tyrannus cubensis.* GIANT KINGBIRD. (Cuba). . . . . _____

❑ *Empidonomus varius.* VARIEGATED FLYCATCHER. (SA). . . . . _____

❑ *Griseotyrannus aurantioatrocristatus.* CROWNED SLATY F. (sc SA). . . _____

❑ *Tyrannopsis sulphurea.* SULPHURY FLYCATCHER. (Amaz). . . . . _____

❑ *Megarynchus pitangua.* BOAT-BILLED FLYCATCHER. (MA, SA). . . . . . _____

❑ *Conopias albovittata.* WHITE-RINGED FLYCATCHER. (s CA, nw SA). . . _____

❑ *Conopias parva.* YELLOW-THROATED FLYCATCHER. (wc SA). . . . . . . _____

❑ *Conopias trivirgata.* THREE-STRIPED FLYCATCHER. (SA). . . . . _____

❑ *Conopias cinchoneti.* LEMON-BROWED FLYCATCHER. (mts w SA). . . . . _____

❑ *Myiodynastes hemichrysus.* GOLDEN-BELLIED FLYCATCHER. (s CA). . . _____

❑ *Myiodynastes chrysocephalus.* GOLDEN-CROWNED F. (mts s CA, SA). _____

❑ *Myiodynastes bairdii.* BAIRD'S FLYCATCHER. (cw SA). . . . . _____

❑ *Myiodynastes maculatus.* STREAKED FLYCATCHER. (MA, SA). . . . . . . _____
  ___*M. (m.) maculatus.* STREAKED FLYCATCHER. (sp)
  ___*M. (m.) solitarius.* SOLITARY FLYCATCHER. (sc SA)

❑ *Myiodynastes luteiventris.* SULPHUR-BELLIED F. (se Ariz, MA; ◊ SA) . _____

❑ *Myiozetetes cayanensis.* RUSTY-MARGINED FLYCATCHER. (Pan, SA). . . _____

❑ *Mylozetetes similis.* SOCIAL FLYCATCHER. (MA, SA). . . . . _____
  ___*M. (s.) texensis.* VERMILION-CROWNED FLYCATCHER. (MA)
  ___*M. (s.) similis.* SOCIAL FLYCATCHER. (s CA, SA)

❑ *Myiozetetes granadensis.* GREY-CAPPED FLYCATCHER. (CA, Amaz). . . _____

❑ *Myiozetetes luteiventris.* DUSKY-CHESTED FLYCATCHER. (Amaz). . . . . _____

❑ *Legatus leucophaius.* PIRATIC FLYCATCHER. (MA, SA). . . . . _____

❑ *Philohydor lictor.* LESSER KISKADEE. (e Pan, SA). . . . . _____

❑ *Pitangus sulphuratus.* GREAT KISKADEE. (s Tex, MA, SA; ♦ Berm) . _____

❑ *Phelpsia inornata.* WHITE-BEARDED FLYCATCHER. (wc,n Ven). . . . . . _____

Subfamily Tityrinae [4/23]
Tribe Schiffornithini [1/3]

❑ *Schiffornis major.* Greater Schiffornis. (Amaz). . . . . _____

❑ *Schiffornis turdinus.* Thrush-like Schiffornis. (MA, SA). . . . . _____
   ___*S. (t.) veraepacis.* Brown Schiffornis. (MA)
   ___*S. (t.) turdinus.* Thrush-like Schiffornis. (s CA, SA)

❑ *Schiffornis virescens.* Greenish Schiffornis. (se SA). . . . . _____

Tribe Tityrini [3/20]

❑ *Xenopsaris albinucha.* White-naped Xenopsaris. (SA). . . . . _____

❑ *Pachyramphus viridis.* Green-backed Becard. (SA). . . . . _____
   ___*P. (v.) viridis.* Green-backed Becard. (sp)
   ___*P. (v.) xanthogenys.* Yellow-cheeked Becard. (wc SA)

❑ *Pachyramphus versicolor.* Barred Becard. (mts s CA, w SA). . . . . . _____

❑ *Pachyramphus cinnamomeus.* Cinnamon Becard. (MA, nw SA). . . _____

❑ *Pachyramphus castaneus.* Chestnut-crowned Becard. (SA). . . . . . _____

❑ *Pachyramphus polychopterus.* White-winged Becard. (CA, SA). . . _____

❑ *Pachyramphus major.* Grey-collared Becard. (MA). . . . . _____

❑ *Pachyramphus albogriseus.* Black-and-white Becard. (s CA-w,n SA)_____

❑ *Pachyramphus marginatus.* Black-capped Becard. (c,se SA). . . . . . _____

❑ *Pachyramphus surinamus.* Glossy-backed Becard. (ne SA). . . . . . _____

❑ *Pachyramphus rufus.* Cinereous Becard. (Pan, Amaz). . . . . _____

❑ *Pachyramphus spodiurus.* Slaty Becard. (cw SA). . . . . _____

❑ *Pachyramphus aglaiae.* Rose-throated Becard. (sw US, MA). . . . . _____

❑ *Pachyramphus homochrous.* One-colored Becard. (Pan, nw SA) . _____

❑ *Pachyramphus minor.* Pink-throated Becard. (Amaz). . . . . _____

❑ *Pachyramphus niger.* Jamaican Becard. (Jam). . . . . _____

❑ *Pachyramphus validus.* Crested Becard. (sc SA). . . . . _____

❑ *Tityra cayana.* Black-tailed Tityra. (SA). . . . . _____

❑ *Tityra semifasciata.* Masked Tityra. (MA, Amaz). . . . . _____

❑ *Tityra inquisitor.* Black-crowned Tityra. (MA, SA). . . . . _____

Subfamily Cotinginae [28/69]

❑ *Phoenicircus nigricollis.* Black-necked Red-Cotinga. (Amaz). . . . . _____

❑ *Phoenicircus carnifex.* Guianan Red-Cotinga. (Amaz). . . . . _____

❑ *Laniisoma elegans.* Shrike-like Cotinga. (w,se SA). . . . . _____
   ___*L. (e.) buckleyi.* Buckley's Cotinga. (w SA)
   ___*L. (e.) elegans.* Shrike-like Cotinga. (se Braz)

❏ *Phibalura flavirostris.* SWALLOW-TAILED COTINGA. (sc,se SA). . . . . . _____

❏ *Tijuca atra.* BLACK-AND-GOLD COTINGA. (mts se Braz). . . . . _____

❏ *Tijuca condita.* GREY-WINGED COTINGA. (mts se Braz). . . . . _____

❏ *Carpornis cucullatus.* HOODED BERRYEATER. (se Braz). . . . . _____

❏ *Carpornis melanocephalus.* BLACK-HEADED BERRYEATER. (se Braz) . _____

❏ *Doliornis sclateri.* BAY-VENTED COTINGA. (Andes c Peru). . . . . _____

❏ *Ampelion rubrocristata.* RED-CRESTED COTINGA. (mts w SA). . . . . . . _____

❏ *Ampelion rufaxilla.* CHESTNUT-CRESTED COTINGA. (Andes w SA). . . . _____

❏ *Phytotoma raimondii.* PERUVIAN PLANTCUTTER. (nw Peru). . . . . _____

❏ *Phytotoma rutila.* WHITE-TIPPED PLANTCUTTER. (s SA). . . . . _____

❏ *Phytotoma rara.* RUFOUS-TAILED PLANTCUTTER. (s SA). . . . . _____

❏ *Zaratornis stresemanni.* WHITE-CHEEKED COTINGA. (Andes wc Peru). _____

❏ *Pipreola riefferii.* GREEN-AND-BLACK FRUITEATER. (mts w,n SA). . . . . _____
   ___*P. (r.) riefferii.* GREEN-AND-BLACK FRUITEATER. (sp)
   ___*P. (r.) tallmanorum.* BLACK-HEADED FRUITEATER. (c Peru)

❏ *Pipreola intermedia.* BAND-TAILED FRUITEATER. (Andes sw SA). . . . . _____

❏ *Pipreola arcuata.* BARRED FRUITEATER. (mts w SA). . . . . _____

❏ *Pipreola aureopectus.* GOLDEN-BREASTED FRUITEATER. (mts nw SA) . _____

❏ *Pipreola jucunda.* ORANGE-BREASTED FRUITEATER. (Andes nw SA) . _____

❏ *Pipreola lubomirskii.* BLACK-CHESTED FRUITEATER. (Andes nw SA) . _____

❏ *Pipreola pulchra.* MASKED FRUITEATER. (Andes e Peru). . . . . _____

❏ *Pipreola chlorolepidota.* FIERY-THROATED FRUITEATER. (w SA). . . . . . _____

❏ *Pipreola frontalis.* SCARLET-BREASTED FRUITEATER. (w,sw SA). . . . . . _____
   ___*P. (f.) squamipectus.* BLUISH-CROWNED FRUITEATER. (cw SA)
   ___*P. (f.) frontalis.* SCARLET-BREASTED FRUITEATER. (sw SA)

❏ *Pipreola formosa.* HANDSOME FRUITEATER. (mts n Ven). . . . . _____

❏ *Pipreola whitelyi.* RED-BANDED FRUITEATER. (Pant nc NA). . . . . _____

❏ *Ampelioides tschudii.* SCALED FRUITEATER. (mts w SA). . . . . _____

❏ *Iodopleura pipra.* BUFF-THROATED PURPLETUFT. (se Braz). . . . . _____

❏ *Iodopleura isabellae.* WHITE-BROWED PURPLETUFT. (Amaz). . . . . _____

❏ *Iodopleura fusca.* DUSKY PURPLETUFT. (n SA). . . . . _____

❏ *Calyptura cristata.* KINGLET CALYPTURA. (se Braz). . . . . _____

❏ *Lipaugus subalaris.* GREY-TAILED PIHA. (Andes wc SA). . . . . _____

❏ *Lipaugus cryptolophus.* OLIVACEOUS PIHA. (Andes w SA). . . . . _____

❏ *Lipaugus fuscocinereus.* DUSKY PIHA. (Andes nw SA). . . . . _____

❏ *Lipaugus uropygialis.* SCIMITAR-WINGED PIHA. (Andes sw SA). . . . . . _____

❑ *Lipaugus vociferans.* SCREAMING PIHA. (n,c,e SA). . . . . _____

❑ *Lipaugus unirufus.* RUFOUS PIHA. (MA, nw SA). . . . . _____

❑ *Lipaugus lanioides.* CINNAMON-VENTED PIHA. (mts se Braz). . . . . _____

❑ *Lipaugus streptophorus.* ROSE-COLLARED PIHA. (Pant sc SA). . . . . _____

❑ *Porphyrolaema porphyrolaema.* PURPLE-THROATED COTINGA. (w Amaz)_____

❑ *Cotinga amabilis.* LOVELY COTINGA. (MA). . . . . _____

❑ *Cotinga ridgwayi.* TURQUOISE COTINGA. (sw CR, w Pan). . . . . _____

❑ *Cotinga nattererii.* BLUE COTINGA. (Pan, nw SA). . . . . _____

❑ *Cotinga maynana.* PLUM-THROATED COTINGA. (w Amaz). . . . . _____

❑ *Cotinga cotinga.* PURPLE-BREASTED COTINGA. (Amaz). . . . . _____

❑ *Cotinga maculata.* BANDED COTINGA. (se Braz). . . . . _____

❑ *Cotinga cayana.* SPANGLED COTINGA. (Amaz). . . . . _____

❑ *Xipholena punicea.* POMPADOUR COTINGA. (Amaz). . . . . _____

❑ *Xipholena lamellipennis.* WHITE-TAILED COTINGA. (e Braz). . . . . _____

❑ *Xipholena atropurpurea.* WHITE-WINGED COTINGA. (e Braz). . . . . _____

❑ *Carpodectes nitidus.* SNOWY COTINGA. (CA). . . . . _____

❑ *Carpodectes antoniae.* YELLOW-BILLED COTINGA. (sw CR, w Pan). . . . _____

❑ *Carpodectes hopkei.* BLACK-TIPPED COTINGA. (e Pan, nw SA). . . . . . . _____

❑ *Conioptilon mcilhennyi.* BLACK-FACED COTINGA. (se Peru). . . . . _____

❑ *Gymnoderus foetidus.* BARE-NECKED FRUITCROW. (Amaz). . . . . _____

❑ *Haematoderus militaris.* CRIMSON FRUITCROW. (ne Amaz). . . . . _____

❑ *Querula purpurata.* PURPLE-THROATED FRUITCROW. (s CA, Amaz). . . _____

❑ *Pyroderus scutatus.* RED-RUFFED FRUITCROW. (mts w,n SA). . . . . _____

❑ *Cephalopterus glabricollis.* BARE-NECKED UMBRELLABIRD. (s CA). . . _____

❑ *Cephalopterus penduliger.* LONG-WATTLED UMBRELLABIRD. (nw SA). _____

❑ *Cephalopterus ornatus.* AMAZONIAN UMBRELLABIRD. (Amaz). . . . . . . _____

❑ *Perissocephalus tricolor.* CAPUCHINBIRD. (n Amaz). . . . . _____

❑ *Procnias tricarunculata.* THREE-WATTLED BELLBIRD. (mts CA). . . . . . _____

❑ *Procnias alba.* WHITE BELLBIRD. (n,c Amaz). . . . . _____

❑ *Procnias averano.* BEARDED BELLBIRD. (n,c Amaz). . . . . _____

❑ *Procnias nudicollis.* BARE-THROATED BELLBIRD. (se SA). . . . . _____

❑ *Rupicola rupicola.* GUIANAN COCK-OF-THE-ROCK. (n Amaz). . . . . _____

❑ *Rupicola peruviana.* ANDEAN COCK-OF-THE-ROCK. (Andes w SA). . . . _____

❑ *Oxyruncus cristatus.* SHARPBILL. (mts s CA, SA). . . . . _____

Subfamily Piprinae [12/53]

❑ *Pipra aureola.* CRIMSON-HOODED MANAKIN. (Amaz). . . . . _____

❑ *Pipra fasciicauda.* BAND-TAILED MANAKIN. (sc SA). . . . . _____

❑ *Pipra filicauda.* WIRE-TAILED MANAKIN. (w Amaz). . . . . _____

❑ *Pipra mentalis.* RED-CAPPED MANAKIN. (MA, nw SA). . . . . _____

❑ *Pipra erythrocephala.* GOLDEN-HEADED MANAKIN. (e Pan, Amaz). . . . _____

❑ *Pipra rubrocapilla.* RED-HEADED MANAKIN. (s Amaz). . . . . _____

❑ *Pipra chloromeros.* ROUND-TAILED MANAKIN. (w Amaz). . . . . _____

❑ *Pipra cornuta.* SCARLET-HORNED MANAKIN. (Pant nc SA). . . . . _____

❑ *Pipra pipra.* WHITE-CROWNED MANAKIN. (s CA, SA). . . . . _____
   ___*P. (p.) anthracina.* ZELEDON'S MANAKIN. (s CA)
   ___*P. (p.) pipra.* WHITE-CROWNED MANAKIN. (SA)

❑ *Pipra coronata.* BLUE-CROWNED MANAKIN. (s CA, w Amaz). . . . . _____
   ___*P. (c.) velutina.* VELVETY MANAKIN. (s CA, nw SA)
   ___*P. (c.) coronata.* BLUE-CROWNED MANAKIN. (w Amaz)
   ___*P. (c.) exquisita.* EXQUISITE MANAKIN. (sw Amaz)

❑ *Pipra suavissima.* TEPUI MANAKIN. (Pant nc SA). . . . . _____

❑ *Pipra serena.* WHITE-FRONTED MANAKIN. (n SA). . . . . _____

❑ *Pipra iris.* OPAL-CROWNED MANAKIN. (se Amaz), ... _____

❑ *Pipra vilasboasi.* GOLDEN-CROWNED MANAKIN. (sw Amaz Braz). . . . . _____

❑ *Pipra nattereri.* SNOW-CAPPED MANAKIN. (s Amaz). . . . . _____

❑ *Pipra isidorei.* BLUE-RUMPED MANAKIN. (Andes w SA). . . . . _____

❑ *Pipra coeruleocapilla.* CERULEAN-CAPPED MANAKIN. (c,e Peru). . . . . _____

❑ *Antilophia galeata.* HELMETED MANAKIN. (mts sc SA). . . . . _____

❑ *Chiroxiphia linearis.* LONG-TAILED MANAKIN. (MA). . . . . _____

❑ *Chiroxiphia lanceolata.* LANCE-TAILED MANAKIN. (s CA, nw SA). . . . _____

❑ *Chiroxiphia pareola.* BLUE-BACKED MANAKIN. (Tob, SA). . . . . _____

❑ *Chiroxiphia boliviana.* YUNGAS MANAKIN. (Andes sw SA). . . . . _____

❑ *Chiroxiphia caudata.* SWALLOW-TAILED MANAKIN. (se SA). . . . . _____

❑ *Masius chrysopterus.* GOLDEN-WINGED MANAKIN. (Andes nw SA). . . _____

❑ *Ilicura militaris.* PIN-TAILED MANAKIN. (se Braz). . . . . _____

❑ *Corapipo gutturalis.* WHITE-THROATED MANAKIN. (Pant nc SA). . . . . _____

❑ *Corapipo altera.* WHITE-RUFFED MANAKIN. (CA, nw Colom). . . . . . . _____

❑ *Corapipo leucorrhoa.* WHITE-BIBBED MANAKIN. (nw SA). . . . . _____

❑ *Manacus candei.* WHITE-COLLARED MANAKIN. (MA). . . . . _____

❑ *Manacus aurantiacus.* ORANGE-COLLARED MANAKIN. (s CA-nw SA) . _____
   ___*M. (a.) aurantiacus.* ORANGE-COLLARED MANAKIN. (s CA)
   ___*M. (a.) viridiventris.* GREENISH-BELLIED MANAKIN. (nw SA)

❑ *Manacus vitellinus.* GOLDEN-COLLARED MANAKIN. (Pan, n Colom). . . _____
   ___*M. (v.) cerritus.* ALMIRANTE MANAKIN. (nw Pan)
   ___*M. (v.) vitellinus.* GOLDEN-COLLARED MANAKIN. (sp)

❑ *Manacus manacus.* WHITE-BEARDED MANAKIN. (SA). . . . . _____

❑ *Machaeropterus pyrocephalus.* FIERY-CAPPED MANAKIN. (Amaz). . . . _____

❑ *Machaeropterus regulus.* STRIPED MANAKIN. (n,c SA). . . . . _____

❑ *Machaeropterus deliciosus.* CLUB-WINGED MANAKIN. (nw SA). . . . . _____

❑ *Xenopipo atronitens.* BLACK MANAKIN. (Amaz). . . . . _____

❑ *Chloropipo unicolor.* JET MANAKIN. (Andes wc SA). . . . . _____

❑ *Chloropipo uniformis.* OLIVE MANAKIN. (Pant nc SA). . . . . _____

❑ *Chloropipo holochlora.* GREEN MANAKIN. (e Pan, nw SA). . . . . _____

❑ *Chloropipo flavicapilla.* YELLOW-HEADED MANAKIN. (mts Colom). . . _____

❑ *Neopipo cinnamomea.* CINNAMON TYRANT-MANAKIN. (Amaz). . . . . . _____

❑ *Heterocercus flavivertex.* YELLOW-CRESTED MANAKIN. (n Amaz). . . . _____

❑ *Heterocercus aurantiivertex.* ORANGE-CRESTED MANAKIN. (w Amaz). _____

❑ *Heterocercus linteatus.* FLAME-CRESTED MANAKIN. (Amaz). . . . . _____

❑ *Neopelma chrysocephalum.* SAFFRON-CRESTED TYRANT-M. (n Amaz). _____

❑ *Neopelma sulphureiventer.* SULPHUR-BELLIED TYRANT-M. (w Amaz). _____

❑ *Neopelma pallescens.* PALE-BELLIED TYRANT-MANAKIN. (n.c SA). . . . _____

❑ *Neopelma aurifrons.* WIED'S TYRANT-MANAKIN. (e Braz). . . . . _____

❑ *Tyranneutes stolzmanni.* DWARF TYRANT-MANAKIN. (Amaz). . . . . . _____

❑ *Tyranneutes virescens.* TINY TYRANT-MANAKIN. (n Amaz). . . . . _____

❑ *Piprites pileatus.* BLACK-CAPPED PIPRITES. (se SA). . . . . _____

❑ *Piprites griseiceps.* GREY-HEADED PIPRITES. (CA). . . . . _____

❑ *Piprites chloris.* WING-BARRED PIPRITES. (SA). . . . . _____

Parvorder THAMNOPHILIDA [45/190]
Family **Thamnophilidae** [45/190]

❑ *Cymbilaimus lineatus.* FASCIATED ANTSHRIKE. (CA, Amaz). . . . . _____

❑ *Cymbilaimus sanctaemariae.* BAMBOO ANTSHRIKE. (w Amaz). . . . . . _____

❑ *Hypoedaleus guttatus.* SPOT-BACKED ANTSHRIKE. (se SA). . . . . _____

❑ *Batara cinerea.* GIANT ANTSHRIKE. (sc,se SA). . . . . _____

❑ *Mackenziaena severa.* TUFTED ANTSHRIKE. (se SA). . . . . _____

❑ *Mackenziaena leachii.* LARGE-TAILED ANTSHRIKE. (se SA). . . . . _____

❑ *Frederickena viridis.* BLACK-THROATED ANTSHRIKE. (n Amaz). . . . . . _____

❑ *Frederickena unduligera.* UNDULATED ANTSHRIKE. (w Amaz). . . . . . . _____

❏ *Taraba major.* GREAT ANTSHRIKE. (MA, SA)................... _____

❏ *Sakesphorus canadensis.* BLACK-CRESTED ANTSHRIKE. (n Amaz).... _____

❏ *Sakesphorus cristatus.* SILVERY-CHEEKED ANTSHRIKE. (e Braz)...... _____

❏ *Sakesphorus bernardi.* COLLARED ANTSHRIKE. (cw SA)........... _____

❏ *Sakesphorus melanonotus.* BLACK-BACKED ANTSHRIKE. (nw SA).... _____

❏ *Sakesphorus melanothorax.* BAND-TAILED ANTSHRIKE. (Amaz)...... _____

❏ *Sakesphorus luctuosus.* GLOSSY ANTSHRIKE. (Amaz)............. _____

❏ *Biatas nigropectus.* WHITE-BEARDED ANTSHRIKE. (se SA)......... _____

❏ *Thamnophilus doliatus.* BARRED ANTSHRIKE. (MA, SA).......... _____
   ___*T. (d.) doliatus.* BARRED ANTSHRIKE. (sp)
   ___*T. (d.) zarumae.* CHAPMAN'S ANTSHRIKE. (cw SA)

❏ *Thamnophilus multistriatus.* BAR-CRESTED ANTSHRIKE. (Colom).... _____

❏ *Thamnophilus palliatus.* LINED ANTSHRIKE. (nw SA, Amaz)....... _____
   ___*T. (p.) tenuepunctatus.* LINED ANTSHRIKE. (nw SA)
   ___*T. (p.) palliatus.* CHESTNUT-BACKED ANTSHRIKE. (Amaz)

❏ *Thamnophilus bridgesi.* BLACK-HOODED ANTSHRIKE. (CR, w Pan)... _____

❏ *Thamnophilus nigriceps.* BLACK ANTSHRIKE. (e Pan, n,c Colom).... _____

❏ *Thamnophilus praecox.* COCHA ANTSHRIKE. (ne Ecua)............ _____

❏ *Thamnophilus nigrocinereus.* BLACKISH-GREY ANTSHRIKE. (Amaz) . _____

❏ *Thamnophilus cryptoleucus.* CASTELNAU'S ANTSHRIKE. (w Amaz)... _____

❏ *Thamnophilus aethiops.* WHITE-SHOULDERED ANTSHRIKE. (n,c,e SA). _____

❏ *Thamnophilus unicolor.* UNIFORM ANTSHRIKE. (Andes w SA)....... _____

❏ *Thamnophilus schistaceus.* PLAIN-WINGED ANTSHRIKE. (w Amaz)... _____

❏ *Thamnophilus murinus.* MOUSE-COLORED ANTSHRIKE. (Amaz)...... _____

❏ *Thamnophilus aroyae.* UPLAND ANTSHRIKE. (Andes sw SA)....... _____

❏ *Thamnophilus punctatus.* SLATY ANTSHRIKE. (CA, SA)........... _____
   ___*T. (p.) atrinucha.* WESTERN SLATY-ANTSHRIKE. (CA, nw SA)
   ___*T. (p.) punctatus.* EASTERN SLATY-ANTSHRIKE. (SA)

❏ *Thamnophilus insignis.* STREAK-BACKED ANTSHRIKE. (Pant s Ven)... _____

❏ *Thamnophilus amazonicus.* AMAZONIAN ANTSHRIKE. (Amaz)....... _____
   ___*T. (a.) cinereiceps.* GREY-CAPPED ANTSHRIKE. (n Amaz)
   ___*T. (a.) amazonicus.* AMAZONIAN ANTSHRIKE. (c,s Amaz)

❏ *Thamnophilus caerulescens.* VARIABLE ANTSHRIKE. (c,se SA)...... _____
   ___*T. (c.) melanochrous.* MOUNTAIN ANTSHRIKE. (mts e Peru)
   ___*T. (c.) aspersiventer.* BAR-BELLIED ANTSHRIKE. (mts wc Bol)
   ___*T. (c.) connectens.* BOLIVIAN ANTSHRIKE. (e Bol)
   ___*T. (c.) caerulescens.* VARIABLE ANTSHRIKE. (c,sc SA)
   ___*T. (c.) gilvigaster.* TAWNY-BELLIED ANTSHRIKE. (se SA)

❏ *Thamnophilus torquatus.* RUFOUS-WINGED ANTSHRIKE. (sc,se SA)... _____

❑ *Thamnophilus ruficapillus.* RUFOUS-CAPPED ANTSHRIKE. (sw,se SA). _____
   ___*T. (r.) marcapatae.* MARCAPATA ANTSHRIKE. (mts sw SA)
   ___*T. (r.) ruficapillus.* RUFOUS-CAPPED ANTSHRIKE. (se SA)

❑ *Pygiptila stellaris.* SPOT-WINGED ANTSHRIKE. (Amaz). . . . . _____

❑ *Megastictus margaritatus.* PEARLY ANTSHRIKE. (w Amaz). . . . . _____

❑ *Neoctantes niger.* BLACK BUSHBIRD. (w Amaz). . . . . _____

❑ *Clytoctantes alixii.* RECURVE-BILLED BUSHBIRD. (nw SA). . . . . _____

❑ *Clytoctantes atrogularis.* RONDONIA BUSHBIRD. (sw Braz). . . . . _____

❑ *Xenornis setifrons.* SPECKLED ANTSHRIKE. (e Pan, nw Colom). . . . . . _____

❑ *Thamnistes anabatinus.* RUSSET ANTSHRIKE. (MA, w SA). . . . . _____
   ___*T. (a.) anabatinus.* RUSSET ANTSHRIKE. (MA, nw SA)
   ___*T. (a.) rufescens.* PERUVIAN ANTSHRIKE. (s SA)

❑ *Dysithamnus stictothorax.* SPOT-BREASTED ANTVIREO. (se Braz). . . . . _____

❑ *Dysithamnus mentalis.* PLAIN ANTVIREO. (MA, SA). . . . . _____

❑ *Dysithamnus striaticeps.* STREAK-CROWNED ANTVIREO. (CA). . . . . . . _____

❑ *Dysithamnus puncticeps.* SPOT-CROWNED ANTVIREO. (s CA, nw SA) . _____

❑ *Dysithamnus xanthopterus.* RUFOUS-BACKED ANTVIREO. (se Braz). . . _____

❑ *Dysithamnus leucostictus.* WHITE-SPOTTED ANTVIREO. (nw,cn SA). . . _____

❑ *Dysithamnus plumbeus.* PLUMBEOUS ANTVIREO. (n Bol, se Braz). . . . _____

❑ *Dysithamnus occidentalis.* BICOLORED ANTVIREO. (Andes nw SA). . . _____

❑ *Thamnomanes ardesiacus.* SATURNINE ANTSHRIKE. (Amaz). . . . . _____
   ___*T. (a.) ardesiacus.* DUSKY-THROATED ANTSHRIKE. (sp)
   ___*T. (a.) saturninus.* SATURNINE ANTSHRIKE. (sw Amaz)

❑ *Thamnomanes caesius.* CINEREOUS ANTSHRIKE. (wc,c,e, SA). . . . . . . _____

❑ *Thamnomanes schistogynus.* BLUISH-SLATE ANTSHRIKE. (sw Amaz) . _____

❑ *Myrmotherula brachyura.* PYGMY ANTWREN. (Pan, Amaz). . . . . _____
   ___*M. (b.) ignota.* GRISCOM'S ANTWREN. (Pan, w Colom)
   ___*M. (b.) brachyura.* PYGMY ANTWREN. (Amaz)

❑ *Myrmotherula obscura.* SHORT-BILLED ANTWREN. (w Amaz). . . . . . . _____

❑ *Myrmotherula sclateri.* SCLATER'S ANTWREN. (sw Amaz). . . . . _____

❑ *Myrmotherula klagesi.* KLAGES'S ANTWREN. (w Amaz Braz). . . . . . . _____

❑ *Myrmotherula ambigua.* YELLOW-THROATED ANTWREN. (nw Amaz) . _____

❑ *Myrmotherula surinamensis.* STREAKED ANTWREN. (Pan, Amaz). . . . _____

❑ *Myrmotherula cherriei.* CHERRIE'S ANTWREN. (w Amaz). . . . . _____

❑ *Myrmotherula longicauda.* STRIPE-CHESTED ANTWREN. (w Amaz). . . _____

❑ *Myrmotherula hauxwelli.* PLAIN-THROATED ANTWREN. (Amaz). . . . . . _____

❑ *Myrmotherula guttata.* RUFOUS-BELLIED ANTWREN. (n Amaz). . . . . . _____

❑ *Myrmotherula gularis.* STAR-THROATED ANTWREN. (se Braz)...... _____

❑ *Myrmotherula gutturalis.* BROWN-BELLIED ANTWREN. (n Amaz)..... _____

❑ *Myrmotherula fulviventris.* CHECKER-THROATED A. (CA-Colom)..... _____

❑ *Myrmotherula leucophthalma.* WHITE-EYED ANTWREN. (s Amaz).... _____

❑ *Myrmotherula haematonota.* STIPPLE-THROATED ANTWREN. (w Amaz)_____

❑ *Myrmotherula spodionota.* FOOTHILL ANTWREN. (nw Amaz)....... _____

❑ *Myrmotherula ornata.* ORNATE ANTWREN. (Amaz)............... _____
   ___*M. (o.) ornata.* CHESTNUT-SADDLED ANTWREN. (n,c Amaz)
   ___*M. (o.) atrogularis.* BLACK-THROATED ANTWREN. (sw Amaz)

❑ *Myrmotherula erythrura.* RUFOUS-TAILED ANTWREN. (w Amaz)..... _____

❑ *Myrmotherula axillaris.* WHITE-FLANKED ANTWREN. (CA, n,c,e SA) . _____

❑ *Myrmotherula fluminensis.* RIO DE JANEIRO ANTWREN. (mts se Braz). _____

❑ *Myrmotherula schisticolor.* SLATY ANTWREN. (MA, w SA)........ _____

❑ *Myrmotherula sunensis.* RIO SUNO ANTWREN. (w Amaz).......... _____

❑ *Myrmotherula longipennis.* LONG-WINGED ANTWREN. (Amaz)...... _____
   ___*M. (l.) longipennis.* LONG-WINGED ANTWREN. (sp)
   ___*M. (l.) garbei.* GARBE'S ANTWREN. (sw Amaz)

❑ *Myrmotherula minor.* SALVADORI'S ANTWREN. (w Amaz)......... _____

❑ *Myrmotherula iheringi.* IHERING'S ANTWREN. (sc Amaz).......... _____

❑ *Myrmotherula grisea.* ASHY ANTWREN. (c Bol).................. _____

❑ *Myrmotherula unicolor.* UNICOLORED ANTWREN. (se Braz)........ _____

❑ *Myrmotherula behni.* PLAIN-WINGED ANTWREN. (mts n SA)........ _____

❑ *Myrmotherula urosticta.* BAND-TAILED ANTWREN. (se Braz)....... _____

❑ *Myrmotherula menetriesii.* GREY ANTWREN. (Amaz)............. _____

❑ *Myrmotherula assimilis.* LEADEN ANTWREN. (Amaz)............. _____

❑ *Dichrozona cincta.* BANDED ANTBIRD. (Amaz)................. _____

❑ *Myrmorchilus strigilatus.* STRIPE-BACKED ANTBIRD. (sc,e SA)...... _____

❑ *Herpsilochmus parkeri.* ASH-THROATED ANTWREN. (Andes nc Peru) . _____

❑ *Herpsilochmus motacilloides.* CREAMY-BELLIED ANTWREN. (c Peru) . _____

❑ *Herpsilochmus atricapillus.* BLACK-CAPPED ANTWREN. (sc SA)...... _____

❑ *Herpsilochmus pileatus.* BAHIA ANTWREN. (e Braz)............. _____

❑ *Herpsilochmus sticturus.* SPOT-TAILED ANTWREN. (n Amaz)....... _____
   ___*H. (s.) dugandi.* DUGAND'S ANTWREN. (nw Amaz)
   ___*H. (s.) sticturus.* SPOT-TAILED ANTWREN. (cn Amaz)

❑ *Herpsilochmus stictocephalus.* TODD'S ANTWREN. (cn SA)......... _____

❑ *Herpsilochmus dorsimaculatus.* SPOT-BACKED ANTWREN. (w Amaz). _____

❑ *Herpsilochmus roraimae.* RORAIMAN ANTWREN. (Pant nc SA)....... _____

❑ *Herpsilochmus pectoralis.* PECTORAL ANTWREN. (e Braz)......... _____

❑ *Herpsilochmus longirostris.* LARGE-BILLED ANTWREN. (s Amaz)..... _____

❑ *Herpsilochmus axillaris.* YELLOW-BREASTED ANTWREN. (w SA)..... _____

❑ *Herpsilochmus rufimarginatus.* RUFOUS-WINGED ANTWREN. (e Pan-SA)_____

❑ *Microrhopias quixensis.* DOT-WINGED ANTWREN. (MA, Amaz)...... _____
   ___*M. (q.) boucardi.* BOUCARD'S ANTWREN. (MA, nw SA)
   ___*M. (q.) quixensis.* UPPER AMAZONIAN ANTWREN. (n Amaz)
   ___*M. (q.) emiliae.* LOWER AMAZONIAN ANTWREN. (s Amaz)

❑ *Formicivora iheringi.* NARROW-BILLED ANTWREN. (e Braz)........ _____

❑ *Formicivora grisea.* WHITE-FRINGED ANTWREN. (Pan, Amaz)........ _____

❑ *Formicivora melanogaster.* BLACK-BELLIED ANTWREN. (mts sc SA) . _____

❑ *Formicivora serrana.* SERRA ANTWREN. (mts se Braz)............ _____

❑ *Formicivora erythronotos.* BLACK-HOODED ANTWREN. (se Braz)..... _____

❑ *Formicivora rufa.* RUSTY-BACKED ANTWREN. (SA)................ _____

❑ *Drymophila ferruginea.* FERRUGINOUS ANTBIRD. (se Braz)......... _____

❑ *Drymophila rubricollis.* BERTONI'S ANTBIRD. (mts se SA).......... _____

❑ *Drymophila genei.* RUFOUS-TAILED ANTBIRD. (se Braz)........... _____

❑ *Drymophila ochropyga.* OCHRE-RUMPED ANTBIRD. (se Braz)....... _____

❑ *Drymophila devillei.* STRIATED ANTBIRD. (w,s Amaz)............. _____

❑ *Drymophila caudata.* LONG-TAILED ANTBIRD. (mts w SA)......... _____

❑ *Drymophila malura.* DUSKY-TAILED ANTBIRD. (se SA)............ _____

❑ *Drymophila squamata.* SCALED ANTBIRD. (se Braz)............. _____

❑ *Terenura maculata.* STREAK-CAPPED ANTWREN. (se SA).......... _____

❑ *Terenura sicki.* ALAGOAS ANTWREN. (e Braz).................. _____

❑ *Terenura callinota.* RUFOUS-RUMPED ANTWREN. (mts s CA, w SA)... _____
   ___*T. (c.) callinota.* RUFOUS-RUMPED ANTWREN. (sp)
   ___*T. (c.) venezuelana.* PERIJA ANTWREN. (nw Ven)

❑ *Terenura humeralis.* CHESTNUT-SHOULDERED ANTWREN. (w Amaz) . _____

❑ *Terenura sharpei.* YELLOW-RUMPED ANTWREN. (Andes sw SA)...... _____

❑ *Terenura spodioptila.* ASH-WINGED ANTWREN. (Amaz)............ _____

❑ *Cercomacra cinerascens.* GREY ANTBIRD. (Amaz).............. _____
   ___*C. (c.) cinerascens.* GREY ANTBIRD. (sp)
   ___*C. (c.) sclateri.* SCLATER'S ANTBIRD. (w Amaz)

❑ *Cercomacra brasiliana.* RIO DE JANEIRO ANTBIRD. (se Braz)....... _____

❑ *Cercomacra tyrannina.* DUSKY ANTBIRD. (MA, Amaz)........... _____

❑ *Cercomacra nigrescens.* BLACKISH ANTBIRD. (Amaz)............ _____

❑ *Cercomacra ferdinandi.* BANANAL ANTBIRD. (c Braz)............. _____

❑ *Cercomacra serva.* BLACK ANTBIRD. (w Amaz)................. _____

❑ *Cercomacra nigricans.* JET ANTBIRD. (Pan, nw,cn SA)............ _____

❑ *Cercomacra carbonaria.* RIO BRANCO ANTBIRD. (nw Amaz Braz).... _____

❑ *Cercomacra manu.* MANU ANTBIRD. (sw Amaz)................. _____

❑ *Cercomacra melanaria.* MATO GROSSO ANTBIRD. (sw,sc SA)....... _____

❑ *Pyriglena leuconota.* WHITE-BACKED FIRE-EYE. (w,c SA).......... _____

❑ *Pyriglena leucoptera.* WHITE-SHOULDERED FIRE-EYE. (se SA)...... _____

❑ *Pyriglena atra.* FRINGE-BACKED FIRE-EYE. (e Braz)............. _____

❑ *Rhopornis ardesiaca.* SLENDER ANTBIRD. (mts e Braz)........... _____

❑ *Myrmoborus leucophrys.* WHITE-BROWED ANTBIRD. (Amaz)....... _____

❑ *Myrmoborus lugubris.* ASH-BREASTED ANTBIRD. (Amaz)......... _____

❑ *Myrmoborus myotherinus.* BLACK-FACED ANTBIRD. (Amaz)....... _____

❑ *Myrmoborus melanurus.* BLACK-TAILED ANTBIRD. (ne Peru)....... _____

❑ *Hypocnemis cantator.* WARBLING ANTBIRD. (Amaz).............. _____
   ___*H. (c.) cantator.* WARBLING ANTBIRD. (sp)
   ___*H. (c.) flavescens.* YELLOW-TIPPED ANTBIRD. (nw Amaz)
   ___*H. (c.) subflava.* SULPHUR-BREASTED ANTBIRD. (sw Amaz)

❑ *Hypocnemis hypoxantha.* YELLOW-BROWED ANTBIRD. (Amaz)...... _____

❑ *Hypocnemoides melanopogon.* BLACK-CHINNED ANTBIRD. (Amaz)... _____

❑ *Hypocnemoides maculicauda.* BAND-TAILED ANTBIRD. (Amaz)...... _____

❑ *Myrmochanes hemileucus.* BLACK-AND-WHITE ANTBIRD. (w Amaz) . _____

❑ *Gymnocichla nudiceps.* BARE-CROWNED ANTBIRD. (CA, n Colom)... _____

❑ *Sclateria naevia.* SILVERED ANTBIRD. (Amaz).................. _____

❑ *Percnostola rufifrons.* BLACK-HEADED ANTBIRD. (w,n Amaz)....... _____

❑ *Percnostola schistacea.* SLATE-COLORED ANTBIRD. (w Amaz)....... _____

❑ *Percnostola leucostigma.* SPOT-WINGED ANTBIRD. (Amaz)......... _____

❑ *Percnostola caurensis.* CAURA ANTBIRD. (n Amaz)............... _____

❑ *Percnostola lophotes.* WHITE-LINED ANTBIRD. (e Peru, n Bol)....... _____

❑ *Myrmeciza berlepschi.* STUB-TAILED ANTBIRD. (nw SA)........... _____

❑ *Myrmeciza longipes.* WHITE-BELLIED ANTBIRD. (Pan, n SA)........ _____

❑ *Myrmeciza exsul.* CHESTNUT-BACKED ANTBIRD. (CA, nw SA)....... _____
   ___*M. (e.) exsul.* CHESTNUT-BACKED ANTBIRD. (CA)
   ___*M. (e.) maculifer.* WING-SPOTTED ANTBIRD. (e Pan, nw SA)

❑ *Myrmeciza ferruginea.* FERRUGINOUS-BACKED ANTBIRD. (Amaz).... _____

❑ *Myrmeciza ruficauda.* SCALLOPED ANTBIRD. (e Braz)............. _____

❑ *Myrmeciza loricata.* WHITE-BIBBED ANTBIRD. (se Braz).......... _____

❏ *Myrmeciza squamosa.* SQUAMATE ANTBIRD. (se Braz). . . . . _____

❏ *Myrmeciza laemosticta.* DULL-MANTLED ANTBIRD. (s CA, nw SA). . . . _____

❏ *Myrmeciza nigricauda.* ESMERALDAS ANTBIRD. (nw SA). . . . . _____

❏ *Myrmeciza disjuncta.* YAPACANA ANTBIRD. (s Ven). . . . . _____

❏ *Myrmeciza pelzelni.* GREY-BELLIED ANTBIRD. (n Amaz). . . . . _____

❏ *Myrmeciza hemimelaena.* CHESTNUT-TAILED ANTBIRD. (w,s Amaz) . _____

❏ *Myrmeciza hyperythra.* PLUMBEOUS ANTBIRD. (w Amaz). . . . . _____

❏ *Myrmeciza melanoceps.* WHITE-SHOULDERED ANTBIRD. (w Amaz). . . _____

❏ *Myrmeciza goeldii.* GOELDI'S ANTBIRD. (sw Amaz). . . . . _____

❏ *Myrmeciza fortis.* SOOTY ANTBIRD. (w Amaz). . . . . _____

❏ *Myrmeciza immaculata.* IMMACULATE ANTBIRD. (s CA, nw SA). . . . . _____

❏ *Myrmeciza griseiceps.* GREY-HEADED ANTBIRD. (Andes nw SA). . . . . _____

❏ *Myrmeciza atrothorax.* BLACK-THROATED ANTBIRD. (Amaz). . . . . . . _____

❏ *Pithys albifrons.* WHITE-PLUMED ANTBIRD. (w,n Amaz). . . . . _____

❏ *Pithys castanea.* WHITE-MASKED ANTBIRD. (n Peru). . . . . _____

❏ *Gymnopithys rufigula.* RUFOUS-THROATED ANTBIRD. (n Amaz). . . . . . _____

❏ *Gymnopithys bicolor.* BICOLORED ANTBIRD. (CA, nw SA). . . . . _____

❏ *Gymnopithys leucaspis.* WHITE-CHEEKED ANTBIRD. (nw SA). . . . . . . _____

❏ *Gymnopithys lunulata.* LUNULATED ANTBIRD. (e Ecua, e Peru). . . . . . _____

❏ *Gymnopithys salvini.* WHITE-THROATED ANTBIRD. (w Amaz). . . . . . . _____

❏ *Myrmornis torquata.* WING-BANDED ANTBIRD. (s CA, w,s Amaz). . . . _____
   ___*M. (t.) stictoptera.* BUFF-BANDED ANTBIRD. (s CA, n Colom)
   ___*M. (t.) torquata.* WING-BANDED ANTBIRD. (w,s Amaz)

❏ *Rhegmatorhina melanosticta.* HAIRY-CRESTED ANTBIRD. (w Amaz) . _____

❏ *Rhegmatorhina cristata.* CHESTNUT-CRESTED ANTBIRD. (nw Amaz). . . _____

❏ *Rhegmatorhina hoffmannsi.* WHITE-BREASTED ANTBIRD. (w Amaz) . _____

❏ *Rhegmatorhina berlepschi.* HARLEQUIN ANTBIRD. (c Amaz Braz). . . . _____

❏ *Rhegmatorhina gymnops.* SANTAREM ANTBIRD. (sc Amaz Braz). . . . . _____

❏ *Hylophylax naevioides.* SPOTTED ANTBIRD. (s CA, nw SA). . . . . _____

❏ *Hylophylax naevia.* SPOT-BACKED ANTBIRD. (Amaz). . . . . _____

❏ *Hylophylax punctulata.* DOT-BACKED ANTBIRD. (Amaz). . . . . _____

❏ *Hylophylax poecilonota.* SCALE-BACKED ANTBIRD. (Amaz). . . . . _____
   ___*H. (p.) poecilonota.* SCALE-BACKED ANTBIRD. (w,n Amaz)
   ___*H. (p.) griseiventris.* PLAIN-BACKED ANTBIRD. (s Amaz)

❏ *Phlegopsis nigromaculata.* BLACK-SPOTTED BARE-EYE. (Amaz). . . . . . _____

❏ *Phlegopsis barringeri.* ARGUS BARE-EYE. (se Colom). . . . . _____

❏ *Phlegopsis erythroptera.* REDDISH-WINGED BARE-EYE. (w Amaz). . . . . _____

❏ *Skutchia borbae.* PALE-FACED BARE-EYE. (w Amaz Braz). . . . . _____

❏ *Phaenostictus mcleannani.* OCELLATED ANTBIRD. (CA, nw SA). . . . . _____

Parvorder FURNARIIDA [86/376]
Superfamily FURNARIOIDEA [66/279]
Family **Furnariidae** [66/279]
Subfamily Furnariinae [53/231]

❏ *Geobates poecilopterus.* CAMPO MINER. (sc SA). . . . . _____

❏ *Geositta cunicularia.* COMMON MINER. (s SA). . . . . _____

❏ *Geositta maritima.* GREYISH MINER. (sw SA). . . . . _____

❏ *Geositta peruviana.* COASTAL MINER. (w Peru). . . . . _____

❏ *Geositta punensis.* PUNA MINER. (Andes sw SA). . . . . _____

❏ *Geositta saxicolina.* DARK-WINGED MINER. (Andes c Peru). . . . . _____

❏ *Geositta isabellina.* CREAMY-RUMPED MINER. (Andes sw SA). . . . . . . _____

❏ *Geositta antarctica.* SHORT-BILLED MINER. (s SA). . . . . _____

❏ *Geositta rufipennis.* RUFOUS-BANDED MINER. (Andes sw SA). . . . . . . _____

❏ *Geositta crassirostris.* THICK-BILLED MINER. (Andes w Peru). . . . . . . _____

❏ *Geositta tenuirostris.* SLENDER-BILLED MINER. (Andes sw SA). . . . . . . _____

❏ *Upucerthia harterti.* BOLIVIAN EARTHCREEPER. (Andes c,se Bol). . . . . _____

❏ *Upucerthia certhioides.* CHACO EARTHCREEPER. (sc SA). . . . . _____

❏ *Upucerthia ruficauda.* STRAIGHT-BILLED EARTHCREEPER. (s SA). . . . . _____

❏ *Upucerthia andaecola.* ROCK EARTHCREEPER. (Andes sw SA). . . . . . . _____

❏ *Upucerthia serrana.* STRIATED EARTHCREEPER. (Andes Peru). . . . . . . _____

❏ *Upucerthia dumetaria.* SCALE-THROATED EARTHCREEPER. (SA). . . . . _____

❏ *Upucerthia albigula.* WHITE-THROATED EARTHCREEPER. (sw SA). . . . _____

❏ *Upucerthia jelskii.* PLAIN-BREASTED EARTHCREEPER. (Andes sw SA) . _____

❏ *Upucerthia validirostris.* BUFF-BREASTED EARTHCREEPER. (sw SA). . . _____

❏ *Cinclodes fuscus.* BAR-WINGED CINCLODES. (mts w,s SA). . . . . _____

❏ *Cinclodes comechingonus.* CORDOBA CINCLODES. (mts nc Argen). . . . _____

❏ *Cinclodes pabsti.* LONG-TAILED CINCLODES. (mts se Braz). . . . . _____

❏ *Cinclodes oustaleti.* GREY-FLANKED CINCLODES. (mts s SA, JF). . . . . _____

❏ *Cinclodes olrogi.* OLROG'S CINCLODES. (mts c Argen). . . . . _____

❏ *Cinclodes excelsior.* STOUT-BILLED CINCLODES. (Andes w SA). . . . . . _____
___*C. (e.) excelsior.* STOUT-BILLED CINCLODES. (nw SA)
___*C. (e.) aricomae.* ROYAL CINCLODES. (se Peru)

❏ *Cinclodes patagonicus.* DARK-BELLIED CINCLODES. (mts s SA). . . . . . _____

❑ *Cinclodes taczanowskii.* SURF CINCLODES. (c,s Peru). . . . . _____

❑ *Cinclodes nigrofumosus.* SEASIDE CINCLODES. (n,c Chile). . . . . _____

❑ *Cinclodes antarcticus.* BLACKISH CINCLODES. (is s SA). . . . . _____

❑ *Cinclodes atacamensis.* WHITE-WINGED CINCLODES. (Andes sw SA) . _____

❑ *Cinclodes palliatus.* WHITE-BELLIED CINCLODES. (Andes n,c Peru). . . . _____

❑ *Chilia melanura.* CRAG CHILIA. (mts Chile). _____

❑ *Furnarius minor.* LESSER HORNERO. (Amaz). . . . . _____

❑ *Furnarius figulus.* WING-BANDED HORNERO. (Braz). . . . . _____
    ___*F. (f.) pileatus.* PILEATED HORNERO. (Amaz Braz)
    ___*F. (f.) figulus.* WING-BANDED HORNERO. (e,se Braz)

❑ *Furnarius leucopus.* PALE-LEGGED HORNERO. (n,c,e SA). . . . . _____
    ___*F. (l.) leucopus.* PALE-LEGGED HORNERO. (sp)
    ___*F. (l.) cinnamomeus.* PACIFIC HORNERO. (cw SA)

❑ *Furnarius torridus.* PALE-BILLED HORNERO. (w Amaz). . . . . _____

❑ *Furnarius rufus.* RUFOUS HORNERO. (sc SA). . . . . _____

❑ *Furnarius cristatus.* CRESTED HORNERO. (sc SA). . . . . _____

❑ *Sylviorthorhynchus desmursii.* DES MURS'S WIRETAIL. (s SA). . . . . . . _____

❑ *Aphrastura spinicauda.* THORN-TAILED RAYADITO. (s SA). . . . . _____

❑ *Aphrastura masafuerae.* MAS AFUERA RAYADITO. (†JF). . . . . _____

❑ *Leptasthenura fuliginiceps.* BROWN-CAPPED TIT-SPINETAIL. (sw SA). _____

❑ *Leptasthenura yanacensis.* TAWNY TIT-SPINETAIL. (Andes sw SA). . . _____

❑ *Leptasthenura platensis.* TUFTED TIT-SPINETAIL. (se,s SA). . . . . _____

❑ *Leptasthenura aegithaloides.* PLAIN-MANTLED TIT-SPINETAIL. (s SA). _____

❑ *Leptasthenura striolata.* STRIOLATED TIT-SPINETAIL. (se Braz). . . . . . _____

❑ *Leptasthenura pileata.* RUSTY-CROWNED TIT-SPINETAIL. (mts Peru). . . _____
    ___*L. (p.) cajabambae.* STREAK-CROWNED TIT-SPINETAIL. (nw,c Peru)
    ___*L. (p.) pileata.* RUSTY-CROWNED TIT-SPINETAIL. (sc Peru)

❑ *Leptasthenura xenothorax.* WHITE-BROWED TIT-SPINETAIL. (c Peru) . _____

❑ *Leptasthenura striata.* STREAKED TIT-SPINETAIL. (Andes sw SA). . . . . _____

❑ *Leptasthenura andicola.* ANDEAN TIT-SPINETAIL. (mts w SA). . . . . . . _____

❑ *Leptasthenura setaria.* ARAUCARIA TIT-SPINETAIL. (se SA). . . . . _____

❑ *Schizoeaca perijana.* PERIJA THISTLETAIL. (mts nw SA). . . . . _____

❑ *Schizoeaca coryi.* OCHRE-BROWED THISTLETAIL. (Andes nw Ven). . . . _____

❑ *Schizoeaca fuliginosa.* WHITE-CHINNED THISTLETAIL. (Andes nw SA). _____

❑ *Schizoeaca griseomurina.* MOUSE-COLORED THISTLETAIL. (nw SA). . . _____

❑ *Schizoeaca palpebralis.* EYE-RINGED THISTLETAIL. (Andes c Peru). . . . _____

❑ *Schizoeaca vilcabambae.* VILCABAMBA THISTLETAIL. (Andes c Peru). _____

❑ *Schizoeaca helleri.* PUNA THISTLETAIL. (Andes se Peru). . . . . _____

❑ *Schizoeaca harterti.* BLACK-THROATED THISTLETAIL. (Andes c Bol). . . . _____

❑ *Schizoeaca moreirae.* ITATIAIA THISTLETAIL. (mts se Braz). . . . . _____

❑ *Schoeniophylax phryganophila.* CHOTOY SPINETAIL. (sc,se SA). . . . . _____

❑ *Synallaxis ruficapilla.* RUFOUS-CAPPED SPINETAIL. (se SA). . . . . _____

❑ *Synallaxis frontalis.* SOOTY-FRONTED SPINETAIL. (sc,se SA). . . . . _____

❑ *Synallaxis azarae.* AZARA'S SPINETAIL. (Andes w SA). . . . . _____
   ___*S. (a.) elegantior.* ELEGANT SPINETAIL. (nw SA)
   ___*S. (a.) azarae.* AZARA'S SPINETAIL. (cw SA)
   ___*S. (a.) superciliosa.* BUFF-BROWED SPINETAIL. (sw SA)

❑ *Synallaxis courseni.* APURIMAC SPINETAIL. (Andes sc Peru). . . . . _____

❑ *Synallaxis albescens.* PALE-BREASTED SPINETAIL. (s CA, SA). . . . . _____

❑ *Synallaxis spixi.* CHICLI SPINETAIL. (se SA). . . . . _____

❑ *Synallaxis brachyura.* SLATY SPINETAIL. (CA, nw SA). . . . . _____

❑ *Synallaxis albigularis.* DARK-BREASTED SPINETAIL. (w Amaz). . . . . . . _____

❑ *Synallaxis hypospodia.* CINEREOUS-BREASTED SPINETAIL. (c SA). . . . . _____

❑ *Synallaxis infuscata.* PINTO'S SPINETAIL. (e Braz). . . . . _____

❑ *Synallaxis moesta.* DUSKY SPINETAIL. (nw Amaz). . . . . _____
   ___*S. (m.) moesta.* DUSKY SPINETAIL. (se Colom)
   ___*S. (m.) brunneicaudalis.* BROWN-TAILED SPINETAIL. (sp)

❑ *Synallaxis macconnelli.* MACCONNELL'S SPINETAIL. (Pant nc SA). . . . _____

❑ *Synallaxis cabanisi.* CABANIS'S SPINETAIL. (Andes wc SA). . . . . _____

❑ *Synallaxis subpudica.* SILVERY-THROATED SPINETAIL. (ce Colom). . . . _____

❑ *Synallaxis tithys.* BLACKISH-HEADED SPINETAIL. (Andes cw SA). . . . . _____

❑ *Synallaxis cinerascens.* GREY-BELLIED SPINETAIL. (se SA). . . . . _____

❑ *Synallaxis propinqua.* WHITE-BELLIED SPINETAIL. (Amaz). . . . . _____

❑ *Synallaxis hellmayri.* RED-SHOULDERED SPINETAIL. (e Braz). . . . . . . _____

❑ *Synallaxis maranonica.* MARANON SPINETAIL. (n Peru). . . . . _____

❑ *Synallaxis gujanensis.* PLAIN-CROWNED SPINETAIL. (Amaz). . . . . _____

❑ *Synallaxis albilora.* WHITE-LORED SPINETAIL. (sc SA). . . . . _____

❑ *Synallaxis rutilans.* RUDDY SPINETAIL. (Amaz). . . . . _____

❑ *Synallaxis cherriei.* CHESTNUT-THROATED SPINETAIL. (w Amaz). . . . . _____

❑ *Synallaxis unirufa.* RUFOUS SPINETAIL. (mts w SA). . . . . _____

❑ *Synallaxis castanea.* BLACK-THROATED SPINETAIL. (mts nc Ven). . . . . _____

❑ *Synallaxis fuscorufa.* RUSTY-HEADED SPINETAIL. (mts ne Colom). . . . _____

❑ *Synallaxis zimmeri.* RUSSET-BELLIED SPINETAIL. (Andes c Peru). . . . . _____

❏ *Synallaxis erythrothorax.* RUFOUS-BREASTED SPINETAIL. (c MA). . . . . _____

❏ *Synallaxis cinnamomea.* STRIPE-BREASTED SPINETAIL. (Tob-n SA). . . _____

❏ *Synallaxis stictothorax.* NECKLACED SPINETAIL. (cw SA). . . . . _____
   ___*S. (s.) stictothorax.* NECKLACED SPINETAIL. (sp)
   ___*S. (s.) chinchipensis.* CHINCHIPE SPINETAIL. (nw Peru)

❏ *Synallaxis candei.* WHITE-WHISKERED SPINETAIL. (nw SA). . . . . _____

❏ *Synallaxis kollari.* HOARY-THROATED SPINETAIL. (n Amaz Braz). . . . . _____

❏ *Synallaxis scutata.* OCHRE-CHEEKED SPINETAIL. (sc,e SA). . . . . _____

❏ *Hellmayrea gularis.* WHITE-BROWED SPINETAIL. (mts w SA). . . . . _____

❏ *Cranioleuca erythrops.* RED-FACED SPINETAIL. (s CA, nw SA). . . . . . . _____

❏ *Cranioleuca antisiensis.* LINE-CHEEKED SPINETAIL. (Andes cw SA). . . _____
   ___*C. (a.) antisiensis.* FRASER'S SPINETAIL. (sp)
   ___*C. (a.) baroni.* BARON'S SPINETAIL. (n,c Peru)

❏ *Cranioleuca pallida.* PALLID SPINETAIL. (se Braz). . . . . _____

❏ *Cranioleuca curtata.* ASH-BROWED SPINETAIL. (Andes w SA). . . . . . . _____

❏ *Cranioleuca demissa.* TEPUI SPINETAIL. (Pant nc SA). . . . . _____

❏ *Cranioleuca hellmayri.* STREAK-CAPPED SPINETAIL. (mts ne Colom) . _____

❏ *Cranioleuca subcristata.* CRESTED SPINETAIL. (n SA). . . . . _____

❏ *Cranioleuca pyrrhophia.* STRIPE-CROWNED SPINETAIL. (sc SA). . . . . . _____

❏ *Cranioleuca obsoleta.* OLIVE SPINETAIL. (se SA). . . . . _____

❏ *Cranioleuca marcapatae.* MARCAPATA SPINETAIL. (Andes se Peru). . . _____

❏ *Cranioleuca albiceps.* LIGHT-CROWNED SPINETAIL. (Andes sw SA). . . _____

❏ *Cranioleuca semicinerea.* GREY-HEADED SPINETAIL. (e Braz). . . . . . . _____

❏ *Cranioleuca albicapilla.* CREAMY-CRESTED SPINETAIL. (c,se Peru). . . . _____

❏ *Cranioleuca dissita.* COIBA SPINETAIL. (is w Pan). . . . . _____

❏ *Cranioleuca vulpina.* RUSTY-BACKED SPINETAIL. (Amaz). . . . . _____

❏ *Cranioleuca muelleri.* SCALED SPINETAIL. (e Amaz Braz). . . . . _____

❏ *Cranioleuca gutturata.* SPECKLED SPINETAIL. (Amaz). . . . . _____

❏ *Cranioleuca sulphurifera.* SULPHUR-BEARDED SPINETAIL. (se SA). . . . _____

❏ *Certhiaxis cinnamomea.* YELLOW-CHINNED SPINETAIL. (SA). . . . . _____

❏ *Certhiaxis mustelina.* RED-AND-WHITE SPINETAIL. (Amaz). . . . . _____

❏ *Asthenes pyrrholeuca.* LESSER CANASTERO. (Andes s SA; ◊-sc SA). . . _____

❏ *Asthenes baeri.* SHORT-BILLED CANASTERO. (s SA). . . . . _____

❏ *Asthenes pudibunda.* CANYON CANASTERO. (Andes w Peru). . . . . _____

❏ *Asthenes ottonis.* RUSTY-FRONTED CANASTERO. (Andes se Peru). . . . . _____

❏ *Asthenes heterura.* MAQUIS CANASTERO. (Andes wc Bol). . . . . _____

❑ *Asthenes cactorum.* CACTUS CANASTERO. (Pac c Peru)............ _____

❑ *Asthenes modesta.* CORDILLERAN CANASTERO. (Andes sw,s SA)..... _____

❑ *Asthenes luizae.* CIPO CANASTERO. (se Braz).................... _____

❑ *Asthenes dorbignyi.* CREAMY-BREASTED CANASTERO. (Andes sw SA). _____
   ___*A. (d.) huancavelicae.* PALE-TAILED CANASTERO. (wc Peru)
   ___*A. (d.) usheri.* WHITE-TAILED CANASTERO. (sw Peru)
   ___*A. (d.) dorbignyi.* CREAMY-BREASTED CANASTERO. (sp)

❑ *Asthenes berlepschi.* BERLEPSCH'S CANASTERO. (Andes cw Bol)..... _____

❑ *Asthenes steinbachi.* CHESTNUT CANASTERO. (Andes w Argen)...... _____

❑ *Asthenes humicola.* DUSKY-TAILED CANASTERO. (s SA)........... _____

❑ *Asthenes patagonica.* PATAGONIAN CANASTERO. (w Argen)........ _____

❑ *Asthenes humilis.* STREAK-THROATED CANASTERO. (Andes sw SA)... _____

❑ *Asthenes wyatti.* STREAK-BACKED CANASTERO. (mts w SA)........ _____

❑ *Asthenes punensis.* PUNO CANASTERO. (Andes sw SA)............ _____
   ___*A. (p.) punensis.* PUNO CANASTERO. (se Peru, cw Bol)
   ___*A. (p.) cuchacanchae.* BOLIVIAN CANASTERO. (sw Bol)
   ___*A. (p.) lilloi.* LILLO'S CANASTERO. (nw Argen)
   ___*A. (p.) sclateri.* CORDOBA CANASTERO. (Andes nc Argen)

❑ *Asthenes anthoides.* AUSTRAL CANASTERO. (s SA)............... _____

❑ *Asthenes urubambensis.* LINE-FRONTED CANASTERO. (Andes sw SA). _____

❑ *Asthenes flammulata.* MANY-STRIPED CANASTERO. (Andes w SA).... _____

❑ *Asthenes virgata.* JUNIN CANASTERO. (Andes c,se Peru)........... _____

❑ *Asthenes maculicauda.* SCRIBBLE-TAILED CANASTERO. (sw SA)...... _____

❑ *Asthenes hudsoni.* HUDSON'S CANASTERO. (sc,s SA)............. _____

❑ *Thripophaga cherriei.* ORINOCO SOFTTAIL. (sw Ven)............. _____

❑ *Thripophaga macroura.* STRIATED SOFTTAIL. (se Braz)........... _____

❑ *Thripophaga berlepschi.* RUSSET-MANTLED SOFTTAIL. (nc Peru)..... _____

❑ *Thripophaga fusciceps.* PLAIN SOFTTAIL. (w Amaz).............. _____

❑ *Siptornopsis hypochondriacus.* GREAT SPINETAIL. (Andes nw Peru) . _____

❑ *Phacellodomus rufifrons.* RUFOUS-FRONTED THORNBIRD. (SA)...... _____
   ___*P. (r.) inornatus.* NORTHERN THORNBIRD. (cn SA)
   ___*P. (r.) peruvianus.* PERUVIAN THORNBIRD. (ne Peru)
   ___*P. (r.) rufifrons.* RUFOUS-FRONTED THORNBIRD. (sc,e SA)

❑ *Phacellodomus sibilatrix.* LITTLE THORNBIRD. (sc SA)............ _____

❑ *Phacellodomus striaticeps.* STREAK-FRONTED THORNBIRD. (sw SA)... _____

❑ *Phacellodomus striaticollis.* FRECKLE-BREASTED THORNBIRD. (sw,se SA)_____
   ___*P. (s.) maculipectus.* SPOT-BREASTED THORNBIRD. (sw SA)
   ___*P. (s.) striaticollis.* FRECKLE-BREASTED THORNBIRD. (se SA)

❑ *Phacellodomus ruber.* GREATER THORNBIRD. (sc SA)............. _____

❑ *Phacellodomus dorsalis.* CHESTNUT-BACKED THORNBIRD. (nw Peru) . _____

❑ *Phacellodomus erythrophthalmus.* RED-EYED THORNBIRD. (se Braz) . _____
___*P. (e.) erythrophthalmus.* RED-EYED THORNBIRD. (e Braz)
___*P. (e.) ferrugineigula.* ORANGE-EYED THORNBIRD. (se Braz)

❑ *Clibanornis dendrocolaptoides.* CANEBRAKE GROUNDCREEPER. (se SA) _____

❑ *Spartonoica maluroides.* BAY-CAPPED WREN-SPINETAIL. (se SA). . . . . _____

❑ *Phleocryptes melanops.* WREN-LIKE RUSHBIRD. (w,sc,s SA). . . . . _____

❑ *Limnornis curvirostris.* CURVE-BILLED REEDHAUNTER. (se SA). . . . . _____

❑ *Limnornis rectirostris.* STRAIGHT-BILLED REEDHAUNTER. (sc SA). . . . _____

❑ *Anumbius annumbi.* FIREWOOD-GATHERER. (s SA). . . . . _____

❑ *Coryphistera alaudina.* LARK-LIKE BRUSHRUNNER. (sc SA). . . . . _____

❑ *Eremobius phoenicurus.* BAND-TAILED EARTHCREEPER. (w,s Argen) . _____

❑ *Siptornis striaticollis.* SPECTACLED PRICKLETAIL. (Andes nw SA). . . . . _____

❑ *Metopothrix aurantiacus.* ORANGE-FRONTED PLUSHCROWN. (w Amaz). _____

❑ *Xenerpestes minlosi.* DOUBLE-BANDED GREYTAIL. (e Pan, n Colom). . _____

❑ *Xenerpestes singularis.* EQUATORIAL GREYTAIL. (Andes nw SA). . . . . _____

❑ *Roraimia adusta.* RORAIMAN BARBTAIL. (Pant nc SA). . . . . _____

❑ *Premnornis guttuligera.* RUSTY-WINGED BARBTAIL. (mts w SA). . . . . _____

❑ *Premnoplex brunnescens.* SPOTTED BARBTAIL. (s CA, w,n SA). . . . . . _____

❑ *Premnoplex tatei.* WHITE-THROATED BARBTAIL. (mts n Ven). . . . . . . _____
___*P. (t.) tatei.* WHITE-THROATED BARBTAIL. (cn Ven)
___*P. (t.) pariae.* PARIA BARBTAIL. (ne Ven)

❑ *Margarornis rubiginosus.* RUDDY TREERUNNER. (mts CR, w Pan). . . . _____

❑ *Margarornis stellatus.* FULVOUS-DOTTED TREERUNNER. (nw SA). . . . . _____

❑ *Margarornis bellulus.* BEAUTIFUL TREERUNNER. (mts e Pan). . . . . . . _____

❑ *Margarornis squamiger.* PEARLED TREERUNNER. (mts w SA). . . . . . . _____

❑ *Lochmias nematura.* SHARP-TAILED STREAMCREEPER. (e Pan, SA). . . . _____

❑ *Pseudoseisura cristata.* RUFOUS CACHOLOTE. (sc,e SA). . . . . _____

❑ *Pseudoseisura lophotes.* BROWN CACHOLOTE. (sc SA). . . . . _____

❑ *Pseudoseisura gutturalis.* WHITE-THROATED CACHOLOTE. (w,c Argen). _____

❑ *Pseudocolaptes lawrencii.* BUFFY TUFTEDCHEEK. (mts s CA, nw SA) . _____
___*P. (l.) lawrencii.* BUFFY TUFTEDCHEEK. (s CA)
___*P. (l.) johnsoni.* PACIFIC TUFTEDCHEEK. (nw SA)

❑ *Pseudocolaptes boissonneautii.* STREAKED TUFTEDCHEEK. (w SA). . . . _____

❑ *Berlepschia rikeri.* POINT-TAILED PALMCREEPER. (Amaz). . . . . _____

❑ *Ancistrops strigilatus.* CHESTNUT-WINGED HOOKBILL. (w Amaz). . . . . _____

❑ *Cichlocolaptes leucophrus.* PALE-BROWED TREEHUNTER. (se Braz). . . _____

❑ *Hyloctistes subulatus.* STRIPED WOODHAUNTER. (s CA, w,n Amaz). . . _____

❑ *Syndactyla guttulata.* GUTTULATED FOLIAGE-GLEANER. (mts n Ven). . _____

❑ *Syndactyla subalaris.* LINEATED FOLIAGE-GLEANER. (s CA, w SA). . . . _____

❑ *Syndactyla rufosuperciliata.* BUFF-BROWED FOLIAGE-GLEANER. (sc SA)_____

❑ *Syndactyla ruficollis.* RUFOUS-NECKED FOLIAGE-GLEANER. (nw SA) . _____

❑ *Anabacerthia variegaticeps.* SCALY-BREASTED F. (mts MA, nw SA). . _____
   ___*A. (v.) variegaticeps.* SCALY-BREASTED FOLIAGE-GLEANER. (MA)
   ___*A. (v.) temporalis.* SPOT-BREASTED FOLIAGE-GLEANER. (nw SA)

❑ *Anabacerthia striaticollis.* MONTANE FOLIAGE-GLEANER. (w,n SA). . . _____

❑ *Philydor ruficaudatus.* RUFOUS-TAILED FOLIAGE-GLEANER. (Amaz). . . _____

❑ *Philydor pyrrhodes.* CINNAMON-RUMPED FOLIAGE-GLEANER. (Amaz) . _____

❑ *Philydor dimidiatus.* RUSSET-MANTLED FOLIAGE-GLEANER. (sc SA). . . _____
   ___*P. (d.) dimidiatus.* RUSSET-MANTLED FOLIAGE-GLEANER. (sp)
   ___*P. (d.) baeri.* BAER'S FOLIAGE-GLEANER. (sc Braz)

❑ *Philydor fuscipennis.* SLATY-WINGED FOLIAGE-GLEANER. (Pan, nw SA) _____
   ___*P. (f.) fuscipennis.* DUSKY-WINGED FOLIAGE-GLEANER. (w,c Pan)
   ___*P. (f.) erythronotus.* RUFOUS-BACKED FOLIAGE-GLEANER. (e Pan, nw SA)

❑ *Philydor erythrocercus.* RUFOUS-RUMPED FOLIAGE-GLEANER. (Amaz). _____

❑ *Philydor ochrogaster.* OCHRE-BELLIED FOLIAGE-GLEANER. (sw SA). . . _____

❑ *Philydor erythropterus.* CHESTNUT-WINGED FOLIAGE-GLEANER. (Amaz)_____

❑ *Philydor amaurotis.* WHITE-BROWED FOLIAGE-GLEANER. (se SA). . . . . _____

❑ *Philydor lichtensteini.* OCHRE-BREASTED FOLIAGE-GLEANER. (se SA) . _____

❑ *Philydor rufus.* BUFF-FRONTED FOLIAGE-GLEANER. (s CA, SA). . . . . . . _____

❑ *Philydor atricapillus.* BLACK-CAPPED FOLIAGE-GLEANER. (se SA). . . . _____

❑ *Philydor novaesi.* ALAGOAS FOLIAGE-GLEANER. (ne Braz). . . . . _____

❑ *Simoxenops ucayalae.* PERUVIAN RECURVEBILL. (sw Amaz). . . . . _____

❑ *Simoxenops striatus.* BOLIVIAN RECURVEBILL. (Andes c Bol). . . . . . . _____

❑ *Anabazenops fuscus.* WHITE-COLLARED FOLIAGE-GLEANER. (se Braz). _____

❑ *Thripadectes ignobilis.* UNIFORM TREEHUNTER. (nw SA). . . . . _____

❑ *Thripadectes rufobrunneus.* STREAK-BREASTED TREEHUNTER. (s CA). _____

❑ *Thripadectes virgaticeps.* STREAK-CAPPED TREEHUNTER. (mts nw SA). _____

❑ *Thripadectes melanorhynchus.* BLACK-BILLED TREEHUNTER. (nw SA). _____

❑ *Thripadectes holostictus.* STRIPED TREEHUNTER. (Andes w SA). . . . . . _____

❑ *Thripadectes flammulatus.* FLAMMULATED TREEHUNTER. (nw SA). . . _____

❑ *Thripadectes scrutator.* BUFF-THROATED TREEHUNTER. (sw SA). . . . . _____

❑ *Automolus ochrolaemus.* BUFF-THROATED FOLIAGE-GL. (MA, Amaz). _____

❑ *Automolus dorsalis.* CRESTED FOLIAGE-GLEANER. (w Amaz). . . . . _____

❏ *Automolus infuscatus.* OLIVE-BACKED FOLIAGE-GLEANER. (Amaz). . . _____

❏ *Automolus leucophthalmus.* WHITE-EYED FOLIAGE-GLEANER. (se SA). _____

❏ *Automolus roraimae.* WHITE-THROATED FOLIAGE-GLEANER. (nc SA). . _____

❏ *Automolus melanopezus.* BROWN-RUMPED FOLIAGE-GL. (w Amaz). . . _____

❏ *Automolus rubiginosus.* RUDDY FOLIAGE-GLEANER. (MA, w,n SA). . . _____

❏ *Automolus rufipileatus.* CHESTNUT-CROWNED FOLIAGE-GL. (Amaz). . . _____

❏ *Hylocryptus rectirostris.* CHESTNUT-CAPPED FOLIAGE-GLEANER. (sc SA)_____

❏ *Hylocryptus erythrocephalus.* HENNA-HOODED FOLIAGE-GL. (cw SA). _____

❏ *Sclerurus mexicanus.* TAWNY-THROATED LEAFTOSSER. (MA, n,c SA). _____

❏ *Sclerurus rufigularis.* SHORT-BILLED LEAFTOSSER. (Amaz). . . . . _____

❏ *Sclerurus albigularis.* GREY-THROATED LEAFTOSSER. (s CA-w,n SA). _____

❏ *Sclerurus caudacutus.* BLACK-TAILED LEAFTOSSER. (n,c,e SA). . . . . . . _____

❏ *Sclerurus scansor.* RUFOUS-BREASTED LEAFTOSSER. (se SA). . . . . _____

❏ *Sclerurus guatemalensis.* SCALY-THROATED LEAFTOSSER. (MA-nw SA)_____

❏ *Heliobletus contaminatus.* SHARP-BILLED TREEHUNTER. (se SA). . . . . _____

❏ *Xenops milleri.* RUFOUS-TAILED XENOPS. (Amaz). . . . . _____

❏ *Xenops tenuirostris.* SLENDER-BILLED XENOPS. (Amaz). . . . . _____

❏ *Xenops minutus.* PLAIN XENOPS. (MA, SA). _____

❏ *Xenops rutilans.* STREAKED XENOPS. (mts s CA, SA). . . . . _____

❏ *Megaxenops parnaguae.* GREAT XENOPS. (e Braz). . . . . _____

❏ *Pygarrhichas albogularis.* WHITE-THROATED TREERUNNER. (s SA). . . _____

Subfamily Dendrocolaptinae [13/48]

❏ *Dendrocincla tyrannina.* TYRANNINE WOODCREEPER. (Andes w SA) . _____

❏ *Dendrocincla fuliginosa.* PLAIN-BROWN WOODCREEPER. (CA, Amaz). _____
   ___*D. (f.) meruloides.* PLAIN-BROWN WOODCREEPER. (CA, w,n Amaz)
   ___*D. (f.) fuliginosa.* LINE-THROATED WOODCREEPER. (c,ne Amaz)
   ___*D. (f.) atrirostris.* D'ORBIGNY'S WOODCREEPER. (sw Amaz)

❏ *Dendrocincla turdina.* THRUSH-LIKE WOODCREEPER. (se SA). . . . . . . _____

❏ *Dendrocincla anabatina.* TAWNY-WINGED WOODCREEPER. (MA). . . . . _____

❏ *Dendrocincla merula.* WHITE-CHINNED WOODCREEPER. (w,c Amaz) . _____
   ___*D. (m.) castanoptera.* BLUE-EYED WOODCREEPER. (sp)
   ___*D. (m.) merula.* WHITE-CHINNED WOODCREEPER. (ne SA)

❏ *Dendrocincla homochroa.* RUDDY WOODCREEPER. (MA, nw SA). . . . _____

❑ *Deconychura longicauda.* LONG-TAILED WOODCREEPER. (CA-Amaz). _____

❑ *Deconychura stictolaema.* SPOT-THROATED WOODCREEPER. (n,c Amaz)_____
___*D. (s.) secunda.* ECUADORIAN WOODCREEPER. (nw Amaz)
___*D. (s.) stictolaema.* SPOT-THROATED WOODCREEPER. (n,c Amaz)

❑ *Sittasomus griseicapillus.* OLIVACEOUS WOODCREEPER. (MA, SA). . . _____

❑ *Glyphorynchus spirurus.* WEDGE-BILLED WOODCREEPER. (MA, Amaz)_____

❑ *Drymornis bridgesii.* SCIMITAR-BILLED WOODCREEPER. (sc SA). . . . . . _____

❑ *Nasica longirostris.* LONG-BILLED WOODCREEPER. (Amaz). . . . . _____

❑ *Dendrexetastes rufigula.* CINNAMON-THROATED WOODCREEPER. (Amaz)_____
___*D. (r.) devillei.* CINNAMON-THROATED WOODCREEPER. (w Amaz)
___*D. (r.) rufigula.* STREAK-THROATED WOODCREEPER. (n,c Amaz)

❑ *Hylexetastes stresemanni.* BAR-BELLIED WOODCREEPER. (w Amaz). . . _____

❑ *Hylexetastes perrotii.* RED-BILLED WOODCREEPER. (Amaz). . . . . _____
___*H. (p.) perrotii.* RED-BILLED WOODCREEPER. (n Amaz)
___*H. (p.) uniformis.* UNIFORM WOODCREEPER. (s Amaz)

❑ *Xiphocolaptes promeropirhynchus.* STRONG-BILLED W. (MA, SA). . . _____
___*X. (p.) promeropirhynchus.* STRONG-BILLED WOODCREEPER. (sp)
___*X. (p.) orenocensis.* RUSTY-BREASTED WOODCREEPER. (c Amaz)

❑ *Xiphocolaptes albicollis.* WHITE-THROATED WOODCREEPER. (se SA) . _____
___*X. (a.) albicollis.* WHITE-THROATED WOODCREEPER. (sp)
___*X. (a.) vlllanovae.* VILA NOVA WOODCREEPER. (se Braz)

❑ *Xiphocolaptes falcirostris.* MOUSTACHED WOODCREEPER. (ne,e Braz). _____
___*X. (f.) falcirostris.* MOUSTACHED WOODCREEPER. (ne Braz)
___*X. (f.) franciscanus.* SNETHLAGE'S WOODCREEPER. (e Braz)

❑ *Xiphocolaptes major.* GREAT RUFOUS WOODCREEPER. (sc SA). . . . . . _____

❑ *Dendrocolaptes certhia.* BARRED WOODCREEPER. (MA, Amaz). . . . . . _____
___*D. (c.) sanctithomae.* NORTHERN BARRED-WOODCREEPER. (MA, nw SA)
___*D. (c.) certhia.* SOUTHERN BARRED-WOODCREEPER. (Amaz)

❑ *Dendrocolaptes hoffmannsi.* HOFFMANNS'S WOODCR. (w Amaz Braz). _____

❑ *Dendrocolaptes picumnus.* BLACK-BANDED WOODCREEPER. (MA, SA)_____
___*D. (p.) picumnus.* BLACK-BANDED WOODCREEPER. (MA, Amaz)
___*D. (p.) transfasciatus.* CROSS-BARRED WOODCREEPER. (c Amaz Braz)
___*D. (p.) pallescens.* PALE-BILLED WOODCREEPER. (sw SA)

❑ *Dendrocolaptes platyrostris.* PLANALTO WOODCREEPER. (e,se SA). . . . _____

❑ *Xiphorhynchus picus.* STRAIGHT-BILLED WOODCREEPER. (Pan-Amaz). _____

❑ *Xiphorhynchus necopinus.* ZIMMER'S WOODCREEPER. (Amaz Braz). . . _____

❑ *Xiphorhynchus obsoletus.* STRIPED WOODCREEPER. (w Amaz). . . . . . _____

❑ *Xiphorhynchus ocellatus.* OCELLATED WOODCREEPER. (Amaz). . . . . . _____

❑ *Xiphorhynchus spixii.* SPIX'S WOODCREEPER. (Amaz). . . . . _____
___*X. (s.) spixii.* SPIX'S WOODCREEPER. (nw,c Amaz)
___*X. (s.) insignis.* HELLMAYR'S WOODCREEPER. (e Peru)
___*X. (s.) juruanus.* IHERING'S WOODCREEPER. (sw Amaz)

❑ *Xiphorhynchus elegans.* ELEGANT WOODCREEPER. (Amaz)........ _____
  ___*X. (e.) ornatus.* ORNATE WOODCREEPER. (nw Amaz)
  ___*X. (e.) elegans.* ELEGANT WOODCREEPER. (s Amaz)

❑ *Xiphorhynchus pardalotus.* CHESTNUT-RUMPED WOODCR. (n,c Amaz). _____

❑ *Xiphorhynchus guttatus.* BUFF-THROATED WOODCREEPER. (MA, SA). _____
  ___*X. (g.) guttatus.* BUFF-THROATED WOODCREEPER. (sp)
  ___*X. (g.) susurrans.* COCOA WOODCREEPER. (Tob-ne Ven)

❑ *Xiphorhynchus eytoni.* DUSKY-BILLED WOODCREEPER. (e,c Amaz Braz)_____

❑ *Xiphorhynchus flavigaster.* IVORY-BILLED WOODCREEPER. (MA)..... _____

❑ *Xiphorhynchus lachrymosus.* BLACK-STRIPED W. (s CA, nw SA).... _____

❑ *Xiphorhynchus erythropygius.* SPOTTED WOODCREEPER. (MA, nw SA)_____
  ___*X. (e.) erythropygius.* SPOTTED WOODCREEPER. (n,c MA)
  ___*X. (e.) aequatorialis.* BERLEPSCH'S WOODCREEPER. (s CA, nw SA)

❑ *Xiphorhynchus triangularis.* OLIVE-BACKED WOODCREEPER. (w SA). _____

❑ *Lepidocolaptes leucogaster.* WHITE-STRIPED WOODCREEPER. (Mex)... _____

❑ *Lepidocolaptes souleyetii.* STREAK-HEADED WOODCR. (MA, w,n SA) . _____

❑ *Lepidocolaptes angustirostris.* NARROW-BILLED WOODCR. (sc,e SA) . _____

❑ *Lepidocolaptes affinis.* SPOT-CROWNED WOODCREEPER. (MA, w,n SA)_____
  ___*L. (a.) affinis.* SPOT-CROWNED WOODCREEPER. (MA)
  ___*L. (a.) lachrymiger.* MONTANE WOODCREEPER. (w,n SA)

❑ *Lepidocolaptes squamatus.* SCALED WOODCREEPER. (se SA)....... _____

❑ *Lepidocolaptes fuscus.* LESSER WOODCREEPER. (se SA)........... _____

❑ *Lepidocolaptes albolineatus.* LINEATED WOODCREEPER. (Amaz)..... _____

❑ *Campylorhamphus pucherani.* GREATER SCYTHEBILL. (Andes w SA). _____

❑ *Campylorhamphus trochilirostris.* RED-BILLED SCYTHEBILL. (Pan-SA). _____

❑ *Campylorhamphus falcularius.* BLACK-BILLED SCYTHEBILL. (se SA) . _____

❑ *Campylorhamphus pusillus.* BROWN-BILLED SCYTHEBILL.(s CA, nw SA)_____

❑ *Campylorhamphus procurvoides.* CURVE-BILLED SCYTHEBILL. (Amaz) _____

Superfamily FORMICARIOIDEA [20/97]
Family **Formicariidae** [7/60]

❑ *Formicarius colma.* RUFOUS-CAPPED ANTTHRUSH. (nc,c,e,se SA)..... _____

❑ *Formicarius analis.* BLACK-FACED ANTTHRUSH. (MA, Amaz)....... _____
  ___*F. (a.) moniliger.* MEXICAN ANTTHRUSH. (c MA)
  ___*F. (a.) hoffmanni.* HOFFMANN'S ANTTHRUSH. (s CA, n Amaz)
  ___*F. (a.) analis.* BLACK-FACED ANTTHRUSH. (Amaz)

❑ *Formicarius rufifrons.* RUFOUS-FRONTED ANTTHRUSH. (se Peru)..... _____

❑ *Formicarius nigricapillus.* BLACK-HEADED ANTTHRUSH. (s CA, nw SA)_____

❑ *Formicarius rufipectus.* RUFOUS-BREASTED ANTTHRUSH. (s CA, w SA)_____

❑ *Chamaeza campanisona.* SHORT-TAILED ANTTHRUSH. (SA)........ _____
    ___*C. (c.) olivacea.* NORTHERN SHORT-TAILED ANTTHRUSH. (w,n SA)
    ___*C. (c.) campanisona.* SOUTHERN SHORT-TAILED ANTTHRUSH. (se,e SA)

❑ *Chamaeza nobilis.* STRIATED ANTTHRUSH. (w Amaz)............. _____

❑ *Chamaeza turdina.* SCHWARTZ'S ANTTHRUSH. (mts n SA).......... _____

❑ *Chamaeza meruloides.* SUCH'S ANTTHRUSH. (mts se Braz)......... _____

❑ *Chamaeza ruficauda.* RUFOUS-TAILED ANTTHRUSH. (mts se Braz).... _____

❑ *Chamaeza mollissima.* BARRED ANTTHRUSH. (Andes w SA)......... _____

❑ *Pittasoma michleri.* BLACK-CROWNED ANTPITTA. (s CA, nw Colom) . _____

❑ *Pittasoma rufopileatum.* RUFOUS-CROWNED ANTPITTA. (nw SA)..... _____

❑ *Grallaria squamigera.* UNDULATED ANTPITTA. (Andes w SA)....... _____

❑ *Grallaria gigantea.* GIANT ANTPITTA. (Andes nw SA)............. _____
    ___*G. (g.) gigantea.* GIANT ANTPITTA. (sp)
    ___*G. (g.) hylodroma.* PICHINCHA ANTPITTA. (nw Ecua)

❑ *Grallaria excelsa.* GREAT ANTPITTA. (mts w,nc Ven)............. _____

❑ *Grallaria varia.* VARIEGATED ANTPITTA. (SA).................. _____

❑ *Grallaria guatimalensis.* SCALED ANTPITTA. (mts MA, w,n SA)...... _____

❑ *Grallaria alleni.* MOUSTACHED ANTPITTA. (Andes c Colom)........ _____

❑ *Grallaria chthonia.* TACHIRA ANTPITTA. (Andes sw Ven).......... _____

❑ *Grallaria haplonota.* PLAIN-BACKED ANTPITTA. (mts nw,n SA)...... _____

❑ *Grallaria dignissima.* OCHRE-STRIPED ANTPITTA. (nw Amaz)....... _____

❑ *Grallaria eludens.* ELUSIVE ANTPITTA. (ne Peru)................ _____

❑ *Grallaria kaestneri.* CUNDIMARCA ANTPITTA. (mts c Colom)........ _____

❑ *Grallaria bangsi.* SANTA MARTA ANTPITTA. (mts ne Colom)....... _____

❑ *Grallaria ruficapilla.* CHESTNUT-CROWNED ANTPITTA. (mts w,n SA) . _____

❑ *Grallaria watkinsi.* SCRUB ANTIPITTA. (Andes nw SA)............ _____

❑ *Grallaria andicola.* STRIPE-HEADED ANTPITTA. (Andes sw SA)...... _____
    ___*G. (a.) andicola.* STRIPE-HEADED ANTPITTA. (n,c Peru)
    ___*G. (a.) punensis.* PUNO ANTPITTA. (se Peru, wc Bol)

❑ *Grallaria rufocinerea.* BICOLORED ANTPITTA. (Andes c Colom)...... _____

❑ *Grallaria nuchalis.* CHESTNUT-NAPED ANTPITTA. (Andes nw SA)..... _____
    ___*G. (n.) ruficeps.* RUSSET-CAPPED ANTPITTA. (Colom)
    ___*G. (n.) nuchalis.* CHESTNUT-NAPED ANTPITTA. (Ecua, nw Peru)

❑ *Grallaria carrikeri.* PALE-BILLED ANTPITTA. (Andes n Peru)........ _____

❑ *Grallaria albigula.* WHITE-THROATED ANTPITTA. (Andes sw SA)..... _____

❑ *Grallaria flavotincta.* YELLOW-BREASTED ANTPITTA. (Andes nw SA) . _____

❑ *Grallaria hypoleuca.* WHITE-BELLIED ANTPITTA. (Andes nw SA)..... _____

❏ *Grallaria przewalskii.* RUSTY-TINGED ANTPITTA. (Andes n Peru). . . . . _____

❏ *Grallaria capitalis.* BAY ANTPITTA. (Andes c Peru). . . . . _____

❏ *Grallaria erythroleuca.* RED-AND-WHITE ANTPITTA. (Andes se Peru) . _____

❏ *Grallaria griseonucha.* GREY-NAPED ANTPITTA. (Andes w Ven). . . . . _____

❏ *Grallaria rufula.* RUFOUS ANTPITTA. (mts w SA). . . . . _____

❏ *Grallaria blakei.* CHESTNUT ANTPITTA. (Andes c Peru). . . . . _____

❏ *Grallaria erythrotis.* RUFOUS-FACED ANTPITTA. (Andes c Bol). . . . . . . _____

❏ *Grallaria quitensis.* TAWNY ANTPITTA. (Andes nw SA). . . . . _____

❏ *Grallaria milleri.* BROWN-BANDED ANTPITTA. (Andes c Colom). . . . . . _____

❏ *Hylopezus perspicillatus.* SPECTACLED ANTPITTA. (s CA, nw SA). . . . _____

❏ *Hylopezus macularius.* SPOTTED ANTPITTA. (w,n Amaz). . . . . _____

❏ *Hylopezus dives.* FULVOUS-BELLIED ANTPITTA. (CA, nw SA). . . . . _____
　　___*H. (d.) dives.* FULVOUS-BELLIED ANTPITTA. (sp)
　　___*H. (d.) flammulatus.* FLAMMULATED ANTPITTA. (w Pan)

❏ *Hylopezus fulviventris.* WHITE-LORED ANTPITTA. (nw Amaz). . . . . . . _____

❏ *Hylopezus berlepschi.* AMAZONIAN ANTPITTA. (w Amaz). . . . . _____

❏ *Hylopezus ochroleucus.* WHITE-BROWED ANTPITTA. (se Braz). . . . . . . _____

❏ *Hylopezus nattereri.* SPECKLE-BREASTED ANTPITTA. (se SA). . . . . _____

❏ *Myrmothera campanisona.* THRUSH-LIKE ANTPITTA. (Amaz). . . . . _____

❏ *Myrmothera simplex.* BROWN-BREASTED ANTPITTA. (Pant nc SA). . . . _____

❏ *Grallaricula flavirostris.* OCHRE-BREASTED ANTPITTA. (s CA, w SA) . _____

❏ *Grallaricula ferrugineipectus.* RUSTY-BREASTED ANTPITTA. (w,n SA). _____
　　___*G. (f.) ferrugineipectus.* RUSTY-BREASTED ANTPITTA. (cn SA)
　　___*G. (f.) rara.* RUFOUS-BREASTED ANTPITTA. (nw SA)
　　___*G. (f.) leymebambae.* LEYMEBAMBA ANTPITTA. (sw SA)

❏ *Grallaricula nana.* SLATE-CROWNED ANTPITTA. (mts w,n SA). . . . . . . _____

❏ *Grallaricula loricata.* SCALLOP-BREASTED ANTPITTA. (mts nc Ven). . . _____

❏ *Grallaricula peruviana.* PERUVIAN ANTPITTA. (Andes nw SA). . . . . . . _____

❏ *Grallaricula ochraceifrons.* OCHRE-FRONTED ANTPITTA. (n Peru). . . . _____

❏ *Grallaricula lineifrons.* CRESCENT-FACED ANTPITTA. (Andes nw SA). _____

❏ *Grallaricula cucullata.* HOODED ANTPITTA. (Andes nw SA). . . . . _____

Family **Conopophagidae** [1/8]

❏ *Conopophaga lineata.* RUFOUS GNATEATER. (e,se SA). . . . . _____
　　___*C. (l.) cearae.* CAATINGA GNATEATER. (e Braz)
　　___*C. (l.) lineata.* SILVERY-TUFTED GNATEATER. (se SA)

❏ *Conopophaga aurita.* CHESTNUT-BELTED GNATEATER. (Amaz). . . . . . . _____

❑ *Conopophaga roberti.* HOODED GNATEATER. (ce Amaz)........... _____

❑ *Conopophaga peruviana.* ASH-THROATED GNATEATER. (sw Amaz)... _____

❑ *Conopophaga ardesiaca.* SLATY GNATEATER. (Andes sw SA)....... _____

❑ *Conopophaga castaneiceps.* CHESTNUT-CROWNED G. (mts w SA).... _____

❑ *Conopophaga melanops.* BLACK-CHEEKED GNATEATER. (e Braz)..... _____

❑ *Conopophaga melanogaster.* BLACK-BELLIED GNATEATER. (s Amaz). _____

Family **Rhinocryptidae** [12/29]

❑ *Pteroptochos tarnii.* HUET-HUET. (s SA)...................... _____
   ___*P. (t.) castaneus.* CHESTNUT-THROATED HUET-HUET. (c,s Chile)
   ___*P. (t.) tarnii.* BLACK-THROATED HUET-HUET. (s Chile, sw Argen)

❑ *Pteroptochos megapodius.* MOUSTACHED TURCA. (nc,c Chile)...... _____

❑ *Scelorchilus albicollis.* WHITE-THROATED TAPACULO. (nc,c Chile).... _____

❑ *Scelorchilus rubecula.* CHUCAO TAPACULO. (s SA)............... _____

❑ *Rhinocrypta lanceolata.* CRESTED GALLITO. (sc SA)............. _____

❑ *Teledromas fuscus.* SANDY GALLITO. (w Argen)................. _____

❑ *Liosceles thoracicus.* RUSTY-BELTED TAPACULO. (w Amaz)........ _____

❑ *Melanopareia torquata.* COLLARED CRESCENT-CHEST. (sc SA)....... _____

❑ *Melanopareia maximiliani.* OLIVE-CROWNED CRESCENT-CHEST. (sc SA) _____

❑ *Melanopareia elegans.* ELEGANT CRESCENT-CHEST. (nw SA)....... _____
   ___*M. (e.) elegans.* ELEGANT CRESCENT-CHEST. (sp)
   ___*M. (e.) maranonica.* MARANON CRESCENT-CHEST. (nc Peru)

❑ *Psilorhamphus guttatus.* SPOTTED BAMBOOWREN. (se SA)......... _____

❑ *Merulaxis ater.* SLATY BRISTLEFRONT. (se Braz)................ _____

❑ *Merulaxis stresemanni.* STRESEMANN'S BRISTLEFRONT. (e Braz)..... _____

❑ *Eugralla paradoxa.* OCHRE-FLANKED TAPACULO. (s Chile)......... _____

❑ *Myornis senilis.* ASH-COLORED TAPACULO. (Andes nw SA)........ _____

❑ *Scytalopus unicolor.* UNICOLORED TAPACULO. (Andes w SA)....... _____
   ___*S. (u.) latrans.* BLACKISH TAPACULO. (nw SA)
   ___*S. (u.) unicolor.* UNICOLORED TAPACULO. (sw SA)

❑ *Scytalopus macropus.* LARGE-FOOTED TAPACULO. (Andes n Peru).... _____

❑ *Scytalopus femoralis.* RUFOUS-VENTED TAPACULO. (mts w SA)..... _____
   ___*S. (f.) sanctaemartae.* SANTA MARTA TAPACULO. (ne Colom)
   ___*S. (f.) atratus.* NORTHERN WHITE-CROWNED TAPACULO. (c Colom)
   ___*S. (f.) femoralis.* RUFOUS-VENTED TAPACULO. (w SA)
   ___*S. (f.) bolivianus.* SOUTHERN WHITE-CROWNED TAPACULO. (sw SA)

❑ *Scytalopus panamensis.* TACARCUNA TAPACULO. (mts e Pan)....... _____

❑ *Scytalopus vicinior.* NARINO TAPACULO. (mts e Pan, nw SA)....... _____

❑ *Scytalopus argentifrons.* SILVERY-FRONTED TAPACULO. (mts s CA)... _____
   ___*S. (a.) argentifrons.* SILVERY-FRONTED TAPACULO. (CR)
   ___*S. (a.) chiriquensis.* CHIRIQUI TAPACULO. (w Pan)

❑ *Scytalopus latebricola.* BROWN-RUMPED TAPACULO. (mts nw,n SA)... _____
   ___*S. (l.) latebricola.* BROWN-RUMPED TAPACULO. (nw SA)
   ___*S. (l.) caracae.* VENEZUELAN TAPACULO. (n Ven)

❑ *Scytalopus magellanicus.* ANDEAN TAPACULO. (Andes SA)......... _____
   ___*S. (m.) griseicollis.* ANDEAN TAPACULO. (nw SA)
   ___*S. (m.) acutirostris.* SHARP-BILLED TAPACULO. (cw SA)
   ___*S. (m.) fuscus.* DUSKY TAPACULO. (sw SA)
   ___*S. (m.) magellanicus.* MAGELLANIC TAPACULO. (s SA)

❑ *Scytalopus superciliaris.* WHITE-BROWED TAPACULO. (Andes sw SA). _____

❑ *Scytalopus speluncae.* MOUSE-COLORED TAPACULO. (mts se SA)..... _____

❑ *Scytalopus novacapitalis.* BRASILIA TAPACULO. (ec Braz)......... _____

❑ *Scytalopus psychopompus.* CHESTNUT-SIDED TAPACULO. (se Braz)... _____

❑ *Scytalopus indigoticus.* WHITE-BREASTED TAPACULO. (se Braz)...... _____

❑ *Acropternis orthonyx.* OCELLATED TAPACULO. (Andes w SA)....... _____

Suborder PASSERI [876/4580]
Parvorder CORVIDA [228/1103]
Superfamily Menuroidea [11/31]
Family **Climacteridae** [2/7]

❑ *Cormobates placens.* PAPUAN TREECREEPER. (mts NG)............. _____

❑ *Cormobates leucophaea.* WHITE-THROATED TREECREEPER. (e Aust)... _____
   ___*C. (l.) minor.* LITTLE TREECREEPER. (ne Aust)
   ___*C. (l.) leucophaea.* WHITE-THROATED TREECREEPER. (e,se Aust)

❑ *Climacteris affinis.* WHITE-BROWED TREECREEPER. (int Aust)....... _____

❑ *Climacteris erythrops.* RED-BROWED TREECREEPER. (se Aust)....... _____

❑ *Climacteris picumnus.* BROWN TREECREEPER. (ne,e Aust)......... _____
   ___*C. (p.) melanota.* BLACK TREECREEPER. (ne Aust)
   ___*C. (p.) picumnus.* BROWN TREECREEPER. (e Aust)

❑ *Climacteris melanura.* BLACK-TAILED TREECREEPER. (n,wc Aust).... _____
   ___*C. (m.) melanura.* BLACK-TAILED TREECREEPER. (n Aust)
   ___*C. (m.) wellsi.* ALLIED TREECREEPER. (wc Aust)

❑ *Climacteris rufa.* RUFOUS TREECREEPER. (sw Aust).............. _____

Family **Menuridae** [2/4]
Subfamily Menurinae [1/2]

❑ *Menura alberti.* ALBERT'S LYREBIRD. (mts ce Aust).............. _____

❑ *Menura novaehollandiae.* SUPERB LYREBIRD. (e,se Aust).......... _____

Subfamily Atrichornithinae [1/2]

☐ *Atrichornis rufescens*. RUFOUS SCRUB-BIRD. (mts ce Aust)......... _____

☐ *Atrichornis clamosus*. NOISY SCRUB-BIRD. (sw Aust)............. _____

Family **Ptilonorhynchidae** [7/20]

☐ *Ailuroedus buccoides*. WHITE-EARED CATBIRD. (NG)............. _____

☐ *Ailuroedus melanotis*. SPOTTED CATBIRD. (Aru-NG, ne Aust)....... _____

☐ *Ailuroedus crassirostris*. GREEN CATBIRD. (ce Aust)............. _____

☐ *Ailuroedus dentirostris*. TOOTH-BILLED CATBIRD. (mts ne Aust)..... _____

☐ *Archboldia papuensis*. ARCHBOLD'S BOWERBIRD. (mts NG)........ _____

☐ *Archboldia sanfordi*. SANFORD'S BOWERBIRD. (mts c NG)......... _____

☐ *Amblyornis inornatus*. VOGELKOP BOWERBIRD. (mts nw NG)....... _____

☐ *Amblyornis macgregoriae*. MACGREGOR'S BOWERBIRD. (mts c,e NG). _____

☐ *Amblyornis subalaris*. STREAKED BOWERBIRD. (mts se NG)........ _____

☐ *Amblyornis flavifrons*. GOLDEN-FRONTED BOWERBIRD. (mts nc NG) . _____

☐ *Prionodura newtoniana*. GOLDEN BOWERBIRD. (mts ne Aust)....... _____

☐ *Sericulus aureus*. FLAME BOWERBIRD. (nw,sc NG).............. _____

☐ *Sericulus bakeri*. FIRE-MANED BOWERBIRD. (mts ne NG).......... _____

☐ *Sericulus chrysocephalus*. REGENT BOWERBIRD. (ce Aust)......... _____

☐ *Ptilonorhynchus violaceus*. SATIN BOWERBIRD. (mts e Aust)....... _____

☐ *Chlamydera guttata*. WESTERN BOWERBIRD. (int w,c Aust)......... _____

☐ *Chlamydera maculata*. SPOTTED BOWERBIRD. (int e,se Aust)....... _____

☐ *Chlamydera nuchalis*. GREAT BOWERBIRD. (n Aust)............. _____

☐ *Chlamydera lauterbachi*. YELLOW-BREASTED BOWERBIRD. (NG)..... _____
  ___*C. (l.) uniformis*. UNIFORM BOWERBIRD. (nw,s NG)
  ___*C. (l.) lauterbachi*. YELLOW-BREASTED BOWERBIRD. (nc NG)

☐ *Chlamydera cerviniventris*. FAWN-BREASTED BOWERBIRD. (NG, ne Aust)_____

Superfamily MELIPHAGOIDEA [63/276]
Family **Maluridae** [5/26]
Subfamily Malurinae [4/18]
Tribe Malurini [3/15]

☐ *Clytomyias insignis*. ORANGE-CROWNED FAIRYWREN. (mts NG)...... _____

☐ *Sipodotus wallacii*. WALLACE'S FAIRYWREN. (Aru-NG)............ _____

☐ *Malurus grayi*. BROAD-BILLED FAIRYWREN. (w Pap, nw NG)....... _____

☐ *Malurus campbelli*. CAMPBELL'S FAIRYWREN. (sc NG)............ _____

☐ *Malurus alboscapulatus*. WHITE-SHOULDERED FAIRYWREN. (NG).... _____

❑ *Malurus melanocephalus.* RED-BACKED FAIRYWREN. (n,e Aust). . . . . _____

❑ *Malurus leucopterus.* WHITE-WINGED FAIRYWREN. (int Aust). . . . . . . _____
 ___*M. (l.) leuconotus.* BLUE-AND-WHITE FAIRYWREN. (sp)
 ___*M. (l.) leucopterus.* BLACK-AND-WHITE FAIRYWREN. (cw Aust)

❑ *Malurus cyaneus.* SUPERB FAIRYWREN. (se Aust). . . . . _____

❑ *Malurus splendens.* SPLENDID FAIRYWREN. (int Aust). . . . . _____
 ___*M. (s.) splendens.* SPLENDID FAIRYWREN. (sw Aust)
 ___*M. (s.) callainus.* TURQUOISE FAIRYWREN. (c Aust)
 ___*M. (s.) melanotus.* BLACK-BACKED FAIRYWREN. (se Aust)

❑ *Malurus lamberti.* VARIEGATED FAIRYWREN. (int Aust). . . . . _____
 ___*M. (l.) rogersi.* ROGERS'S FAIRYWREN. (ne W Aust)
 ___*M. (l.) dulcis.* LAVENDER-FLANKED FAIRYWREN. (cn Aust)
 ___*M. (l.) assimilis.* PURPLE-BACKED FAIRYWREN. (sp)
 ___*M. (l.) lamberti.* VARIEGATED FAIRYWREN. (ce Aust)

❑ *Malurus amabilis.* LOVELY FAIRYWREN. (ne Aust). . . . . _____

❑ *Malurus elegans.* RED-WINGED FAIRYWREN. (sw Aust). . . . . _____

❑ *Malurus pulcherrimus.* BLUE-BREASTED FAIRYWREN. (sw,sc Aust). . . _____

❑ *Malurus coronatus.* PURPLE-CROWNED FAIRYWREN. (cn,ne Aust). . . . . _____
 ___*M. (c.) coronatus.* PURPLE-CROWNED FAIRYWREN. (cn Aust)
 ___*M. (c.) macgillivrayi.* MACGILLIVRAY'S FAIRYWREN. (ne Aust)

❑ *Malurus cyanocephalus.* EMPEROR FAIRYWREN. (Aru-NG). . . . . _____

Tribe Stipiturini [1/3]

❑ *Stipiturus ruficeps.* RUFOUS-CROWNED EMUWREN. (w,c Aust). . . . . . . _____

❑ *Stipiturus malachurus.* SOUTHERN EMUWREN. (e,s Aust). . . . . _____

❑ *Stipiturus mallee.* MALLEE EMUWREN. (int se Aust). . . . . _____

Subfamily Amytornithinae [1/8]

❑ *Amytornis barbatus.* GREY GRASSWREN. (ec Aust). . . . . _____

❑ *Amytornis woodwardi.* WHITE-THROATED GRASSWREN. (cn Aust). . . . _____

❑ *Amytornis dorotheae.* CARPENTARIAN GRASSWREN. (cn Aust). . . . . . . _____

❑ *Amytornis striatus.* STRIATED GRASSWREN. (int Aust). . . . . _____
 ___*A. (s.) whitei.* RUFOUS GRASSWREN. (sp)
 ___*A. (s.) striatus.* STRIATED GRASSWREN. (se Aust)

❑ *Amytornis goyderi.* EYREAN GRASSWREN. (c Aust). . . . . _____

❑ *Amytornis textilis.* THICK-BILLED GRASSWREN. (c,sw Aust). . . . . _____
 ___*A. (t.) textilis.* WESTERN GRASSWREN. (sw,sc Aust)
 ___*A. (t.) modestus.* THICK-BILLED GRASSWREN. (c Aust)

❑ *Amytornis purnelli.* DUSKY GRASSWREN. (c Aust). . . . . _____

❑ *Amytornis housei.* BLACK GRASSWREN. (ne W Aust). . . . . _____

Family **Meliphagidae** [42/182]

❑ *Myzomela blasii.* DRAB MYZOMELA. (s Moluc)................... _____

❑ *Myzomela albigula.* WHITE-CHINNED MYZOMELA. (se NG)......... _____

❑ *Myzomela eques.* RED-THROATED MYZOMELA. (w Pap-w Bism)..... _____
  ___*M. (e.) eques.* RED-THROATED MYZOMELA. (w Pap-NG)
  ___*M. (e.) cineracea.* ASHY MYZOMELA. (w Bism)

❑ *Myzomela obscura.* DUSKY MYZOMELA. (Moluc-NG, n,ne Aust)..... _____
  ___*M. (o.) simplex.* MOLUCCAN MYZOMELA. (n Moluc)
  ___*M. (o.) obscura.* DUSKY MYZOMELA. (Aru-sNG, n,ne Aust)
  ___*M. (o.) rubrobrunnea.* RED-BROWN MYZOMELA. (nw NG)

❑ *Myzomela cruentata.* RED MYZOMELA. (NG-Bism).............. _____

❑ *Myzomela nigrita.* BLACK MYZOMELA. (Aru-NG)............... _____

❑ *Myzomela pulchella.* OLIVE-YELLOW MYZOMELA. (e Bism)........ _____

❑ *Myzomela adolphinae.* MOUNTAIN MYZOMELA. (mts NG)......... _____

❑ *Myzomela kuehni.* CRIMSON-HOODED MYZOMELA. (Sumba)........ _____

❑ *Myzomela dammermani.* SUMBA MYZOMELA. (Wetar)............ _____

❑ *Myzomela erythrocephala.* RED-HEADED MYZOMELA. (Aru, s NG, n Aust)_____

❑ *Myzomela chloroptera.* SULAWESI MYZOMELA. (mts Sulaw, n Moluc). _____

❑ *Myzomela wakoloensis.* WAKOLO MYZOMELA. (mts s Moluc)....... _____

❑ *Myzomela boiei.* BANDA MYZOMELA. (mts L Sunda).............. _____

❑ *Myzomela sanguinolenta.* SCARLET MYZOMELA. (e Aust).......... _____

❑ *Myzomela caledonica.* NEW CALEDONIAN MYZOMELA. (N Cal)...... _____

❑ *Myzomela rubratra.* MICRONESIAN MYZOMELA. (Micro)........... _____

❑ *Myzomela cardinalis.* CARDINAL MYZOMELA. (Solom-Samoa)...... _____

❑ *Myzomela chermesina.* ROTUMA MYZOMELA. (nw Fiji)........... _____

❑ *Myzomela sclateri.* SCARLET-BIBBED MYZOMELA. (is NG, Bism).... _____

❑ *Myzomela pammelaena.* EBONY MYZOMELA. (is Bism)............ _____

❑ *Myzomela lafargei.* SCARLET-NAPED MYZOMELA. (Solom)......... _____

❑ *Myzomela eichhorni.* YELLOW-VENTED MYZOMELA. (c Solom)...... _____

❑ *Myzomela melanocephala.* BLACK-HEADED MYZOMELA. (Solom).... _____

❑ *Myzomela malaitae.* RED-BELLIED MYZOMELA. (se Solom)......... _____

❑ *Myzomela tristrami.* SOOTY MYZOMELA. (s Solom).............. _____

❑ *Myzomela jugularis.* ORANGE-BREASTED MYZOMELA. (Fiji)........ _____

❑ *Myzomela erythromelas.* BLACK-BELLIED MYZOMELA. (cs Bism)..... _____

❑ *Myzomela vulnerata.* RED-RUMPED MYZOMELA. (Timor).......... _____

❑ *Myzomela rosenbergii.* RED-COLLARED MYZOMELA. (mts NG)...... _____

❑ *Certhionyx pectoralis.* BANDED HONEYEATER. (n Aust)............ _____

❑ *Certhionyx niger.* BLACK HONEYEATER. (Aust)............... _____

❑ *Certhionyx variegatus.* PIED HONEYEATER. (int w,c Aust).......... _____

❑ *Timeliopsis fulvigula.* OLIVE STRAIGHTBILL. (mts NG)............ _____

❑ *Timeliopsis griseigula.* TAWNY STRAIGHTBILL. (nw,se NG)........ _____

❑ *Melilestes megarhynchus.* LONG-BILLED HONEYEATER. (Aru-NG).... _____

❑ *Stresemannia bougainvillei.* BOUGAINVILLE HONEYEATER. (nw Solom)_____

❑ *Glycichaera fallax.* GREEN-BACKED HONEYEATER. (Aru-NG, ne Aust). _____
   ___*G. (f.) poliocephala.* PALE-EYED HONEYEATER. (Aru-nw NG)
   ___*G. (f.) fallax.* WHITE-EYED HONEYEATER. (c,e NG)
   ___*G. (f.) claudi.* GREEN-BACKED HONEYEATER. (ne Aust)

❑ *Lichmera lombokia.* SCALY-CROWNED HONEYEATER. (wc L Sunda)... _____

❑ *Lichmera argentauris.* OLIVE HONEYEATER. (Wall).............. _____

❑ *Lichmera limbata.* INDONESIAN HONEYEATER. (L Sunda).......... _____

❑ *Lichmera indistincta.* BROWN HONEYEATER. (Aru, cs NG, Aust)..... _____

❑ *Lichmera incana.* DARK-BROWN HONEYEATER. (N Cal-Vanu)....... _____

❑ *Lichmera squamata.* WHITE-TUFTED HONEYEATER. (L Sunda-Kai)... _____

❑ *Lichmera alboauricularis.* SILVER-EARED HONEYEATER. (nc,se NG) . _____

❑ *Lichmera deningeri.* BURU HONEYEATER. (s Moluc).............. _____

❑ *Lichmera monticola.* SERAM HONEYEATER. (s Moluc)............ _____

❑ *Lichmera flavicans.* YELLOW-EARED HONEYEATER. (Timor)........ _____

❑ *Lichmera notabilis.* BLACK-CHESTED HONEYEATER. (Wetar)........ _____

❑ *Trichodere cockerelli.* WHITE-STREAKED HONEYEATER. (ne Aust).... _____

❑ *Meliphaga montana.* FOREST HONEYEATER. (w Pap, n NG)........ _____

❑ *Meliphaga mimikae.* MOTTLE-BREASTED HONEYEATER. (mts s NG)... _____

❑ *Meliphaga orientalis.* HILL-FOREST HONEYEATER. (mts w Pap, NG)... _____

❑ *Meliphaga albonotata.* SCRUB HONEYEATER. (NG)............... _____

❑ *Meliphaga aruensis.* PUFF-BACKED HONEYEATER. (Aru-NG)....... _____

❑ *Meliphaga analoga.* MIMIC HONEYEATER. (Aru-NG).............. _____

❑ *Meliphaga vicina.* TAGULA HONEYEATER. (sw NG).............. _____

❑ *Meliphaga gracilis.* GRACEFUL HONEYEATER. (Aru-NG, ne Aust).... _____
   ___*M. (g.) gracilis.* GRACEFUL HONEYEATER. (sp)
   ___*M. (g.) stevensi.* STEVENS'S HONEYEATER. (se NG)

❑ *Meliphaga notata.* YELLOW-SPOTTED HONEYEATER. (ne Aust)....... _____

❑ *Meliphaga flavirictus.* YELLOW-GAPED HONEYEATER. (NG)........ _____

❑ *Meliphaga lewinii.* LEWIN'S HONEYEATER. (e Aust).............. _____

❑ *Meliphaga albilineata.* WHITE-LINED HONEYEATER. (n Aust)....... _____

❑ *Meliphaga reticulata.* STREAKY-BREASTED HONEYEATER. (Timor). . . . _____

❑ *Guadalcanaria inexpectata.* GUADALCANAL HONEYEATER. (se Solom) _____

❑ *Foulehaio carunculata.* WATTLED HONEYEATER. (mts s Polyn). . . . . . _____

❑ *Lichenostomus subfrenatus.* BLACK-THROATED HONEYEATER. (NG) . _____

❑ *Lichenostomus obscurus.* OBSCURE HONEYEATER. (NG). . . . . _____

❑ *Lichenostomus frenatus.* BRIDLED HONEYEATER. (mts ne Aust). . . . . . _____

❑ *Lichenostomus hindwoodi.* EUNGELLA HONEYEATER. (mts ne Aust) . _____

❑ *Lichenostomus chrysops.* YELLOW-FACED HONEYEATER. (e Aust). . . . _____

❑ *Lichenostomus versicolor.* VARIED HONEYEATER. (w Pap, NG, ne Aust)_____

❑ *Lichenostomus fasciogularis.* MANGROVE HONEYEATER. (ne Aust). . . _____

❑ *Lichenostomus virescens.* SINGING HONEYEATER. (Aust). . . . . _____

❑ *Lichenostomus flavus.* YELLOW HONEYEATER. (ne Aust). . . . . _____

❑ *Lichenostomus unicolor.* WHITE-GAPED HONEYEATER. (n Aust). . . . . . _____

❑ *Lichenostomus leucotis.* WHITE-EARED HONEYEATER. (sw,s,e Aust) . _____

❑ *Lichenostomus flavicollis.* YELLOW-THROATED HONEYEATER. (Tas) . _____

❑ *Lichenostomus melanops.* YELLOW-TUFTED HONEYEATER. (e,se Aust). _____
   ___*L. (m.) melanops.* YELLOW-TUFTED HONEYEATER. (sp)
   ___*L. (m.) cassidix.* HELMETED HONEYEATER. (se Aust)

❑ *Lichenostomus cratitius.* PURPLE-GAPED HONEYEATER. (sw,sc Aust) . _____

❑ *Lichenostomus keartlandi.* GREY-HEADED HONEYEATER. (w,c Aust) . _____

❑ *Lichenostomus flavescens.* YELLOW-TINTED H. (se NG, n Aust). . . . . . _____

❑ *Lichenostomus fuscus.* FUSCOUS HONEYEATER. (e Aust). . . . . _____

❑ *Lichenostomus plumulus.* GREY-FRONTED HONEYEATER. (w,int Aust). _____

❑ *Lichenostomus ornatus.* YELLOW-PLUMED HONEYEATER. (s Aust). . . . _____

❑ *Lichenostomus penicillatus.* WHITE-PLUMED HONEYEATER. (int Aust). _____

❑ *Xanthotis flaviventer.* TAWNY-BREASTED H. (Aru-NG, ne Aust). . . . . . _____

❑ *Xanthotis polygramma.* SPOTTED HONEYEATER. (w Pap-NG). . . . . . . _____

❑ *Xanthotis macleayana.* MACLEAY HONEYEATER. (ne Aust). . . . . _____

❑ *Xanthotis provocator.* KADAVU HONEYEATER. (sw Fiji). . . . . _____

❑ *Oreornis chrysogenys.* ORANGE-CHEEKED HONEYEATER. (wc NG). . . . _____

❑ *Apalopteron familiare.* BONIN HONEYEATER. (Bonin). . . . . _____

❑ *Melithreptus lunatus.* WHITE-NAPED HONEYEATER. (sw,e Aust). . . . . . _____

❑ *Melithreptus affinis.* BLACK-HEADED HONEYEATER. (Tas). . . . . _____

❑ *Melithreptus albogularis.* WHITE-THROATED H. (s NG, n,ne Aust). . . . _____

❑ *Melithreptus laetior.* GOLDEN-BACKED HONEYEATER. (w,n,c Aust). . . . _____

❑ *Melithreptus gularis.* BLACK-CHINNED HONEYEATER. (e,se Aust). . . . . _____

❑ *Melithreptus alidirostris.* STRONG-BILLED HONEYEATER. (Tas). . . . . . . _____

❑ *Melithreptus brevirostris.* BROWN-HEADED HONEYEATER. (sw,s,ec Aust)_____

❑ *Notiomystis cincta.* STITCHBIRD. (NZ). . . . . _____

❑ *Pycnopygius ixoides.* PLAIN HONEYEATER. (n,sc NG). . . . . _____

❑ *Pycnopygius cinereus.* MARBLED HONEYEATER. (mts NG). . . . . _____

❑ *Pycnopygius stictocephalus.* STREAK-HEADED HONEYEATER. (Aru-NG) _____

❑ *Melitograis gilolensis.* WHITE-STREAKED FRIARBIRD. (n Moluc). . . . . . _____

❑ *Philemon meyeri.* MEYER'S FRIARBIRD. (NG). . . . . _____

❑ *Philemon inornatus.* PLAIN FRIARBIRD. (Timor). . . . . _____

❑ *Philemon kisserensis.* GREY FRIARBIRD. (ec L Sunda). . . . . _____

❑ *Philemon brassi.* BRASS'S FRIARBIRD. (nw NG). . . . . _____

❑ *Philemon citreogularis.* LITTLE FRIARBIRD. (cs NG, n,e Aust). . . . . . . _____

❑ *Philemon fuscicapillus.* DUSKY FRIARBIRD. (n Moluc). . . . . _____

❑ *Philemon moluccensis.* BLACK-FACED FRIARBIRD. (e Wall). . . . . _____

❑ *Philemon subcorniculatus.* GREY-NECKED FRIARBIRD. (s Moluc). . . . . _____

❑ *Philemon buceroides.* HELMETED FRIARBIRD. (w,c L Sunda, cn Aust). _____
    ___*P. (b.) buceroides.* HELMETED FRIARBIRD. (w,c L Sunda)
    ___*P. (b.) gordoni.* MELVILLE ISLAND FRIARBIRD. (cn Aust)

❑ *Philemon novaeguineae.* NEW GUINEA FRIARBIRD. (Aru-NG, ne Aust) _____
    ___*P. (n.) novaeguineae.* NEW GUINEA FRIARBIRD. (Aru-NG)
    ___*P. (n.) yorki.* CAPE YORK FRIARBIRD. (ne Aust)

❑ *Philemon albitorques.* WHITE-NAPED FRIARBIRD. (nw Bism). . . . . _____

❑ *Philemon cockerelli.* NEW BRITAIN FRIARBIRD. (sw Bism). . . . . _____

❑ *Philemon eichhorni.* NEW IRELAND FRIARBIRD. (e Bism). . . . . _____

❑ *Philemon argenticeps.* SILVER-CROWNED FRIARBIRD. (n Aust). . . . . . . _____

❑ *Philemon corniculatus.* NOISY FRIARBIRD. (sc NG, e Aust). . . . . _____

❑ *Philemon diemenensis.* NEW CALEDONIAN FRIARBIRD. (N Cal, Loy) . _____

❑ *Ptiloprora plumbea.* LEADEN HONEYEATER. (mts NG). . . . . _____

❑ *Ptiloprora meekiana.* OLIVE-STREAKED HONEYEATER. (mts NG). . . . . _____

❑ *Ptiloprora erythropleura.* RUFOUS-SIDED HONEYEATER. (mts w NG) . _____

❑ *Ptiloprora mayri.* MAYR'S HONEYEATER. (mts n NG). . . . . _____

❑ *Ptiloprora guisei.* RUFOUS-BACKED HONEYEATER. (mts c,se NG). . . . . _____

❑ *Ptiloprora perstriata.* BLACK-BACKED HONEYEATER. (mts c,se NG). . . _____

❑ *Melidectes fuscus.* SOOTY MELIDECTES. (mts c,se NG). . . . . _____

❑ *Melidectes whitemanensis.* BISMARCK MELIDECTES. (mts sw Bism). . . _____

❑ *Melidectes nouhuysi.* SHORT-BEARDED MELIDECTES. (mts w NG). . . . _____

❑ *Melidectes princeps.* LONG-BEARDED MELIDECTES. (mts ec NG). . . . . . _____

❑ *Melidectes ochromelas.* CINNAMON-BROWED MELIDECTES. (mts NG) . _____

❑ *Melidectes leucostephes.* VOGELKOP MELIDECTES. (mts nw NG). . . . . _____

❑ *Melidectes belfordi.* BELFORD'S MELIDECTES. . . . . _____

❑ *Melidectes rufocrissalis.* YELLOW-BROWED MELIDECTES. (mts c NG) . _____

❑ *Melidectes foersteri.* HUON MELIDECTES. (mts ne NG). . . . . _____

❑ *Melidectes torquatus.* ORNATE MELIDECTES. (mts NG). . . . . _____

❑ *Melidectes sclateri.* SAN CRISTOBAL MELIDECTES. (c Solom). . . . . . . _____

❑ *Melipotes gymnops.* ARFAK HONEYEATER. (mts w NG). . . . . _____

❑ *Melipotes fumigatus.* SMOKY HONEYEATER. (mts c,se NG). . . . . _____

❑ *Melipotes ater.* SPANGLED HONEYEATER. (mts ne NG). . . . . _____

❑ *Myza celebensis.* DARK-EARED MYZA. (mts Sulaw). . . . . _____

❑ *Myza sarasinorum.* WHITE-EARED MYZA. (mts Sulaw). . . . . _____

❑ *Gymnomyza viridis.* GIANT HONEYEATER. (mts Fiji). . . . . _____

❑ *Gymnomyza samoensis.* MAO. (mts Samoa). . . . . _____

❑ *Gymnomyza aubryana.* CROW HONEYEATER. (mts N Cal). . . . . _____

❑ *Moho braccatus.* KAUAI OO. (mts Kauai). . . . . _____

   Moho apicalis. OAHU OO. (†mts Oahu). . . . . _____

❑ *Moho bishopi.* BISHOP'S OO. (mts Maui). . . . . _____

   Moho nobilis. HAWAII OO. (†mts Hawaii). . . . . _____

   Chaetoptila angustipluma. KIOEA. (†Hawaii). . . . . _____

❑ *Phylidonyris pyrrhoptera.* CRESCENT HONEYEATER. (se Aust). . . . . . . _____

❑ *Phylidonyris novaehollandiae.* NEW HOLLAND H. (sw,se Aust). . . . . . _____

❑ *Phylidonyris nigra.* WHITE-CHEEKED HONEYEATER. (sw,ne,se Aust). . . _____

❑ *Phylidonyris albifrons.* WHITE-FRONTED HONEYEATER. (Aust). . . . . . . _____

❑ *Phylidonyris undulata.* BARRED HONEYEATER. (mts N Cal). . . . . _____

❑ *Phylidonyris notabilis.* NEW HEBRIDES HONEYEATER. (s Melan). . . . . . _____

❑ *Phylidonyris melanops.* TAWNY-CROWNED HONEYEATER. (sw,se Aust) _____

❑ *Ramsayornis modestus.* BROWN-BACKED H. (Aru-NG, ne Aust). . . . . . _____

❑ *Ramsayornis fasciatus.* BAR-BREASTED HONEYEATER. (n Aust). . . . . . _____

❑ *Plectorhyncha lanceolata.* STRIPED HONEYEATER. (e,se Aust). . . . . . . _____

❑ *Conopophila albogularis.* RUFOUS-BANDED H. (Aru-NG, n Aust). . . . . _____

❑ *Conopophila rufogularis.* RUFOUS-THROATED H. (int n Aust). . . . . _____

❑ *Conopophila whitei.* GREY HONEYEATER. (wc Aust). . . . . _____

❏ *Grantiella picta.* PAINTED HONEYEATER. (e Aust). . . . . _____

❏ *Xanthomyza phrygia.* REGENT HONEYEATER. (se Aust). . . . . _____

❏ *Acanthorhynchus tenuirostris.* EASTERN SPINEBILL. (e,se Aust). . . . . . _____

❏ *Acanthorhynchus superciliosus.* WESTERN SPINEBILL. (sw Aust). . . . . _____

❏ *Entomyzon cyanotis.* BLUE-FACED HONEYEATER. (sc NG, n,e Aust). . . _____
   ___*E. (c.) albipennis.* WHITE-WINGED HONEYEATER. (sc NG, n Aust)
   ___*E. (c.) cyanotis.* BLUE-FACED HONEYEATER. (e Aust)

❏ *Manorina melanophrys.* BELL MINER. (se Aust). . . . . _____

❏ *Manorina melanocephala.* NOISY MINER. (e,se Aust). . . . . _____

❏ *Manorina flavigula.* YELLOW-THROATED MINER. (Aust). . . . . _____
   ___*M. (f.) obscura.* DUSKY MINER. (sw Aust)
   ___*M. (f.) flavigula.* YELLOW-THROATED MINER. (sp)
   ___*M. (f.) melanotis.* BLACK-EARED MINER. (sc Aust)

❏ *Anthornis melanura.* NEW ZEALAND BELLBIRD. (NZ). . . . . _____

❏ *Acanthagenys rufogularis.* SPINY-CHEEKED HONEYEATER. (Aust). . . . _____

❏ *Anthochaera lunulata.* LITTLE WATTLEBIRD. (sw Aust). . . . . _____

❏ *Anthochaera chrysoptera.* BRUSH WATTLEBIRD. (se Aust). . . . . _____

❏ *Anthochaera carunculata.* RED WATTLEBIRD. (s Aust). . . . . _____

❏ *Anthochaera paradoxa.* YELLOW WATTLEBIRD. (Tas). . . . . _____

❏ *Prosthemadera novaeseelandiae.* TUI. (NZ-Chatham). . . . . _____

❏ *Epthianura tricolor.* CRIMSON CHAT. (int Aust). . . . . _____

❏ *Epthianura aurifrons.* ORANGE CHAT. (int c,s Aust). . . . . _____

❏ *Epthianura crocea.* YELLOW CHAT. (n,ne Aust). . . . . _____

❏ *Epthianura albifrons.* WHITE-FRONTED CHAT. (s Aust). . . . . _____

❏ *Ashbyia lovensis.* GIBBERBIRD. (ec Aust). _____

Family **Pardalotidae** [16/68]
Subfamily Pardalotinae [1/4]

❏ *Pardalotus punctatus.* SPOTTED PARDALOTE. (e,s Aust). . . . . _____
   ___*P. (p.) punctatus.* SPOTTED PARDALOTE. (sw,e,se Aust)
   ___*P. (p.) xanthopygus.* YELLOW-RUMPED PARDALOTE. (s Aust)

❏ *Pardalotus quadragintus.* FORTY-SPOTTED PARDALOTE. (Tas). . . . . . _____

❏ *Pardalotus rubricatus.* RED-BROWED PARDALOTE. (n,c Aust). . . . . . . _____

❏ *Pardalotus striatus.* STRIATED PARDALOTE. (Aust). . . . . _____
   ___*P. (s.) uropygialis.* NORTHERN PARDALOTE. (n Aust)
   ___*P. (s.) melanocephalus.* BLACK-HEADED PARDALOTE. (ne Aust)
   ___*P. (s.) substriatus.* STRIATED PARDALOTE. (c Aust)
   ___*P. (s.) ornatus.* RED-TIPPED PARDALOTE. (se Aust)
   ___*P. (s.) striatus.* YELLOW-TIPPED PARDALOTE. (Tas)

Subfamily Dasyornithinae [1/3]

❑ *Dasyornis longirostris*. WESTERN BRISTLEBIRD. (sw Aust)......... _____

❑ *Dasyornis brachypterus*. EASTERN BRISTLEBIRD. (se Aust)......... _____

❑ *Dasyornis broadbenti*. RUFOUS BRISTLEBIRD. (sw,se Aust)......... _____

Subfamily Acanthizinae [14/61]
Tribe Sericornithini [10/26]

❑ *Pycnoptilus floccosus*. PILOTBIRD. (se Aust).................... _____

❑ *Origma solitaria*. ORIGMA. (ce Aust)........................ _____

❑ *Oreoscopus gutturalis*. FERNWREN. (ne Aust)................... _____

❑ *Crateroscelis murina*. RUSTY MOUSE-WARBLER. (Aru-NG)......... _____

❑ *Crateroscelis nigrorufa*. BICOLORED MOUSE-WARBLER. (mts NG).... _____

❑ *Crateroscelis robusta*. MOUNTAIN MOUSE-WARBLER. (mts NG)...... _____

❑ *Sericornis citreogularis*. YELLOW-THROATED SCRUBWREN. (e Aust)... _____

❑ *Sericornis frontalis*. WHITE-BROWED SCRUBWREN. (s,e Aust)....... _____
   ___*S. (f.) maculatus*. SPOTTED SCRUBWREN. (sw,s Aust)
   ___*S. (f.) laevigaster*. BUFF-BREASTED SCRUBWREN. (ne Aust)
   ___*S. (f.) frontalis*. WHITE-BROWED SCRUBWREN. (e,se Aust)

❑ *Sericornis humilis*. BROWN SCRUBWREN. (Tas)................. _____

❑ *Sericornis keri*. ATHERTON SCRUBWREN. (mts ne Aust)............ _____

❑ *Sericornis beccarii*. BECCARI'S SCRUBWREN. (Aru-s NG, ne Aust).... _____

❑ *Sericornis virgatus*. PERPLEXING SCRUBWREN. (mts w,n NG)....... _____

❑ *Sericornis nouhuysi*. LARGE SCRUBWREN. (mts NG).............. _____

❑ *Sericornis magnirostris*. LARGE-BILLED SCRUBWREN. (e Aust)...... _____

❑ *Sericornis rufescens*. VOGELKOP SCRUBWREN. (mts w NG)........ _____

❑ *Sericornis perspicillatus*. BUFF-FACED SCRUBWREN. (mts c,e NG).... _____

❑ *Sericornis arfakianus*. GREY-GREEN SCRUBWREN. (mts NG)........ _____

❑ *Sericornis papuensis*. PAPUAN SCRUBWREN. (mts c,e NG)......... _____

❑ *Sericornis spilodera*. PALE-BILLED SCRUBWREN. (Aru-NG)......... _____

❑ *Acanthornis magnus*. SCRUBTIT. (Tas)....................... _____

❑ *Pyrrholaemus brunneus*. REDTHROAT. (s Aust)................. _____

❑ *Chthonicola sagittatus*. SPECKLED WARBLER. (e Aust)............ _____

❑ *Calamanthus campestris*. RUFOUS CALAMANTHUS. (s Aust)........ _____
   ___*C. (c.) isabellinus*. RUSTY CALAMANTHUS. (sc,cs Aust)
   ___*C. (c.) montanellus*. ROCK CALAMANTHUS. (sw Aust)
   ___*C. (c.) campestris*. RUFOUS CALAMANTHUS. (se Aust)

❑ *Calamanthus fuliginosus*. STRIATED CALAMANTHUS. (se Aust)...... _____

❑ *Hylacola pyrrhopygia*. CHESTNUT-RUMPED HYLACOLA. (se Aust). . . . . _____

❑ *Hylacola cautus*. SHY HYLACOLA. (s Aust). . . . . _____

Tribe Acanthizini [4/35]

❑ *Acanthiza murina*. PAPUAN THORNBILL. (mts c,e NG). . . . . _____

❑ *Acanthiza katherina*. MOUNTAIN THORNBILL. (mts ne Aust). . . . . _____

❑ *Acanthiza pusilla*. BROWN THORNBILL. (Aust). . . . . _____
___*A. (p.) apicalis*. BROAD-TAILED THORNBILL. (w Aust)
___*A. (p.) tanami*. TANAMI THORNBILL. (nc Aust)
___*A. (p.) whitlocki*. WHITLOCK'S THORNBILL. (cs Aust)
___*A. (p.) albiventris*. INLAND THORNBILL. (c Aust)
___*A. (p.) pusilla*. BROWN THORNBILL. (e,se Aust)

❑ *Acanthiza ewingii*. TASMANIAN THORNBILL. (Tas). . . . . _____

❑ *Acanthiza reguloides*. BUFF-RUMPED THORNBILL. (e,se Aust). . . . . . . _____
___*A. (r.) squamata*. VARIED THORNBILL. (e Aust)
___*A. (r.) reguloides*. BUFF-RUMPED THORNBILL. (se Aust)

❑ *Acanthiza inornata*. WESTERN THORNBILL. (sw Aust). . . . . _____

❑ *Acanthiza iredalei*. SLENDER-BILLED THORNBILL. (int w,s Aust). . . . . . _____

❑ *Acanthiza chrysorrhoa*. YELLOW-RUMPED THORNBILL. (c,s Aust). . . . . _____

❑ *Acanthiza uropygialis*. CHESTNUT-RUMPED THORNBILL. (int s Aust). . . _____

❑ *Acanthiza nana*. YELLOW THORNBILL. (ne,e Aust). . . . . _____

❑ *Acanthiza lineata*. STRIATED THORNBILL. (se Aust). . . . . _____

❑ *Acanthiza robustirostris*. SLATY-BACKED THORNBILL. (int c,w Aust) . _____

❑ *Smicrornis brevirostris*. WEEBILL. (Aust). _____
___*S. (b.) flavescens*. YELLOW WEEBILL. (n Aust)
___*S. (b.) brevirostris*. BROWN WEEBILL. (c,s Aust)

❑ *Gerygone cinerea*. MOUNTAIN GERYGONE. (mts NG). . . . . _____

❑ *Gerygone chloronotus*. GREEN-BACKED GERYGONE. (Aru-NG, nw Aust)_____

❑ *Gerygone palpebrosa*. FAIRY GERYGONE. (Aru-NG, e Aust). . . . . _____
___*G. (p.) palpebrosa*. BLACK-HEADED GERYGONE. (Aru-NG, ne Aust)
___*G. (p.) personata*. BLACK-THROATED GERYGONE. (ne Aust)
___*G. (p.) flavida*. FAIRY GERYGONE. (ce Aust)

❑ *Gerygone olivacea*. WHITE-THROATED GERYGONE. (se NG, n,e Aust) . _____

❑ *Gerygone chrysogaster*. YELLOW-BELLIED GERYGONE. (Aru-NG). . . . . _____
___*G. (c.) neglecta*. WAIGEO GERYGONE. (w Pap)
___*G. (c.) notata*. WHITE-BELLIED GERYGONE. (Aru-w NG)
___*G. (c.) chrysogaster*. YELLOW-BELLIED GERYGONE. (c,e NG)

❑ *Gerygone magnirostris*. LARGE-BILLED GERYGONE. (Aru-NG, n Aust). _____
___*G. (m.) magnirostris*. LARGE-BILLED GERYGONE. (sp)
___*G. (m.) hypoxantha*. BIAK GERYGONE. (w NG)

❑ *Gerygone tenebrosa*. DUSKY GERYGONE. (nw Aust). . . . . _____

❏ *Gerygone sulphurea.* GOLDEN-BELLIED GERYGONE. (se Asia-Wall)... _____

❏ *Gerygone inornata.* PLAIN GERYGONE. (L Sunda).............. _____

❏ *Gerygone dorsalis.* RUFOUS-SIDED GERYGONE. (Wall)............ _____

❏ *Gerygone ruficollis.* BROWN-BREASTED GERYGONE. (mts NG)...... _____

❏ *Gerygone levigaster.* MANGROVE GERYGONE. (s NG, n Aust)....... _____
   ___*G. (l.) levigaster.* BUFF-BREASTED GERYGONE. (sp)
   ___*G. (l.) cantator.* MANGROVE GERYGONE. (ne Aust)

❏ *Gerygone fusca.* WESTERN GERYGONE. (int Aust)............... _____

  Gerygone insularis. LORD HOWE ISLAND GERYGONE. (†L Howe)..... _____

❏ *Gerygone mouki.* BROWN GERYGONE. (e Aust)................ _____
   ___*G. (m.) mouki.* NORTHERN GERYGONE. (ne Aust)
   ___*G. (m.) richmondi.* BROWN GERYGONE. (se Aust)

❏ *Gerygone modesta.* NORFOLK ISLAND GERYGONE. (Norfolk)........ _____

❏ *Gerygone igata.* GREY GERYGONE. (NZ)..................... _____

❏ *Gerygone albofrontata.* CHATHAM ISLANDS GERYGONE. (Chatham)... _____

❏ *Gerygone flavolateralis.* FAN-TAILED GERYGONE. (Solom-Vanu)..... _____

❏ *Aphelocephala leucopsis.* SOUTHERN WHITEFACE. (s Aust)......... _____

❏ *Aphelocephala pectoralis.* CHESTNUT-BREASTED WHITEFACE. (sc Aust) _____

❏ *Aphelocephala nigricincta.* BANDED WHITEFACE. (int c Aust)....... _____

Superfamily CORVOIDEA [154/796]
Family **Petroicidae** [13/44]

❏ *Amalocichla sclateriana.* GREATER GROUND-ROBIN. (mts c,se NG)... _____

❏ *Amalocichla incerta.* LESSER GROUND-ROBIN. (mts NG).......... _____

❏ *Monachella muelleriana.* TORRENT ROBIN. (NG, cs Bism)......... _____

❏ *Microeca fascinans.* JACKY-WINTER. (se NG, Aust).............. _____

❏ *Microeca hemixantha.* GOLDEN-BELLIED FLYROBIN. (Tanim)....... _____

❏ *Microeca flavigaster.* LEMON-BELLIED FLYROBIN. (NG, n Aust)...... _____
   ___*M. (f.) tormenti.* KIMBERLEY FLYROBIN. (ne W Aust)
   ___*M. (f.) flavigaster.* LEMON-BELLIED FLYROBIN. (sp)

❏ *Microeca griseoceps.* YELLOW-LEGGED FLYROBIN. (mts NG, ne Aust). _____

❏ *Microeca flavovirescens.* OLIVE FLYROBIN. (Aru-NG)............ _____

❏ *Microeca papuana.* CANARY FLYROBIN. (mts NG)............... _____

❏ *Eugerygone rubra.* GARNET ROBIN. (mts NG)................. _____

❏ *Petroica bivittata.* ALPINE ROBIN. (mts NG)................... _____

❏ *Petroica archboldi.* SNOW MOUNTAIN ROBIN. (mts wc NG)........ _____

❏ *Petroica multicolor.* SCARLET ROBIN. (Solom-Samoa, s,e Aust)..... _____

❑ *Petroica macrocephala.* TOMTIT. (NZ-Chatham, Snares). . . . . _____

❑ *Petroica goodenovii.* RED-CAPPED ROBIN. (int Aust). . . . . _____

❑ *Petroica phoenicea.* FLAME ROBIN. (se Aust). . . . . _____

❑ *Petroica rosea.* ROSE ROBIN. (se Aust). _____

❑ *Petroica rodinogaster.* PINK ROBIN. (se Aust). . . . . _____

❑ *Petroica australis.* NEW ZEALAND ROBIN. (NZ). . . . . _____

❑ *Petroica traversi.* CHATHAM ISLANDS ROBIN. (Chatham). . . . . _____

❑ *Melanodryas cucullata.* HOODED ROBIN. (Aust). . . . . _____

❑ *Melanodryas vittata.* DUSKY ROBIN. (Tas). . . . . _____

❑ *Tregellasia leucops.* WHITE-FACED ROBIN. (NG, ne Aust). . . . . _____

❑ *Tregellasia capito.* PALE-YELLOW ROBIN. (e Aust). . . . . _____
   ___*T. (c.) nana.* NORTHERN PALE-YELLOW ROBIN. (ne Aust)
   ___*T. (c.) capito.* SOUTHERN PALE-YELLOW ROBIN. (ce Aust)

❑ *Eopsaltria australis.* YELLOW ROBIN. (e,se Aust). . . . . _____
   ___*E. (a.) chrysorrhos.* NORTHERN YELLOW-ROBIN. (e Aust)
   ___*E. (a.) australis.* EASTERN YELLOW-ROBIN. (se Aust)

❑ *Eopsaltria griseogularis.* GREY-BREASTED ROBIN. (sw Aust). . . . . _____

❑ *Eopsaltria flaviventris.* YELLOW-BELLIED ROBIN. (N Cal). . . . . _____

❑ *Eopsaltria georgiana.* WHITE-BREASTED ROBIN. (sw Aust). . . . . _____

❑ *Eopsaltria pulverulenta.* MANGROVE ROBIN. (Aru, nw,s NG, n Aust) . _____
   ___*E. (p.) pulverulenta.* NEW GUINEA MANGROVE-ROBIN. (nw,s NG)
   ___*E. (p.) leucura.* AUSTRALIAN MANGROVE-ROBIN. (Aru, n Aust)

❑ *Poecilodryas brachyura.* BLACK-CHINNED ROBIN. (nw,n NG). . . . . _____

❑ *Poecilodryas hypoleuca.* BLACK-SIDED ROBIN. (w Pap, NG). . . . . _____

❑ *Poecilodryas superciliosa.* WHITE-BROWED ROBIN. (n,ne Aust). . . . . . . _____
   ___*P. (s.) cerviniventris.* BUFF-SIDED ROBIN. (n Aust)
   ___*P. (s.) superciliosa.* WHITE-BROWED ROBIN. (ne Aust)

❑ *Poecilodryas placens.* OLIVE-YELLOW ROBIN. (w Pap, NG). . . . . _____

❑ *Poecilodryas albonotata.* BLACK-THROATED ROBIN. (mts NG). . . . . . . _____

❑ *Peneothello sigillatus.* WHITE-WINGED ROBIN. (mts c,e NG). . . . . _____

❑ *Peneothello cryptoleucus.* SMOKY ROBIN. (mts w NG). . . . . _____

❑ *Peneothello cyanus.* BLUE-GREY ROBIN. (mts NG). . . . . _____

❑ *Peneothello bimaculatus.* WHITE-RUMPED ROBIN. (mts NG). . . . . _____

❑ *Heteromyias albispecularis.* ASHY ROBIN. (mts NG). . . . . _____

❑ *Heteromyias cinereifrons.* GREY-HEADED ROBIN. (mts ne Aust). . . . . . _____

❑ *Pachycephalopsis hattamensis.* GREEN-BACKED ROBIN. (mts w,c NG). _____

❑ *Pachycephalopsis poliosoma.* WHITE-EYED ROBIN. (mts c,e NG). . . . . _____

❑ *Drymodes superciliaris.* NORTHERN SCRUB-ROBIN. (Aru-NG, ne Aust). _____

❑ *Drymodes brunneopygia.* SOUTHERN SCRUB-ROBIN. (s Aust). . . . . _____

Family **Irenidae** [2/10]

❑ *Irena puella.* ASIAN FAIRY-BLUEBIRD. (s Asia-sw Phil). . . . . _____

❑ *Irena cyanogaster.* PHILIPPINE FAIRY-BLUEBIRD. (Phil). . . . . _____

❑ *Chloropsis flavipennis.* PHILIPPINE LEAFBIRD. (c,s Phil). . . . . _____

❑ *Chloropsis palawanensis.* YELLOW-THROATED LEAFBIRD. (sw Phil). . . _____

❑ *Chloropsis sonnerati.* GREATER GREEN LEAFBIRD. (se Asia). . . . . _____

❑ *Chloropsis cyanopogon.* LESSER GREEN LEAFBIRD. (se Asia). . . . . _____

❑ *Chloropsis cochinchinensis.* BLUE-WINGED LEAFBIRD. (s,se Asia). . . . _____
    ___*C. (c.) jerdoni.* JERDON'S LEAFBIRD. (s India)
    ___*C. (c.) cochinchinensis.* YELLOW-HEADED LEAFBIRD. (se Asia)

❑ *Chloropsis aurifrons.* GOLDEN-FRONTED LEAFBIRD. (s,se Asia). . . . . . _____

❑ *Chloropsis hardwickii.* ORANGE-BELLIED LEAFBIRD. (s,se Asia). . . . . . _____

❑ *Chloropsis venusta.* BLUE-MASKED LEAFBIRD. (Sum). . . . . _____

Family **Orthonychidae** [1/2]

❑ *Orthonyx temminckii.* LOGRUNNER. (NG, e Aust). . . . . _____
    ___*O. (t.) novaeguineae.* NEW GUINEA LOGRUNNER. (mts NG)
    ___*O. (t.) temminckii.* SOUTHERN LOGRUNNER. (e Aust)

❑ *Orthonyx spaldingii.* CHOWCHILLA. (ne Aust). . . . . _____

Family **Pomatostomidae** [1/5]

❑ *Pomatostomus isidorei.* NEW GUINEA BABBLER. (w Pap, NG). . . . . _____

❑ *Pomatostomus temporalis.* GREY-CROWNED BABBLER. (sc NG, Aust). _____
    ___*P. (t.) rubeculus.* RED-BREASTED BABBLER. (sc NG, wc,n Aust)
    ___*P. (t.) temporalis.* GREY-CROWNED BABBLER. (e,se Aust)

❑ *Pomatostomus superciliosus.* WHITE-BROWED BABBLER. (s Aust). . . . _____

❑ *Pomatostomus halli.* HALL'S BABBLER. (ce Aust). . . . . _____

❑ *Pomatostomus ruficeps.* CHESTNUT-CROWNED BABBLER. (ec Aust). . . _____

Family **Laniidae** [3/30]

❑ *Lanius tigrinus.* TIGER SHRIKE. (e Asia; ◊-se Asia). . . . . _____

❑ *Lanius bucephalus.* BULL-HEADED SHRIKE. (e Asia). . . . . _____

❑ *Lanius collurio.* RED-BACKED SHRIKE. (Palea; ◊-s Afr). . . . . _____

❑ *Lanius isabellinus.* RUFOUS-TAILED SHRIKE. (sc Eura; ◊ e Afr-s Asia). _____
    ___*L. (i.) pheonicuroides.* RUFOUS-TAILED SHRIKE. (sp)
    ___*L. (i.) isabellinus.* ISABELLINE SHRIKE. (w China)

❑ *Lanius cristatus.* BROWN SHRIKE. (e Asia; ◊ ne Afr-s,se Asia)...... _____
   ___*L. (c.) cristatus.* BROWN SHRIKE. (sp)
   ___*L. (c.) superciliosus.* JAPANESE SHRIKE. (n Japan; ◊ s,se Asia)

❑ *Lanius collurioides.* BURMESE SHRIKE. (mts s,se Asia)........... _____

❑ *Lanius gubernator.* EMIN'S SHRIKE. (subsah Afr)................. _____

❑ *Lanius souzae.* SOUZA'S SHRIKE. (c Afr)...................... _____

❑ *Lanius vittatus.* BAY-BACKED SHRIKE. (s Asia)................. _____

❑ *Lanius schach.* LONG-TAILED SHRIKE. (s Asia-Phil, L Sunda; NG).... _____
   ___*L. (s.) nigriceps.* BLACK-HEADED SHRIKE. (Himal)
   ___*L. (s.) schach.* RUFOUS-BACKED SHRIKE. (s Asia-L Sunda)
   ___*L. (s.) nasutus.* PHILIPPINE SHRIKE. (n Born, Phil)

❑ *Lanius tephronotus.* GREY-BACKED SHRIKE. (Himal; ◊ se Asia)...... _____

❑ *Lanius validirostris.* MOUNTAIN SHRIKE. (mts Phil).............. _____

❑ *Lanius minor.* LESSER GREY SHRIKE. (c Palea; ◊ Afr)............ _____

❑ *Lanius ludovicianus.* LOGGERHEAD SHRIKE. (NA, Mex)........... _____

❑ *Lanius excubitor.* NORTHERN SHRIKE. (Hol-nc Afr, s Asia)........ _____
   ___*L. (e.) excubitor.* GREAT GREY SHRIKE. (Palea, n NA; ◊-Med, c US)
   ___*L. (e.) meridionalis.* SOUTHERN GREY SHRIKE. (s Palea, s Asia)
   ___*L. (e.) leucopygos.* SAHARAN SHRIKE. (nc Afr)

❑ *Lanius sphenocercus.* CHINESE GREY SHRIKE. (mts e Asia)........ _____

❑ *Lanius excubitoroides.* GREY-BACKED FISCAL. (c,ne Afr).......... _____

❑ *Lanius cabanisi.* LONG-TAILED FISCAL. (ne Afr)................. _____

❑ *Lanius dorsalis.* TEITA FISCAL. (ne Afr)...................... _____

❑ *Lanius somalicus.* SOMALI FISCAL. (ne Afr).................... _____

❑ *Lanius mackinnoni.* MACKINNON'S SHRIKE. (c Afr).............. _____

❑ *Lanius collaris.* COMMON FISCAL. (Afr)...................... _____
   ___*L. (c.) collaris.* COMMON FISCAL. (sp)
   ___*L. (c.) subcoronatus.* LATAKOO FISCAL. (sw Afr)

❑ *Lanius newtoni.* NEWTON'S FISCAL. (ST)..................... _____

❑ *Lanius marwitzi.* UHEHE FISCAL. (mts Tanz).................... _____

❑ *Lanius senator.* WOODCHAT SHRIKE. (w Palea; ◊-trop Afr)......... _____

❑ *Lanius nubicus.* MASKED SHRIKE. (sc Eura; ◊-ne Afr)............ _____

❑ *Corvinella corvina.* YELLOW-BILLED SHRIKE. (subsah Afr)......... _____

❑ *Corvinella melanoleuca.* MAGPIE SHRIKE. (c,e Afr)............... _____

❑ *Eurocephalus rueppelli.* WHITE-RUMPED SHRIKE. (e Afr).......... _____

❑ *Eurocephalus anguitimens.* WHITE-CROWNED SHRIKE. (s Afr)....... _____

Family **Vireonidae** [4/52]

❑ *Cyclarhis gujanensis*. RUFOUS-BROWED PEPPERSHRIKE. (MA, SA). . . . _____
　___*C. (g.) gujanensis*. RUFOUS-BROWED PEPPERSHRIKE. (sp)
　___*C. (g.) virenticeps*. YELLOW-BACKED PEPPERSHRIKE. (nw SA)
　___*C. (g.) viridis*. CHACO PEPPERSHRIKE. (sc SA)
　___*C. (g.) ochrocephala*. OCHRE-CROWNED PEPPERSHRIKE. (se SA)

❑ *Cyclarhis nigrirostris*. BLACK-BILLED PEPPERSHRIKE. (nw SA). . . . . . . _____

❑ *Vireolanius melitophrys*. CHESTNUT-SIDED SHRIKE-VIREO. (nc MA) . _____

❑ *Vireolanius pulchellus*. GREEN SHRIKE-VIREO. (MA). . . . . _____

❑ *Vireolanius eximius*. YELLOW-BROWED SHRIKE-VIREO. (Pan-nw SA). _____

❑ *Vireolanius leucotis*. SLATY-CAPPED SHRIKE-VIREO. (Amaz). . . . . . . _____

❑ *Vireo brevipennis*. SLATY VIREO. (Amaz). _____

❑ *Vireo bellii*. BELL'S VIREO. (sw,sc US, n Mex; ◊ n MA). . . . . _____

❑ *Vireo atricapillus*. BLACK-CAPPED VIREO. (sc US, cn Mex; ◊ Mex). . . _____

❑ *Vireo nelsoni*. DWARF VIREO. (mts c Mex). _____

❑ *Vireo huttoni*. HUTTON'S VIREO. (sw Can-w Guat). . . . . _____

❑ *Vireo carmioli*. YELLOW-WINGED VIREO. (mts CR, w Pan). . . . . _____

❑ *Vireo griseus*. WHITE-EYED VIREO. (e NA, e Mex; ◊-W Indies, CA). . . _____
　___*V. (g.) griseus*. WHITE-EYED VIREO. (sp)
　___*V. (g.) perquisitor*. VERACRUZ VIREO. (ce Mex)

❑ *Vireo pallens*. MANGROVE VIREO. (MA). . . . . _____
　___*V. (p.) pallens*. MANGROVE VIREO. (Pac MA)
　___*V. (p.) semiflavus*. MAYAN VIREO. (Carib MA)

❑ *Vireo bairdi*. COZUMEL VIREO. (Coz). . . . . _____

❑ *Vireo gundlachii*. CUBAN VIREO. (Cuba). . . . . _____

❑ *Vireo crassirostris*. THICK-BILLED VIREO. (W Indies). . . . . _____
　___*V. (c.) crassirostris*. THICK-BILLED VIREO. (Bah-Cay)
　___*V. (c.) approximans*. OLD PROVIDENCE VIREO. (Providencia)

❑ *Vireo caribaeus*. ST. ANDREW VIREO. (San Andrés). . . . . _____

❑ *Vireo vicinior*. GREY VIREO. (sw US, nw Mex). . . . . _____

❑ *Vireo hypochryseus*. GOLDEN VIREO. (w Mex). . . . . _____

❑ *Vireo modestus*. JAMAICAN VIREO. (Jam). _____

❑ *Vireo nanus*. FLAT-BILLED VIREO. (Hisp). _____

❑ *Vireo latimeri*. PUERTO RICAN VIREO. (PR). . . . . _____

❑ *Vireo osburni*. BLUE MOUNTAIN VIREO. (mts Jam). . . . . _____

❑ *Vireo cassinii*. CASSIN'S VIREO. (mts w NA; ◊-Guat). . . . . _____

❑ *Vireo plumbeus*. PLUMBEOUS VIREO. (mts cw NA, n MA). . . . . _____

❑ *Vireo solitarius*. BLUE-HEADED VIREO. (nc,e NA; ◊-CR, Cuba). . . . . . . _____

❑ *Vireo flavifrons.* YELLOW-THROATED VIREO. (e NA; ◊-n SA)........ _____

❑ *Vireo philadelphicus.* PHILADELPHIA VIREO. (n NA; ◊ MA, nw SA)... _____

❑ *Vireo olivaceus.* RED-EYED VIREO. (NA, SA).................... _____
   ___*V. (o.) olivaceus.* RED-EYED VIREO. (NA; ◊ SA)
   ___*V. (o.) chivi.* CHIVI VIREO. (SA)

❑ *Vireo flavoviridis.* YELLOW-GREEN VIREO. (s Tex, MA; ◊ SA)...... _____

❑ *Vireo gracilirostris.* NORONHA VIREO. (FdeN)................. _____

❑ *Vireo altiloquus.* BLACK-WHISKERED VIREO. (se US, W Indies, n SA). _____

❑ *Vireo magister.* YUCATAN VIREO. (Cay, c MA)................. _____

❑ *Vireo swainsonii.* WESTERN WARBLING-VIREO. (w NA, nw Mex)..... _____

❑ *Vireo gilvus.* EASTERN WARBLING-VIREO. (e NA; ◊ MA).......... _____

❑ *Vireo leucophrys.* BROWN-CAPPED VIREO. (mts MA, w SA)........ _____

❑ *Hylophilus amaurocephalus.* GREY-EYED GREENLET. (e Braz)....... _____

❑ *Hylophilus poicilotis.* RUFOUS-CROWNED GREENLET. (sc,se SA)...... _____

❑ *Hylophilus thoracicus.* LEMON-CHESTED GREENLET. (c,se SA)...... _____

❑ *Hylophilus semicinereus.* GREY-CHESTED GREENLET. (Amaz)...... _____

❑ *Hylophilus pectoralis.* ASHY-HEADED GREENLET. (n,c Amaz)....... _____

❑ *Hylophilus sclateri.* TEPUI GREENLET. (Pant nc SA)............. _____

❑ *Hylophilus muscicapinus.* BUFF-CHEEKED GREENLET. (Amaz)...... _____
   ___*H. (m.) muscicapinus.* BUFF-CHEEKED GREENLET. (n Amaz)
   ___*H. (m.) griseifrons.* GREY-FRONTED GREENLET. (c,s Amaz)

❑ *Hylophilus brunneiceps.* BROWN-HEADED GREENLET. (w Amaz)..... _____

❑ *Hylophilus hypoxanthus.* DUSKY-CAPPED GREENLET. (Amaz)...... _____
   ___*H. (h.) hypoxanthus.* DUSKY-CAPPED GREENLET. (n Amaz)
   ___*H. (h.) flaviventris.* YELLOW-BELLIED GREENLET. (c Peru)
   ___*H. (h.) inornatus.* AMAZON GREENLET. (s Amaz)

❑ *Hylophilus semibrunneus.* RUFOUS-NAPED GREENLET. (mts nw SA) . _____

❑ *Hylophilus aurantiifrons.* GOLDEN-FRONTED GREENLET. (Pan, n SA) . _____

❑ *Hylophilus flavipes.* SCRUB GREENLET. (s CA, n SA, Tob)......... _____
   ___*H. (f.) viridiflavus.* YELLOW-GREEN GREENLET. (s CA)
   ___*H. (f.) flavipes.* SCRUB GREENLET. (n SA, Tob)

❑ *Hylophilus olivaceus.* OLIVACEOUS GREENLET. (Andes wc SA)...... _____

❑ *Hylophilus ochraceiceps.* TAWNY-CROWNED GREENLET. (MA-Amaz). _____
   ___*H. (o.) ochraceiceps.* TAWNY-CROWNED GREENLET. (sp)
   ___*H. (o.) rubrifrons.* RED-FRONTED GREENLET. (s Amaz)

❑ *Hylophilus decurtatus.* LESSER GREENLET. (MA, nw SA).......... _____
   ___*H. (d.) decurtatus.* GREY-HEADED GREENLET. (MA)
   ___*H. (d.) minor.* LESSER GREENLET. (e Pan, nw SA)

Family **Corvidae** [127/650]
Subfamily Cinclosomatinae [6/15]

❏ *Androphobus viridis.* PAPUAN WHIPBIRD. (mts w NG). . . . . _____

❏ *Psophodes olivaceus.* EASTERN WHIPBIRD. (e Aust). . . . . _____
   ___*P. (o.) lateralis.* NORTHERN WHIPBIRD. (ne Aust)
   ___*P. (o.) olivaceus.* EASTERN WHIPBIRD. (e,se Aust)

❏ *Psophodes nigrogularis.* WESTERN WHIPBIRD. (sw,sc Aust). . . . . _____

❏ *Psophodes occidentalis.* CHIMING WEDGEBILL. (w,c Aust). . . . . _____

❏ *Psophodes cristatus.* CHIRRUPING WEDGEBILL. (int se Aust). . . . . _____

❏ *Cinclosoma punctatum.* SPOTTED QUAIL-THRUSH. (se Aust). . . . . _____

❏ *Cinclosoma castanotus.* CHESTNUT QUAIL-THRUSH. (sw,s Aust). . . . . . _____

❏ *Cinclosoma castaneothorax.* CHESTNUT-BREASTED QUAIL-T. (c Aust). _____
   ___*C. (c.) marginatum.* WESTERN QUAIL-THRUSH. (sp)
   ___*C. (c.) castaneothorax.* CHESTNUT-BREASTED QUAIL-THRUSH. (ec Aust)

❏ *Cinclosoma cinnamomeum.* CINNAMON QUAIL-THRUSH. (Aust). . . . . . _____
   ___*C. (c.) cinnamomeum.* CINNAMON QUAIL-THRUSH. (n,ne Aust)
   ___*C. (c.) alisteri.* NULLARBOR QUAIL-THRUSH. (cs Aust)

❏ *Cinclosoma ajax.* PAINTED QUAIL-THRUSH. (w,s,se NG). . . . . _____

❏ *Ptilorrhoa leucosticta.* SPOTTED JEWEL-BABBLER. (mts NG). . . . . _____

❏ *Ptilorrhoa caerulescens.* BLUE JEWEL-BABBLER. (w Pap, NG). . . . . . . _____

❏ *Ptilorrhoa castanonota.* CHESTNUT-BACKED JEWEL-BABBLER. (NG reg)_____

❏ *Eupetes macrocerus.* MALAYSIAN RAIL-BABBLER. (se Asia). . . . . _____

❏ *Ifrita kowaldi.* IFRIT. (mts c,e NG). . . . . _____

Subfamily Corcoracinae [2/2]

❏ *Corcorax melanorhamphos.* WHITE-WINGED CHOUGH. (e,se Aust). . . . _____

❏ *Struthidea cinerea.* APOSTLEBIRD. (int e Aust). . . . . _____

Subfamily Pachycephalinae [14/59]
Tribe Neosittini [1/2]

❏ *Daphoenositta chrysoptera.* VARIED SITTELLA. (NG, Aust). . . . . _____
   ___*D. (c.) papuensis.* PAPUAN SITTELLA. (mts NG)
   ___*D. (c.) leucoptera.* WHITE-WINGED SITTELLA. (nc Aust)
   ___*D. (c.) striata.* STRIATED SITTELLA. (ne Aust)
   ___*D. (c.) pileata.* BLACK-CAPPED SITTELLA. (w,s Aust)
   ___*D. (c.) leucocephala.* WHITE-HEADED SITTELLA. (ce Aust)
   ___*D. (c.) chrysoptera.* ORANGE-WINGED SITTELLA. (se Aust)

❏ *Daphoenositta miranda.* BLACK SITTELLA. (mts c,e NG). . . . . _____

Tribe Mohouini [1/3]

❑ *Mohoua albicilla.* WHITEHEAD. (n NZ). . . . . _____

❑ *Mohoua ochrocephala.* YELLOWHEAD. (s NZ). . . . . _____

❑ *Mohoua novaeseelandiae.* PIPIPI. (s NZ). . . . . _____

Tribe Falcunculini [3/3]

❑ *Falcunculus frontatus.* CRESTED SHRIKE-TIT. (Aust). . . . . _____
  ___*F. (f.) whitei.* NORTHERN SHRIKE-TIT. (cn Aust)
  ___*F. (f.) frontatus.* EASTERN SHRIKE-TIT. (e Aust)
  ___*F. (f.) leucogaster.* WESTERN SHRIKE-TIT. (sw Aust)

❑ *Oreoica gutturalis.* CRESTED BELLBIRD. (Aust). . . . . _____

❑ *Rhagologus leucostigma.* MOTTLED WHISTLER. (mts NG). . . . . _____

Tribe Pachycephalini [9/51]

❑ *Pachycare flavogrisea.* GOLDENFACE. (mts NG). . . . . _____

❑ *Hylocitrea bonensis.* OLIVE-FLANKED WHISTLER. (mts Sulaw). . . . . . . _____

❑ *Coracornis raveni.* MAROON-BACKED WHISTLER. (mts Sulaw). . . . . . . _____

❑ *Aleadryas rufinucha.* RUFOUS-NAPED WHISTLER. (mts NG). . . . . _____

❑ *Pachycephala olivacea.* OLIVE WHISTLER. (se Aust). . . . . _____

❑ *Pachycephala rufogularis.* RED-LORED WHISTLER. (se Aust). . . . . _____

❑ *Pachycephala inornata.* GILBERT'S WHISTLER. (s Aust). . . . . _____

❑ *Pachycephala grisola.* MANGROVE WHISTLER. (s Asia-Wall). . . . . _____
  ___*P. (g.) grisola.* MANGROVE WHISTLER. (s Asia-L Sunda)
  ___*P. (g.) plateni.* PALAWAN WHISTLER. (sw Phil)

❑ *Pachycephala albiventris.* GREEN-BACKED WHISTLER. (mts n,nc Phil). _____

❑ *Pachycephala homeyeri.* WHITE-VENTED WHISTLER. (c,s Phil). . . . . . . _____

❑ *Pachycephala phaionotus.* ISLAND WHISTLER. (Moluc, Kai-nw NG) . _____

❑ *Pachycephala hyperythra.* RUSTY WHISTLER. (nw,se NG). . . . . _____

❑ *Pachycephala modesta.* BROWN-BACKED WHISTLER. (mts c,e NG). . . . _____

❑ *Pachycephala hypoxantha.* BORNEAN WHISTLER. (mts Born). . . . . _____

❑ *Pachycephala sulfuriventer.* SULPHUR-BELLIED WHISTLER. (Sulaw). . . _____

❑ *Pachycephala philippinensis.* YELLOW-BELLIED WHISTLER. (Phil). . . . _____

❑ *Pachycephala meyeri.* VOGELKOP WHISTLER. (mts w NG). . . . . _____

❑ *Pachycephala griseiceps.* GREY-HEADED WHISTLER. (Kai-NG, ne Aust)_____

❑ *Pachycephala simplex.* BROWN WHISTLER. (n Aust). . . . . _____

❑ *Pachycephala orpheus.* FAWN-BREASTED WHISTLER. (c L Sunda). . . . _____

❑ *Pachycephala pectoralis.* GOLDEN WHISTLER. (Wall-sw Melan, Aust). _____
  ___*P. (p.) pectoralis.* GOLDEN WHISTLER. (sp)
  ___*P. (p.) balim.* BALIM WHISTLER. (mts c NG)
  ___*P. (p.) xanthoprocta.* NORFOLK ISLAND WHISTLER. (Norfolk)

❏ *Pachycephala soror.* SCLATER'S WHISTLER. (mts NG). . . . . _____

❏ *Pachycephala lorentzi.* LORENTZ'S WHISTLER. (mts c NG). . . . . _____

❏ *Pachycephala melanura.* BLACK-TAILED WHISTLER. (NG reg-n Aust). _____
   ___*P. (m.) spinicauda.* ROBUST WHISTLER. (s NG-Solom, ne Aust)
   ___*P. (m.) melanura.* BLACK-TAILED WHISTLER. (nw Aust)

❏ *Pachycephala caledonica.* NEW CALEDONIAN WHISTLER. (N Cal). . . . _____

❏ *Pachycephala flavifrons.* SAMOAN WHISTLER. (w Samoa). . . . . _____

❏ *Pachycephala jacquinoti.* TONGAN WHISTLER. (n Tonga). . . . . _____

❏ *Pachycephala schlegelii.* REGENT WHISTLER. (mts NG). . . . . _____

❏ *Pachycephala nudigula.* BARE-THROATED WHISTLER. (w L Sunda). . . _____

❏ *Pachycephala implicata.* HOODED WHISTLER. (mts Solom). . . . . _____

❏ *Pachycephala aurea.* GOLDEN-BACKED WHISTLER. (NG). . . . . _____

❏ *Pachycephala griseonota.* DRAB WHISTLER. (Wall). . . . . _____

❏ *Pachycephala arctitorquis.* WALLACEAN WHISTLER. (L Sunda-Kai). . . _____

❏ *Pachycephala monacha.* BLACK-HEADED WHISTLER. (Aru, c NG). . . . _____

❏ *Pachycephala leucogastra.* WHITE-BELLIED WHISTLER. (cn,se NG). . . _____

❏ *Pachycephala rufiventris.* RUFOUS WHISTLER. (Aust, N Cal). . . . . . . _____

❏ *Pachycephala lanioides.* WHITE-BREASTED WHISTLER. (n Aust). . . . . . _____

❏ *Colluricincla umbrina.* SOOTY SHRIKE-THRUSH. (mts c NG). . . . . _____

❏ *Colluricincla megarhyncha.* LITTLE SHRIKE-THRUSH. (NG, n Aust). . . _____
   ___*C. (m.) megarhyncha.* RUFOUS SHRIKE-THRUSH. (NG, ne Aust)
   ___*C. (m.) parvula.* LITTLE SHRIKE-THRUSH. (cn Aust)

❏ *Colluricincla boweri.* BOWER'S SHRIKE-THRUSH. (mts ne Aust). . . . . . _____

❏ *Colluricincla woodwardi.* SANDSTONE SHRIKE-THRUSH. (n Aust). . . . . _____

❏ *Colluricincla harmonica.* GREY SHRIKE-THRUSH. (e NG, Aust). . . . . . _____
   ___*C. (h.) harmonica.* GREY SHRIKE-THRUSH. (e NG, e,se Aust)
   ___*C. (h.) brunnea.* BROWN SHRIKE-THRUSH. (n Aust)
   ___*C. (h.) rufiventris.* WESTERN SHRIKE-THRUSH. (w,c Aust)

❏ *Colluricincla tenebrosa.* MORNINGBIRD. (Palau). . . . . _____

❏ *Pitohui kirhocephalus.* VARIABLE PITOHUI. (Aru-NG). . . . . _____

❏ *Pitohui dichrous.* HOODED PITOHUI. (mts NG). . . . . _____

❏ *Pitohui incertus.* WHITE-BELLIED PITOHUI. (s NG). . . . . _____

❏ *Pitohui ferrugineus.* RUSTY PITOHUI. (Aru-NG). . . . . _____

❏ *Pitohui cristatus.* CRESTED PITOHUI. (mts NG). . . . . _____

❏ *Pitohui nigrescens.* BLACK PITOHUI. (mts NG). . . . . _____

❏ *Eulacestoma nigropectus.* WATTLED PLOUGHBILL. (mts NG). . . . . _____

❏ *Turnagra capensis.* PIOPIO. (NZ). . . . . _____
   ___*T. (c.) tanagra.* NORTH ISLAND PIOPIO. (n NZ)
   ___*T. (c.) capensis.* SOUTH ISLAND PIOPIO. (s NZ)

Subfamily Corvinae [56/299]
Tribe Corvini [25/118]

❏ *Platylophus galericulatus*. CRESTED JAY. (se Asia). . . . . _____
___*P. (g.) ardesiacus*. MALAY CRESTED-JAY. (Malay pen)
___*P. (g.) coronatus*. SUMATRAN CRESTED-JAY. (Sum, Born)
___*P. (g.) galericulatus*. JAVAN CRESTED-JAY. (Java)

❏ *Platysmurus leucopterus*. BLACK MAGPIE. (se Asia). . . . . _____

❏ *Gymnorhinus cyanocephalus*. PINYON JAY. (w NA). . . . . _____

❏ *Cyanocitta cristata*. BLUE JAY. (NA). . . . . _____

❏ *Cyanocitta stelleri*. STELLER'S JAY. (mts w NA, MA). . . . . _____

❏ *Aphelocoma insularis*. SANTA CRUZ JAY. (is w Calif). . . . . _____

❏ *Aphelocoma californica*. SCRUB JAY. (w US, Mex). . . . . _____
___*A. (c.) californica*. CALIFORNIA JAY. (w US, nw Mex)
___*A. (c.) woodhouseii*. WOODHOUSE'S JAY. (mts wc US-nc Mex)
___*A. (c.) sumichrasti*. SUMICHRAST'S JAY. (mts c Mex)

❏ *Aphelocoma coerulescens*. FLORIDA JAY. (c pen Fla). . . . . _____

❏ *Aphelocoma ultramarina*. MEXICAN JAY. (mts sw US, Mex). . . . . _____

❏ *Aphelocoma unicolor*. UNICOLORED JAY. (mts n MA). . . . . _____

❏ *Cyanolyca armillata*. BLACK-COLLARED JAY. (Andes nw SA). . . . . _____

❏ *Cyanolyca turcosa*. TURQUOISE JAY. (Andes nw SA). . . . . _____

❏ *Cyanolyca viridicyana*. WHITE-COLLARED JAY. (Andes sw SA). . . . . . _____

❏ *Cyanolyca cucullata*. AZURE-HOODED JAY. (mts MA). . . . . _____

❏ *Cyanolyca pulchra*. BEAUTIFUL JAY. (Andes nw SA). . . . . _____

❏ *Cyanolyca pumilo*. BLACK-THROATED JAY. (mts c MA). . . . . _____

❏ *Cyanolyca nana*. DWARF JAY. (mts se Mex). . . . . _____

❏ *Cyanolyca mirabilis*. WHITE-THROATED JAY. (mts sw Mex). . . . . _____

❏ *Cyanolyca argentigula*. SILVERY-THROATED JAY. (mts CR, w Pan). . . _____

❏ *Cyanocorax melanocyaneus*. BUSHY-CRESTED JAY. (n CA). . . . . _____

❏ *Cyanocorax sanblasianus*. SAN BLAS JAY. (w Mex). . . . . _____

❏ *Cyanocorax yucatanicus*. YUCATAN JAY. (c MA). . . . . _____

❏ *Cyanocorax beecheii*. PURPLISH-BACKED JAY. (nw Mex). . . . . _____

❏ *Cyanocorax cyanomelas*. PURPLISH JAY. (sc SA). . . . . _____

❏ *Cyanocorax caeruleus*. AZURE JAY. (se SA). . . . . _____

❏ *Cyanocorax violaceus*. VIOLACEOUS JAY. (w Amaz). . . . . _____

❏ *Cyanocorax cristatellus*. CURL-CRESTED JAY. (se SA). . . . . _____

❏ *Cyanocorax heilprini*. AZURE-NAPED JAY. (nw Amaz). . . . . _____

❏ *Cyanocorax cayanus*. CAYENNE JAY. (n Amaz). . . . . _____

❏ *Cyanocorax affinis.* BLACK-CHESTED JAY. (s CA, nw SA). . . . . _____

❏ *Cyanocorax dickeyi.* TUFTED JAY. (mts nw Mex). . . . . _____

❏ *Cyanocorax chrysops.* PLUSH-CRESTED JAY. (sc,e SA). . . . . _____

❏ *Cyanocorax cyanopogon.* WHITE-NAPED JAY. (se SA). . . . . _____

❏ *Cyanocorax mystacalis.* WHITE-TAILED JAY. (cw SA). . . . . _____

❏ *Cyanocorax yncas.* GREEN JAY. (n MA, w,n Amaz). . . . . _____
   ___*C. (y.) luxuosus.* GREEN JAY. (n MA)
   ___*C. (y.) yncas.* INCA JAY. (w,n Amaz)

❏ *Psilorhinus morio.* BROWN JAY. (MA). . . . . _____

❏ *Calocitta colliei.* BLACK-THROATED MAGPIE-JAY. (nw Mex). . . . . _____

❏ *Calocitta formosa.* WHITE-THROATED MAGPIE-JAY. (Pac n,c MA). . . . _____

❏ *Garrulus glandarius.* EURASIAN JAY. (Palea, s,se Asia). . . . . _____
   ___*G. (g.) glandarius.* EURASIAN JAY. (w Eura)
   ___*G. (g.) cervicalis.* BLACK-CROWNED JAY. (nw Afr)
   ___*G. (g.) atricapillus.* BLACK-CAPPED JAY. (sw Asia)
   ___*G. (g.) hyrcanus.* IRANIAN JAY. (n Iran)
   ___*G. (g.) brandtii.* BRANDT'S JAY. (ne Eura)
   ___*G. (g.) japonicus.* JAPANESE JAY. (c,s Japan)
   ___*G. (g.) bispecularis.* HIMALAYAN JAY. (Himal)
   ___*G. (g.) leucotis.* WHITE-FACED JAY. (se Asia)

❏ *Garrulus lanceolatus.* BLACK-HEADED JAY. (Himal). . . . . _____

❏ *Garrulus lidthi.* LIDTH'S JAY. (n Ryu). . . . . _____

❏ *Perisoreus infaustus.* SIBERIAN JAY. (n Eura). . . . . _____

❏ *Perisoreus internigrans.* SICHUAN JAY. (mts wc China). . . . . _____

❏ *Perisoreus canadensis.* GREY JAY. (w,n NA; ◊-nc,ne US). . . . . _____

❏ *Urocissa ornata.* CEYLON MAGPIE. (Ceylon). . . . . _____

❏ *Urocissa caerulea.* FORMOSAN MAGPIE. (Taiwan). . . . . _____

❏ *Urocissa flavirostris.* GOLD-BILLED MAGPIE. (Himal). . . . . _____

❏ *Urocissa erythrorhyncha.* BLUE MAGPIE. (s,se Asia). . . . . _____

❏ *Urocissa whiteheadi.* WHITE-WINGED MAGPIE. (mts se Asia). . . . . _____

❏ *Cissa chinensis.* GREEN MAGPIE. (s,se Asia). . . . . _____

❏ *Cissa hypoleuca.* YELLOW-BREASTED MAGPIE. (se Asia). . . . . _____

❏ *Cissa thalassina.* SHORT-TAILED MAGPIE. (G Sunda). . . . . _____
   ___*C. (t.) jefferyi.* BORNEAN MAGPIE. (Born)
   ___*C. (t.) thalassina.* SHORT-TAILED MAGPIE. (Java)

❏ *Cyanopica cyana.* AZURE-WINGED MAGPIE. (se Euro, e Asia). . . . . . . _____

❏ *Dendrocitta vagabunda.* RUFOUS TREEPIE. (s,se Asia). . . . . _____

❏ *Dendrocitta formosae.* GREY TREEPIE. (s Asia). . . . . _____

❑ *Dendrocitta occipitalis.* SUNDA TREEPIE. (mts G Sunda). . . . . _____
   ___*D. (o.) occipitalis.* SUMATRAN TREEPIE. (Sum)
   ___*D. (o.) cinerascens.* BORNEAN TREEPIE. (Born)

❑ *Dendrocitta leucogastra.* WHITE-BELLIED TREEPIE. (sw India). . . . . . . _____

❑ *Dendrocitta frontalis.* COLLARED TREEPIE. (s Asia). . . . . _____

❑ *Dendrocitta bayleyi.* ANDAMAN TREEPIE. (And). . . . . _____

❑ *Crypsirina temia.* RACKET-TAILED TREEPIE. (se Asia). . . . . _____

❑ *Crypsirina cucullata.* HOODED TREEPIE. (Burma). . . . . _____

❑ *Temnurus temnurus.* RATCHET-TAILED TREEPIE. (se Asia). . . . . _____

❑ *Pica pica.* BLACK-BILLED MAGPIE. (Palea, w NA). . . . . _____
   ___*P. (p.) pica.* BLACK-BILLED MAGPIE. (sp)
   ___*P. (p.) mauritanica.* NORTH AFRICAN MAGPIE. (nw Afr)

❑ *Pica nuttalli.* YELLOW-BILLED MAGPIE. (c Calif). . . . . _____

❑ *Zavattariornis stresemanni.* STRESEMANN'S BUSH-CROW. (s Eth). . . . . _____

❑ *Podoces hendersoni.* MONGOLIAN GROUND-JAY. (c Asia). . . . . _____

❑ *Podoces biddulphi.* XINJIANG GROUND-JAY. (nw China). . . . . _____

❑ *Podoces panderi.* TURKESTAN GROUND-JAY. (sc Asia). . . . . _____

❑ *Podoces pleskei.* IRANIAN GROUND-JAY. (c,e Iran). . . . . _____

❑ *Pseudopodoces humilis.* TIBETAN GROUND-JAY. (Himal). . . . . _____

❑ *Nucifraga columbiana.* CLARK'S NUTCRACKER. (mts w NA). . . . . _____

❑ *Nucifraga caryocatactes.* SPOTTED NUTCRACKER. (Eura). . . . . _____
   ___*N. (c.) caryocatactes.* EURASIAN NUTCRACKER. (sp)
   ___*N. (c.) multipunctata.* INDIAN NUTCRACKER. (Himal)

❑ *Pyrrhocorax pyrrhocorax.* RED-BILLED CHOUGH. (Palea, c Eth). . . . . . _____

❑ *Pyrrhocorax graculus.* YELLOW-BILLED CHOUGH. (s Palea). . . . . _____

❑ *Ptilostomus afer.* PIAPIAC. (subsah Afr). . . . . _____

❑ *Corvus monedula.* EURASIAN JACKDAW. (Palea). . . . . _____

❑ *Corvus dauuricus.* DAURIAN JACKDAW. (e Asia). . . . . _____

❑ *Corvus splendens.* HOUSE CROW. (s Asia; ◆ Afr, se Asia). . . . . _____

❑ *Corvus moneduloides.* NEW CALEDONIAN CROW. (N Cal). . . . . _____

❑ *Corvus enca.* SLENDER-BILLED CROW. (se Asia, Phil). . . . . _____

❑ *Corvus typicus.* PIPING CROW. (c,s Sulaw). . . . . _____

❑ *Corvus unicolor.* BANGGAI CROW. (is e Sulaw). . . . . _____

❑ *Corvus florensis.* FLORES CROW. (Flores). _____

❑ *Corvus kubaryi.* MARIANA CROW. (Mari). _____

❑ *Corvus validus.* LONG-BILLED CROW. (Moluc). . . . . _____

❑ *Corvus meeki.* BOUGAINVILLE CROW. (n Solom). . . . . _____

❏ *Corvus woodfordi.* WHITE-BILLED CROW. (s Solom) . . . . _____

❏ *Corvus fuscicapillus.* BROWN-HEADED CROW. (Aru-nw NG) . . . . _____

❏ *Corvus tristis.* GREY CROW. (w Pap, NG) . . . . _____

❏ *Corvus capensis.* CAPE CROW. (ne,s Afr) . . . . _____

❏ *Corvus frugilegus.* ROOK. (Eura; ◆ NZ) . . . . _____

❏ *Corvus caurinus.* NORTHWESTERN CROW. (nw NA) . . . . _____

❏ *Corvus brachyrhynchos.* AMERICAN CROW. (NA) . . . . _____

❏ *Corvus ossifragus.* FISH CROW. (e,se US) . . . . _____

❏ *Corvus imparatus.* TAMAULIPAS CROW. (s Tex, ne Mex) . . . . _____

❏ *Corvus sinaloae.* SINALOA CROW. (w Mex) . . . . _____

❏ *Corvus palmarum.* PALM CROW. (w Cuba, Hisp) . . . . _____

❏ *Corvus jamaicensis.* JAMAICAN CROW. (Jam) . . . . _____

❏ *Corvus nasicus.* CUBAN CROW. (Cuba, s Bah) . . . . _____

❏ *Corvus leucognaphalus.* WHITE-NECKED CROW. (Hisp, PR) . . . . _____

❏ *Corvus corone.* CARRION CROW. (Eura) . . . . _____
   ___*C. (c.) corone.* CARRION CROW. (n,sw,e Eura)
   ___*C. (c.) cornix.* HOODED CROW. (c,s Eura)

❏ *Corvus macrorhynchos.* LARGE-BILLED CROW. (e,s Asia-Phil) . . . . . . _____

❏ *Corvus levaillantii.* JUNGLE CROW. (s Asia) . . . . _____

❏ *Corvus orru.* TORRESIAN CROW. (Wall-Bism, n,e Aust) . . . . _____
   ___*C. (o.) orru.* NEW GUINEA CROW. (n Moluc-Bism)
   ___*C. (o.) latirostris.* TANIMBAR CROW. (e L Sunda, Tanim)
   ___*C. (o.) cecilae.* AUSTRALIAN CROW. (n,c Aust)

❏ *Corvus bennetti.* LITTLE CROW. (w,int Aust) . . . . _____

❏ *Corvus coronoides.* AUSTRALIAN RAVEN. (int sw,c,e Aust) . . . . _____

❏ *Corvus mellori.* LITTLE RAVEN. (se Aust) . . . . _____

❏ *Corvus boreus.* RELICT RAVEN. (se Aust) . . . . _____

❏ *Corvus tasmanicus.* FOREST RAVEN. (se Aust) . . . . _____

❏ *Corvus torquatus.* COLLARED CROW. (s Asia) . . . . _____

❏ *Corvus hawaiiensis.* HAWAIIAN CROW. (mts Hawaii) . . . . _____

❏ *Corvus cryptoleucus.* CHIHUAHUAN RAVEN. (sw US, n,c Mex) . . . . . . _____

❏ *Corvus albus.* PIED CROW. (Afr, Mad reg) . . . . _____

❏ *Corvus ruficollis.* BROWN-NECKED RAVEN. (s Palea, n Afr) . . . . _____
   ___*C. (r.) ruficollis.* BROWN-NECKED RAVEN. (s Palea)
   ___*C. (r.) edithae.* DWARF RAVEN. (n Afr)

❏ *Corvus corax.* COMMON RAVEN. (Palea, w,n NA, MA) . . . . _____

❏ *Corvus rhipidurus.* FAN-TAILED RAVEN. (sw Palea, subsah Afr) . . . . . . _____

❏ *Corvus albicollis.* White-necked Raven. (e,s Afr). . . . . _____

❏ *Corvus crassirostris.* Thick-billed Raven. (mts ne Afr). . . . . _____

Tribe Paradisaeini [17/46]

❏ *Melampitta lugubris.* Lesser Melampitta. (mts NG). . . . . _____

❏ *Melampitta gigantea.* Greater Melampitta. (mts NG). . . . . _____

❏ *Loboparadisea sericea.* Yellow-breasted Bird-of-Paradise. (NG). _____

❏ *Cnemophilus macgregorii.* Crested Bird-of-Paradise. (mts e NG) . _____

❏ *Cnemophilus loriae.* Loria's Bird-of-Paradise. (mts c NG). . . . . . . _____

❏ *Macgregoria pulchra.* Macgregor's Bird-of-Paradise. (wc,se NG). _____

❏ *Lycocorax pyrrhopterus.* Paradise-crow. (n Moluc). . . . . _____

❏ *Manucodia atra.* Glossy-mantled Manucode. (Aru-NG). . . . . _____

❏ *Manucodia chalybata.* Crinkle-collared Manucode. (w Pap, NG). _____

❏ *Manucodia comrii.* Curl-crested Manucode. (se NG). . . . . _____

❏ *Manucodia jobiensis.* Jobi Manucode. (n NG). . . . . _____

❏ *Manucodia keraudrenii.* Trumpet Manucode. (Aru, NG, ne Aust) . _____
 ___*M. (k.) keraudrenii.* Trumpet Manucode. (sp)
 ___*M. (k.) hunsteini.* Hunstein's Manucode. (se NG)

❏ *Semioptera wallacii.* Standardwing. (mts n Moluc). . . . . _____

❏ *Paradigalla carunculata.* Long-tailed Paradigalla. (mts w NG). . . _____

❏ *Paradigalla brevicauda.* Short-tailed Paradigalla. (mts w,c NG). _____

❏ *Epimachus fastuosus.* Black Sicklebill. (mts w,c NG). . . . . _____

❏ *Epimachus meyeri.* Brown Sicklebill. (mts c,e NG). . . . . _____

❏ *Epimachus albertisi.* Black-billed Sicklebill. (mts NG). . . . . _____

❏ *Epimachus bruijnii.* Pale-billed Sicklebill. (nw NG). . . . . _____

❏ *Lophorina superba.* Superb Bird-of-Paradise. (mts NG). . . . . _____

❏ *Parotia sefilata.* Western Parotia. (mts w NG). . . . . _____

❏ *Parotia carolae.* Carola's Parotia. (mts w,c NG). . . . . _____

❏ *Parotia lawesii.* Lawes's Parotia. (mts e,se NG). . . . . _____

❏ *Parotia helenae.* Eastern Parotia. (mts se NG). . . . . _____

❏ *Parotia wahnesi.* Wahnes's Parotia. (mts se NG). . . . . _____

❏ *Ptiloris magnificus.* Magnificent Riflebird. (w,c NG, ne Aust). . . . . _____

❏ *Ptiloris intercedens.* Eastern Riflebird. (e NG). . . . . _____

❏ *Ptiloris victoriae.* Victoria's Riflebird. (ne Aust). . . . . _____

❏ *Ptiloris paradiseus.* Paradise Riflebird. (mts ne Aust). . . . . _____

❏ *Cicinnurus magnificus.* Magnificent Bird-of-Paradise. (w Pap, NG)_____

❏ *Cicinnurus respublica.* Wilson's Bird-of-Paradise. (mts w Pap). . . . _____

❑ *Cicinnurus regius.* KING BIRD-OF-PARADISE. (Aru-NG)............ _____

❑ *Astrapia nigra.* ARFAK ASTRAPIA. (mts nw NG)................. _____

❑ *Astrapia splendidissima.* SPLENDID ASTRAPIA. (mts w,c NG)....... _____

❑ *Astrapia mayeri.* RIBBON-TAILED ASTRAPIA. (mts ec NG).......... _____

❑ *Astrapia stephaniae.* STEPHANIE'S ASTRAPIA. (mts e,se NG)........ _____

❑ *Astrapia rothschildi.* HUON ASTRAPIA. (mts se NG)............... _____

❑ *Pteridophora alberti.* KING-OF-SAXONY BIRD-OF-PARADISE. (c NG)... _____

❑ *Seleucidis melanoleuca.* TWELVE-WIRED BIRD-OF-PARADISE.(w Pap-NG)_____

❑ *Paradisaea rubra.* RED BIRD-OF-PARADISE. (w Pap).............. _____

❑ *Paradisaea minor.* LESSER BIRD-OF-PARADISE. (w Pap, w,n NG)..... _____

❑ *Paradisaea apoda.* GREATER BIRD-OF-PARADISE. (Aru, s NG)....... _____

❑ *Paradisaea raggiana.* RAGGIANA BIRD-OF-PARADISE. (ne,se NG)..... _____

❑ *Paradisaea decora.* GOLDIE'S BIRD-OF-PARADISE. (se NG)......... _____

❑ *Paradisaea guilielmi.* EMPEROR BIRD-OF-PARADISE. (mts se NG)..... _____

❑ *Paradisaea rudolphi.* BLUE BIRD-OF-PARADISE. (mts c,se NG)....... _____

Tribe Artamini [6/24]

❑ *Cracticus mentalis.* BLACK-BACKED BUTCHERBIRD. (se NG, ne Aust) . _____

❑ *Cracticus torquatus.* GREY BUTCHERBIRD. (Aust)............... _____
   ___*C. (t.) argenteus.* SILVER-BACKED BUTCHERBIRD. (n Aust)
   ___*C. (t.) torquatus.* GREY BUTCHERBIRD. (c,s,e Aust)

❑ *Cracticus cassicus.* HOODED BUTCHERBIRD. (Aru-NG)............ _____

❑ *Cracticus louisiadensis.* TAGULA BUTCHERBIRD. (se NG).......... _____

❑ *Cracticus nigrogularis.* PIED BUTCHERBIRD. (Aust)............... _____

❑ *Cracticus quoyi.* BLACK BUTCHERBIRD. (Aru-NG, n,ne Aust)....... _____

❑ *Gymnorhina tibicen.* AUSTRALASIAN MAGPIE. (sc NG-Aust; ◆ NZ) . _____
   ___*G. (t.) papuana.* NEW GUINEA MAGPIE. (sc NG)
   ___*G. (t.) tibicen.* BLACK-BACKED MAGPIE. (Aust)
   ___*G. (t.) dorsalis.* WESTERN MAGPIE. (sw Aust)
   ___*G. (t.) hypoleuca.* WHITE-BACKED MAGPIE. (se Aust)

❑ *Strepera graculina.* PIED CURRAWONG. (ne,e Aust)............... _____
   ___*S. (g.) magnirostris.* GREAT-BILLED CURRAWONG. (ne Aust)
   ___*S. (g.) graculina.* PIED CURRAWONG. (e Aust)

❑ *Strepera fuliginosa.* BLACK CURRAWONG. (Tas)................. _____

❑ *Strepera versicolor.* GREY CURRAWONG. (s Aust)............... _____
   ___*S. (v.) versicolor.* GREY CURRAWONG. (sp)
   ___*S. (v.) intermedia.* BROWN CURRAWONG. (se S Aust)
   ___*S. (v.) melanoptera.* BLACK-WINGED CURRAWONG. (cs Aust)
   ___*S. (v.) arguta.* CLINKING CURRAWONG. (Tas)

❑ *Artamus fuscus.* ASHY WOODSWALLOW. (s,se Asia). . . . . _____

❑ *Artamus leucorynchus.* WHITE-BREASTED W. (se Asia-sw Pac, Aust). _____

❑ *Artamus monachus.* IVORY-BACKED WOODSWALLOW. (Sulaw). . . . . . . _____

❑ *Artamus maximus.* GREAT WOODSWALLOW. (mts NG). . . . . _____

❑ *Artamus insignis.* BISMARCK WOODSWALLOW. (Bism). . . . . _____

❑ *Artamus mentalis.* FIJI WOODSWALLOW. (n Fiji). . . . . _____

❑ *Artamus personatus.* MASKED WOODSWALLOW. (Aust). . . . . _____

❑ *Artamus superciliosus.* WHITE-BROWED WOODSWALLOW. (int Aust) . _____

❑ *Artamus cinereus.* BLACK-FACED WOODSWALLOW. (L Sunda, Aust) . _____
___*A. (c.) cinereus.* BLACK-FACED WOODSWALLOW. (sp)
___*A. (c.) albiventris.* WHITE-VENTED WOODSWALLOW. (ne Aust)

❑ *Artamus cyanopterus.* DUSKY WOODSWALLOW. (sw,e,se Aust). . . . . . . _____

❑ *Artamus minor.* LITTLE WOODSWALLOW. (n,c Aust). . . . . _____

❑ *Pityriasis gymnocephala.* BORNEAN BRISTLEHEAD. (Born). . . . . _____

❑ *Peltops blainvillii.* LOWLAND PELTOPS. (w Pap, NG). . . . . _____

❑ *Peltops montanus.* MOUNTAIN PELTOPS. (mts NG). . . . . _____

Tribe Oriolini [8/111]

❑ *Oriolus melanotis.* OLIVE-BROWN ORIOLE. (c L Sunda). . . . . _____

❑ *Oriolus bouroensis.* BLACK-EARED ORIOLE. (s Moluc, Tanim). . . . . . . _____

❑ *Oriolus forsteni.* GREY-COLLARED ORIOLE. (s Moluc). . . . . _____

❑ *Oriolus phaeochromus.* DUSKY-BROWN ORIOLE. (n Moluc). . . . . _____

❑ *Oriolus szalayi.* BROWN ORIOLE. (w Pap, NG). . . . . _____

❑ *Oriolus sagittatus.* OLIVE-BACKED ORIOLE. (n,e,se Aust). . . . . _____

❑ *Oriolus flavocinctus.* GREEN ORIOLE. (L Sunda-s NG, n Aust). . . . . . . _____

❑ *Oriolus xanthonotus.* DARK-THROATED ORIOLE. (se Asia, sw Phil). . . _____

❑ *Oriolus steerii.* PHILIPPINE ORIOLE. (Phil). . . . . _____

❑ *Oriolus albiloris.* WHITE-LORED ORIOLE. (mts n Phil). . . . . _____

❑ *Oriolus isabellae.* ISABELA ORIOLE. (mts n Phil). . . . . _____

❑ *Oriolus oriolus.* EURASIAN GOLDEN-ORIOLE. (Palea; ◊ Afr, s Asia). . . _____

❑ *Oriolus auratus.* AFRICAN GOLDEN-ORIOLE. (Afr). . . . . _____

❑ *Oriolus chinensis.* BLACK-NAPED ORIOLE. (e,se Asia, Phil; ◊-s Asia) . _____

❑ *Oriolus tenuirostris.* SLENDER-BILLED ORIOLE. (e India, se Asia). . . . . _____

❑ *Oriolus chlorocephalus.* GREEN-HEADED ORIOLE. (mts e Afr). . . . . . . _____

❑ *Oriolus crassirostris.* SAO TOME ORIOLE. (ST). . . . . _____

❑ *Oriolus brachyrhynchus.* WESTERN BLACK-HEADED ORIOLE. (w,c Afr) _____

❑ *Oriolus monacha.* DARK-HEADED ORIOLE. (mts Eth). . . . . _____

❑ *Oriolus larvatus.* AFRICAN BLACK-HEADED ORIOLE. (e,s Afr). . . . . . . _____

❑ *Oriolus percivali.* BLACK-TAILED ORIOLE. (mts e Afr). . . . . _____

❑ *Oriolus nigripennis.* BLACK-WINGED ORIOLE. (w,c Afr). . . . . _____

❑ *Oriolus xanthornus.* BLACK-HOODED ORIOLE. (s,se Asia). . . . . _____

❑ *Oriolus hosii.* BLACK ORIOLE. (mts n Born). . . . . _____

❑ *Oriolus cruentus.* BLACK-AND-CRIMSON ORIOLE. (mts se Asia). . . . . . _____

❑ *Oriolus traillii.* MAROON ORIOLE. (s,se Asia). . . . . _____

❑ *Oriolus mellianus.* SILVER ORIOLE. (mts s,c China). . . . . _____

❑ *Sphecotheres hypoleucus.* WETAR FIGBIRD. (Wetar). . . . . _____

❑ *Sphecotheres viridis.* GREEN FIGBIRD. (c L Sunda-se NG, n,e Aust). . . _____
   ___*S. (v.) viridis.* TIMOR FIGBIRD. (c L Sunda)
   ___*S. (v.) flaviventris.* YELLOW FIGBIRD. (Kai, n,ne Aust)
   ___*S. (v.) vieilloti.* GREEN FIGBIRD. (se NG, e Aust)

❑ *Coracina maxima.* GROUND CUCKOOSHRIKE. (int Aust). . . . . _____

❑ *Coracina larvata.* SUNDA CUCKOOSHRIKE. (mts G Sunda). . . . . _____

❑ *Coracina macei.* LARGE CUCKOOSHRIKE. (s,se Asia). . . . . _____

❑ *Coracina javensis.* JAVAN CUCKOOSHRIKE. (Java, Bali). . . . . _____

❑ *Coracina schistacea.* SLATY CUCKOOSHRIKE. (is e Sulaw). . . . . _____

❑ *Coracina personata.* WALLACEAN CUCKOOSHRIKE. (L Sunda-Kai). . . . _____
   ___*C. (p.) personata.* TIMOR CUCKOOSHRIKE. (L Sunda)
   ___*C. (p.) pollens.* KAI CUCKOOSHRIKE. (Tanim, Kai)

❑ *Coracina atriceps.* MOLUCCAN CUCKOOSHRIKE. (Moluc). . . . . _____

❑ *Coracina fortis.* BURU CUCKOOSHRIKE. (s Moluc). . . . . _____

❑ *Coracina caledonica.* MELANESIAN CUCKOOSHRIKE. (Solom-Loy). . . . _____

❑ *Coracina novaehollandiae.* BLACK-FACED C. (Aust; ◊-Indon, NG). . . . _____

❑ *Coracina caeruleogrisea.* STOUT-BILLED CUCKOOSHRIKE. (Aru, NG) . _____

❑ *Coracina temminckii.* CERULEAN CUCKOOSHRIKE. (Sulaw). . . . . _____

❑ *Coracina striata.* BAR-BELLIED CUCKOOSHRIKE. (se Asia, Phil). . . . . . _____

❑ *Coracina bicolor.* PIED CUCKOOSHRIKE. (n Sulaw). . . . . _____

❑ *Coracina lineata.* YELLOW-EYED C. (w Pap-Solom, ne Aust). . . . . _____

❑ *Coracina boyeri.* BOYER'S CUCKOOSHRIKE. (w Pap, NG). . . . . _____

❑ *Coracina leucopygia.* WHITE-RUMPED CUCKOOSHRIKE. (Sulaw). . . . . . _____

❑ *Coracina papuensis.* WHITE-BELLIED C. (Wall-Solom, n,e Aust). . . . . _____
   ___*C. (p.) papuensis.* PAPUAN CUCKOOSHRIKE. (Wall-Solom)
   ___*C. (p.) hypoleuca.* WHITE-BELLIED CUCKOOSHRIKE. (n Aust)
   ___*C. (p.) robusta.* LITTLE CUCKOOSHRIKE. (e Aust)

❏ *Coracina longicauda.* HOODED CUCKOOSHRIKE. (mts NG). . . . . _____

❏ *Coracina parvula.* HALMAHERA CUCKOOSHRIKE. (mts n Moluc). . . . . . _____

❏ *Coracina abbotti.* PYGMY CUCKOOSHRIKE. (mts Sulaw). . . . . _____

❏ *Coracina analis.* NEW CALEDONIAN CUCKOOSHRIKE. (mts N Cal). . . . _____

❏ *Coracina pectoralis.* WHITE-BREASTED CUCKOOSHRIKE. (Afr). . . . . . . _____

❏ *Coracina caesia.* GREY CUCKOOSHRIKE. (Afr). . . . . _____

❏ *Coracina azurea.* BLUE CUCKOOSHRIKE. (w,c Afr). . . . . _____

❏ *Coracina graueri.* GRAUER'S CUCKOOSHRIKE. (mts ec Afr). . . . . _____

❏ *Coracina cinerea.* ASHY CUCKOOSHRIKE. (Com, Mad). . . . . _____

❏ *Coracina typica.* MAURITIUS CUCKOOSHRIKE. (Maur). . . . . _____

❏ *Coracina newtoni.* REUNION CUCKOOSHRIKE. (Réun). . . . . _____

❏ *Coracina coerulescens.* BLACKISH CUCKOOSHRIKE. (n Phil). . . . . _____

❏ *Coracina tenuirostris.* SLENDER-BILLED CICADABIRD. (Aust reg-Micro)_____

❏ *Coracina dohertyi.* SUMBA CICADABIRD. (wc L Sunda). . . . . _____

❏ *Coracina sula.* SULA CICADABIRD. (is e Sulaw). . . . . _____

❏ *Coracina dispar.* KAI CICADABIRD. (Kai). _____

❏ *Coracina mindanensis.* BLACK-BIBBED CICADABIRD. (Phil). . . . . _____

❏ *Coracina orio.* SULAWESI CICADABIRD. (Sulaw). . . . . _____

❏ *Coracina ceramensis.* PALE CICADABIRD. (Moluc). . . . . _____

❏ *Coracina incerta.* BLACK-SHOULDERED CICADABIRD. (w Pap, NG). . . . _____

❏ *Coracina schisticeps.* GREY-HEADED CUCKOOSHRIKE. (w Pap, NG). . . _____

❏ *Coracina melas.* NEW GUINEA CUCKOOSHRIKE. (Aru-NG). . . . . _____

❏ *Coracina montana.* BLACK-BELLIED CUCKOOSHRIKE. (mts NG). . . . . . _____

❏ *Coracina holopolia.* SOLOMON ISLANDS CUCKOOSHRIKE. (Solom). . . . _____

❏ *Coracina mcgregori.* MCGREGOR'S CUCKOOSHRIKE. (mts s Phil). . . . . _____

❏ *Coracina ostenta.* WHITE-WINGED CUCKOOSHRIKE. (c Phil). . . . . _____

❏ *Coracina polioptera.* INDOCHINESE CUCKOOSHRIKE. (mts se Asia). . . . _____

❏ *Coracina melaschistos.* BLACK-WINGED CUCKOOSHRIKE. (s,se Asia) . _____

❏ *Coracina fimbriata.* LESSER CUCKOOSHRIKE. (se Asia). . . . . _____

❏ *Coracina melanoptera.* BLACK-HEADED CUCKOOSHRIKE. (India). . . . . _____
    ___*C. (m.) melanoptera.* HIMALAYAN CUCKOOSHRIKE. (n India)
    ___*C. (m.) sykesi.* BLACK-HEADED CUCKOOSHRIKE. (c,s,e India)

❏ *Campochaera sloetii.* GOLDEN CUCKOOSHRIKE. (NG). . . . . _____

❏ *Lalage melanoleuca.* BLACK-AND-WHITE TRILLER. (Phil). . . . . _____

❏ *Lalage nigra.* PIED TRILLER. (se Asia, Phil). . . . . _____

❑ *Lalage leucopygialis.* WHITE-RUMPED TRILLER. (Sulaw). . . . . _____

❑ *Lalage sueurii.* WHITE-SHOULDERED TRILLER. (Indon). . . . . _____

❑ *Lalage tricolor.* WHITE-WINGED TRILLER. (s NG, Aust). . . . . _____

❑ *Lalage aurea.* RUFOUS-BELLIED TRILLER. (n Moluc). . . . . _____

❑ *Lalage moesta.* WHITE-BROWED TRILLER. (Tanim). . . . . _____

❑ *Lalage atrovirens.* BLACK-BROWED TRILLER. (w Pap, n NG). . . . . _____

❑ *Lalage leucomela.* VARIED TRILLER. (Kai-Bism, n,e Aust). . . . . _____
___*L. (l.) leucomela.* VARIED TRILLER. (sp)
___*L. (l.) conjuncta.* MUSSAU TRILLER. (n Bism)

❑ *Lalage maculosa.* POLYNESIAN TRILLER. (Vanu-w Samoa). . . . . _____

❑ *Lalage sharpei.* SAMOAN TRILLER. (mts w Samoa). . . . . _____

❑ *Lalage leucopyga.* LONG-TAILED TRILLER. (se Solom-N Cal, Loy). . . . _____

❑ *Campephaga petiti.* PETIT'S CUCKOOSHRIKE. (c Afr). . . . . _____

❑ *Campephaga flava.* BLACK CUCKOOSHRIKE. (ne,c,s Afr). . . . . _____

❑ *Campephaga phoenicea.* RED-SHOULDERED CUCKOOSHRIKE. (Afr). . . . _____

❑ *Campephaga quiscalina.* PURPLE-THROATED C. (w,c Afr). . . . . _____

❑ *Campephaga lobata.* GHANA CUCKOOSHRIKE. (w Afr). . . . . _____

❑ *Campephaga oriolina.* ORIOLE CUCKOOSHRIKE. (c Afr). . . . . _____

❑ *Pericrocotus roseus.* ROSY MINIVET. (Himal; ◊-s,se Asia). . . . . _____

❑ *Pericrocotus cantonensis.* BROWN-RUMPED M. (ce China; ◊-se Asia) . _____

❑ *Pericrocotus divaricatus.* ASHY MINIVET. (e Asia; ◊ se Asia-Indon). . . _____

❑ *Pericrocotus tegimae.* RYUKYU MINIVET. (s Japan, Ryu). . . . . _____

❑ *Pericrocotus cinnamomeus.* SMALL MINIVET. (s,se Asia). . . . . _____
___*P. (c.) peregrinus.* LITTLE MINIVET. (sp)
___*P. (c.) cinnamomeus.* SMALL MINIVET. (s India)

❑ *Pericrocotus igneus.* FIERY MINIVET. (se Asia, w Phil). . . . . _____

❑ *Pericrocotus lansbergei.* FLORES MINIVET. (wc L Sunda). . . . . _____

❑ *Pericrocotus erythropygius.* WHITE-BELLIED MINIVET. (sc Asia). . . . . _____

❑ *Pericrocotus solaris.* GREY-CHINNED MINIVET. (s,se Asia). . . . . _____

❑ *Pericrocotus ethologus.* LONG-TAILED MINIVET. (mts s,se Asia). . . . . . _____

❑ *Pericrocotus brevirostris.* SHORT-BILLED MINIVET. (mts s,se Asia). . . . _____

❑ *Pericrocotus miniatus.* SUNDA MINIVET. (mts Sum, Java). . . . . _____

❑ *Pericrocotus flammeus.* SCARLET MINIVET. (s Asia-Phil). . . . . _____
___*P. (f.) flammeus.* FLAME MINIVET. (pen sw India)
___*P. (f.) speciosus.* SCARLET MINIVET. (sp)

❑ *Hemipus picatus.* BAR-WINGED FLYCATCHER-SHRIKE. (mts s,se Asia) . _____

❑ *Hemipus hirundinaceus.* BLACK-WINGED FLYCATCHER-S. (G Sunda) . _____

Subfamily Dicrurinae [21/164]
Tribe Rhipidurini [1/42]

❏ *Rhipidura hypoxantha.* YELLOW-BELLIED FANTAIL. (mts s,se Asia). . . _____

❏ *Rhipidura superciliaris.* BLUE FANTAIL. (Phil). . . . . _____

❏ *Rhipidura cyaniceps.* BLUE-HEADED FANTAIL. (Phil). . . . . _____

❏ *Rhipidura phoenicura.* RUFOUS-TAILED FANTAIL. (mts Java). . . . . _____

❏ *Rhipidura nigrocinnamomea.* BLACK-AND-CINNAMON FANTAIL. (s Phil)_____

❏ *Rhipidura albicollis.* WHITE-THROATED FANTAIL. (s,se Asia). . . . . _____
___*R. (a.) albicollis.* WHITE-THROATED FANTAIL. (n India, se Asia)
___*R. (a.) albogularis.* SPOT-BREASTED FANTAIL. (c,s India)

❏ *Rhipidura euryura.* WHITE-BELLIED FANTAIL. (mts Java). . . . . _____

❏ *Rhipidura aureola.* WHITE-BROWED FANTAIL. (s,se Asia). . . . . _____

❏ *Rhipidura javanica.* PIED FANTAIL. (se Asia, Phil). . . . . _____

❏ *Rhipidura perlata.* SPOTTED FANTAIL. (se Asia). . . . . _____

❏ *Rhipidura leucophrys.* WILLIE-WAGTAIL. (Moluc-Solom, Aust). . . . . . _____

❏ *Rhipidura diluta.* BROWN-CAPPED FANTAIL. (wc L Sunda). . . . . _____

❏ *Rhipidura rufiventris.* NORTHERN FANTAIL. (L Sunda-Bism, n Aust) . _____

❏ *Rhipidura fuscorufa.* CINNAMON-TAILED FANTAIL. (Tanim). . . . . _____

❏ *Rhipidura cockerelli.* WHITE-WINGED FANTAIL. (Solom). . . . . _____

❏ *Rhipidura threnothorax.* SOOTY THICKET-FANTAIL. (Aru-NG). . . . . . . _____

❏ *Rhipidura maculipectus.* BLACK THICKET-FANTAIL. (Aru-NG). . . . . . . _____

❏ *Rhipidura leucothorax.* WHITE-BELLIED THICKET-FANTAIL. (NG). . . . _____
___*R. (l.) leucothorax.* WHITE-BELLIED THICKET-FANTAIL. (sp)
___*R. (l.) clamosa.* KARIMUI THICKET-FANTAIL. (mts ec NG)

❏ *Rhipidura atra.* BLACK FANTAIL. (mts w Pap, NG). . . . . _____

❏ *Rhipidura hyperythra.* CHESTNUT-BELLIED FANTAIL. (Aru, NG). . . . . . _____

❏ *Rhipidura albolimbata.* FRIENDLY FANTAIL. (mts NG). . . . . _____

❏ *Rhipidura phasiana.* MANGROVE FANTAIL. (s NG, n Aust). . . . . _____

❏ *Rhipidura fuliginosa.* GREY FANTAIL. (s Solom-Loy, Aust, NZ). . . . . . _____

❏ *Rhipidura drownei.* BROWN FANTAIL. (mts Solom). . . . . _____

❏ *Rhipidura tenebrosa.* DUSKY FANTAIL. (mts s Solom). . . . . _____

❏ *Rhipidura rennelliana.* RENNELL FANTAIL. (e Solom). . . . . _____

❏ *Rhipidura spilodera.* STREAKED FANTAIL. (N Cal-Fiji). . . . . _____

❏ *Rhipidura personata.* KADAVU FANTAIL. (sw Fiji). . . . . _____

❏ *Rhipidura nebulosa.* SAMOAN FANTAIL. (mts w Samoa). . . . . _____

❏ *Rhipidura brachyrhyncha.* DIMORPHIC FANTAIL. (mts NG). . . . . _____

❑ *Rhipidura teysmanni.* RUSTY-BELLIED FANTAIL. (Sulaw). . . . . _____
   ___*R. (t.) teysmanni.* RUSTY-BELLIED FANTAIL. (mts Sulaw)
   ___*R. (t.) sulaensis.* SULA FANTAIL. (Sula Is)

❑ *Rhipidura superflua.* TAWNY-BACKED FANTAIL. (s Moluc). . . . . _____

❑ *Rhipidura dedemi.* STREAKY-BREASTED FANTAIL. (mts s Moluc). . . . . _____

❑ *Rhipidura opistherythra.* LONG-TAILED FANTAIL. (Tanim). . . . . _____

❑ *Rhipidura lepida.* PALAU FANTAIL. (Palau). _____

❑ *Rhipidura rufidorsa.* RUFOUS-BACKED FANTAIL. (w Pap, NG). . . . . . . _____

❑ *Rhipidura dahli.* BISMARCK FANTAIL. (mts Bism). . . . . _____

❑ *Rhipidura matthiae.* MATTHIAS FANTAIL. (n Bism). . . . . _____

❑ *Rhipidura malaitae.* MALAITA FANTAIL. (mts se Solom). . . . . _____

❑ *Rhipidura kubaryi.* POHNPEI FANTAIL. (e Carol). . . . . _____

❑ *Rhipidura rufifrons.* RUFOUS FANTAIL. (Wall-Micro, Solom, Aust). . . _____

❑ *Rhipidura semirubra.* MANUS FANTAIL. (n Bism). . . . . _____

Tribe Dicrurini [2/24]

❑ *Chaetorhynchus papuensis.* PYGMY DRONGO. (mts NG). . . . . _____

❑ *Dicrurus ludwigii.* SQUARE-TAILED DRONGO. (Afr). . . . . _____
   ___*D. (l.) sharpei.* SHARPE'S DRONGO. (n,c Afr)
   ___*D. (l.) ludwigii.* SQUARE-TAILED DRONGO. (s Afr)

❑ *Dicrurus atripennis.* SHINING DRONGO. (w,c Afr). . . . . _____

❑ *Dicrurus adsimilis.* FORK-TAILED DRONGO. (Afr). . . . . _____

❑ *Dicrurus modestus.* VELVET-MANTLED DRONGO. (w,c Afr). . . . . _____
   ___*D. (m.) coracinus.* VELVET-MANTLED DRONGO. (sp)
   ___*D. (m.) modestus.* PRINCIPE DRONGO. (Prín)

❑ *Dicrurus aldabranus.* ALDABRA DRONGO. (Ald). . . . . _____

❑ *Dicrurus fuscipennis.* COMORO DRONGO. (Com). . . . . _____

❑ *Dicrurus forficatus.* CRESTED DRONGO. (Com, Mad). . . . . _____

❑ *Dicrurus waldenii.* MAYOTTE DRONGO. (Com). . . . . _____

❑ *Dicrurus macrocercus.* BLACK DRONGO. (s,se Asia; ♦ Mari). . . . . _____

❑ *Dicrurus leucophaeus.* ASHY DRONGO. (s Asia-sw Phil). . . . . _____
   ___*D. (l.) longicaudatus.* GREY DRONGO. (sc Asia)
   ___*D. (l.) leucophaeus.* ASHY DRONGO. (sp)

❑ *Dicrurus caerulescens.* WHITE-BELLIED DRONGO. (India). . . . . _____

❑ *Dicrurus annectans.* CROW-BILLED DRONGO. (sc Asia; ◊-Phil). . . . . . _____

❑ *Dicrurus aeneus.* BRONZED DRONGO. (s,se Asia). . . . . _____

❑ *Dicrurus remifer.* LESSER RACKET-TAILED DRONGO. (s,se Asia). . . . . . _____

❑ *Dicrurus hottentottus.* HAIR-CRESTED DRONGO. (s,se Asia-c Moluc) . _____

❏ *Dicrurus sumatranus.* SUMATRAN DRONGO. (Sum). . . . . _____

❏ *Dicrurus montanus.* SULAWESI DRONGO. (mts Sulaw). . . . . _____

❏ *Dicrurus densus.* WALLACEAN DRONGO. (L Sunda-Kai). . . . . _____

❏ *Dicrurus balicassius.* BALICASSIAO. (n,c Phil). . . . . _____

❏ *Dicrurus bracteatus.* SPANGLED DRONGO. (Wall-Bism, ne Aust). . . . . . _____

❏ *Dicrurus megarhynchus.* RIBBON-TAILED DRONGO. (e Bism). . . . . _____

❏ *Dicrurus andamanensis.* ANDAMAN DRONGO. (And). . . . . _____

❏ *Dicrurus paradiseus.* GREATER RACKET-TAILED DRONGO. (s,se Asia). _____

Tribe Monarchini [18/98]

❏ *Erythrocercus mccallii.* CHESTNUT-CAPPED FLYCATCHER. (w,c Afr). . . _____

❏ *Erythrocercus holochlorus.* YELLOW FLYCATCHER. (e Afr). . . . . _____

❏ *Erythrocercus livingstonei.* LIVINGSTONE'S FLYCATCHER. (ce,se Afr) . _____
  ___*E. (l.) thomsoni.* THOMSON'S FLYCATCHER. (ce Afr)
  ___*E. (l.) livingstonei.* LIVINGSTONE'S FLYCATCHER. (se Afr)

❏ *Elminia longicauda.* AFRICAN BLUE-FLYCATCHER. (w,c Afr). . . . . . . _____

❏ *Elminia albicauda.* WHITE-TAILED BLUE-FLYCATCHER. (sc Afr). . . . . . _____

❏ *Trochocercus nigromitratus.* DUSKY CRESTED-FLYCATCHER. (w,c Afr) _____

❏ *Trochocercus albiventris.* WHITE-BELLIED CRESTED-FLYCATCHER. (c Afr)_____

❏ *Trochocercus albonotatus.* WHITE-TAILED CRESTED-FLYC. (e,se Afr). _____

❏ *Trochocercus nitens.* BLUE-HEADED CRESTED-FLYCATCHER. (w,c Afr) _____

❏ *Trochocercus cyanomelas.* AFRICAN CRESTED-FLYCATCHER. (e,se Afr)_____

❏ *Hypothymis helenae.* SHORT-CRESTED MONARCH. (Phil). . . . . _____
  ___*H. (h.) personata.* CAMIGUIN MONARCH. (n Phil)
  ___*H. (h.) helenae.* SHORT-CRESTED MONARCH. (sp)

❏ *Hypothymis coelestis.* CELESTIAL MONARCH. (Phil). . . . . _____

❏ *Hypothymis azurea.* BLACK-NAPED MONARCH. (s Asia-Wall, Phil). . . . _____
  ___*H. (a.) azurea.* BLACK-NAPED MONARCH. (sp)
  ___*H. (a.) puella.* PACIFIC MONARCH. (Sulaw)

❏ *Eutrichomyias rowleyi.* CERULEAN PARADISE-FLYCATCHER. (Sangihe). _____

❏ *Terpsiphone rufiventer.* BLACK-HEADED PARADISE-FLYC. (w,c Afr). . . _____
  ___*T. (r.) rufiventer.* BLACK-HEADED PARADISE-FLYCATCHER. (sp)
  ___*T. (r.) smithii.* ANNOBON PARADISE-FLYCATCHER. (Pagalu)

❏ *Terpsiphone bedfordi.* BEDFORD'S PARADISE-FLYCATCHER. (e Zaire) . _____

❏ *Terpsiphone rufocinerea.* RUFOUS-VENTED PARADISE-FLYC. (Afr). . . . _____
  ___*T. (r.) rufocinerea.* RUFOUS-VENTED PARADISE-FLYCATCHER. (wc Afr)
  ___*T. (r.) batesi.* BATES'S PARADISE-FLYCATCHER. (c,ec Afr)
  ___*T. (r.) bannermani.* BANNERMAN'S PARADISE-FLYCATCHER. (Angola)

❑ *Terpsiphone viridis.* AFRICAN PARADISE-FLYCATCHER. (Afr reg). . . . . _____
   ___*T. (v.) viridis.* AFRICAN PARADISE-FLYCATCHER. (n,c Afr reg)
   ___*T. (v.) plumbeiceps.* GREY-HEADED PARADISE-FLYCATCHER. (s Afr)

❑ *Terpsiphone atrochalybeia.* SAO TOME PARADISE-FLYCATCHER. (ST). _____

❑ *Terpsiphone mutata.* MADAGASCAR PARADISE-FLYC. (Com, Mad). . . . _____

❑ *Terpsiphone corvina.* SEYCHELLES PARADISE-FLYCATCHER. (Seyc). . . _____

❑ *Terpsiphone bourbonnensis.* MASCARENE PARADISE-FLYC. (Maur). . . _____

❑ *Terpsiphone paradisi.* ASIAN PARADISE-FLYC. (s,se Asia; ◊-Indon). . . _____

❑ *Terpsiphone atrocaudata.* JAPANESE PARADISE-FLYC. (e Asia-n Phil). _____

❑ *Terpsiphone cinnamomea.* RUFOUS PARADISE-FLYCATCHER. (Phil). . . _____
   ___*T. (c.) unirufa.* LUZON PARADISE-FLYCATCHER. (n,c Phil)
   ___*T. (c.) cinnamomea.* RUFOUS PARADISE-FLYCATCHER. (sw,s Phil)
   ___*T. (c.) talautensis.* TALAUD PARADISE-FLYCATCHER. (Talaud)

❑ *Terpsiphone cyanescens.* BLUE PARADISE-FLYCATCHER. (sw Phil). . . . _____

❑ *Chasiempis sandwichensis.* ELEPAIO. (mts Haw Is). . . . . _____

❑ *Pomarea dimidiata.* RAROTONGA MONARCH. (sw Cook). . . . . _____

❑ *Pomarea nigra.* TAHITI MONARCH. (mts Tahiti). . . . . _____

❑ *Pomarea iphis.* IPHIS MONARCH. (n Marq). _____

❑ *Pomarea mendozae.* MARQUESAN MONARCH. (c,s Marq). . . . . _____

❑ *Pomarea whitneyi.* FATUHIVA MONARCH. (s Marq). . . . . _____

❑ *Mayrornis versicolor.* OGEA MONARCH. (se Fiji). . . . . _____

❑ *Mayrornis lessoni.* SLATY MONARCH. (Fiji). _____

❑ *Mayrornis schistaceus.* VANIKORO MONARCH. (Santa Cruz). . . . . _____

❑ *Neolalage banksiana.* BUFF-BELLIED MONARCH. (Vanu). . . . . _____

❑ *Clytorhynchus pachycephaloides.* SOUTHERN SHRIKEBILL. (sw Pac) . _____

❑ *Clytorhynchus vitiensis.* FIJI SHRIKEBILL. (Samoa, Fiji, Tonga). . . . . . _____

❑ *Clytorhynchus nigrogularis.* BLACK-THROATED S. (Fiji, Santa Cruz) . _____

❑ *Clytorhynchus hamlini.* RENNELL SHRIKEBILL. (se Solom). . . . . _____

❑ *Metabolus rugensis.* TRUK MONARCH. (e Carol). . . . . _____

❑ *Monarcha axillaris.* BLACK MONARCH. (mts NG). . . . . _____

❑ *Monarcha rubiensis.* RUFOUS MONARCH. (n,sw NG). . . . . _____

❑ *Monarcha cinerascens.* ISLAND MONARCH. (Wall-Solom). . . . . _____

❑ *Monarcha frater.* BLACK-WINGED MONARCH. (NG, ne Aust). . . . . _____
   ___*M. (f.) frater.* BLACK-WINGED MONARCH. (mts NG)
   ___*M. (f.) canescens.* PEARLY MONARCH. (ne Aust)

❑ *Monarcha melanopsis.* BLACK-FACED MONARCH. (e Aust). . . . . _____

❑ *Monarcha erythrostictus.* BOUGAINVILLE MONARCH. (nw Solom). . . . _____

❏ *Monarcha castaneiventris.* CHESTNUT-BELLIED MONARCH. (Solom). . _____

❏ *Monarcha richardsii.* WHITE-CAPPED MONARCH. (c Solom). . . . . _____

❏ *Monarcha pileatus.* WHITE-NAPED MONARCH. (Moluc). . . . . _____

❏ *Monarcha castus.* LOETOE MONARCH. (Tanim). . . . . _____

❏ *Monarcha leucotis.* WHITE-EARED MONARCH. (ne Aust). . . . . _____

❏ *Monarcha guttulus.* SPOT-WINGED MONARCH. (Aru-NG). . . . . _____

❏ *Monarcha mundus.* BLACK-BIBBED MONARCH. (L Sunda). . . . . _____

❏ *Monarcha trivirgatus.* SPECTACLED MONARCH. (Wall-s NG, ne Aust). _____

❏ *Monarcha sacerdotum.* FLORES MONARCH. (Flores). . . . . _____

❏ *Monarcha everetti.* WHITE-TIPPED MONARCH. (sw Wall). . . . . _____

❏ *Monarcha loricatus.* BLACK-TIPPED MONARCH. (s Moluc). . . . . _____

❏ *Monarcha boanensis.* BLACK-CHINNED MONARCH. (s Moluc). . . . . . . _____

❏ *Monarcha leucurus.* WHITE-TAILED MONARCH. (Kai). . . . . _____

❏ *Monarcha julianae.* BLACK-BACKED MONARCH. (w Pap). . . . . _____

❏ *Monarcha manadensis.* HOODED MONARCH. (NG). . . . . _____

❏ *Monarcha brehmii.* BIAK MONARCH. (nw NG). . . . . _____

❏ *Monarcha infelix.* MANUS MONARCH. (n Bism). . . . . _____

❏ *Monarcha menckei.* WHITE-BREASTED MONARCH. (n Bism). . . . . _____

❏ *Monarcha verticalis.* BLACK-TAILED MONARCH. (Bism). . . . . _____
    ___*M. (v.) verticalis.* BLACK-TAILED MONARCH. (sp)
    ___*M. (v.) ateralbus.* DJAUL MONARCH. (ec Bism)

❏ *Monarcha barbatus.* BLACK-AND-WHITE MONARCH. (Solom). . . . . . . _____

❏ *Monarcha browni.* KULAMBANGRA MONARCH. (wc Solom). . . . . _____

❏ *Monarcha viduus.* WHITE-COLLARED MONARCH. (s Solom). . . . . _____

❏ *Monarcha godeffroyi.* YAP MONARCH. (nw Carol). . . . . _____

❏ *Monarcha takatsukasae.* TINIAN MONARCH. (Mari). . . . . _____

❏ *Monarcha chrysomela.* GOLDEN MONARCH. (Aru-Bism). . . . . _____

❏ *Arses telescophthalmus.* FRILLED MONARCH. (Aru-NG, ne Aust). . . . . _____
    ___*A. (t.) telescophthalmus.* FRILLED MONARCH. (Aru-NG)
    ___*A. (t.) lorealis.* FRILL-NECKED MONARCH. (ne Aust)

❏ *Arses insularis.* RUFOUS-COLLARED MONARCH. (n NG). . . . . _____

❏ *Arses kaupi.* PIED MONARCH. (ne Aust). . . . . _____

❏ *Myiagra freycineti.* GUAM FLYCATCHER. (s Mari). . . . . _____

❏ *Myiagra erythrops.* MANGROVE FLYCATCHER. (Palau). . . . . _____

❏ *Myiagra oceanica.* OCEANIC FLYCATCHER. (w Carol). . . . . _____

❏ *Myiagra pluto.* POHNPEI FLYCATCHER. (e Carol). . . . . _____

❏ *Myiagra atra.* BIAK FLYCATCHER. (nw NG)..................... _____

❏ *Myiagra galeata.* DARK-GREY FLYCATCHER. (Moluc, Kai)......... _____

❏ *Myiagra rubecula.* LEADEN FLYCATCHER. (ne,s NG, n,e Aust)...... _____

❏ *Myiagra ferrocyanea.* STEEL-BLUE FLYCATCHER. (Solom)......... _____

❏ *Myiagra cervinicauda.* OCHRE-HEADED FLYCATCHER. (s Solom)..... _____

❏ *Myiagra caledonica.* MELANESIAN FLYCATCHER. (s Solom-Loy)..... _____

❏ *Myiagra vanikorensis.* VANIKORO FLYCATCHER. (Fiji, Santa Cruz)... _____

❏ *Myiagra albiventris.* SAMOAN FLYCATCHER. (w Samoa)........... _____

❏ *Myiagra azureocapilla.* BLUE-CRESTED FLYCATCHER. (mts Fiji)...... _____

❏ *Myiagra ruficollis.* BROAD-BILLED FLYCATCHER. (Wall-s NG, n Aust). _____

❏ *Myiagra cyanoleuca.* SATIN FLYCATCHER. (se Aust).............. _____

❏ *Myiagra inquieta.* RESTLESS FLYCATCHER. (sc NG, Aust).......... _____
   ___*M. (i.) nana.* PAPERBARK FLYCATCHER. (sc NG, n Aust)
   ___*M. (i.) inquieta.* RESTLESS FLYCATCHER. (e,se,sw Aust)

❏ *Myiagra alecto.* SHINING FLYCATCHER. (n Moluc-Bism, n Aust)...... _____

❏ *Myiagra hebetior.* DULL FLYCATCHER. (Bism).................. _____

❏ *Lamprolia victoriae.* SILKTAIL. (mts Fiji)..................... _____

❏ *Machaerirhynchus flaviventer.* YELLOW-BREASTED BOATBILL. (NG reg)_____

❏ *Machaerirhynchus nigripectus.* BLACK-BREASTED BOATBILL. (NG).. _____

❏ *Grallina cyanoleuca.* MAGPIE-LARK. (sc NG, Aust; ◊-s Indon)...... _____

❏ *Grallina bruijni.* TORRENT-LARK. (mts NG)................... _____

Subfamily Aegithininae [1/4]

❏ *Aegithina tiphia.* COMMON IORA. (s Asia-sw Phil)............... _____

❏ *Aegithina nigrolutea.* WHITE-TAILED IORA. (s Asia)............. _____

❏ *Aegithina viridissima.* GREEN IORA. (se Asia).................. _____

❏ *Aegithina lafresnayei.* GREAT IORA. (se Asia).................. _____

Subfamily Malaconotinae [27/107]
Tribe Malaconotini [8/49]

❏ *Lanioturdus torquatus.* CHATSHRIKE. (sw Afr).................. _____

❏ *Nilaus afer.* BRUBRU. (Afr)................................ _____
   ___*N. (a.) afer.* NORTHERN BRUBRU. (w,nc,ne Afr)
   ___*N. (a.) nigritemporalis.* BLACK-BROWED BRUBRU. (se Afr)
   ___*N. (a.) affinis.* ANGOLA BRUBRU. (cw Afr)
   ___*N. (a.) brubru.* SOUTHERN BRUBRU. (s Afr)

❏ *Dryoscopus gambensis.* NORTHERN PUFFBACK. (mts w,c Afr)....... _____

❏ *Dryoscopus pringlii.* PRINGLE'S PUFFBACK. (ne Afr)............. _____

❑ *Dryoscopus cubla.* BLACK-BACKED PUFFBACK. (c,e,s Afr)........... _____
   ___*D. (c.) cubla.* BLACK-BACKED PUFFBACK. (c,s Afr)
   ___*D. (c.) affinis.* ZANZIBAR PUFFBACK. (e Afr)

❑ *Dryoscopus senegalensis.* RED-EYED PUFFBACK. (c Afr)........... _____

❑ *Dryoscopus angolensis.* PINK-FOOTED PUFFBACK. (c,e Afr)......... _____

❑ *Dryoscopus sabini.* LARGE-BILLED PUFFBACK. (w,c Afr)........... _____

❑ *Tchagra minuta.* MARSH TCHAGRA. (w,c Afr)................. _____

❑ *Tchagra anchietae.* ANCHIETA'S TCHAGRA. (c Afr)............. _____

❑ *Tchagra senegala.* BLACK-CROWNED TCHAGRA. (Afr reg).......... _____
   ___*T. (s.) cucullata.* MOROCCAN TCHAGRA. (nw Afr)
   ___*T. (s.) senegala.* BLACK-CROWNED TCHAGRA. (sp)

❑ *Tchagra australis.* BROWN-CROWNED TCHAGRA. (Afr)............ _____
   ___*T. (a.) australis.* BROWN-CROWNED TCHAGRA. (sp)
   ___*T. (a.) souzae.* SOUZA'S TCHAGRA. (sc Afr)

❑ *Tchagra jamesi.* THREE-STREAKED TCHAGRA. (ne Afr)............ _____

❑ *Tchagra tchagra.* SOUTHERN TCHAGRA. (s Afr)................ _____

❑ *Laniarius ruficeps.* RED-NAPED BUSHSHRIKE. (ne Afr)........... _____
   ___*L. (r.) ruficeps.* RED-CROWNED BUSHSHRIKE. (nw Som)
   ___*L. (r.) rufinuchalis.* RED-NAPED BUSHSHRIKE. (sp)

❑ *Laniarius luehderi.* LUEHDER'S BUSHSHRIKE. (c Afr)............. _____

❑ *Laniarius brauni.* ORANGE-BREASTED BUSHSHRIKE. (nw Ang)....... _____

❑ *Laniarius amboinensis.* GABELA BUSHSHRIKE. (cw Ang).......... _____

❑ *Laniarius liberatus.* BULO BURTI BOUBOU. (c Som)............. _____

❑ *Laniarius turatii.* TURATI'S BOUBOU. (w Afr)................ _____

❑ *Laniarius aethiopicus.* TROPICAL BOUBOU. (Afr)............... _____

❑ *Laniarius bicolor.* GABON BOUBOU. (wc Afr)................. _____

❑ *Laniarius ferrugineus.* SOUTHERN BOUBOU. (s Afr)............. _____

❑ *Laniarius barbarus.* COMMON GONOLEK. (w Afr)............... _____
   ___*L. (b.) barbarus.* COMMON GONOLEK. (sp)
   ___*L. (b.) helenae.* SIERRA LEONE GONOLEK. (SL)

❑ *Laniarius erythrogaster.* BLACK-HEADED GONOLEK. (c Afr)........ _____

❑ *Laniarius atrococcineus.* CRIMSON-BREASTED GONOLEK. (s Afr)..... _____

❑ *Laniarius mufumbiri.* PAPYRUS GONOLEK. (ec Afr)............. _____

❑ *Laniarius atroflavus.* YELLOW-BREASTED BOUBOU. (mts wc Afr)..... _____

❑ *Laniarius funebris.* SLATE-COLORED BOUBOU. (ne Afr)........... _____

❑ *Laniarius leucorhynchus.* SOOTY BOUBOU. (w,c Afr)............ _____

❑ *Laniarius poensis.* MOUNTAIN BOUBOU. (mts c Afr)............. _____

❑ *Laniarius fuelleborni.* FUELLEBORN'S BOUBOU. (mts ce Afr)....... _____

❏ *Rhodophoneus cruentus.* ROSY-PATCHED BUSHSHRIKE. (ne,ce Afr)... _____
   ___*R. (c.) cruentus.* ROSY-PATCHED BUSHSHRIKE. (ne Afr)
   ___*R. (c.) cathemagmenus.* TSAVO BUSHSHRIKE. (ce Afr)

❏ *Telophorus zeylonus.* BOKMAKIERIE BUSHSHRIKE. (s Afr).......... _____

❏ *Telophorus bocagei.* GREY-GREEN BUSHSHRIKE. (c Afr)........... _____

❏ *Telophorus sulfureopectus.* SULPHUR-BREASTED BUSHSHRIKE. (Afr) . _____

❏ *Telophorus olivaceus.* OLIVE BUSHSHRIKE. (se Afr)............. _____

❏ *Telophorus multicolor.* MANY-COLORED BUSHSHRIKE. (w,c Afr)..... _____

❏ *Telophorus nigrifrons.* BLACK-FRONTED BUSHSHRIKE. (mts e Afr).... _____

❏ *Telophorus kupeensis.* SERLE'S BUSHSHRIKE. (mts sw Camer)...... _____

❏ *Telophorus viridis.* PERRIN'S BUSHSHRIKE. (wc,c Afr)............ _____

❏ *Telophorus dohertyi.* DOHERTY'S BUSHSHRIKE. (mts ec Afr)........ _____

❏ *Telophorus quadricolor.* FOUR-COLORED BUSHSHRIKE. (e,se Afr)..... _____

❏ *Malaconotus cruentus.* FIERY-BREASTED BUSHSHRIKE. (w,c Afr)..... _____

❏ *Malaconotus lagdeni.* LAGDEN'S BUSHSHRIKE. (w,c Afr)........... _____

❏ *Malaconotus gladiator.* GREEN-BREASTED BUSHSHRIKE. (mts wc Afr). _____

❏ *Malaconotus blanchoti.* GREY-HEADED BUSHSHRIKE. (Afr)......... _____

❏ *Malaconotus monteiri.* MONTEIRO'S BUSHSHRIKE. (wc,ec Afr)...... _____

❏ *Malaconotus alius.* ULUGURU BUSHSHRIKE. (mts c Tanz).......... _____

Tribe Vangini [19/58]

❏ *Prionops plumatus.* WHITE HELMETSHRIKE. (Afr)............... _____
   ___*P. (p.) plumatus.* STRAIGHT-CRESTED HELMETSHRIKE. (w Afr)
   ___*P. (p.) cristatus.* CURLY-CRESTED HELMETSHRIKE. (nc,ne Afr)
   ___*P. (p.) poliocephalus.* SOUTHERN HELMETSHRIKE. (ec,s Afr)

❏ *Prionops poliolophus.* GREY-CRESTED HELMETSHRIKE. (e Afr)....... _____

❏ *Prionops alberti.* YELLOW-CRESTED HELMETSHRIKE. (mts ec Afr)..... _____

❏ *Prionops caniceps.* CHESTNUT-BELLIED HELMETSHRIKE. (w Afr)...... _____

❏ *Prionops rufiventris.* GABON HELMETSHRIKE. (c Afr)............ _____

❏ *Prionops retzii.* RETZ'S HELMETSHRIKE. (c Afr)................ _____

❏ *Prionops gabela.* ANGOLA HELMETSHRIKE. (wc Ang)............. _____

❏ *Prionops scopifrons.* CHESTNUT-FRONTED HELMETSHRIKE. (e Afr).... _____

❏ *Bias flammulatus.* AFRICAN SHRIKE-FLYCATCHER. (w,c Afr)....... _____

❏ *Bias musicus.* BLACK-AND-WHITE SHRIKE-FLYCATCHER. (w,c,se Afr) . _____

❏ *Pseudobias wardi.* WARD'S SHRIKE-FLYCATCHER. (e Mad)......... _____

❏ *Batis diops.* RUWENZORI BATIS. (mts ec Afr)................... _____

❏ *Batis margaritae.* BOULTON'S BATIS. (mts wc Afr)............... _____

❏ *Batis mixta.* SHORT-TAILED BATIS. (e,se Afr)..................... _____
   ___*B. (m.) ultima.* SOKOKE BATIS. (se Kenya)
   ___*B. (m.) mixta.* SHORT-TAILED BATIS. (se Afr)

❏ *Batis reichenowi.* REICHENOW'S BATIS. (se Tanz)............... _____

❏ *Batis dimorpha.* MALAWI BATIS. (mts ce Afr).................... _____

❏ *Batis capensis.* CAPE BATIS. (s Afr)........................... _____

❏ *Batis fratrum.* ZULULAND BATIS. (se Afr)...................... _____

❏ *Batis molitor.* CHINSPOT BATIS. (e,s Afr)...................... _____

❏ *Batis soror.* PALE BATIS. (e Afr).............................. _____

❏ *Batis pririt.* PRIRIT BATIS. (sw Afr)........................... _____

❏ *Batis senegalensis.* SENEGAL BATIS. (w Afr).................... _____

❏ *Batis orientalis.* GREY-HEADED BATIS. (ne Afr)................. _____

❏ *Batis minor.* BLACK-HEADED BATIS. (c,e Afr)................... _____

❏ *Batis perkeo.* PYGMY BATIS. (ne Afr).......................... _____

❏ *Batis minima.* VERREAUX'S BATIS. (wc Afr)..................... _____

❏ *Batis ituriensis.* ITURI BATIS. (n,e Zaire)...................... _____

❏ *Batis occultus.* WEST AFRICAN BATIS. (w Afr)................. _____

❏ *Batis poensis.* FERNANDO PO BATIS. (Bioko)................... _____

❏ *Batis minulla.* ANGOLA BATIS. (cw Afr)....................... _____

❏ *Platysteira cyanea.* BROWN-THROATED WATTLE-EYE. (w,c Afr)...... _____

❏ *Platysteira laticincta.* BANDED WATTLE-EYE. (mts s Camer)........ _____

❏ *Platysteira albifrons.* WHITE-FRONTED WATTLE-EYE. (w Ang)...... _____

❏ *Platysteira peltata.* BLACK-THROATED WATTLE-EYE. (c,e,se Afr)..... _____

❏ *Platysteira castanea.* CHESTNUT WATTLE-EYE. (w,c Afr)........... _____

❏ *Platysteira tonsa.* WHITE-SPOTTED WATTLE-EYE. (c Afr)........... _____

❏ *Platysteira blissetti.* RED-CHEEKED WATTLE-EYE. (w Afr).......... _____

❏ *Platysteira chalybea.* BLACK-NECKED WATTLE-EYE. (wc Afr)....... _____

❏ *Platysteira jamesoni.* JAMESON'S WATTLE-EYE. (c Afr)............ _____

❏ *Platysteira concreta.* YELLOW-BELLIED WATTLE-EYE. (w,c Afr)...... _____
   ___*P. (c.) concreta.* YELLOW-BELLIED WATTLE-EYE. (sp)
   ___*P. (c.) kungwensis.* KUNGWE WATTLE-EYE. (mts w Tanz)

❏ *Philentoma pyrhopterum.* RUFOUS-WINGED PHILENTOMA. (se Asia)... _____

❏ *Philentoma velatum.* MAROON-BREASTED PHILENTOMA. (se Asia).... _____

❏ *Tephrodornis gularis.* LARGE WOODSHRIKE. (s,se Asia)............ _____

❏ *Tephrodornis pondicerianus.* COMMON WOODSHRIKE. (s,se Asia).... _____

❏ *Calicalicus madagascariensis.* RED-TAILED VANGA. (w,n,e Mad)..... _____

❑ *Schetba rufa.* RUFOUS VANGA. (w,n Mad)...................... _____

❑ *Vanga curvirostris.* HOOK-BILLED VANGA. (Mad)............... _____

❑ *Xenopirostris xenopirostris.* LAFRESNAYE'S VANGA. (sw,s Mad)..... _____

❑ *Xenopirostris damii.* VAN DAM'S VANGA. (nw Mad)............. _____

❑ *Xenopirostris polleni.* POLLEN'S VANGA. (nw,e Mad)............ _____

❑ *Falculea palliata.* SICKLE-BILLED VANGA. (w,s Mad)............ _____

❑ *Artamella viridis.* WHITE-HEADED VANGA. (Mad)............... _____

❑ *Leptopterus chabert.* CHABERT'S VANGA. (Mad)................ _____

❑ *Cyanolanius madagascarinus.* BLUE VANGA. (Com, Mad)......... _____

❑ *Oriolia bernieri.* BERNIER'S VANGA. (n,e Mad)................. _____

❑ *Euryceros prevostii.* HELMET VANGA. (ne Mad)................ _____

❑ *Tylas eduardi.* TYLAS VANGA. (cw,e Mad).................... _____

❑ *Hypositta corallirostris.* NUTHATCH VANGA. (e Mad)............ _____

Family **Callaeatidae** [3/3]

❑ *Callaeas cinerea.* KOKAKO. (NZ)............................ _____
  ___*C. (c.) wilsoni.* NORTH ISLAND KOKAKO. (n NZ)
  ___*C. (c.) cinerea.* SOUTH ISLAND KOKAKO. (s NZ)

❑ *Philesturnus carunculatus.* SADDLEBACK. (n NZ)................ _____

  Heteralocha acutirostris. HUIA. (†mts n NZ)................... _____

Parvorder *Incertae sedis* [2/4]
Family **Picathartidae** [2/4]

❑ *Chaetops frenatus.* RUFOUS ROCK-JUMPER. (sw S Afr)............ _____

❑ *Chaetops aurantius.* ORANGE-BREASTED ROCK-JUMPER. (e S Afr).... _____

❑ *Picathartes gymnocephalus.* WHITE-NECKED ROCKFOWL. (w Afr).... _____

❑ *Picathartes oreas.* GREY-NECKED ROCKFOWL. (w Afr)............ _____

Parvorder PASSERIDA [646/3473]
Superfamily MUSCICAPOIDEA [113/613]
Family **Bombycillidae** [5/8]
Tribe Dulini [1/1]

❑ *Dulus dominicus.* PALMCHAT. (Hisp)......................... _____

Tribe Ptilogonatini [3/4]

❑ *Ptilogonys cinereus.* GREY SILKY-FLYCATCHER. (mts Mex)......... _____

❑ *Ptilogonys caudatus.* LONG-TAILED SILKY-FLYCATCHER. (mts s CA) . _____

❑ *Phainopepla nitens.* PHAINOPEPLA. (sw US, n,c Mex)............ _____

❑ *Phainoptila melanoxantha.* BLACK-AND-YELLOW SILKY-FLYC. (s CA)._____

Tribe Bombycillini [1/3]

❑ *Bombycilla garrulus.* BOHEMIAN WAXWING. (n Hol; ◊-Medit, c US) . _____

❑ *Bombycilla japonica.* JAPANESE WAXWING. (e Asia). . . . . _____

❑ *Bombycilla cedrorum.* CEDAR WAXWING. (NA; ◊-G Ant, n SA). . . . . . _____

Family **Cinclidae** [1/5]

❑ *Cinclus cinclus.* WHITE-THROATED DIPPER. (mts Palea). . . . . _____

❑ *Cinclus pallasii.* BROWN DIPPER. (mts Asia). . . . . _____

❑ *Cinclus mexicanus.* AMERICAN DIPPER. (mts w NA, MA). . . . . _____

❑ *Cinclus leucocephalus.* WHITE-CAPPED DIPPER. (mts SA). . . . . _____
   ___*C. (l.) leuconotus.* WHITE-BACKED DIPPER. (w SA)
   ___*C. (l.) leucocephalus.* WHITE-CAPPED DIPPER. (sw SA)

❑ *Cinclus schulzi.* RUFOUS-THROATED DIPPER. (Andes sw SA). . . . . _____

Family **Muscicapidae** [69/452]
Subfamily Turdinae [21/179]

❑ *Neocossyphus finschii.* FINSCH'S FLYCATCHER-THRUSH. (w Afr). . . . . _____

❑ *Neocossyphus fraseri.* RUFOUS FLYCATCHER-THRUSH. (c Afr). . . . . . . _____

❑ *Neocossyphus rufus.* RED-TAILED ANT-THRUSH. (c,e Afr). . . . . _____

❑ *Neocossyphus poensis.* WHITE-TAILED ANT-THRUSH. (w,c Afr). . . . . . _____

❑ *Pseudocossyphus sharpei.* FOREST ROCK-THRUSH. (Mad). . . . . _____

❑ *Pseudocossyphus bensoni.* BENSON'S ROCK-THRUSH. (sc Mad). . . . . . _____

❑ *Pseudocossyphus imerinus.* LITTORAL ROCK-THRUSH. (sw,s Mad). . . . _____

❑ *Monticola rupestris.* CAPE ROCK-THRUSH. (mts s Afr). . . . . _____

❑ *Monticola explorator.* SENTINEL ROCK-THRUSH. (s,e S Afr). . . . . _____

❑ *Monticola brevipes.* SHORT-TOED ROCK-THRUSH. (s Afr). . . . . _____

❑ *Monticola pretoriae.* TRANSVAAL ROCK-THRUSH. (mts s Afr). . . . . . . _____

❑ *Monticola angolensis.* MIOMBO ROCK-THRUSH. (c Afr). . . . . _____

❑ *Monticola saxatilis.* RUFOUS-TAILED ROCK-THRUSH. (s Palea; ◊ n Afr). _____

❑ *Monticola rufocinereus.* LITTLE ROCK-THRUSH. (mts ne Afr). . . . . _____

❑ *Monticola cinclorhynchus.* BLUE-CAPPED ROCK-THRUSH. (Himal). . . . _____

❑ *Monticola gularis.* WHITE-THROATED ROCK-THRUSH. (mts ne Asia). . . _____

❑ *Monticola rufiventris.* CHESTNUT-BELLIED ROCK-THRUSH. (s Asia). . . _____

❑ *Monticola solitarius.* BLUE ROCK-THRUSH. (s Palea, s Asia; ◊-n Afr) . _____
   ___*M. (s.) solitarius.* BLUE ROCK-THRUSH. (sp)
   ___*M. (s.) philippensis.* RED-BELLIED ROCK-THRUSH. (e Asia; ◊-Indon)

❑ *Myiophonus blighi.* CEYLON WHISTLING-THRUSH. (mts Ceylon). . . . . _____

❏ *Myiophonus melanurus.* SHINY WHISTLING-THRUSH. (mts Sum). . . . . _____

❏ *Myiophonus glaucinus.* SUNDA WHISTLING-THRUSH. (G Sunda). . . . . _____
 ___*M. (g.) castaneus.* BROWN-WINGED WHISTLING-THRUSH. (Sum)
 ___*M. (g.) glaucinus.* SUNDA WHISTLING-THRUSH. (Born, Java, Bali)

❏ *Myiophonus robinsoni.* MALAYAN WHISTLING-THRUSH. (c Malaya) . _____

❏ *Myiophonus horsfieldii.* MALABAR WHISTLING-THRUSH. (w,c India) . _____

❏ *Myiophonus caeruleus.* BLUE WHISTLING-THRUSH. (s,se Asia). . . . . . _____
 ___*M. (c.) caeruleus.* BLUE WHISTLING-THRUSH. (sp)
 ___*M. (c.) flavirostris.* LARGE WHISTLING-THRUSH. (G Sunda)

❏ *Myiophonus insularis.* FORMOSAN WHISTLING-THRUSH. (mts Taiwan). _____

❏ *Geomalia heinrichi.* GEOMALIA. (mts Sulaw). . . . . _____

❏ *Zoothera schistacea.* SLATY-BACKED THRUSH. (Tanim). . . . . _____

❏ *Zoothera dumasi.* MOLUCCAN THRUSH. (s Moluc). . . . . _____
 ___*Z. (d.) dumasi.* BURU THRUSH. (Buru)
 ___*Z. (d.) joiceyi.* SERAM THRUSH. (Seram)

❏ *Zoothera interpres.* CHESTNUT-CAPPED THRUSH. (se Asia-s Phil). . . . . _____
 ___*Z. (i.) interpres.* CHESTNUT-CAPPED THRUSH. (sp)
 ___*Z. (i.) leucolaema.* ENGGANO THRUSH. (Enggano)

❏ *Zoothera erythronota.* RED-BACKED THRUSH. (Sulaw). . . . . _____

❏ *Zoothera dohertyi.* CHESTNUT-BACKED THRUSH. (L Sunda). . . . . _____

❏ *Zoothera wardii.* PIED THRUSH. (Himal n,ne India; ◊ Ceylon). . . . . _____

❏ *Zoothera cinerea.* ASHY THRUSH. (Phil). . . . . _____

❏ *Zoothera peronii.* ORANGE-BANDED THRUSH. (L Sunda). . . . . _____

❏ *Zoothera citrina.* ORANGE-HEADED THRUSH. (s,se Asia). . . . . _____

❏ *Zoothera everetti.* EVERETT'S THRUSH. (mts n Born). . . . . _____

❏ *Zoothera sibirica.* SIBERIAN THRUSH. (e Asia; ◊-se Asia, w Indon). . . . _____

❏ *Zoothera naevia.* VARIED THRUSH. (nw NA; ◊-nw Mex). . . . . _____

❏ *Zoothera pinicola.* AZTEC THRUSH. (mts w,c Mex). . . . . _____

❏ *Zoothera piaggiae.* ABYSSINIAN GROUND-THRUSH. (mts ne Afr). . . . . . _____

❏ *Zoothera tanganjicae.* KIVU GROUND-THRUSH. (mts ec Afr). . . . . _____

❏ *Zoothera crossleyi.* CROSSLEY'S GROUND-THRUSH. (mts wc Afr). . . . . _____

❏ *Zoothera gurneyi.* ORANGE GROUND-THRUSH. (e,s Afr). . . . . _____

❏ *Zoothera oberlaenderi.* OBERLAENDER'S GROUND-THRUSH. (ec Afr) . _____

❏ *Zoothera cameronensis.* BLACK-EARED GROUND-THRUSH. (c Afr). . . . _____
 ___*Z. (c.) cameronensis.* CAMEROON GROUND-THRUSH. (wc Afr)
 ___*Z. (c.) graueri.* GRAUER'S GROUND-THRUSH. (ec Afr)

❏ *Zoothera princei.* GREY GROUND-THRUSH. (w,c Afr). . . . . _____

❏ *Zoothera kibalensis.* KIBALE GROUND-THRUSH. (mts w Uganda). . . . . _____

❑ *Zoothera guttata.* SPOTTED GROUND-THRUSH. (se,s Afr). . . . . _____

❑ *Zoothera spiloptera.* SPOT-WINGED THRUSH. (mts Ceylon). . . . . _____

❑ *Zoothera andromedae.* SUNDA THRUSH. (Sum-L Sunda; Phil). . . . . . . _____

❑ *Zoothera mollissima.* PLAIN-BACKED THRUSH. (Himal; ◊-se Asia). . . . _____

❑ *Zoothera dixoni.* LONG-TAILED THRUSH. (Himal). . . . . _____

❑ *Zoothera dauma.* SCALY THRUSH. (e Eura, se Asia). . . . . _____

❑ *Zoothera major.* AMAMI THRUSH. (Ryu). _____

❑ *Zoothera horsfieldi.* HORSFIELD'S THRUSH. (mts Sum-Lombok). . . . . . _____

❑ *Zoothera machiki.* FAWN-BREASTED THRUSH. (Tanim). . . . . _____

❑ *Zoothera lunulata.* OLIVE-TAILED THRUSH. (NG-Solom, n,ne Aust). . . _____
    ___*Z. (l.) papuensis.* PAPUAN OLIVE-TAILED THRUSH. (NG-nw Solom)
    ___*Z. (l.) lunulata.* AUSTRALIAN OLIVE-TAILED THRUSH. (n,ne Aust)

❑ *Zoothera heinei.* RUSSET-TAILED THRUSH. (ne Aust). . . . . _____

❑ *Zoothera talaseae.* NEW BRITAIN THRUSH. (cs Bism, n Solom). . . . . . . _____

❑ *Zoothera margaretae.* SAN CRISTOBAL THRUSH. (mts Solom). . . . . . . _____

❑ *Zoothera monticola.* LONG-BILLED THRUSH. (Himal). . . . . _____

❑ *Zoothera marginata.* DARK-SIDED THRUSH. (Himal). . . . . _____

  Zoothera terrestris. BONIN THRUSH. (†Bonin). . . . . _____

❑ *Cataponera turdoides.* SULAWESI THRUSH. (mts Sulaw). . . . . _____

❑ *Nesocichla eremita.* TRISTAN THRUSH. (TdaC). . . . . _____

❑ *Cichlherminia lherminieri.* FOREST THRUSH. (L Ant). . . . . _____

❑ *Sialia sialis.* EASTERN BLUEBIRD. (c,e NA, MA). . . . . _____

❑ *Sialia mexicana.* WESTERN BLUEBIRD. (w NA, n,c Mex). . . . . _____

❑ *Sialia currucoides.* MOUNTAIN BLUEBIRD. (w NA; ◊-c Mex). . . . . _____

❑ *Myadestes myadestinus.* KAMAO. (mts Kauai). . . . . _____

  Myadestes oahensis. AMAUI. (†Oahu). . . . . _____

❑ *Myadestes lanaiensis.* OLOMAO. (mts Molokai). . . . . _____

❑ *Myadestes obscurus.* OMAO. (mts Hawaii). _____

❑ *Myadestes palmeri.* PUAIOHI. (Kauai). . . . . _____

❑ *Myadestes townsendi.* TOWNSEND'S SOLITAIRE. (w NA, Mex). . . . . . . _____

❑ *Myadestes occidentalis.* BROWN-BACKED SOLITAIRE. (mts n,c MA). . . _____

❑ *Myadestes elisabeth.* CUBAN SOLITAIRE. (mts w,e Cuba). . . . . _____

❑ *Myadestes genibarbis.* RUFOUS-THROATED SOLITAIRE. (W Indies). . . . _____
    ___*M. (g.) genibarbis.* RUFOUS-THROATED SOLITAIRE. (Jam-c L Ant)
    ___*M. (g.) sibilans.* ST. VINCENT SOLITAIRE. (s L Ant)

❏ *Myadestes melanops.* BLACK-FACED SOLITAIRE. (mts CR, w Pan). . . . . _____

❏ *Myadestes coloratus.* VARIED SOLITAIRE. (mts e Pan, nw Colom). . . . . _____

❏ *Myadestes ralloides.* ANDEAN SOLITAIRE. (mts w SA). . . . . _____

❏ *Myadestes unicolor.* SLATE-COLORED SOLITAIRE. (mts n,c MA). . . . . . _____

❏ *Cichlopsis leucogenys.* RUFOUS-BROWN SOLITAIRE. (w,n,se SA). . . . . . _____
  ___*C. (l.) gularis.* GUYANAN SOLITAIRE. (mts w,n SA)
  ___*C. (l.) leucogenys.* RUFOUS-BROWN SOLITAIRE. (se Braz)

❏ *Entomodestes leucotis.* WHITE-EARED SOLITAIRE. (Andes wc SA). . . . _____

❏ *Entomodestes coracinus.* BLACK SOLITAIRE. (Andes nw SA). . . . . _____

❏ *Catharus gracilirostris.* BLACK-BILLED NIGHTINGALE-THRUSH. (s CA). _____

❏ *Catharus aurantiirostris.* ORANGE-BILLED NIGHTINGALE-T. (MA-n SA) _____
  ___*C. (a.) aurantiirostris.* ORANGE-BILLED NIGHTINGALE-THRUSH. (sp)
  ___*C. (a.) griseiceps.* GREY-HEADED NIGHTINGALE-THRUSH. (s CA, nw SA)

❏ *Catharus fuscater.* SLATY-BACKED NIGHTINGALE-THRUSH. (s CA, w SA)_____
  ___*C. (f.) hellmayri.* BLACK-BACKED NIGHTINGALE-THRUSH. (CR, w Pan)
  ___*C. (f.) fuscater.* SLATY-BACKED NIGHTINGALE-THRUSH. (e Pan, w SA)

❏ *Catharus occidentalis.* RUSSET NIGHTINGALE-THRUSH. (mts Mex). . . . _____
  ___*C. (o.) olivascens.* OLIVE NIGHTINGALE-THRUSH. (nw Mex)
  ___*C. (o.) occidentalis.* RUSSET NIGHTINGALE-THRUSH. (c Mex)

❏ *Catharus frantzii.* RUDDY-CAPPED NIGHTINGALE-THRUSH. (mts MA) . _____

❏ *Catharus mexicanus.* BLACK-HEADED NIGHTINGALE-THRUSH. (MA) . _____

❏ *Catharus dryas.* SPOTTED NIGHTINGALE-THRUSH. (mts c MA, w SA) . _____

❏ *Catharus fuscescens.* VEERY. (n,c NA; ◊ SA). . . . . _____

❏ *Catharus minimus.* GREY-CHEEKED THRUSH. (ne Sib, n NA; ◊-SA). . . _____
  ___*C. (m.) minimus.* GREY-CHEEKED THRUSH. (ne Sib, n NA; ◊ SA)
  ___*C. (m.) bicknelli.* BICKNELL'S THRUSH. (ce NA; ◊ Hisp)

❏ *Catharus ustulatus.* SWAINSON'S THRUSH. (n,c NA; ◊ MA, SA). . . . . _____
  ___*C. (u.) swainsoni.* OLIVE-BACKED THRUSH. (n,c NA; ◊ SA)
  ___*C. (u.) ustulatus.* RUSSET-BACKED THRUSH. (nw NA; ◊ MA)

❏ *Catharus guttatus.* HERMIT THRUSH. (n,c NA; ◊ US, Bah). . . . . _____

❏ *Catharus mustelinus.* WOOD THRUSH. (e NA; ◊ Mex-nw SA). . . . . . . _____

❏ *Platycichla flavipes.* YELLOW-LEGGED THRUSH. (mts n,se SA). . . . . . _____

❏ *Platycichla leucops.* PALE-EYED THRUSH. (mts w SA). . . . . _____

❏ *Psophocichla litsipsirupa.* GROUNDSCRAPER THRUSH. (e,s Afr). . . . . . _____
  ___*P. (l.) simensis.* ETHIOPIAN THRUSH. (sp)
  ___*P. (l.) litsipsirupa.* GROUNDSCRAPER THRUSH. (mts Eth)

❏ *Turdus pelios.* AFRICAN THRUSH. (w,c Afr). _____
  ___*T. (p.) pelios.* AFRICAN THRUSH. (sp)
  ___*T. (p.) nigrilorum.* CAMEROON MOUNTAIN THRUSH. (mts sw CAMER)
  ___*T. (p.) poensis.* FERNANDO PO THRUSH. (Bioko)

❑ *Turdus tephronotus.* BARE-EYED THRUSH. (ne Afr). . . . . _____

❑ *Turdus libonyanus.* KURRICHANE THRUSH. (c,s Afr). . . . . _____

❑ *Turdus olivaceofuscus.* OLIVACEOUS THRUSH. (ST, Prín). . . . . _____

❑ *Turdus olivaceus.* OLIVE THRUSH. (mts e,s Afr). . . . . _____
   ___*T. (o.) abyssinicus.* ABYSSINIAN THRUSH. (e Afr)
   ___*T. (o.) ludoviciae.* SOMALI THRUSH. (n Som)
   ___*T. (o.) helleri.* TEITA THRUSH. (se Kenya)
   ___*T. (o.) oldeani.* OLDEAN'S THRUSH. (nc Tanz)
   ___*T. (o.) roehli.* ROEHL'S THRUSH. (ne Tanz)
   ___*T. (o.) swynnertoni.* SWYNNERTON'S THRUSH. (se Afr)
   ___*T. (o.) olivaceus.* CAPE THRUSH. (s Afr)

❑ *Turdus menachensis.* YEMEN THRUSH. (mts sw Arabia). . . . . _____

❑ *Turdus bewsheri.* COMORO THRUSH. (Com). _____
   ___*T. (b.) comorensis.* GRAND COMORO THRUSH. (nw Com)
   ___*T. (b.) moheliensis.* MOHELI THRUSH. (sw Com)
   ___*T. (b.) bewsheri.* ANJOUAN THRUSH. (c Com)

❑ *Turdus hortulorum.* GREY-BACKED THRUSH. (ne Asia; ◊ se Asia). . . . _____

❑ *Turdus unicolor.* TICKELL'S THRUSH. (Himal; ◊-pen India). . . . . _____

❑ *Turdus dissimilis.* BLACK-BREASTED THRUSH. (mts s,se Asia). . . . . . . _____

❑ *Turdus cardis.* JAPANESE THRUSH. (e Asia; ◊-se Asia). . . . . _____

❑ *Turdus albocinctus.* WHITE-COLLARED BLACKBIRD. (Himal). . . . . . . _____

❑ *Turdus torquatus.* RING OUZEL. (w,sw Palea; ◊-n Afr). . . . . _____

❑ *Turdus boulboul.* GREY-WINGED BLACKBIRD. (Himal). . . . . _____

❑ *Turdus merula.* EURASIAN BLACKBIRD. (Palea, India; ◆ e Aust, NZ) . _____
   ___*T. (m.) merula.* EURASIAN BLACKBIRD. (Palea; ◆ e Aust, NZ)
   ___*T. (m.) simillimus.* NILGIRI BLACKBIRD. (mts pen India)

❑ *Turdus poliocephalus.* ISLAND THRUSH. (Chris, se Asia-s Melan). . . . . _____
   ___*T. (p.) poliocephalus.* ISLAND THRUSH. (sp)
   ___*T. (p.) papuensis.* NEW GUINEA BLACKBIRD. (mts NG)
   ___*T. (p.) canescens.* GOODENOUGH BLACKBIRD. (is se NG)
   ___*T. (p.) xanthopus.* VINOUS-TINTED BLACKBIRD. (N Cal)

❑ *Turdus rubrocanus.* CHESTNUT THRUSH. (Himal). . . . . _____

❑ *Turdus kessleri.* WHITE-BACKED THRUSH. (Himal w China). . . . . _____

❑ *Turdus feae.* GREY-SIDED THRUSH. (mts ne China; ◊ se Asia). . . . . . . _____

❑ *Turdus obscurus.* EYEBROWED THRUSH. (e Asia; ◊-Indon, w Micro) . _____

❑ *Turdus pallidus.* PALE THRUSH. (e Asia; ◊ se Asia). . . . . _____

❑ *Turdus chrysolaus.* BROWN-HEADED THRUSH. (e Asia; ◊-Phil). . . . . . _____

❑ *Turdus celaenops.* IZU THRUSH. (is s Japan). . . . . _____

❑ *Turdus ruficollis.* DARK-THROATED THRUSH. (nc,ec Eura; ◊ s Asia). . . _____
   ___*T. (r.) atrogularis.* BLACK-THROATED THRUSH. (nc Eura)
   ___*T. (r.) ruficollis.* RED-THROATED THRUSH. (ec Eura)

❑ *Turdus naumanni.* DUSKY THRUSH. (n,c,se Sib; ◊ s Asia, Japan). . . . . _____
   ___*T. (n.) eunomus.* DUSKY THRUSH. (n Sib)
   ___*T. (n.) naumanni.* NAUMANN'S THRUSH. (c,se Sib)

❑ *Turdus pilaris.* FIELDFARE. (Palea; ◊-n Afr). . . . . _____

❑ *Turdus iliacus.* REDWING. (Palea; ◊-n Afr). . . . . _____

❑ *Turdus philomelos.* SONG THRUSH. (Palea; ◊-n Afr; ♦ se Aust, NZ) . _____

❑ *Turdus mupinensis.* CHINESE THRUSH. (mts n,w,sw China). . . . . _____

❑ *Turdus viscivorus.* MISTLE THRUSH. (Palea). . . . . _____

❑ *Turdus aurantius.* WHITE-CHINNED THRUSH. (mts Jam). . . . . _____

   Turdus ravidus. GRAND CAYMAN THRUSH. (†Cay). . . . . _____

❑ *Turdus plumbeus.* RED-LEGGED THRUSH. (n,c W Indies). . . . . _____
   ___*T. (p.) plumbeus.* WESTERN RED-LEGGED THRUSH. (n Bah, Cuba, Cay)
   ___*T. (p.) ardosiaceus.* EASTERN RED-LEGGED THRUSH. (Hisp-n L Ant)

❑ *Turdus chiguanco.* CHIGUANCO THRUSH. (w,sw SA). . . . . _____
   ___*T. (c.) chiguanco.* CHIGUANCO THRUSH. (w SA)
   ___*T. (c.) anthracinus.* DARK THRUSH. (Andes sw SA)

❑ *Turdus nigrescens.* SOOTY THRUSH. (mts CR, w Pan), , ... _____

❑ *Turdus fuscater.* GREAT THRUSH. (mts w SA). . . . . _____
   ___*T. (f.) gigas.* GIANT THRUSH. (sp)
   ___*T. (f.) fuscater.* GREAT THRUSH. (wc Bol)

❑ *Turdus infuscatus.* BLACK THRUSH. (mts n,c MA). . . . . _____

❑ *Turdus serranus.* GLOSSY-BLACK THRUSH. (mts w SA). . . . . _____

❑ *Turdus nigriceps.* ANDEAN SLATY-THRUSH. (Andes w SA). . . . . _____

❑ *Turdus subalaris.* EASTERN SLATY-THRUSH. (e,se SA). . . . . _____

❑ *Turdus reevei.* PLUMBEOUS-BACKED THRUSH. (cw SA). . . . . _____

❑ *Turdus olivater.* BLACK-HOODED THRUSH. (mts n SA). . . . . _____
   ___*T. (o.) caucae.* CAUCA THRUSH. (se Colom)
   ___*T. (o.) olivater.* BLACK-HOODED THRUSH. (sp)

❑ *Turdus maranonicus.* MARANON THRUSH. (Andes n Peru). . . . . _____

❑ *Turdus fulviventris.* CHESTNUT-BELLIED THRUSH. (mts w SA). . . . . . . _____

❑ *Turdus rufiventris.* RUFOUS-BELLIED THRUSH. (sc,e SA). . . . . _____

❑ *Turdus falcklandii.* AUSTRAL THRUSH. (s SA). . . . . _____

❑ *Turdus leucomelas.* PALE-BREASTED THRUSH. (SA). . . . . _____

❑ *Turdus amaurochalinus.* CREAMY-BELLIED THRUSH. (sc,se SA). . . . . . _____

❑ *Turdus plebejus.* AMERICAN MOUNTAIN THRUSH. (mts c,s MA). . . . . . _____

❑ *Turdus ignobilis.* BLACK-BILLED THRUSH. (w Amaz). . . . . _____

❑ *Turdus lawrencii.* LAWRENCE'S THRUSH. (w Amaz). . . . . _____

❑ *Turdus obsoletus.* PALE-VENTED THRUSH. (s CA, nw SA). . . . . _____

❑ *Turdus fumigatus.* COCOA THRUSH. (s L Ant, Amaz)............. _____
   ___*T. (f.) personus.* LESSER ANTILLEAN THRUSH. (s L Ant)
   ___*T. (f.) fumigatus.* COCOA THRUSH. (Amaz)

❑ *Turdus hauxwelli.* HAUXWELL'S THRUSH. (w Amaz).............. _____

❑ *Turdus grayi.* CLAY-COLORED THRUSH. (MA, nw SA)............. _____

❑ *Turdus nudigenis.* YELLOW-EYED THRUSH. (s L Ant, n Amaz)....... _____

❑ *Turdus maculirostris.* ECUADORIAN THRUSH. (cw SA)............ _____

❑ *Turdus haplochrous.* UNICOLORED THRUSH. (n,e Bol)............. _____

❑ *Turdus jamaicensis.* WHITE-EYED THRUSH. (Jam)................ _____

❑ *Turdus assimilis.* WHITE-THROATED THRUSH. (mts MA, nw SA)..... _____
   ___*T. (a.) assimilis.* WHITE-THROATED THRUSH. (MA)
   ___*T. (a.) daguae.* DAGUA THRUSH. (e Pan, nw SA)

❑ *Turdus albicollis.* WHITE-NECKED THRUSH. (SA)................. _____
   ___*T. (a.) phaeopygos.* GREY-FLANKED THRUSH. (Amaz)
   ___*T. (a.) paraguayensis.* PARAGUAYAN THRUSH. (sc SA)
   ___*T. (a.) albicollis.* RUFOUS-FLANKED THRUSH. (se Braz)
   ___*T. (a.) crotopezus.* WHITE-NECKED THRUSH. (e Braz)

❑ *Turdus rufopalliatus.* RUFOUS-BACKED THRUSH. (w Mex)......... _____

❑ *Turdus graysoni.* GRAYSON'S THRUSH. (Tres Marias)............. _____

❑ *Turdus swalesi.* LA SELLE THRUSH. (mts Hisp)................. _____

❑ *Turdus migratorius.* AMERICAN ROBIN. (NA, Mex; ◊-W Indies)...... _____
   ___*T. (m.) migratorius.* AMERICAN ROBIN. (sp)
   ___*T. (m.) confinis.* SAN LUCAS ROBIN. (s Baja)

❑ *Turdus rufitorques.* RUFOUS-COLLARED ROBIN. (mts c MA)........ _____

❑ *Chlamydochaera jefferyi.* BLACK-BREASTED FRUIT-HUNTER. (n Born). _____

❑ *Brachypteryx stellata.* GOULD'S SHORTWING. (Himal)............ _____

❑ *Brachypteryx hyperythra.* RUSTY-BELLIED SHORTWING. (ne India).... _____

❑ *Brachypteryx major.* WHITE-BELLIED SHORTWING. (sw pen India).... _____

❑ *Brachypteryx leucophrys.* LESSER SHORTWING. (s,se Asia, L Sunda) . _____
   ___*B. (l.) carolinae.* CAROLINE'S SHORTWING. (s,se Asia)
   ___*B. (l.) leucophrys.* LESSER SHORTWING. (Sunda)

❑ *Brachypteryx montana.* WHITE-BROWED SHORTWING. (s,se Asia-Phil). _____
   ___*B. (m.) cruralis.* INDIGO-BLUE SHORTWING. (s,se Asia)
   ___*B. (m.) montana.* WHITE-BROWED SHORTWING. (G Sunda-Phil)

❑ *Heinrichia calligyna.* GREAT SHORTWING. (mts Sulaw)........... _____

❑ *Alethe poliocephala.* BROWN-CHESTED ALETHE. (w,c Afr)......... _____

❑ *Alethe poliophrys.* RED-THROATED ALETHE. (mts ec Afr).......... _____

❑ *Alethe fuelleborni.* WHITE-CHESTED ALETHE. (mts ce Afr)......... _____

❑ *Alethe choloensis.* CHOLO ALETHE. (mts se Afr)................ _____

❑ *Alethe diademata.* WHITE-TAILED ALETHE. (w Afr). . . . . _____

❑ *Alethe castanea.* FIRE-CRESTED ALETHE. (c Afr). . . . . _____

Subfamily Muscicapinae [48/273]
Tribe Muscicapini [18/117]

❑ *Empidornis semipartitus.* SILVERBIRD. (e Afr). . . . . _____

❑ *Bradornis pallidus.* PALE FLYCATCHER. (Afr). . . . . _____
___*B. (p.) pallidus.* PALE FLYCATCHER. (sp)
___*B. (p.) bafirawari.* WAJIR FLYCATCHER. (ne Kenya)

❑ *Bradornis infuscatus.* CHAT FLYCATCHER. (s Afr). . . . . _____

❑ *Bradornis mariquensis.* MARIQUA FLYCATCHER. (s Afr). . . . . _____

❑ *Bradornis pumilus.* LITTLE GREY FLYCATCHER. (ne Afr). . . . . _____

❑ *Bradornis microrhynchus.* LARGE FLYCATCHER. (ne Afr). . . . . _____

❑ *Dioptrornis chocolatinus.* ABYSSINIAN SLATY-FLYCATCHER. (w,c Eth). _____

❑ *Dioptrornis fischeri.* WHITE-EYED SLATY-FLYCATCHER. (mts e Afr). . . _____

❑ *Dioptrornis brunneus.* ANGOLA SLATY-FLYCATCHER. (mts w Ang). . . _____

❑ *Melaenornis edolioides.* NORTHERN BLACK-FLYCATCHER. (subsah Afr). _____

❑ *Melaenornis pammelaina.* SOUTHERN BLACK-FLYCATCHER. (s,e Afr). . _____

❑ *Melaenornis ardesiacus.* YELLOW-EYED BLACK-FLYCATCHER. (ec Afr). _____

❑ *Melaenornis annamarulae.* WEST AFRICAN BLACK-FLYC. (w Afr). . . . _____

❑ *Fraseria ocreata.* AFRICAN FOREST-FLYCATCHER. (w,c Afr). . . . . _____

❑ *Fraseria cinerascens.* WHITE-BROWED FOREST-FLYCATCHER. (w,c Afr)_____

❑ *Sigelus silens.* FISCAL FLYCATCHER. (s Afr). _____

❑ *Rhinomyias addita.* STREAKY-BREASTED JUNGLE-FLYCATCHER. (Buru) _____

❑ *Rhinomyias oscillans.* RUSSET-BACKED JUNGLE-FLYCATCHER. (Flores) _____

❑ *Rhinomyias brunneata.* BROWN-CHESTED JUNGLE-FLYCATCHER. (s Asia)_____

❑ *Rhinomyias olivacea.* FULVOUS-CHESTED JUNGLE-FLYC. (s,se Asia). . . _____

❑ *Rhinomyias umbratilis.* GREY-CHESTED JUNGLE-FLYCATCHER. (se Asia)_____

❑ *Rhinomyias ruficauda.* RUFOUS-TAILED JUNGLE-FLYC. (n Born-Phil) . _____

❑ *Rhinomyias colonus.* HENNA-TAILED JUNGLE-FLYCATCHER. (e Sulaw). _____

❑ *Rhinomyias gularis.* EYEBROWED JUNGLE-FLYCATCHER. (n Born). . . . _____

❑ *Rhinomyias insignis.* WHITE-BROWED JUNGLE-FLYCATCHER. (n Phil) . _____

❑ *Rhinomyias albigularis.* WHITE-THROATED JUNGLE-FLYC. (sc Phil). . . _____

❑ *Rhinomyias goodfellowi.* SLATY-BACKED JUNGLE-FLYCATCHER. (s Phil) _____

❑ *Muscicapa striata.* SPOTTED FLYCATCHER. (Palea; ◊ Afr). . . . . _____

❑ *Muscicapa gambagae.* GAMBAGA FLYCATCHER. (subsah Afr reg). . . . . _____

❏ *Muscicapa griseisticta*. GREY-STREAKED FLYCATCHER. (e Asia; ◊-Indon)_____

❏ *Muscicapa sibirica*. DARK-SIDED FLYC. (s,e Asia; s,se Asia, Phil). . . . . _____
   ___*M. (s.) cacabata*. HIMALAYAN FLYCATCHER. (Himal; ◊ India)
   ___*M. (s.) sibirica*. DARK-SIDED FLYCATCHER. (e Asia; ◊ se Asia, Phil)

❏ *Muscicapa dauurica*. ASIAN BROWN FLYCATCHER. (s,e,se Asia; ◊-Phil)_____
   ___*M. (d.) dauurica*. ASIAN BROWN FLYCATCHER. (s,e Asia; ◊-se Asia, Phil)
   ___*M. (d.) williamsoni*. BROWN-STREAKED FLYCATCHER. (se Asia)

❏ *Muscicapa randi*. ASHY-BREASTED FLYCATCHER. (n,c Phil). . . . . _____

❏ *Muscicapa segregata*. SUMBA BROWN FLYCATCHER. (Sumba). . . . . . . _____

❏ *Muscicapa ruficauda*. RUSTY-TAILED FLYCATCHER. (Himal; ◊ s India). _____

❏ *Muscicapa muttui*. BROWN-BREASTED FLYCATCHER. (s,se Asia). . . . . _____

❏ *Muscicapa ferruginea*. FERRUGINOUS FLYCATCHER. (Himal; ◊-Phil) . _____

❏ *Muscicapa ussheri*. USSHER'S FLYCATCHER. (w Afr). . . . . _____

❏ *Muscicapa infuscata*. SOOTY FLYCATCHER. (c Afr). . . . . _____

❏ *Muscicapa boehmi*. BOEHM'S FLYCATCHER. (s Afr). . . . . _____

❏ *Muscicapa aquatica*. SWAMP ALSEONAX. (w,c Afr). . . . . _____

❏ *Muscicapa olivascens*. OLIVACEOUS ALSEONAX. (w,c Afr). . . . . _____

❏ *Muscicapa lendu*. CHAPIN'S ALSEONAX. (mts ec Afr). . . . . _____

❏ *Muscicapa itombwensis*. ITOMBWE ALSEONAX. (ce Zaire). . . . . _____

❏ *Muscicapa adusta*. DUSKY ALSEONAX. (wc,e,s Afr). . . . . _____

❏ *Muscicapa epulata*. LITTLE GREY ALSEONAX. (w,c Afr). . . . . _____

❏ *Muscicapa sethsmithi*. YELLOW-FOOTED ALSEONAX. (c Afr). . . . . _____

❏ *Muscicapa comitata*. DUSKY-BLUE FLYCATCHER. (w,c Afr). . . . . _____

❏ *Muscicapa tessmanni*. TESSMANN'S FLYCATCHER. (w,c Afr). . . . . _____

❏ *Muscicapa cassini*. CASSIN'S ALSEONAX. (w,c Afr). . . . . _____

❏ *Muscicapa caerulescens*. ASHY ALSEONAX. (Afr). . . . . _____

❏ *Myioparus griseigularis*. GREY-THROATED TIT-FLYCATCHER. (c Afr) . _____

❏ *Myioparus plumbeus*. GREY TIT-FLYCATCHER. (Afr). . . . . _____

❏ *Humblotia flavirostris*. HUMBLOT'S FLYCATCHER. (Com). . . . . _____

❏ *Ficedula hypoleuca*. EUROPEAN PIED FLYCATCHER. (Palea; ◊-c Afr). . . _____

❏ *Ficedula albicollis*. COLLARED FLYCATCHER. (c,se Euro; ◊-s Afr). . . . . _____

❏ *Ficedula semitorquata*. SEMICOLLARED FLYCATCHER. (sc Eura; ◊ e Afr)_____

❏ *Ficedula zanthopygia*. YELLOW-RUMPED FLYC. (e Asia; ◊ se Asia). . . . _____

❏ *Ficedula narcissina*. NARCISSUS FLYCATCHER. (e Asia; ◊-Phil). . . . . . _____

❏ *Ficedula mugimaki*. MUGIMAKI FLYCATCHER. (e Asia; ◊-Wall, Phil) . _____

❏ *Ficedula hodgsonii*. SLATY-BACKED FLYCATCHER. (mts s Asia). . . . . . _____

❏ *Ficedula strophiata.* RUFOUS-GORGETED FLYCATCHER. (mts s Asia)... _____

❏ *Ficedula parva.* RED-BREASTED FLYCATCHER. (Eura; ◊ ne Afr, s,se Asia)_____
   ___*F. (p.) parva.* RED-BREASTED FLYCATCHER. (w Eura; ◊ ne Afr, s Asia)
   ___*F. (p.) albicilla.* RED-THROATED FLYCATCHER. (e Eura; ◊s,se Asia)

❏ *Ficedula subrubra.* KASHMIR FLYCATCHER. (n India; ◊-Ceylon)...... _____

❏ *Ficedula monileger.* WHITE-GORGETED FLYCATCHER. (s,se Asia)..... _____

❏ *Ficedula solitaris.* RUFOUS-BROWED FLYCATCHER. (mts se Asia)..... _____
   ___*F. (s.) submoniliger.* RUFOUS-BROWED FLYCATCHER. (Indoc)
   ___*F. (s.) solitaris.* MALAYSIAN FLYCATCHER. (Malay, Sum)

❏ *Ficedula hyperythra.* SNOWY-BROWED FLYCATCHER. (s Asia-Wall)... _____

❏ *Ficedula dumetoria.* RUFOUS-CHESTED FLYCATCHER. (se Asia, Wall) . _____

❏ *Ficedula rufigula.* RUFOUS-THROATED FLYCATCHER. (Sulaw)....... _____

❏ *Ficedula buruensis.* CINNAMON-CHESTED FLYCATCHER. (s Moluc, Kai)_____

❏ *Ficedula basilanica.* LITTLE SLATY FLYCATCHER. (c,s Phil)........ _____

❏ *Ficedula henrici.* DAMAR FLYCATCHER. (Damar)............... _____

❏ *Ficedula harterti.* SUMBA FLYCATCHER. (Sumba)............... _____

❏ *Ficedula platenae.* PALAWAN FLYCATCHER. (sw Phil)............ _____

❏ *Ficedula crypta.* CRYPTIC FLYCATCHER. (n,s Phil)............... _____

❏ *Ficedula bonthaina.* LOMPOBATTANG FLYCATCHER. (mts sw Sulaw) . _____

❏ *Ficedula westermanni.* LITTLE PIED FLYCATCHER. (s,se Asia, Phil)... _____

❏ *Ficedula superciliaris.* ULTRAMARINE FLYCATCHER. (Himal; ◊-se Asia) _____

❏ *Ficedula tricolor.* SLATY-BLUE FLYCATCHER. (mts s,se Asia)....... _____

❏ *Ficedula sapphira.* SAPPHIRE FLYCATCHER. (mts s,se Asia)........ _____

❏ *Ficedula nigrorufa.* BLACK-AND-RUFOUS FLYCATCHER. (sw India).... _____

❏ *Ficedula timorensis.* BLACK-BANDED FLYCATCHER. (Timor)........ _____

❏ *Cyanoptila cyanomelana.* BLUE-AND-WHITE FLYCATCHER. (e,se Asia). _____

❏ *Eumyias thalassina.* VERDITER FLYCATCHER. (s Asia; ◊-se Asia)..... _____

❏ *Eumyias sordida.* DULL-BLUE FLYCATCHER. (mts Ceylon)......... _____

❏ *Eumyias panayensis.* ISLAND FLYCATCHER. (Sulaw, Phil, s Moluc)... _____

❏ *Eumyias albicaudata.* NILGIRI FLYCATCHER. (mts sw India)........ _____

❏ *Eumyias indigo.* INDIGO FLYCATCHER. (mts G Sunda)............ _____

❏ *Niltava grandis.* LARGE NILTAVA. (mts s,se Asia)............... _____

❏ *Niltava macgrigoriae.* SMALL NILTAVA. (mts s,se Asia)........... _____

❏ *Niltava davidi.* FUJIAN NILTAVA. (mts s,se Asia)............... _____

❏ *Niltava sundara.* RUFOUS-BELLIED NILTAVA. (Himal)............ _____

❏ *Niltava sumatrana.* RUFOUS-VENTED NILTAVA. (mts Malaya, Sum)... _____

❑ *Niltava vivida.* Vivid Niltava. (mts s,se Asia)................. _____

❑ *Cyornis sanfordi.* Matinan Flycatcher. (mts n Sulaw).......... _____

❑ *Cyornis hoevelli.* Blue-fronted Flycatcher. (mts c,se Sulaw)..... _____

❑ *Cyornis hyacinthinus.* Timor Blue-Flycatcher. (c L Sunda)...... _____

❑ *Cyornis concretus.* White-tailed Flycatcher. (mts se Asia)...... _____

❑ *Cyornis ruckii.* Rueck's Blue-Flycatcher. (Sum).............. _____

❑ *Cyornis herioti.* Blue-breasted Flycatcher. (mts n Phil)........ _____

❑ *Cyornis hainanus.* Hainan Blue-Flycatcher. (s Asia).......... _____

❑ *Cyornis pallipes.* White-bellied Blue-Flycatcher. (sw India)..... _____

❑ *Cyornis poliogenys.* Pale-chinned Flycatcher. (s Asia)......... _____

❑ *Cyornis unicolor.* Pale Blue-Flycatcher. (s,se Asia)........... _____

❑ *Cyornis rubeculoides.* Blue-throated Flycatcher. (s,se Asia)..... _____

❑ *Cyornis banyumas.* Hill Blue-Flycatcher. (s,se Asia).......... _____

❑ *Cyornis lemprieri.* Palawan Blue-Flycatcher. (sw Phil)........ _____

❑ *Cyornis superbus.* Bornean Blue-Flycatcher. (mts Born)....... _____

❑ *Cyornis caerulatus.* Large-billed Blue-Flycatcher. (Sum, Born) . _____

❑ *Cyornis turcosus.* Malaysian Blue-Flycatcher. (se Asia)....... _____

❑ *Cyornis tickelliae.* Tickell's Blue-Flycatcher. (s,se Asia)....... _____

❑ *Cyornis rufigaster.* Mangrove Blue-Flycatcher. (se Asia, Phil)... _____

❑ *Cyornis omissus.* Sulawesi Blue-Flycatcher. (Sulaw).......... _____
   ___*C. (o.) omissus.* Sulawesi Blue-Flycatcher. (sp)
   ___*C. (o.) djampeanus.* Tanahjampea Blue-Flycatcher. (is Flores Sea)

❑ *Muscicapella hodgsoni.* Pygmy Blue-Flycatcher. (mts s,se Asia) . _____

❑ *Culicicapa ceylonensis.* Grey-headed Canary-Flyc. (s Asia-Wall). _____

❑ *Culicicapa helianthea.* Citrine Canary-Flycatcher. (G Sunda, Phil) _____

❑ *Horizorhinus dohrni.* Dohrn's Flycatcher. (Prín).............. _____

Tribe Saxicolini [30/156]

❑ *Pogonocichla stellata.* White-starred Robin. (mts ce,se Afr)...... _____

❑ *Swynnertonia swynnertoni.* Swynnerton's Robin. (mts se Afr)..... _____

❑ *Stiphrornis erythrothorax.* Forest Robin. (w,c Afr).............. _____

❑ *Sheppardia poensis.* Alexander's Akalat. (mts c Afr)........... _____

❑ *Sheppardia bocagei.* Bocage's Akalat. (sc Afr)................ _____

❑ *Sheppardia cyornithopsis.* Lowland Akalat. (w,c Afr)........... _____

❑ *Sheppardia aequatorialis.* Equatorial Akalat. (mts ec Afr)....... _____

❑ *Sheppardia sharpei.* Sharpe's Akalat. (mts ec Afr)............. _____

❑ *Sheppardia gunningi.* EAST COAST AKALAT. (e Afr). . . . . _____

   ___**S. (g.) gunningi.* EAST COAST AKALAT. (sp)

   ___**S. (g.) bensoni.* MALAWI AKALAT. (nw Malawi)

❑ *Sheppardia gabela.* GABELA AKALAT. (wc Ang). . . . . _____

❑ *Sheppardia montana.* USAMBARA AKALAT. (mts ne Tanz). . . . . _____

❑ *Sheppardia lowei.* IRINGA AKALAT. (mts sc Tanz). . . . . _____

❑ *Erithacus rubecula.* EUROPEAN ROBIN. (Palea; ◊-n Afr). . . . . _____

❑ *Erithacus akahige.* JAPANESE ROBIN. (mts e Asia). . . . . _____

❑ *Erithacus komadori.* RYUKYU ROBIN. (Ryu). . . . . _____

❑ *Luscinia sibilans.* RUFOUS-TAILED ROBIN. (e Asia; ◊ se Asia). . . . . . . _____

❑ *Luscinia luscinia.* THRUSH NIGHTINGALE. (n Eura; ◊ e,s Afr). . . . . . . _____

❑ *Luscinia megarhynchos.* COMMON NIGHTINGALE. (Palea; ◊ trop Afr). . . _____

❑ *Luscinia calliope.* SIBERIAN RUBYTHROAT. (c,e Asia; ◊s Asia-Phil). . . _____

❑ *Luscinia pectoralis.* WHITE-TAILED RUBYTHROAT. (Himal). . . . . _____

❑ *Luscinia svecica.* BLUETHROAT. (mts Eura, w,n Alas; ◊ n Afr, s Asia). _____

❑ *Luscinia ruficeps.* RUFOUS-HEADED ROBIN. (mts nc China). . . . . _____

❑ *Luscinia obscura.* BLACK-THROATED BLUE ROBIN. (mts w China). . . . _____

❑ *Luscinia pectardens.* FIRETHROAT. (mts c China; ◊ se Asia). . . . . _____

❑ *Luscinia brunnea.* INDIAN BLUE ROBIN. (Himal). . . . . _____

❑ *Luscinia cyane.* SIBERIAN BLUE ROBIN. (e Eura; ◊ se Asia-Phil). . . . . . _____

❑ *Tarsiger cyanurus.* ORANGE-FLANKED BUSH-ROBIN. (n Palea, s Asia). _____

❑ *Tarsiger chrysaeus.* GOLDEN BUSH-ROBIN. (Himal; ◊ se Asia). . . . . . . _____

❑ *Tarsiger indicus.* WHITE-BROWED BUSH-ROBIN. (Himal). . . . . _____

❑ *Tarsiger hyperythrus.* RUFOUS-BREASTED BUSH-ROBIN. (Himal). . . . . _____

❑ *Tarsiger johnstoniae.* COLLARED BUSH-ROBIN. (mts Taiwan). . . . . _____

❑ *Irania gutturalis.* WHITE-THROATED ROBIN. (sc Eura). . . . . _____

❑ *Cossypha isabellae.* MOUNTAIN ROBIN-CHAT. (mts wc Afr). . . . . _____

❑ *Cossypha roberti.* WHITE-BELLIED ROBIN-CHAT. (mts c Afr). . . . . _____

❑ *Cossypha archeri.* ARCHER'S ROBIN-CHAT. (mts ec Afr). . . . . _____

❑ *Cossypha anomala.* OLIVE-FLANKED ROBIN-CHAT. (mts ce,se Afr). . . . _____

   ___**C. (a.) mbuluensis.* MBULU ROBIN-CHAT. (nc Tanz)

   ___**C. (a.) albigularis.* MACCLOUNIE'S ROBIN-CHAT. (sp)

   ___**C. (a.) anomala.* MALAWI ROBIN-CHAT. (nc Malawi)

   ___**C. (a.) gurue.* MOZAMBIQUE ROBIN-CHAT. (nc Moz)

❑ *Cossypha caffra.* CAPE ROBIN-CHAT. (mts e,s Afr). . . . . _____

❑ *Cossypha humeralis.* WHITE-THROATED ROBIN-CHAT. (se Afr). . . . . . . _____

❑ *Cossypha cyanocampter.* BLUE-SHOULDERED ROBIN-CHAT. (w,c Afr). _____

❏ *Cossypha polioptera.* GREY-WINGED ROBIN-CHAT. (w,c Afr)....... _____

❏ *Cossypha semirufa.* RUEPPELL'S ROBIN-CHAT. (mts ne Afr)........ _____

❏ *Cossypha heuglini.* WHITE-BROWED ROBIN-CHAT. (c,e,s Afr)....... _____

❏ *Cossypha natalensis.* RED-CAPPED ROBIN-CHAT. (c,e,s Afr)........ _____

❏ *Cossypha dichroa.* CHORISTER ROBIN-CHAT. (e,s S Afr)........... _____

❏ *Cossypha heinrichi.* WHITE-HEADED ROBIN-CHAT. (cw Afr)........ _____

❏ *Cossypha niveicapilla.* SNOWY-CROWNED ROBIN-CHAT. (w,c Afr).... _____

❏ *Cossypha albicapilla.* WHITE-CROWNED ROBIN-CHAT. (subsah Afr)... _____

❏ *Xenocopsychus ansorgei.* ANGOLA CAVE-CHAT. (mts w Ang)....... _____

❏ *Cichladusa arquata.* COLLARED PALM-THRUSH. (e Afr)........... _____

❏ *Cichladusa ruficauda.* RUFOUS-TAILED PALM-THRUSH. (wc Afr)..... _____

❏ *Cichladusa guttata.* SPOTTED MORNING-THRUSH. (ne Afr)......... _____

❏ *Cercotrichas leucosticta.* FOREST SCRUB-ROBIN. (w,c Afr)......... _____

❏ *Cercotrichas quadrivirgata.* BEARDED SCRUB-ROBIN. (e,s Afr)....... _____
    ___*C. (q.) quadrivirgata.* EASTERN BEARDED SCRUB-ROBIN. (sp)
    ___*C. (q.) greenwayi.* ZANZIBAR BEARDED SCRUB-ROBIN. (is Tanz)

❏ *Cercotrichas barbata.* MIOMBO SCRUB-ROBIN. (c Afr)............ _____

❏ *Cercotrichas signata.* BROWN SCRUB-ROBIN. (se Afr)............. _____

❏ *Cercotrichas hartlaubi.* BROWN-BACKED SCRUB-ROBIN. (c Afr)...... _____

❏ *Cercotrichas leucophrys.* RED-BACKED SCRUB-ROBIN. (c,s,ne Afr).... _____
    ___*C. (l.) leucophrys.* WHITE-BROWED SCRUB-ROBIN. (c,s Afr)
    ___*C. (l.) zambesiana.* RED-BACKED SCRUB-ROBIN. (ec Afr)
    ___*C. (l.) leucoptera.* WHITE-WINGED SCRUB-ROBIN. (ne Afr)

❏ *Cercotrichas galactotes.* RUFOUS-TAILED SCRUB-ROBIN. (s Palea-ncAfr)_____
    ___*C. (g.) galactotes.* RUFOUS-TAILED SCRUB-ROBIN. (s Palea)
    ___*C. (g.) familiaris.* GREYISH SCRUB-ROBIN. (sc Eura)
    ___*C. (g.) minor.* AFRICAN SCRUB-ROBIN. (subsah Afr)

❏ *Cercotrichas paena.* KALAHARI SCRUB-ROBIN. (sw,sc Afr)......... _____

❏ *Cercotrichas coryphaeus.* KAROO SCRUB-ROBIN. (sw Afr)......... _____

❏ *Cercotrichas podobe.* BLACK SCRUB-ROBIN. (n Afr reg)........... _____

❏ *Namibornis herero.* HERERO CHAT. (wc Namibia)............... _____

❏ *Copsychus sechellarum.* SEYCHELLES MAGPIE-ROBIN. (Seyc)....... _____

❏ *Copsychus albospecularis.* MADAGASCAR MAGPIE-ROBIN. (Mad)..... _____

❏ *Copsychus saularis.* ORIENTAL MAGPIE-ROBIN. (s,se Asia, Phil)...... _____

❏ *Copsychus malabaricus.* WHITE-RUMPED SHAMA. (s,se Asia; ◆ Haw Is) _____

❏ *Copsychus stricklandii.* WHITE-CROWNED SHAMA. (n Born)........ _____

❏ *Copsychus luzoniensis.* WHITE-BROWED SHAMA. (Phil)............ _____

❑ *Copsychus niger.* WHITE-VENTED SHAMA. (sw Phil). . . . . _____

❑ *Copsychus cebuensis.* BLACK SHAMA. (sc Phil). . . . . _____

❑ *Trichixos pyrropyga.* RUFOUS-TAILED SHAMA. (se Asia). . . . . _____

❑ *Saxicoloides fulicata.* INDIAN ROBIN. (s Asia). . . . . _____
    ___*S. (f.) cambaiensis.* BROWN-BACKED ROBIN. (sp)
    ___*S. (f.) fulicata.* BLACK-BACKED ROBIN. (s India)

❑ *Phoenicurus alaschanicus.* ALA SHAN REDSTART. (mts w,nc China) . . _____

❑ *Phoenicurus erythronota.* RUFOUS-BACKED REDSTART. (mts c Asia) . _____

❑ *Phoenicurus caeruleocephalus.* BLUE-CAPPED REDSTART. (Himal). . . _____

❑ *Phoenicurus ochruros.* BLACK REDSTART. (Palea; ◊-n Afr, s,se Asia). _____

❑ *Phoenicurus phoenicurus.* COMMON REDSTART. (Palea; ◊-n Afr). . . . . _____

❑ *Phoenicurus hodgsoni.* HODGSON'S REDSTART. (Himal w,c China). . . _____

❑ *Phoenicurus schisticeps.* WHITE-THROATED REDSTART. (w,c China) . _____

❑ *Phoenicurus auroreus.* DAURIAN REDSTART. (mts Asia; ◊-se Asia). . . _____

❑ *Phoenicurus moussieri.* MOUSSIER'S REDSTART. (nw Afr). . . . . _____

❑ *Phoenicurus erythrogaster.* WHITE-WINGED REDSTART. (mts s Asia) . _____

❑ *Phoenicurus frontalis.* BLUE-FRONTED REDSTART. (Himal). . . . . _____

❑ *Chaimarriornis leucocephalus.* WHITE-CAPPED WATER-R. (Himal). . . _____

❑ *Rhyacornis fuliginosus.* PLUMBEOUS WATER-REDSTART. (Himal). . . . _____

❑ *Rhyacornis bicolor.* LUZON WATER-REDSTART. (mts n Phil). . . . . _____

❑ *Hodgsonius phaenicuroides.* WHITE-BELLIED REDSTART. (Himal). . . . _____

❑ *Cinclidium leucurum.* WHITE-TAILED ROBIN. (mts s,se Asia). . . . . . . _____

❑ *Cinclidium diana.* SUNDA ROBIN. (mts Sum, Java). . . . . _____

❑ *Cinclidium frontale.* BLUE-FRONTED ROBIN. (Himal). . . . . _____

❑ *Grandala coelicolor.* GRANDALA. (Himal). . . . . _____

❑ *Enicurus scouleri.* LITTLE FORKTAIL. (mts s Asia). . . . . _____
    ___*E. (s.) scouleri.* LITTLE FORKTAIL. (sp)
    ___*E. (s.) fortis.* FORMOSAN FORKTAIL. (Taiwan)

❑ *Enicurus velatus.* SUNDA FORKTAIL. (mts Sum, Java). . . . . _____

❑ *Enicurus ruficapillus.* CHESTNUT-NAPED FORKTAIL. (se Asia). . . . . . . _____

❑ *Enicurus immaculatus.* BLACK-BACKED FORKTAIL. (s Asia). . . . . _____

❑ *Enicurus schistaceus.* SLATY-BACKED FORKTAIL. (mts s,se Asia). . . . . _____

❑ *Enicurus leschenaulti.* WHITE-CROWNED FORKTAIL. (s,se Asia). . . . . . _____

❑ *Enicurus maculatus.* SPOTTED FORKTAIL. (mts s Asia). . . . . _____

❑ *Cochoa purpurea.* PURPLE COCHOA. (mts s Asia). . . . . _____

❑ *Cochoa viridis.* GREEN COCHOA. (mts s,se Asia). . . . . _____

❑ *Cochoa beccarii.* SUMATRAN COCHOA. (mts w Sum). . . . . _____

❑ *Cochoa azurea.* JAVAN COCHOA. (mts w,c Java). . . . . _____

❑ *Saxicola rubetra.* WHINCHAT. (Palea; ◊ trop,s Afr). . . . . _____

❑ *Saxicola macrorhyncha.* WHITE-BROWED BUSHCHAT. (s Asia). . . . . . . _____

❑ *Saxicola insignis.* WHITE-THROATED BUSHCHAT. (c Asia; ◊ n,c India). _____

❑ *Saxicola dacotiae.* CANARY ISLANDS CHAT. (Can Is). . . . . _____

❑ *Saxicola torquata.* COMMON STONECHAT. (Palea, Afr; ◊-se Asia). . . . . _____
   ___*S. (t.) torquata.* COMMON STONECHAT. (s Palea, Afr)
   ___*S. (t.) maura.* SIBERIAN STONECHAT. (c,e Eura; ◊-ne Afr, se Asia)
   ___*S. (t.) albofasciata.* ETHIOPIAN STONECHAT. (ne Afr)

❑ *Saxicola tectes.* REUNION STONECHAT. (Réun). . . . . _____

❑ *Saxicola leucura.* WHITE-TAILED STONECHAT. (s Asia). . . . . _____

❑ *Saxicola caprata.* PIED BUSHCHAT. (s Eura-Phil, Wall, Bism). . . . . . . _____
   ___*S. (c.) caprata.* PIED BUSHCHAT. (s Eura-Phil, Wall)
   ___*S. (c.) aethiops.* BLACK BUSHCHAT. (NG, Bism)

❑ *Saxicola jerdoni.* JERDON'S BUSHCHAT. (s,se Asia). . . . . _____

❑ *Saxicola ferrea.* GREY BUSHCHAT. (s Asia). _____

❑ *Saxicola gutturalis.* WHITE-BELLIED BUSHCHAT. (ce L Sunda). . . . . . _____

❑ *Saxicola bifasciata.* BUFF-STREAKED CHAT. (mts e S Afr). . . . . _____

❑ *Oenanthe leucopyga.* WHITE-TAILED WHEATEAR. (n Afr reg). . . . . . . _____

❑ *Oenanthe monacha.* HOODED WHEATEAR. (ne Afr, sc Palea). . . . . . . _____

❑ *Oenanthe alboniger.* HUME'S WHEATEAR. (sc Eura). . . . . _____

❑ *Oenanthe leucura.* BLACK WHEATEAR. (sw Palea). . . . . _____

❑ *Oenanthe monticola.* MOUNTAIN WHEATEAR. (sw Afr). . . . . _____

❑ *Oenanthe phillipsi.* SOMALI WHEATEAR. (mts ne Afr). . . . . _____

❑ *Oenanthe oenanthe.* NORTHERN WHEATEAR. (Palea, n NA; ◊-s Afr) . _____
   ___*O. (o.) oenanthe.* NORTHERN WHEATEAR. (sp)
   ___*O. (o.) seebohmi.* BLACK-THROATED WHEATEAR. (nw Afr)

❑ *Oenanthe lugens.* MOURNING WHEATEAR. (s Palea). . . . . _____

❑ *Oenanthe lugentoides.* ARABIAN WHEATEAR. (Arabia). . . . . _____

❑ *Oenanthe lugubris.* SCHALOW'S WHEATEAR. (mts ne Afr). . . . . _____

❑ *Oenanthe finschii.* FINSCH'S WHEATEAR. (sc Eura). . . . . _____

❑ *Oenanthe picata.* VARIABLE WHEATEAR. (sc Eura). . . . . _____

❑ *Oenanthe moesta.* RED-RUMPED WHEATEAR. (sw Palea). . . . . _____

❑ *Oenanthe hispanica.* BLACK-EARED WHEATEAR. (s Palea). . . . . _____

❑ *Oenanthe pleschanka.* PIED WHEATEAR. (sc Eura). . . . . _____

❑ *Oenanthe cypriaca.* CYPRUS WHEATEAR. (Cyprus). . . . . _____

❑ *Oenanthe xanthoprymna.* RUFOUS-TAILED WHEATEAR. (sc Eura). . . . . _____
   ___*O. (x.) xanthoprymna. RUFOUS-TAILED WHEATEAR. (Asia Minor)
   ___*O. (x.) chrysopygia. AFGHAN WHEATEAR. (sp)

❑ *Oenanthe deserti.* DESERT WHEATEAR. (sw,s,c Palea; ◊-n Afr, India) . _____

❑ *Oenanthe pileata.* CAPPED WHEATEAR. (c,s Afr). . . . . _____

❑ *Oenanthe isabellina.* ISABELLINE WHEATEAR. (sc Eura; ◊ ne Afr, s Asia)_____

❑ *Oenanthe bottae.* BOTTA'S WHEATEAR. (mts Eth, Arabia). . . . . _____

❑ *Oenanthe heuglini.* HEUGLIN'S WHEATEAR. (subsah Afr). . . . . _____

❑ *Cercomela sinuata.* SICKLEWING CHAT. (s Afr). . . . . _____

❑ *Cercomela schlegelii.* KAROO CHAT. (sw Afr). . . . . _____

❑ *Cercomela tractrac.* TRACTRAC CHAT. (sw Afr). . . . . _____

❑ *Cercomela familiaris.* FAMILIAR CHAT. (c,s Afr). . . . . _____

❑ *Cercomela scotocerca.* BROWN-TAILED CHAT. (ne Afr). . . . . _____

❑ *Cercomela fusca.* INDIAN CHAT. (s Asia). . . . . _____

❑ *Cercomela dubia.* SOMBRE CHAT. (mts ne Afr). . . . . _____

❑ *Cercomela melanura.* BLACKSTART. (subsah Afr, cs Eura). . . . . _____

❑ *Cercomela sordida.* MOORLAND CHAT. (mts e Afr). . . . . _____

❑ *Myrmecocichla tholloni.* CONGO MOOR-CHAT. (w Afr). . . . . _____

❑ *Myrmecocichla aethiops.* NORTHERN ANTEATER-CHAT. (subsah Afr) , _____

❑ *Myrmecocichla formicivora.* SOUTHERN ANTEATER-CHAT. (s Afr). . . . _____

❑ *Myrmecocichla nigra.* SOOTY CHAT. (w,c Afr). . . . . _____

❑ *Myrmecocichla melaena.* RUEPPELL'S CHAT. (mts n Eth). . . . . _____

❑ *Myrmecocichla albifrons.* WHITE-FRONTED BLACK-CHAT. (subsah Afr)_____

❑ *Myrmecocichla arnotti.* WHITE-HEADED BLACK-CHAT. (cs Afr). . . . . . _____

❑ *Thamnolaea cinnamomeiventris.* MOCKING CLIFF-CHAT. (cw,e,s Afr). _____
   ___*T. (c.) bambarae. BAMBARA CLIFF-CHAT. (mts cw Afr)
   ___*T. (c.) albiscapulata. ABYSSINIAN CLIFF-CHAT. (mts ne Afr)
   ___*T. (c.) cinnamomeiventris. MOCKING CLIFF-CHAT. (e,s Afr)

❑ *Thamnolaea coronata.* WHITE-CROWNED CLIFF-CHAT. (subsah nc Afr) _____

❑ *Thamnolaea semirufa.* WHITE-WINGED CLIFF-CHAT. (mts Eth). . . . . . . _____

❑ *Pinarornis plumosus.* BOULDER CHAT. (se Afr). . . . . _____

Family **Sturnidae** [38/148]
Tribe Sturnini [27/114]

❑ *Aplonis zelandica.* RUSTY-WINGED STARLING. (Vanu-Santa Cruz). . . . _____

❑ *Aplonis santovestris.* MOUNTAIN STARLING. (mts Vanu). . . . . _____

❑ *Aplonis pelzelni.* POHNPEI STARLING. (mts e Carol). . . . . _____

❑ *Aplonis atrifusca.* SAMOAN STARLING. (Samoa)................ _____

   Aplonis corvina. KOSRAE STARLING. (†e Carol)................ _____

❑ *Aplonis mavornata.* MYSTERIOUS STARLING. (Cook)............. _____

❑ *Aplonis cinerascens.* RAROTONGA STARLING. (mts sw Cook)....... _____

❑ *Aplonis tabuensis.* POLYNESIAN STARLING. (s Polyn)............. _____

❑ *Aplonis striata.* STRIATED STARLING. (N Cal, Loy)............. _____
   ___*A. (s.) striata.* STRIATED STARLING. (N Cal)
   ___*A. (s.) atronitens.* LOYALTY ISLANDS STARLING. (Loy)

   Aplonis fusca. NORFOLK STARLING. (†L Howe, Norfolk)........... _____

❑ *Aplonis opaca.* MICRONESIAN STARLING. (Micro)............... _____

❑ *Aplonis crassa.* TANIMBAR STARLING. (Tanim)................ _____

❑ *Aplonis cantoroides.* SINGING STARLING. (Aru-Solom)............ _____

❑ *Aplonis feadensis.* ATOLL STARLING. (nw Bism, Solom).......... _____

❑ *Aplonis insularis.* RENNELL STARLING. (s Solom)............... _____

❑ *Aplonis grandis.* BROWN-WINGED STARLING. (Solom)............ _____

❑ *Aplonis dichroa.* SAN CRISTOBAL STARLING. (s Solom)............ _____

❑ *Aplonis mysolensis.* MOLUCCAN STARLING. (Wall)............... _____

❑ *Aplonis minor.* SHORT-TAILED STARLING. (Sulaw, L Sunda, s Phil)... _____

❑ *Aplonis panayensis.* ASIAN GLOSSY STARLING. (s,se Asia, Phil)...... _____
   ___*A. (p.) panayensis.* ASIAN GLOSSY STARLING. (sp)
   ___*A. (p.) eustathis.* BORNEAN STARLING. (e Born)

❑ *Aplonis metallica.* METALLIC STARLING. (Moluc-Solom, ne Aust).... _____

❑ *Aplonis magna.* LONG-TAILED STARLING. (nw NG)............... _____

❑ *Aplonis mystacea.* YELLOW-EYED STARLING. (s NG)............. _____

❑ *Aplonis brunneicapilla.* WHITE-EYED STARLING. (Solom).......... _____

❑ *Poeoptera stuhlmanni.* STUHLMANN'S STARLING. (mts ne Afr)....... _____

❑ *Poeoptera kenricki.* KENRICK'S STARLING. (mts e Afr)............. _____

❑ *Poeoptera lugubris.* NARROW-TAILED STARLING. (w,c Afr)......... _____

❑ *Grafisia torquata.* WHITE-COLLARED STARLING. (w,c Afr)......... _____

❑ *Onychognathus walleri.* WALLER'S STARLING. (mts c,e Afr)........ _____

❑ *Onychognathus nabouroup.* PALE-WINGED STARLING. (sw,s Afr)..... _____

❑ *Onychognathus tristramii.* TRISTRAM'S STARLING. (sw Palea)....... _____

❑ *Onychognathus morio.* RED-WINGED STARLING. (Afr)............ _____

❑ *Onychognathus blythii.* SOMALI STARLING. (n Eth, n Som)......... _____

❑ *Onychognathus frater.* SOCOTRA STARLING. (Socotra)........... _____

❑ *Onychognathus fulgidus.* CHESTNUT-WINGED STARLING. (w,c Afr)... _____

❑ *Onychognathus tenuirostris.* SLENDER-BILLED STARLING. (mts e Afr). _____

❑ *Onychognathus albirostris.* WHITE-BILLED STARLING. (mts n,c Eth). . . _____

❑ *Onychognathus salvadorii.* BRISTLE-CROWNED STARLING. (ne Afr). . . _____

❑ *Coccycolius iris.* IRIS GLOSSY-STARLING. (w Afr). . . . . _____

❑ *Lamprotornis cupreocauda.* COPPER-TAILED GLOSSY-STARLING. (w Afr)_____

❑ *Lamprotornis purpureiceps.* PURPLE-HEADED GLOSSY-ST. (w,c Afr) . _____

❑ *Lamprotornis corruscus.* BLACK-BELLIED GLOSSY-STARLING. (e,se Afr) _____

❑ *Lamprotornis purpureus.* PURPLE GLOSSY-STARLING. (w,c Afr). . . . . . _____

❑ *Lamprotornis nitens.* RED-SHOULDERED GLOSSY-STARLING. (c,s Afr). _____

❑ *Lamprotornis chalcurus.* BRONZE-TAILED GLOSSY-ST . (subsah Afr) . _____

❑ *Lamprotornis chalybaeus.* GREATER BLUE-EARED GLOSSY-ST. (Afr) . _____

❑ *Lamprotornis chloropterus.* LESSER BLUE-EARED GLOSSY-ST. (nc Afr) _____

❑ *Lamprotornis elisabeth.* SOUTHERN BLUE-EARED GLOSSY-ST. (e Afr). _____

❑ *Lamprotornis acuticaudus.* SHARP-TAILED GLOSSY-STARLING. (c Afr). _____

❑ *Lamprotornis splendidus.* SPLENDID GLOSSY-STARLING. (subsah Afr). _____

❑ *Lamprotornis ornatus.* PRINCIPE GLOSSY-STARLING. (Prín). . . . . _____

❑ *Lamprotornis australis.* BURCHELL'S GLOSSY-STARLING. (sc Afr). . . . _____

❑ *Lamprotornis mevesii.* MEVES'S GLOSSY-STARLING. (s Afr). . . . . _____
　　___*L. (m.) benguelensis.* ANGOLA GLOSSY-STARLING. (sw,c Ang)
　　___*L. (m.) mevesii.* MEVES'S GLOSSY-STARLING. (sp)

❑ *Lamprotornis caudatus.* LONG-TAILED GLOSSY-STARLING. (subsah Afr)_____

❑ *Lamprotornis purpuropterus.* RUEPPELL'S GLOSSY-STARLING. (ne Afr)_____

❑ *Lamprotornis superbus.* SUPERB STARLING. (ne Afr). . . . . _____

❑ *Lamprotornis pulcher.* CHESTNUT-BELLIED STARLING. (subsah Afr). . . _____

❑ *Lamprotornis shelleyi.* SHELLEY'S STARLING. (ne Afr). . . . . _____

❑ *Lamprotornis hildebrandti.* HILDEBRANDT'S STARLING. (e Afr). . . . . . _____

❑ *Cinnyricinclus sharpii.* SHARPE'S STARLING. (mts e Afr). . . . . _____

❑ *Cinnyricinclus femoralis.* ABBOTT'S STARLING. (mts e Afr). . . . . _____

❑ *Cinnyricinclus leucogaster.* VIOLET-BACKED STARLING. (Afr reg). . . . _____

❑ *Speculipastor bicolor.* MAGPIE STARLING. (ne Afr). . . . . _____

❑ *Neocichla gutturalis.* BABBLING STARLING. (c Afr). . . . . _____

❑ *Spreo fischeri.* FISCHER'S STARLING. (ne Afr). . . . . _____

❑ *Spreo bicolor.* AFRICAN PIED STARLING. (s Afr). . . . . _____

❑ *Spreo albicapillus.* WHITE-CROWNED STARLING. (ne Afr). . . . . _____

❑ *Cosmopsarus regius.* GOLDEN-BREASTED STARLING. (ne Afr). . . . . . . _____

❑ *Cosmopsarus unicolor.* ASHY STARLING. (e Afr)................ _____

❑ *Saroglossa aurata.* MADAGASCAR STARLING. (Mad)............. _____

❑ *Saroglossa spiloptera.* SPOT-WINGED STARLING. (nc India; ◊-se Asia). _____

❑ *Creatophora cinerea.* WATTLED STARLING. (e,s Afr)............. _____

   Necropsar rodericanus. RODRIGUEZ STARLING. (†is Rod).......... _____

   Fregilupus varius. REUNION STARLING. (†Réun)................ _____

❑ *Sturnus senex.* WHITE-FACED STARLING. (sw Ceylon)............. _____

❑ *Sturnus malabaricus.* CHESTNUT-TAILED STARLING. (s Asia)....... _____

❑ *Sturnus erythropygius.* WHITE-HEADED STARLING. (And, Nico)...... _____

❑ *Sturnus pagodarum.* BRAHMINY STARLING. (s Asia).............. _____

❑ *Sturnus sericeus.* RED-BILLED STARLING. (c,s China)............. _____

❑ *Sturnus sturninus.* PURPLE-BACKED STARLING. (e Asia; ◊ se Asia).... _____

❑ *Sturnus philippensis.* CHESTNUT-CHEEKED ST. (e Asia; ◊-Indon, Phil). _____

❑ *Sturnus sinensis.* WHITE-SHOULDERED STARLING. (s Asia)......... _____

❑ *Sturnus roseus.* ROSY STARLING. (sc Eura; ◊-India).............. _____

❑ *Sturnus vulgaris.* COMMON STARLING. (Palea; ◆ cosm)........... _____

❑ *Sturnus unicolor.* SPOTLESS STARLING. (s Palea)................ _____

❑ *Sturnus cineraceus.* WHITE-CHEEKED STARLING. (e Asia; ◊-s Asia)... _____

❑ *Sturnus contra.* ASIAN PIED STARLING. (s,se Asia).............. _____

❑ *Sturnus nigricollis.* BLACK-COLLARED STARLING. (s,se Asia)....... _____

❑ *Sturnus burmannicus.* VINOUS-BREASTED STARLING. (se Asia)..... _____

❑ *Sturnus melanopterus.* BLACK-WINGED STARLING. (Java-Lombok)... _____

❑ *Leucopsar rothschildi.* BALI MYNA. (Bali)..................... _____

❑ *Acridotheres tristis.* COMMON MYNA. (s,se Asia; ◆ Afr, Aust, Haw Is). _____

❑ *Acridotheres ginginianus.* BANK MYNA. (s Asia)............... _____

❑ *Acridotheres fuscus.* JUNGLE MYNA. (s,se Asia; ◆ Polyn)......... _____

❑ *Acridotheres grandis.* WHITE-VENTED MYNA. (s,se Asia)......... _____

❑ *Acridotheres cinereus.* PALE-BELLIED MYNA. (Java, Sulaw, Bali)..... _____

❑ *Acridotheres albocinctus.* COLLARED MYNA. (s Asia)............. _____

❑ *Acridotheres cristatellus.* CRESTED MYNA. (s,se Asia; ◆ Phil, BC)... _____

❑ *Ampeliceps coronatus.* GOLDEN-CRESTED MYNA. (s,se Asia)....... _____

❑ *Mino anais.* GOLDEN MYNA. (w Pap-NG)..................... _____
   ___*M. (a.) anais.* WESTERN GOLDEN-MYNA. (w Pap, w NG)
   ___*M. (a.) orientalis.* EASTERN GOLDEN-MYNA. (NG)

❑ *Mino dumontii.* YELLOW-FACED MYNA. (Aru-Solom)............. _____

❑ *Basilornis celebensis.* SULAWESI MYNA. (Sulaw). . . . . _____

❑ *Basilornis galeatus.* HELMETED MYNA. (is e Sulaw). . . . . _____

❑ *Basilornis corythaix.* LONG-CRESTED MYNA. (Seram). . . . . _____

❑ *Basilornis miranda.* APO MYNA. (mts s Phil). . . . . _____

❑ *Streptocitta albicollis.* WHITE-NECKED MYNA. (Sulaw). . . . . _____

❑ *Streptocitta albertinae.* BARE-EYED MYNA. (is e Sulaw). . . . . _____

❑ *Sarcops calvus.* COLETO. (Phil). . . . . _____

❑ *Gracula ptilogenys.* CEYLON MYNA. (Ceylon). . . . . _____

❑ *Gracula religiosa.* HILL MYNA. (s Asia-L Sunda, Phil; ♦ Chris, PR) . _____
   ___*G. (r.) religiosa.* EASTERN HILL-MYNA. (sp)
   ___*G. (r.) indica.* SOUTHERN HILL-MYNA. (sw pen India)

❑ *Enodes erythrophris.* FIERY-BROWED MYNA. (mts Sulaw). . . . . _____

❑ *Scissirostrum dubium.* FINCH-BILLED MYNA. (Sulaw). , , , , , , , , , , , , _____

❑ *Buphagus africanus.* YELLOW-BILLED OXPECKER. (Afr). . . . . _____

❑ *Buphagus erythrorhynchus.* RED-BILLED OXPECKER. (e,s Afr). . . . . . . _____

Tribe Mimini [11/34]

❑ *Dumetella carolinensis.* GREY CATBIRD. (NA; ◊ s US, MA, G Ant). . . _____

❑ *Melanoptila glabrirostris.* BLACK CATBIRD. (c MA). . . . . _____

❑ *Melanotis caerulescens.* BLUE MOCKINGBIRD. (Mex). . . . . _____

❑ *Melanotis hypoleucus.* BLUE-AND-WHITE MOCKINGBIRD. (mts c MA). _____

❑ *Mimus polyglottos.* NORTHERN MOCKINGBIRD. (NA, Mex, G Ant). . . . _____

❑ *Mimus gilvus.* TROPICAL MOCKINGBIRD. (c MA, s L Ant, n,e SA). . . . _____
   ___*M. (g.) gilvus.* TROPICAL MOCKINGBIRD. (sp)
   ___*M. (g.) magnirostris.* ST. ANDREW MOCKINGBIRD. (San Andrés)
   ___*M. (g.) antelius.* BLUE-GREY MOCKINGBIRD. (e Braz)

❑ *Mimus gundlachii.* BAHAMA MOCKINGBIRD. (Bah, is n Cuba, s Jam) . _____

❑ *Mimus saturninus.* CHALK-BROWED MOCKINGBIRD. (Amaz, se SA). . . _____

❑ *Mimus patagonicus.* PATAGONIAN MOCKINGBIRD. (s SA). . . . . _____

❑ *Mimus dorsalis.* BROWN-BACKED MOCKINGBIRD. (mts sw SA). . . . . . _____

❑ *Mimus triurus.* WHITE-BANDED MOCKINGBIRD. (s SA). . . . . _____

❑ *Mimus longicaudatus.* LONG-TAILED MOCKINGBIRD. (cw SA). . . . . . . _____

❑ *Mimus thenca.* CHILEAN MOCKINGBIRD. (c Chile). . . . . _____

❑ *Nesomimus parvulus.* GALAPAGOS MOCKINGBIRD. (Galap). . . . . _____
   ___*N. (p.) personatus.* BLACK-EARED MOCKINGBIRD. (n Galap)
   ___*N. (p.) parvulus.* ISABELA MOCKINGBIRD. (c,s Galap)

❑ *Nesomimus trifasciatus.* CHARLES MOCKINGBIRD. (cs Galap). . . . . . . _____

❏ *Nesomimus macdonaldi.* HOOD MOCKINGBIRD. (se Galap)......... _____

❏ *Nesomimus melanotis.* SAN CRISTOBAL MOCKINGBIRD. (ce Galap).... _____

❏ *Mimodes graysoni.* SOCORRO MOCKINGBIRD. (Revil)............. _____

❏ *Oreoscoptes montanus.* SAGE THRASHER. (w NA; ◊-n Mex)........ _____

❏ *Toxostoma rufum.* BROWN THRASHER. (e NA; ◊ se US)........... _____

❏ *Toxostoma longirostre.* LONG-BILLED THRASHER. (s Tex, n,c Mex)... _____

❏ *Toxostoma guttatum.* COZUMEL THRASHER. (Coz)............... _____

❏ *Toxostoma bendirei.* BENDIRE'S THRASHER. (sw US, nw Mex)...... _____

❏ *Toxostoma cinereum.* GREY THRASHER. (Baja)................. _____

❏ *Toxostoma curvirostre.* CURVE-BILLED THRASHER. (sw US, Mex).... _____

❏ *Toxostoma ocellatum.* OCELLATED THRASHER. (mts sc Mex)....... _____

❏ *Toxostoma lecontei.* LE CONTE'S THRASHER. (sw US, nw Mex)...... _____

❏ *Toxostoma redivivum.* CALIFORNIA THRASHER. (Calif, nw Baja)..... _____

❏ *Toxostoma crissale.* CRISSAL THRASHER. (sw US, n,c Mex)........ _____

❏ *Cinclocerthia ruficauda.* BROWN TREMBLER. (n,s L Ant).......... _____

❏ *Cinclocerthia gutturalis.* GREY TREMBLER. (c L Ant)............. _____

❏ *Ramphocinclus brachyurus.* WHITE-BREASTED THRASHER. (c L Ant) . _____

❏ *Margarops fuscus.* SCALY-BREASTED THRASHER. (L Ant).......... _____

❏ *Margarops fuscatus.* PEARLY-EYED THRASHER. (W Indies)......... _____

Superfamily SYLVIOIDEA [203/1204]
Family **Sittidae** [2/25]
Subfamily Sittinae [1/24]

❏ *Sitta europaea.* WOOD NUTHATCH. (Palea)..................... _____
___*S. (e.) caesia.* SOUTHERN NUTHATCH. (w Palea)
___*S. (e.) europaea.* EURASIAN NUTHATCH. (c,e Palea)
___*S. (e.) sinensis.* ORIENTAL NUTHATCH. (sc,e China)

❏ *Sitta nagaensis.* CHESTNUT-VENTED NUTHATCH. (mts s Asia)........ _____

❏ *Sitta cashmirensis.* KASHMIR NUTHATCH. (Himal)............... _____

❏ *Sitta castanea.* CHESTNUT-BELLIED NUTHATCH. (s,se Asia)......... _____

❏ *Sitta himalayensis.* WHITE-TAILED NUTHATCH. (Himal)........... _____

❏ *Sitta victoriae.* WHITE-BROWED NUTHATCH. (Himal w Burma)...... _____

❏ *Sitta pygmaea.* PYGMY NUTHATCH. (w NA, Mex)................ _____

❏ *Sitta pusilla.* BROWN-HEADED NUTHATCH. (se US, n Bah).......... _____

❏ *Sitta whiteheadi.* CORSICAN NUTHATCH. (mts Corsica)............ _____

❏ *Sitta ledanti.* KABYLIE NUTHATCH. (mts ne Algeria).............. _____

❑ *Sitta krueperi.* KRUEPER'S NUTHATCH. (Asia Minor). . . . . _____

❑ *Sitta villosa.* SNOWY-BROWED NUTHATCH. (mts e Asia). . . . . _____

❑ *Sitta yunnanensis.* YUNNAN NUTHATCH. (Himal sw China). . . . . _____

❑ *Sitta canadensis.* RED-BREASTED NUTHATCH. (w,n NA; ◊-n Mex). . . . . _____

❑ *Sitta leucopsis.* WHITE-CHEEKED NUTHATCH. (Himal). . . . . _____

❑ *Sitta carolinensis.* WHITE-BREASTED NUTHATCH. (NA, Mex). . . . . _____

❑ *Sitta neumayer.* WESTERN ROCK-NUTHATCH. (s Eura). . . . . _____

❑ *Sitta tephronota.* EASTERN ROCK-NUTHATCH. (sc Eura). . . . . _____

❑ *Sitta frontalis.* VELVET-FRONTED NUTHATCH. (mts s,se Asia, sw Phil). _____

❑ *Sitta solangiae.* YELLOW-BILLED NUTHATCH. (mts Vietnam). . . . . _____

❑ *Sitta oenochlamys.* SULPHUR-BILLED NUTHATCH. (mts Phil). . . . . _____

❑ *Sitta azurea.* BLUE NUTHATCH. (mts se Asia). . . . . _____

❑ *Sitta magna.* GIANT NUTHATCH. (mts se Asia). . . . . _____

❑ *Sitta formosa.* BEAUTIFUL NUTHATCH. (Himal). . . . . _____

Subfamily Tichodrominae [1/1]

❑ *Tichodroma muraria.* WALLCREEPER. (s Palea). . . . . _____

Family **Certhiidae** [23/97]
Subfamily Certhiinae [2/7]
Tribe Certhiini [1/6]

❑ *Certhia familiaris.* EURASIAN TREE-CREEPER. (Eura). . . . . _____

❑ *Certhia americana.* AMERICAN TREE-CREEPER. (NA, mts n,c MA). . . . _____

❑ *Certhia brachydactyla.* SHORT-TOED TREE-CREEPER. (w Palea). . . . . . _____

❑ *Certhia himalayana.* BAR-TAILED TREE-CREEPER. (Himal). . . . . _____

❑ *Certhia nipalensis.* RUSTY-FLANKED TREE-CREEPER. (Himal). . . . . . . _____

❑ *Certhia discolor.* BROWN-THROATED TREE-CREEPER. (mts s,se Asia) . _____

Tribe Salpornithini [1/1]

❑ *Salpornis spilonotus.* SPOTTED CREEPER. (subsah,e,c Afr). . . . . _____

Subfamily Troglodytinae [17/75]

❑ *Donacobius atricapillus.* BLACK-CAPPED DONACOBIUS. (e Pan, SA). . . _____

❑ *Campylorhynchus gularis.* SPOTTED WREN. (mts w,c Mex). . . . . _____

❑ *Campylorhynchus brunneicapillus.* CACTUS WREN. (sw US-n,c Mex). . _____

❑ *Campylorhynchus jocosus.* BOUCARD'S WREN. (mts sc Mex). . . . . _____

❑ *Campylorhynchus yucatanicus.* YUCATAN WREN. (n Yucatán). . . . . . . _____

❑ *Campylorhynchus chiapensis.* GIANT WREN. (Chiapas). . . . . _____

❑ *Campylorhynchus griseus.* BICOLORED WREN. (n SA)............ _____

❑ *Campylorhynchus rufinucha.* RUFOUS-NAPED WREN. (MA)........ _____
___*C. (r.) humilis.* SCLATER'S WREN. (w Mex)
___*C. (r.) rufinucha.* RUFOUS-NAPED WREN. (int sc Mex)
___*C. (r.) capistratus.* RUFOUS-BACKED WREN. (c MA)

❑ *Campylorhynchus turdinus.* THRUSH-LIKE WREN. (Amaz)......... _____
___*C. (t.) turdinus.* THRUSH-LIKE WREN. (sp)
___*C. (t.) unicolor.* PLAIN-BREASTED WREN. (sw Amaz)

❑ *Campylorhynchus megalopterus.* GREY-BARRED WREN. (mts c Mex). _____

❑ *Campylorhynchus zonatus.* BAND-BACKED WREN. (MA, nw SA)..... _____

❑ *Campylorhynchus albobrunneus.* WHITE-HEADED WREN. (Pan-Colom)_____

❑ *Campylorhynchus nuchalis.* STRIPE-BACKED WREN. (nw SA)....... _____

❑ *Campylorhynchus fasciatus.* FASCIATED WREN. (cw SA).......... _____

❑ *Odontorchilus branickii.* GREY-MANTLED WREN. (Andes w SA)..... _____

❑ *Odontorchilus cinereus.* TOOTH-BILLED WREN. (sw Amaz)........ _____

❑ *Salpinctes obsoletus.* ROCK WREN. (mts w NA, MA)............. _____

❑ *Catherpes mexicanus.* CANYON WREN. (mts w US, Mex).......... _____

❑ *Hylorchilus sumichrasti.* SLENDER-BILLED WREN. (sc Mex)....... _____
___*H. (s.) sumichrasti.* SUMICHRAST'S WREN. (sp)
___*H. (s.) navai.* NAVA'S WREN. (w Chiapas)

❑ *Cinnycerthia unirufa.* RUFOUS WREN. (mts nw SA).............. _____

❑ *Cinnycerthia peruana.* SEPIA-BROWN WREN. (Andes w SA)........ _____

❑ *Cistothorus platensis.* SEDGE WREN. (e NA, MA, SA)............ _____
___*C. (p.) stellaris.* SEDGE WREN. (e NA, MA)
___*C. (p.) platensis.* GRASS WREN. (SA)

❑ *Cistothorus apolinari.* APOLINAR'S WREN. (Andes Colom)......... _____

❑ *Cistothorus meridae.* MERIDA WREN. (Andes nw Ven)............ _____

❑ *Cistothorus palustris.* MARSH WREN. (NA, Mex)................ _____
___*C. (p.) paludicola.* WESTERN MARSH-WREN. (w NA, Mex)
___*C. (p.) palustris.* EASTERN MARSH-WREN. (e NA)

❑ *Thryomanes bewickii.* BEWICK'S WREN. (NA).................. _____

❑ *Thryomanes sissonii.* SOCORRO WREN. (Revil)................. _____

❑ *Ferminia cerverai.* ZAPATA WREN. (sw Cuba)................. _____

❑ *Thryothorus atrogularis.* BLACK-THROATED WREN. (c CA)........ _____

❑ *Thryothorus spadix.* SOOTY-HEADED WREN. (e Pan, w,c Colom)..... _____

❑ *Thryothorus fasciatoventris.* BLACK-BELLIED WREN. (s CA-Colom) . _____

❑ *Thryothorus euophrys.* PLAIN-TAILED WREN. (Andes w SA)....... _____
___*T. (e.) euophrys.* SPOT-CHESTED WREN. (nw SA)
___*T. (e.) atriceps.* BLACK-CROWNED WREN. (n Peru)

❑ *Thryothorus eisenmanni.* INCA WREN. (Andes ec Peru)........... _____

❑ *Thryothorus mystacalis.* WHISKERED WREN. (mts nw SA)......... _____
    ___*T. (m.) mystacalis.* WHISKERED WREN. (sp)
    ___*T. (m.) macrurus.* DUSKY-TAILED WREN. (c Colom)

❑ *Thryothorus genibarbis.* MOUSTACHED WREN. (Amaz, e SA)....... _____

❑ *Thryothorus coraya.* CORAYA WREN. (n,c Amaz)............... _____

❑ *Thryothorus felix.* HAPPY WREN. (w,s Mex)................... _____

❑ *Thryothorus maculipectus.* SPOT-BREASTED WREN. (MA)......... _____

❑ *Thryothorus rutilus.* RUFOUS-BREASTED WREN. (s CA, Tob-n SA).... _____

❑ *Thryothorus sclateri.* SPECKLE-BREASTED WREN. (Andes nw SA).... _____

❑ *Thryothorus semibadius.* RIVERSIDE WREN. (sw CR, w Pan)....... _____

❑ *Thryothorus nigricapillus.* BAY WREN. (s CA, nw SA)............ _____
    ___*T. (n.) castaneus.* BAY WREN. (s CA)
    ___*T. (n.) nigricapillus.* BLACK-CAPPED WREN. (e Pan, nw SA)

❑ *Thryothorus thoracicus.* STRIPE-BREASTED WREN. (s CA)......... _____

❑ *Thryothorus leucopogon.* STRIPE-THROATED WREN. (e Pan, nw SA) . _____

❑ *Thryothorus pleurostictus.* BANDED WREN. (Pac MA)............ _____

❑ *Thryothorus ludovicianus.* CAROLINA WREN. (e NA, e Mex, n CA)... _____
    ___*T. (l.) ludovicianus.* CAROLINA WREN. (e NA, ne Mex)
    ___*T. (l.) albinucha.* WHITE-BROWED WREN. (se Mex, n CA)

❑ *Thryothorus rufalbus.* RUFOUS-AND-WHITE WREN. (c,s MA, n SA)... _____

❑ *Thryothorus nicefori.* NICEFORO'S WREN. (Andes n Colom)........ _____

❑ *Thryothorus sinaloa.* SINALOA WREN. (w Mex)................. _____

❑ *Thryothorus modestus.* PLAIN WREN. (c,s MA)................. _____
    ___*T. (m.) modestus.* PLAIN WREN. (sp)
    ___*T. (m.) zeledoni.* CANEBRAKE WREN. (Carib s CA)

❑ *Thryothorus leucotis.* BUFF-BREASTED WREN. (c,e Pan, Amaz)...... _____

❑ *Thryothorus superciliaris.* SUPERCILIATED WREN. (cw SA)........ _____

❑ *Thryothorus guarayanus.* FAWN-BREASTED WREN. (sc SA)........ _____

❑ *Thryothorus longirostris.* LONG-BILLED WREN. (int e Braz)........ _____

❑ *Thryothorus griseus.* GREY WREN. (w Amaz Braz)............... _____

❑ *Troglodytes troglodytes.* WINTER WREN. (Hol; ◊-n Mex)........... _____
    ___*T. (t.) troglodytes.* NORTHERN WREN. (Palea)
    ___*T. (t.) hiemalis.* WINTER WREN. (NA; ◊-n Mex)

❑ *Troglodytes aedon.* HOUSE WREN. (NA, MA, L Ant, SA)........... _____
    ___*T. (a.) aedon.* NORTHERN HOUSE-WREN. (NA; ◊-s Mex)
    ___*T. (a.) brunneicollis.* BROWN-THROATED WREN. (mts se Ariz, Mex)
    ___*T. (a.) beani.* COZUMEL WREN. (Coz)
    ___*T. (a.) martinicensis.* ANTILLEAN HOUSE-WREN. (L Ant)
    ___*T. (a.) musculus.* SOUTHERN HOUSE-WREN. (MA, SA)

❑ *Troglodytes tanneri.* CLARION WREN. (Revil). . . . . _____

❑ *Troglodytes rufociliatus.* RUFOUS-BROWED WREN. (mts c MA). . . . . . . _____

❑ *Troglodytes ochraceus.* OCHRACEOUS WREN. (mts s CA). . . . . _____

❑ *Troglodytes monticola.* SANTA MARTA WREN. (mts ne Colom). . . . . . . _____

❑ *Troglodytes solstitialis.* MOUNTAIN WREN. (mts w SA). . . . . _____

❑ *Troglodytes rufulus.* TEPUI WREN. (Pant nc SA). . . . . _____

❑ *Thryorchilus browni.* TIMBERLINE WREN. (mts CR, w Pan). . . . . _____

❑ *Uropsila leucogastra.* WHITE-BELLIED WREN. (c MA). . . . . _____

❑ *Henicorhina leucosticta.* WHITE-BREASTED WOOD-WREN. (MA, SA). _____

❑ *Henicorhina leucophrys.* GREY-BREASTED WOOD-WREN. (MA-w,n SA)_____

❑ *Henicorhina leucoptera.* BAR-WINGED WOOD-WREN. (Andes n Peru). _____

❑ *Microcerculus philomela.* NORTHERN NIGHTINGALE-WREN. (c MA) . _____

❑ *Microcerculus marginatus.* SOUTHERN NIGHTINGALE-W. (s CA-c SA) _____
   ___*M. (m.) luscinia.* WHISTLING WREN. (s CA)
   ___*M. (m.) taeniatus.* SCALY NIGHTINGALE-WREN. (nw SA)
   ___*M. (m.) marginatus.* SOUTHERN NIGHTINGALE-WREN. (Amaz)

❑ *Microcerculus ustulatus.* FLUTIST WREN. (Pant nc SA). . . . . _____

❑ *Microcerculus bambla.* WING-BANDED WREN. (Amaz). . . . . _____

❑ *Cyphorhinus phaeocephalus.* SONG WREN. (CA, nw SA). . . . . _____

❑ *Cyphorhinus thoracicus.* CHESTNUT-BREASTED WREN. (w SA). . . . . . _____

❑ *Cyphorhinus aradus.* MUSICIAN WREN. (Amaz). . . . . _____
   ___*C. (a.) modulator.* MUSICIAN WREN. (nw,c,s Amaz)
   ___*C. (a.) aradus.* ORGAN WREN. (n Amaz)

Subfamily Polioptilinae [4/15]

❑ *Auriparus flaviceps.* VERDIN. (sw US, nw Mex). . . . . _____

❑ *Microbates collaris.* COLLARED GNATWREN. (n,c Amaz). . . . . _____

❑ *Microbates cinereiventris.* TAWNY-FACED GNATWREN. (s CA, w SA) . _____

❑ *Ramphocaenus melanurus.* LONG-BILLED GNATWREN. (MA, SA). . . . _____
   ___*R. (m.) rufiventris.* LONG-BILLED GNATWREN. (MA, nw SA)
   ___*R. (m.) melanurus.* BLACK-TAILED GNATWREN. (Amaz, e SA)

❑ *Polioptila caerulea.* BLUE-GREY GNATC. (NA-c MA, Bah; ◊-G Ant). . . _____

❑ *Polioptila californica.* CALIFORNIA GNATCATCHER. (sw US, nw Mex). _____

❑ *Polioptila melanura.* BLACK-TAILED GNATCATCHER. (sw US, n Mex). _____

❑ *Polioptila lembeyei.* CUBAN GNATCATCHER. (Cuba). . . . . _____

❑ *Polioptila nigriceps.* BLACK-CAPPED GNATCATCHER. (sw US, n Mex). _____

❑ *Polioptila albiloris.* WHITE-LORED GNATCATCHER. (Pac, int MA). . . . . _____

❑ *Polioptila plumbea.* TROPICAL GNATCATCHER. (MA, SA). . . . . _____
   ___*P. (p.) bilineata.* WHITE-BROWED GNATCATCHER. (MA, w SA)
   ___*P. (p.) plumbea.* TROPICAL GNATCATCHER. (Amaz, e SA)
   ___*P. (p.) maior.* MARANON GNATCATCHER. (n Peru)

❑ *Polioptila lactea.* CREAMY-BELLIED GNATCATCHER. (se SA). . . . . _____

❑ *Polioptila guianensis.* GUIANAN GNATCATCHER. (n Amaz). . . . . _____

❑ *Polioptila schistaceigula.* SLATE-THROATED GNATC. (e Pan, nw SA). . _____

❑ *Polioptila dumicola.* MASKED GNATCATCHER. (c,se SA). . . . . _____
   ___*P. (d.) berlepschi.* BERLEPSCH'S GNATCATCHER. (c SA)
   ___*P. (d.) dumicola.* MASKED GNATCATCHER. (sc SA)

Family **Paridae** [7/65]
Subfamily Remizinae [4/12]

❑ *Remiz pendulinus.* EURASIAN PENDULINE-TIT. (Palea). . . . . _____
   ___*R. (p.) pendulinus.* WHITE-THROATED PENDULINE-TIT. (w,n Palea)
   ___*R. (p.) macronyx.* BLACK-HEADED PENDULINE-TIT. (sc Asia)

❑ *Remiz coronatus.* WHITE-CROWNED PENDULINE-TIT. (sc Eura). . . . . . _____

❑ *Remiz consobrinus.* CHINESE PENDULINE-TIT. (n China). . . . . _____

❑ *Anthoscopus punctifrons.* SENNAR PENDULINE-TIT. (subsah Afr). . . . . _____

❑ *Anthoscopus parvulus.* YELLOW PENDULINE-TIT. (subsah Afr). . . . . . . _____

❑ *Anthoscopus musculus.* MOUSE-COLORED PENDULINE-TIT. (ne Afr). . . _____

❑ *Anthoscopus flavifrons.* FOREST PENDULINE-TIT. (w,c Afr). . . . . _____

❑ *Anthoscopus caroli.* AFRICAN PENDULINE-TIT. (c,s Afr). . . . . _____
   ___*A. (c.) caroli.* AFRICAN PENDULINE-TIT. (sp)
   ___*A. (c.) rankinei.* ZAMBESI PENDULINE-TIT. (se Afr)

❑ *Anthoscopus sylviella.* BUFF-BELLIED PENDULINE-TIT. (e Afr). . . . . . _____

❑ *Anthoscopus minutus.* SOUTHERN PENDULINE-TIT. (sw Afr). . . . . _____

❑ *Cephalopyrus flammiceps.* FIRE-CAPPED TIT. (Himal). . . . . _____

❑ *Pholidornis rushiae.* TIT-HYLIA. (w,c Afr). . . . . _____

Subfamily Parinae [3/53]

❑ *Parus palustris.* MARSH TIT. (Eura). . . . . _____
   ___*P. (p.) palustris.* EURASIAN MARSH-TIT. (w Eura)
   ___*P. (p.) brevirostris.* ASIAN MARSH-TIT. (ne Eura)
   ___*P. (p.) hypermelaena.* BLACK-BIBBED MARSH-TIT. (s Asia)

❑ *Parus lugubris.* SOMBRE TIT. (sc Eura). . . . . _____
   ___*P. (l.) lugubris.* WILLOW TIT. (sp)
   ___*P. (l.) hyrcanus.* HYRCANIAN TIT. (n Iran)

❑ *Parus montanus.* WILLOW TIT. (Palea). . . . . _____
   ___*P. (m.) montanus.* WILLOW TIT. (w,c,n Palea)
   ___*P. (m.) songarus.* SONGAR TIT. (sc Eura)

❑ *Parus carolinensis.* CAROLINA CHICKADEE. (se US). . . . . _____

❑ *Parus atricapillus.* BLACK-CAPPED CHICKADEE. (n NA). . . . . _____

❑ *Parus gambeli.* MOUNTAIN CHICKADEE. (mts w NA, nw Mex). . . . . . . _____

❑ *Parus sclateri.* MEXICAN CHICKADEE. (mts sw US, Mex). . . . . _____

❑ *Parus superciliosus.* WHITE-BROWED TIT. (Himal w China). . . . . _____

❑ *Parus davidi.* RUSTY-BREASTED TIT. (Himal w China). . . . . _____

❑ *Parus cinctus.* SIBERIAN TIT. (n Eura, nw NA). . . . . _____

❑ *Parus hudsonicus.* BOREAL CHICKADEE. (n NA; ◊-n US). . . . . _____

❑ *Parus rufescens.* CHESTNUT-BACKED CHICKADEE. (w NA). . . . . _____

❑ *Parus rufonuchalis.* DARK-GREY TIT. (Himal). . . . . _____

❑ *Parus rubidiventris.* RUFOUS-VENTED TIT. (Himal). . . . . _____
   ___*P. (r.) rubidiventris.* RUFOUS-BELLIED TIT. (sw India)
   ___*P. (r.) beavani.* SIKKIM TIT. (sp)

❑ *Parus melanolophus.* BLACK-CRESTED TIT. (Himal). . . . . _____

❑ *Parus ater.* COAL TIT. (Palea). . . . . _____

❑ *Parus venustulus.* YELLOW-BELLIED TIT. (e,c,s China). . . . . _____

❑ *Parus elegans.* ELEGANT TIT. (Phil). . . . . _____

❑ *Parus amabilis.* PALAWAN TIT. (sw Phil). . . . . _____

❑ *Parus cristatus.* CRESTED TIT. (Euro). . . . . _____

❑ *Parus dichrous.* GREY-CRESTED TIT. (Himal). . . . . _____

❑ *Parus guineensis.* WHITE-SHOULDERED TIT. (w,c Afr). . . . . _____

❑ *Parus leucomelas.* WHITE-WINGED TIT. (c,s Afr). . . . . _____
   ___*P. (l.) leucomelas.* WHITE-WINGED TIT. (sp)
   ___*P. (l.) carpi.* CARP'S TIT. (sw Afr)

❑ *Parus niger.* BLACK TIT. (se Afr). . . . . _____

❑ *Parus albiventris.* WHITE-BELLIED TIT. (wc,e Afr). . . . . _____

❑ *Parus leuconotus.* WHITE-BACKED TIT. (mts Eth). . . . . _____

❑ *Parus funereus.* DUSKY TIT. (c Afr). . . . . _____

❑ *Parus rufiventris.* RUFOUS-BELLIED TIT. (se Afr). . . . . _____

❑ *Parus pallidiventris.* CINNAMON-BREASTED TIT. (se Afr). . . . . _____

❑ *Parus fringillinus.* RED-THROATED TIT. (e Afr). . . . . _____

❑ *Parus fasciiventer.* STRIPE-BREASTED TIT. (mts ec Afr). . . . . _____

❑ *Parus thruppi.* SOMALI TIT. (ne Afr). . . . . _____

❑ *Parus griseiventris.* MIOMBO TIT. (sc Afr). . . . . _____

❑ *Parus cinerascens.* ASHY TIT. (s Afr). . . . . _____

❑ *Parus afer.* GREY TIT. (s Afr). . . . . _____

❑ *Parus major.* GREAT TIT. (Palea, s,se Asia, L Sunda). . . . . _____

   ___*P. (m.) major.* GREAT TIT. (w,c,n Palea)

   ___*P. (m.) cinereus.* CINEREOUS TIT. (s,se Asia, L Sunda)

   ___*P. (m.) minor.* JAPANESE TIT. (e Asia)

❑ *Parus bokharensis.* TURKESTAN TIT. (mts sc Asia). . . . . _____

❑ *Parus monticolus.* GREEN-BACKED TIT. (Himal). . . . . _____

❑ *Parus nuchalis.* WHITE-NAPED TIT. (c,s India). . . . . _____

❑ *Parus xanthogenys.* BLACK-LORED TIT. (Himal). . . . . _____

❑ *Parus spilonotus.* YELLOW-CHEEKED TIT. (Himal). . . . . _____

❑ *Parus holsti.* YELLOW TIT. (mts Taiwan). . . . . _____

❑ *Parus caeruleus.* BLUE TIT. (Palea). . . . . _____

   ___*P. (c.) caeruleus.* EURASIAN BLUE-TIT. (sp)

   ___*P. (c.) teneriffae.* AFRICAN BLUE-TIT. (Can Is, nw Afr)

❑ *Parus cyanus.* AZURE TIT. (Eura). . . . . _____

❑ *Parus flavipectus.* YELLOW-BREASTED TIT. (mts sc Eura). . . . . _____

   ___*P. (f.) flavipectus.* YELLOW-BREASTED TIT. (sp)

   ___*P. (f.) berezowskii.* CHINESE TIT. (nw China)

❑ *Parus varius.* VARIED TIT. (e Asia). . . . . _____

❑ *Parus semilarvatus.* WHITE-FRONTED TIT. (n,s Phil). . . . . _____

❑ *Parus wollweberi.* BRIDLED TITMOUSE. (mts sw US, Mex). . . . . _____

❑ *Parus inornatus.* PLAIN TITMOUSE. (w US, nw Mex). . . . . _____

   ___*P. (i.) inornatus.* PLAIN TITMOUSE. (w US, Baja)

   ___*P. (i.) ridgwayi.* RIDGWAY'S TITMOUSE. (wc US, ne Sonora)

❑ *Parus bicolor.* TUFTED TITMOUSE. (e,se US). . . . . _____

❑ *Parus atricristatus.* BLACK-CRESTED TITMOUSE. (w,c Tex, ne Mex). . . _____

❑ *Sylviparus modestus.* YELLOW-BROWED TIT. (Himal). . . . . _____

❑ *Melanochlora sultanea.* SULTAN TIT. (s,se Asia). . . . . _____

Family **Aegithalidae** [3/8]

❑ *Aegithalos caudatus.* LONG-TAILED TIT. (Palea). . . . . _____

   ___*A. (c.) europaeus.* EUROPEAN TIT. (w,sw,ce Eura)

   ___*A. (c.) caudatus.* LONG-TAILED TIT. (n,c,ne Eura)

   ___*A. (c.) alpinus.* ALPINE TIT. (s Palea)

❑ *Aegithalos leucogenys.* WHITE-CHEEKED TIT. (Himal). . . . . _____

❑ *Aegithalos concinnus.* BLACK-THROATED TIT. (mts s,se Asia). . . . . . . _____

❑ *Aegithalos niveogularis.* WHITE-THROATED TIT. (Himal). . . . . _____

❑ *Aegithalos iouschistos.* BLACK-BROWED TIT. (Himal). . . . . _____

   ___*A. (i.) iouschistos.* BLACK-BROWED TIT. (sp)

   ___*A. (i.) bonvaloti.* BLACK-HEADED TIT. (sw China, Burma)

❑ *Aegithalos fuliginosus.* WHITE-NECKLACED TIT. (mts w,c China). . . . . _____

❑ *Psaltriparus minimus.* BUSHTIT. (w NA, n,c MA) . . . . _____
   ___*P. (m.) minimus.* COMMON BUSHTIT. (w NA, Baja)
   ___*P. (m.) plumbeus.* LEAD-COLORED BUSHTIT. (int w NA)
   ___*P. (m.) melanotis.* BLACK-EARED BUSHTIT. (mts w Tex, Mex, Guat)

❑ *Psaltria exilis.* PYGMY TIT. (mts w,c Java) . . . . _____

Family **Hirundinidae** [14/89]
Subfamily Pseudochelidoninae [1/2]

❑ *Pseudochelidon eurystomina.* AFRICAN RIVER-MARTIN. (Zaire) . . . . . . _____

❑ *Pseudochelidon sirintarae.* WHITE-EYED RIVER-MARTIN. (se Asia) . . . _____

Subfamily Hirundininae [13/87]

❑ *Tachycineta bicolor.* TREE SWALLOW. (NA; ◊-n SA) . . . . _____

❑ *Tachycineta albilinea.* MANGROVE SWALLOW. (MA, nw Peru) . . . . _____
   ___*T. (a.) albilinea.* MANGROVE SWALLOW. (MA)
   ___*T. (a.) stolzmanni.* WEST PERUVIAN SWALLOW. (nw Peru)

❑ *Tachycineta albiventer.* WHITE-WINGED SWALLOW. (SA) . . . . _____

❑ *Tachycineta leucorrhoa.* WHITE-RUMPED SWALLOW. (sc SA) . . . . _____

❑ *Tachycineta meyeni.* CHILEAN SWALLOW. (s SA; ◊-sc SA) . . . . _____

❑ *Tachycineta thalassina.* VIOLET-GREEN SWALLOW. (w NA-CA) . . . . . . _____

❑ *Tachycineta cyaneoviridis.* BAHAMA SWALLOW. (n Bah) . . . . _____

❑ *Tachycineta euchrysea.* GOLDEN SWALLOW. (mts Hisp, Jam) . . . . _____

❑ *Phaeoprogne tapera.* BROWN-CHESTED MARTIN. (SA; ◊-Pan) . . . . _____

❑ *Progne subis.* PURPLE MARTIN. (NA, Mex; ◊ SA) . . . . _____

❑ *Progne cryptoleuca.* CUBAN MARTIN. (Cuba; ◊ SA) . . . . _____

❑ *Progne dominicensis.* CARIBBEAN MARTIN. (W Indies; ◊ SA) . . . . _____

❑ *Progne sinaloae.* SINALOA MARTIN. (mts w Mex; ◊ SA) . . . . _____

❑ *Progne chalybea.* GREY-BREASTED MARTIN. (MA, SA) . . . . _____

❑ *Progne modesta.* SOUTHERN MARTIN. (Galap, cw,s SA; ◊-n SA) . . . . . _____
   ___*P. (m.) modesta.* GALAPAGOS MARTIN. (Galap)
   ___*P. (m.) murphyi.* PERUVIAN MARTIN. (cw SA)
   ___*P. (m.) elegans.* SOUTHERN MARTIN. (s SA; ◊-n SA)

❑ *Notiochelidon murina.* BROWN-BELLIED SWALLOW. (mts w SA) . . . . . _____

❑ *Notiochelidon cyanoleuca.* BLUE-AND-WHITE SWALLOW. (s CA, SA) . _____
   ___*N. (c.) cyanoleuca.* BLUE-AND-WHITE SWALLOW. (sp)
   ___*N. (c.) patagonica.* PATAGONIAN SWALLOW. (s SA; ◊-s CA)

❑ *Notiochelidon flavipes.* PALE-FOOTED SWALLOW. (Andes w SA) . . . . . _____

❑ *Notiochelidon pileata.* BLACK-CAPPED SWALLOW. (mts c MA) . . . . . . _____

❑ *Atticora fasciata.* WHITE-BANDED SWALLOW. (Amaz) . . . . _____

❑ *Atticora melanoleuca.* BLACK-COLLARED SWALLOW. (Amaz). . . . . _____

❑ *Neochelidon tibialis.* WHITE-THIGHED SWALLOW. (s CA, n,c,e SA). . . _____

❑ *Stelgidopteryx fucata.* TAWNY-HEADED SWALLOW. (SA). . . . . _____

❑ *Stelgidopteryx serripennis.* NORTHERN ROUGH-WINGED SW. (NA-MA). _____

❑ *Stelgidopteryx ridgwayi.* RIDGWAY'S ROUGH-WINGED SWALLOW. (c MA)_____

❑ *Stelgidopteryx ruficollis.* SOUTHERN ROUGH-WINGED SW. (s CA, SA). _____

❑ *Cheramoeca leucosternus.* WHITE-BACKED SWALLOW. (c,s Aust). . . . . _____

❑ *Riparia riparia.* SAND MARTIN. (Palea, NA; ◊-s Afr, s,se Asia, SA). . . _____
   ___**R. (r.) riparia.* COMMON SAND-MARTIN. (sp)
   ___**R. (r.) diluta.* EASTERN SAND-MARTIN. (c,s Asia)

❑ *Riparia paludicola.* PLAIN MARTIN. (Afr, Mad, s,se Asia, Phil). . . . . . _____

❑ *Riparia congica.* CONGO MARTIN. (w Afr). . . . . _____

❑ *Riparia cincta.* BANDED MARTIN. (Afr). _____

❑ *Phedina borbonica.* MASCARENE MARTIN. (Mad, Masc). . . . . _____

❑ *Phedina brazzae.* BRAZZA'S MARTIN. (wc Afr). . . . . _____

❑ *Hirundo griseopyga.* GREY-RUMPED SWALLOW. (Afr). . . . . _____

❑ *Hirundo rupestris.* EURASIAN CRAG-MARTIN. (s Palea; ◊-n Afr, s Asia)_____

❑ *Hirundo obsoleta.* PALE CRAG-MARTIN. (n Afr, cs Palea). . . . . _____

❑ *Hirundo fuligula.* ROCK MARTIN. (Afr). _____
   ___**H. (f.) pusilla.* RED-THROATED ROCK-MARTIN. (n,c,se Afr)
   ___**H. (f.) fuligula.* AFRICAN ROCK-MARTIN. (s Afr)

❑ *Hirundo concolor.* DUSKY CRAG-MARTIN. (s,se Asia). . . . . _____

❑ *Hirundo rustica.* BARN SWALLOW. (Hol-Mex, ne Argen; ◊-S Hem). . . _____
   ___**H. (r.) rustica.* EURASIAN SWALLOW. (Palea; ◊-s Afr, n Aust)
   ___**H. (r.) erythrogaster.* BARN SWALLOW. (NA, Mex, ne Argen; ◊-s SA)

❑ *Hirundo lucida.* RED-CHESTED SWALLOW. (w,c,ne Afr). . . . . _____

❑ *Hirundo aethiopica.* ETHIOPIAN SWALLOW. (subsah Afr). . . . . _____

❑ *Hirundo angolensis.* ANGOLA SWALLOW. (c Afr). . . . . _____

❑ *Hirundo albigularis.* WHITE-THROATED SWALLOW. (s Afr). . . . . _____

❑ *Hirundo domicola.* HILL SWALLOW. (mts sw pen India). . . . . _____

❑ *Hirundo tahitica.* PACIFIC SWALLOW. (se Asia, Phil, Indon-s Polyn). . . _____
   ___**H. (t.) javanica.* SMALL HOUSE-SWALLOW. (se Asia, Phil, Indon-NG)
   ___**H. (t.) tahitica.* EASTERN HOUSE-SWALLOW. (Bism-s Polyn)

❑ *Hirundo neoxena.* WELCOME SWALLOW. (sw,s,e Aust, NZ). . . . . _____

❑ *Hirundo smithii.* WIRE-TAILED SWALLOW. (Afr, s,se Asia). . . . . _____
   ___**H. (s.) smithii.* AFRICAN WIRE-TAILED SWALLOW. (Afr)
   ___**H. (s.) filifera.* ASIAN WIRE-TAILED SWALLOW. (s,se Asia)

❑ *Hirundo nigrita.* WHITE-THROATED BLUE SWALLOW. (w,c Afr). . . . . . _____

❑ *Hirundo nigrorufa.* BLACK-AND-RUFOUS SWALLOW. (c Afr)........ _____

❑ *Hirundo atrocaerulea.* BLUE SWALLOW. (mts se Afr; ◊-c,ne Afr)..... _____

❑ *Hirundo leucosoma.* PIED-WINGED SWALLOW. (w Afr)............ _____

❑ *Hirundo megaensis.* WHITE-TAILED SWALLOW. (mts s Eth)......... _____

❑ *Hirundo dimidiata.* PEARL-BREASTED SWALLOW. (s Afr)........... _____

❑ *Hirundo cucullata.* GREATER STRIPED-SWALLOW. (s Afr; ◊-c Afr).... _____

❑ *Hirundo abyssinica.* LESSER STRIPED-SWALLOW. (Afr)........... _____

❑ *Hirundo semirufa.* RUFOUS-CHESTED SWALLOW. (Afr)........... _____

❑ *Hirundo senegalensis.* MOSQUE SWALLOW. (Afr)............... _____

❑ *Hirundo daurica.* RED-RUMPED SWALLOW. (s Eura- w,e Afr)....... _____
   ___*H. (d.) rufula.* RED-RUMPED SWALLOW. (s Palea, w,e Afr; ◊-s Asia)
   ___*H. (d.) melanocrissus.* BLACK-VENTED SWALLOW. (w,c Eth)
   ___*H. (d.) daurica.* LESSER STRIATED SWALLOW. (s,e Asia; ◊-NG)
   ___*H. (d.) hyperythra.* CEYLON SWALLOW. (Ceylon)

❑ *Hirundo domicella.* WEST AFRICAN SWALLOW. (subsah Afr)....... _____

❑ *Hirundo striolata.* STRIATED SWALLOW. (se Asia, L Sunda, n,c Phil) . _____

❑ *Hirundo perdita.* RED SEA SWALLOW. (Sudan).................. _____

❑ *Hirundo preussi.* PREUSS'S SWALLOW. (w Afr).................. _____

❑ *Hirundo rufigula.* RED-THROATED SWALLOW. (cw Afr)........... _____

❑ *Hirundo spilodera.* SOUTH AFRICAN SWALLOW. (s Afr; ◊-c Afr)...... _____

❑ *Hirundo andecola.* ANDEAN SWALLOW. (Andes sw SA)........... _____

❑ *Hirundo pyrrhonota.* CLIFF SWALLOW. (NA, Mex; ◊ SA)

❑ *Hirundo fulva.* CAVE SWALLOW. (s US, Mex, G Ant, se Ecua; ◊-SA) . _____
   ___*H. (f.) pelodoma.* CAVE SWALLOW. (sw US, n Mex)
   ___*H. (f.) fulva.* CINNAMON-THROATED SWALLOW. (s Mex, G Ant; ◊-SA)
   ___*H. (f.) aequatorialis.* ECUADORIAN SWALLOW. (sw Ecua)

❑ *Hirundo rufocollaris.* CHESTNUT-COLLARED SWALLOW. (cw SA)..... _____

❑ *Hirundo nigricans.* TREE MARTIN. (c L Sunda, Aust; ◊-Indo, Solom). _____

❑ *Hirundo fluvicola.* STREAK-THROATED SWALLOW. (s Asia)......... _____

❑ *Hirundo ariel.* FAIRY MARTIN. (Aust; ◊-L Sunda, NG)............ _____

❑ *Hirundo fuliginosa.* FOREST SWALLOW. (wc Afr)............... _____

❑ *Delichon urbica.* NORTHERN HOUSE-MARTIN. (Palea; ◊-s Afr, se Asia). _____

❑ *Delichon dasypus.* ASIAN HOUSE-MARTIN. (s,e Asia; ◊ se Asia-Phil) . _____

❑ *Delichon nipalensis.* NEPAL HOUSE-MARTIN. (Himal)............. _____

❑ *Psalidoprocne nitens.* SQUARE-TAILED SAWWING. (w,c Afr)........ _____

❑ *Psalidoprocne fuliginosa.* MOUNTAIN SAWWING. (mts sw Camer).... _____

❑ *Psalidoprocne albiceps.* WHITE-HEADED SAWWING. (c,ne Afr)....... _____

❑ *Psalidoprocne chalybea.* SHARI SAWWING. (c Afr)............... _____

❑ *Psalidoprocne petiti.* PETIT'S SAWWING. (wc Afr)................ _____

❑ *Psalidoprocne mangbettorum.* MANGBETTU SAWWING. (ec Afr)...... _____

❑ *Psalidoprocne oleaginea.* ETHIOPIAN SAWWING. (sw Eth).......... _____

❑ *Psalidoprocne pristoptera.* BLUE SAWWING. (n Eth).............. _____

❑ *Psalidoprocne antinorii.* BROWN SAWWING. (mts Eth)............ _____
   ___*P. (a.) blanfordi.* BLANFORD'S SAWWING. (wc Eth)
   ___*P. (a.) antinorii.* BROWN SAWWING. (c,s,ne Eth)

❑ *Psalidoprocne orientalis.* EASTERN SAWWING. (wc Afr)........... _____

❑ *Psalidoprocne holomelas.* BLACK SAWWING. (mts e,s Afr)......... _____

❑ *Psalidoprocne obscura.* FANTI SAWWING. (w Afr)................ _____

Family **Regulidae** [1/6]

❑ *Regulus calendula.* RUBY-CROWNED KINGLET. (w,n NA; ◊-n CA).... _____

❑ *Regulus regulus.* GOLDCREST. (Pale; ◊-Medit, s Asia)............. _____

❑ *Regulus teneriffae.* CANARY ISLANDS KINGLET. (Can Is)........... _____

❑ *Regulus goodfellowi.* FLAMECREST. (mts Taiwan)............... _____

❑ *Regulus ignicapillus.* FIRECREST. (w Palea).................... _____

❑ *Regulus satrapa.* GOLDEN-CROWNED KINGLET. (w,n NA-Guat; ◊-s US)_____

Family **Pycnonotidae** [21/138]

❑ *Spizixos canifrons.* CRESTED FINCHBILL. (mts s Asia)............. _____

❑ *Spizixos semitorques.* COLLARED FINCHBILL. (s Asia)............. _____

❑ *Pycnonotus zeylanicus.* STRAW-HEADED BULBUL. (se Asia)........ _____

❑ *Pycnonotus striatus.* STRIATED BULBUL. (Himal)................ _____

❑ *Pycnonotus leucogrammicus.* CREAM-STRIPED BULBUL. (mts Sum)... _____

❑ *Pycnonotus tympanistrigus.* SPOT-NECKED BULBUL. (Sum)........ _____

❑ *Pycnonotus melanoleucus.* BLACK-AND-WHITE BULBUL. (se Asia).... _____

❑ *Pycnonotus priocephalus.* GREY-HEADED BULBUL. (pen sw India).... _____

❑ *Pycnonotus atriceps.* BLACK-HEADED BULBUL. (s,se Asia, sw Phil)... _____

❑ *Pycnonotus melanicterus.* BLACK-CRESTED BULBUL. (s,se Asia)..... _____
   ___*P. (m.) flaviventris.* BLACK-CRESTED YELLOW BULBUL. (s Asia)
   ___*P. (m.) gularis.* RUBY-THROATED BULBUL. (pen India)
   ___*P. (m.) melanicterus.* BLACK-HEADED YELLOW BULBUL. (Ceylon)
   ___*P. (m.) dispar.* YELLOW BULBUL. (se Asia)

❑ *Pycnonotus squamatus.* SCALY-BREASTED BULBUL. (se Asia)....... _____

❏ *Pycnonotus cyaniventris.* GREY-BELLIED BULBUL. (se Asia)........ _____

❏ *Pycnonotus jocosus.* RED-WHISKERED B. (s,se Asia; ◆ Aust, Haw Is). _____

❏ *Pycnonotus xanthorrhous.* BROWN-BREASTED BULBUL. (s Asia)..... _____

❏ *Pycnonotus sinensis.* LIGHT-VENTED BULBUL. (s Asia)............ _____

❏ *Pycnonotus taivanus.* STYAN'S BULBUL. (e,s Taiwan)............. _____

❏ *Pycnonotus barbatus.* GARDEN BULBUL. (n,w,c,ne Afr)........... _____
   ___*P. (b.) barbatus.* WHITE-VENTED BULBUL. (n,w,c Afr)
   ___*P. (b.) arsinoe.* EGYPTIAN BULBUL. (ne Afr)

❏ *Pycnonotus somaliensis.* SOMALI BULBUL. (ne Afr)............... _____

❏ *Pycnonotus dodsoni.* DODSON'S BULBUL. (e Afr)................. _____

❏ *Pycnonotus tricolor.* DARK-CAPPED BULBUL. (c,e,se Afr).......... _____

❏ *Pycnonotus nigricans.* BLACK-FRONTED BULBUL. (sw Afr)......... _____

❏ *Pycnonotus capensis.* CAPE BULBUL. (sw S Afr)................. _____

❏ *Pycnonotus xanthopygos.* WHITE-SPECTACLED BULBUL. (sc Eura).... _____

❏ *Pycnonotus leucotis.* WHITE-EARED BULBUL. (sw Asia)........... _____

❏ *Pycnonotus leucogenys.* HIMALAYAN BULBUL. (Himal)........... _____

❏ *Pycnonotus cafer.* RED-VENTED BULBUL. (s Asia; ◆ Polyn, Haw Is) . _____

❏ *Pycnonotus aurigaster.* SOOTY-HEADED BULBUL. (se Asia)......... _____

❏ *Pycnonotus eutilotus.* PUFF-BACKED BULBUL. (se Asia)........... _____

❏ *Pycnonotus nieuwenhuisii.* BLUE-WATTLED BULBUL. (Sum, Born).... _____

❏ *Pycnonotus urostictus.* YELLOW-WATTLED BULBUL. (Phil)......... _____

❏ *Pycnonotus bimaculatus.* ORANGE-SPOTTED BULBUL. (mts G Sunda) . _____

❏ *Pycnonotus finlaysoni.* STRIPE-THROATED BULBUL. (se Asia)....... _____

❏ *Pycnonotus xantholaemus.* YELLOW-THROATEDBULBUL. (s India).... _____

❏ *Pycnonotus penicillatus.* YELLOW-EARED BULBUL. (mts Ceylon)..... _____

❏ *Pycnonotus flavescens.* FLAVESCENT BULBUL. (mts s,se Asia)...... _____

❏ *Pycnonotus luteolus.* WHITE-BROWED BULBUL. (s India).......... _____

❏ *Pycnonotus goiavier.* YELLOW-VENTED BULBUL. (se Asia, Phil)..... _____

❏ *Pycnonotus plumosus.* OLIVE-WINGED BULBUL. (se Asia, sw Phil).... _____

❏ *Pycnonotus blanfordi.* STREAK-EARED BULBUL. (se Asia).......... _____

❏ *Pycnonotus simplex.* CREAM-VENTED BULBUL. (se Asia).......... _____

❏ *Pycnonotus brunneus.* RED-EYED BULBUL. (se Asia)............. _____

❏ *Pycnonotus erythropthalmos.* SPECTACLED BULBUL. (se Asia)....... _____

❏ *Andropadus montanus.* CAMEROON GREENBUL. (mts w Afr)....... _____

❑ *Andropadus kakamegae.* KAKAMEGA GREENBUL. (mts ec Afr)...... _____

❑ *Andropadus masukuensis.* SHELLEY'S GREENBUL. (mts ec Afr)..... _____

❑ *Andropadus virens.* LITTLE GREENBUL. (w,c,e Afr)............. _____

❑ *Andropadus hallae.* HALL'S GREENBUL. (e Zaire)............... _____

❑ *Andropadus gracilis.* GREY GREENBUL. (w,c Afr)............... _____

❑ *Andropadus ansorgei.* ANSORGE'S GREENBUL. (w,c Afr).......... _____

❑ *Andropadus curvirostris.* PLAIN GREENBUL. (w,c Afr)........... _____

❑ *Andropadus gracilirostris.* SLENDER-BILLED GREENBUL. (w,c Afr).... _____

❑ *Andropadus importunus.* SOMBRE GREENBUL. (e,s Afr)........... _____
    ___*A. (i.) insularis.* ZANZIBAR SOMBRE-GREENBUL. (e,se Afr)
    ___*A. (i.) fricki.* FRICK'S SOMBRE-GREENBUL. (mts c Kenya)
    ___*A. (i.) importunus.* SOUTHERN SOMBRE-GREENBUL. (s Afr)

❑ *Andropadus latirostris.* YELLOW-WHISKERED GREENBUL. (w,c Afr)... _____

❑ *Andropadus tephrolaemus.* GREY-THROATED GREENBUL. (mts wc Afr). _____

❑ *Andropadus nigriceps.* MOUNTAIN GREENBUL. (mts e Afr)......... _____

❑ *Andropadus chlorigula.* GREEN-THROATED GREENBUL. (mts Tanz)... _____

❑ *Andropadus olivaceiceps.* OLIVE-HEADED GREENBUL. (mts e Afr).... _____

❑ *Andropadus milanjensis.* STRIPE-CHEEKED GREENBUL. (mts se Afr)... _____

❑ *Calyptocichla serina.* GOLDEN GREENBUL. (w,c Afr)............. _____

❑ *Baeopogon indicator.* HONEYGUIDE GREENBUL. (w,c Afr)......... _____

❑ *Baeopogon clamans.* WHITE-TAILED GREENBUL. (c Afr)........... _____

❑ *Ixonotus guttatus.* SPOTTED GREENBUL. (w,c Afr)............... _____

❑ *Chlorocichla simplex.* SIMPLE GREENBUL. (w,c Afr)............. _____

❑ *Chlorocichla flavicollis.* YELLOW-THROATED GREENBUL. (w,c Afr)... _____

❑ *Chlorocichla falkensteini.* YELLOW-NECKED GREENBUL. (wc Afr).... _____

❑ *Chlorocichla flaviventris.* YELLOW-BELLIED GREENBUL. (e,s,wc Afr) . _____

❑ *Chlorocichla laetissima.* JOYFUL GREENBUL. (mts ec Afr)......... _____

❑ *Chlorocichla prigoginei.* PRIGOGINE'S GREENBUL. (mts ne Zaire)..... _____

❑ *Thescelocichla leucopleura.* SWAMP GREENBUL. (w,c Afr)......... _____

❑ *Phyllastrephus scandens.* LEAF-LOVE. (w,c Afr)................ _____

❑ *Phyllastrephus cabanisi.* CABANIS'S GREENBUL. (mts ec,sc Afr)...... _____

❑ *Phyllastrephus fischeri.* FISCHER'S GREENBUL. (e Afr)............ _____

❑ *Phyllastrephus placidus.* PLACID GREENBUL. (mts e Afr).......... _____

❑ *Phyllastrephus terrestris.* TERRESTRIAL BROWNBUL. (e,se Afr)...... _____

❑ *Phyllastrephus strepitans.* NORTHERN BROWNBUL. (e Afr)......... _____

❑ *Phyllastrephus fulviventris.* PALE-OLIVE GREENBUL. (wc Afr)....... _____

❑ *Phyllastrephus cerviniventris.* GREY-OLIVE GREENBUL. (e,sc Afr). . . . _____

❑ *Phyllastrephus baumanni.* BAUMANN'S OLIVE-GREENBUL. (w Afr). . . _____

❑ *Phyllastrephus poensis.* CAMEROON OLIVE-GREENBUL. (mts wc Afr) . _____

❑ *Phyllastrephus hypochloris.* TORO OLIVE-GREENBUL. (ec Afr). . . . . . . _____

❑ *Phyllastrephus lorenzi.* SASSI'S GREENBUL. (e Zaire). . . . . _____

❑ *Phyllastrephus poliocephalus.* GREY-HEADED GREENBUL. (wc Afr). . . _____

❑ *Phyllastrephus flavostriatus.* YELLOW-STREAKED GREENBUL. (e,se Afr) _____

❑ *Phyllastrephus alfredi.* SHARPE'S GREENBUL. (mts ec Afr). . . . . _____

❑ *Phyllastrephus debilis.* TINY GREENBUL. (e Afr). . . . . _____
   ___*P. (d.) debilis.* TINY GREENBUL. (sp)
   ___*P. (d.) albigula.* USAMBARA GREENBUL. (mts ne Tanz)

❑ *Phyllastrephus albigularis.* WHITE-THROATED GREENBUL. (w,c Afr). . _____

❑ *Phyllastrephus icterinus.* ICTERINE GREENBUL. (w,c Afr). . . . . _____

❑ *Phyllastrephus leucolepis.* LIBERIAN GREENBUL. (se Liberia). . . . . . . _____

❑ *Phyllastrephus xavieri.* XAVIER'S GREENBUL. (c Afr). . . . . _____

❑ *Phyllastrephus madagascariensis.* LONG-BILLED GREENBUL. (Mad). . . _____

❑ *Phyllastrephus zosterops.* SPECTACLED GREENBUL. (Mad). . . . . _____

❑ *Phyllastrephus apperti.* APPERT'S GREENBUL. (sw Mad). . . . . _____

❑ *Phyllastrephus tenebrosus.* DUSKY GREENBUL. (ne,ce Mad). . . . . _____

❑ *Phyllastrephus cinereiceps.* GREY-CROWNED GREENBUL. (ce Mad). . . _____

❑ *Bleda syndactyla.* COMMON BRISTLEBILL. (w,c Afr). . . . . _____

❑ *Bleda eximia.* GREEN-TAILED BRISTLEBILL. (w,c Afr). . . . . _____

❑ *Bleda canicapilla.* GREY-HEADED BRISTLEBILL. (w Afr). . . . . _____

❑ *Nicator chloris.* YELLOW-SPOTTED NICATOR. (w,c Afr). . . . . _____

❑ *Nicator gularis.* EASTERN NICATOR. (e Afr). _____

❑ *Nicator vireo.* YELLOW-THROATED NICATOR. (c Afr). . . . . _____

❑ *Criniger barbatus.* BEARDED BULBUL. (w,c Afr). . . . . _____

❑ *Criniger chloronotus.* GREEN-BACKED BULBUL. (c Afr). . . . . _____

❑ *Criniger calurus.* RED-TAILED BULBUL. (w,c Afr). . . . . _____

❑ *Criniger olivaceus.* YELLOW-BEARDED BULBUL. (w Afr). . . . . _____

❑ *Criniger ndussumensis.* WHITE-BEARDED BULBUL. (c Afr). . . . . _____

❑ *Alophoixus finschii.* FINSCH'S BULBUL. (se Asia). . . . . _____

❑ *Alophoixus flaveolus.* WHITE-THROATED BULBUL. (s Asia). . . . . _____

❑ *Alophoixus pallidus.* PUFF-THROATED BULBUL. (se Asia). . . . . _____

❑ *Alophoixus ochraceus.* OCHRACEOUS BULBUL. (se Asia). . . . . _____

❏ *Alophoixus bres.* GREY-CHEEKED BULBUL. (se Asia-sw Phil)....... _____
   ___*A. (b.) tephrogenys.* GREY-CHEEKED BULBUL. (Malay)
   ___*A. (b.) bres.* SCRUB BULBUL. (G Sunda-sw Phil)

❏ *Alophoixus phaeocephalus.* YELLOW-BELLIED BULBUL. (s Asia)..... _____

❏ *Alophoixus affinis.* GOLDEN BULBUL. (is e Sulaw, Moluc)......... _____

❏ *Setornis criniger.* HOOK-BILLED BULBUL. (e Sum, Born)........... _____

❏ *Tricholestes criniger.* HAIRY-BACKED BULBUL. (se Asia).......... _____

❏ *Iole virescens.* OLIVE BULBUL. (s Asia)..................... _____

❏ *Iole propinqua.* GREY-EYED BULBUL. (se Asia)................. _____

❏ *Iole olivacea.* BUFF-VENTED BULBUL. (se Asia)................. _____

❏ *Iole indica.* YELLOW-BROWED BULBUL. (mts s India)............. _____

❏ *Ixos palawanensis.* SULPHUR-BELLIED BULBUL. (mts sw Phil)....... _____

❏ *Ixos philippinus.* PHILIPPINE BULBUL. (Phil).................... _____

❏ *Ixos rufigularis.* ZAMBOANGA BULBUL. (s Phil).................. _____

❏ *Ixos siquijorensis.* STREAK-BREASTED BULBUL. (c Phil)........... _____

❏ *Ixos amaurotis.* BROWN-EARED BULBUL. (e Asia)................. _____

❏ *Ixos everetti.* YELLOWISH BULBUL. (c,s Phil).................... _____

❏ *Ixos malaccensis.* STREAKED BULBUL. (se Asia)................. _____

❏ *Hemixos flavala.* ASHY BULBUL. (s,se Asia).................... _____

❏ *Hemixos castanonotus.* CHESTNUT BULBUL. (s Asia)............. _____

❏ *Hypsipetes mcclellandii.* MOUNTAIN BULBUL. (mts s,se Asia)....... _____

❏ *Hypsipetes virescens.* SUNDA BULBUL. (Sum, Java)............... _____

❏ *Hypsipetes madagascariensis.* MADAGASCAR BULBUL. (Mad reg).... _____

❏ *Hypsipetes crassirostris.* SEYCHELLES BULBUL. (Seyc)............. _____

❏ *Hypsipetes parvirostris.* COMORO BULBUL. (Com)................ _____

❏ *Hypsipetes borbonicus.* OLIVACEOUS BULBUL. (Masc)............. _____
   ___*H. (b.) olivaceus.* MAURITIUS BULBUL. (Maur)
   ___*H. (b.) borbonicus.* REUNION BULBUL. (Réun)

❏ *Hypsipetes leucocephalus.* BLACK BULBUL. (s,se Asia)............. _____

❏ *Hypsipetes nicobariensis.* NICOBAR BULBUL. (Nico).............. _____

❏ *Hypsipetes thompsoni.* WHITE-HEADED BULBUL. (se Asia)......... _____

❏ *Neolestes torquatus.* BLACK-COLLARED BULBUL. (c Afr)........... _____

❏ *Malia grata.* MALIA. (mts Sulaw)........................... _____

Family **Hypocoliidae** [1/1]

❏ *Hypocolius ampelinus.* GREY HYPOCOLIUS. (sw Asia)............. _____

Family **Cisticolidae** [17/120]

❏ *Cisticola erythrops*. RED-FACED CISTICOLA. (Afr)................. _____

❏ *Cisticola lepe*. LEPE CISTICOLA. (wc Afr)...................... _____

❏ *Cisticola cantans*. SINGING CISTICOLA. (w,c,se Afr).............. _____

❏ *Cisticola lateralis*. WHISTLING CISTICOLA. (w,c Afr)............. _____

❏ *Cisticola anonymus*. CHATTERING CISTICOLA. (wc Afr)............ _____

❏ *Cisticola woosnami*. TRILLING CISTICOLA. (ec Afr)............... _____

❏ *Cisticola bulliens*. BUBBLING CISTICOLA. (wc Afr)............... _____

❏ *Cisticola discolor*. BROWN-BACKED CISTICOLA. (mts wc Afr)....... _____

❏ *Cisticola chubbi*. CHUBB'S CISTICOLA. (mts ec Afr).............. _____

❏ *Cisticola hunteri*. HUNTER'S CISTICOLA. (mts ne Afr)............. _____

❏ *Cisticola nigriloris*. BLACK-LORED CISTICOLA. (mts se Afr)......... _____

❏ *Cisticola emini*. ROCK-LOVING CISTICOLA. (w,c Afr).............. _____

❏ *Cisticola aberrans*. LAZY CISTICOLA. (se,e Afr)................. _____

❏ *Cisticola bodessa*. BORAN CISTICOLA. (ne Afr)................. _____

❏ *Cisticola chinianus*. RATTLING CISTICOLA. (c,e,s Afr)............. _____

❏ *Cisticola cinereolus*. ASHY CISTICOLA. (ne Afr)................. _____

❏ *Cisticola ruficeps*. RED-PATE CISTICOLA. (subsah Afr)............. _____

❏ *Cisticola mongalla*. MONGALLA CISTICOLA. (ne Afr)............. _____

❏ *Cisticola dorsti*. DORST'S CISTICOLA. (wc Afr).................. _____

❏ *Cisticola rufilatus*. GREY CISTICOLA. (s Afr)................... _____

❏ *Cisticola subruficapillus*. RED-HEADED CISTICOLA. (sw Afr)........ _____

❏ *Cisticola lais*. WAILING CISTICOLA. (c,s Afr).................. _____

❏ *Cisticola distinctus*. LYNES'S CISTICOLA. (mts e Afr)............. _____

❏ *Cisticola restrictus*. TANA RIVER CISTICOLA. (ne Kenya)........... _____

❏ *Cisticola njombe*. CHURRING CISTICOLA. (mts ec Afr)............. _____

❏ *Cisticola galactotes*. WINDING CISTICOLA. (Afr)................ _____
   ___*C. (g.) galactotes*. WINDING CISTICOLA. (sp)
   ___*C. (g.) luapula*. LUAPULA CISTICOLA. (Zambia)

❏ *Cisticola pipiens*. CHIRPING CISTICOLA. (wc Afr)................ _____

❏ *Cisticola carruthersi*. CARRUTHERS'S CISTICOLA. (ec Afr).......... _____

❏ *Cisticola tinniens*. TINKLING CISTICOLA. (ec,s Afr).............. _____

❏ *Cisticola angolensis*. ANGOLA CISTICOLA. (c Afr)............... _____
   ___*C. (a.) angolensis*. ANGOLA CISTICOLA. (wc Afr)
   ___*C. (a.) awemba*. AWEMBA CISTICOLA. (ec Afr)

❏ *Cisticola robustus*. STOUT CISTICOLA. (mts e Afr)............... _____

❏ *Cisticola aberdare.* ABERDARE CISTICOLA. (mts c Kenya). . . . . _____

❏ *Cisticola natalensis.* CROAKING CISTICOLA. (Afr). . . . . _____

❏ *Cisticola fulvicapillus.* PIPING CISTICOLA. (c,s Afr). . . . . _____

❏ *Cisticola angusticauda.* TABORA CISTICOLA. (ec Afr). . . . . _____

❏ *Cisticola melanurus.* BLACK-TAILED CISTICOLA. (c Afr). . . . . _____

❏ *Cisticola brachypterus.* SIFFLING CISTICOLA. (Afr). . . . . _____

❏ *Cisticola rufus.* RUFOUS CISTICOLA. (w Afr). . . . . _____

❏ *Cisticola troglodytes.* FOXY CISTICOLA. (nc,ne Afr). . . . . _____

❏ *Cisticola nanus.* TINY CISTICOLA. (ne Afr). . . . . _____

❏ *Cisticola incanus.* SOCOTRA CISTICOLA. (Socotra). . . . . _____

❏ *Cisticola juncidis.* ZITTING CISTICOLA. (s Eura-Afr, Aust). . . . . _____

❏ *Cisticola haesitatus.* ISLAND CISTICOLA. (Socotra). . . . . _____

❏ *Cisticola cherinus.* MADAGASCAR CISTICOLA. (Ald, Mad). . . . . _____

❏ *Cisticola aridulus.* DESERT CISTICOLA. (Afr). . . . . _____

❏ *Cisticola textrix.* TINK-TINK CISTICOLA. (s Afr). . . . . _____

❏ *Cisticola eximius.* BLACK-NECKED CISTICOLA. (subsah Afr). . . . . _____

❏ *Cisticola dambo.* CLOUD-SCRAPING CISTICOLA. (c Afr). . . . . _____

❏ *Cisticola brunnescens.* PECTORAL-PATCH CISTICOLA. (mts c,e,s Afr) . _____

❏ *Cisticola ayresii.* WING-SNAPPING CISTICOLA. (c,s Afr). . . . . _____

❏ *Cisticola exilis.* GOLDEN-HEADED CISTICOLA. (s Asia-Bism, n,e Aust). _____

❏ *Scotocerca inquieta.* STREAKED SCRUB-WARBLER. (s Palea). . . . . _____

❏ *Rhopophilus pekinensis.* WHITE-BROWED CHINESE W. (w,n China). . . _____

❏ *Prinia burnesii.* RUFOUS-VENTED PRINIA. (s Asia). . . . . _____
  ___*P. (b.) burnesii.* LONG-TAILED PRINIA. (Pakistan)
  ___*P. (b.) cinerascens.* SWAMP PRINIA. (e India)

❏ *Prinia criniger.* STRIATED PRINIA. (s Asia). . . . . _____

❏ *Prinia polychroa.* BROWN PRINIA. (se Asia). . . . . _____

❏ *Prinia atrogularis.* HILL PRINIA. (mts s,se Asia). . . . . _____

❏ *Prinia cinereocapilla.* GREY-CROWNED PRINIA. (n India). . . . . _____

❏ *Prinia buchanani.* RUFOUS-FRONTED PRINIA. (sc Asia). . . . . _____

❏ *Prinia rufescens.* RUFESCENT PRINIA. (s,se Asia). . . . . _____

❏ *Prinia hodgsonii.* GREY-BREASTED PRINIA. (s,se Asia). . . . . _____

❏ *Prinia gracilis.* GRACEFUL PRINIA. (ne Afr, sc Asia). . . . . _____

❏ *Prinia sylvatica.* JUNGLE PRINIA. (s Asia). _____

❑ *Prinia familiaris.* BAR-WINGED PRINIA. (Sum-Bali). . . . . _____

❑ *Prinia flaviventris.* YELLOW-BELLIED PRINIA. (s,se Asia). . . . . _____

❑ *Prinia socialis.* ASHY PRINIA. (India). . . . . _____

❑ *Prinia subflava.* TAWNY-FLANKED PRINIA. (Afr). . . . . _____

❑ *Prinia somalica.* PALE PRINIA. (ne Afr). _____

❑ *Prinia inornata.* PLAIN PRINIA. (s,se Asia). . . . . _____

❑ *Prinia fluviatilis.* RIVER PRINIA. (w Afr). _____

❑ *Prinia flavicans.* BLACK-CHESTED PRINIA. (s Afr). . . . . _____

❑ *Prinia maculosa.* KAROO PRINIA. (s Afr). _____
    ___*P. (m.) maculosa.* KAROO PRINIA. (sw Afr)
    ___*P. (m.) hypoxantha.* DRAKENSBURG PRINIA. (S Afr)

❑ *Prinia molleri.* SAO TOME PRINIA. (ST). . . . . _____

❑ *Prinia leontica.* SIERRA LEONE PRINIA. (mts w Afr). . . . . _____

❑ *Prinia leucopogon.* WHITE-CHINNED PRINIA. (c Afr). . . . . _____

❑ *Prinia bairdii.* BANDED PRINIA. (c Afr). . . . . _____

❑ *Prinia melanops.* BLACK-FACED PRINIA. (mts ec Afr). . . . . _____

❑ *Phragmacia substriata.* NAMAQUA WARBLER. (s Afr). . . . . _____

❑ *Oreophilais robertsi.* BRIAR WARBLER. (mts se Afr). . . . . _____

❑ *Heliolais erythroptera.* RED-WINGED WARBLER. (w,c,e Afr). . . . . _____

❑ *Malcorus pectoralis.* RUFOUS-EARED WARBLER. (s Afr). . . . . _____

❑ *Drymocichla incana.* RED-WINGED GREY WARBLER. (c Afr). . . . . _____

❑ *Urolais epichlora.* GREEN LONGTAIL. (mts wc Afr). . . . . _____

❑ *Spiloptila clamans.* CRICKET LONGTAIL. (Saharan Afr). . . . . _____

❑ *Apalis pulchra.* BLACK-COLLARED APALIS. (mts c,e Afr). . . . . _____

❑ *Apalis ruwenzorii.* COLLARED APALIS. (mts e Afr). . . . . _____

❑ *Apalis thoracica.* BAR-THROATED APALIS. (mts e,s Afr). . . . . _____
    ___*A. (t.) griseiceps.* GREY-HEADED APALIS. (sp)
    ___*A. (t.) fuscigularis.* TEITA APALIS. (se Kenya)
    ___*A. (t.) murinus.* MOUSE APALIS. (se Afr)
    ___*A. (t.) flavigularis.* YELLOW-THROATED APALIS. (nc Moz)
    ___*A. (t.) lynesi.* NAMULI APALIS. (ne Moz)
    ___*A. (t.) thoracica.* BAR-THROATED APALIS. (s S Afr)

❑ *Apalis nigriceps.* BLACK-CAPPED APALIS. (subsah Afr). . . . . _____

❑ *Apalis jacksoni.* BLACK-THROATED APALIS. (c,e Afr). . . . . _____

❑ *Apalis chariessa.* WHITE-WINGED APALIS. (e Afr). . . . . _____

❑ *Apalis binotata.* MASKED APALIS. (c Afr). _____

❑ *Apalis personata.* BLACK-FACED APALIS. (mts ec Afr). . . . . _____

❑ *Apalis flavida.* YELLOW-BREASTED APALIS. (Afr)................ _____

❑ *Apalis viridiceps.* BROWN-TAILED APALIS. (ne Afr).............. _____

❑ *Apalis ruddi.* RUDD'S APALIS. (se Afr)......................... _____

❑ *Apalissharpei.* SHARPE'S APALIS. (w Afr)...................... _____

❑ *Apalis rufogularis.* BUFF-THROATED APALIS. (mts w,c Afr)......... _____
   ___*A. (r.) rufogularis.* BUFF-THROATED APALIS. (w,wc Afr)
   ___*A. (r.) nigrescens.* BLACK-BACKED APALIS. (ec Afr)

❑ *Apalis argentea.* KUNGWE APALIS. (mts ec Afr)................. _____
   ___*A. (a.) eidos.* PETERS'S APALIS. (ce Zaire)
   ___*A. (a.) argentea.* KUNGWE APALIS. (se Zaire, w Tanz)

❑ *Apalis bamendae.* BAMENDA APALIS. (mts Camer)............... _____

❑ *Apalis goslingi.* GOSLING'S APALIS. (mts wc Afr)............... _____

❑ *Apalis porphyrolaema.* CHESTNUT-THROATED APALIS. (mts ec Afr)... _____

❑ *Apalis kaboboensis.* KABOBO APALIS. (mts se Zaire)............. _____

❑ *Apalis chapini.* CHAPIN'S APALIS. (mts ec Afr).................. _____
   ___*A. (c.) strausae.* STRAUS'S APALIS. (sp)
   ___*A. (c.) chapini.* CHAPIN'S APALIS. (ec Tanz)

❑ *Apalis melanocephala.* BLACK-HEADED APALIS. (e Afr)........... _____

❑ *Apalis chirindensis.* CHIRINDA APALIS. (mts se Afr)............. _____

❑ *Apalis cinerea.* GREY APALIS. (mts c,e Afr).................... _____

❑ *Apalis alticola.* BROWN-HEADED APALIS. (mts c Afr)............. _____

❑ *Apalis karamojae.* KARAMOJA APALIS. (mts e Afr).............. _____

❑ *Apalis rufifrons.* RED-FACED APALIS. (ne Afr).................. _____

❑ *Hypergerus atriceps.* ORIOLE WARBLER. (w Afr)................ _____

❑ *Eminia lepida.* GREY-CAPPED WARBLER. (mts e Afr)............. _____

❑ *Camaroptera brevicaudata.* GREY-BACKED CAMAROPTERA. (Afr)..... _____

❑ *Camaroptera harterti.* HARTERT'S CAMAROPTERA. (nw Ang)....... _____

❑ *Camaroptera brachyura.* GREEN-BACKED CAMAROPTERA. (e,s Afr)... _____

❑ *Camaroptera superciliaris.* YELLOW-BROWED CAM. (w,c Afr)....... _____

❑ *Camaroptera chloronota.* OLIVE-GREEN CAMAROPTERA. (w,c Afr).... _____

❑ *Calamonastes simplex.* GREY WREN-WARBLER. (c,ne Afr)......... _____
   ___*C. (s.) cinereus.* WESTERN WREN-WARBLER. (sc Afr)
   ___*C. (s.) undosus.* ZAMBIA WREN-WARBLER. (ec Afr)
   ___*C. (s.) simplex.* GREY WREN-WARBLER. (ne Afr)

❑ *Calamonastes stierlingi.* STIERLING'S WREN-WARBLER. (se Afr)...... _____

❑ *Calamonastes fasciolatus.* BARRED WREN-WARBLER. (s Afr)....... _____

❑ *Euryptila subcinnamomea.* KOPJE WARBLER. (sw Afr)............ _____

Family **Zosteropidae** [13/95]

❑ *Speirops melanocephalus.* CAMEROON SPEIROPS. (mts sw Camer). . . . _____

❑ *Speirops lugubris.* BLACK-CAPPED SPEIROPS. (mts ST). . . . . _____

❑ *Speirops brunneus.* FERNANDO PO SPEIROPS. (mts Bioko). . . . . _____

❑ *Speirops leucophoeus.* PRINCIPE SPEIROPS. (Prín)). . . . . _____

❑ *Zosterops senegalensis.* AFRICAN YELLOW WHITE-EYE. (Afr). . . . . _____

❑ *Zosterops aughani.* PEMBA WHITE-EYE. (is se Tanz). . . . . _____

❑ *Zosterops mayottensis.* CHESTNUT-SIDED WHITE-EYE. (Seyc, Com). . . _____
    Z. (m.) semiflavus. SEYCHELLES YELLOW WHITE-EYE. (†Seyc)
   ___*Z. (m.) mayottensis.* MAYOTTE WHITE-EYE. (Com)

❑ *Zosterops poliogaster.* BROAD-RINGED WHITE-EYE. (mts ne Afr). . . . . . _____
   ___*Z. (p.) poliogaster.* HEUGLIN'S WHITE-EYE. (w,c Eth)
   ___*Z. (p.) kikuyuensis.* KIKUYU WHITE-EYE. (c Kenya)
   ___*Z. (p.) silvanus.* TEITA WHITE-EYE. (se Kenya)
   ___*Z. (p.) eurycricotus.* BROAD-RINGED WHITE-EYE. (ne Tanz)

❑ *Zosterops abyssinicus.* WHITE-BREASTED WHITE-EYE. (ne,ce Afr reg). . _____
   ___*Z. (a.) abyssinicus.* ABYSSINIAN WHITE-EYE. (ne Afr reg)
   ___*Z. (a.) flavilateralis.* KENYA WHITE-EYE. (ce Afr)

❑ *Zosterops pallidus.* PALE WHITE-EYE. (s Afr). . . . . _____
   ___*Z. (p.) pallidus.* PALE WHITE-EYE. (sw Afr)
   ___*Z. (p.) virens.* GREEN WHITE-EYE. (se Afr)
   ___*Z. (p.) capensis.* CAPE WHITE-EYE. (s S Afr)

❑ *Zosterops maderaspatanus.* MADAGASCAR WHITE-EYE. (Mad reg). . . . _____
   ___*Z. (m.) kirki.* KIRK'S WHITE-EYE. (Com)
   ___*Z. (m.) maderaspatanus.* MALAGASY WHITE-EYE. (sp)

❑ *Zosterops mouroniensis.* COMORO WHITE-EYE. (mts Com). . . . . _____

❑ *Zosterops ficedulinus.* PRINCIPE WHITE-EYE. (Prín, ST). . . . . _____

❑ *Zosterops griseovirescens.* ANNOBON WHITE-EYE. (Pagalu). . . . . _____

❑ *Zosterops borbonicus.* MASCARENE GREY WHITE-EYE. (Réun, Maur) . _____

❑ *Zosterops olivaceus.* REUNION OLIVE WHITE-EYE. (Réun). . . . . _____

❑ *Zosterops chloronothos.* MAURITIUS OLIVE WHITE-EYE. (Maur). . . . . . _____

❑ *Zosterops modestus.* SEYCHELLES GREY WHITE-EYE. (Seyc). . . . . _____

❑ *Zosterops ceylonensis.* CEYLON WHITE-EYE. (mts Ceylon). . . . . _____

❑ *Zosterops erythropleurus.* CHESTNUT-FLANKED WHITE-EYE. (e,s Asia). _____

❑ *Zosterops palpebrosus.* ORIENTAL WHITE-EYE. (s,se Asia-w L Sunda) . _____

❑ *Zosterops japonicus.* JAPANESE WHITE-EYE. (e,se Asia; ◆ Haw Is). . . . _____ _____

❑ *Zosterops meyeni.* LOWLAND WHITE-EYE. (n Phil). . . . . _____

❑ *Zosterops salvadorii.* ENGGANO WHITE-EYE. (is w Sum). . . . . _____

❑ *Zosterops conspicillatus.* BRIDLED WHITE-EYE. (Mari). . . . . _____
   ___*Z. (c.) saypani.* SAIPAN WHITE-EYE. (sc Mari)
   ___*Z. (c.) rotensis.* ROTA WHITE-EYE. (cs Mari)
   ___*Z. (c.) conspicillatus.* BRIDLED WHITE-EYE. (s Mari)

❑ *Zosterops hypolais.* PLAIN WHITE-EYE. (nw Carol). . . . . _____

❑ *Zosterops semperi.* CAROLINE ISLANDS WHITE-EYE. (Palau, Carol). . . . _____

❑ *Zosterops atricapillus.* BLACK-CAPPED WHITE-EYE. (mts Sum, Born) . _____

❑ *Zosterops everetti.* EVERETT'S WHITE-EYE. (se Asia, c,w Phil). . . . . . . _____

❑ *Zosterops nigrorum.* GOLDEN-GREEN WHITE-EYE. (Phil). . . . . _____

❑ *Zosterops montanus.* MOUNTAIN WHITE-EYE. (mts Sum-Moluc, Phil). _____

❑ *Zosterops natalis.* CHRISTMAS ISLAND WHITE-EYE. (Chris). . . . . _____

❑ *Zosterops flavus.* JAVAN WHITE-EYE. (nw Java, se Born). . . . . _____

❑ *Zosterops chloris.* LEMON-BELLIED WHITE-EYE. (Wall). . . . . _____

❑ *Zosterops citrinellus.* ASHY-BELLIED WHITE-EYE. (L Sunda, ne Aust) . _____
   ___*Z. (c.) citrinellus.* ASHY-BELLIED WHITE-EYE. (wc L Sunda)
   ___*Z. (c.) harterti.* ALOR WHITE-EYE. (c L Sunda)
   ___*Z. (c.) albiventris.* WHITE-BELLIED WHITE-EYE. (e L Sunda, ne Aust)

❑ *Zosterops grayi.* PEARL-BELLIED WHITE-EYE. (w Kai). . . . . _____

❑ *Zosterops uropygialis.* GOLDEN-BELLIED WHITE-EYE. (e Kai). . . . . . . _____

❑ *Zosterops consobrinorum.* PALE-BELLIED WHITE-EYE. (se Sulaw). . . . _____

❑ *Zosterops anomalus.* LEMON-THROATED WHITE-EYE. (sw Sulaw). . . . . _____

❑ *Zosterops wallacei.* YELLOW-SPECTACLED WHITE-EYE. (L Sunda). . . . . _____

❑ *Zosterops atrifrons.* BLACK-CROWNED WHITE-EYE. (mts n,c Sulaw). . . _____

❑ *Zosterops atriceps.* CREAMY-THROATED WHITE-EYE. (n Moluc). . . . . . _____

❑ *Zosterops minor.* BLACK-FRONTED WHITE-EYE. (mts NG). . . . . _____
   ___*Z. (m.) chrysolaemus.* ARFAK BLACK-FRONTED WHITE-EYE. (w NG)
   ___*Z. (m.) minor.* PAPUAN BLACK-FRONTED WHITE-EYE. (n NG)
   ___*Z. (m.) delicatulus.* SMALL BLACK-FRONTED WHITE-EYE. (e NG)

❑ *Zosterops meeki.* WHITE-THROATED WHITE-EYE. (se NG). . . . . _____

❑ *Zosterops hypoxanthus.* BLACK-HEADED WHITE-EYE. (Bism). . . . . _____

❑ *Zosterops mysorensis.* BIAK WHITE-EYE. (mts nw NG). . . . . _____

❑ *Zosterops fuscicapillus.* CAPPED WHITE-EYE. (mts NG). . . . . _____
   ___*Z. (f.) fuscicapillus.* CAPPED WHITE-EYE. (w,c NG)
   ___*Z. (f.) crookshanki.* CROOKSHANK'S WHITE-EYE. (se NG)

❑ *Zosterops buruensis.* BURU YELLOW WHITE-EYE. (mts Buru). . . . . _____

❑ *Zosterops kuehni.* AMBON YELLOW WHITE-EYE. (Ambon). . . . . _____

❑ *Zosterops novaeguineae.* NEW GUINEA WHITE-EYE. (Aru, NG). . . . . . . _____

❑ *Zosterops luteus.* AUSTRALIAN YELLOW WHITE-EYE. (n Aust). . . . . . . _____

❑ *Zosterops griseotinctus.* LOUISIADE WHITE-EYE. (is e NG, Bism). . . . . _____

❑ *Zosterops rennellianus.* RENNELL WHITE-EYE. (se Solom). . . . . _____

❑ *Zosterops vellalavella.* BANDED WHITE-EYE. (c Solom). . . . . _____

❑ *Zosterops splendidus.* GANONGGA WHITE-EYE. (wc Solom). . . . . _____

❑ *Zosterops luteirostris.* SPLENDID WHITE-EYE. (c Solom). . . . . _____

❑ *Zosterops kulambangrae.* SOLOMON ISLANDS WHITE-EYE. (c Solom) . _____

❑ *Zosterops murphyi.* HERMIT WHITE-EYE. (mts c Solom). . . . . _____

❑ *Zosterops metcalfii.* YELLOW-THROATED WHITE-EYE. (Solom). . . . . . _____

❑ *Zosterops rendovae.* GREY-THROATED WHITE-EYE. (mts Solom). . . . . _____

❑ *Zosterops stresemanni.* MALAITA WHITE-EYE. (se Solom). . . . . _____

❑ *Zosterops sanctaecrucis.* SANTA CRUZ WHITE-EYE. (Santa Cruz). . . . . _____

❑ *Zosterops lateralis.* SILVEREYE. (Aust, NZ, sw Oceania). . . . . _____
   ___*Z. (l.) gouldi.* WESTERN SILVEREYE. (sw Aust)
   ___*Z. (l.) halmaturinus.* GREY-BACKED SILVEREYE. (cs Aust)
   ___*Z. (l.) lateralis.* GREY-BREASTED SILVEREYE. (e Aust, NZ, sw Oceania)

❑ *Zosterops tephropleurus.* LORD HOWE ISLAND WHITE-EYE. (L Howe). _____

  Zosterops strenuus. ROBUST WHITE-EYE. (†L Howe). . . . . _____

  Zosterops tenuirostris. SLENDER-BILLED WHITE-EYE. (†Norfolk). . . . . . _____

❑ *Zosterops albogularis.* WHITE-CHESTED WHITE-EYE. (Norfolk). . . . . . . _____

❑ *Zosterops inornatus.* LARGE LIFOU WHITE-EYE. (Loy). . . . . _____

❑ *Zosterops explorator.* LAYARD'S WHITE-EYE. (mts Fiji). . . . . _____

❑ *Zosterops flavifrons.* YELLOW-FRONTED WHITE-EYE. (Vanu). . . . . _____

❑ *Zosterops xanthochrous.* GREEN-BACKED WHITE-EYE. (N Cal-Loy). . . _____

❑ *Zosterops minutus.* SMALL LIFOU WHITE-EYE. (Loy). . . . . _____

❑ *Zosterops samoensis.* SAMOAN WHITE-EYE. (mts w Samoa). . . . . _____

❑ *Zosterops finschii.* DUSKY WHITE-EYE. (Palau). . . . . _____

❑ *Zosterops cinereus.* GREY-BROWN WHITE-EYE. (e Carol). . . . . _____
   ___*Z. (c.) ponapensis.* GREY-BROWN WHITE-EYE. (Pohnpei)
   ___*Z. (c.) cinereus.* KOSRAE WHITE-EYE. (Kosrae)

❑ *Zosterops oleagineus.* YAP OLIVE WHITE-EYE. (nw Carol). . . . . _____

❑ *Rukia longirostra.* LONG-BILLED WHITE-EYE. (mts e Carol). . . . . _____

❑ *Rukia ruki.* TRUK WHITE-EYE. (e Carol). . . . . _____

❑ *Cleptornis marchei.* GOLDEN WHITE-EYE. (s Mari). . . . . _____

❑ *Tephrozosterops stalkeri.* BICOLORED WHITE-EYE. (mts s Moluc). . . . . _____

❑ *Madanga ruficollis.* RUFOUS-THROATED WHITE-EYE. (mts s Moluc). . . _____

❑ *Lophozosterops javanicus.* JAVAN GREY-THROATED W. (Java, Bali). . . _____

❑ *Lophozosterops squamiceps.* STREAKY-HEADED WHITE-EYE. (Sulaw) . _____

❑ *Lophozosterops goodfellowi.* BLACK-MASKED WHITE-EYE. (s Phil). . . . _____

❑ *Lophozosterops superciliaris.* YELLOW-BROWED W. (wc L Sunda). . . . _____

❑ *Lophozosterops pinaiae.* GREY-HOODED WHITE-EYE. (mts s Moluc). . . _____

❑ *Lophozosterops dohertyi.* CRESTED WHITE-EYE. (mts c L Sunda). . . . . _____

❑ *Oculocincta squamifrons.* PYGMY WHITE-EYE. (mts Born). . . . . _____

❑ *Heleia crassirostris.* THICK-BILLED WHITE-EYE. (c L Sunda). . . . . _____

❑ *Heleia muelleri.* SPOT-BREASTED WHITE-EYE. (Timor). . . . . _____

❑ *Chlorocharis emiliae.* MOUNTAIN BLACKEYE. (mts n Born). . . . . _____

❑ *Woodfordia superciliosa.* BARE-EYED WHITE-EYE. (se Solom). . . . . . . _____

❑ *Woodfordia lacertosa.* SANFORD'S WHITE-EYE. (Santa Cruz). . . . . _____

❑ *Megazosterops palauensis.* GIANT WHITE-EYE. (Palau). . . . . _____

❑ *Hypocryptadius cinnamomeus.* CINNAMON IBON. (mts s Phil). . . . . . . _____

Family **Sylviidae** [101/560]
Sufamily Acrocephalinae [36/223]

❑ *Tesia castaneocoronata.* CHESTNUT-HEADED TESIA. (s Asia). . . . . _____

❑ *Tesia olivea.* SLATY-BELLIED TESIA. (s Asia). . . . . _____

❑ *Tesia cyaniventer.* GREY-BELLIED TESIA. (s Asia, Java). . . . . _____

❑ *Tesia superciliaris.* JAVAN TESIA. (Java). . . . . _____

❑ *Tesia everetti.* RUSSET-CAPPED TESIA. (wc L Sunda). . . . . _____

❑ *Urosphena subulata.* TIMOR STUBTAIL. (Timor). . . . . _____

❑ *Urosphena whiteheadi.* BORNEAN STUBTAIL. (mts Born). . . . . _____

❑ *Urosphena squameiceps.* ASIAN STUBTAIL. (ne Asia; ◊-se Asia). . . . . . _____

❑ *Cettia pallidipes.* PALE-FOOTED BUSH-WARBLER. (s Asia). . . . . _____

❑ *Cettia canturians.* MANCHURIAN BUSH-WARBLER. (ce Asia; ◊ se Asia). _____

❑ *Cettia diphone.* JAPANESE BUSH-WARBLER. (e Asia; ◆ Haw Is). . . . . . _____

❑ *Cettia seebohmi.* PHILIPPINE BUSH-WARBLER. (mts n Phil). . . . . _____

❑ *Cettia annae.* PALAU BUSH-WARBLER. (Palau). . . . . _____

❑ *Cettia parens.* SHADE WARBLER. (mts s Solom). . . . . _____

❑ *Cettia ruficapilla.* FIJI BUSH-WARBLER. (mts Fiji). . . . . _____

❑ *Cettia fortipes.* BROWNISH-FLANKED BUSH-WARBLER. (s Asia). . . . . . _____

❑ *Cettia vulcania.* SUNDA BUSH-WARBLER. (mts Sunda, sw Phil). . . . . . _____

❑ *Cettia carolinae.* TANIMBAR BUSH-WARBLER. (Tanim). . . . . _____

❏ *Cettia major.* CHESTNUT-CROWNED BUSH-WARBLER. (Himal). . . . . . . _____

❏ *Cettia flavolivacea.* ABERRANT BUSH-WARBLER. (mts s Asia). . . . . . . _____

❏ *Cettia acanthizoides.* YELLOWISH-BELLIED BUSH-WARBLER. (s Asia) . _____
   ___*C. (a.) acanthizoides.* YELLOWISH-BELLIED BUSH-WARBLER. (sp)
   ___*C. (a.) concolor.* FORMOSAN BUSH-WARBLER. (Taiwan)

❏ *Cettia brunnifrons.* GREY-SIDED BUSH-WARBLER. (Himal). . . . . _____

❏ *Cettia cetti.* CETTI'S WARBLER. (s Eura). _____

❏ *Bradypterus baboecala.* AFRICAN BUSH-WARBLER. (Afr). . . . . _____

❏ *Bradypterus grandis.* JA RIVER SCRUB-WARBLER. (cw Afr). . . . . _____

❏ *Bradypterus carpalis.* WHITE-WINGED SCRUB-WARBLER. (c Afr). . . . . _____

❏ *Bradypterus graueri.* GRAUER'S SCRUB-WARBLER. (mts c Afr). . . . . . . _____

❏ *Bradypterus alfredi.* BAMBOO SCRUB-WARBLER. (mts c Afr). . . . . _____

❏ *Bradypterus sylvaticus.* KNYSNA SCRUB-WARBLER. (s,e S Afr). . . . . . . _____

❏ *Bradypterus lopezi.* CAMEROON SCRUB-WARBLER. (s Camer, Bioko) . _____
   ___*B. (l.) camerunensis.* CAMEROON SCRUB-WARBLER. (s Camer)
   ___*B. (l.) lopezi.* FERNANDO PO SCRUB-WARBLER. (Bioko)

❏ *Bradypterus mariae.* EVERGREEN FOREST WARBLER. (mts ec,e Afr). . . _____
   ___*B. (m.) barakae.* RUWENZORI SCRUB-WARBLER. (ec Afr)
   ___*B. (m.) mariae.* EVERGREEN FOREST WARBLER. (e Afr)

❏ *Bradypterus barratti.* AFRICAN SCRUB-WARBLER. (mts se Afr). . . . . . . _____

❏ *Bradypterus cinnamomeus.* CINNAMON BRACKEN-WARBLER. (cw-e Afr) _____

❏ *Bradypterus victorini.* VICTORIN'S SCRUB-WARBLER. (mts s S Afr). . . . _____

❏ *Bradypterus thoracicus.* SPOTTED BUSH-WARBLER. (Himal). . . . . _____

❏ *Bradypterus major.* LONG-BILLED BUSH-WARBLER. (Himal). . . . . _____

❏ *Bradypterus tacsanowskius.* CHINESE BUSH-WARBLER. (mts s,e Asia). _____

❏ *Bradypterus luteoventris.* BROWN BUSH-WARBLER. (mts s Asia). . . . . _____

❏ *Bradypterus seebohmi.* RUSSET BUSH-WARBLER. (s Asia-Phil, Wall) . _____
   ___*B. (s.) seebohmi.* RUSSET BUSH-WARBLER. (s Asia, Phil)
   ___*B. (s.) montis.* JAVAN BUSH-WARBLER. (e Java)
   ___*B. (s.) timoriensis.* TIMOR BUSH-WARBLER. (Timor)

❏ *Bradypterus palliseri.* CEYLON BUSH-WARBLER. (mts Ceylon). . . . . . . _____

❏ *Bradypterus caudatus.* LONG-TAILED BUSH-WARBLER. (mts n,s Phil) . _____

❏ *Bradypterus accentor.* FRIENDLY BUSH-WARBLER. (mts n Born). . . . . _____

❏ *Bradypterus castaneus.* CHESTNUT-BACKED BUSH-WARBLER. (c,s Moluc)_____

❏ *Dromaeocercus brunneus.* BROWN EMU-TAIL. (e Mad). . . . . _____

❏ *Bathmocercus cerviniventris.* BLACK-CAPPED RUFOUS WARBLER. (w Afr)_____

❏ *Bathmocercus rufus.* BLACK-FACED RUFOUS WARBLER. (c Afr). . . . . . _____

❏ *Scepomycter winifredae.* MRS. MOREAU'S WARBLER. (mts ec Tanz). . . _____

❑ *Nesillas aldabrana.* ALDABRA BRUSH-WARBLER. (Ald)............ _____

❑ *Nesillas longicaudata.* ANJOUAN BRUSH-WARBLER. (Com)......... _____

❑ *Nesillas typica.* MADAGASCAR BRUSH-WARBLER. (Mad)........... _____

❑ *Nesillas brevicaudata.* GRAND COMORO BRUSH-WARBLER. (Com).... _____

❑ *Nesillas mariae.* MOHELI BRUSH-WARBLER. (Com).............. _____

❑ *Thamnornis chloropetoides.* THAMNORNIS WARBLER. (sw Mad)..... _____

❑ *Melocichla mentalis.* MOUSTACHED GRASS-WARBLER. (Afr)........ _____

❑ *Achaetops pycnopygius.* DAMARA ROCK-JUMPER. (sw Afr)......... _____

❑ *Sphenoeacus afer.* CAPE GRASS-WARBLER. (s Afr).............. _____

❑ *Locustella lanceolata.* LANCEOLATED WARBLER. (c Eura; ◊ s-Asia)... _____

❑ *Locustella naevia.* COMMON GRASSHOPPER-WARBLER. (Eura; ◊-n Afr). _____

❑ *Locustella certhiola.* PALLAS'S GRASSHOPPER-W. (e Asia; ◊ se Asia) . _____

❑ *Locustella ochotensis.* MIDDENDORFF'S GRASSH.-W. (e Asia; ◊-Phil) . _____

❑ *Locustella pleskei.* PLESKE'S GRASSHOPPER-W. (e Asia; ◊ se China)... _____

❑ *Locustella fluviatilis.* EURASIAN RIVER WARBLER. (c,e Euro; ◊-se Afr). _____

❑ *Locustella luscinioides.* SAVI'S WARBLER. (Eura; ◊ trop Afr)....... _____

❑ *Locustella fasciolata.* GRAY'S GRASSHOPPER-WARBLER. (e Asia; ◊ Indon)_____
   ___*L. (f.) fasciolata.* GRAY'S GRASSHOPPER-WARBLER. (sp)
   ___*L. (f.) amnicola.* SAKHALIN GRASSHOPPER-WARBLER. (ce Asia)

❑ *Acrocephalus melanopogon.* MOUSTACHED WARBLER. (s Palea)..... _____

❑ *Acrocephalus paludicola.* AQUATIC WARBLER. (Euro; ◊ n,trop Afr)... _____

❑ *Acrocephalus schoenobaenus.* SEDGE WARBLER. (Eura; ◊ trop,s Afr). _____

❑ *Acrocephalus sorghophilus.* STREAKED REED-W. (ne China; ◊ Phil) . _____

❑ *Acrocephalus bistrigiceps.* BLACK-BROWED REED-WARBLER. (e,se Asia)_____

❑ *Acrocephalus agricola.* PADDYFIELD WARBLER. (c Eura; ◊ s,se Asia) . _____
   ___*A. (a.) agricola.* PADDYFIELD WARBLER. (sp)
   ___*A. (a.) tangorum.* MANCHURIAN REED-WARBLER. (ne China)

❑ *Acrocephalus concinens.* BLUNT-WINGED WARBLER. (s,se Asia)..... _____

❑ *Acrocephalus scirpaceus.* EURASIAN REED-WARBLER. (w Palea; ◊-c Afr)_____

❑ *Acrocephalus baeticatus.* AFRICAN REED-WARBLER. (Afr reg)....... _____
   ___*A. (b.) cinnamomeus.* RUFESCENT REED-WARBLER. (sp)
   ___*A. (b.) baeticatus.* SOUTH AFRICAN REED-WARBLER. (s Afr)

❑ *Acrocephalus dumetorum.* BLYTH'S REED-WARBLER. (Eura; ◊ s Asia). _____

❑ *Acrocephalus palustris.* MARSH WARBLER. (w Eura; ◊ e,se Afr)...... _____

❑ *Acrocephalus arundinaceus.* GREAT REED-W. (Eura; ◊-s Afr, Indon). _____
   ___*A. (a.) arundinaceus.* GREAT REED-WARBLER. (w,c Eura; ◊-s Afr)
   ___*A. (a.) orientalis.* ORIENTAL REED-WARBLER. (e Asia; ◊-Indon)

❑ *Acrocephalus stentoreus.* CLAMOROUS REED-WARBLER. (Palea-Aust reg)_____
   ___*A. (s.) stentoreus.* CLAMOROUS REED-WARBLER. (sp)
   ___*A. (s.) orinus.* LARGE-BILLED REED-WARBLER. (Himal n India)
   ___*A. (s.) celebensis.* HEINROTH'S REED-WARBLER. (s Sulaw)

❑ *Acrocephalus griseldis.* BASRA REED-WARBLER. (s Iraq). . . . . _____

❑ *Acrocephalus australis.* AUSTRALIAN REED-WARBLER. (Aust). . . . . . . _____

❑ *Acrocephalus luscinia.* NIGHTINGALE REED-WARBLER. (Mari). . . . . . . _____

❑ *Acrocephalus syrinx.* CAROLINE ISLANDS REED-WARBLER. (Carol). . . _____

❑ *Acrocephalus rehsei.* NAURU REED-WARBLER. (Nauru). . . . . _____

❑ *Acrocephalus familiaris.* MILLERBIRD. (Haw Is). . . . . _____
   ___*A. (f.) kingi.* NIHOA MILLERBIRD. (Nihoa)
    A. (f.) familiaris. LAYSAN MILLERBIRD. (†Laysan)

❑ *Acrocephalus aequinoctialis.* BOKIKOKIKO. (n Line Is). . . . . _____

❑ *Acrocephalus caffer.* TAHITI REED-WARBLER. (Soc). . . . . _____

❑ *Acrocephalus mendanae.* MARQUESAN REED-WARBLER. (Marq). . . . . _____

❑ *Acrocephalus atyphus.* TUAMOTU REED-WARBLER. (Tuam). . . . . _____

❑ *Acrocephalus kerearako.* COOK ISLANDS REED-WARBLER. (Cook). . . . _____

❑ *Acrocephalus rimatarae.* RIMATARA REED-WARBLER. (Tubuai). . . . . . _____

❑ *Acrocephalus vaughani.* PITCAIRN REED-WARBLER. (Pitcairn). . . . . . . _____

❑ *Acrocephalus taiti.* HENDERSON ISLAND REED-WARBLER. (Henderson). _____

❑ *Acrocephalus rufescens.* GREATER SWAMP-WARBLER. (w,c Afr). . . . . _____

❑ *Acrocephalus brevipennis.* CAPE VERDE SWAMP-WARBLER. (C Verde) _____

❑ *Acrocephalus gracilirostris.* LESSER SWAMP-WARBLER. (e,s Afr). . . . . _____

❑ *Acrocephalus newtoni.* MADAGASCAR SWAMP-WARBLER. (Mad). . . . . _____

❑ *Acrocephalus aedon.* THICK-BILLED WARBLER. (e Asia; ◊ s,se Asia) . _____

❑ *Bebrornis rodericanus.* RODRIGUEZ BRUSH-WARBLER. (Rodr). . . . . . _____

❑ *Bebrornis sechellensis.* SEYCHELLES BRUSH-WARBLER. (Seyc). . . . . . _____

❑ *Hippolais caligata.* BOOTED WARBLER. (c,e Eura; ◊ s Asia). . . . . _____

❑ *Hippolais rama.* SYKES'S WARBLER. (sc Eura; ◊ s Asia). . . . . _____

❑ *Hippolais pallida.* OLIVACEOUS WARBLER. (s Palea; ◊ trop Afr). . . . . _____

❑ *Hippolais languida.* UPCHER'S WARBLER. (sc Asia; ◊-ne Afr). . . . . . . _____

❑ *Hippolais olivetorum.* OLIVE-TREE WARBLER. (wc Palea; ◊ e,se Afr) . _____

❑ *Hippolais polyglotta.* MELODIOUS WARBLER. (w Palea; ◊ w Afr). . . . . _____

❑ *Hippolais icterina.* ICTERINE WARBLER. (Eura; ◊ trop,s Afr). . . . . _____

❑ *Chloropeta natalensis.* YELLOW FLYCATCHER-WARBLER. (mts Afr). . . _____

❑ *Chloropeta similis.* MOUNTAIN FLYCATCHER-WARBLER. (mts e Afr) . _____

❑ *Chloropeta gracilirostris.* THIN-BILLED FLYCATCHER-WARBLER. (e Afr) _____

❑ *Stenostira scita.* FAIRY WARBLER. (s Afr)...................... _____

❑ *Phyllolais pulchella.* BUFF-BELLIED WARBLER. (n Afr)............. _____

❑ *Orthotomus metopias.* AFRICAN TAILORBIRD. (mts e Afr).......... _____

❑ *Orthotomus moreaui.* LONG-BILLED TAILORBIRD. (mts se Afr)....... _____

❑ *Orthotomus cuculatus.* MOUNTAIN TAILORBIRD. (s Asia-Wall, Phil) . _____

❑ *Orthotomus heterolaemus.* RUFOUS-HEADED TAILORBIRD. (s Phil).... _____

❑ *Orthotomus sutorius.* COMMON TAILORBIRD. (s,se Asia)........... _____

❑ *Orthotomus atrogularis.* DARK-NECKED TAILORBIRD. (s,se Asia)..... _____

❑ *Orthotomus castaneiceps.* PHILIPPINE TAILORBIRD. (n,c Phil)....... _____

❑ *Orthotomus frontalis.* RUFOUS-FRONTED TAILORBIRD. (s Phil)....... _____

❑ *Orthotomus derbianus.* GREY-BACKED TAILORBIRD. (n,sw Phil)..... _____

❑ *Orthotomus sericeus.* RUFOUS-TAILED TAILORBIRD. (se Asia, sw Phil). _____

❑ *Orthotomus ruficeps.* ASHY TAILORBIRD. (se Asia, sw Phil)........ _____

❑ *Orthotomus sepium.* OLIVE-BACKED TAILORBIRD. (Java-Lombok).... _____

❑ *Orthotomus samarensis.* YELLOW-BREASTED TAILORBIRD. (c Phil).... _____

❑ *Orthotomus nigriceps.* BLACK-HEADED TAILORBIRD. (s Phil)........ _____

❑ *Orthotomus cinereiceps.* WHITE-EARED TAILORBIRD. (s Phil)....... _____

❑ *Poliolais lopezi.* WHITE-TAILED WARBLER. (mts wc Afr)........... _____

❑ *Graueria vittata.* GRAUER'S WARBLER. (mts ec Afr).............. _____

❑ *Eremomela icteropygialis.* YELLOW-BELLIED EREMOMELA. (Afr)..... _____

❑ *Eremomela salvadorii.* SALVADORI'S EREMOMELA. (mts wc Afr)..... _____

❑ *Eremomela flavicrissalis.* YELLOW-VENTED EREMOMELA. (ne Afr).... _____

❑ *Eremomela pusilla.* SENEGAL EREMOMELA. (w Afr)............. _____

❑ *Eremomela canescens.* GREEN-BACKED EREMOMELA. (subsah Afr)... _____

❑ *Eremomela scotops.* GREENCAP EREMOMELA. (c,se Afr)........... _____

❑ *Eremomela gregalis.* YELLOW-RUMPED EREMOMELA. (sw Afr)....... _____

❑ *Eremomela badiceps.* RUFOUS-CROWNED EREMOMELA. (w,c Afr)..... _____

❑ *Eremomela turneri.* TURNER'S EREMOMELA. (ec Afr)............. _____

❑ *Eremomela atricollis.* BLACK-NECKED EREMOMELA. (sc Afr)........ _____

❑ *Eremomela usticollis.* BURNT-NECK EREMOMELA. (s Afr).......... _____

❑ *Randia pseudozosterops.* RAND'S WARBLER. (e Mad)............. _____

❑ *Newtonia amphichroa.* DARK NEWTONIA. (mts e Mad)............ _____

❑ *Newtonia brunneicauda.* COMMON NEWTONIA. (Mad)............ _____

❑ *Newtonia archboldi.* ARCHBOLD'S NEWTONIA. (sw,s Mad)......... _____

❑ *Newtonia fanovanae.* RED-TAILED NEWTONIA. (e Mad)............ _____

❑ *Sylvietta virens.* GREEN CROMBEC. (w,c Afr).................. _____
    ___*S. (v.) flaviventris.* YELLOW-BELLIED CROMBEC. (w Afr)
    ___*S. (v.) virens.* GREEN CROMBEC. (c Afr)

❑ *Sylvietta denti.* LEMON-BELLIED CROMBEC. (w,c Afr)............. _____

❑ *Sylvietta chapini.* CHAPIN'S CROMBEC. (mts ne Zaire)............ _____

❑ *Sylvietta leucophrys.* WHITE-BROWED CROMBEC. (mts e Afr)....... _____

❑ *Sylvietta brachyura.* NORTHERN CROMBEC. (subsah Afr)........... _____

❑ *Sylvietta philippae.* SHORT-BILLED CROMBEC. (ne Afr)............ _____

❑ *Sylvietta ruficapilla.* RED-CAPPED CROMBEC. (sc Afr)............. _____

❑ *Sylvietta whytii.* RED-FACED CROMBEC. (e Afr)................. _____

❑ *Sylvietta isabellina.* SOMALI CROMBEC. (ne Afr)................ _____

❑ *Sylvietta rufescens.* CAPE CROMBEC. (sc,s Afr)................. _____
    ___*S. (r.) ansorgei.* ANSORGE'S CROMBEC. (w Ang)
    ___*S. (r.) rufescens.* CAPE CROMBEC. (sp)

❑ *Hemitesia neumanni.* NEUMANN'S WARBLER. (mts ec Afr)......... _____

❑ *Macrosphenus kempi.* KEMP'S LONGBILL. (w Afr)............... _____

❑ *Macrosphenus flavicans.* YELLOW LONGBILL. (c Afr)............. _____

❑ *Macrosphenus concolor.* GREY LONGBILL. (w,c Afr)............. _____

❑ *Macrosphenus pulitzeri.* PULITZER'S LONGBILL. (cw Ang)......... _____

❑ *Macrosphenus kretschmeri.* KRETSCHMER'S LONGBILL. (ce Afr)..... _____

❑ *Amaurocichla bocagii.* BOCAGE'S LONGBILL. (ST)............... _____

❑ *Hylia prasina.* GREEN HYLIA. (w,c Afr)..................... _____

❑ *Leptopoecile sophiae.* WHITE-BROWED TIT-WARBLER. (Himal)....... _____

❑ *Leptopoecile elegans.* CRESTED TIT-WARBLER. (Himal nc,c China)... _____

❑ *Phylloscopus laetus.* RED-FACED WOODLAND-WARBLER. (mts ec Afr). _____

❑ *Phylloscopus laurae.* LAURA'S WOODLAND-WARBLER. (sc Afr)...... _____

❑ *Phylloscopus ruficapillus.* YELLOW-THROATED WOODLAND-W. (e,s Afr)_____

❑ *Phylloscopus herberti.* BLACK-CAPPED WOODLAND-W. (mts wc Afr) . _____

❑ *Phylloscopus budongoensis.* UGANDA WOODLAND-W. (mts ec Afr)... _____

❑ *Phylloscopus umbrovirens.* BROWN WOODLAND-W. (mts e Afr reg) . _____

❑ *Phylloscopus trochilus.* WILLOW WARBLER. (Eura; ◊ trop,s Afr)..... _____

❑ *Phylloscopus collybita.* COMMON CHIFFCHAFF. (Eura; ◊-n Afr, s Asia). _____
    ___*P. (c.) collybita.* EURASIAN CHIFFCHAFF. (w,c Eura; ◊ sp)
    ___*P. (c.) tristis.* SIBERIAN CHIFFCHAFF. (Sib; ◊ s Asia)
    ___*P. (c.) sindianus.* MOUNTAIN CHIFFCHAFF. (Himal)

❑ *Phylloscopus lorenzii.* CAUCASIAN CHIFFCHAFF. (mts sw Asia)....... _____

❑ *Phylloscopus neglectus.* PLAIN LEAF-WARBLER. (mts sc Asia)....... _____

❑ *Phylloscopus bonelli.* BONELLI'S WARBLER. (sw,sc Palea; ◊ n,ne Afr). _____
   ___*P. (b.) bonelli.* WESTERN BONELLI'S-WARBLER. (sw Palea; ◊ n Afr)
   ___*P. (b.) orientalis.* EASTERN BONELLI'S-WARBLER. (sc Palea; ◊ ne Afr)

❑ *Phylloscopus sibilatrix.* WOOD WARBLER. (Euro; ◊ trop Afr)....... _____

❑ *Phylloscopus fuscatus.* DUSKY WARBLER. (e Asia; ◊ s Asia)........ _____

❑ *Phylloscopus fuligiventer.* SMOKY WARBLER. (Himal)............. _____
   ___*P. (f.) fuligiventer.* SMOKY WARBLER. (s India, s Tibet)
   ___*P. (f.) tibetanus.* SIKANG WARBLER. (e Tibet)

❑ *Phylloscopus affinis.* TICKELL'S LEAF-WARBLER. (Himal; ◊ s Asia)... _____

❑ *Phylloscopus subaffinis.* BUFF-THROATED W. (c,s China; ◊-se Asia).. _____

❑ *Phylloscopus griseolus.* SULPHUR-BELLIED WARBLER. (s Asia; ◊ India) _____

❑ *Phylloscopus armandii.* YELLOW-STREAKED W. (ne,c China; ◊-se Asia) _____

❑ *Phylloscopus schwarzi.* RADDE'S WARBLER. (e Asia; ◊ se Asia)...... _____

❑ *Phylloscopus pulcher.* BUFF-BARRED WARBLER. (Himal; ◊ s Asia).... _____

❑ *Phylloscopus maculipennis.* ASHY-THROATED WARBLER. (Himal).... _____

❑ *Phylloscopus proregulus.* LEMON-RUMPED WARBLER. (e Asia; ◊ se Asia)_____

❑ *Phylloscopus chloronotus.* PALE-RUMPED WARBLER. (Himal; ◊-se Asia)_____

❑ *Phylloscopus subviridis.* BROOKS'S LEAF-WARBLER. (Himal)....... _____

❑ *Phylloscopus inornatus.* INORNATE WARBLER. (e Eura; ◊-se Asia).... _____
   ___*P. (i.) inornatus.* YELLOW-BROWED WARBLER. (taiga e Eura)
   ___*P. (i.) humei.* BUFF-BROWED WARBLER. (mts sc Asia)

❑ *Phylloscopus borealis.* ARCTIC WARBLER. (n Eura; ◊ se Asia-Wall)... _____

❑ *Phylloscopus trochiloides.* GREENISH WARBLER. (Eura; ◊ s,se Asia)... _____
   ___*P. (t.) trochiloides.* GREENISH WARBLER. (w,c Eura; ◊ s Asia)
   ___*P. (t.) plumbeitarsus.* TWO-BARRED WARBLER. (e Asia; ◊ se Asia)
   ___*P. (t.) nitidus.* BRIGHT-GREEN WARBLER. (mts sc Asia; ◊ India)

❑ *Phylloscopus tenellipes.* PALE-LEGGED LEAF-WARBLER. (e,se Asia)... _____

❑ *Phylloscopus borealoides.* SAKHALIN LEAF-WARBLER. (e,se Asia).... _____

❑ *Phylloscopus magnirostris.* LARGE-BILLED LEAF-W. (Himal; ◊-s Asia). _____

❑ *Phylloscopus tytleri.* TYTLER'S LEAF-WARBLER. (Himal n India; ◊ s Asia)_____

❑ *Phylloscopus occipitalis.* WESTERN CROWNED-W. (Himal; ◊ India)... _____

❑ *Phylloscopus coronatus.* EASTERN CROWNED-W. (e Asia; ◊ se Asia) . _____

❑ *Phylloscopus ijimae.* IJIMA'S LEAF-WARBLER. (Izu; ◊ n Phil)....... _____

❑ *Phylloscopus reguloides.* BLYTH'S LEAF-WARBLER. (Himal; ◊ se Asia) _____

❑ *Phylloscopus davisoni.* WHITE-TAILED LEAF-WARBLER. (Himal)..... _____

❑ *Phylloscopus cantator.* YELLOW-VENTED WARBLER. (s,se Asia)...... _____

❑ *Phylloscopus ricketti.* SULPHUR-BREASTED WARBLER. (s,se Asia)..... _____

❏ *Phylloscopus olivaceus.* Philippine Leaf-Warbler. (Phil). . . . . _____

❏ *Phylloscopus cebuensis.* Lemon-throated Leaf-Warbler. (n,c Phil) _____

❏ *Phylloscopus trivirgatus.* Mountain Leaf-Warbler. (se Asia, Phil). _____

❏ *Phylloscopus sarasinorum.* Sulawesi Leaf-Warbler. (mts Sulaw) . _____

❏ *Phylloscopus presbytes.* Timor Leaf-Warbler. (c L Sunda). . . . . . . _____

❏ *Phylloscopus poliocephala.* Island Leaf-Warbler. (Moluc-Solom). _____
___*P. (p.) poliocephala.* New Guinea Leaf-Warbler. (sp)
___*P. (p.) maforensis.* Numfor Leaf-Warbler. (nw NG)

❏ *Phylloscopus makirensis.* San Cristobal Leaf-Warbler. (s Solom). _____

❏ *Phylloscopus amoenus.* Sombre Leaf-Warbler. (nw Solom). . . . . . _____

❏ *Seicercus burkii.* Golden-spectacled Warbler. (Himal; ◊ s Asia) . _____

❏ *Seicercus xanthoschistos.* Grey-hooded Warbler. (Himal). . . . . . . _____

❏ *Seicercus affinis.* White-spectacled Warbler. (Himal). . . . . _____

❏ *Seicercus poliogenys.* Grey-cheeked Warbler. (Himal). . . . . _____

❏ *Seicercus castaniceps.* Chestnut-crowned Warbler. (mts se Asia). _____

❏ *Seicercus montis.* Yellow-breasted Warbler. (Malay-sw Phil, w Pap)_____

❏ *Seicercus grammiceps.* Sunda Warbler. (Sum-Bali). . . . . _____

❏ *Tickellia hodgsoni.* Broad-billed Warbler. (mts se Asia). . . . . _____

❏ *Abroscopus albogularis.* Rufous-faced Warbler. (mts se Asia). . . . _____

❏ *Abroscopus schisticeps.* Black-faced Warbler. (mts se Asia). . . . . . _____

❏ *Abroscopus superciliaris.* Yellow-bellied Warbler. (se Asia). . . . . _____

❏ *Hyliota flavigaster.* Yellow-bellied Hyliota. (Afr). . . . . _____

❏ *Hyliota australis.* Southern Hyliota. (sc Afr). . . . . _____

❏ *Hyliota violacea.* Violet-backed Hyliota. (c Afr). . . . . _____

Subfamily Megalurinae [10/22]

❏ *Amphilais seebohmi.* Grey Emu-tail. (mts c Mad). . . . . _____

❏ *Megalurus pryeri.* Marsh Grassbird. (e Asia; ◊ se China). . . . . _____

❏ *Megalurus timoriensis.* Tawny Grassbird. (Phil, Wall-Bism, Aust) . _____

❏ *Megalurus palustris.* Striated Grassbird. (s,se Asia, Phil). . . . . _____

❏ *Megalurus albolimbatus.* Fly River Grassbird. (se NG). . . . . _____

❏ *Megalurus gramineus.* Little Grassbird. (NG, Aust). . . . . _____

❏ *Megalurus punctatus.* New Zealand Fernbird. (NZ, Snares). . . . . . . _____

 Megalurus rufescens. Chatham Islands Fernbird. (†Chatham). . . . . _____

❏ *Cincloramphus cruralis.* Brown Songlark. (Aust). . . . . _____

❑ *Cincloramphus mathewsi.* RUFOUS SONGLARK. (Aust)............ _____

❑ *Eremiornis carteri.* SPINIFEX-BIRD. (int Aust)................. _____

❑ *Buettikoferella bivittata.* BUFF-BANDED GRASSBIRD. (Timor)....... _____

❑ *Megalurulus mariei.* NEW CALEDONIAN GRASSBIRD. (N Cal)....... _____

❑ *Megalurulus grosvenori.* BISMARCK THICKETBIRD. (mts cs Bism).... _____

❑ *Megalurulus llaneae.* BOUGAINVILLE THICKETBIRD. (mts c Solom)... _____

❑ *Megalurulus whitneyi.* GUADALCANAL THICKETBIRD. (se Solom-Vanu)_____
   ___*M. (w.) turipavae.* GUADALCANAL THICKETBIRD. (se Solom)
   ___*M. (w.) whitneyi.* NEW HEBRIDES THICKETBIRD. (ne Vanu)

❑ *Megalurulus rubiginosus.* RUSTY THICKETBIRD. (cs Bism)......... _____

❑ *Trichocichla rufa.* LONG-LEGGED THICKETBIRD. (mts Fiji)......... _____

❑ *Chaetornis striatus.* BRISTLED GRASSBIRD. (s Asia)............. _____

❑ *Graminicola bengalensis.* RUFOUS-RUMPED GRASSBIRD. (s,se Asia)... _____

❑ *Schoenicola brevirostris.* FAN-TAILED GRASSBIRD. (Afr)........... _____

❑ *Schoenicola platyura.* BROAD-TAILED GRASSBIRD. (sw India)....... _____

Subfamily Garrulacinae [2/54]

❑ *Garrulax cinereifrons.* ASHY-HEADED LAUGHINGTHRUSH. (Ceylon)... _____

❑ *Garrulax palliatus.* SUNDA LAUGHINGTHRUSH. (mts w Sum, n Born) . _____

❑ *Garrulax rufifrons.* RUFOUS-FRONTED LAUGHINGTHRUSH. (w Java)... _____

❑ *Garrulax perspicillatus.* MASKED LAUGHINGTHRUSH. (s Asia)....... _____

❑ *Garrulax albogularis.* WHITE-THROATED LAUGHINGTHRUSH. (s Asia). _____

❑ *Garrulax leucolophus.* WHITE-CRESTED LAUGHINGTHRUSH. (s,se Asia) _____

❑ *Garrulax monileger.* LESSER NECKLACED LAUGHINGTHRUSH. (s,se Asia)_____

❑ *Garrulax pectoralis.* GREATER NECKLACED LAUGHINGTHRUSH. (Himal) _____

❑ *Garrulax lugubris.* BLACK LAUGHINGTHRUSH. (Malaya, Sum)....... _____

❑ *Garrulax calvus.* BARE-HEADED LAUGHINGTHRUSH. (mts ne Born).... _____

❑ *Garrulax striatus.* STRIATED LAUGHINGTHRUSH. (Himal).......... _____

❑ *Garrulax strepitans.* WHITE-NECKED LAUGHINGTHRUSH. (s,se Asia)... _____

❑ *Garrulax milleti.* BLACK-HOODED LAUGHINGTHRUSH. (mts s Viet).... _____

❑ *Garrulax maesi.* GREY LAUGHINGTHRUSH. (mts s Asia)............ _____

❑ *Garrulax ruficollis.* RUFOUS-NECKED LAUGHINGTHRUSH. (s Asia).... _____

❑ *Garrulax nuchalis.* CHESTNUT-BACKED LAUGHINGTHRUSH. (s Asia)... _____

❑ *Garrulax chinensis.* BLACK-THROATED LAUGHINGTHRUSH. (se Asia) . _____

❑ *Garrulax vassali.* WHITE-CHEEKED LAUGHINGTHRUSH. (mts se Asia) . _____

❏ *Garrulax galbanus.* YELLOW-THROATED LAUGHINGTHRUSH. (Himal) . _____
___*G. (g.) galbanus.* YELLOW-THROATED LAUGHINGTHRUSH. (sp)
___*G. (g.) courtoisi.* COURTOIS'S LAUGHINGTHRUSH. (ec China)

❏ *Garrulax delesserti.* WYNAAD LAUGHINGTHRUSH. (sw India)....... _____

❏ *Garrulax gularis.* RUFOUS-VENTED LAUGHINGTHRUSH. (s Asia)..... _____

❏ *Garrulax davidi.* PLAIN LAUGHINGTHRUSH. (mts n,nc China)....... _____

❏ *Garrulax sukatschewi.* SNOWY-CHEEKED LAUGHINGTHRUSH. (n China) _____

❏ *Garrulax cineraceus.* MOUSTACHED LAUGHINGTHRUSH. (Himal)..... _____

❏ *Garrulax rufogularis.* RUFOUS-CHINNED LAUGHINGTHRUSH. (Himal) . _____

❏ *Garrulax lunulatus.* BARRED LAUGHINGTHRUSH. (Himal c China).... _____

❏ *Garrulax bieti.* WHITE-SPECKLED LAUGHINGTHRUSH. (Himal sw China)_____

❏ *Garrulax maximus.* GIANT LAUGHINGTHRUSH. (Himal w,nc China)... _____

❏ *Garrulax ocellatus.* SPOTTED LAUGHINGTHRUSH. (Himal).......... _____

❏ *Garrulax caerulatus.* GREY-SIDED LAUGHINGTHRUSH. (Himal)...... _____

❏ *Garrulax poecilorhynchus.* RUSTY LAUGHINGTHRUSH. (mts s Asia)... _____

❏ *Garrulax mitratus.* CHESTNUT-CAPPED LAUGHINGTHRUSH. (se Asia) . _____

❏ *Garrulax merulinus.* SPOT-BREASTED LAUGHINGTHRUSH. (Himal).... _____

❏ *Garrulax canorus.* HWAMEI. (s Asia; ◆ Haw Is)................. _____

❏ *Garrulax sannio.* WHITE-BROWED LAUGHINGTHRUSH. (s Asia)....... _____

❏ *Garrulax cachinnans.* RUFOUS-BREASTED LAUGHINGTHRUSH. (sw India)_____

❏ *Garrulax jerdoni.* GREY-BREASTED LAUGHINGTHRUSH. (mts sw India). _____

❏ *Garrulax lineatus.* STREAKED LAUGHINGTHRUSH. (Himal)......... _____

❏ *Garrulax virgatus.* STRIPED LAUGHINGTHRUSH. (Himal)........... _____

❏ *Garrulax austeni.* BROWN-CAPPED LAUGHINGTHRUSH. (Himal)...... _____

❏ *Garrulax squamatus.* BLUE-WINGED LAUGHINGTHRUSH. (Himal)..... _____

❏ *Garrulax subunicolor.* SCALY LAUGHINGTHRUSH. (Himal)......... _____

❏ *Garrulax elliotii.* ELLIOT'S LAUGHINGTHRUSH. (Himal wc China)..... _____

❏ *Garrulax variegatus.* VARIEGATED LAUGHINGTHRUSH. (Himal)...... _____

❏ *Garrulax henrici.* BROWN-CHEEKED LAUGHINGTHRUSH. (Himal)..... _____

❏ *Garrulax affinis.* BLACK-FACED LAUGHINGTHRUSH. (Himal)........ _____

❏ *Garrulax morrisonianus.* WHITE-WHISKERED LAUGHINGT. (Taiwan) . _____

❏ *Garrulax erythrocephalus.* CHESTNUT-CROWNED LAUGHINGT. (s,se Asia)_____
___*G. (e.) erythrocephalus.* CHESTNUT-CROWNED LAUGHINGTHRUSH. (s Asia)
___*G. (e.) nigrimentum.* BLACK-EARED LAUGHINGTHRUSH. (ne India)
___*G. (e.) chrysopterus.* GREY-EARED LAUGHINGTHRUSH. (se Asia)

❏ *Garrulax yersini.* COLLARED LAUGHINGTHRUSH. (mts c Viet)....... _____

❑ *Garrulax formosus.* RED-WINGED LAUGHINGTHRUSH. (Himal)...... _____

❑ *Garrulax milnei.* RED-TAILED LAUGHINGTHRUSH. (Himal)......... _____

❑ *Liocichla phoenicea.* RED-FACED LIOCICHLA. (Himal s,se Asia)...... _____
   ___*L. (phoenicea) phoenicea.* CRIMSON-WINGED LIOCICHLA. (s Asia)
   ___*L. (phoenicea) ripponi.* CRIMSON-HEADED LIOCICHLA. (se Asia)

❑ *Liocichla omeiensis.* OMEI SHAN LIOCICHLA. (Himal c China)...... _____

❑ *Liocichla steerii.* STEERE'S LIOCICHLA. (mts Taiwan)............. _____

Subfamily Sylviinae [53/261]
Tribe Timaliini [51/236]

❑ *Modulatrix stictigula.* SPOT-THROAT. (mts se Afr)............... _____

❑ *Arcanator orostruthus.* DAPPLE-THROAT. (ne Tanz, nc Moz)....... _____

❑ *Trichastoma rostratum.* WHITE-CHESTED BABBLER. (se Asia)....... _____

❑ *Trichastoma celebense.* SULAWESI BABBLER. (Sulaw)............. _____

❑ *Trichastoma bicolor.* FERRUGINOUS BABBLER. (se Asia)........... _____

❑ *Trichastoma woodi.* BAGOBO BABBLER. (mts s Phil)............. _____

❑ *Malacocincla abbotti.* ABBOTT'S BABBLER. (s,se Asia)............ _____

❑ *Malacocincla sepiarium.* HORSFIELD'S BABBLER. (se Asia)......... _____

❑ *Malacocincla vanderbilti.* VANDERBILT'S BABBLER. (mts n Sum)..... _____

❑ *Malacocincla perspicillata.* BLACK-BROWED BABBLER. (s Born)...... _____

❑ *Malacocincla malaccensis.* SHORT-TAILED BABBLER. (se Asia)...... _____
   ___*M. (m.) malaccensis.* SHORT-TAILED BABBLER. (sp)
   ___*M. (m.) feriatum.* OCHRACEOUS-THROATED BABBLER. (ne Born)

❑ *Malacocincla cinereiceps.* ASHY-HEADED BABBLER. (sw Phil)...... _____

❑ *Pellorneum tickelli.* BUFF-BREASTED BABBLER. (s,se Asia)......... _____

❑ *Pellorneum pyrrogenys.* TEMMINCK'S BABBLER. (mts n Born, Java)... _____

❑ *Pellorneum albiventre.* SPOT-THROATED BABBLER. (mts se Asia)..... _____

❑ *Pellorneum palustre.* MARSH BABBLER. (mts ne India)............ _____

❑ *Pellorneum ruficeps.* PUFF-THROATED BABBLER. (mts s,se Asia)..... _____

❑ *Pellorneum fuscocapillum.* BROWN-CAPPED BABBLER. (Ceylon)..... _____

❑ *Pellorneum capistratum.* BLACK-CAPPED BABBLER. (se Asia)....... _____

❑ *Malacopteron magnirostre.* MOUSTACHED BABBLER. (se Asia)...... _____

❑ *Malacopteron affine.* SOOTY-CAPPED BABBLER. (se Asia).......... _____

❑ *Malacopteron cinereum.* SCALY-CROWNED BABBLER. (se Asia)..... _____

❑ *Malacopteron magnum.* RUFOUS-CROWNED BABBLER. (se Asia)..... _____

❑ *Malacopteron palawanense.* MELODIOUS BABBLER. (sw Phil)....... _____

❑ *Malacopteron albogulare.* GREY-BREASTED BABBLER. (se Asia)...... _____

❑ *Illadopsis cleaveri.* BLACKCAP ILLADOPSIS. (w,wc Afr)............ _____

❑ *Illadopsis albipectus.* SCALY-BREASTED ILLADOPSIS. (c Afr)........ _____

❑ *Illadopsis rufescens.* RUFOUS-WINGED ILLADOPSIS. (w Afr)......... _____

❑ *Illadopsis puveli.* PUVEL'S ILLADOPSIS. (w,c Afr)................ _____

❑ *Illadopsis rufipennis.* PALE-BREASTED ILLADOPSIS. (w,c Afr)....... _____

❑ *Illadopsis fulvescens.* BROWN ILLADOPSIS. (w,c Afr).............. _____
    ___*I. (f.) fulvescens.* BROWN ILLADOPSIS. (sp)
    ___*I. (f.) moloneyanum.* MOLONEY'S ILLADOPSIS. (wc Afr)

❑ *Illadopsis pyrrhoptera.* MOUNTAIN ILLADOPSIS. (mts ec Afr)....... _____

❑ *Illadopsis atriceps.* RUWENZORI HILL-BABBLER. (mts w,ec Afr)...... _____

❑ *Illadopsis abyssinica.* ABYSSINIAN HILL-BABBLER. (mts w,e Afr)..... _____

❑ *Kakamega poliothorax.* GREY-CHESTED ILLADOPSIS. (mts c Afr)..... _____

❑ *Ptyrticus turdinus.* THRUSH BABBLER. (c Afr).................... _____

❑ *Pomatorhinus hypoleucos.* LARGE SCIMITAR-BABBLER. (s,se Asia)... _____

❑ *Pomatorhinus erythrocnemis.* SPOT-BREASTED SCIMITAR-B. (s Asia) . _____

❑ *Pomatorhinus erythrogenys.* RUSTY-CHEEKED SCIMITAR-B. (se Asia). _____

❑ *Pomatorhinus horsfieldii.* INDIAN SCIMITAR-BABBLER. (s India)..... _____

❑ *Pomatorhinus schisticeps.* WHITE-BROWED SCIMITAR-B. (s,se Asia) . _____

❑ *Pomatorhinus montanus.* CHESTNUT-BACKED SCIMITAR-B. (se Asia) . _____

❑ *Pomatorhinus ruficollis.* STREAK-BREASTED SCIMITAR-B. (s Asia).... _____

❑ *Pomatorhinus ochraceiceps.* RED-BILLED SCIMITAR-BABBLER. (s Asia) _____

❑ *Pomatorhinus ferruginosus.* CORAL-BILLED SCIMITAR-B. (s Asia).... _____

❑ *Xiphirhynchus superciliaris.* SLENDER-BILLED SCIMITAR-B. (s Asia) . _____

❑ *Jabouilleia danjoui.* SHORT-TAILED SCIMITAR-BABBLER. (mts c Viet). _____

❑ *Rimator malacoptilus.* LONG-BILLED WREN-BABBLER. (s,se Asia).... _____
    ___*R. (m.) malacoptilus.* LONG-BILLED WREN-BABBLER. (s Asia)
    ___*R. (m.) pasquieri.* WHITE-THROATED WREN-BABBLER. (n Viet)
    ___*R. (m.) albostriatus.* SUMATRAN WREN-BABBLER. (w Sum)

❑ *Ptilocichla leucogrammica.* BORNEAN WREN-BABBLER. (Born)...... _____

❑ *Ptilocichla mindanensis.* STRIATED WREN-BABBLER. (se Phil)....... _____

❑ *Ptilocichla falcata.* FALCATED WREN-BABBLER. (sw Phil).......... _____

❑ *Kenopia striata.* STRIPED WREN-BABBLER. (se Asia).............. _____

❑ *Napothera macrodactyla.* LARGE WREN-BABBLER. (se Asia)....... _____

❑ *Napothera rufipectus.* RUSTY-BREASTED WREN-BABBLER. (w Sum)... _____

❑ *Napothera atrigularis.* BLACK-THROATED WREN-BABBLER. (Born)... _____

❑ *Napothera marmorata.* MARBLED WREN-BABBLER. (Malaya, Sum)... _____

❏ *Napothera crispifrons.* LIMESTONE WREN-BABBLER. (se Asia). . . . . . . _____

❏ *Napothera brevicaudata.* STREAKED WREN-BABBLER. (se Asia). . . . . . _____

❏ *Napothera crassa.* MOUNTAIN WREN-BABBLER. (mts n Born). . . . . . . _____

❏ *Napothera rabori.* RABOR'S WREN-BABBLER. (n,nc Phil). . . . . _____
   ___*N. (r.) rabori.* RABOR'S WREN-BABBLER. (n Phil)
   ___*N. (r.) sorsogonensis.* SORSOGON WREN-BABBLER. (mts cn Phil)

❏ *Napothera epilepidota.* EYEBROWED WREN-BABBLER. (s,se Asia). . . . . _____

❏ *Pnoepyga albiventer.* SCALY-BREASTED WREN-BABBLER. (Himal). . . . _____

❏ *Pnoepyga immaculata.* NEPAL WREN-BABBLER. (Nepal). . . . . _____

❏ *Pnoepyga pusilla.* PYGMY WREN-BABBLER. (s,se Asia-c L Sunda). . . . _____

❏ *Spelaeornis caudatus.* RUFOUS-THROATED WREN-BABBLER. (ne India) _____

❏ *Spelaeornis badeigularis.* RUSTY-THROATED WREN-BABBLER. (ne India)_____

❏ *Spelaeornis troglodytoides.* BAR-WINGED WREN-BABBLER. (Himal). . . _____

❏ *Spelaeornis formosus.* SPOTTED WREN-BABBLER. (Himal). . . . . _____

❏ *Spelaeornis chocolatinus.* LONG-TAILED WREN-BABBLER. (Himal). . . _____

❏ *Spelaeornis longicaudatus.* TAWNY-BREASTED WREN-B. (ne India). . . _____

❏ *Sphenocichla humei.* WEDGE-BILLED WREN-BABBLER. (Himal). . . . . . _____

❏ *Neomixis tenella.* COMMON JERY. (Mad). . . . . _____

❏ *Neomixis viridis.* GREEN JERY. (e Mad). . . . . _____

❏ *Neomixis striatigula.* STRIPE-THROATED JERY. (sw,e Mad). . . . . _____

❏ *Neomixis flavoviridis.* WEDGE-TAILED JERY. (e Mad). . . . . _____

❏ *Stachyris rodolphei.* DEIGNAN'S BABBLER. (Himal nw Thai). . . . . _____

❏ *Stachyris ambigua.* BUFF-CHESTED BABBLER. (s Asia). . . . . _____

❏ *Stachyris rufifrons.* RUFOUS-FRONTED BABBLER. (se Asia). . . . . _____

❏ *Stachyris ruficeps.* RUFOUS-CAPPED BABBLER. (Himal). . . . . _____

❏ *Stachyris pyrrhops.* BLACK-CHINNED BABBLER. (Himal). . . . . _____

❏ *Stachyris chrysaea.* GOLDEN BABBLER. (mts s,se Asia). . . . . _____

❏ *Stachyris plateni.* PYGMY BABBLER. (se Phil). . . . . _____

❏ *Stachyris dennistouni.* GOLDEN-CROWNED BABBLER. (n Phil). . . . . . . _____

❏ *Stachyris nigrocapitata.* BLACK-CROWNED BABBLER. (c Phil). . . . . . . _____

❏ *Stachyris capitalis.* RUSTY-CROWNED BABBLER. (s Phil). . . . . _____

❏ *Stachyris speciosa.* FLAME-TEMPLED BABBLER. (sc Phil). . . . . _____

❏ *Stachyris whiteheadi.* CHESTNUT-FACED BABBLER. (n Phil). . . . . _____

❏ *Stachyris striata.* LUZON STRIPED-BABBLER. (n Phil). . . . . _____

❏ *Stachyris latistriata.* PANAY STRIPED-BABBLER. (mts c Phil). . . . . _____

❏ *Stachyris nigrorum.* NEGROS STRIPED-BABBLER. (mts sc Phil)...... _____

❏ *Stachyris hypogrammica.* PALAWAN STRIPED-BABBLER. (w Phil)..... _____

❏ *Stachyris grammiceps.* WHITE-BREASTED BABBLER. (w Java)....... _____

❏ *Stachyris herberti.* SOOTY BABBLER. (c Laos)................. _____

❏ *Stachyris nigriceps.* GREY-THROATED BABBLER. (mts s,se Asia)...... _____

❏ *Stachyris poliocephala.* GREY-HEADED BABBLER. (se Asia)........ _____

❏ *Stachyris oglei.* SNOWY-THROATED BABBLER. (Himal ne India)..... _____

❏ *Stachyris striolata.* SPOT-NECKED BABBLER. (mts se Asia)......... _____

❏ *Stachyris leucotis.* WHITE-NECKED BABBLER. (se Asia)........... _____

❏ *Stachyris nigricollis.* BLACK-THROATED BABBLER. (se Asia)........ _____

❏ *Stachyris thoracica.* WHITE-BIBBED BABBLER. (Java)............. _____

❏ *Stachyris maculata.* CHESTNUT-RUMPED BABBLER. (se Asia)....... _____

❏ *Stachyris erythroptera.* CHESTNUT-WINGED BABBLER. (se Asia)...... _____

❏ *Stachyris melanothorax.* CRESCENT-CHESTED BABBLER. (Java, Bali) . _____

❏ *Dumetia hyperythra.* TAWNY-BELLIED BABBLER. (India)........... _____
    ___*D. (h.) hyperythra.* RUFOUS-BELLIED BABBLER. (n,c India)
    ___*D. (h.) albogularis.* TAWNY-BELLIED BABBLER. (s India)

❏ *Rhopocichla atriceps.* DARK-FRONTED BABBLER. (sw India)........ _____

❏ *Macronous gularis.* STRIPED TIT-BABBLER. (s,se Asia, sw Phil)...... _____

❏ *Macronous flavicollis.* GREY-CHEEKED TIT-BABBLER. (Java)....... _____

❏ *Macronous kelleyi.* GREY-FACED TIT-BABBLER. (se Asia).......... _____

❏ *Macronous striaticeps.* BROWN TIT-BABBLER. (se Phil)........... _____

❏ *Macronous ptilosus.* FLUFFY-BACKED TIT-BABBLER. (se Asia)....... _____

❏ *Micromacronus leytensis.* MINIATURE TIT-BABBLER. (ce,s Phil)...... _____

❏ *Timalia pileata.* CHESTNUT-CAPPED BABBLER. (s,se Asia).......... _____

❏ *Chrysomma sinense.* YELLOW-EYED BABBLER. (s,se Asia)......... _____

❏ *Chrysomma altirostre.* JERDON'S BABBLER. (s Asia)............. _____

❏ *Chrysomma poecilotis.* RUFOUS-TAILED BABBLER. (Himal cw China) . _____

❏ *Turdoides nipalensis.* SPINY BABBLER. (Himal Nepal)............ _____

❏ *Turdoides altirostris.* IRAQ BABBLER. (se Iraq, sw Iran)............ _____

❏ *Turdoides caudatus.* COMMON BABBLER. (s Eura)............... _____

❏ *Turdoides earlei.* STRIATED BABBLER. (s Asia)................. _____

❏ *Turdoides gularis.* WHITE-THROATED BABBLER. (Burma).......... _____

❏ *Turdoides longirostris.* SLENDER-BILLED BABBLER. (s Asia)........ _____

❏ *Turdoides malcolmi.* LARGE GREY BABBLER. (c,pen India)......... _____

❑ *Turdoides squamiceps.* ARABIAN BABBLER. (Near East-s Arabia)..... _____

❑ *Turdoides fulvus.* FULVOUS CHATTERER. (n Afr)................. _____

❑ *Turdoides aylmeri.* SCALY CHATTERER. (ne Afr)................. _____

❑ *Turdoides rubiginosus.* RUFOUS CHATTERER. (ne Afr)............. _____

❑ *Turdoides subrufus.* RUFOUS BABBLER. (sw India)................ _____

❑ *Turdoides striatus.* JUNGLE BABBLER. (s Asia)................... _____
   ___*T. (s.) striatus.* JUNGLE BABBLER. (sp)
   ___*T. (s.) somervillei.* DECCAN BABBLER. (sw India)

❑ *Turdoides rufescens.* ORANGE-BILLED BABBLER. (Ceylon)......... _____

❑ *Turdoides affinis.* YELLOW-BILLED BABBLER. (s India)............ _____

❑ *Turdoides reinwardtii.* BLACKCAP BABBLER. (w,wc Afr)........... _____

❑ *Turdoides tenebrosus.* DUSKY BABBLER. (ce Afr)................ _____

❑ *Turdoides melanops.* BLACK-LORED BABBLER. (sw Afr)........... _____

❑ *Turdoides squamulatus.* SCALY BABBLER. (e Afr)................ _____

❑ *Turdoides leucopygius.* WHITE-RUMPED BABBLER. (ne Afr)........ _____

❑ *Turdoides hartlaubii.* ANGOLA BABBLER. (c Afr)................. _____

❑ *Turdoides bicolor.* SOUTHERN PIED-BABBLER. (s Afr)............. _____

❑ *Turdoides sharpei.* SHARPE'S PIED-BABBLER. (e Afr).............. _____

❑ *Turdoides hypoleucus.* NORTHERN PIED-BABBLER. (mts e Afr)....... _____

❑ *Turdoides hindei.* HINDE'S PIED-BABBLER. (ec Kenya)............ _____

❑ *Turdoides plebejus.* BROWN BABBLER. (subsah Afr).............. _____

❑ *Turdoides leucocephalus.* CRETSCHMAR'S BABBLER. (ne Afr)....... _____

❑ *Turdoides jardineii.* ARROW-MARKED BABBLER. (e,c,se Afr)........ _____

❑ *Turdoides gymnogenys.* BARE-CHEEKED BABBLER. (sw Afr)........ _____

❑ *Babax lanceolatus.* CHINESE BABAX. (Himal)................... _____

❑ *Babax waddelli.* GIANT BABAX. (Himal)....................... _____

❑ *Babax koslowi.* TIBETAN BABAX. (Himal)..................... _____

❑ *Leiothrix argentauris.* SILVER-EARED MESIA. (mts s,se Asia)....... _____

❑ *Leiothrix lutea.* RED-BILLED LEIOTHRIX. (Himal; ◆ Haw Is)........ _____

❑ *Cutia nipalensis.* CUTIA. (mts s,se Asia)...................... _____

❑ *Pteruthius rufiventer.* BLACK-HEADED SHRIKE-BABBLER. (Himal).... _____

❑ *Pteruthius flaviscapis.* WHITE-BROWED SHRIKE-BABBLER. (s,se Asia). _____

❑ *Pteruthius xanthochlorus.* GREEN SHRIKE-BABBLER. (Himal)....... _____

❑ *Pteruthius melanotis.* BLACK-EARED SHRIKE-BABBLER. (s,se Asia)... _____

❑ *Pteruthius aenobarbus.* CHESTNUT-FRONTED SHRIKE-B. (s,se Asia)... _____

❑ *Gampsorhynchus rufulus.* WHITE-HOODED BABBLER. (s,se Asia)..... _____

❑ *Actinodura egertoni.* RUSTY-FRONTED BARWING. (Himal).......... _____

❑ *Actinodura ramsayi.* SPECTACLED BARWING. (Himal)............. _____

❑ *Actinodura nipalensis.* HOARY-THROATED BARWING. (Himal)...... _____

❑ *Actinodura waldeni.* STREAK-THROATED BARWING. (Himal)........ _____

❑ *Actinodura souliei.* STREAKED BARWING. (Himal)............... _____

❑ *Actinodura morrisoniana.* FORMOSAN BARWING. (mts Taiwan)..... _____

❑ *Minla cyanouroptera.* BLUE-WINGED MINLA. (mts s,se Asia)....... _____

❑ *Minla strigula.* CHESTNUT-TAILED MINLA. (mts s,se Asia).......... _____

❑ *Minla ignotincta.* RED-TAILED MINLA. (Himal)................. _____

❑ *Alcippe chrysotis.* GOLDEN-BREASTED FULVETTA. (Himal)......... _____

❑ *Alcippe variegaticeps.* GOLD-FRONTED FULVETTA. (Himal s China)... _____

❑ *Alcippe cinerea.* YELLOW-THROATED FULVETTA. (Himal).......... _____

❑ *Alcippe castaneceps.* RUFOUS-WINGED FULVETTA. (mts s,se Asia).... _____

❑ *Alcippe vinipectus.* WHITE-BROWED FULVETTA. (Himal)........... _____

❑ *Alcippe striaticollis.* CHINESE FULVETTA. (Himal c,sw China)....... _____

❑ *Alcippe ruficapilla.* SPECTACLED FULVETTA. (Himal)............. _____

❑ *Alcippe cinereiceps.* STREAK-THROATED FULVETTA. (Himal)........ _____

❑ *Alcippe ludlowi.* LUDLOW'S FULVETTA. (Himal)................. _____

❑ *Alcippe rufogularis.* RUFOUS-THROATED FULVETTA. (mts s,se Asia)... _____

❑ *Alcippe brunnea.* DUSKY FULVETTA. (Himal).................. _____

❑ *Alcippe dubia.* RUSTY-CAPPED FULVETTA. (mts s Burma).......... _____

❑ *Alcippe brunneicauda.* BROWN FULVETTA. (se Asia).............. _____

❑ *Alcippe poioicephala.* BROWN-CHEEKED FULVETTA. (s,se Asia)...... _____

❑ *Alcippe pyrrhoptera.* JAVAN FULVETTA. (w,c Java)............... _____

❑ *Alcippe peracensis.* MOUNTAIN FULVETTA. (mts se Asia).......... _____

❑ *Alcippe morrisonia.* GREY-CHEEKED FULVETTA. (Himal).......... _____

❑ *Alcippe nipalensis.* NEPAL FULVETTA. (Himal)................. _____

❑ *Lioptilus nigricapillus.* BLACKCAP MOUNTAIN-BABBLER. (e S Afr)... _____

❑ *Kupeornis gilberti.* WHITE-THROATED MOUNTAIN-BABBLER. (wc Afr). _____

❑ *Kupeornis rufocinctus.* RED-COLLARED MOUNTAIN-BABBLER. (c Afr). _____

❑ *Kupeornis chapini.* CHAPIN'S MOUNTAIN-BABBLER. (e Zaire)....... _____

❑ *Parophasma galinieri.* ABYSSINIAN CATBIRD. (mts Eth)........... _____

❑ *Phyllanthus atripennis.* CAPUCHIN BABBLER. (w,c Afr)........... _____

❑ *Crocias langbianis.* GREY-CROWNED CROCIAS. (mts c Viet)........ _____

❑ *Crocias albonotatus.* SPOTTED CROCIAS. (mts w,c Java)............ _____

❑ *Heterophasia annectens.* RUFOUS-BACKED SIBIA. (Himal)......... _____

❑ *Heterophasia capistrata.* RUFOUS SIBIA. (Himal)................ _____

❑ *Heterophasia gracilis.* GREY SIBIA. (Himal).................... _____

❑ *Heterophasia melanoleuca.* BLACK-HEADED SIBIA. (mts s,se Asia)... _____
   ___*H. (m.) desgodinsi.* BLACK-EARED SIBIA. (s Asia)
   ___*H. (m.) melanoleuca.* BLACK-CAPPED SIBIA. (Burma, Thai)
   ___*H. (m.) robinsoni.* WHITE-SPECTACLED SIBIA. (Viet, Laos)

❑ *Heterophasia auricularis.* WHITE-EARED SIBIA. (mts Taiwan)....... _____

❑ *Heterophasia pulchella.* BEAUTIFUL SIBIA. (Himal)............... _____

❑ *Heterophasia picaoides.* LONG-TAILED SIBIA. (mts s,se Asia)....... _____

❑ *Yuhina castaniceps.* STRIATED YUHINA. (mts s,se Asia)........... _____
   ___*Y. (c.) castaniceps.* WHITE-BROWED YUHINA. (s Asia)
   ___*Y. (c.) torqueola.* COLLARED YUHINA. (se Asia)

❑ *Yuhina everetti.* CHESTNUT-CRESTED YUHINA. (mts n Born)........ _____

❑ *Yuhina bakeri.* WHITE-NAPED YUHINA. (Himal)................. _____

❑ *Yuhina flavicollis.* WHISKERED YUHINA. (Himal)................ _____

❑ *Yuhina humilis.* BURMESE YUHINA. (mts se Asia)................ _____

❑ *Yuhina gularis.* STRIPE-THROATED YUHINA. (Himal)............. _____

❑ *Yuhina diademata.* WHITE-COLLARED YUHINA. (Himal)........... _____

❑ *Yuhina occipitalis.* RUFOUS-VENTED YUHINA. (Himal)............ _____

❑ *Yuhina brunneiceps.* FORMOSAN YUHINA. (mts Taiwan)........... _____

❑ *Yuhina nigrimenta.* BLACK-CHINNED YUHINA. (Himal)............ _____

❑ *Yuhina zantholeuca.* WHITE-BELLIED YUHINA. (mts s,se Asia)....... _____

❑ *Myzornis pyrrhoura.* FIRE-TAILED MYZORNIS. (Himal)............ _____

❑ *Oxylabes madagascariensis.* WHITE-THROATED OXYLABES. (Mad).... _____

❑ *Crossleyia xanthophrys.* YELLOW-BROWED OXYLABES. (n,ce Mad)... _____

❑ *Mystacornis crossleyi.* CROSSLEY'S BABBLER. (e Mad)............ _____

❑ *Panurus biarmicus.* BEARDED PARROTBILL. (Palea).............. _____

❑ *Conostoma oemodium.* GREAT PARROTBILL. (Himal)............. _____

❑ *Paradoxornis paradoxus.* THREE-TOED PARROTBILL. (c,sw China).... _____

❑ *Paradoxornis unicolor.* BROWN PARROTBILL. (Himal)............. _____

❑ *Paradoxornis gularis.* GREY-HEADED PARROTBILL. (s Asia)........ _____

❑ *Paradoxornis flavirostris.* BLACK-BREASTED PARROTBILL. (Himal)... _____

❑ *Paradoxornis guttaticollis.* SPOT-BREASTED PARROTBILL. (Himal).... _____

❑ *Paradoxornis conspicillatus.* SPECTACLED PARROTBILL. (c China).... _____

❑ *Paradoxornis webbianus.* VINOUS-THROATED PARROTBILL. (mts e Asia)_____

❑ *Paradoxornis brunneus.* BROWN-WINGED PARROTBILL. (Himal)...... _____

❑ *Paradoxornis alphonsianus.* ASHY-THROATED PARROTBILL. (Himal) . _____

❑ *Paradoxornis zappeyi.* GREY-HOODED PARROTBILL. (Himal sw China). _____

❑ *Paradoxornis przewalskii.* RUSTY-THROATED PARROTBILL. (nc China). _____

❑ *Paradoxornis fulvifrons.* FULVOUS PARROTBILL. (Himal).......... _____

❑ *Paradoxornis nipalensis.* BLACK-THROATED PARROTBILL. (Himal).... _____
   ___*P. (n.) nipalensis.* ASHY-EARED PARROTBILL. (n India)
   ___*P. (n.) poliotis.* BLYTH'S PARROTBILL. (ne India-Thai)

❑ *Paradoxornis verreauxi.* GOLDEN PARROTBILL. (Himal)........... _____

❑ *Paradoxornis davidianus.* SHORT-TAILED PARROTBILL. (s Asia)...... _____

❑ *Paradoxornis atrosuperciliaris.* BLACK-BROWED PARROTBILL. (Himal) _____

❑ *Paradoxornis ruficeps.* RUFOUS-HEADED PARROTBILL. (s Asia)...... _____

❑ *Paradoxornis heudei.* REED PARROTBILL. (e Asia).............. _____

❑ *Rhabdornis mystacalis.* STRIPE-SIDED RHABDORNIS. (Phil)......... _____

❑ *Rhabdornis grandis.* LONG-BILLED RHABDORNIS. (mts n Phil)...... _____

❑ *Rhabdornis inornatus.* STRIPE-BREASTED RHABDORNIS. (ec,s Phil).... _____

Tribe Chamaeini [1/1]

❑ *Chamaea fasciata.* WRENTIT. (w US, nw Baja)................. _____

Tribe Sylviini [1/24]

❑ *Sylvia buryi.* YEMEN WARBLER. (s Arabia).................... _____

❑ *Sylvia lugens.* BROWN WARBLER. (mts ne Afr)................. _____

❑ *Sylvia boehmi.* BANDED WARBLER. (ne Afr)................... _____

❑ *Sylvia layardi.* LAYARD'S WARBLER. (sw Afr)................. _____

❑ *Sylvia subcaeruleum.* RUFOUS-VENTED WARBLER. (s Afr)......... _____

❑ *Sylvia atricapilla.* BLACKCAP. (Palea; ◊-trop Afr).............. _____

❑ *Sylvia borin.* GARDEN WARBLER. (Eura; ◊ trop,s Afr)............ _____

❑ *Sylvia communis.* GREATER WHITETHROAT. (Palea; ◊ trop,s Afr)..... _____

❑ *Sylvia curruca.* LESSER WHITETHROAT. (Palea; ◊ trop,e Afr-India).... _____

❑ *Sylvia minula.* SMALL WHITETHROAT. (sc Asia)................ _____

❑ *Sylvia althaea.* HUME'S WHITETHROAT. (mts s Asia; ◊ s Asia)....... _____

❑ *Sylvia nana.* DESERT WARBLER. (nw Afr, sc Asia).............. _____

❑ *Sylvia nisoria.* BARRED WARBLER. (c Eura; ◊-e Afr)............. _____

❑ *Sylvia hortensis.* ORPHEAN WARBLER. (s Palea; ◊-trop Afr, India).... _____

❑ *Sylvia leucomelaena.* RED SEA WARBLER. (ne Afr reg)............ _____

❑ *Sylvia rueppelli.* RUEPPELL'S WARBLER. (sw Eura; ◊ ne Afr)........ _____

❑ *Sylvia melanocephala.* SARDINIAN WARBLER. (sw Palea; ◊-n Afr).... _____

❑ *Sylvia melanothorax.* CYPRUS WARBLER. (Cyprus; ◊-Egypt)........ _____

❑ *Sylvia cantillans.* SUBALPINE WARBLER. (sw Palea; ◊ n Afr reg)...... _____

❑ *Sylvia mystacea.* MENETRIES'S WARBLER. (sc Asia; ◊ ne Afr-cs Palea). _____

❑ *Sylvia conspicillata.* SPECTACLED WARBLER. (sw Palea; ◊-nw,n Afr) . _____

❑ *Sylvia deserticola.* TRISTRAM'S WARBLER. (nw Afr)............... _____
  ___*S. (d.) deserticola.* TRISTRAM'S WARBLER. (sp)
  ___*S. (d.) ticehursti.* MEINERTZHAGEN'S WARBLER. (Mor)

❑ *Sylvia undata.* DARTFORD WARBLER. (sw Palea)................. _____

❑ *Sylvia sarda.* MARMORA'S WARBLER. (sw Palea; ◊ nw Afr)........ _____

Superfamily PASSEROIDEA [330/1656]
Family **Alaudidae** [19/91]

❑ *Mirafra passerina.* MONOTONOUS LARK. (s Afr)................ _____

❑ *Mirafra cantillans.* SINGING LARK. (n Afr, s Asia)............. _____

❑ *Mirafra javanica.* AUSTRALASIAN LARK. (se Asia-Phil, NG, Aust).... _____
  ___*M. (j.) javanica.* HORSFIELD'S LARK. (sp)
  ___*M. (j.) woodwardi.* CINNAMON LARK. (cw Aust)

❑ *Mirafra cheniana.* LATAKOO LARK. (se Afr)...................... _____

❑ *Mirafra albicauda.* WHITE-TAILED LARK. (nc,ne Afr)............. _____

❑ *Mirafra hova.* MADAGASCAR LARK. (Mad)..................... _____

❑ *Mirafra cordofanica.* KORDOFAN LARK. (subsah Afr)............. _____

❑ *Mirafra williamsi.* WILLIAMS'S LARK. (nc Kenya)................ _____

❑ *Mirafra pulpa.* FRIEDMANN'S LARK. (ne Afr).................... _____

❑ *Mirafra hypermetra.* RED-WINGED LARK. (ne Afr)................ _____

❑ *Mirafra somalica.* SOMALI LONG-BILLED LARK. (Som)............ _____

❑ *Mirafra ashi.* ASH'S LARK. (s Som)........................... _____

❑ *Mirafra africana.* RUFOUS-NAPED LARK. (Afr)................. _____

❑ *Mirafra sharpii.* SOMALI LARK. (n Som)...................... _____

❑ *Mirafra angolensis.* ANGOLA LARK. (mts sc Afr)................ _____

❑ *Mirafra rufocinnamomea.* FLAPPET LARK. (Afr)................. _____
  ___*M. (r.) buckleyi.* BUCKLEY'S LARK. (w Afr)
  ___*M. (r.) rufocinnamomea.* FLAPPET LARK. (c,e,s Afr)

❑ *Mirafra apiata.* CLAPPER LARK. (s Afr)....................... _____
  ___*M. (a.) damarensis.* DAMARA CLAPPER-LARK. (sc Afr)
  ___*M. (a.) apiata.* CAPE CLAPPER-LARK. (sp)
  ___*M. (a.) rufipilea.* NAMAQUA CLAPPER-LARK. (e S Afr)

❏ *Mirafra collaris.* COLLARED LARK. (ne Afr)..................... _____

❏ *Mirafra africanoides.* FAWN-COLORED LARK. (ne,s Afr)........... _____

❏ *Mirafra alopex.* ABYSSINIAN LARK. (ne Afr)..................... _____

❏ *Mirafra erythroptera.* INDIAN LARK. (cs Asia)................... _____

❏ *Mirafra assamica.* RUFOUS-WINGED LARK. (s,se Asia)............. _____

❏ *Mirafra rufa.* RUSTY LARK. (subsah Afr)...................... _____

❏ *Mirafra gilletti.* GILLETT'S LARK. (ne Afr)..................... _____

❏ *Mirafra poecilosterna.* PINK-BREASTED LARK. (ne Afr)............ _____

❏ *Mirafra degodiensis.* DEGODI LARK. (se Eth)................... _____

❏ *Mirafra naevia.* BRADFIELD'S LARK. (sw Afr)................... _____

❏ *Mirafra sabota.* SABOTA LARK. (se Afr)...................... _____

❏ *Pinarocorys erythropygia.* RUFOUS-RUMPED LARK. (subsah w,c Afr) . _____

❏ *Pinarocorys nigricans.* DUSKY LARK. (c,s Afr).................. _____

❏ *Heteromirafra archeri.* ARCHER'S LARK. (mts nw Som)........... _____

❏ *Heteromirafra sidamoensis.* SIDAMO LARK. (mts cs Eth).......... _____

❏ *Heteromirafra ruddi.* RUDD'S LARK. (e S Afr)................... _____

❏ *Certhilauda curvirostris.* LONG-BILLED LARK. (s Afr)............. _____

❏ *Certhilauda chuana.* SHORT-CLAWED LARK. (s Afr).............. _____

❏ *Certhilauda erythrochlamys.* DUNE LARK. (s Afr)................ _____

❏ *Certhilauda albescens.* KAROO LARK. (s Afr).................. _____

❏ *Certhilauda burra.* FERRUGINOUS LARK. (sw Afr)............... _____

❏ *Chersomanes albofasciata.* SPIKE-HEELED LARK. (s Afr)........... _____

❏ *Eremopterix leucotis.* CHESTNUT-BACKED SPARROW-LARK. (Afr)..... _____

❏ *Eremopterix australis.* BLACK-EARED SPARROW-LARK. (cs Afr)..... _____

❏ *Eremopterix verticalis.* GREY-BACKED SPARROW-LARK. (sw Afr)..... _____

❏ *Eremopterix leucopareia.* FISCHER'S SPARROW-LARK. (e Afr)........ _____

❏ *Eremopterix signata.* CHESTNUT-HEADED SPARROW-LARK. (ne Afr)... _____

❏ *Eremopterix nigriceps.* BLACK-CROWNED SPARROW-L. (n Afr, sc Asia) _____

❏ *Eremopterix grisea.* ASHY-CROWNED SPARROW-LARK. (s Asia)...... _____

❏ *Ammomanes cincturus.* BAR-TAILED LARK. (n Afr, cs Asia)........ _____

❏ *Ammomanes phoenicurus.* RUFOUS-TAILED LARK. (pen India)....... _____

❏ *Ammomanes deserti.* DESERT LARK. (n Afr, cs Asia)............. _____

❏ *Ammomanes grayi.* GRAY'S LARK. (sw Afr).................... _____

❏ *Alaemon alaudipes.* GREATER HOOPOE-LARK. (n Afr, cs Asia)...... _____

❏ *Alaemon hamertoni.* LESSER HOOPOE-LARK. (ne Som)............ _____

❏ *Ramphocoris clotbey.* THICK-BILLED LARK. (n Afr reg). . . . . _____

❏ *Melanocorypha calandra.* CALANDRA LARK. (s Palea). . . . . _____

❏ *Melanocorypha bimaculata.* BIMACULATED LARK. (s Eura; ◊-ne Afr). _____

❏ *Melanocorypha maxima.* TIBETAN LARK. (Himal). . . . . _____

❏ *Melanocorypha mongolica.* MONGOLIAN LARK. (e Eura; ◊-c China) . _____

❏ *Melanocorypha leucoptera.* WHITE-WINGED LARK. (c Eura; ◊-sc Asia). _____

❏ *Melanocorypha yeltoniensis.* BLACK LARK. (c Eura). . . . . _____

❏ *Calandrella brachydactyla.* GREATER SHORT-TOED LARK. (s Palea). . . _____

❏ *Calandrella blanfordi.* BLANFORD'S LARK. (ne Afr reg). . . . . _____

❏ *Calandrella erlangeri.* ERLANGER'S LARK. (mts Eth). . . . . _____

❏ *Calandrella cinerea.* RED-CAPPED LARK. (wc,e,s Afr). . . . . _____

❏ *Calandrella acutirostris.* HUME'S LARK. (mts s Eura). . . . . _____

❏ *Calandrella rufescens.* LESSER SHORT-TOED LARK. (s Palea). . . . . . . _____

❏ *Calandrella cheleensis.* ASIAN SHORT-TOED LARK. (sc Asia). . . . . . . _____

❏ *Calandrella raytal.* INDIAN SHORT-TOED LARK. (s Eura). . . . . _____

❏ *Calandrella somalica.* RUFOUS SHORT-TOED LARK. (ne Afr). . . . . . . _____

❏ *Calandrella athensis.* ATHI SHORT-TOED LARK. (e Afr). . . . . _____

❏ *Spizocorys conirostris.* PINK-BILLED LARK. (sc Afr). . . . . _____

❏ *Spizocorys sclateri.* SCLATER'S LARK. (sw Afr). . . . . _____

❏ *Spizocorys obbiensis.* OBBIA LARK. (ce Som). . . . . _____

❏ *Spizocorys personata.* MASKED LARK. (ne Afr). . . . . _____

❏ *Spizocorys fringillaris.* BOTHA'S LARK. (ec S Afr). . . . . _____

❏ *Eremalauda starki.* STARK'S LARK. (s Afr). . . . . _____

❏ *Eremalauda dunni.* DUNN'S LARK. (n Afr reg). . . . . _____

❏ *Chersophilus duponti.* DUPONT'S LARK. (sw Palea). . . . . _____

❏ *Galerida cristata.* CRESTED LARK. (Palea, subsah Afr). . . . . _____

❏ *Galerida theklae.* THEKLA LARK. (sw Palea, ne Afr). . . . . _____

❏ *Galerida malabarica.* MALABAR LARK. (w pen India). . . . . _____

❏ *Galerida deva.* TAWNY LARK. (India). . . . . _____

❏ *Galerida modesta.* SUN LARK. (subsah Afr). . . . . _____

❏ *Galerida magnirostris.* LARGE-BILLED LARK. (S Afr). . . . . _____

❏ *Pseudalaemon fremantlii.* SHORT-TAILED LARK. (ne Afr). . . . . _____

❏ *Lullula arborea.* WOOD LARK. (w Palea; ◊-n Afr). . . . . _____

❏ *Alauda arvensis.* EURASIAN SKYLARK. (Palea; ◆ NZ, Haw Is, BC). . . _____

❏ *Alauda japonica.* JAPANESE SKYLARK. (Japan; ◊-Ryu). . . . . _____

❏ *Alauda gulgula.* ORIENTAL SKYLARK. (c,e Eura, Phil; ◊-s Asia). . . . . . _____

❏ *Alauda razae.* RAZO LARK. (C Verde)........................ _____

❏ *Eremophila alpestris.* HORNED LARK. (Hol-Mex, mts ce Colom)..... _____
   ___*E. (a.) alpestris.* HORNED LARK. (sp)
   ___*E. (a.) teleschowi.* PRZEWALSKI'S LARK. (wc China)

❏ *Eremophila bilopha.* TEMMINCK'S LARK. (sw Palea).............. _____

Family **Nectariniidae** [8/170]
Subfamily Promeropinae [1/2]

❏ *Promerops gurneyi.* GURNEY'S SUGARBIRD. (mts s Afr)............ _____

❏ *Promerops cafer.* CAPE SUGARBIRD. (mts s S Afr)................ _____

Subfamily Nectariniinae [7/168]
Tribe Dicaeini [2/44]

❏ *Prionochilus olivaceus.* OLIVE-BACKED FLOWERPECKER. (Phil)...... _____

❏ *Prionochilus maculatus.* YELLOW-BREASTED FLOWERPECKER. (se Asia)_____

❏ *Prionochilus percussus.* CRIMSON-BREASTED FLOWERPECKER. (se Asia)_____

❏ *Prionochilus plateni.* PALAWAN FLOWERPECKER. (sw Phil)......... _____

❏ *Prionochilus xanthopygius.* YELLOW-RUMPED FLOWERPECKER. (Born) _____

❏ *Prionochilus thoracicus.* SCARLET-BREASTED FLOWERPECKER. (se Asia)_____

❏ *Dicaeum annae.* GOLDEN-RUMPED FLOWERPECKER. (c L Sunda)..... _____

❏ *Dicaeum agile.* THICK-BILLED FLOWERPECKER. (s,se Asia, wc L Sunda)_____
   ___*D. (a.) agile.* THICK-BILLED FLOWERPECKER. (s Asia)
   ___*D. (a.) modestum.* STREAK-BREASTED FLOWERPECKER. (sp)

❏ *Dicaeum aeruginosum.* STRIPED FLOWERPECKER. (Phil)........... _____

❏ *Dicaeum everetti.* BROWN-BACKED FLOWERPECKER. (se Asia)....... _____

❏ *Dicaeum proprium.* WHISKERED FLOWERPECKER. (mts s Phil)...... _____

❏ *Dicaeum chrysorrheum.* YELLOW-VENTED FLOWERPECKER. (s,se Asia)_____

❏ *Dicaeum melanoxanthum.* YELLOW-BELLIED FLOWERPECKER. (s Asia)_____

❏ *Dicaeum vincens.* WHITE-THROATED FLOWERPECKER. (Ceylon)...... _____

❏ *Dicaeum aureolimbatum.* YELLOW-SIDED FLOWERPECKER. (Sulaw)... _____

❏ *Dicaeum nigrilore.* OLIVE-CAPPED FLOWERPECKER. (s Phil)........ _____

❏ *Dicaeum anthonyi.* FLAME-CROWNED FLOWERPECKER. (n,s Phil)..... _____
   ___*D. (a.) anthonyi.* YELLOW-CROWNED FLOWERPECKER. (n Phil)
   ___*D. (a.) kampalili.* RED-CROWNED FLOWERPECKER. (s Phil)

❏ *Dicaeum bicolor.* BICOLORED FLOWERPECKER. (Phil)............. _____

  Dicaeum quadricolor. CEBU FLOWERPECKER. (†sc Phil)........... _____

❏ *Dicaeum australe.* RED-STRIPED FLOWERPECKER. (Phil)........... _____

❏ *Dicaeum retrocinctum.* SCARLET-COLLARED FLOWERPECKER. (cw Phil)_____

❏ *Dicaeum trigonostigma.* ORANGE-BELLIED FLOWERP. (s,se Asia, Phil). . _____
   ___*D. (t.) trigonostigma.* ORANGE-BELLIED FLOWERPECKER. (s,se Asia)
   ___*D. (t.) dorsale.* SULU FLOWERPECKER. (Phil)

❏ *Dicaeum hypoleucum.* BUZZING FLOWERPECKER. (Phil). . . . . _____

❏ *Dicaeum erythrorhynchos.* PALE-BILLED FLOWERPECKER. (s Asia). . . . _____

❏ *Dicaeum concolor.* PLAIN FLOWERPECKER. (s,se Asia). . . . . _____
   ___*D. (c.) concolor.* PLAIN FLOWERPECKER. (sw pen India)
   ___*D. (c.) minullum.* OLIVACEOUS FLOWERPECKER. (sp)

❏ *Dicaeum pygmaeum.* PYGMY FLOWERPECKER. (Phil). . . . . _____

❏ *Dicaeum nehrkorni.* CRIMSON-CROWNED FLOWERPECKER. (Sulaw). . . _____

❏ *Dicaeum erythrothorax.* FLAME-BREASTED FLOWERPECKER. (Moluc). _____

❏ *Dicaeum vulneratum.* ASHY FLOWERPECKER. (mts s Moluc). . . . . _____

❏ *Dicaeum pectorale.* OLIVE-CROWNED FLOWERPECKER. (w Pap, nw NG)_____

❏ *Dicaeum geelvinkianum.* RED-CAPPED FLOWERPECKER. (NG). . . . . . . _____

❏ *Dicaeum nitidum.* LOUISIADE FLOWERPECKER. (is se NG). . . . . _____

❏ *Dicaeum eximium.* RED-BANDED FLOWERPECKER. (Bism). . . . . _____

❏ *Dicaeum aeneum.* MIDGET FLOWERPECKER. (Solom). . . . . _____

❏ *Dicaeum tristrami.* MOTTLED FLOWERPECKER. (se Solom). . . . . _____

❏ *Dicaeum igniferum.* BLACK-FRONTED FLOWERPECKER. (c L Sunda). . . _____

❏ *Dicaeum maugei.* RED-CHESTED FLOWERPECKER. (L Sunda). . . . . _____

❏ *Dicaeum ignipectus.* FIRE-BREASTED FLOWERPECKER. (s Asia-Phil). . . _____
   ___*D. (i.) ignipectus.* FIRE-BREASTED FLOWERPECKER. (s,se Asia)
   ___*D. (i.) cambodianum.* CAMBODIAN FLOWERPECKER. (Indoc)
   ___*D. (i.) beccarii.* BUFF-BELLIED FLOWERPECKER. (n Sum)
   ___*D. (i.) luzoniense.* LUZON FLOWERPECKER. (Phil)

❏ *Dicaeum monticolum.* BLACK-SIDED FLOWERPECKER. (mts n Born). . . _____

❏ *Dicaeum celebicum.* GREY-SIDED FLOWERPECKER. (Sulaw). . . . . _____

❏ *Dicaeum sanguinolentum.* BLOOD-BREASTED FLOWERP. (Java-L Sunda)_____

❏ *Dicaeum hirundinaceum.* MISTLETOEBIRD. (s Wall, Aust). . . . . _____
   ___*D. (h.) ignicolle.* WALLACEAN FLOWERPECKER. (s Wall)
   ___*D. (h.) hirundinaceum.* MISTLETOEBIRD. (Aust)

❏ *Dicaeum cruentatum.* SCARLET-BACKED FLOWERPECKER. (s,se Asia) . _____

❏ *Dicaeum trochileum.* SCARLET-HEADED FLOWERP. (G Sunda-Lombok)_____

Tribe Nectariniini [5/124]

❏ *Anthreptes fraseri.* SCARLET-TUFTED SUNBIRD. (w,wc Afr). . . . . _____

❏ *Anthreptes axillaris.* GREY-HEADED SUNBIRD. (c Afr). . . . . _____

❏ *Anthreptes reichenowi.* PLAIN-BACKED SUNBIRD. (e,se Afr). . . . . _____
   ___*A. (r.) yokanae.* KENYA SUNBIRD. (e Afr)
   ___*A. (r.) reichenowi.* PLAIN-BACKED SUNBIRD. (se Afr)

❑ *Anthreptes anchietae.* ANCHIETA'S SUNBIRD. (sc Afr)............. _____

❑ *Anthreptes simplex.* PLAIN SUNBIRD. (se Asia)................. _____

❑ *Anthreptes malacensis.* PLAIN-THROATED SUNBIRD. (se Asia-Wall)... _____
   ___*A. (m.) malacensis.* BROWN-THROATED SUNBIRD. (se Asia, sw Phil)
   ___*A. (m.) chlorigaster.* PLAIN-THROATED SUNBIRD. (Wall, wc Phil)
   ___*A. (m.) griseigularis.* GREY-THROATED SUNBIRD. (n,ec,s Phil)

❑ *Anthreptes rhodolaema.* RED-THROATED SUNBIRD. (se Asia)....... _____

❑ *Anthreptes singalensis.* RUBY-CHEEKED SUNBIRD. (s,se Asia)....... _____

❑ *Anthreptes gabonicus.* MOUSE-BROWN SUNBIRD. (w Afr).......... _____

❑ *Anthreptes longuemarei.* WESTERN VIOLET-BACKED SUNBIRD. (Afr) . _____

❑ *Anthreptes orientalis.* KENYA VIOLET-BACKED SUNBIRD. (ne Afr).... _____

❑ *Anthreptes neglectus.* ULUGURU VIOLET-BACKED SUNBIRD. (e Afr)... _____

❑ *Anthreptes aurantium.* VIOLET-TAILED SUNBIRD. (c Afr).......... _____

❑ *Anthreptes pallidigaster.* AMANI SUNBIRD. (e Afr)............... _____

❑ *Anthreptes rectirostris.* GREEN SUNBIRD. (w,c Afr)............... _____
   ___*A. (r.) rectirostris.* YELLOW-CHINNED SUNBIRD. (w Afr)
   ___*A. (r.) tephrolaema.* GREY-CHINNED SUNBIRD. (c Afr)

❑ *Anthreptes rubritorques.* BANDED SUNBIRD. (mts ne Tanz)......... _____

❑ *Anthreptes collaris.* COLLARED SUNBIRD. (Afr)................. _____

❑ *Anthreptes platurus.* PYGMY SUNBIRD. (subsah Afr).............. _____

❑ *Anthreptes metallicus.* NILE VALLEY SUNBIRD. (ne Afr reg)........ _____

❑ *Hypogramma hypogrammicum.* PURPLE-NAPED SUNBIRD. (s,se Asia). _____

❑ *Nectarinia seimundi.* LITTLE GREEN SUNBIRD. (w,c Afr)........... _____

❑ *Nectarinia batesi.* BATES'S SUNBIRD. (w,c Afr)................. _____

❑ *Nectarinia olivacea.* OLIVE SUNBIRD. (Afr).................... _____

❑ *Nectarinia violacea.* ORANGE-BREASTED SUNBIRD. (mts s S Afr)..... _____

❑ *Nectarinia veroxii.* MOUSE-COLORED SUNBIRD. (e,se Afr).......... _____

❑ *Nectarinia reichenbachii.* REICHENBACH'S SUNBIRD. (w,c Afr)...... _____

❑ *Nectarinia hartlaubii.* PRINCIPE SUNBIRD. (Prín)................. _____

❑ *Nectarinia newtonii.* NEWTON'S SUNBIRD. (ST)................. _____

❑ *Nectarinia thomensis.* SAO TOME SUNBIRD. (mts ST)............. _____

❑ *Nectarinia oritis.* CAMEROON SUNBIRD. (mts wc Afr)............. _____

❑ *Nectarinia alinae.* BLUE-HEADED SUNBIRD. (mts ec Afr).......... _____

❑ *Nectarinia verticalis.* GREEN-HEADED SUNBIRD. (w,c Afr)......... _____

❑ *Nectarinia bannermani.* BANNERMAN'S SUNBIRD. (wc Afr)........ _____

❑ *Nectarinia cyanolaema.* BLUE-THROATED BROWN SUNBIRD. (w,c Afr) . _____

❏ *Nectarinia balfouri.* SOCOTRA SUNBIRD. (Socotra). . . . . _____

❏ *Nectarinia dussumieri.* SEYCHELLES SUNBIRD. (Seyc). . . . . _____

❏ *Nectarinia fuliginosa.* CARMELITE SUNBIRD. (w Afr). . . . . _____

❏ *Nectarinia amethystina.* AMETHYST SUNBIRD. (e,c,se Afr). . . . . _____

❏ *Nectarinia rubescens.* GREEN-THROATED SUNBIRD. (c Afr). . . . . _____

❏ *Nectarinia senegalensis.* SCARLET-CHESTED SUNBIRD. (Afr). . . . . _____

❏ *Nectarinia hunteri.* HUNTER'S SUNBIRD. (ne Afr). . . . . _____

❏ *Nectarinia adelberti.* BUFF-THROATED SUNBIRD. (w Afr). . . . . _____

❏ *Nectarinia zeylonica.* PURPLE-RUMPED SUNBIRD. (s Asia). . . . . _____

❏ *Nectarinia minima.* CRIMSON-BACKED SUNBIRD. (w,sw India). . . . . . . _____

❏ *Nectarinia sperata.* PURPLE-THROATED SUNBIRD. (s,se Asia, Phil). . . . _____
   ___*N. (s.) brasiliana.* PURPLE-THROATED SUNBIRD. (s,se Asia)
   ___*N. (s.) sperata.* VAN HASSELT'S SUNBIRD. (is e Born, c Phil)
   ___*N. (s.) henkei.* HENKE'S SUNBIRD. (n Phil)
   ___*N. (s.) juliae.* MINDANAO SUNBIRD. (s Phil)

❏ *Nectarinia aspasia.* BLACK SUNBIRD. (Wall-Bism). . . . . _____

❏ *Nectarinia calcostetha.* COPPER-THROATED SUNBIRD. (se Asia). . . . . . _____

❏ *Nectarinia jugularis.* OLIVE-BACKED SUNBIRD. (s Asia-Solom, ne Aust)_____
   ___*N. (j.) jugularis.* YELLOW-BELLIED SUNBIRD. (s,se Asia, Wall)
   ___*N. (j.) idenburgi.* BLACK-BREASTED SUNBIRD. (n NG)
   ___*N. (j.) frenata.* YELLOW-BREASTED SUNBIRD. (n Moluc-Solom, ne Aust)

❏ *Nectarinia buettikoferi.* APRICOT-BREASTED SUNBIRD. (Sumba). . . . . . _____

❏ *Nectarinia solaris.* FLAME-BREASTED SUNBIRD. (L Sunda). . . . . _____

❏ *Nectarinia sovimanga.* SOUIMANGA SUNBIRD. (Ald, Mad). . . . . _____

❏ *Nectarinia humbloti.* HUMBLOT'S SUNBIRD. (w Com). . . . . _____

❏ *Nectarinia comorensis.* ANJOUAN SUNBIRD. (c Com). . . . . _____

❏ *Nectarinia coquerellii.* MAYOTTE SUNBIRD. (se Com). . . . . _____

❏ *Nectarinia venusta.* VARIABLE SUNBIRD. (w,c,e Afr). . . . . _____
   ___*N. (v.) venusta.* VARIABLE SUNBIRD. (sp)
   ___*N. (v.) albiventris.* WHITE-BELLIED SUNBIRD. (ne Afr)
   ___*N. (v.) igneiventris.* ORANGE-BELLIED SUNBIRD. (mts ec Afr)

❏ *Nectarinia ursulae.* URSULA'S SUNBIRD. (mts Camer). . . . . _____

❏ *Nectarinia talatala.* WHITE-BREASTED SUNBIRD. (sc Afr). . . . . _____

❏ *Nectarinia oustaleti.* OUSTALET'S SUNBIRD. (c Afr). . . . . _____
   ___*N. (o.) oustaleti.* OUSTALET'S SUNBIRD. (c Ang)
   ___*N. (o.) rhodesiae.* ZAMBIAN SUNBIRD. (Zamb, Tanz)

❏ *Nectarinia bouvieri.* ORANGE-TUFTED SUNBIRD. (c Afr). . . . . _____

❏ *Nectarinia osea.* PALESTINE SUNBIRD. (nc Afr, sw Palea). . . . . _____

❏ *Nectarinia asiatica.* PURPLE SUNBIRD. (s,se Asia). . . . . _____

❑ *Nectarinia habessinica.* SHINING SUNBIRD. (ne Afr reg)........... _____

❑ *Nectarinia lotenia.* LONG-BILLED SUNBIRD. (s Asia).............. _____

❑ *Nectarinia manoensis.* MIOMBO DOUBLE-COLLARED SUNB. (sc,s Afr). _____
   ___*N. (m.) pintoi.* PINTO'S DOUBLE-COLLARED SUNBIRD. (sc Afr)
   ___*N. (m.) manoensis.* MIOMBO DOUBLE-COLLARED SUNBIRD. (s Afr)

❑ *Nectarinia chalybea.* SOUTHERN DOUBLE-COLLARED SUNBIRD. (S Afr). _____

❑ *Nectarinia ludovicensis.* MONTANE DOUBLE-COLLARED SUNBIRD. (Ang)_____

❑ *Nectarinia prigoginei.* PRIGOGINE'SDOUBLE-COLLARED SUNBIRD. (c Afr)_____

❑ *Nectarinia stuhlmanni.* STUHLMANN'S DOUBLE-COLLARED S. (ce Zaire) _____

❑ *Nectarinia preussi.* NORTHERN DOUBLE-COLLARED SUNBIRD. (wc,ne Afr)_____

❑ *Nectarinia afra.* GREATER DOUBLE-COLLARED SUNBIRD. (ne,e,s Afr) . _____

❑ *Nectarinia mediocris.* EASTERN DOUBLE-COLLARED SUNBIRD. (e Afr). _____

❑ *Nectarinia neergaardi.* NEERGAARD'S SUNBIRD. (se Afr)........... _____

❑ *Nectarinia chloropygia.* OLIVE-BELLIED SUNBIRD. (w,c Afr)........ _____

❑ *Nectarinia minulla.* TINY SUNBIRD. (w Afr)................... _____

❑ *Nectarinia regia.* REGAL SUNBIRD. (mts ec Afr)................ _____

❑ *Nectarinia loveridgei.* LOVERIDGE'S SUNBIRD. (mts ce Tanz)........ _____

❑ *Nectarinia moreaui.* MOREAU'S SUNBIRD. (mts ce Tanz)........... _____

❑ *Nectarinia rockefelleri.* ROCKEFELLER'S SUNBIRD. (mts ce Zaire)..... _____

❑ *Nectarinia cuprea.* COPPER SUNBIRD. (c Afr).................... _____

❑ *Nectarinia fusca.* DUSKY SUNBIRD. (sw Afr)................... _____

❑ *Nectarinia rufipennis.* RUFOUS-WINGED SUNBIRD. (mts ec Tanz)..... _____

❑ *Nectarinia tacazze.* TACAZZE SUNBIRD. (mts ne Afr).............. _____

❑ *Nectarinia purpureiventris.* PURPLE-BREASTED SUNBIRD. (c Afr)..... _____

❑ *Nectarinia bocagii.* BOCAGE'S SUNBIRD. (mts wc Afr)............. _____

❑ *Nectarinia kilimensis.* BRONZE SUNBIRD. (mts c,e Afr)........... _____
   ___*N. (k.) gadowi.* GADOW'S SUNBIRD. (c Ang)
   ___*N. (k.) kilimensis.* BRONZE SUNBIRD. (e Afr)

❑ *Nectarinia reichenowi.* GOLDEN-WINGED SUNBIRD. (mts e Afr)...... _____

❑ *Nectarinia famosa.* MALACHITE SUNBIRD. (mts e,s Afr)........... _____

❑ *Nectarinia johnstoni.* RED-TUFTED SUNBIRD. (mts e Afr).......... _____

❑ *Nectarinia shelleyi.* SHELLEY'S SUNBIRD. (e Afr)................ _____

❑ *Nectarinia erythrocerca.* RED-CHESTED SUNBIRD. (e Afr).......... _____

❑ *Nectarinia congensis.* CONGO SUNBIRD. (nw,nc Zaire)............ _____

❑ *Nectarinia mariquensis.* MARIQUA SUNBIRD. (e,s Afr)............ _____
   ___*N. (m.) osiris.* SWAHILI SUNBIRD. (e Afr)
   ___*N. (m.) mariquensis.* MARIQUA SUNBIRD. (s Afr)

❏ *Nectarinia bifasciata.* PURPLE-BANDED SUNBIRD. (e,c,se Afr). . . . . _____
　___*N. (b.) tsavoensis.* TSAVO PURPLE-BANDED SUNBIRD. (e Afr)
　___*N. (b.) bifasciata.* LITTLE PURPLE-BANDED SUNBIRD. (c,se Afr)

❏ *Nectarinia pembae.* VIOLET-BREASTED SUNBIRD. (e Afr). . . . . _____
　___*N. (p.) chalcomelas.* VIOLET-BREASTED SUNBIRD. (sp)
　___*N. (p.) pembae.* PEMBA SUNBIRD. (is se Tanz)

❏ *Nectarinia notata.* LONG-BILLED GREEN SUNBIRD. (Com, Mad). . . . . . _____

❏ *Nectarinia coccinigastra.* SPLENDID SUNBIRD. (c Afr). . . . . _____

❏ *Nectarinia johannae.* JOHANNA'S SUNBIRD. (w Afr). . . . . _____

❏ *Nectarinia superba.* SUPERB SUNBIRD. (w,c Afr). . . . . _____

❏ *Nectarinia pulchella.* BEAUTIFUL SUNBIRD. (subsah,ne Afr). . . . . _____

❏ *Nectarinia nectarinioides.* BLACK-BELLIED SUNBIRD. (ne Afr). . . . . . . _____

❏ *Aethopyga primigenius.* GREY-HOODED SUNBIRD. (mts s Phil). . . . . . . _____

❏ *Aethopyga boltoni.* APO SUNBIRD. (mts s Phil). . . . . _____

❏ *Aethopyga flagrans.* FLAMING SUNBIRD. (n,c Phil). . . . . _____

❏ *Aethopyga pulcherrima.* METALLIC-WINGED SUNBIRD. (Phil). . . . . _____

❏ *Aethopyga duyvenbodei.* ELEGANT SUNBIRD. (Sangihe). . . . . _____

❏ *Aethopyga shelleyi.* LOVELY SUNBIRD. (Phil). . . . . _____

❏ *Aethopyga gouldiae.* GOULD'S SUNBIRD. (s,se Asia). . . . . _____

❏ *Aethopyga nipalensis.* GREEN-TAILED SUNBIRD. (Himal). . . . . _____

❏ *Aethopyga eximia.* WHITE-FLANKED SUNBIRD. (mts Java). . . . . _____

❏ *Aethopyga christinae.* FORK-TAILED SUNBIRD. (e China, Viet). . . . . . . _____

❏ *Aethopyga saturata.* BLACK-THROATED SUNBIRD. (mts s,se Asia). . . . . _____

❏ *Aethopyga siparaja.* CRIMSON SUNBIRD. (s,se Asia, wc Phil). . . . . _____

❏ *Aethopyga mystacalis.* SCARLET SUNBIRD. (se Asia). . . . . _____
　___*A. (m.) tenuirostris.* SCARLET SUNBIRD. (sp)
　___*A. (m.) mystacalis.* JAVAN SUNBIRD. (Java)

❏ *Aethopyga ignicauda.* FIRE-TAILED SUNBIRD. (Himal). . . . . _____

❏ *Arachnothera longirostra.* LITTLE SPIDERHUNTER. (s,se Asia-s Phil) . _____

❏ *Arachnothera crassirostris.* THICK-BILLED SPIDERHUNTER. (se Asia) . _____

❏ *Arachnothera robusta.* LONG-BILLED SPIDERHUNTER. (se Asia). . . . . . _____

❏ *Arachnothera flavigaster.* SPECTACLED SPIDERHUNTER. (se Asia). . . . . _____

❏ *Arachnothera chrysogenys.* YELLOW-EARED SPIDERHUNTER. (se Asia) _____

❏ *Arachnothera clarae.* NAKED-FACED SPIDERHUNTER. (Phil). . . . . _____

❏ *Arachnothera affinis.* GREY-BREASTED SPIDERHUNTER. (se Asia). . . . . _____

❏ *Arachnothera everetti.* BORNEAN SPIDERHUNTER. (mts n,c Born). . . . . _____

❏ *Arachnothera magna.* STREAKED SPIDERHUNTER. (mts s,se Asia). . . . . _____

❏ *Arachnothera juliae.* WHITEHEAD'S SPIDERHUNTER. (mts n Born). . . . . _____

Family **Melanocharitidae** [3/10]
Tribe Melanocharitinae [1/6]

❑ *Melanocharis arfakiana.* OBSCURE BERRYPECKER. (mts se NG)...... _____

❑ *Melanocharis nigra.* BLACK BERRYPECKER. (Aru-NG)............ _____

❑ *Melanocharis longicauda.* LEMON-BREASTED BERRYPECKER. (NG)... _____

❑ *Melanocharis versteri.* FAN-TAILED BERRYPECKER. (mts NG)....... _____

❑ *Melanocharis striativentris.* STREAKED BERRYPECKER. (mts c,e NG) . _____

❑ *Melanocharis crassirostris.* SPOTTED BERRYPECKER. (mts NG)...... _____

Tribe Toxorhamphini [2/4]

❑ *Toxorhamphus novaeguineae.* GREEN-CROWNED LONGBILL. (Aru-NG)_____

❑ *Toxorhamphus poliopterus.* GREY-WINGED LONGBILL. (mts c,e NG) . _____

❑ *Toxorhamphus iliolophus.* PLUMED LONGBILL. (w Pap, NG)....... _____

❑ *Oedistoma pygmaeum.* PYGMY LONGBILL. (w Pap, NG)........... _____

Family **Paramythiidae** [2/2]

❑ *Oreocharis arfaki.* TIT BERRYPECKER. (mts NG)................. _____

❑ *Paramythia montium.* CRESTED BERRYPECKER. (mts c,e NG)....... _____
___*P. (m.) olivaceum.* OLIVACEOUS BERRYPECKER. (c NG)
___*P. (m.) montium.* CRESTED BERRYPECKER. (ec,se NG)

Family **Passeridae** [57/388]
Subfamily Passerinae [4/36]

❑ *Passer ammodendri.* SAXAUL SPARROW. (sc Eura).............. _____

❑ *Passer domesticus.* HOUSE SPARROW. (Palea-s Asia; ◆ cosm)...... _____
___*P. (d.) domesticus.* HOUSE SPARROW. (Palea; ◆ cosm)
___*P. (d.) indicus.* INDIAN SPARROW. (s Eura; ◆ Afr reg)

❑ *Passer hispaniolensis.* SPANISH SPARROW. (s Palea; ◊-n Afr, n India) . _____

❑ *Passer pyrrhonotus.* SIND SPARROW. (s Eura)................... _____

❑ *Passer castanopterus.* SOMALI SPARROW. (ne Afr).............. _____

❑ *Passer rutilans.* RUSSET SPARROW. (s,e Asia)................... _____

❑ *Passer flaveolus.* PLAIN-BACKED SPARROW. (se Asia)............ _____

❑ *Passer moabiticus.* DEAD SEA SPARROW. (sc Palea).............. _____

❑ *Passer iagoensis.* IAGO SPARROW. (C Verde)................... _____

❑ *Passer rufocinctus.* KENYA RUFOUS-SPARROW. (ne Afr)........... _____
___*P. (r.) cordofanicus.* KORDOFAN RUFOUS-SPARROW. (cw Sudan)
___*P. (r.) shelleyi.* SHELLEY'S RUFOUS-SPARROW. (s Sudan-Som, Uganda)
___*P. (r.) rufocinctus.* KENYA RUFOUS-SPARROW. (Kenya, ne Tanz)

❑ *Passer insularis.* SOCOTRA SPARROW. (Socotra)................ _____

❑ *Passer motitensis.* SOUTHERN RUFOUS-SPARROW. (s Afr)........... _____

❑ *Passer melanurus.* MOSSIE. (s Afr)............................. _____

❑ *Passer griseus.* GREY-HEADED SPARROW. (w,c Afr)............... _____

❑ *Passer swainsonii.* SWAINSON'S SPARROW. (mts ne Afr)........... _____

❑ *Passer gongonensis.* PARROT-BILLED SPARROW. (ne Afr)........... _____

❑ *Passer suahelicus.* SWAHILI SPARROW. (s Kenya, Tanz)........... _____

❑ *Passer diffusus.* CAPE SPARROW. (se,s Afr)..................... _____

❑ *Passer simplex.* DESERT SPARROW. (s Palea)..................... _____

❑ *Passer montanus.* EURASIAN TREE SPARROW. (Palea-s Asia; ♦ cosm). _____

❑ *Passer luteus.* SUDAN GOLDEN-SPARROW. (subsah Afr)............. _____

❑ *Passer euchlorus.* ARABIAN GOLDEN-SPARROW. (sw Arabia, n Som) . _____

❑ *Passer eminibey.* CHESTNUT SPARROW. (ne Afr)................. _____

❑ *Petronia pyrgita.* YELLOW-SPOTTED PETRONIA. (subsah,ne Afr)...... _____

❑ *Petronia xanthocollis.* CHESTNUT-SHOULDERED PETRONIA. (s Asia)... _____

❑ *Petronia superciliaris.* YELLOW-THROATED PETRONIA. (c,se Afr).... _____

❑ *Petronia dentata.* BUSH PETRONIA. (n Afr reg).................. _____

❑ *Petronia petronia.* ROCK SPARROW. (s Palea).................... _____

❑ *Carpospiza brachydactyla.* PALE ROCKFINCH. (cs Eura; ◊-ne Afr)..... _____

❑ *Montifringilla nivalis.* WHITE-WINGED SNOWFINCH. (mts s Eura)..... _____

❑ *Montifringilla adamsi.* BLACK-WINGED SNOWFINCH. (Himal)........ _____

❑ *Montifringilla taczanowskii.* WHITE-RUMPED SNOWFINCH. (w China). _____

❑ *Montifringilla davidiana.* SMALL SNOWFINCH. (mts c Asia)........ _____

❑ *Montifringilla ruficollis.* RUFOUS-NECKED SNOWFINCH. (w China).... _____

❑ *Montifringilla blanfordi.* PLAIN-BACKED SNOWFINCH. (w China)..... _____

❑ *Montifringilla theresae.* AFGHAN SNOWFINCH. (mts n Afgh)........ _____

Subfamily Motacillinae [5/65]

❑ *Dendronanthus indicus.* FOREST WAGTAIL. (e,s Asia; ◊-Phil)....... _____

❑ *Motacilla alba.* WHITE WAGTAIL. (Palea-w Alas; ◊-s Afr, Indon)..... _____
   ___*M. (a.) alba.* WHITE WAGTAIL. (sp)
   ___*M. (a.) yarrelli.* BRITISH PIED WAGTAIL. (nw Euro; ◊-nw Afr)
   ___*M. (a.) subpersonata.* MOROCCAN WAGTAIL. (Mor)
   ___*M. (a.) personata.* MASKED WAGTAIL. (s Eura; ◊-s Asia)

❑ *Motacilla lugens.* BLACK-BACKED WAGTAIL. (e Asia; ◊-s,se Asia).... _____

❑ *Motacilla grandis.* JAPANESE WAGTAIL. (Japan)................. _____

❑ *Motacilla madaraspatensis.* WHITE-BROWED WAGTAIL. (s Asia)..... _____

❏ *Motacilla aguimp.* AFRICAN PIED WAGTAIL. (Afr)................ _____

❏ *Motacilla capensis.* CAPE WAGTAIL. (s,e Afr).................. _____
   ___*M. (c.) simplicissima.* ANGOLA WAGTAIL. (sc,se Afr)
   ___*M. (c.) wellsi.* WELLS'S WAGTAIL. (e Afr)
   ___*M. (c.) capensis.* CAPE WAGTAIL. (s Afr)

❏ *Motacilla flaviventris.* MADAGASCAR WAGTAIL. (Mad)............ _____

❏ *Motacilla citreola.* CITRINE WAGTAIL. (c Eura; ◊ s Asia)........... _____

❏ *Motacilla flava.* YELLOW WAGTAIL. (Palea, w,n Alas; ◊-s Afr, Aust) . _____
   ___*M. (f.) flavissima.* YELLOWISH-CROWNED WAGTAIL. (nw Euro)
   ___*M. (f.) flava.* BLUE-HEADED WAGTAIL. (c,se Palea)
   ___*M. (f.) cinereocapilla.* ASHY-HEADED WAGTAIL. (sc Euro)
   ___*M. (f.) leucocephala.* WHITE-HEADED WAGTAIL. (c Asia)
   ___*M. (f.) lutea.* YELLOW-HEADED WAGTAIL. (sc Eura)
   ___*M. (f.) feldegg.* BLACK-HEADED WAGTAIL. (sc Eura)
   ___*.M (f.) melanogrisea.* WHITE-CHINNED WAGTAIL. (c Asia)
   ___*M. (f.) thunbergi.* GREY-HEADED WAGTAIL. (n Eura)
   ___*M. (f.) taivana.* GREEN-HEADED WAGTAIL. (ne Asia)
   ___*M. (f.) simillima.* SIBERIAN YELLOW-WAGTAIL. (e Sib)
   ___*M. (f.) tschutschensis.* ALASKA YELLOW-WAGTAIL. (ne Sib, w,n Alas)

❏ *Motacilla cinerea.* GREY WAGTAIL. (Pale; ◊-s Afr, Indon, NG)....... _____

❏ *Motacilla clara.* MOUNTAIN WAGTAIL. (Afr).................... _____

❏ *Tmetothylacus tenellus.* GOLDEN PIPIT. (ne Afr)................. _____

❏ *Macronyx croceus.* YELLOW-THROATED LONGCLAW. (Afr)......... _____

❏ *Macronyx fuellebornii.* FUELLEBORN'S LONGCLAW. (c Afr)......... _____

❏ *Macronyx capensis.* CAPE LONGCLAW. (se Afr)................. _____

❏ *Macronyx flavicollis.* ABYSSINIAN LONGCLAW. (mts w,c Eth)....... _____

❏ *Macronyx ameliae.* ROSY-THROATED LONGCLAW. (c,ne,se Afr)...... _____

❏ *Macronyx aurantiigula.* PANGANI LONGCLAW. (ne Afr)........... _____

❏ *Macronyx grimwoodi.* GRIMWOOD'S LONGCLAW. (wc Afr)......... _____

❏ *Anthus sharpei.* SHARPE'S PIPIT. (mts w,c Kenya)............... _____

❏ *Anthus chloris.* YELLOW-BREASTED PIPIT. (mts e S Afr)........... _____

❏ *Anthus lineiventris.* STRIPED PIPIT. (mts wc,ce,s Afr)............. _____

❏ *Anthus crenatus.* YELLOW-TUFTED PIPIT. (mts e S Afr)........... _____

❏ *Anthus cinnamomeus.* AFRICAN PIPIT. (e,s Afr reg)............... _____

❏ *Anthus camaroonensis.* CAMEROON PIPIT. (mts Camer)........... _____

❏ *Anthus hoeschi.* MOUNTAIN PIPIT. (mts c,s Afr)................. _____

❏ *Anthus richardi.* RICHARD'S PIPIT. (e Asia; ◊ s,se Asia)........... _____

❏ *Anthus rufulus.* PADDYFIELD PIPIT. (s,se Asia, Wall, Phil)......... _____

❏ *Anthus novaeseelandiae.* AUSTRALASIAN PIPIT. (Aust, NG, NZ reg) . _____
   ___*A. (n.) australis.* AUSTRALIAN PIPIT. (Aust, c NG)
   ___*A. (n.) novaeseelandiae.* NEW ZEALAND PIPIT. (NZ-Antipodes)

❑ *Anthus leucophrys.* PLAIN-BACKED PIPIT. (Afr)................ _____
   ___*A. (l.) leucophrys.* PLAIN-BACKED PIPIT. (sp)
   ___*A. (l.) goodsoni.* GOODSON'S PIPIT. (mts ne Afr)

❑ *Anthus vaalensis.* BUFFY PIPIT. (c,s Afr)..................... _____

❑ *Anthus pallidiventris.* LONG-LEGGED PIPIT. (cw Afr).............. _____

❑ *Anthus melindae.* MALINDI PIPIT. (e Afr)..................... _____

❑ *Anthus campestris.* TAWNY PIPIT. (w,c Palea; ◊-n Afr, s Asia)....... _____

❑ *Anthus godlewskii.* BLYTH'S PIPIT. (e Asia; ◊-s Asia).............. _____

❑ *Anthus berthelotii.* BERTHELOT'S PIPIT. (e Atl).................. _____

❑ *Anthus bannermani.* BANNERMAN'S PIPIT. (w Afr)............... _____

❑ *Anthus latistriatus.* JACKSON'S PIPIT. (mts e Afr)............... _____

❑ *Anthus similis.* LONG-BILLED PIPIT. (Afr,s Eurasia).............. _____
   ___*A. (s.) similis.* LONG-BILLED PIPIT. (sp)
   ___*A. (s.) moco.* MOCO PIPIT. (mts cw Ang)

❑ *Anthus nyassae.* WOODLAND PIPIT. (c Afr).................... _____

❑ *Anthus brachyurus.* SHORT-TAILED PIPIT. (c,s Afr).............. _____

❑ *Anthus caffer.* BUSH PIPIT. (e,s Afr)......................... _____

❑ *Anthus sokokensis.* SOKOKE PIPIT. (ce Afr)................... _____

❑ *Anthus trivialis.* TREE PIPIT. (Eura; ◊-s Afr, s Asia)............. _____

❑ *Anthus hodgsoni.* OLIVE-BACKED PIPIT. (e Eura; ◊ s,se Asia, Phil).... _____

❑ *Anthus gustavi.* PECHORA PIPIT. (n Palea; ◊-Indon, Phil).......... _____
   ___*A. (g.) gustavi.* PECHORA PIPIT. (sp)
   ___*A. (g.) menzbieri.* MENZBIER'S PIPIT. (se Sib; ◊ s China)

❑ *Anthus pratensis.* MEADOW PIPIT. (w Palea; ◊-n Afr)............. _____

❑ *Anthus cervinus.* RED-THROATED PIPIT. (n Palea-Alas; ◊-Afr, Indon) . _____

❑ *Anthus roseatus.* ROSY PIPIT. (Himal; ◊-se Asia)................ _____

❑ *Anthus petrosus.* ROCK PIPIT. (w Palea; ◊-nw Mex)............. _____

❑ *Anthus spinoletta.* WATER PIPIT. (mts Palea; ◊ s Asia)........... _____

❑ *Anthus rubescens.* AMERICAN PIPIT. (e Sib-w,n NA; ◊-se Asia, n CA). _____

❑ *Anthus sylvanus.* UPLAND PIPIT. (Himal)..................... _____

❑ *Anthus nilghiriensis.* NILGIRI PIPIT. (mts sw India).............. _____

❑ *Anthus correndera.* CORRENDERA PIPIT. (mts sc,s SA)............ _____

❑ *Anthus antarcticus.* SOUTH GEORGIA PIPIT. (S Georgia).......... _____

❑ *Anthus spragueii.* SPRAGUE'S PIPIT. (nc NA; ◊-c Mex)........... _____

❑ *Anthus furcatus.* SHORT-BILLED PIPIT. (mts s SA)............... _____

❑ *Anthus hellmayri.* HELLMAYR'S PIPIT. (sc,se,s SA).............. _____

❑ *Anthus bogotensis.* PARAMO PIPIT. (Andes w SA)............... _____

❑ *Anthus lutescens.* YELLOWISH PIPIT. (Pan, SA). . . . . _____

❑ *Anthus chacoensis.* CHACO PIPIT. (sc SA). . . . . _____

❑ *Anthus nattereri.* OCHRE-BREASTED PIPIT. (se SA). . . . . _____

❑ *Anthus gutturalis.* ALPINE PIPIT. (mts NG). _____

Subfamily Prunellinae [1/13]

❑ *Prunella collaris.* ALPINE ACCENTOR. (Palea). . . . . _____

❑ *Prunella himalayana.* RUFOUS-STREAKED ACCENTOR. (mts c Asia). . . _____

❑ *Prunella rubeculoides.* ROBIN ACCENTOR. (Himal). . . . . _____

❑ *Prunella strophiata.* RUFOUS-BREASTED ACCENTOR. (Himal). . . . . . . _____

❑ *Prunella montanella.* SIBERIAN ACCENTOR. (ne Eura). . . . . _____

❑ *Prunella ocularis.* RADDE'S ACCENTOR. (mts sc Eura). . . . . _____

❑ *Prunella fagani.* YEMEN ACCENTOR. (mts sw Arabia). . . . . _____

❑ *Prunella fulvescens.* BROWN ACCENTOR. (mts s Eura). . . . . _____

❑ *Prunella atrogularis.* BLACK-THROATED ACCENTOR. (mts c Eura). . . . _____

❑ *Prunella koslowi.* MONGOLIAN ACCENTOR. (mts c Asia). . . . . _____

❑ *Prunella modularis.* HEDGE ACCENTOR. (w Eura; ◊-nw Afr, M East) . _____

❑ *Prunella rubida.* JAPANESE ACCENTOR. (s Kuril, Japan). . . . . _____

❑ *Prunella immaculata.* MAROON-BACKED ACCENTOR. (Himal). . . . . . . _____

Subfamily Ploceinae [17/118]

❑ *Bubalornis albirostris.* WHITE-BILLED BUFFALO-WEAVER. (subsah Afr)_____

❑ *Bubalornis niger.* RED-BILLED BUFFALO-WEAVER. (ne,s Afr). . . . . . . _____
    ___*B. (n.) intermedius.* NORTHERN RED-BILLED BUFFALO-WEAVER. (ne Afr)
    ___*B. (n.) niger.* SOUTHERN RED-BILLED BUFFALO-WEAVER. (s Afr)

❑ *Dinemellia dinemelli.* WHITE-HEADED BUFFALO-WEAVER. (e Afr). . . . _____

❑ *Sporopipes frontalis.* SPECKLE-FRONTED WEAVER. (subsah,ne Afr). . . _____

❑ *Sporopipes squamifrons.* SCALY WEAVER. (s Afr). . . . . _____

❑ *Plocepasser mahali.* WHITE-BROWED SPARROW-WEAVER. (e,s Afr). . . _____

❑ *Plocepasser superciliosus.* CHESTNUT-CROWNED SP.-W. (subsah Afr). _____

❑ *Plocepasser rufoscapulatus.* CHESTNUT-BACKED SP.-W. (sc Afr). . . . . _____

❑ *Plocepasser donaldsoni.* DONALDSON-SMITH'S SPARROW-W. (ne Afr). _____

❑ *Histurgops ruficauda.* RUFOUS-TAILED WEAVER. (n Tanz). . . . . _____

❑ *Pseudonigrita arnaudi.* GREY-HEADED SOCIAL-WEAVER. (ne Afr). . . . _____

❑ *Pseudonigrita cabanisi.* BLACK-CAPPED SOCIAL-WEAVER. (ne Afr). . . _____

❑ *Philetairus socius.* SOCIABLE WEAVER. (sw Afr). . . . . _____

❑ *Ploceus bannermani.* BANNERMAN'S WEAVER. (mts wc Afr). . . . . _____

❑ *Ploceus batesi.* BATES'S WEAVER. (se Camer). . . . . _____

❑ *Ploceus nigrimentum.* BLACK-CHINNED WEAVER. (w Afr). . . . . _____

❑ *Ploceus baglafecht.* BAGLAFECHT WEAVER. (c,e Afr). . . . . _____
   ___*P. (b.) baglafecht.* BAGLAFECHT WEAVER. (c Afr)
   ___*P. (b.) emini.* EMIN'S WEAVER. (ne Afr)
   ___*P. (b.) reichenowi.* REICHENOW'S WEAVER. (e Afr)
   ___*P. (b.) stuhlmanni.* STUHLMANN'S WEAVER. (se Afr)

❑ *Ploceus bertrandi.* BERTRAND'S WEAVER. (mts se Afr). . . . . _____

❑ *Ploceus pelzelni.* SLENDER-BILLED WEAVER. (w,c Afr). . . . . _____
   ___*P. (p.) monachus.* WEST AFRICAN WEAVER. (w,wc Afr)
   ___*P. (p.) pelzelni.* SLENDER-BILLED WEAVER. (ec Afr)

❑ *Ploceus subpersonatus.* LOANGO WEAVER. (wc Afr). . . . . _____

❑ *Ploceus luteolus.* LITTLE WEAVER. (subsah,ne Afr). . . . . _____

❑ *Ploceus intermedius.* LESSER MASKED WEAVER. (e,s Afr). . . . . _____

❑ *Ploceus ocularis.* SPECTACLED WEAVER. (c,se Afr). . . . . _____

❑ *Ploceus nigricollis.* BLACK-NECKED WEAVER. (w,c,e Afr). . . . . _____
   ___*P. (n.) brachypterus.* SWAINSON'S WEAVER. (w Afr)
   ___*P. (n.) nigricollis.* BLACK-NECKED WEAVER. (c,e Afr)

❑ *Ploceus melanogaster.* BLACK-BILLED WEAVER. (mts c Afr). . . . . _____

❑ *Ploceus alienus.* STRANGE WEAVER. (mts ec Afr). . . . . _____

❑ *Ploceus temporalis.* BOCAGE'S WEAVER. (wc Afr). . . . . _____

❑ *Ploceus capensis.* CAPE WEAVER. (S Afr). . . . . _____

❑ *Ploceus subaureus.* AFRICAN GOLDEN-WEAVER. (e,se Afr). . . . . _____

❑ *Ploceus xanthops.* HOLUB'S GOLDEN-WEAVER. (c,se Afr). . . . . _____

❑ *Ploceus princeps.* PRINCIPE GOLDEN WEAVER. (Prín). . . . . _____

❑ *Ploceus aurantius.* ORANGE WEAVER. (w,c Afr). . . . . _____

❑ *Ploceus bojeri.* GOLDEN PALM WEAVER. (e Afr). . . . . _____

❑ *Ploceus castaneiceps.* TAVETA GOLDEN WEAVER. (e Afr). . . . . _____

❑ *Ploceus xanthopterus.* SOUTHERN BROWN-THROATED W. (s Afr). . . . . _____

❑ *Ploceus castanops.* NORTHERN BROWN-THROATED WEAVER. (e Afr) . _____

❑ *Ploceus burnieri.* KILOMBERO WEAVER. (ec Tanz). . . . . _____

❑ *Ploceus galbula.* RUEPPELL'S WEAVER. (ne Afr reg). . . . . _____

❑ *Ploceus heuglini.* HEUGLIN'S MASKED-WEAVER. (subsah Afr). . . . . . . _____

❑ *Ploceus taeniopterus.* NORTHERN MASKED-WEAVER. (ne Afr). . . . . . . _____

❑ *Ploceus victoriae.* VICTORIA MASKED-WEAVER. (s Uganda). . . . . _____

❑ *Ploceus vitellinus.* VITELLINE MASKED-WEAVER. (n,e Afr). . . . . _____

❑ *Ploceus velatus.* SOUTHERN MASKED-WEAVER. (s Afr). . . . . _____

❑ *Ploceus katangae.* KATANGA MASKED-WEAVER. (ec Afr). . . . . _____

❑ *Ploceus ruweti.* RUWET'S MASKED-WEAVER. (se Zaire). . . . . _____

❑ *Ploceus reichardi.* TANZANIA MASKED-WEAVER. (sw Tanz). . . . . _____

❑ *Ploceus cucullatus.* VILLAGE WEAVER. (Afr; ◆ ST, Hisp, Masc). . . . . _____
   ___*P. (c.) cucullatus.* VILLAGE WEAVER. (w,nc Afr; ◆ ST, Hisp)
   ___*P. (c.) collaris.* MOTTLED WEAVER. (wc Afr)
   ___*P. (c.) nigriceps.* LAYARD'S WEAVER. (se Afr)
   ___*P. (c.) spilonotus.* SPOT-BACKED WEAVER. (s Afr; ◆ Masc)

❑ *Ploceus grandis.* GIANT WEAVER. (ST). . . . . _____

❑ *Ploceus spekei.* SPEKE'S WEAVER. (mts ne Afr). . . . . _____

❑ *Ploceus spekeoides.* FOX'S WEAVER. (ec Uganda). . . . . _____

❑ *Ploceus nigerrimus.* VIEILLOT'S BLACK WEAVER. (w,c Afr). . . . . _____
   ___*P. (n.) castaneofuscus.* CHESTNUT-AND-BLACK WEAVER. (w Afr)
   ___*P. (n.) nigerrimus.* VIEILLOT'S BLACK WEAVER. (c Afr)

❑ *Ploceus weynsi.* WEYNS'S WEAVER. (c Afr). . . . . _____

❑ *Ploceus golandi.* CLARKE'S WEAVER. (e Kenya). . . . . _____

❑ *Ploceus melanocephalus.* BLACK-HEADED WEAVER. (w,c,ne Afr). . . . . _____
   ___*P. (m.) melanocephalus.* BLACK-HEADED WEAVER. (w,sc Afr)
   ___*P. (m.) capitalis.* YELLOW-COLLARED WEAVER. (nc,ne Afr)

❑ *Ploceus dicrocephalus.* SALVADORI'S WEAVER. (ne Afr). . . . . _____

❑ *Ploceus jacksoni.* GOLDEN-BACKED WEAVER. (e Afr). . . . . _____

❑ *Ploceus badius.* CINNAMON WEAVER. (e,s Sudan). . . . . _____

❑ *Ploceus rubiginosus.* CHESTNUT WEAVER. (sw,ne Afr). . . . . _____

❑ *Ploceus aureonucha.* GOLDEN-NAPED WEAVER. (ne Zaire). . . . . _____

❑ *Ploceus tricolor.* YELLOW-MANTLED WEAVER. (w,c Afr). . . . . _____

❑ *Ploceus albinucha.* MAXWELL'S BLACK WEAVER. (w,c Afr). . . . . _____

❑ *Ploceus nelicourvi.* NELICOURVI WEAVER. (n,e Mad). . . . . _____

❑ *Ploceus sakalava.* SAKALAVA WEAVER. (Mad). . . . . _____

❑ *Ploceus benghalensis.* BLACK-BREASTED WEAVER. (s Asia). . . . . _____

❑ *Ploceus manyar.* STREAKED WEAVER. (s,se Asia; ◆ Egypt). . . . . _____

❑ *Ploceus philippinus.* BAYA WEAVER. (s,se Asia). . . . . _____

❑ *Ploceus hypoxanthus.* ASIAN GOLDEN WEAVER. (se Asia). . . . . _____

❑ *Ploceus megarhynchus.* YELLOW WEAVER. (n India). . . . . _____

❑ *Ploceus bicolor.* FOREST WEAVER. (c,e,se Afr). . . . . _____
   ___*P. (b.) amaurocephalus.* GREY-BACKED WEAVER. (c Afr)
   ___*P. (b.) kersteni.* BLACK-BACKED WEAVER. (ce Afr)
   ___*P. (b.) stictifrons.* SPOT-HEADED WEAVER. (se Afr)
   ___*P. (b.) bicolor.* DARK-BACKED WEAVER. (se S Afr)

❏ *Ploceus preussi.* PREUSS'S WEAVER. (w,c Afr). . . . . _____

❏ *Ploceus dorsomaculatus.* YELLOW-CAPPED WEAVER. (c Afr). . . . . _____

❏ *Ploceus nicolli.* USAMBARA WEAVER. (mts ne Tanz). . . . . _____

❏ *Ploceus olivaceiceps.* OLIVE-HEADED WEAVER. (mts se Afr). . . . . _____

❏ *Ploceus insignis.* BROWN-CAPPED WEAVER. (mts c Afr). . . . . _____

❏ *Ploceus angolensis.* BAR-WINGED WEAVER. (c Afr). . . . . _____

❏ *Ploceus sanctithomae.* SAO TOME WEAVER. (ST). . . . . _____

❏ *Pachyphantes superciliosus.* COMPACT WEAVER. (w,c Afr). . . . . _____

❏ *Malimbus flavipes.* YELLOW-LEGGED MALIMBE. (ne Zaire). . . . . _____

❏ *Malimbus coronatus.* RED-CROWNED MALIMBE. (c Afr). . . . . _____

❏ *Malimbus cassini.* BLACK-THROATED MALIMBE. (wc Afr). . . . . _____

❏ *Malimbus ballmanni.* BALLMANN'S MALIMBE. (w Afr). . . . . _____

❏ *Malimbus racheliae.* RACHEL'S MALIMBE. (wc Afr). . . . . _____

❏ *Malimbus scutatus.* RED-VENTED MALIMBE. (w Afr). . . . . _____

❏ *Malimbus ibadanensis.* IBADAN MALIMBE. (sw Nigeria). . . . . _____

❏ *Malimbus erythrogaster.* RED-BELLIED MALIMBE. (c Afr). . . . . _____

❏ *Malimbus nitens.* GRAY'S MALIMBE. (c Afr), , , , , , , , , , , , , , , , , , _____

❏ *Malimbus malimbicus.* CRESTED MALIMBE. (w,c Afr). . . . . _____

❏ *Malimbus rubricollis.* RED-HEADED MALIMBE. (w,c Afr). . . . . _____

❏ *Anaplectes rubriceps.* RED-HEADED WEAVER. (Afr). . . . . _____
    ___*A. (r.) leuconotus.* RED-WINGED WEAVER. (w,c,e Afr)
    ___*A. (r.) rubriceps.* RED-HEADED WEAVER. (sc,s Afr)

❏ *Brachycope anomala.* BOB-TAILED WEAVER. (wc Afr). . . . . _____

❏ *Quelea cardinalis.* CARDINAL QUELEA. (e Afr). . . . . _____

❏ *Quelea erythrops.* RED-HEADED QUELEA. (Afr). . . . . _____

❏ *Quelea quelea.* RED-BILLED QUELEA. (Afr). . . . . _____

❏ *Foudia madagascariensis.* MADAGASCAR RED FODY. (Mad reg). . . . . _____

❏ *Foudia eminentissima.* RED-HEADED FODY. (Ald, Com). . . . . _____

❏ *Foudia omissa.* FOREST FODY. (e Mad). . . . . _____

❏ *Foudia rubra.* MAURITIUS FODY. (Maur). . . . . _____

❏ *Foudia sechellarum.* SEYCHELLES FODY. (Seyc). . . . . _____

❏ *Foudia flavicans.* YELLOW FODY. (Rodr). . . . . _____

❏ *Euplectes afer.* YELLOW-CROWNED BISHOP. (Afr). . . . . _____
    ___*E. (a.) afer.* YELLOW-CROWNED BISHOP. (w,c Afr)
    ___*E. (a.) taha.* TAHA BISHOP. (e,s Afr)

❏ *Euplectes diadematus.* FIRE-FRONTED BISHOP. (e Afr). . . . . _____

❑ *Euplectes gierowii.* BLACK BISHOP. (c,ne Afr)................... _____
   ___*E. (g.) gierowii.* ANGOLA BLACK-BISHOP. (wc Afr)
   ___*E. (g.) ansorgei.* NORTHERN BLACK-BISHOP. (nc,ne Afr)
   ___*E. (g.) friedrichseni.* SOUTHERN BLACK-BISHOP. (ec Afr)

❑ *Euplectes hordeaceus.* BLACK-WINGED BISHOP. (Afr)............. _____

❑ *Euplectes franciscanus.* ORANGE BISHOP. (subsah Afr; ♦ PR)....... _____

❑ *Euplectes orix.* RED BISHOP. (s,e Afr)......................... _____

❑ *Euplectes nigroventris.* ZANZIBAR BISHOP. (ce Afr)............... _____

❑ *Euplectes aureus.* GOLDEN-BACKED BISHOP. (cw Ang)........... _____

❑ *Euplectes capensis.* YELLOW BISHOP. (c,e,s Afr)................. _____

❑ *Euplectes axillaris.* FAN-TAILED WIDOWBIRD. (Afr)............... _____

❑ *Euplectes macrourus.* YELLOW-SHOULDERED WIDOWBIRD. (Afr)..... _____
   ___*E. (m.) macrourus.* YELLOW-MANTLED WIDOWBIRD. (w,c Afr)
   ___*E. (m.) macrocercus.* YELLOW-SHOULDERED WIDOWBIRD. (mts ne Afr)

❑ *Euplectes albonotatus.* WHITE-WINGED WIDOWBIRD. (wc,e,ne Afr)... _____
   ___*E. (a.) eques.* CINNAMON-SHOULDERED WIDOWBIRD. (ne Afr)
   ___*E. (a.) albonotatus.* WHITE-SHOULDERED WIDOWBIRD. (w,c Afr)

❑ *Euplectes ardens.* RED-COLLARED WIDOWBIRD. (Afr)............. _____
   ___*E. (a.) concolor.* BLACK WIDOWBIRD. (w,c Afr)
   ___*E. (a.) laticauda.* RED-NAPED WIDOWBIRD. (ne Afr)
   ___*E. (a.) ardens.* RED-COLLARED WIDOWBIRD. (sc,s Afr)

❑ *Euplectes hartlaubi.* MARSH WIDOWBIRD. (c Afr)............... _____

❑ *Euplectes psammocromius.* BUFF-SHOULDERED WIDOWBIRD. (ec Afr). _____

❑ *Euplectes progne.* LONG-TAILED WIDOWBIRD. (e,c,s Afr).......... _____

❑ *Euplectes jacksoni.* JACKSON'S WIDOWBIRD. (mts e Afr)........... _____

❑ *Anomalospiza imberbis.* PARASITIC WEAVER. (Afr)............... _____

❑ *Amblyospiza albifrons.* GROSBEAK WEAVER. (Afr)............... _____

Subfamily Estrildinae [30/156]
Tribe Estrildini [29/140]

❑ *Parmoptila rubrifrons.* JAMESON'S ANTPECKER. (w,c,e Afr)........ _____
   ___*P. (r.) rubrifrons.* RED-FRONTED ANTPECKER. (w,c Afr)
   ___*P. (r.) jamesoni.* JAMESON'S ANTPECKER. (n,ne,c,ce Afr)

❑ *Parmoptila woodhousei.* WOODHOUSE'S ANTPECKER. (c Afr)....... _____

❑ *Nigrita fusconota.* WHITE-BREASTED NEGROFINCH. (c Afr)......... _____

❑ *Nigrita bicolor.* CHESTNUT-BREASTED NEGROFINCH. (c Afr)........ _____

❑ *Nigrita luteifrons.* PALE-FRONTED NEGROFINCH. (c Afr)........... _____

❑ *Nigrita canicapilla.* GREY-HEADED NEGROFINCH. (w,c Afr)......... _____
   ___*N. (c.) emiliae.* WESTERN NEGROFINCH. (w Afr)
   ___*N. (c.) canicapilla.* GREY-CROWNED NEGROFINCH. (c Afr)
   ___*N. (c.) candida.* KUNGWE NEGROFINCH. (mts sw Tanz)

❑ *Nesocharis shelleyi.* FERNANDO PO OLIVEBACK. (Camer). . . . . _____

❑ *Nesocharis ansorgei.* WHITE-COLLARED OLIVEBACK. (mts ec Afr). . . . _____

❑ *Nesocharis capistrata.* GREY-HEADED OLIVEBACK. (c Afr). . . . . _____

❑ *Pytilia phoenicoptera.* RED-WINGED PYTILIA. (w,c Afr). . . . . _____

❑ *Pytilia lineata.* LINEATED PYTILIA. (mts w,c Eth). . . . . _____

❑ *Pytilia afra.* ORANGE-WINGED PYTILIA. (e,c Afr). . . . . _____

❑ *Pytilia melba.* GREEN-WINGED PYTILIA. (Afr). . . . . _____

❑ *Pytilia hypogrammica.* RED-FACED PYTILIA. (w,c Afr). . . . . _____

❑ *Mandingoa nitidula.* GREEN-BACKED TWINSPOT. (Afr). . . . . _____

❑ *Cryptospiza reichenovii.* RED-FACED CRIMSON-WING. (mts c,e Afr). . . _____

❑ *Cryptospiza salvadorii.* ABYSSINIAN CRIMSON-WING. (mts ne Afr). . . . _____

❑ *Cryptospiza jacksoni.* DUSKY CRIMSON-WING. (mts ec Afr). . . . . _____

❑ *Cryptospiza shelleyi.* SHELLEY'S CRIMSON-WING. (mts ec Afr). . . . . . . _____

❑ *Pyrenestes sanguineus.* CRIMSON SEEDCRACKER. (w Afr). . . . . _____

❑ *Pyrenestes ostrinus.* BLACK-BELLIED SEEDCRACKER. (wc,c,se Afr). . . . _____
    ___*P. (o.) ostrinus.* BLACK-BELLIED SEEDCRACKER. (wc,c Afr)
    ___*P. (o.) rothschildi.* ROTHSCHILD'S SEEDCRACKER. (wc,c Afr)
    ___*P. (o.) frommi.* URUNGU SEEDCRACKER. (s Tanz)
    ___*P. (o.) maximus.* LARGE-BILLED SEEDCRACKER. (wc,nc Afr)

❑ *Pyrenestes minor.* LESSER SEEDCRACKER. (se Afr). . . . . _____

❑ *Spermophaga poliogenys.* GRANT'S BLUEBILL. (c Afr). . . . . _____

❑ *Spermophaga haematina.* WESTERN BLUEBILL. (w,c Afr). . . . . _____

❑ *Spermophaga ruficapilla.* RED-HEADED BLUEBILL. (c,e Afr). . . . . _____
    ___*S. (r.) ruficapilla.* RED-HEADED BLUEBILL. (sp)
    ___*S. (r.) cana.* USAMBARA BLUEBILL. (mts ne Tanz)

❑ *Clytospiza monteiri.* BROWN TWINSPOT. (c Afr). . . . . _____

❑ *Hypargos niveoguttatus.* PETERS'S TWINSPOT. (sc,e Afr). . . . . _____

❑ *Hypargos margaritatus.* PINK-THROATED TWINSPOT. (se Afr). . . . . _____

❑ *Euschistospiza dybowskii.* DYBOWSKI'S TWINSPOT. (w,c Afr). . . . . _____

❑ *Euschistospiza cinereovinacea.* DUSKY TWINSPOT. (mts c Afr). . . . . . . _____

❑ *Lagonosticta rufopicta.* BAR-BREASTED FIREFINCH. (w,c Afr). . . . . _____

❑ *Lagonosticta nitidula.* BROWN FIREFINCH. (sc Afr). . . . . _____

❑ *Lagonosticta senegala.* RED-BILLED FIREFINCH. (Afr). . . . . _____

❑ *Lagonosticta rara.* BLACK-BELLIED FIREFINCH. (subsah Afr). . . . . _____

❑ *Lagonosticta rubricata.* AFRICAN FIREFINCH. (Afr). . . . . _____

❑ *Lagonosticta landanae.* PALE-BILLED FIREFINCH. (wc Afr). . . . . _____

❑ *Lagonosticta virata.* MALI FIREFINCH. (s Mali). . . . . _____

❏ *Lagonosticta umbrinodorsalis.* REICHENOW'S FIREFINCH. (wc Afr). . . . _____

❏ *Lagonosticta rhodopareia.* JAMESON'S FIREFINCH. (s,e Afr). . . . . _____

❏ *Lagonosticta vinacea.* BLACK-FACED FIREFINCH. (w,nc Afr). . . . . _____
    ___*L. (v.) vinacea.* VINACEOUS FIREFINCH. (w Afr)
    ___*L. (v.) nigricollis.* BLACK-FACED FIREFINCH. (nc Afr)

❏ *Lagonosticta larvata.* BLACK-THROATED FIREFINCH. (e Sudan-w Eth). _____

❏ *Uraeginthus angolensis.* BLUE-BREASTED CORDONBLEU. (c,s Afr). . . . _____

❏ *Uraeginthus bengalus.* RED-CHEEKED CORDONBLEU. (w,c Afr; ♦ Haw Is)_____

❏ *Uraeginthus cyanocephala.* BLUE-CAPPED CORDONBLEU. (e Afr). . . . . _____

❏ *Uraeginthus ianthinogaster.* PURPLE GRENADIER. (ne Afr). . . . . _____

❏ *Uraeginthus granatina.* COMMON GRENADIER. (s Afr). . . . . _____

❏ *Estrilda caerulescens.* LAVENDER WAXBILL. (w Afr; ♦ Haw Is). . . . . . _____

❏ *Estrilda perreini.* BLACK-TAILED WAXBILL. (c,se Afr). . . . . _____

❏ *Estrilda thomensis.* CINDERELLA WAXBILL. (w Afr). . . . . _____

❏ *Estrilda quartinia.* YELLOW-BELLIED WAXBILL. (mts cw,e,se Afr). . . . _____
    ___*E. (q.) quartinia.* SWEE WAXBILL. (e,se Afr)
    ___*E. (q.) bocagei.* BOCAGE'S WAXBILL. (w Ang)

❏ *Estrilda melanotis.* SWEE WAXBILL. (s Afr). . . . . _____

❏ *Estrilda poliopareia.* ANAMBRA WAXBILL. (s Nigeria). . . . . _____

❏ *Estrilda paludicola.* FAWN-BREASTED WAXBILL. (ne,c Afr). . . . . _____

❏ *Estrilda ochrogaster.* ABYSSINIAN WAXBILL. (mts ne Afr). . . . . _____

❏ *Estrilda melpoda.* ORANGE-CHEEKED WAXBILL. (w,c Afr). . . . . _____

❏ *Estrilda rhodopyga.* CRIMSON-RUMPED WAXBILL. (e Afr). . . . . _____

❏ *Estrilda rufibarba.* ARABIAN WAXBILL. (sw Arabia). . . . . _____

❏ *Estrilda troglodytes.* BLACK-RUMPED WAXBILL. (c Afr; ♦ Haw Is, PR) _____

❏ *Estrilda astrild.* COMMON WAXBILL. (c,s Afr; ♦ is cosm, Euro, Braz). _____

❏ *Estrilda nigriloris.* BLACK-FACED WAXBILL. (se Zaire). . . . . _____

❏ *Estrilda nonnula.* BLACK-CROWNED WAXBILL. (c Afr). . . . . _____

❏ *Estrilda atricapilla.* BLACK-HEADED WAXBILL. (c Afr). . . . . _____

❏ *Estrilda kandti.* KANDT'S WAXBILL. (mts ec Afr). . . . . _____

❏ *Estrilda charmosyna.* RED-RUMPED WAXBILL. (ne Afr). . . . . _____

❏ *Estrilda erythronotos.* BLACK-CHEEKED WAXBILL. (s,e Afr). . . . . _____

❏ *Amandava amandava.* RED AVADAVAT. (s,se Asia; ♦ cosm). . . . . _____

❏ *Amandava formosa.* GREEN AVADAVAT. (c India). . . . . _____

❏ *Amandava subflava.* ZEBRA WAXBILL. (Afr reg). . . . . _____

❏ *Ortygospiza atricollis.* AFRICAN QUAILFINCH. (w,c,s Afr)........... _____
___*O. (a.) atricollis. AFRICAN QUAILFINCH. (w,c Afr)
___*O. (a.) fuscocrissa. ETHIOPIAN QUAILFINCH. (sc,s Afr)

❏ *Ortygospiza gabonensis.* RED-BILLED QUAILFINCH. (c Afr)......... _____

❏ *Ortygospiza locustella.* LOCUSTFINCH. (sc,se Afr)............... _____
___*O. (l.) uelensis. ZAIRE LOCUSTFINCH. (Zaire)
___*O. (l.) locustella. COMMON LOCUSTFINCH. (sp)

❏ *Emblema pictum.* PAINTED FIRETAIL. (int w,c Aust)............. _____

❏ *Stagonopleura bella.* BEAUTIFUL FIRETAIL. (se Aust)............. _____

❏ *Stagonopleura oculata.* RED-EARED FIRETAIL. (sw Aust).......... _____

❏ *Stagonopleura guttata.* DIAMOND FIRETAIL. (e,se Aust).......... _____

❏ *Oreostruthus fuliginosus.* MOUNTAIN FIRETAIL. (mts NG)......... _____

❏ *Neochmia temporalis.* RED-BROWED FIRETAIL. (e,se Aust; ◆ Polyn) . _____

❏ *Neochmia phaeton.* CRIMSON FINCH. (sc NG, n Aust)............. _____
___*N. (p.) evangelinae. PALE CRIMSON-FINCH. (sc NG, ne Aust)
___*N. (p.) phaeton. COMMON CRIMSON-FINCH. (n Aust)

❏ *Neochmia ruficauda.* STAR FINCH. (nw,n,se Aust)............... _____

❏ *Neochmia modesta.* PLUM-HEADED FINCH. (e Aust)............... _____

❏ *Taeniopygia guttata.* ZEBRA FINCH. (L Sunda, Aust)............., _____
___*T. (g.) guttata. ZEBRA FINCH. (L Sunda)
___*T. (g.) castanotis. CHESTNUT-EARED FINCH. (Aust)

❏ *Taeniopygia bichenovii.* DOUBLE-BARRED FINCH. (n,ne Aust)....... _____
___*T. (b.) annulosa. BLACK-RINGED FINCH. (n Aust)
___*T. (b.) bichenovii. DOUBLE-BARRED FINCH. (ne Aust)

❏ *Poephila personata.* MASKED FINCH. (n Aust)................... _____

❏ *Poephila acuticauda.* LONG-TAILED FINCH. (n Aust)............. _____

❏ *Poephila cincta.* BLACK-THROATED FINCH. (ne,e Aust)............ _____
___*P. (c.) atropygialis. BLACK-TAILED FINCH. (ne Aust)
___*P. (c.) cincta. BLACK-THROATED FINCH. (e Aust)

❏ *Erythrura hyperythra.* TAWNY-BREASTED PARROTFINCH. (se Asia-Wall)_____

❏ *Erythrura prasina.* PIN-TAILED PARROTFINCH. (se Asia)........... _____

❏ *Erythrura viridifacies.* GREEN-FACED PARROTFINCH. (n,c Phil)....... _____

❏ *Erythrura tricolor.* TRICOLORED PARROTFINCH. (L Sunda).......... _____

❏ *Erythrura trichroa.* BLUE-FACED PARROTFINCH. (Wall-Oceania, ne Aust) _____

❏ *Erythrura coloria.* RED-EARED PARROTFINCH. (mts s Phil)......... _____

❏ *Erythrura papuana.* PAPUAN PARROTFINCH. (mts NG)............. _____

❏ *Erythrura psittacea.* RED-THROATED PARROTFINCH. (N Cal)........ _____

❏ *Erythrura pealii.* FIJI PARROTFINCH. (Fiji)..................... _____

❏ *Erythrura cyaneovirens.* RED-HEADED PARROTFINCH. (w Samoa)..... _____

❏ *Erythrura regia.* ROYAL PARROTFINCH. (Banks, Vanu)............. _____

❏ *Erythrura kleinschmidti.* PINK-BILLED PARROTFINCH. (mts Fiji)...... _____

❏ *Chloebia gouldiae.* GOULDIAN FINCH. (n Aust).................. _____

❏ *Lemuresthes nana.* MADAGASCAR MUNIA. (Mad)................ _____

❏ *Lonchura cantans.* AFRICAN SILVERBILL. (Afr reg; ◆ Haw Is, PR)... _____

❏ *Lonchura malabarica.* WHITE-THROATED SILVERBILL. (s Asia)...... _____

❏ *Lonchura griseicapilla.* GREY-HEADED SILVERBILL. (ne Afr)........ _____

❏ *Lonchura cucullata.* BRONZE MUNIA. (Afr, Com; ◆ PR).......... _____

❏ *Lonchura bicolor.* BLACK-AND-WHITE MUNIA. (w,c,e Afr)......... _____
   ___*L. (b.) bicolor.* RED-BACKED MUNIA. (w Afr)
   ___*L. (b.) poensis.* BLACK-AND-WHITE MUNIA. (c,e Afr)

❏ *Lonchura nigriceps.* BROWN-BACKED MUNIA. (s Afr)............. _____

❏ *Lonchura fringilloides.* MAGPIE MUNIA. (Afr)................. _____

❏ *Lonchura striata.* WHITE-RUMPED MUNIA. (s,se Asia)............ _____
   ___*L. (s.) striata.* WHITE-RUMPED MUNIA. (c,s India)
   ___*L. (s.) acuticauda.* BENGALESE MUNIA. (sp)

❏ *Lonchura leucogastroides.* JAVAN MUNIA. (Sum-Lombok)......... _____

❏ *Lonchura fuscans.* DUSKY MUNIA. (Born, sw Phil).............. _____

❏ *Lonchura molucca.* BLACK-FACED MUNIA. (Wall).............. _____

❏ *Lonchura kelaarti.* BLACK-THROATED MUNIA. (s India)........... _____

❏ *Lonchura punctulata.* SCALY-BREASTED MUNIA. (s Asia-Sulaw, Phil). _____

❏ *Lonchura leucogastra.* WHITE-BELLIED MUNIA. (se Asia, Phil)...... _____

❏ *Lonchura tristissima.* STREAK-HEADED MUNIA. (w,c NG).......... _____

❏ *Lonchura leucosticta.* WHITE-SPOTTED MUNIA. (s NG)........... _____

❏ *Lonchura malacca.* BLACK-HEADED MUNIA. (s Asia-Phil; ◆ is)...... _____
   ___*L. (m.) malacca.* INDIAN BLACK-HEADED MUNIA. (s India)
   ___*L. (m.) atricapilla.* SOUTHERN BLACK-HEADED MUNIA. (sp)

❏ *Lonchura ferruginosa.* WHITE-CAPPED MUNIA. (Java)........... _____

❏ *Lonchura quinticolor.* FIVE-COLORED MUNIA. (L Sunda).......... _____

❏ *Lonchura maja.* WHITE-HEADED MUNIA. (se Asia).............. _____

❏ *Lonchura pallida.* PALE-HEADED MUNIA. (Sulaw, L Sunda)........ _____

❏ *Lonchura grandis.* GRAND MUNIA. (e NG).................... _____

❏ *Lonchura vana.* GREY-BANDED MUNIA. (mts nw NG)............. _____

❏ *Lonchura caniceps.* GREY-HEADED MUNIA. (e NG).............. _____

❏ *Lonchura nevermanni.* GREY-CROWNED MUNIA. (s NG).......... _____

❏ *Lonchura spectabilis.* HOODED MUNIA. (n NG, e Bism).......... _____

❏ *Lonchura hunsteini.* MOTTLED MUNIA. (e Bism)............... _____

❑ *Lonchura forbesi.* NEW IRELAND MUNIA. (e Bism). . . . . _____

❑ *Lonchura nigerrima.* NEW HANOVER MUNIA. (ne Bism). . . . . _____

❑ *Lonchura flaviprymna.* YELLOW-RUMPED MUNIA. (nw Aust). . . . . . . _____

❑ *Lonchura castaneothorax.* CHESTNUT-BREASTED M. (NG-n,e Aust). . . _____

❑ *Lonchura stygia.* BLACK MUNIA. (s NG). . . . . _____

❑ *Lonchura teerinki.* BLACK-BREASTED MUNIA. (mts wc NG). . . . . _____

❑ *Lonchura montana.* SNOW MOUNTAIN MUNIA. (mts wc NG). . . . . . . _____

❑ *Lonchura monticola.* ALPINE MUNIA. (mts se NG). . . . . _____

❑ *Lonchura melaena.* BISMARCK MUNIA. (sc Bism). . . . . _____

❑ *Heteromunia pectoralis.* PICTORELLA MUNIA. (n Aust). . . . . _____

❑ *Padda oryzivora.* JAVA SPARROW. (Java, Bali; ♦ cosm trop). . . . . . . _____

❑ *Padda fuscata.* TIMOR SPARROW. (c L Sunda). . . . . _____

❑ *Amadina fasciata.* CUT-THROAT. (subsah,e Afr). . . . . _____

❑ *Amadina erythrocephala.* RED-HEADED FINCH. (s Afr). . . . . _____

Tribe Viduini [1/16]

❑ *Vidua chalybeata.* VILLAGE INDIGOBIRD. (w,c,s Afr). . . . . _____
___*V. (c.) chalybeata.* GREEN INDIGOBIRD. (w Afr)
___*V. (c.) ultramarina.* PURPLE INDIGOBIRD. (nc Afr)
___*V. (c.) amauropteryx.* SOUTH AFRICAN INDIGOBIRD. (sc,s Afr)

❑ *Vidua raricola.* JAMBANDU INDIGOBIRD. (w,nc Afr). . . . . _____

❑ *Vidua larvaticola.* BAKA INDIGOBIRD. (w,nc Afr). . . . . _____

❑ *Vidua funerea.* VARIABLE INDIGOBIRD. (w,c,s Afr). . . . . _____

❑ *Vidua codringtoni.* TWINSPOT INDIGOBIRD. (se Afr). . . . . _____

❑ *Vidua purpurascens.* DUSKY INDIGOBIRD. (e,s Afr). . . . . _____

❑ *Vidua wilsoni.* PALE-WINGED INDIGOBIRD. (subsah,ec Afr). . . . . _____
___*V. (w.) wilsoni.* PALE-WINGED INDIGOBIRD. (sp)
___*V. (w.) incognita.* ZAIRE INDIGOBIRD. (se Zaire)

❑ *Vidua hypocherina.* STEEL-BLUE WHYDAH. (ne Afr). . . . . _____

❑ *Vidua fischeri.* STRAW-TAILED WHYDAH. (ne Afr). . . . . _____

❑ *Vidua regia.* QUEEN WHYDAH. (s Afr). . . . . _____

❑ *Vidua macroura.* PIN-TAILED WHYDAH. (Afr; ♦ PR). . . . . _____

❑ *Vidua orientalis.* NORTHERN PARADISE-WHYDAH. (subsah Afr). . . . . . _____

❑ *Vidua togoensis.* TOGO PARADISE-WHYDAH. (w Afr). . . . . _____

❑ *Vidua interjecta.* LONG-TAILED PARADISE-WHYDAH. (w,c Afr). . . . . . _____

❑ *Vidua paradisaea.* EASTERN PARADISE-WHYDAH. (e,s Afr). . . . . _____

❑ *Vidua obtusa.* BROAD-TAILED PARADISE-WHYDAH. (c,s Afr). . . . . . . _____

Family **Fringillidae** [241/995]
Subfamily Peucedraminae [1/1]

❑ *Peucedramus taeniatus.* Olive Warbler. (sw US, MA)........... _____

Subfamily Fringillinae [39/170]
Tribe Fringillini [1/3]

❑ *Fringilla coelebs.* Chaffinch. (Palea; ◊-n Afr, s Asia; ◆ S Afr, NZ) . _____
❑ *Fringilla teydea.* Teydefinch. (mts Can Is)..................... _____
❑ *Fringilla montifringilla.* Brambling. (n Eura; ◊-Medit, s Asia)...... _____

Tribe Carduelini [20/137]

❑ *Serinus pusillus.* Fire-fronted Serin. (mts s Eura).............. _____
❑ *Serinus serinus.* European Serin. (s Palea; ◊-n Afr)............. _____
❑ *Serinus syriacus.* Syrian Serin. (mts Near East)................ _____
❑ *Serinus canaria.* Island Canary. (e Atl)...................... _____
❑ *Serinus citrinella.* Citril Finch. (mts s,c Euro)................. _____
　　___*S. (c.) citrinella.* European Citril. (sp)
　　___*S. (c.) corsicana.* Corsican Citril. (Sard, Cors)
❑ *Serinus thibetanus.* Tibetan Serin. (mts s Asia)................ _____
❑ *Serinus canicollis.* Cape Canary. (e,sc,s Afr).................. _____
　　___*S. (c.) canicollis.* Cape Canary. (e,sc Afr)
　　___*S. (c.) flavivertex.* Yellow-crowned Canary. (s Afr)
❑ *Serinus nigriceps.* Abyssinian Siskin. (mts w,c Eth)............. _____
❑ *Serinus frontalis.* Western Citril. (mts e Afr)................. _____
　　___*S. (f.) frontalis.* Western Citril. (sp)
　　___*S. (f.) kikuyuensis.* Kenya Citril. (w,c Kenya)
❑ *Serinus citrinelloides.* African Citril. (mts s Sudan, w,c Eth)...... _____
❑ *Serinus hypostictus.* East African Citril. (mts e Afr)........... _____
❑ *Serinus capistratus.* Black-faced Canary. (c Afr).............. _____
❑ *Serinus koliensis.* Papyrus Canary. (ec Afr).................. _____
❑ *Serinus scotops.* Forest Canary. (S Afr)..................... _____
❑ *Serinus leucopygius.* White-rumped Seedeater. (subsah Afr)...... _____
❑ *Serinus rothschildi.* Olive-rumped Serin. (mts sw Arabia)........ _____
❑ *Serinus flavigula.* Yellow-throated Seedeater. (mts c Eth)...... _____
❑ *Serinus xanthopygius.* Abyssinian Yellow-rumped Seedeater. (Eth)_____
❑ *Serinus reichenowi.* Kenya Yellow-rumped Seedeater. (e Afr).... _____
❑ *Serinus atrogularis.* Southern Yellow-rumped Seedeater. (e,s Afr)_____
❑ *Serinus citrinipectus.* Lemon-breasted Seedeater. (se Afr)...... _____

❑ *Serinus mozambicus.* YELLOW-FRONTED CANARY. (Afr; ◆ is). . . . . . . _____

❑ *Serinus donaldsoni.* ABYSSINIAN GROSBEAK-CANARY. (ne Afr). . . . . . _____

❑ *Serinus buchanani.* KENYA GROSBEAK-CANARY. (e Afr). . . . . _____

❑ *Serinus dorsostriatus.* WHITE-BELLIED CANARY. (ne Afr). . . . . _____

❑ *Serinus flaviventris.* YELLOW CANARY. (s Afr). . . . . _____

❑ *Serinus sulphuratus.* BRIMSTONE CANARY. (e,s Afr). . . . . _____

❑ *Serinus albogularis.* WHITE-THROATED CANARY. (sw Afr). . . . . _____

❑ *Serinus canicapillus.* WEST AFRICAN SEEDEATER. (wc Afr). . . . . _____

❑ *Serinus reichardi.* REICHARD'S SEEDEATER. (mts e Afr). . . . . _____

❑ *Serinus gularis.* STREAKY-HEADED SEEDEATER. (s Afr). . . . . _____

❑ *Serinus mennelli.* BLACK-EARED SEEDEATER. (sc Afr). . . . . _____

❑ *Serinus tristriatus.* BROWN-RUMPED SEEDEATER. (mts ne Afr). . . . . . . _____

❑ *Serinus menachensis.* YEMEN SERIN. (mts sw Arabia). . . . . _____

❑ *Serinus ankoberensis.* ANKOBER SERIN. (mts c Eth). . . . . _____

❑ *Serinus striolatus.* STREAKY SEEDEATER. (mts e Afr). . . . . _____

❑ *Serinus whytii.* YELLOW-BROWED SEEDEATER. (mts e Afr). . . . . _____

❑ *Serinus burtoni.* THICK-BILLED SEEDEATER. (mts c Afr). . . . . _____

❑ *Serinus rufobrunneus.* PRINCIPE SEEDEATER. (Prín, ST). . . . . _____

❑ *Serinus melanochrous.* KIPENGERE SEEDEATER. (mts sw Tanz). . . . . . _____

❑ *Serinus leucopterus.* WHITE-WINGED SEEDEATER. (mts sw S Afr). . . . . _____

❑ *Serinus totta.* CAPE SISKIN. (mts s S Afr). . . . . _____

❑ *Serinus symonsi.* DRAKENSBERG SISKIN. (mts e S Afr). . . . . _____

❑ *Serinus leucolaema.* DAMARA CANARY. (s Afr). . . . . _____

❑ *Serinus alario.* BLACK-HEADED CANARY. (S Afr). . . . . _____

❑ *Serinus estherae.* MOUNTAIN SERIN. (G Sunda, s Phil). . . . . _____
   ___*S. (e.) estherae.* INDONESIAN SERIN. (G sunda)
   ___*S. (e.) mindanensis.* MINDANAO SERIN. (s Phil)

❑ *Neospiza concolor.* SAO TOME CANARY. (†ST). . . . . _____

❑ *Linurgus olivaceus.* ORIOLE FINCH. (mts c,e Afr). . . . . _____

❑ *Rhynchostruthus socotranus.* GOLDEN-WINGED GROSBEAK. (ne Afr) . _____

❑ *Carduelis chloris.* EUROPEAN GREENFINCH. (w Palea; ◆ Aust, NZ). . . _____

❑ *Carduelis sinica.* GREY-CAPPED GREENFINCH. (e Asia). . . . . _____

❑ *Carduelis spinoides.* YELLOW-BREASTED GREENFINCH. (Himal). . . . . . _____

❑ *Carduelis ambigua.* BLACK-HEADED GREENFINCH. (Himal). . . . . _____

❑ *Carduelis monguilloti.* VIETNAMESE GREENFINCH. (mts c Viet). . . . . . _____

☐ *Carduelis spinus*. EURASIAN SISKIN. (Palea)..................... _____

☐ *Carduelis pinus*. PINE SISKIN. (w,n NA, Mex; ◊-se US)........... _____

☐ *Carduelis atriceps*. BLACK-CAPPED SISKIN. (mts Chia, w Guat)...... _____

☐ *Carduelis spinescens*. ANDEAN SISKIN. (mts nw SA)............. _____

☐ *Carduelis yarrellii*. YELLOW-FACED SISKIN. (nc Ven, e Braz)....... _____

☐ *Carduelis cucullata*. RED SISKIN. (n SW; ◆ PR)................ _____

☐ *Carduelis crassirostris*. THICK-BILLED SISKIN. (Andes sw SA)...... _____

☐ *Carduelis magellanica*. HOODED SISKIN. (SA).................... _____

☐ *Carduelis siemiradzkii*. SAFFRON SISKIN. (sw Ecua)............. _____

☐ *Carduelis olivacea*. OLIVACEOUS SISKIN. (Andes wc SA).......... _____

☐ *Carduelis notata*. BLACK-HEADED SISKIN. (mts MA)............. _____

☐ *Carduelis barbata*. BLACK-CHINNED SISKIN. (s SA)............. _____

☐ *Carduelis xanthogastra*. YELLOW-BELLIED SISKIN. (mts s CA, w SA). _____

☐ *Carduelis atrata*. BLACK SISKIN. (Andes sw SA)................ _____

☐ *Carduelis uropygialis*. YELLOW-RUMPED SISKIN. (Andes sw SA)..... _____

☐ *Carduelis tristis*. AMERICAN GOLDFINCH. (NA, nw Mex)........... _____

☐ *Carduelis psaltria*. LESSER GOLDFINCH. (w NA, MA, w SA)........ _____

☐ *Carduelis lawrencei*. LAWRENCE'S GOLDFINCH. (sw US; ◊-nw Mex)... _____

☐ *Carduelis dominicensis*. ANTILLEAN SISKIN. (mts Hisp)........... _____

☐ *Carduelis carduelis*. EUROPEAN GOLDFINCH. (Palea; ◆ se Aust, NZ) . _____
   ___*C. (c.) carduelis*. EUROPEAN GOLDFINCH. (sp)
   ___*C. (c.) caniceps*. GREY-CROWNED GOLDFINCH. (s Eura)

☐ *Carduelis hornemanni*. HOARY REDPOLL. (n Hol; ◊-c Eura, n US).... _____
   ___*C. (h.) hornemanni*. HORNEMANN'S REDPOLL. (Arctic NA)
   ___*C. (h.) exilipes*. HOARY REDPOLL. (sp)

☐ *Carduelis flammea*. COMMON REDPOLL. (n Hol; ◊-c Hol; ◆ NZ)..... _____
   ___*C. (f.) flammea*. COMMON REDPOLL. (n Hol; ◊-sp)
   ___*C. (f.) cabaret*. LESSER REDPOLL. (nw Euro; ◆ NZ)

☐ *Carduelis flavirostris*. TWITE. (Eura)........................ _____

☐ *Carduelis cannabina*. EURASIAN LINNET. (Palea; ◊-n Afr)......... _____

☐ *Carduelis yemenensis*. YEMEN LINNET. (mts sw Arabia)........... _____

☐ *Carduelis johannis*. WARSANGLI LINNET. (mts n Som)............ _____

☐ *Leucosticte nemoricola*. PLAIN MOUNTAIN-FINCH. (Himal)......... _____

☐ *Leucosticte brandti*. BLACK-HEADED MOUNTAIN-FINCH. (Himal)..... _____

☐ *Leucosticte arctoa*. ASIAN ROSY-FINCH. (mts c,ne Eura)........... _____

☐ *Leucosticte tephrocotis*. GREY-CROWNED ROSY-FINCH. (w NA)...... _____

❑ *Leucosticte atrata.* BLACK ROSY-FINCH. (mts wc NA). . . . . _____

❑ *Leucosticte australis.* BROWN-CAPPED ROSY-FINCH. (mts wc US). . . . . _____

❑ *Callacanthis burtoni.* SPECTACLED FINCH. (Himal). . . . . _____

❑ *Rhodopechys sanguinea.* CRIMSON-WINGED FINCH. (mts s Palea). . . . . _____

❑ *Rhodopechys githaginea.* TRUMPETER FINCH. (s Palea). . . . . _____

❑ *Rhodopechys mongolica.* MONGOLIAN FINCH. (mts sw,c Asia). . . . . . . _____

❑ *Rhodopechys obsoleta.* DESERT FINCH. (mts s Asia). . . . . _____

❑ *Uragus sibiricus.* LONG-TAILED ROSEFINCH. (mts c Asia). . . . . _____

❑ *Carpodacus rubescens.* CRIMSON ROSEFINCH. (Himal). . . . . _____

❑ *Carpodacus nipalensis.* DARK-BREASTED ROSEFINCH. (Himal). . . . . . . _____

❑ *Carpodacus erythrinus.* COMMON ROSEFINCH. (Eura; ◊-s,se Asia). . . . _____

❑ *Carpodacus purpureus.* PURPLE FINCH. (w,n NA, nw Mex; ◊-se US) . _____

❑ *Carpodacus cassinii.* CASSIN'S FINCH. (mts w NA; ◊-c Mex). . . . . _____

❑ *Carpodacus mexicanus.* HOUSE FINCH. (w NA, Mex; ♦ e NA). . . . . . _____
   ___*C. (m.) mexicanus.* COMMON HOUSE-FINCH. (sp)
   C. (m.) mcgregori. MCGREGOR'S HOUSE-FINCH. (†is Baja)
   ___*C. (m.) amplus.* GUADALUPE HOUSE-FINCH. (Guadalupe)

❑ *Carpodacus pulcherrimus.* BEAUTIFUL ROSEFINCH. (Himal). . . . . _____

❑ *Carpodacus eos.* PINK-RUMPED ROSEFINCH. (Himal c,cs China). . . . . _____

❑ *Carpodacus rodochrous.* PINK-BROWED ROSEFINCH. (Himal). . . . . . . _____

❑ *Carpodacus vinaceus.* VINACEOUS ROSEFINCH. (Himal). . . . . _____

❑ *Carpodacus edwardsii.* DARK-RUMPED ROSEFINCH. (Himal). . . . . _____

❑ *Carpodacus synoicus.* PALE ROSEFINCH. (s Eura). . . . . _____

❑ *Carpodacus roseus.* PALLAS'S ROSEFINCH. (e Asia). . . . . _____

❑ *Carpodacus trifasciatus.* THREE-BANDED ROSEFINCH. (w China). . . . . _____

❑ *Carpodacus rodopeplus.* SPOT-WINGED ROSEFINCH. (Himal). . . . . _____
   ___*C. (r.) rodopeplus.* SPOT-WINGED ROSEFINCH. (n India)
   ___*C. (r.) verreauxii.* SHARPE'S ROSEFINCH. (sc,sw China)

❑ *Carpodacus thura.* WHITE-BROWED ROSEFINCH. (Himal). . . . . _____

❑ *Carpodacus rhodochlamys.* RED-MANTLED ROSEFINCH. (Himal). . . . . _____
   ___*C. (r.) rhodochlamys.* PINKISH-BACKED ROSEFINCH. (c Asia)
   ___*C. (r.) grandis.* BLYTH'S ROSEFINCH. (s Asia)

❑ *Carpodacus rubicilloides.* STREAKED ROSEFINCH. (Himal). . . . . _____

❑ *Carpodacus rubicilla.* GREAT ROSEFINCH. (mts s Eura). . . . . _____

❑ *Carpodacus puniceus.* RED-FRONTED ROSEFINCH. (Himal). . . . . _____

❑ *Carpodacus roborowskii.* TIBETAN ROSEFINCH. (Himal wc China). . . . _____

   Chaunoproctus ferreorostris. BONIN GROSBEAK. (†Bonin). . . . . _____

❑ *Pinicola enucleator.* PINE GROSBEAK. (n Hol; ◊-c Hol). . . . . _____

❑ *Pinicola subhimachalus.* CRIMSON-BROWED FINCH. (Himal). . . . . _____

❑ *Haematospiza sipahi.* SCARLET FINCH. (Himal). . . . . _____

❑ *Loxia pytyopsittacus.* PARROT CROSSBILL. (n Euro). . . . . _____

❑ *Loxia scotica.* SCOTTISH CROSSBILL. (n Brit). . . . . _____

❑ *Loxia curvirostra.* RED CROSSBILL. (Hol-se Asia, n Phil, MA). . . . . . . _____

❑ *Loxia leucoptera.* WHITE-WINGED CROSSBILL. (n Hol, mts Hisp). . . . . _____

❑ *Pyrrhula nipalensis.* BROWN BULLFINCH. (Himal). . . . . _____

❑ *Pyrrhula leucogenis.* WHITE-CHEEKED BULLFINCH. (mts n,s Phil). . . . _____

❑ *Pyrrhula aurantiaca.* ORANGE BULLFINCH. (Himal). . . . . _____

❑ *Pyrrhula erythrocephala.* RED-HEADED BULLFINCH. (Himal). . . . . . . _____

❑ *Pyrrhula erythaca.* GREY-HEADED BULLFINCH. (Himal). . . . . _____

❑ *Pyrrhula pyrrhula.* EURASIAN BULLFINCH. (Eura). . . . . _____
 ___*P. (p.) pyrrhula.* EURASIAN BULLFINCH. (w,n Eura)
 ___*P. (p.) cineracea.* BAIKAL BULLFINCH. (ec Asia)
 ___*P. (p.) griseiventris.* GREY-BELLIED BULLFINCH. (e Asia)
 ___*P. (p.) murina.* AZORES BULLFINCH. (Azores)

❑ *Coccothraustes coccothraustes.* HAWFINCH. (Palea; ◊-n Afr, s Asia) . _____

❑ *Eophona migratoria.* YELLOW-BILLED GROSBEAK. (ce Asia). . . . . _____

❑ *Eophona personata.* JAPANESE GROSBEAK. (e Asia). . . . . _____

❑ *Mycerobas icterioides.* BLACK-AND-YELLOW GROSBEAK. (Himal). . . . . _____

❑ *Mycerobas affinis.* COLLARED GROSBEAK. (Himal). . . . . _____

❑ *Mycerobas melanozanthos.* SPOT-WINGED GROSBEAK. (Himal). . . . . . _____

❑ *Mycerobas carnipes.* WHITE-WINGED GROSBEAK. (mts s Asia). . . . . . . _____

❑ *Hesperiphona vespertina.* EVENING GROSBEAK. (n NA-Mex; ◊-s US). _____

❑ *Hesperiphona abeillei.* HOODED GROSBEAK. (mts MA). . . . . _____

❑ *Pyrrhoplectes epauletta.* GOLD-NAPED FINCH. (Himal). . . . . _____

Tribe Drepanidini [18/30]

❑ *Telespiza ultima.* NIHOA FINCH. (Nihoa). . . . . _____

❑ *Telespiza cantans.* LAYSAN FINCH. (Laysan). . . . . _____

❑ *Psittirostra psittacea.* OU. (mts e Haw Is). _____

 Dysmorodrepanis munroi. LANAI HOOKBILL. (†Lanai). . . . . _____

❑ *Loxioides bailleui.* PALILA. (mst Hawaii). . . . . _____

 Rhodacanthis flaviceps. LESSER KOA-FINCH. (†mts Hawaii). . . . . _____

 Rhodacanthis palmeri. GREATER KOA-FINCH. (†mts Hawaii). . . . . _____

☐ *Chloridops kona.* KONA GROSBEAK. (†mts Hawaii)............... _____

☐ *Pseudonestor xanthophrys.* MAUI PARROTBILL. (mts Maui)........ _____

☐ *Viridonia stejnegeri.* KAUAI AMAKIHI. (mts Kauai)............... _____

☐ *Viridonia virens.* COMMON AMAKIHI. (mts e Haw Is)............. _____

☐ *Viridonia parva.* ANIANIAU. (mts Kauai)....................... _____

Viridonia sagittirostris. GREATER AMAKIHI. (†mts Hawaii)......... _____

☐ *Hemignathus obscurus.* AKIALOA. (mts e Haw Is)............... _____
   ___*H. (o.) ellisianus.* GREATER AKIALOA. (Kauai)
   H. (o.) obscurus. LESSER AKIALOA. (†Hawaii)

☐ *Hemignathus lucidus.* NUKUPUU. (mts Kauai, Maui)............. _____

☐ *Hemignathus wilsoni.* AKIAPOLAAU. (mts Hawaii)............... _____

☐ *Oreomystis bairdi.* KAUAI CREEPER. (mts Kauai)................ _____

☐ *Oreomystis mana.* HAWAII CREEPER. (mts Hawaii).............. _____

☐ *Paroreomyza montana.* MAUI CREEPER. (Maui)................. _____
   ___*P. (m.) newtoni.* MAUI CREEPER. (Maui)
   P. (m.) maculata. LANAI CREEPER. (†Lanai)

☐ *Paroreomyza flammea.* MOLOKAI CREEPER. (Molokai)........... _____

☐ *Paroreomyza maculata.* OAHU CREEPER. (Oahu)................ _____

☐ *Loxops caeruleirostris.* AKEKEE. (mts Kauai).................. _____

☐ *Loxops coccineus.* AKEPA. (mts e Haw Is).................... _____
   ___*L. (c.) rufus.* OAHU AKEPA. (Oahu)
   ___*L. (c.) ochraceus.* MAUI AKEPA. (Maui)
   ___*L. (c.) coccineus.* HAWAII AKEPA. (Hawaii)

Ciridops anna. ULA-AI-HAWANE. (mts †Hawaii)................ _____

☐ *Vestiaria coccinea.* IIWI. (e Haw Is)....................... _____

Drepanis pacifica. HAWAII MAMO. (†Hawaii).................. _____

Drepanis funerea. BLACK MAMO. (†Molokai).................. _____

☐ *Palmeria dolei.* AKOHEKOHE. (mts Maui)..................... _____

☐ *Himatione sanguinea.* APAPANE. (e Haw Is).................. _____
   H. (s.) freethii. LAYSAN HONEYCREEPER. (†Laysan)
   ___*H. (s.) sanguinea.* APAPANE. (e Haw Is)

☐ *Melamprosops phaeosoma.* POO-ULI. (mts Maui)............... _____

Subfamily Emberizinae [201/824]
Tribe Emberizini [32/157]

☐ *Urocynchramus pylzowi.* PINK-TAILED BUNTING. (mts w China)..... _____

☐ *Melophus lathami.* CRESTED BUNTING. (Himal)................ _____

☐ *Latoucheornis siemsseni.* SLATY BUNTING. (mts c China).......... _____

☐ *Emberiza citrinella.* YELLOWHAMMER. (Eura; ◊-nw Afr, e Asia)..... _____

❑ *Emberiza leucocephalos.* PINE BUNTING. (e Asia; ◊-sw,s Asia). . . . . . . _____

❑ *Emberiza stewarti.* CHESTNUT-BREASTED BUNTING. (Himal; ◊-c India) . _____

❑ *Emberiza cirlus.* CIRL BUNTING. (w Palea). . . . . _____

❑ *Emberiza koslowi.* TIBETAN BUNTING. (Himal wc China). . . . . _____

❑ *Emberiza cia.* ROCK BUNTING. (mts s Palea). . . . . _____

❑ *Emberiza godlewskii.* GODLEWSKI'S BUNTING. (mts c Asia). . . . . _____

❑ *Emberiza cioides.* MEADOW BUNTING. (mts e Asia). . . . . _____

❑ *Emberiza jankowskii.* RUFOUS-BACKED BUNTING. (e Asia). . . . . _____

❑ *Emberiza buchanani.* GREY-NECKED BUNTING. (s,c Eura; ◊ India). . . . _____

❑ *Emberiza cineracea.* CINEREOUS BUNTING. (sc Eura; ◊-ne Afr). . . . . . . _____

❑ *Emberiza hortulana.* ORTOLAN BUNTING. (w Eura; ◊-n Afr, s Asia). . . _____

❑ *Emberiza caesia.* CRETZSCHMAR'S BUNTING. (s Eura; ◊-ne Afr). . . . . . _____

❑ *Emberiza striolata.* HOUSE BUNTING. (n Afr, s Palea). . . . . _____

❑ *Emberiza impetuani.* LARK-LIKE BUNTING. (sw Afr). . . . . _____

❑ *Emberiza tahapisi.* CINNAMON-BREASTED BUNTING. (Afr reg). . . . . . . _____

❑ *Emberiza socotrana.* SOCOTRA BUNTING. (mts Socotra). . . . . _____

❑ *Emberiza capensis.* CAPE BUNTING. (s Afr). . . . . _____

❑ *Emberiza tristrami.* TRISTRAM'S BUNTING. (e Asia; ◊-se Asia). . . . . . . _____

❑ *Emberiza fucata.* CHESTNUT-EARED BUNTING. (mts e Asia; ◊-se Asia). _____

❑ *Emberiza pusilla.* LITTLE BUNTING. (n Eura; ◊-Medit, s,se Asia, Phil). _____

❑ *Emberiza chrysophrys.* YELLOW-BROWED BUNTING. (c Sib; ◊-se China) _____

❑ *Emberiza rustica.* RUSTIC BUNTING. (n Eura; ◊ e Asia). . . . . _____

❑ *Emberiza elegans.* YELLOW-THROATED BUNTING. (e Asia; ◊-se Asia) . _____

❑ *Emberiza aureola.* YELLOW-BREASTED BUNTING. (n,e Eura; ◊-se Asia). _____

❑ *Emberiza rutila.* CHESTNUT BUNTING. (e Asia; ◊-s Asia). . . . . _____

❑ *Emberiza flaviventris.* AFRICAN GOLDEN-BREASTED BUNTING. (Afr) . _____

❑ *Emberiza poliopleura.* SOMALI GOLDEN-BREASTED BUNTING. (ne Afr). _____

❑ *Emberiza affinis.* BROWN-RUMPED BUNTING. (subsah Afr). . . . . _____

❑ *Emberiza cabanisi.* CABANIS'S BUNTING. (subsah,c,se Afr). . . . . _____
  ___*E. (c.) cabanisi.* CABANIS'S BUNTING. (subsah Afr)
  ___*E. (c.) cognominata.* ANGOLA BUNTING. (c Afr)
  ___*E. (c.) orientalis.* THREE-STREAKED BUNTING. (se Afr)

❑ *Emberiza melanocephala.* BLACK-HEADED BUNTING. (sc Eura). . . . . . . _____

❑ *Emberiza bruniceps.* RED-HEADED BUNTING. (sc Eura; ◊ India). . . . . . _____

❑ *Emberiza sulphurata.* YELLOW BUNTING. (c Japan; ◊-se China, Phil) . _____

❑ *Emberiza spodocephala.* BLACK-FACED BUNTING. (e Asia; ◊-s Asia) . _____

❑ *Emberiza variabilis.* GREY BUNTING. (e Asia; ◊ Japan, Ryu). . . . . _____

❑ *Emberiza pallasi.* PALLAS'S BUNTING. (e Asia; ◊-c China). . . . . _____
   ___*E. (p.) pallasi.* PALLAS'S BUNTING. (sp)
   ___*E. (p.) lydiae.* MONGOLIAN BUNTING. (c Mong)

❑ *Emberiza schoeniclus.* REED BUNTING. (Palea; ◊-n Afr, s Asia). . . . . . _____
   ___*E. (s.) schoeniclus.* NORTHERN REED-BUNTING. (w,n Palea; ◊ sp)
   ___*E. (s.) intermedia.* DARK REED-BUNTING. (sw Palea)
   ___*E. (s.) pyrrhuloides.* PALE REED-BUNTING. (c Asia)

❑ *Emberiza yessoensis.* OCHRE-RUMPED BUNTING. (e Asia). . . . . _____

❑ *Miliaria calandra.* CORN BUNTING. (w,s Palea). . . . . _____

❑ *Calcarius mccownii.* McCOWN'S LONGSPUR. (c NA; ◊-n Mex). . . . . . . _____

❑ *Calcarius lapponicus.* LAPLAND LONGSPUR. (n Hol; ◊-c Eura, s US) . _____

❑ *Calcarius pictus.* SMITH'S LONGSPUR. (nw,nc NA; ◊ sc US). . . . . _____

❑ *Calcarius ornatus.* CHESTNUT-COLLARED LONGSPUR. (nc NA; ◊-Mex). _____

❑ *Plectrophenax nivalis.* SNOW BUNTING. (n Hol; ◊-Medit, s US). . . . . . _____

❑ *Plectrophenax hyperboreus.* McKAY'S BUNTING. (Alas). . . . . _____

❑ *Calamospiza melanocorys.* LARK BUNTING. (c NA; ◊-nc Mex). . . . . . . _____

❑ *Passerella iliaca.* FOX SPARROW. (w,n NA; ◊-se US, n Mex). . . . . _____

❑ *Melospiza melodia.* SONG SPARROW. (NA, Mex). . . . . _____

❑ *Melospiza lincolnii.* LINCOLN'S SPARROW. (w,n NA; ◊-MA). . . . . _____

❑ *Melospiza georgiana.* SWAMP SPARROW. (nc,ne NA; ◊-ne Mex). . . . . . _____

❑ *Zonotrichia capensis.* RUFOUS-COLLARED SPARROW. (Hisp, c,s MA, SA)_____

❑ *Zonotrichia querula.* HARRIS'S SPARROW. (nc NA; ◊ w,sc US). . . . . . . _____

❑ *Zonotrichia albicollis.* WHITE-THROATED SPARROW. (n NA; ◊-n Mex). _____

❑ *Zonotrichia leucophrys.* WHITE-CROWNED SPARROW. (n NA; ◊-c Mex) _____

❑ *Zonotrichia atricapilla.* GOLDEN-CROWNED SP. (nw NA; ◊-nw Mex). . _____

❑ *Junco vulcani.* VOLCANO JUNCO. (mts CR, w Pan). . . . . _____

❑ *Junco hyemalis.* DARK-EYED JUNCO. (w,n NA-n Mex; ◊-s US). . . . . . . _____
   ___*J. (h.) hyemalis.* SLATE-COLORED JUNCO. (n,ne,ec NA; ◊ sp)
   ___*J. (h.) oreganus.* OREGON JUNCO. (w NA; ◊-n Mex)
   ___*J. (h.) mearnsi.* PINK-SIDED JUNCO. (wc NA; ◊-n Mex)
   ___*J. (h.) aikeni.* WHITE-WINGED JUNCO. (nc US)
   ___*J. (h.) caniceps.* GREY-HEADED JUNCO. (mts wc US; ◊-n Mex)
   ___*J. (h.) dorsalis.* RED-BACKED JUNCO. (sw US; ◊-n Mex)

❑ *Junco insularis.* GUADALUPE JUNCO. (Guadalupe). . . . . _____

❑ *Junco phaeonotus.* YELLOW-EYED JUNCO. (mts sw US, n,c MA). . . . . . _____
   ___*J. (p.) phaeonotus.* MEXICAN JUNCO. (sw US, n,c Mex)
   ___*J. (p.) bairdi.* BAIRD'S JUNCO. (mts s Baja)
   ___*J. (p.) fulvescens.* CHIAPAS JUNCO. (mts int Chia)
   ___*J. (p.) alticola.* GUATEMALA JUNCO. (se Chia, w Guat)

❑ *Passerculus sandwichensis.* SAVANNAH SPARROW. (NA-c MA)...... _____
   ___*P. (s.) sandwichensis.* SAVANNAH SPARROW. (sp)
   ___*P. (s.) princeps.* IPSWICH SPARROW. (s NS)
   ___*P. (s.) beldingi.* BELDING'S SPARROW. (s Calif, nw Baja)

❑ *Passerculus rostratus.* LARGE-BILLED SPARROW. (nw Mex; ◊-s Calif). _____

❑ *Ammodramus maritimus.* SEASIDE SPARROW. (coasts e,s US)....... _____
   ___*A. (m.) maritimus.* COMMON SEASIDE-SPARROW. (sp)
   ___*A. (m.) nigrescens.* DUSKY SEASIDE-SPARROW. (†ce Fla)
   ___*A. (m.) mirabilis.* CAPE SABLE SEASIDE-SPARROW. (sw Fla)

❑ *Ammodramus caudacutus.* SHARP-TAILED SPARROW. (n,c NA; ◊-s US)_____

❑ *Ammodramus leconteii.* LE CONTE'S SPARROW. (nc NA; ◊ sc,se US) . _____

❑ *Ammodramus henslowii.* HENSLOW'S SPARROW. (c NA; ◊ se US)..... _____

❑ *Ammodramus bairdii.* BAIRD'S SPARROW. (nc NA; ◊ sw US, n Mex) . _____

❑ *Ammodramus savannarum.* GRASSHOPPER SP. (NA-nw SA, G Ant)... _____

❑ *Ammodramus humeralis.* GRASSLAND SPARROW. (SA)............ _____

❑ *Ammodramus aurifrons.* YELLOW-BROWED SPARROW. (Amaz)...... _____

❑ *Xenospiza baileyi.* SIERRA MADRE SPARROW. (mts c Mex)......... _____

❑ *Spizella arborea.* AMERICAN TREE SPARROW. (n NA; ◊-s US)........ _____

❑ *Spizella passerina.* CHIPPING SPARROW. (NA, MA).............. _____

❑ *Spizella pallida.* CLAY-COLORED SPARROW. (c NA; ◊-n CA)........ _____

❑ *Spizella taverneri.* TIMBERLINE SPARROW. (mts nw NA; ◊ sw US).... _____

❑ *Spizella breweri.* BREWER'S SPARROW. (wc NA; ◊-c Mex).......... _____

❑ *Spizella pusilla.* FIELD SPARROW. (e NA; ◊-ne Mex)............. _____

❑ *Spizella wortheni.* WORTHEN'S SPARROW. (ne Mex).............. _____

❑ *Spizella atrogularis.* BLACK-CHINNED SPARROW. (sw US, Mex)..... _____

❑ *Pooecetes gramineus.* VESPER SPARROW. (w,n NA; ◊-se US, Mex)... _____

❑ *Chondestes grammacus.* LARK SPARROW. (w,n NA, n Mex; ◊-s Mex). _____

❑ *Amphispiza bilineata.* BLACK-THROATED SPARROW. (w US, n,c Mex). _____

❑ *Amphispiza belli.* SAGE SPARROW. (wc,sw NA, nw Baja; ◊-nw Mex) . _____
   ___*A. (b.) nevadensis.* SAGE SPARROW. (wc NA; ◊-nw Mex)
   ___*A. (b.) belli.* BELL'S SPARROW. (sw NA, nw Baja)

❑ *Aimophila quinquestriata.* FIVE-STRIPED SPARROW. (sw US, nw Mex). _____

❑ *Aimophila mystacalis.* BRIDLED SPARROW. (mts c Mex).......... _____

❑ *Aimophila humeralis.* BLACK-CHESTED SPARROW. (w Mex)........ _____

❑ *Aimophila ruficauda.* STRIPE-HEADED SPARROW. (w Mex, c Guat).... _____

❑ *Aimophila sumichrasti.* CINNAMON-TAILED SPARROW. (sw Mex)..... _____

❑ *Aimophila strigiceps.* STRIPE-CAPPED SPARROW. (sc SA).......... _____

❑ *Aimophila stolzmanni.* TUMBES SPARROW. (cw SA). . . . . _____

❑ *Aimophila aestivalis.* BACHMAN'S SPARROW. (se US). . . . . _____

❑ *Aimophila botterii.* BOTTERI'S SPARROW. (sw US, n,c MA). . . . . _____
   ___*A. (b.) botterii.* BOTTERI'S SPARROW. (sw US, Mex)
   ___*A. (b.) petenica.* PETEN SPARROW. (se Mex, n CA)

❑ *Aimophila cassinii.* CASSIN'S SPARROW. (sc,sw US, n Mex). . . . . _____

❑ *Aimophila carpalis.* RUFOUS-WINGED SPARROW. (sw US, nw Mex). . . _____

❑ *Aimophila ruficeps.* RUFOUS-CROWNED SPARROW. (sw,sc US, Mex) . _____

❑ *Aimophila notosticta.* OAXACA SPARROW. (Oax). . . . . _____

❑ *Aimophila rufescens.* RUSTY SPARROW. (n,c MA). . . . . _____

❑ *Torreornis inexpectata.* ZAPATA SPARROW. (sw,se Cuba). . . . . _____

❑ *Oriturus superciliosus.* STRIPED SPARROW. (mts Mex). . . . . _____

❑ *Pipilo chlorurus.* GREEN-TAILED TOWHEE. (mts w US; ◊-c Mex). . . . . _____

❑ *Pipilo ocai.* COLLARED TOWHEE. (mts c Mex). . . . . _____

❑ *Pipilo erythrophthalmus.* RUFOUS-SIDED TOWHEE. (NA, n,c MA). . . . _____
   ___*P. (e.) maculatus.* SPOTTED TOWHEE. (w NA, n,c MA)
   ___*P. (e.) erythrophthalmus.* EASTERN TOWHEE. (e NA)
   ___*P. (e.) socorroensis.* SOCORRO TOWHEE. (Revilla)
   ___*P. (e.) macronyx.* OLIVE-BACKED TOWHEE. (mts c Mex)

❑ *Pipilo aberti.* ABERT'S TOWHEE. (sw US, nw Mex). . . . . _____

❑ *Pipilo crissalis.* CALIFORNIA TOWHEE. (Pac US, Baja). . . . . _____

❑ *Pipilo fuscus.* CANYON TOWHEE. (sw US, Mex). . . . . _____

❑ *Pipilo albicollis.* WHITE-THROATED TOWHEE. (mts c Mex). . . . . _____

❑ *Melozone kieneri.* RUSTY-CROWNED GROUND-SPARROW. (Mex). . . . . . _____

❑ *Melozone biarcuatum.* PREVOST'S GROUND-SPARROW. (mts Chia-CR). _____

❑ *Melozone leucotis.* WHITE-EARED GROUND-SPARROW. (mts Chia-CR). _____

❑ *Arremon aurantiirostris.* ORANGE-BILLED SPARROW. (MA, w SA). . . . _____

❑ *Arremon schlegeli.* GOLDEN-WINGED SPARROW. (n SA). . . . . _____

❑ *Arremon taciturnus.* PECTORAL SPARROW. (nw SA, Amaz). . . . . _____
   ___*A. (t.) axillaris.* YELLOW-SHOULDERED SPARROW. (nw SA)
   ___*A. (t.) taciturnus.* PECTORAL SPARROW. (Amaz)

❑ *Arremon abeillei.* BLACK-CAPPED SPARROW. (cw SA). . . . . _____
   ___*A. (a.) abeillei.* SLATY-BACKED SPARROW. (sp)
   ___*A. (a.) nigriceps.* BLACK-CAPPED SPARROW. (nc Peru)

❑ *Arremon flavirostris.* SAFFRON-BILLED SPARROW. (se SA). . . . . _____

❑ *Arremonops rufivirgatus.* OLIVE SPARROW. (s Tex, n,c MA). . . . . _____
   ___*A. (r.) superciliosus.* PACIFIC SPARROW. (Pac w MA)
   ___*A. (r.) rufivirgatus.* OLIVE SPARROW. (Carib n,c MA)

❑ *Arremonops tocuyensis.* TOCUYO SPARROW. (n SA). . . . . _____

❑ *Arremonops chloronotus.* GREEN-BACKED SPARROW. (ec MA). . . . . . _____

❑ *Arremonops conirostris.* BLACK-STRIPED SPARROW. (CA, w,n SA). . . _____

❑ *Atlapetes albinucha.* WHITE-NAPED BRUSH-FINCH. (mts Mex). . . . . . _____

❑ *Atlapetes gutturalis.* YELLOW-THROATED BRUSH-FINCH. (c MA-Colom)_____

❑ *Atlapetes pallidinucha.* PALE-NAPED BRUSH-FINCH. (Andes w SA). . . _____

❑ *Atlapetes rufinucha.* RUFOUS-NAPED BRUSH-FINCH. (mts w SA). . . . . _____

❑ *Atlapetes leucopis.* WHITE-RIMMED BRUSH-FINCH. (Andes nw SA). . . . _____

❑ *Atlapetes pileatus.* RUFOUS-CAPPED BRUSH-FINCH. (mts Mex). . . . . . _____

❑ *Atlapetes melanocephalus.* SANTA MARTA BRUSH-FINCH. (ne Colom). _____

❑ *Atlapetes flaviceps.* OLIVE-HEADED BRUSH-FINCH. (Andes c Colom) . _____

❑ *Atlapetes fuscoolivaceus.* DUSKY-HEADED BRUSH-FINCH. (sc Colom) . _____

❑ *Atlapetes tricolor.* TRICOLORED BRUSH-FINCH. (Andes w SA). . . . . . . _____

❑ *Atlapetes albofrenatus.* MOUSTACHED BRUSH-FINCH. (Andes nw SA). _____

❑ *Atlapetes schistaceus.* SLATY BRUSH-FINCH. (mts nw,wc SA). . . . . . . _____
   ___*A. (s.) schistaceus.* SLATY BRUSH-FINCH. (mts nw SA)
   ___*A. (s.) taczanowskii.* TACZANOWSKI'S BRUSH-FINCH. (Andes c Peru)

❑ *Atlapetes seebohmi.* BAY-CROWNED BRUSH-FINCH. (Andes wc SA). . . _____
   ___*A. (s.) celicae.* CELICA BRUSH-FINCH. (s Ecua)
   ___*A. (s.) simonsi.* SIMONS'S BRUSH-FINCH. (s Ecua)
   ___*A. (s.) seebohmi.* BAY-CROWNED BRUSH-FINCH. (nw Peru)

❑ *Atlapetes nationi.* RUSTY-BELLIED BRUSH-FINCH. (Andes Peru). . . . . _____

❑ *Atlapetes leucopterus.* WHITE-WINGED BRUSH-FINCH. (Andes cw SA). _____
   ___*A. (l.) leucopterus.* WHITE-WINGED BRUSH-FINCH. (Ecua)
   ___*A. (l.) dresseri.* WHITE-CHEEKED BRUSH-FINCH. (sw Ecua, nw Peru)
   ___*A. (l.) paynteri.* PAYNTER'S BRUSH-FINCH. (cn Peru)

❑ *Atlapetes albiceps.* WHITE-HEADED BRUSH-FINCH. (cw SA). . . . . _____

❑ *Atlapetes pallidiceps.* PALE-HEADED BRUSH-FINCH. (Andes sw Ecua) . _____

❑ *Atlapetes rufigenis.* RUFOUS-EARED BRUSH-FINCH. (Andes Peru). . . . . _____
   ___*A. (r.) rufigenis.* RUFOUS-EARED BRUSH-FINCH. (nw Peru)
   ___*A. (r.) forbesi.* BLACK-SPECTACLED BRUSH-FINCH. (s Peru)

❑ *Atlapetes semirufus.* OCHRE-BREASTED BRUSH-FINCH. (mts nw SA). . . _____

❑ *Atlapetes personatus.* TEPUI BRUSH-FINCH. (Pant nc SA). . . . . _____

❑ *Atlapetes fulviceps.* FULVOUS-HEADED BRUSH-FINCH. (Andes sw SA). _____

❑ *Atlapetes citrinellus.* YELLOW-STRIPED BRUSH-FINCH. (sc SA). . . . . . _____

❑ *Atlapetes brunneinucha.* CHESTNUT-CAPPED BRUSH-FINCH. (MA-w SA)_____
   ___*A. (b.) apertus.* PLAIN-BREASTED BRUSH-FINCH. (s Ver)
   ___*A. (b.) brunneinucha.* CHESTNUT-CAPPED BRUSH-FINCH. (sp)

❑ *Atlapetes virenticeps.* GREEN-STRIPED BRUSH-FINCH. (mts Mex). . . . . _____

❑ *Atlapetes atricapillus.* BLACK-HEADED BRUSH-FINCH. (s CA, nw SA). _____

❑ *Atlapetes torquatus.* STRIPE-HEADED BRUSH-FINCH. (mts w,n SA).... _____
   ___*A. (t.) assimilis.* GREY-STRIPED BRUSH-FINCH. (nw SA)
   ___*A. (t.) torquatus.* STRIPE-HEADED BRUSH-FINCH. (n,w SA)

❑ *Pezopetes capitalis.* LARGE-FOOTED FINCH. (mts CR-w Pan)........ _____

❑ *Pselliophorus tibialis.* YELLOW-THIGHED FINCH. (mts CR-w Pan)..... _____

❑ *Pselliophorus luteoviridis.* YELLOW-GREEN FINCH. (mts w Pan)...... _____

❑ *Lysurus crassirostris.* SOOTY-FACED FINCH. (mts s CA, nw Colom)... _____

❑ *Lysurus castaneiceps.* OLIVE FINCH. (Andes w SA)............... _____

❑ *Gubernatrix cristata.* YELLOW CARDINAL. (se SA).............. _____

❑ *Paroaria coronata.* RED-CRESTED CARDINAL. (se SA; ♦ Haw Is)..... _____

❑ *Paroaria dominicana.* RED-COWLED CARDINAL. (e Braz).......... _____

❑ *Paroaria gularis.* RED-CAPPED CARDINAL. (Amaz)............... _____
   ___*P. (g.) nigrogenis.* BLACK-EARED CARDINAL. (cn Amaz)
   ___*P. (g.) gularis.* RED-CAPPED CARDINAL. (sp)

❑ *Paroaria baeri.* CRIMSON-FRONTED CARDINAL. (c Braz).......... _____

❑ *Paroaria capitata.* YELLOW-BILLED CARDINAL. (sc SA; ♦ Hawaii).... _____

Tribe Parulini [25/115]

❑ *Vermivora bachmanii.* BACHMAN'S WARBLER. (se US; ◊ Cuba)...... _____

❑ *Vermivora pinus.* BLUE-WINGED WARBLER. (se US; ◊ MA)........ _____

❑ *Vermivora chrysoptera.* GOLDEN-WINGED WARBLER. (e NA; ◊-nw SA) _____

❑ *Vermivora peregrina.* TENNESSEE WARBLER. (n NA; ◊ MA, nw SA) . _____

❑ *Vermivora celata.* ORANGE-CROWNED W. (w,n NA, nw Baja; ◊-n CA). _____

❑ *Vermivora ruficapilla.* NASHVILLE WARBLER. (w,n NA; ◊-n CA, G Ant)_____

❑ *Vermivora virginiae.* VIRGINIA'S WARBLER. (sw US; ◊ Mex)....... _____

❑ *Vermivora crissalis.* COLIMA WARBLER. (w Tex, ne Mex; ◊ w Mex) . _____

❑ *Vermivora luciae.* LUCY'S WARBLER. (sw US, nw Mex; ◊ w Mex).... _____

❑ *Parula americana.* NORTHERN PARULA. (e,sw NA; ◊-MA, W Indies) . _____

❑ *Parula pitiayumi.* TROPICAL PARULA. (s Tex, MA, SA)............ _____
   ___*P. (p.) pitiayumi.* TROPICAL PARULA. (sp)
   ___*P. (p.) graysoni.* SOCORRO PARULA. (Revil)

❑ *Parula superciliosa.* CRESCENT-CHESTED WARBLER. (mts MA)...... _____

❑ *Parula gutturalis.* FLAME-THROATED WARBLER. (mts CR, w Pan).... _____

❑ *Dendroica petechia.* YELLOW WARBLER. (NA, MA, w,n SA)....... _____
   ___*D. (p.) aestiva.* YELLOW WARBLER. (NA, n,c Mex; ◊-c SA)
   ___*D. (p.) petechia.* GOLDEN WARBLER. (s Fla, W Indies, n SA)
   ___*D. (p.) erithachorides.* MANGROVE WARBLER. (coasts MA, w,n SA)

❑ *Dendroica pensylvanica.* CHESTNUT-SIDED W. (n,ne NA; ◊-nw SA) . _____

❑ *Dendroica magnolia.* MAGNOLIA WARBLER. (n,ne NA; ◊-MA, W Indies) _____

❑ *Dendroica tigrina.* CAPE MAY WARBLER. (n NA; ◊-n SA)......... _____

❑ *Dendroica caerulescens.* BLACK-THROATED BLUE W. (e NA; ◊-n SA). _____

❑ *Dendroica coronata.* YELLOW-RUMPED W. (w,n NA-c MA; ◊-MA)... _____
   ___*D. (c.) coronata.* MYRTLE WARBLER. (n,ec NA; ◊-MA, W Indies)
   ___*D. (c.) auduboni.* AUDUBON'S WARBLER. (w NA, n,c MA; ◊-n CA)

❑ *Dendroica nigrescens.* BLACK-THROATED GREY WARBLER. (w NA-Mex)_____

❑ *Dendroica townsendi.* TOWNSEND'S WARBLER. (w NA; ◊-CA)...... _____

❑ *Dendroica occidentalis.* HERMIT WARBLER. (mts w US; ◊-n CA)..... _____

❑ *Dendroica virens.* BLACK-THROATED GREEN W. (n,ne,ec NA; ◊-n SA). _____

❑ *Dendroica chrysoparia.* GOLDEN-CHEEKED W. (c Tex; ◊mts c MA)... _____

❑ *Dendroica fusca.* BLACKBURNIAN WARBLER. (n,e,ec NA; ◊-w,n SA) . _____

❑ *Dendroica dominica.* YELLOW-THROATED WARBLER. (se US, Bah; ◊-MA)_____

❑ *Dendroica graciae.* GRACE'S WARBLER. (mts sw US, n,c MA)...... _____

❑ *Dendroica adelaidae.* ADELAIDE'S WARBLER. (PR, n L Ant)........ _____

❑ *Dendroica pityophila.* OLIVE-CAPPED WARBLER. (Cuba, n Bah)...... _____

❑ *Dendroica pinus.* PINE WARBLER. (e NA, n Bah, Hisp)............ _____

❑ *Dendroica kirtlandii.* KIRTLAND'S WARBLER. (ec NA; ◊ Bah)....... _____

❑ *Dendroica discolor.* PRAIRIE WARBLER. (e NA; ◊ se US, W Indies)... _____

❑ *Dendroica vitellina.* VITELLINE WARBLER. (Cay, Swan)........... _____

❑ *Dendroica palmarum.* PALM WARBLER. (n NA; ◊ s US-n CA, G Ant). _____

❑ *Dendroica castanea.* BAY-BREASTED WARBLER. (n NA; ◊-nw SA).... _____

❑ *Dendroica striata.* BLACKPOLL WARBLER. (n NA; ◊ SA)........... _____

❑ *Dendroica cerulea.* CERULEAN WARBLER. (e NA; ◊ mts w SA)...... _____

❑ *Dendroica plumbea.* PLUMBEOUS WARBLER. (c L Ant)............ _____

❑ *Dendroica pharetra.* ARROWHEAD WARBLER. (Jam).............. _____

❑ *Dendroica angelae.* ELFIN-WOODS WARBLER. (mts e PR).......... _____

❑ *Catharopeza bishopi.* WHISTLING WARBLER. (mts St. Vincent)....... _____

❑ *Mniotilta varia.* BLACK-AND-WHITE WARBLER. (n,e NA; ◊-nw SA)... _____

❑ *Setophaga ruticilla.* AMERICAN REDSTART. (NA; ◊-w,n SA)........ _____

❑ *Protonotaria citrea.* PROTHONOTARY WARBLER. (e US; ◊-n SA)...... _____

❑ *Helmitheros vermivorus.* WORM-EATING W. (e US; ◊ MA, W Indies). _____

❑ *Limnothlypis swainsonii.* SWAINSON'S WARBLER. (se US; ◊ Yuc, G Ant)_____

❑ *Seiurus aurocapillus.* OVENBIRD. (NA; ◊-n SA)................. _____

❑ *Seiurus noveboracensis.* NORTHERN WATERTH.RUSH (n,c NA; ◊-n SA) _____

❏ *Seiurus motacilla.* LOUISIANA WATERTHRUSH. (e NA; ◊-nw SA). . . . . _____

❏ *Oporornis formosus.* KENTUCKY WARBLER. (e US; ◊-nw SA). . . . . . . _____

❏ *Oporornis agilis.* CONNECTICUT WARBLER. (n NA; ◊ SA). . . . . _____

❏ *Oporornis philadelphia.* MOURNING W. (n,ne,ec NA; ◊-nw SA). . . . . . _____

❏ *Oporornis tolmiei.* MACGILLIVRAY'S W. (w NA, n Mex; ◊ mts MA) . _____

❏ *Geothlypis trichas.* COMMON YELLOWTHROAT. (NA, Mex; ◊-w SA). . . _____
    ___*G. (t.) trichas.* COMMON YELLOWTHROAT. (sp)
    ___*G. (t.) chapalensis.* CHAPALA YELLOWTHROAT. (Jalisco)

❏ *Geothlypis beldingi.* BELDING'S YELLOWTHROAT. (s Baja). . . . . _____

❏ *Geothlypis flavovelata.* ALTAMIRA YELLOWTHROAT. (ne Mex). . . . . . _____

❏ *Geothlypis rostrata.* BAHAMA YELLOWTHROAT. (n Bah). . . . . _____

❏ *Geothlypis semiflava.* OLIVE-CROWNED YELLOWTHROAT. (CA, nw SA) _____

❏ *Geothlypis speciosa.* BLACK-POLLED YELLOWTHROAT. (mts c Mex). . . _____

❏ *Geothlypis nelsoni.* HOODED YELLOWTHROAT. (n,ec Mex). . . . . _____

❏ *Geothlypis aequinoctialis.* MASKED YELLOWTHROAT. (s CA, SA). . . . _____
    ___*G. (a.) chiriquensis.* CHIRIQUI YELLOWTHROAT. (s CA)
    ___*G. (a.) auricularis.* BLACK-LORED YELLOWTHROAT. (w SA)
    ___*G. (a.) aequinoctialis.* MASKED YELLOWTHROAT. (SA)

❏ *Geothlypis poliocephala.* GREY-CROWNED YELLOWTHROAT. (MA). . . . _____

❏ *Microligea palustris.* GREEN-TAILED GROUND WARBLER. (Hisp). . . . . _____

❏ *Teretistris fernandinae.* YELLOW-HEADED WARBLER. (w Cuba). . . . . . _____

❏ *Teretistris fornsi.* ORIENTE WARBLER. (e Cuba). . . . . _____

❏ *Leucopeza semperi.* SEMPER'S WARBLER. (mts St. Lucia). . . . . _____

❏ *Wilsonia citrina.* HOODED WARBLER. (e NA; ◊ MA). . . . . _____

❏ *Wilsonia pusilla.* WILSON'S WARBLER. (w,n NA; ◊-n SA). . . . . _____

❏ *Wilsonia canadensis.* CANADA WARBLER. (e,ne,ec NA; ◊-w,n SA). . . . _____

❏ *Cardellina rubrifrons.* RED-FACED WARBLER. (sw US, nw Mex; ◊-n CA)_____

❏ *Ergaticus ruber.* RED WARBLER. (mts Mex). . . . . _____
    ___*E. (r.) melanauris.* BLACK-EARED WARBLER. (nc Mex)
    ___*E. (r.) ruber.* RED WARBLER. (c Mex)

❏ *Ergaticus versicolor.* PINK-HEADED WARBLER. (mts Chia, w Guat). . . . _____

❏ *Myioborus pictus.* PAINTED REDSTART. (mts sw US, MA). . . . . _____

❏ *Myioborus miniatus.* SLATE-THROATED REDSTART. (mts MA, w SA) . _____
    ___*M. (m.) miniatus.* SLATE-THROATED REDSTART. (n,c MA)
    ___*M. (m.) verticalis.* YELLOW-BELLIED REDSTART. (s CA, w SA)

❏ *Myioborus castaneocapillus.* TEPUI REDSTART. (Pant nc SA). . . . . . . _____

❏ *Myioborus brunniceps.* BROWN-CAPPED REDSTART. (Andes sw SA). . . _____

❏ *Myioborus pariae.* YELLOW-FACED REDSTART. (mts ne Ven). . . . . _____

❏ *Myioborus albifacies.* WHITE-FACED REDSTART. (Pant s Ven). . . . . _____

❏ *Myioborus cardonai.* SAFFRON-BREASTED REDSTART. (mts s Ven). . . . _____

❏ *Myioborus torquatus.* COLLARED REDSTART. (mts CR, w Pan). . . . . . . _____

❏ *Myioborus melanocephalus.* SPECTACLED REDSTART. (Andes w SA) . _____
   ___*M. (m.) ruficoronatus.* RUFOUS-CROWNED REDSTART. (nw SA)
   ___*M. (m.) melanocephalus.* SPECTACLED REDSTART. (wc SA)

❏ *Myioborus ornatus.* GOLDEN-FRONTED REDSTART. (Andes nw SA). . . _____
   ___*M. (o.) chrysops.* ANDEAN REDSTART. (w,c Colom)
   ___*M. (o.) ornatus.* GOLDEN-FRONTED REDSTART. (ne Colom, w Ven)

❏ *Myioborus albifrons.* WHITE-FRONTED REDSTART. (Andes w Ven). . . . _____

❏ *Myioborus flavivertex.* YELLOW-CROWNED REDSTART. (ne Colom). . . _____

❏ *Euthlypis lachrymosa.* FAN-TAILED WARBLER. (MA). . . . . _____

❏ *Basileuterus fraseri.* GREY-AND-GOLD WARBLER. (cw SA). . . . . _____

❏ *Basileuterus bivittatus.* TWO-BANDED WARBLER. (mts nc, sw SA). . . . _____
   ___*B. (b.) roraimae.* RORAIMA WARBLER. (Pant nc SA)
   ___*B. (b.) bivittatus.* TWO-BANDED WARBLER. (Andes sw SA)

❏ *Basileuterus chrysogaster.* GOLDEN-BELLIED WARBLER. (nw SA). . . . _____

❏ *Basileuterus signatus.* PALE-LEGGED WARBLER. (Andes w SA). . . . . . _____

❏ *Basileuterus luteoviridis.* CITRINE WARBLER. (Andes w SA). . . . . _____
   ___*B. (l.) richardsoni.* RICHARDSON'S WARBLER. (w Colom)
   ___*B. (l.) luteoviridis.* CITRINE WARBLER. (nw SA)
   ___*B. (l.) euophrys.* BLACK-FRONTED WARBLER. (sw SA)

❏ *Basileuterus nigrocristatus.* BLACK-CRESTED WARBLER. (w,n SA). . . . _____

❏ *Basileuterus griseiceps.* GREY-HEADED WARBLER. (mts n Ven). . . . . . _____

❏ *Basileuterus basilicus.* SANTA MARTA WARBLER. (mts ne Colom). . . . _____

❏ *Basileuterus cinereicollis.* GREY-THROATED WARBLER. (mts nw SA) . _____

❏ *Basileuterus conspicillatus.* WHITE-LORED WARBLER. (ne Colom). . . . _____

❏ *Basileuterus coronatus.* RUSSET-CROWNED WARBLER. (w SA). . . . . . _____
   ___*B. (c.) coronatus.* RUSSET-CROWNED WARBLER. (Andes w SA)
   ___*B. (c.) castaneiceps.* BAY-CROWNED WARBLER. (cw SA)

❏ *Basileuterus culicivorus.* GOLDEN-CROWNED WARBLER. (MA, SA). . . _____
   ___*B. (c.) culicivorus.* STRIPE-CROWNED WARBLER. (MA)
   ___*B. (c.) cabanisi.* CABANIS'S WARBLER. (mts nw,n SA)
   ___*B. (c.) auricapillus.* GOLDEN-CROWNED WARBLER. (SA)

❏ *Basileuterus trifasciatus.* THREE-BANDED WARBLER. (Andes wc SA) . _____

❏ *Basileuterus hypoleucus.* WHITE-BELLIED WARBLER. (sc SA). . . . . . . _____

❏ *Basileuterus rufifrons.* RUFOUS-CAPPED WARBLER. (MA-nw SA). . . . _____
   ___*B. (r.) rufifrons.* RUFOUS-CAPPED WARBLER. (n MA)
   ___*B. (r.) salvini.* SALVIN'S WARBLER. (s Mex, n CA)
   ___*B. (r.) delattrii.* CHESTNUT-CAPPED WARBLER. (CA, nw MA)

❑ *Basileuterus belli.* GOLDEN-BROWED WARBLER. (mts n,c MA). . . . . . . _____

❑ *Basileuterus melanogenys.* BLACK-CHEEKED WARBLER. (CR-w Pan). . _____

❑ *Basileuterus ignotus.* PIRRE WARBLER. (mts e Pan, nw Colom). . . . . . _____

❑ *Basileuterus tristriatus.* THREE-STRIPED WARBLER. (mts s CA, w SA). _____

❑ *Basileuterus leucoblepharus.* WHITE-BROWED WARBLER. (se SA). . . . _____

❑ *Basileuterus leucophrys.* WHITE-STRIPED WARBLER. (c Braz). . . . . _____

❑ *Basileuterus flaveolus.* FLAVESCENT WARBLER. (n,se SA). . . . . _____

❑ *Basileuterus fulvicauda.* BUFF-RUMPED WARBLER. (CA, nw,wc SA) . _____

❑ *Basileuterus rivularis.* NEOTROPICAL RIVER WARBLER. (SA). . . . . . . _____

❑ *Zeledonia coronata.* WRENTHRUSH. (mts CR, w Pan). . . . . _____

❑ *Icteria virens.* YELLOW-BREASTED CHAT. (NA, n,c Mex; ◊-CA). . . . . . _____

❑ *Granatellus venustus.* RED-BREASTED CHAT. (w Mex). . . . . _____
   ___*G. (v.) venustus.* RED-BREASTED CHAT. (sp)
   ___*G. (v.) francescae.* TRES MARIAS CHAT. (Tres Marias)

❑ *Granatellus sallaei.* GREY-THROATED CHAT. (Mex, n CA). . . . . _____

❑ *Granatellus pelzelni.* ROSE-BREASTED CHAT. (Amaz). . . . . _____

❑ *Xenoligea montana.* WHITE-WINGED WARBLER. (mts Hisp). . . . . _____

Tribe Thraupini [105/413]

❑ *Coereba flaveola.* BANANAQUIT. (MA, W Indies, SA). . . . . _____
   ___*C. (f.) bahamensis.* BAHAMA BANANAQUIT. (Bah)
   ___*C. (f.) flaveola.* COMMON BANANAQUIT. (sp)

❑ *Conirostrum speciosum.* CHESTNUT-VENTED CONEBILL. (SA). . . . . . . _____

❑ *Conirostrum leucogenys.* WHITE-EARED CONEBILL. (e Pan, nw SA). . . _____

❑ *Conirostrum bicolor.* BICOLORED CONEBILL. (Amaz). . . . . _____

❑ *Conirostrum margaritae.* PEARLY-BREASTED CONEBILL. (w Amaz). . . _____

❑ *Conirostrum cinereum.* CINEREOUS CONEBILL. (sw SA). . . . . _____

❑ *Conirostrum tamarugensis.* TAMARUGO CONEBILL. (sw SA). . . . . _____

❑ *Conirostrum ferrugineiventre.* WHITE-BROWED CONEBILL. (sw SA) . _____

❑ *Conirostrum rufum.* RUFOUS-BROWED CONEBILL. (mts nw SA). . . . . . _____

❑ *Conirostrum sitticolor.* BLUE-BACKED CONEBILL. (mts w SA). . . . . . . _____
   ___*C. (s.) sitticolor.* BLUE-BACKED CONEBILL. (nw SA)
   ___*C. (s.) cyaneum.* BOLIVIAN CONEBILL. (sw SA)

❑ *Conirostrum albifrons.* CAPPED CONEBILL. (mts w,n SA). . . . . _____
   ___*C. (a.) atrocyaneum.* BLUE-CAPPED CONEBILL. (w SA)
   ___*C. (a.) albifrons.* WHITE-CAPPED CONEBILL. (n SA)

❑ *Oreomanes fraseri.* GIANT CONEBILL. (Andes wc SA). . . . . _____

❑ *Orchesticus abeillei.* BROWN TANAGER. (se Braz). . . . . _____

❑ *Schistochlamys ruficapillus.* CINNAMON TANAGER. (e,c Braz). . . . . . . _____

❑ *Schistochlamys melanopis.* BLACK-FACED TANAGER. (n,c,e SA). . . . . _____

❑ *Neothraupis fasciata.* WHITE-BANDED TANAGER. (sc SA). . . . . _____

❑ *Cypsnagra hirundinacea.* WHITE-RUMPED TANAGER. (sc SA). . . . . . . _____

❑ *Conothraupis speculigera.* BLACK-AND-WHITE TANAGER. (wc SA). . . _____

❑ *Conothraupis mesoleuca.* CONE-BILLED TANAGER. (wc Braz). . . . . . . _____

❑ *Lamprospiza melanoleuca.* RED-BILLED PIED TANAGER. (Amaz). . . . . _____

❑ *Cissopis leveriana.* MAGPIE TANAGER. (SA). _____

❑ *Chlorornis riefferii.* GRASS-GREEN TANAGER. (Andes w SA). . . . . _____

❑ *Compsothraupis loricata.* SCARLET-THROATED TANAGER. (int e Braz). _____

❑ *Sericossypha albocristata.* WHITE-CAPPED TANAGER. (Andes w SA) . _____

❑ *Nesospingus speculiferus.* PUERTO RICAN TANAGER. (mts PR). . . . . . _____

❑ *Chlorospingus ophthalmicus.* COMMON BUSH-TANAGER. (MA-w SA). _____
   ___*C. (o.) ophthalmicus.* BROWN-HEADED BUSH-TANAGER. (sp)
   ___*C. (o.) punctulatus.* DOTTED BUSH-TANAGER. (w Pan)
   ___*C. (o.) flavopectus.* YELLOW-BREASTED BUSH-TANAGER. (nw SA)
   ___*C. (o.) cinereocephalus.* BUFF-BREASTED BUSH-TANAGER. (c Peru)

❑ *Chlorospingus tacarcunae.* TACARCUNA BUSH-T. (e Pan,-w Colom) . _____

❑ *Chlorospingus inornatus.* PIRRE BUSH-TANAGER. (mts e Pan). . . . . . . _____

❑ *Chlorospingus semifuscus.* DUSKY BUSH-TANAGER. (Andes nw SA). . _____

❑ *Chlorospingus pileatus.* SOOTY-CAPPED BUSH-TANAGER. (mts). . . . . . _____

❑ *Chlorospingus parvirostris.* YELLOW-WHISKERED BUSH-T. (w SA). . . _____

❑ *Chlorospingus flavigularis.* YELLOW-THROATED BUSH-T. (Pan-w SA). _____
   ___*C. (f.) hypophaeus.* DRAB-BREASTED BUSH-TANAGER. (w Pan)
   ___*C. (f.) flavigularis.* YELLOW-THROATED BUSH-TANAGER. (w SA)

❑ *Chlorospingus flavovirens.* YELLOW-GREEN BUSH-TANAGER. (nw SA). _____

❑ *Chlorospingus canigularis.* ASHY-THROATED BUSH-T. (s CA, nw SA). _____

❑ *Cnemoscopus rubrirostris.* GREY-HOODED BUSH-TANAGER. (nw SA) . _____
   ___*C. (r.) rubrirostris.* RED-BILLED BUSH-TANAGER. (sp)
   ___*C. (r.) chrysogaster.* GOLDEN-BELLIED BUSH-TANAGER. (n,c Peru)

❑ *Hemispingus atropileus.* BLACK-CAPPED HEMISPINGUS. (nw SA). . . . . _____
   ___*H. (a.) atropileus.* BLACK-CAPPED HEMISPINGUS. (sp)
   ___*H. (a.) auricularis.* PUNO HEMISPINGUS. (e Peru)

❑ *Hemispingus calophrys.* ORANGE-BROWED HEMISPINGUS. (sw SA). . . _____

❑ *Hemispingus parodii.* PARODI'S HEMISPINGUS. (Andes se Peru). . . . . . _____

❑ *Hemispingus superciliaris.* SUPERCILIARIED HEMISPINGUS. (w SA). . . _____
   ___*H. (s.) chrysophrys.* YELLOW-BROWED HEMISPINGUS. (nw Ven)
   ___*H. (s.) superciliaris.* WHITE-BROWED HEMISPINGUS. (sp)
   ___*H. (s.) leucogaster.* WHITE-BELLIED HEMISPINGUS. (e Peru)

❑ *Hemispingus reyi.* GREY-CAPPED HEMISPINGUS. (Andes nw Ven). . . . . _____

❑ *Hemispingus frontalis.* OLEAGINOUS HEMISPINGUS. (mts w SA). . . . . . _____
   ___*H. (f.) frontalis.* OLEAGINOUS HEMISPINGUS. (sp)
   ___*H. (f.) ignobilis.* OCHRACEOUS HEMISPINGUS. (w Ven)

❑ *Hemispingus melanotis.* BLACK-EARED HEMISPINGUS. (Andes w SA). _____

❑ *Hemispingus goeringi.* SLATY-BACKED HEMISPINGUS. (nw Ven). . . . . _____

❑ *Hemispingus rufosuperciliaris.* RUFOUS-BROWED HEMISPINGUS. (e Peru)_____

❑ *Hemispingus verticalis.* BLACK-HEADED HEMISPINGUS. (nw SA). . . . . _____

❑ *Hemispingus xanthophthalmus.* DRAB HEMISPINGUS. (sw SA). . . . . . _____

❑ *Hemispingus trifasciatus.* THREE-STRIPED HEMISPINGUS. (sw SA). . . . _____

❑ *Pyrrhocoma ruficeps.* CHESTNUT-HEADED TANAGER. (se SA). . . . . _____

❑ *Thlypopsis fulviceps.* FULVOUS-HEADED TANAGER. (mts nw SA). . . . . _____

❑ *Thlypopsis ornata.* RUFOUS-CHESTED TANAGER. (Andes w SA). . . . . . _____

❑ *Thlypopsis pectoralis.* BROWN-FLANKED TANAGER. (Andes c Peru). . . _____

❑ *Thlypopsis sordida.* ORANGE-HEADED TANAGER. (SA). . . . . _____

❑ *Thlypopsis inornata.* BUFF-BELLIED TANAGER. (Andes n Peru). . . . . . _____

❑ *Thlypopsis ruficeps.* RUST-AND-YELLOW TANAGER. (Andes sw SA). . . _____

❑ *Hemithraupis guira.* GUIRA TANAGER. (SA). . . . . _____

❑ *Hemithraupis ruficapilla.* RUFOUS-HEADED TANAGER. (se Braz). . . . . _____

❑ *Hemithraupis flavicollis.* YELLOW-BACKED TANAGER. (e Pan, Amaz). _____

❑ *Chrysothlypis chrysomelas.* BLACK-AND-YELLOW TANAGER. (CR, Pan)_____

❑ *Chrysothlypis salmoni.* SCARLET-AND-WHITE TANAGER. (nw SA). . . . _____

❑ *Nemosia pileata.* HOODED TANAGER. (SA). . . . . _____

❑ *Nemosia rourei.* CHERRY-THROATED TANAGER. (se Braz). . . . . _____

❑ *Phaenicophilus palmarum.* BLACK-CROWNED PALM-TANAGER. (Hisp) _____

❑ *Phaenicophilus poliocephalus.* GREY-CROWNED PALM-T. (sw Hisp) . _____

❑ *Calyptophilus frugivorus.* CHAT TANAGER. (Hisp). . . . . _____
   ___*C. (f.) tertius.* HIGHLAND CHAT-TANAGER. (mts sw Hisp)
   ___*C. (f.) frugivorus.* LOWLAND CHAT-TANAGER. (e Hisp)

❑ *Rhodinocichla rosea.* ROSY THRUSH-TANAGER. (MA, n SA). . . . . _____

❑ *Mitrospingus cassinii.* DUSKY-FACED TANAGER. (s CA, nw SA). . . . . . _____

❑ *Mitrospingus oleagineus.* OLIVE-BACKED TANAGER. (Pant nc SA). . . . _____

❑ *Chlorothraupis carmioli.* OLIVE TANAGER. (s CA, w Amaz). . . . . _____
   ___*C. (c.) carmioli.* OLIVE TANAGER. (s CA)
   ___*C. (c.) frenata.* YELLOW-LORED TANAGER. (w Amaz)

❑ *Chlorothraupis olivacea.* LEMON-SPECTACLED TANAGER. (e Pan, nw SA)_____

❑ *Chlorothraupis stolzmanni.* OCHRE-BREASTED TANAGER. (nw SA). . . _____

❑ *Orthogonys chloricterus.* OLIVE-GREEN TANAGER. (mts se Braz)..... _____

❑ *Eucometis penicillata.* GREY-HEADED TANAGER. (MA, SA)......... _____
    ___*E. (p.) cristata.* GREY-CRESTED TANAGER. (MA, nw SA)
    ___*E. (p.) penicillata.* GREY-HEADED TANAGER. (n,c,e SA)

❑ *Lanio fulvus.* FULVOUS SHRIKE-TANAGER. (n Amaz)............. _____

❑ *Lanio versicolor.* WHITE-WINGED SHRIKE-TANAGER. (s Amaz)...... _____

❑ *Lanio aurantius.* BLACK-THROATED SHRIKE-TANAGER. (n,c MA)..... _____

❑ *Lanio leucothorax.* WHITE-THROATED SHRIKE-TANAGER. (s CA)..... _____

❑ *Creurgops verticalis.* RUFOUS-CRESTED TANAGER. (Andes w SA)..... _____

❑ *Creurgops dentata.* SLATY TANAGER. (Andes sw SA)............. _____

❑ *Heterospingus rubrifrons.* SULPHUR-RUMPED TANAGER. (CR, Pan)... _____

❑ *Heterospingus xanthopygius.* SCARLET-BROWED T. (e Pan, nw SA)... _____

❑ *Tachyphonus cristatus.* FLAME-CRESTED TANAGER. (SA)........... _____
    ___*T. (c.) cristatus.* FLAME-CRESTED TANAGER. (sp)
    ___*T. (c.) nattereri.* NATTERER'S TANAGER. (sw Braz)

❑ *Tachyphonus rufiventer.* YELLOW-CRESTED TANAGER. (w Amaz).... _____

❑ *Tachyphonus surinamus.* FULVOUS-CRESTED TANAGER. (Amaz)..... _____
    ___*T. (s.) surinamus.* FULVOUS-CRESTED TANAGER. (n,c Amaz)
    ___*T. (s.) napensis.* NAPO TANAGER. (w Amaz)

❑ *Tachyphonus luctuosus.* WHITE-SHOULDERED TANAGER. (CA, n,c SA) _____

❑ *Tachyphonus delatrii.* TAWNY-CRESTED TANAGER. (CA, nw SA)..... _____

❑ *Tachyphonus coronatus.* RUBY-CROWNED TANAGER. (se SA)....... _____

❑ *Tachyphonus rufus.* WHITE-LINED TANAGER. (s CA, SA).......... _____

❑ *Tachyphonus phoenicius.* RED-SHOULDERED TANAGER. (Amaz)..... _____

❑ *Trichothraupis melanops.* BLACK-GOGGLED TANAGER. (sc SA)..... _____

❑ *Habia rubica.* RED-CROWNED ANT-TANAGER. (MA, SA)........... _____

❑ *Habia fuscicauda.* RED-THROATED ANT-TANAGER. (MA, nw SA).... _____
    ___*H. (f.) salvini.* SALVIN'S ANT-TANAGER. (n,c MA)
    ___*H. (f.) fuscicauda.* RED-THROATED ANT-TANAGER. (s CA, nw SA)

❑ *Habia gutturalis.* SOOTY ANT-TANAGER. (nw,c Colom)........... _____

❑ *Habia atrimaxillaris.* BLACK-CHEEKED ANT-TANAGER. (sw CR)..... _____

❑ *Habia cristata.* CRESTED ANT-TANAGER. (Andes w Colom)........ _____

❑ *Piranga bidentata.* FLAME-COLORED TANAGER. (mts MA)......... _____

❑ *Piranga flava.* HEPATIC TANAGER. (sw US, MA, SA)............. _____
    ___*P. (f.) hepatica.* HEPATIC TANAGER. (sw US, n,c MA)
    ___*P. (f.) lutea.* TOOTH-BILLED TANAGER. (s CA, w SA)
    ___*P. (f.) flava.* RED TANAGER. (SA)

❑ *Piranga rubra.* SUMMER TANAGER. (s,e US-n Mex; ◊ MA-SA)....... _____

❑ *Piranga roseogularis.* ROSE-THROATED TANAGER. (Yuc). . . . . _____

❑ *Piranga olivacea.* SCARLET TANAGER. (e NA; ◊ Pan, w SA). . . . . _____

❑ *Piranga ludoviciana.* WESTERN TANAGER. (w NA, nw Baja; ◊ MA). . . _____

❑ *Piranga leucoptera.* WHITE-WINGED TANAGER. (mts MA, w,n SA). . . . _____

❑ *Piranga erythrocephala.* RED-HEADED TANAGER. (mts w,s Mex). . . . . _____

❑ *Piranga rubriceps.* RED-HOODED TANAGER. (Andes w SA). . . . . _____

❑ *Calochaetes coccineus.* VERMILION TANAGER. (w SA). . . . . _____

❑ *Ramphocelus sanguinolentus.* CRIMSON-COLLARED TANAGER. (MA). _____

❑ *Ramphocelus nigrogularis.* MASKED CRIMSON TANAGER. (w Amaz) . _____

❑ *Ramphocelus dimidiatus.* CRIMSON-BACKED TANAGER. (Pan, nw SA). _____

❑ *Ramphocelus melanogaster.* HUALLAGA TANAGER. (mts e Peru). . . . . _____

❑ *Ramphocelus carbo.* SILVER-BEAKED TANAGER. (n,c,e SA). . . . . _____

❑ *Ramphocelus bresilius.* BRAZILIAN TANAGER. (se SA). . . . . _____

❑ *Ramphocelus passerinii.* SCARLET-RUMPED TANAGER. (MA). . . . . . . _____

❑ *Ramphocelus flammigerus.* FLAME-RUMPED TANAGER. (Pan, nw SA). _____
   ___*R. (f.) icteronotus.* YELLOW-RUMPED TANAGER. (sp)
   ___*R. (f.) flammigerus.* FLAME-RUMPED TANAGER. (w Colom)

❑ *Spindalis zena.* STRIPE-HEADED TANAGER. (Bah, G Ant). . . . . _____
   ___*S. (z.) zena.* STRIPE-HEADED TANAGER. (Bah, Cuba, Cay, Coz)
   ___*S. (z.) dominicensis.* HISPANIOLAN TANAGER. (Hisp, PR)
   ___*S. (z.) nigricephala.* JAMAICAN TANAGER. (Jam)

❑ *Thraupis episcopus.* BLUE-GREY TANAGER. (MA, nw SA, Amaz). . . . . _____

❑ *Thraupis glaucocolpa.* GLAUCOUS TANAGER. (n SA). . . . . _____

❑ *Thraupis sayaca.* SAYACA TANAGER. (e,se SA). . . . . _____

❑ *Thraupis cyanoptera.* AZURE-SHOULDERED TANAGER. (se SA). . . . . . _____

❑ *Thraupis ornata.* GOLDEN-CHEVRONED TANAGER. (se Braz). . . . . _____

❑ *Thraupis abbas.* YELLOW-WINGED TANAGER. (n,c MA). . . . . _____

❑ *Thraupis palmarum.* PALM TANAGER. (s CA, SA). . . . . _____

❑ *Thraupis cyanocephala.* BLUE-CAPPED TANAGER. (mts w,n SA). . . . . . _____
   ___*T. (c.) cyanocephala.* BLUE-CAPPED TANAGER. (w SA)
   ___*T. (c.) olivicyanea.* ARAGUA TANAGER. (n SA)

❑ *Thraupis bonariensis.* BLUE-AND-YELLOW TANAGER. (w,se SA). . . . . _____
   ___*T. (b.) darwinii.* DARWIN'S TANAGER. (w SA)
   ___*T. (b.) bonariensis.* BLUE-AND-YELLOW TANAGER. (se SA)

❑ *Cyanicterus cyanicterus.* BLUE-BACKED TANAGER. (n Amaz). . . . . . . _____

❑ *Bangsia arcaei.* BLUE-AND-GOLD TANAGER. (CR, w,c Pan). . . . . _____

❑ *Bangsia melanochlamys.* BLACK-AND-GOLD TANAGER. (w Colom). . . _____

❑ *Bangsia rothschildi.* GOLDEN-CHESTED TANAGER. (nw SA). . . . . _____

❑ *Bangsia edwardsi.* MOSS-BACKED TANAGER. (nw SA). . . . . _____

❑ *Bangsia aureocincta.* GOLD-RINGED TANAGER. (Andes w Colom). . . . _____

❑ *Buthraupis montana.* HOODED MOUNTAIN-TANAGER. (mts w SA). . . . _____

❑ *Buthraupis eximia.* BLACK-CHESTED MOUNTAIN-TANAGER. (nw,w SA)_____
   ___*B. (e.) eximia.* BLACK-CHESTED MOUNTAIN-TANAGER. (nw SA)
   ___*B. (e.) chloronota.* BLUE-RUMPED MOUNTAIN-TANAGER. (w SA)

❑ *Buthraupis aureodorsalis.* GOLDEN-BACKED MOUNTAIN-T. (c Peru) . _____

❑ *Buthraupis wetmorei.* MASKED MOUNTAIN-TANAGER. (nw SA). . . . . . _____

❑ *Wetmorethraupis sterrhopteron.* ORANGE-THROATED T. (cn Peru). . . . _____

❑ *Anisognathus melanogenys.* SANTA MARTA MOUNTAIN-T. (ne Colom)_____

❑ *Anisognathus lacrymosus.* LACRIMOSE MOUNTAIN-TANAGER. (w SA). _____

❑ *Anisognathus igniventris.* SCARLET-BELLIED MOUNTAIN-T. (w SA). . . _____
   ___*A. (i.) lunulatus.* BLACK-BELLIED MOUNTAIN-TANAGER. (nw SA)
   ___*A. (i.) igniventris.* SCARLET-BELLIED MOUNTAIN-TANAGER. (sw SA)

❑ *Anisognathus somptuosus.* BLUE-WINGED MOUNTAIN-T. (w,n SA). . . _____
   ___*A. (s.) somptuosus.* BLUE-SHOULDERED MOUNTAIN-TANAGER. (sp)
   ___*A. (s.) flavinucha.* BLUE-WINGED MOUNTAIN-TANAGER. (sw SA)

❑ *Anisognathus notabilis.* BLACK-CHINNED MOUNTAIN-T. (nw SA). . . . . _____

❑ *Stephanophorus diadematus.* DIADEMED TANAGER. (se SA). . . . . _____

❑ *Iridosornis porphyrocephala.* PURPLISH-MANTLED TANAGER. (nw SA) _____

❑ *Iridosornis analis.* YELLOW-THROATED TANAGER. (Andes wc SA). . . . _____

❑ *Iridosornis jelskii.* GOLDEN-COLLARED TANAGER. (Andes w SA). . . . . _____

❑ *Iridosornis rufivertex.* GOLDEN-CROWNED TANAGER. (Andes w SA) . _____
   ___*I. (r.) caeruleoventris.* BLUE-BELLIED TANAGER. (nw Colom)
   ___*I. (r.) rufivertex.* GOLDEN-CROWNED TANAGER. (sp)

❑ *Iridosornis reinhardti.* YELLOW-SCARFED TANAGER. (Andes n Peru) . _____

❑ *Dubusia taeniata.* BUFF-BREASTED MOUNTAIN-TANAGER. (w SA). . . . _____
   ___*D. (t.) carrikeri.* CARRIKER'S MOUNTAIN-TANAGER. (ne SA)
   ___*D. (t.) taeniata.* BUFF-BREASTED MOUNTAIN-TANAGER. (w SA)

❑ *Delothraupis castaneoventris.* CHESTNUT-BELLIED MT.-T. (sw SA). . . _____

❑ *Pipraeidea melanonota.* FAWN-BREASTED TANAGER. (w,n,e,se SA). . . _____

❑ *Euphonia jamaica.* JAMAICAN EUPHONIA. (Jam). . . . . _____

❑ *Euphonia plumbea.* PLUMBEOUS EUPHONIA. (n Amaz). . . . . _____

❑ *Euphonia affinis.* SCRUB EUPHONIA. (MA). . . . . _____
   ___*E. (a.) godmani.* PALE-VENTED EUPHONIA. (w Mex)
   ___*E. (a.) affinis.* SCRUB EUPHONIA. (sp)

❑ *Euphonia luteicapilla.* YELLOW-CROWNED EUPHONIA. (s CA). . . . . . _____

❑ *Euphonia chlorotica.* PURPLE-THROATED EUPHONIA. (SA). . . . . _____

❑ *Euphonia trinitatis.* TRINIDAD EUPHONIA. (n SA). . . . . _____

❑ *Euphonia concinna.* VELVET-FRONTED EUPHONIA. (c Colom). . . . . . _____

❑ *Euphonia saturata.* ORANGE-CROWNED EUPHONIA. (mts nw SA). . . . . _____

❑ *Euphonia finschi.* FINSCH'S EUPHONIA. (nc SA). . . . . _____

❑ *Euphonia violacea.* VIOLACEOUS EUPHONIA. (SA). . . . . _____

❑ *Euphonia laniirostris.* THICK-BILLED EUPHONIA. (s CA-Amaz). . . . . . _____
　　___*E. (l.) melanura.* BLACK-TAILED EUPHONIA. (sp)
　　___*E. (l.) laniirostris.* THICK-BILLED EUPHONIA. (cw SA, sw Amaz)

❑ *Euphonia hirundinacea.* YELLOW-THROATED EUPHONIA. (MA). . . . . . _____

❑ *Euphonia chalybea.* GREEN-CHINNED EUPHONIA. (se SA). . . . . _____

❑ *Euphonia elegantissima.* BLUE-RUMPED EUPHONIA. (mts MA). . . . . . . _____

❑ *Euphonia musica.* ANTILLEAN EUPHONIA. (W Indies). . . . . _____

❑ *Euphonia cyanocephala.* GOLDEN-RUMPED EUPHONIA. (SA). . . . . _____

❑ *Euphonia imitans.* SPOT-CROWNED EUPHONIA. (s CA). . . . . _____

❑ *Euphonia fulvicrissa.* FULVOUS-VENTED EUPHONIA. (Pan, nw SA). . . . _____

❑ *Euphonia gouldi.* OLIVE-BACKED EUPHONIA. (MA). . . . . _____

❑ *Euphonia chrysopasta.* WHITE-LORED EUPHONIA. (Amaz). . . . . _____

❑ *Euphonia mesochrysa.* BRONZE-GREEN EUPHONIA. (w Amaz). . . . . . . _____

❑ *Euphonia minuta.* WHITE-VENTED EUPHONIA. (c,s MA, w,n,c SA). . . . _____

❑ *Euphonia anneae.* TAWNY-CAPPED EUPHONIA. (s CA, nw SA). . . . . . . _____

❑ *Euphonia xanthogaster.* ORANGE-BELLIED EUPHONIA. (e Pan, SA). . . _____

❑ *Euphonia rufiventris.* RUFOUS-BELLIED EUPHONIA. (w Amaz). . . . . . . _____

❑ *Euphonia cayennensis.* GOLDEN-SIDED EUPHONIA. (n,e Amaz). . . . . . . _____

❑ *Euphonia pectoralis.* CHESTNUT-BELLIED EUPHONIA. (se SA). . . . . . . _____

❑ *Chlorophonia flavirostris.* YELLOW-COLLARED CH. (e Pan, nw SA). . . _____

❑ *Chlorophonia cyanea.* BLUE-NAPED CHLOROPHONIA. (SA). . . . . _____

❑ *Chlorophonia pyrrhophrys.* CHESTNUT-BREASTED CH. (mts nw SA) . _____

❑ *Chlorophonia occipitalis.* BLUE-CROWNED CHLOROPHONIA. (MA). . . . _____

❑ *Chlorophonia callophrys.* GOLDEN-BROWED CHLOROPHONIA. (s CA) . _____

❑ *Chlorochrysa phoenicotis.* GLISTENING-GREEN TANAGER. (nw SA). . . _____

❑ *Chlorochrysa calliparaea.* ORANGE-EARED TANAGER. (Andes w SA) . _____

❑ *Chlorochrysa nitidissima.* MULTICOLORED TANAGER. (Andes Colom). _____

❑ *Tangara inornata.* PLAIN-COLORED TANAGER. (s CA, nw SA). . . . . . . _____

❑ *Tangara mexicana.* TURQUOISE TANAGER. (Amaz, se Braz). . . . . _____
　　___*T. (m.) mexicana.* TURQUOISE TANAGER. (Amaz)
　　___*T. (m.) brasiliensis.* WHITE-BELLIED TANAGER. (se Braz)

❑ *Tangara cabanisi.* AZURE-RUMPED TANAGER. (mts Chia, w Guat). . . . _____

❑ *Tangara palmeri.* GREY-AND-GOLD TANAGER. (e Pan, nw SA). . . . . . . _____

❑ *Tangara chilensis.* PARADISE TANAGER. (Amaz). . . . . _____

❑ *Tangara fastuosa.* SEVEN-COLORED TANAGER. (e Braz). . . . . _____

❑ *Tangara seledon.* GREEN-HEADED TANAGER. (se SA). . . . . _____

❑ *Tangara cyanocephala.* RED-NECKED TANAGER. (se SA). . . . . _____

❑ *Tangara desmaresti.* BRASSY-BREASTED TANAGER. (se Braz). . . . . _____

❑ *Tangara cyanoventris.* GILT-EDGED TANAGER. (se Braz). . . . . _____

❑ *Tangara johannae.* BLUE-WHISKERED TANAGER. (nw SA). . . . . _____

❑ *Tangara schrankii.* GREEN-AND-GOLD TANAGER. (w Amaz). . . . . _____

❑ *Tangara florida.* EMERALD TANAGER. (s CA, nw SA). . . . . _____

❑ *Tangara arthus.* GOLDEN TANAGER. (mts w,n SA). . . . . _____
   ___*T. (a.) aurulenta.* PERIJA TANAGER. (nw SA)
   ___*T. (a.) sclateri.* SCLATER'S TANAGER. (ec Colom)
   ___*T. (a.) arthus.* GOLDEN TANAGER. (w,n Ven)
   ___*T. (a.) pulchra.* BEAUTIFUL TANAGER. (w SA)

❑ *Tangara icterocephala.* SILVER-THROATED TANAGER. (s CA, nw SA). _____

❑ *Tangara xanthocephala.* SAFFRON-CROWNED TANAGER. (mts w SA) . _____

❑ *Tangara chrysotis.* GOLDEN-EARED TANAGER. (Andes w SA). . . . . . . _____

❑ *Tangara parzudakii.* FLAME-FACED TANAGER. (Andes nw,w SA). . . . . _____
   ___*T. (p.) lunigera.* YELLOW-FACED TANAGER. (nw SA)
   ___*T. (p.) parzudakii.* FLAME-FACED TANAGER. (w SA)

❑ *Tangara xanthogastra.* YELLOW-BELLIED TANAGER. (w,n Amaz). . . . . _____

❑ *Tangara punctata.* SPOTTED TANAGER. (n,e Amaz). . . . . _____

❑ *Tangara guttata.* SPECKLED TANAGER. (s CA, n SA). . . . . _____

❑ *Tangara varia.* DOTTED TANAGER. (n Amaz). . . . . _____

❑ *Tangara rufigula.* RUFOUS-THROATED TANAGER. (nw SA). . . . . _____

❑ *Tangara gyrola.* BAY-HEADED TANAGER. (s CA, n,c SA). . . . . _____
   ___*T. (g.) gyroloides.* BAY-AND-BLUE TANAGER. (s CA, w Amaz)
   ___*T. (g.) viridissima.* BAY-AND-GREEN TANAGER. (n SA)
   ___*T. (g.) gyrola.* BAY-HEADED TANAGER. (n Amaz)

❑ *Tangara lavinia.* RUFOUS-WINGED TANAGER. (CA, nw SA). . . . . _____

❑ *Tangara cayana.* BURNISHED-BUFF TANAGER. (SA). . . . . _____
   ___*T. (c.) cayana.* BURNISHED-BUFF TANAGER. (n SA)
   ___*T. (c.) flava.* OCHRE TANAGER. (sc,e,se SA)

❑ *Tangara cucullata.* LESSER ANTILLEAN TANAGER. (s L Ant). . . . . _____

❑ *Tangara peruviana.* BLACK-BACKED TANAGER. (se SA). . . . . _____

❑ *Tangara preciosa.* CHESTNUT-BACKED TANAGER. (se SA). . . . . _____

❑ *Tangara vitriolina.* SCRUB TANAGER. (nw SA). . . . . _____

❑ *Tangara meyerdeschauenseei.* GREEN-CAPPED TANAGER. (e Peru). . . . _____

❑ *Tangara rufigenis.* RUFOUS-CHEEKED TANAGER. (mts n Ven). . . . . _____

❑ *Tangara ruficervix.* GOLDEN-NAPED TANAGER. (Andes w,sw SA). . . . _____
___*T. (r.) ruficervix.* GOLDEN-NAPED TANAGER. (w SA)
___*T. (r.) fulvicervix.* ORANGE-NAPED TANAGER. (sw SA)

❑ *Tangara labradorides.* METALLIC-GREEN TANAGER. (Andes w SA). . . _____

❑ *Tangara cyanotis.* BLUE-BROWED TANAGER. (Andes w SA). . . . . _____
___*T. (c.) lutleyi.* BLACK-CHEEKED TANAGER. (sp)
___*T. (c.) cyanotis.* BLUE-BROWED TANAGER. (wc Bol)

❑ *Tangara cyanicollis.* BLUE-NECKED TANAGER. (Amaz). . . . . _____

❑ *Tangara larvata.* GOLDEN-HOODED TANAGER. (c,s MA, nw SA). . . . . . _____

❑ *Tangara nigrocincta.* MASKED TANAGER. (w Amaz). . . . . _____

❑ *Tangara dowii.* SPANGLE-CHEEKED TANAGER. (mts CR, w Pan). . . . . . _____

❑ *Tangara fucosa.* GREEN-NAPED TANAGER. (mts e Pan). . . . . _____

❑ *Tangara nigroviridis.* BERYL-SPANGLED TANAGER. (mts w SA). . . . . . _____

❑ *Tangara vassorii.* BLUE-AND-BLACK TANAGER. (Andes w SA). . . . . . . _____
___*T. (v.) vassorii.* BLUE-AND-BLACK TANAGER. (nw SA)
___*T. (v.) branickii.* TAMIAPAMPA TANAGER. (n Peru)
___*T. (v.) atrocerulea.* BUFF-NAPED TANAGER. (sw SA)

❑ *Tangara heinei.* BLACK-CAPPED TANAGER. (mts nw,n SA). . . . . _____

❑ *Tangara phillipsi.* SIRA TANAGER. (Andes ec Peru). . . . . _____

❑ *Tangara viridicollis.* SILVER-BACKED TANAGER. (Andes wc SA). . . . . _____
___*T. (v.) fulvigula.* TAMBILLO TANAGER. (sp)
___*T. (v.) viridicollis.* SILVER-BACKED TANAGER. (Peru)

❑ *Tangara argyrofenges.* STRAW-BACKED TANAGER. (Andes sw SA). . . _____

❑ *Tangara cyanoptera.* BLACK-HEADED TANAGER. (n,nc SA). . . . . _____
___*T. (c.) cyanoptera.* BLACK-HEADED TANAGER. (n SA)
___*T. (c.) whitelyi.* WHITELY'S TANAGER. (n Amaz)

❑ *Tangara velia.* OPAL-RUMPED TANAGER. (SA). . . . . _____
___*T. (v.) velia.* OPAL-RUMPED TANAGER. (Amaz, e SA)
___*T. (v.) cyanomelaena.* SILVERY-BREASTED TANAGER. (se SA)

❑ *Tangara callophrys.* OPAL-CROWNED TANAGER. (w Amaz). . . . . _____

❑ *Iridophanes pulcherrima.* GOLDEN-COLLARED HONEYCREEPER. (w SA) _____

❑ *Pseudodacnis hartlaubi.* TURQUOISE DACNIS-TANAGER. (Colom). . . . . _____

❑ *Dacnis albiventris.* WHITE-BELLIED DACNIS. (w,c Amaz). . . . . _____

❑ *Dacnis lineata.* BLACK-FACED DACNIS. (nw SA, Amaz). . . . . _____
___*D. (l.) egregia.* YELLOW-TUFTED DACNIS. (nw SA)
___*D. (l.) lineata.* BLACK-FACED DACNIS. (Amaz)

❑ *Dacnis flaviventer.* YELLOW-BELLIED DACNIS. (w Amaz). . . . . _____

❑ *Dacnis nigripes.* BLACK-LEGGED DACNIS. (se Braz). . . . . _____

❑ *Dacnis venusta.* SCARLET-THIGHED DACNIS. (s CA, nw SA). . . . . _____

❑ *Dacnis cayana.* BLUE DACNIS. (CA, SA). . . . . _____

❑ *Dacnis viguieri.* VIRIDIAN DACNIS. (e Pan, nw Colom). . . . . _____

❑ *Dacnis berlepschi.* SCARLET-BREASTED DACNIS. (nw SA). . . . . _____

❑ *Chlorophanes spiza.* GREEN HONEYCREEPER. (MA, SA). . . . . _____

❑ *Cyanerpes nitidus.* SHORT-BILLED HONEYCREEPER. (w Amaz). . . . . . . _____

❑ *Cyanerpes lucidus.* SHINING HONEYCREEPER. (c,s MA, nw Colom). . . _____

❑ *Cyanerpes caeruleus.* PURPLE HONEYCREEPER. (e Pan, nw,n,c,e SA) . _____

❑ *Cyanerpes cyaneus.* RED-LEGGED HONEYCREEPER. (MA-SA; ◆ Cuba). _____

❑ *Xenodacnis parina.* TIT-LIKE DACNIS. (Andes wc SA). . . . . _____

❑ *Tersina viridis.* SWALLOW TANAGER. (e Pan, SA). . . . . _____

❑ *Catamblyrhynchus diadema.* PLUSHCAP. (mts w,n SA). . . . . _____

❑ *Oreothraupis arremonops.* TANAGER FINCH. (Andes nw SA). . . . . _____

❑ *Urothraupis stolzmanni.* BLACK-BACKED BUSH-TANAGER. (nw SA). . . _____

❑ *Nephelornis oneillei.* PARDUSCO. (Andes c Peru). . . . . _____

❑ *Charitospiza eucosma.* COAL-CRESTED FINCH. (sc SA). . . . . _____

❑ *Coryphaspiza melanotis.* BLACK-MASKED FINCH. (sc SA). . . . . _____

❑ *Saltatricula multicolor.* MANY-COLORED CHACO-FINCH. (sc SA). . . . . _____

❑ *Coryphospingus pileatus.* PILEATED FINCH. (n,se SA). . . . . _____

❑ *Coryphospingus cucullatus.* RED-CRESTED FINCH. (SA). . . . . _____

❑ *Rhodospingus cruentus.* CRIMSON FINCH-TANAGER. (cw SA). . . . . . . _____

❑ *Phrygilus atriceps.* BLACK-HOODED SIERRA-FINCH. (Andes sw SA). . . _____

❑ *Phrygilus punensis.* PERUVIAN SIERRA-FINCH. (Andes sw SA). . . . . . . _____

❑ *Phrygilus gayi.* GREY-HOODED SIERRA-FINCH. (Andes s SA). . . . . _____

❑ *Phrygilus patagonicus.* PATAGONIAN SIERRA-FINCH. (s SA). . . . . _____

❑ *Phrygilus fruticeti.* MOURNING SIERRA-FINCH. (Andes s SA). . . . . . . _____

❑ *Phrygilus unicolor.* PLUMBEOUS SIERRA-FINCH. (Andes w,s SA). . . . . _____

❑ *Phrygilus dorsalis.* RED-BACKED SIERRA-FINCH. (Andes sw SA). . . . . _____

❑ *Phrygilus erythronotus.* WHITE-THROATED SIERRA-FINCH. (sw SA). . . _____

❑ *Phrygilus plebejus.* ASH-BREASTED SIERRA-FINCH. (Andes w SA). . . . _____

❑ *Phrygilus carbonarius.* CARBONATED SIERRA-FINCH. (c Argen). . . . . . _____

❑ *Phrygilus alaudinus.* BAND-TAILED SIERRA-FINCH. (Andes sw SA). . . _____

❑ *Melanodera melanodera.* CANARY-WINGED FINCH. (s SA). . . . . _____

❑ *Melanodera xanthogramma.* YELLOW-BRIDLED FINCH. (s SA). . . . . . . _____

❑ *Haplospiza rustica.* SLATY FINCH. (mts MA, w SA). . . . . _____

❑ *Haplospiza unicolor.* UNIFORM FINCH. (se SA). . . . . _____

❑ *Acanthidops bairdii.* PEG-BILLED FINCH. (mts CR, w Pan). . . . . _____

❑ *Lophospingus pusillus.* BLACK-CRESTED FINCH. (sc SA). . . . . _____

❑ *Lophospingus griseocristatus.* GREY-CRESTED FINCH. (Andes sw SA). _____

❑ *Donacospiza albifrons.* LONG-TAILED REED-FINCH. (se SA). . . . . _____

❑ *Rowettia goughensis.* GOUGH FINCH. (Gough). . . . . _____

❑ *Nesospiza acunhae.* NIGHTINGALE FINCH. (TdaC). . . . . _____

❑ *Nesospiza wilkinsi.* WILKINS'S FINCH. (TdaC). . . . . _____

❑ *Diuca speculifera.* WHITE-WINGED DIUCA-FINCH. (Andes sw SA). . . . _____

❑ *Diuca diuca.* COMMON DIUCA-FINCH. (s SA). . . . . _____
    ___*D. (d.) diuca.* COMMON DIUCA-FINCH. (Andes s SA)
    ___*D. (d.) minor.* LESSER DIUCA-FINCH. (Argen)

❑ *Idiopsar brachyurus.* SHORT-TAILED FINCH. (Andes sw SA). . . . . _____

❑ *Piezorhina cinerea.* CINEREOUS FINCH. (nw Peru). . . . . _____

❑ *Xenospingus concolor.* SLENDER-BILLED FINCH. (c,s Peru, n Chile). . . _____

❑ *Incaspiza pulchra.* GREAT INCA-FINCH. (Andes c Peru). . . . . _____

❑ *Incaspiza personata.* RUFOUS-BACKED INCA-FINCH. (Andes nw Peru). _____

❑ *Incaspiza ortizi.* GREY-WINGED INCA-FINCH. (Andes nw Peru). . . . . . _____

❑ *Incaspiza laeta.* BUFF-BRIDLED INCA-FINCH. (Andes n Peru). . . . . _____

❑ *Incaspiza watkinsi.* LITTLE INCA-FINCH. (Andes n Peru). . . . . _____

❑ *Poospiza thoracica.* BAY-CHESTED WARBLING-FINCH. (se Braz). . . . . . _____

❑ *Poospiza boliviana.* BOLIVIAN WARBLING-FINCH. (Andes c,se Bol). . . _____

❑ *Poospiza alticola.* PLAIN-TAILED WARBLING-FINCH. (Andes n Peru). . . _____

❑ *Poospiza hypochondria.* RUFOUS-SIDED WARBLING-FINCH. (sw SA) . _____

❑ *Poospiza ornata.* CINNAMON WARBLING-FINCH. (w Argen). . . . . _____

❑ *Poospiza erythrophrys.* RUSTY-BROWED WARBLING-FINCH. (sw SA) . _____

❑ *Poospiza whitii.* BLACK-AND-CHESTNUT WARBLING-FINCH. (sw SA). . . _____

❑ *Poospiza nigrorufa.* BLACK-AND-RUFOUS WARBLING-FINCH. (se SA) . _____

❑ *Poospiza lateralis.* RED-RUMPED WARBLING-FINCH. (se SA). . . . . _____
    ___*P. (l.) cabanisi.* GREY-THROATED WARBLING-FINCH. (se Braz)
    ___*P. (l.) lateralis.* BUFF-THROATED WARBLING-FINCH. (sp)

❑ *Poospiza rubecula.* RUFOUS-BREASTED WARBLING-FINCH. (n Peru). . . _____

❑ *Poospiza garleppi.* COCHABAMBA MOUNTAIN-FINCH. (Andes c Bol). . . _____

❑ *Poospiza baeri.* TUCUMAN MOUNTAIN-FINCH. (Andes nw Argen). . . . . _____

❑ *Poospiza caesar.* CHESTNUT-BREASTED MOUNTAIN-FINCH. (e Peru). . . _____

❑ *Poospiza hispaniolensis.* COLLARED WARBLING-FINCH. (cw SA). . . . . _____

❑ *Poospiza torquata.* RINGED WARBLING-FINCH. (sc SA). . . . . _____

❑ *Poospiza melanoleuca.* BLACK-CAPPED WARBLING-FINCH. (sc SA). . . _____

❑ *Poospiza cinerea.* CINEREOUS WARBLING-FINCH. (c Braz). . . . . _____

❑ *Sicalis citrina.* STRIPE-TAILED YELLOW-FINCH. (SA). . . . . _____

❑ *Sicalis lutea.* PUNA YELLOW-FINCH. (Andes sw SA). . . . . _____

❑ *Sicalis uropygialis.* BRIGHT-RUMPED YELLOW-FINCH. (Andes sw SA). _____

❑ *Sicalis luteocephala.* CITRON-HEADED YELLOW-FINCH. (c,sw Bol). . . . _____

❑ *Sicalis auriventris.* GREATER YELLOW-FINCH. (Andes s SA). . . . . _____

❑ *Sicalis olivascens.* GREENISH YELLOW-FINCH. (Andes sw SA). . . . . . _____

❑ *Sicalis lebruni.* PATAGONIAN YELLOW-FINCH. (s SA). . . . . _____

❑ *Sicalis columbiana.* ORANGE-FRONTED YELLOW-FINCH. (c,e,se Braz) . _____

❑ *Sicalis flaveola.* SAFFRON FINCH. (SA; ◆ Haw Is, Pan, Jam, PR). . . . . _____
   ___*S. (f.) flaveola.* SAFFRON FINCH. (w,n,e SA; ◆ sp)
   ___*S. (f.) pelzelni.* PELZELN'S FINCH. (sc SA)

❑ *Sicalis luteola.* GRASSLAND YELLOW-FINCH. (MA, w,n SA). . . . . _____
   ___*S. (l.) chrysops.* NORTHERN YELLOW-FINCH. (MA)
   ___*S. (l.) luteola.* GRASSLAND YELLOW-FINCH. (n,nc SA)
   ___*S. (l.) bogotensis.* MONTANE YELLOW-FINCH. (Andes wc SA)

❑ *Sicalis luteiventris.* MISTO YELLOW-FINCH. (sc,se US; ◆ L Ant). . . . . _____

❑ *Sicalis raimondii.* RAIMONDI'S YELLOW-FINCH. (Andes w Peru). . . . . . _____

❑ *Sicalis taczanowskii.* SULPHUR-THROATED FINCH. (cw SA). . . . . _____

❑ *Emberizoides herbicola.* WEDGE-TAILED GRASS-FINCH. (s CA, SA). . . _____

❑ *Emberizoides duidae.* DUIDA GRASS-FINCH. (Pant s Ven). . . . . _____

❑ *Emberizoides ypiranganus.* GREY-CHEEKED GRASS-FINCH. (se SA). . . _____

❑ *Embernagra platensis.* GREAT PAMPA-FINCH. (sc,se SA). . . . . _____
   ___*E. (p.) olivascens.* OLIVE PAMPA-FINCH. (sc SA)
   ___*E. (p.) platensis.* RED-BILLED PAMPA-FINCH. (se SA)

❑ *Embernagra longicauda.* PALE-THROATED PAMPA-FINCH. (e Braz). . . _____

❑ *Volatinia jacarina.* BLUE-BLACK GRASSQUIT. (MA, s L Ant, SA). . . . . _____

❑ *Sporophila frontalis.* BUFFY-FRONTED SEEDEATER. (se SA). . . . . _____

❑ *Sporophila falcirostris.* TEMMINCK'S SEEDEATER. (se Braz). . . . . _____

❑ *Sporophila schistacea.* SLATE-COLORED SEEDEATER. (MA-w,n Amaz). _____

❑ *Sporophila intermedia.* GREY SEEDEATER. (n SA). . . . . _____

❑ *Sporophila plumbea.* PLUMBEOUS SEEDEATER. (n,e,sc,se SA). . . . . . . _____

❑ *Sporophila americana.* VARIABLE SEEDEATER. (MA, nw SA, Amaz) . _____
   ___*S. (a.) corvina.* BLACK SEEDEATER. (MA)
   ___*S. (a.) aurita.* VARIABLE SEEDEATER. (s CA, nw SA)
   ___*S. (a.) americana.* WING-BARRED SEEDEATER. (Amaz)

❑ *Sporophila torqueola.* WHITE-COLLARED SEEDEATER. (MA). . . . . _____
   ___*S. (t.) torqueola.* CINNAMON-RUMPED SEEDEATER. (w Mex)
   ___*S. (t.) morelleti.* WHITE-COLLARED SEEDEATER. (sp)

❑ *Sporophila collaris.* RUSTY-COLLARED SEEDEATER. (sc,se SA). . . . . . _____

❑ *Sporophila bouvronides.* LESSON'S SEEDEATER. (n SA; ◊-Amaz). . . . . _____

❑ *Sporophila lineola.* LINED SEEDEATER. (sc,se Braz; ◊-n SA). . . . . _____

❑ *Sporophila luctuosa.* BLACK-AND-WHITE SEEDEATER. (wc SA). . . . . . _____

❑ *Sporophila nigricollis.* YELLOW-BELLIED SEEDEATER. (s CA-SA). . . . . _____

❑ *Sporophila ardesiaca.* DUBOIS'S SEEDEATER. (e Braz). . . . . _____

❑ *Sporophila melanops.* HOODED SEEDEATER. (se Braz). . . . . _____

❑ *Sporophila caerulescens.* DOUBLE-COLLARED SEEDEATER. (c,se SA) . _____

❑ *Sporophila albogularis.* WHITE-THROATED SEEDEATER. (e Braz). . . . . _____

❑ *Sporophila leucoptera.* WHITE-BELLIED SEEDEATER. (SA). . . . . _____
   ___*S. (l.) leucoptera.* GREY-BACKED SEEDEATER. (sp)
   ___*S. (l.) bicolor.* BLACK-BACKED SEEDEATER. (sw Amaz)

❑ *Sporophila peruviana.* PARROT-BILLED SEEDEATER. (cw SA). . . . . . . _____

❑ *Sporophila simplex.* DRAB SEEDEATER. (Peru). . . . . _____

❑ *Sporophila nigrorufa.* BLACK-AND-TAWNY SEEDEATER. (sw SA). . . . . _____

❑ *Sporophila bouvreuil.* CAPPED SEEDEATER. (e,se SA). . . . . _____
   ___*S. (b.) bouvreuil.* CAPPED SEEDEATER. (sp)
   ___*S. (b.) saturata.* SAO PAULO SEEDEATER. (se Braz)

❑ *Sporophila minuta.* RUDDY-BREASTED SEEDEATER. (c SA-n Amaz). . . _____

❑ *Sporophila hypoxantha.* TAWNY-BELLIED SEEDEATER. (sc,se SA). . . . _____

❑ *Sporophila ruficollis.* DARK-THROATED SEEDEATER. (sc SA). . . . . . . _____

❑ *Sporophila palustris.* MARSH SEEDEATER. (sc SA). . . . . _____

❑ *Sporophila castaneiventris.* CHESTNUT-BELLIED SEEDEATER. (Amaz) . _____

❑ *Sporophila hypochroma.* GREY-AND-CHESTNUT SEEDEATER. (sc SA) . _____

❑ *Sporophila cinnamomea.* CHESTNUT SEEDEATER. (sc SA). . . . . _____

❑ *Sporophila zelichi.* NAROSKY'S SEEDEATER. (ne Argen). . . . . _____

❑ *Sporophila melanogaster.* BLACK-BELLIED SEEDEATER. (se Braz). . . . . _____

❑ *Sporophila telasco.* CHESTNUT-THROATED SEEDEATER. (cw SA). . . . . . _____

❑ *Sporophila insulata.* TUMACO SEEDEATER. (sw Colom). . . . . _____

❑ *Oryzoborus nuttingi.* NICARAGUAN SEED-FINCH. (s CA). . . . . _____

❑ *Oryzoborus crassirostris.* LARGE-BILLED SEED-FINCH. (nw,n SA). . . . . _____

❑ *Oryzoborus atrirostris.* BLACK-BILLED SEED-FINCH. (sw SA). . . . . _____

❑ *Oryzoborus maximiliani.* GREAT-BILLED SEED-F. (e,se Braz; ◊-n SA). _____

❑ *Oryzoborus angolensis.* LESSER SEED-FINCH. (MA, SA). . . . . _____
   ___*O. (a.) funereus.* THICK-BILLED SEED-FINCH. (MA, nw SA)
   ___*O. (a.) angolensis.* CHESTNUT-BELLIED SEED-FINCH. (SA)

❑ *Amaurospiza concolor.* BLUE SEEDEATER. (mts MA, nw SA). . . . . . . _____
   ___*A. (c.) relicta.* SLATE-BLUE SEEDEATER. (c Mex)
   ___*A. (c.) concolor.* BLUE SEEDEATER. (sp)

❑ *Amaurospiza moesta.* BLACKISH-BLUE SEEDEATER. (se SA). . . . . _____

❑ *Melopyrrha nigra.* CUBAN BULLFINCH. (Cuba, Cay). . . . . _____

❑ *Dolospingus fringilloides.* WHITE-NAPED SEEDEATER. (nw,n Amaz). . . _____

❑ *Catamenia analis.* BAND-TAILED SEEDEATER. (mts w SA). . . . . _____

❑ *Catamenia inornata.* PLAIN-COLORED SEEDEATER. (Andes w SA). . . . _____

❑ *Catamenia homochroa.* PARAMO SEEDEATER. (mts w SA). . . . . _____
   ___*C. (h.) oreophila.* SANTA MARTA SEEDEATER. (ne Colom)
   ___*C. (h.) homochroa.* PARAMO SEEDEATER. (sp)

❑ *Tiaris obscura.* DULL-COLORED GRASSQUIT. (w,wc NA). . . . . _____

❑ *Tiaris canora.* CUBAN GRASSQUIT. (Cuba; ◆ Bah). . . . . _____

❑ *Tiaris olivacea.* YELLOW-FACED GRASSQUIT. (G Ant, MA-nw SA). . . . _____

❑ *Tiaris bicolor.* BLACK-FACED GRASSQUIT. (W Indies, n SA). . . . . _____

❑ *Tiaris fuliginosa.* SOOTY GRASSQUIT. (n,se SA). . . . . _____

❑ *Loxipasser anoxanthus.* YELLOW-SHOULDERED GRASSQUIT. (Jam). . . . _____

❑ *Loxigilla portoricensis.* PUERTO RICAN BULLFINCH. (PR). . . . . _____

❑ *Loxigilla violacea.* GREATER ANTILLEAN BULLFINCH. (Bah, Hisp). . . . _____

❑ *Loxigilla noctis.* LESSER ANTILLEAN BULLFINCH. (L Ant). . . . . _____

❑ *Diglossa baritula.* CINNAMON-BELLIED FLOWER-PIERCER. (mts MA). . . _____

❑ *Diglossa plumbea.* SLATY FLOWER-PIERCER. (mts CR, w Pan). . . . . . . _____

❑ *Diglossa sittoides.* RUSTY FLOWER-PIERCER. (mts w,n SA). . . . . _____

❑ *Diglossa venezuelensis.* VENEZUELAN FLOWER-PIERCER. (ne Ven). . . . _____

❑ *Diglossa albilatera.* WHITE-SIDED FLOWER-PIERCER. (mts w,n SA). . . . _____

❑ *Diglossa gloriosissima.* CHESTNUT-BELLIED FLOWER-P. (w Colom). . . _____

❑ *Diglossa lafresnayii.* GLOSSY FLOWER-PIERCER. (Andes w SA). . . . . . _____

❑ *Diglossa mystacalis.* MOUSTACHED FLOWER-PIERCER. (sw SA). . . . . . _____

❑ *Diglossa gloriosa.* MERIDA FLOWER-PIERCER. (Andes w Ven). . . . . . . _____

❑ *Diglossa humeralis.* BLACK FLOWER-PIERCER. (mts w,n SA). . . . . _____
   ___*D. (h.) aterrima.* ALL-BLACK FLOWER-PIERCER. (w SA)
   ___*D. (h.) humeralis.* BLACK FLOWER-PIERCER. (nw SA)
   ___*D. (h.) nocticolor.* SANTA MARTA FLOWER-PIERCER. (n SA)

❑ *Diglossa brunneiventris.* BLACK-THROATED FLOWER-PIERCER. (w SA). _____
   ___*D. (b.) vuilleumieri.* VUILLEUMIER'S FLOWER-PIERCER. (n Colom)
   ___*D. (b.) brunneiventris.* BLACK-THROATED FLOWER-PIERCER. (sw SA)

❑ *Diglossa carbonaria.* GREY-BELLIED FLOWER-PIERCER. (wc Bol). . . . . _____

❑ *Diglossa duidae.* SCALED FLOWER-PIERCER. (Pant nc SA). . . . . _____

❑ *Diglossa major.* GREATER FLOWER-PIERCER. (Pant nc SA). . . . . _____

❑ *Diglossopis indigotica.* INDIGO FLOWER-PIERCER. (Andes nw SA). . . . _____

❑ *Diglossopis glauca.* DEEP-BLUE FLOWER-PIERCER. (Andes w SA). . . . . _____

❑ *Diglossopis caerulescens.* BLUISH FLOWER-PIERCER. (mts w,n SA). . . . _____

❑ *Diglossopis cyanea.* MASKED FLOWER-PIERCER. (mts w,n SA). . . . . . . _____

❑ *Euneornis campestris.* ORANGEQUIT. (mts Jam). . . . . _____

❑ *Melanospiza richardsoni.* ST. LUCIA BLACK FINCH. (St. Lucia). . . . . . _____

❑ *Geospiza magnirostris.* LARGE GROUND-FINCH. (Galap). . . . . _____

❑ *Geospiza fortis.* MEDIUM GROUND-FINCH. (Galap). . . . . _____

❑ *Geospiza fuliginosa.* SMALL GROUND-FINCH. (Galap). . . . . _____

❑ *Geospiza difficilis.* SHARP-BEAKED GROUND-FINCH. (nw Galap). . . . . . _____

❑ *Geospiza scandens.* COMMON CACTUS-FINCH. (Galap). . . . . _____

❑ *Geospiza conirostris.* LARGE CACTUS-FINCH. (Galap). . . . . _____

❑ *Camarhynchus crassirostris.* VEGETARIAN FINCH. (Galap). . . . . _____

❑ *Camarhynchus psittacula.* LARGE TREE-FINCH. (Galap). . . . . _____

❑ *Camarhynchus pauper.* MEDIUM TREE-FINCH. (cs Galap). . . . . _____

❑ *Camarhynchus parvulus.* SMALL TREE-FINCH. (Galap). . . . . _____

❑ *Camarhynchus pallidus.* WOODPECKER FINCH. (Galap). . . . . _____

❑ *Camarhynchus heliobates.* MANGROVE FINCH. (w Galap). . . . . _____

❑ *Certhidea olivacea.* WARBLER FINCH. (Galap). . . . . _____

❑ *Pinaroloxias inornata.* COCOS FINCH. (Cocos). . . . . _____

Tribe Cardinalini [13/42]

❑ *Spiza americana.* DICKCISSEL. (c,e SA; ◊-n SA). . . . . _____

❑ *Pheucticus chrysopeplus.* YELLOW GROSBEAK. (mts Mex, c Guat). . . . _____

❑ *Pheucticus chrysogaster.* GOLDEN-BELLIED GROSBEAK. (w,n SA). . . . _____

❑ *Pheucticus tibialis.* BLACK-THIGHED GROSBEAK. (mts CR, w Pan). . . . _____

❑ *Pheucticus aureoventris.* BLACK-BACKED GROSBEAK. (w,sc SA). . . . . _____
   ___*P. (a.) uropygialis.* YELLOW-RUMPED GROSBEAK. (mts nw SA)
   ___*P. (a.) crissalis.* RIOBAMBA GROSBEAK. (cw SA)
   ___*P. (a.) terminalis.* CHAPMAN'S GROSBEAK. (e Peru)
   ___*P. (a.) aureoventris.* BLACK-BACKED GROSBEAK. (sw,sc SA)

❑ *Pheucticus ludovicianus.* ROSE-BREASTED GR. (c,ce NA; ◊-w,n SA) . _____

❑ *Pheucticus melanocephalus.* BLACK-HEADED GROSBEAK. (w NA, Mex)_____

❏ *Cardinalis cardinalis.* NORTHERN CARDINAL. (s,e NA-c MA; ◆ Haw Is)_____
   ___*C. (c.) cardinalis.* NORTHERN CARDINAL. (sp)
   ___*C. (c.) carneus.* LONG-CRESTED CARDINAL. (w Mex)

❏ *Cardinalis phoeniceus.* VERMILION CARDINAL. (n SA). . . . . _____

❏ *Cardinalis sinuatus.* PYRRHULOXIA. (sw US, n,c Mex). . . . . _____

❏ *Caryothraustes poliogaster.* BLACK-FACED GROSBEAK. (MA). . . . . . . _____

❏ *Caryothraustes canadensis.* YELLOW-GREEN GROSBEAK. (e Pan-se SA)_____

❏ *Caryothraustes humeralis.* YELLOW-SHOULDERED GROSBEAK. (w Amaz)_____

❏ *Rhodothraupis celaeno.* CRIMSON-COLLARED GROSBEAK. (ne Mex). . . _____

❏ *Periporphyrus erythromelas.* RED-AND-BLACK GROSBEAK. (n,e Amaz) _____

❏ *Pitylus grossus.* SLATE-COLORED GROSBEAK. (CA, nw SA, Amaz). . . . _____

❏ *Pitylus fuliginosus.* BLACK-THROATED GROSBEAK. (se SA). . . . . _____

❏ *Saltator atriceps.* BLACK-HEADED SALTATOR. (MA). . . . . _____

❏ *Saltator maximus.* BUFF-THROATED SALTATOR. (MA, SA). . . . . _____

❏ *Saltator atripennis.* BLACK-WINGED SALTATOR. (Andes nw SA). . . . . . _____

❏ *Saltator coerulescens.* GREYISH SALTATOR. (MA, SA). . . . . _____
   ___*S. (c.) grandis.* MIDDLE AMERICAN SALTATOR. (MA)
   ___*S. (c.) coerulescens.* GREYISH SALTATOR. (SA)

❏ *Saltator similis.* GREEN-WINGED SALTATOR. (sc SA). . . . . _____

❏ *Saltator orenocensis.* ORINOCAN SALTATOR. (n SA). . . . . _____

❏ *Saltator nigriceps.* BLACK-COWLED SALTATOR. (Andes wc SA). . . . . . _____

❏ *Saltator aurantiirostris.* GOLDEN-BILLED SALTATOR. (sc SA). . . . . . . _____

❏ *Saltator maxillosus.* THICK-BILLED SALTATOR. (se SA). . . . . _____

❏ *Saltator cinctus.* MASKED SALTATOR. (Andes wc SA). . . . . _____

❏ *Saltator atricollis.* BLACK-THROATED SALTATOR. (sc SA). . . . . _____

❏ *Saltator rufiventris.* RUFOUS-BELLIED SALTATOR. (Andes sw SA). . . . _____

❏ *Saltator albicollis.* STREAKED SALTATOR. (L Ant, s CA, w,n SA). . . . . _____
   ___*S. (a.) albicollis.* LESSER ANTILLEAN SALTATOR. (L Ant)
   ___*S. (a.) striatipectus.* STREAKED SALTATOR. (s CA, w,n SA)

❏ *Cyanoloxia glaucocaerulea.* INDIGO GROSBEAK. (sc,se SA). . . . . _____

❏ *Cyanocompsa cyanoides.* BLUE-BLACK GROSBEAK. (MA, Amaz). . . . . _____

❏ *Cyanocompsa parellina.* BLUE BUNTING. (n,c MA). . . . . _____

❏ *Cyanocompsa brissonii.* ULTRAMARINE GROSBEAK. (SA). . . . . _____

❏ *Guiraca caerulea.* BLUE GROSBEAK. (NA, MA; ◊-n SA). . . . . _____

❏ *Passerina amoena.* LAZULI BUNTING. (w NA, nw Baja; ◊-Mex). . . . . . _____

❏ *Passerina cyanea.* INDIGO BUNTING. (c,e NA; ◊-n SA). . . . . _____

❏ *Passerina versicolor.* VARIED BUNTING. (w NA, Mex, Guat). . . . . _____

❏ *Passerina ciris.* PAINTED BUNTING. (se US-nc Mex; ◊-MA, W Indies). _____
  ___*P. (c.) pallidior.* WESTERN PAINTED-BUNTING. (sc US, nc Mex; ◊-MA)
  ___*P. (c.) ciris.* EASTERN PAINTED-BUNTING. (se US; ◊-W Indies)

❏ *Passerina rositae.* ROSE-BELLIED BUNTING. (se Mex). . . . . _____

❏ *Passerina leclancherii.* ORANGE-BREASTED BUNTING. (w Mex). . . . . . _____

❏ *Porphyrospiza caerulescens.* YELLOW-BILLED BLUE FINCH. (sc SA). . . _____

Tribe Icterini [26/97]

❏ *Psarocolius oseryi.* CASQUED OROPENDOLA. (wc SA). . . . . _____

❏ *Psarocolius decumanus.* CRESTED OROPENDOLA. (Pan, SA). . . . . _____

❏ *Psarocolius viridis.* GREEN OROPENDOLA. (Amaz). . . . . _____

❏ *Psarocolius atrovirens.* DUSKY-GREEN OROPENDOLA. (Andes wc SA). _____

❏ *Psarocolius angustifrons.* RUSSET-BACKED OROPENDOLA. (w,n SA) . _____
  ___*P. (a.) alfredi.* RUSSET-BACKED OROPENDOLA. (mts w SA)
  ___*P. (a.) angustifrons.* BLACK-BILLED OROPENDOLA. (n,wc SA)

❏ *Psarocolius wagleri.* CHESTNUT-HEADED OROPENDOLA. (MA, nw SA). _____

❏ *Ocyalus latirostris.* BAND-TAILED OROPENDOLA. (wc SA). . . . . _____

❏ *Gymnostinops montezuma.* MONTEZUMA OROPENDOLA. (MA). . . . . . . _____

❏ *Gymnostinops cassini.* BAUDO OROPENDOLA. (nw Colom). . . . . _____

❏ *Gymnostinops bifasciatus.* AMAZONIAN OROPENDOLA. (Amaz). . . . . . _____
  ___*G. (b.) yuracares.* OLIVE OROPENDOLA. (w,n Amaz)
  ___*G. (b.) bifasciatus.* PARA OROPENDOLA. (e,s Amaz)

❏ *Gymnostinops guatimozinus.* BLACK OROPENDOLA. (Pan-nw Colom). _____

❏ *Cacicus cela.* YELLOW-RUMPED CACIQUE. (Pan, n,c SA). . . . . _____
  ___*C. (c.) vitellinus.* SAFFRON-RUMPED CACIQUE. (Pan, nw SA)
  ___*C. (c.) cela.* YELLOW-RUMPED CACIQUE. (n,c SA)

❏ *Cacicus haemorrhous.* RED-RUMPED CACIQUE. (SA). . . . . _____

❏ *Cacicus uropygialis.* SCARLET-RUMPED CACIQUE. (CA, w SA). . . . . . . _____
  ___*C. (u.) microrhynchus.* SCARLET-RUMPED CACIQUE. (CA)
  ___*C. (u.) pacificus.* PACIFIC CACIQUE. (e Pan, nw SA)
  ___*C. (u.) uropygialis.* SUBTROPICAL CACIQUE. (mts w SA)

❏ *Cacicus koepckeae.* SELVA CACIQUE. (e Peru). . . . . _____

❏ *Cacicus chrysopterus.* GOLDEN-WINGED CACIQUE. (s SA). . . . . _____

❏ *Cacicus chrysonotus.* MOUNTAIN CACIQUE. (Andes w SA). . . . . _____
  ___*C. (c.) leucoramphus.* NORTHERN MOUNTAIN-CACIQUE. (nw,wc SA)
  ___*C. (c.) chrysonotus.* SOUTHERN MOUNTAIN-CACIQUE. (sw SA)

❏ *Cacicus sclateri.* ECUADORIAN CACIQUE. (e Ecua, n Peru). . . . . _____

❏ *Cacicus solitarius.* SOLITARY CACIQUE. (SA). . . . . _____

❏ *Cacicus melanicterus.* YELLOW-WINGED CACIQUE. (w Mex). . . . . _____

❑ *Amblycercus holosericeus.* YELLOW-BILLED CACIQUE. (MA, w SA). . . _____
     ___*A. (h.) holosericeus.* YELLOW-BILLED CACIQUE. (MA, nw SA)
     ___*A. (h.) australis.* CHAPMAN'S CACIQUE. (w SA)

❑ *Icterus chrysocephalus.* MORICHE ORIOLE. (w,n Amaz). . . . . _____

❑ *Icterus cayanensis.* EPAULET ORIOLE. (SA). _____
     ___*I. (c.) cayanensis.* EPAULET ORIOLE. (n,c SA)
     ___*I. (c.) pyrrhopterus.* YELLOW-SHOULDERED ORIOLE. (sc SA)

❑ *Icterus graduacauda.* AUDUBON'S ORIOLE. (s Tex, Mex). . . . . _____

❑ *Icterus chrysater.* YELLOW-BACKED ORIOLE. (MA, nw SA). . . . . _____

❑ *Icterus nigrogularis.* YELLOW ORIOLE. (n SA). . . . . _____

❑ *Icterus leucopteryx.* JAMAICAN ORIOLE. (Jam, Cay, San Andrés). . . . . _____

❑ *Icterus auratus.* ORANGE ORIOLE. (Yuc). . . . . _____

❑ *Icterus mesomelas.* YELLOW-TAILED ORIOLE. (MA, w SA). . . . . _____

❑ *Icterus auricapillus.* ORANGE-CROWNED ORIOLE. (e Pan, n SA). . . . . . _____

❑ *Icterus graceannae.* WHITE-EDGED ORIOLE. (cw SA). . . . . _____

❑ *Icterus pectoralis.* SPOT-BREASTED ORIOLE. (MA; ◆ se Fla). . . . . _____

❑ *Icterus gularis.* ALTAMIRA ORIOLE. (s Tex, n,c MA). . . . . _____

❑ *Icterus pustulatus.* STREAK-BACKED ORIOLE. (MA). . . . . _____
     ___*I. (p.) pustulatus.* SCARLET-HEADED ORIOLE. (w Mex)
     ___*I. (p.) graysonii.* TRES MARIAS ORIOLE. (Tres Marías)
     ___*I. (p.) sclateri.* STREAK-BACKED ORIOLE. (sp)

❑ *Icterus icterus.* TROUPIAL. (n SA; ◆ PR). . . . . _____

❑ *Icterus jamacaii.* CAMPO ORIOLE. (SA). . . . . _____
     ___*I. (i.) croconotus.* ORANGE-BACKED ORIOLE. (n,w Amaz)
     ___*I. (i.) jamacaii.* CAMPO ORIOLE. (c,sc SA)

❑ *Icterus galbula.* NORTHERN ORIOLE. (NA, Mex; ◊-w SA, G Ant). . . . . _____
     ___*I. (g.) bullockii.* BULLOCK'S ORIOLE. (w NA, n Mex; ◊-CA)
     ___*I. (g.) galbula.* BALTIMORE ORIOLE. (e NA; ◊-w SA, G Ant)
     ___*I. (g.) abeillei.* BLACK-BACKED ORIOLE. (mts c Mex)

❑ *Icterus cucullatus.* HOODED ORIOLE. (sw US, Mex). . . . . _____

❑ *Icterus spurius.* ORCHARD ORIOLE. (e NA, ne,c Mex; ◊-nw SA). . . . . . _____
     ___*I. (s.) spurius.* ORCHARD ORIOLE. (e NA, c Mex; ◊-nw SA)
     ___*I. (s.) fuertesi.* OCHRE ORIOLE. (ne Mex; ◊ c Mex)

❑ *Icterus wagleri.* BLACK-VENTED ORIOLE. (MA). . . . . _____

❑ *Icterus dominicensis.* BLACK-COWLED ORIOLE. (MA, G Ant, Bah). . . . _____
     ___*I. (d.) prosthemelas.* BLACK-COWLED ORIOLE. (MA)
     ___*I. (d.) dominicensis.* GREATER ANTILLEAN ORIOLE. (G Ant, Bah)

❑ *Icterus oberi.* MONTSERRAT ORIOLE. (mts Montserrat). . . . . _____

❑ *Icterus bonana.* MARTINIQUE ORIOLE. (Martinique). . . . . _____

❑ *Icterus laudabilis.* ST. LUCIA ORIOLE. (St. Lucia). . . . . _____

❑ *Icterus maculialatus.* BAR-WINGED ORIOLE. (c MA). . . . . _____

❑ *Icterus parisorum.* SCOTT'S ORIOLE. (sw US, Mex). . . . . _____

❑ *Nesopsar nigerrimus.* JAMAICAN BLACKBIRD. (Jam). . . . . _____

❑ *Gymnomystax mexicanus.* ORIOLE BLACKBIRD. (Amaz). . . . . _____

❑ *Xanthocephalus xanthocephalus.* YELLOW-HEADED B. (w,c NA). . . . . _____

❑ *Agelaius flavus.* SAFFRON-COWLED BLACKBIRD. (sc SA). . . . . _____

❑ *Agelaius xanthophthalmus.* PALE-EYED BLACKBIRD. (wc SA). . . . . . . _____

❑ *Agelaius thilius.* YELLOW-WINGED BLACKBIRD. (sw,sc SA). . . . . _____

❑ *Agelaius cyanopus.* UNICOLORED BLACKBIRD. (sc SA). . . . . _____

❑ *Agelaius phoeniceus.* RED-WINGED BLACKBIRD. (NA-MA). . . . . _____

❑ *Agelaius tricolor.* TRICOLORED BLACKBIRD. (w US, n Baja). . . . . _____

❑ *Agelaius icterocephalus.* YELLOW-HOODED BLACKBIRD. (n,c SA). . . . _____

❑ *Agelaius humeralis.* TAWNY-SHOULDERED BLACKBIRD. (Cuba-Hisp). _____

❑ *Agelaius xanthomus.* YELLOW-SHOULDERED BLACKBIRD. (PR). . . . . . _____

❑ *Agelaius ruficapillus.* CHESTNUT-CAPPED BLACKBIRD. (SA). . . . . _____

❑ *Leistes militaris.* RED-BREASTED BLACKBIRD. (s CA, n,c SA). . . . . . . _____

❑ *Leistes superciliaris.* WHITE-BROWED BLACKBIRD. (sc SA). . . . . _____

❑ *Sturnella bellicosa.* PERUVIAN MEADOWLARK. (w SA). . . . . _____

❑ *Sturnella militaris.* PAMPAS MEADOWLARK. (se SA). . . . . _____

❑ *Sturnella loyca.* LONG-TAILED MEADOWLARK. (s SA). . . . . _____

❑ *Sturnella magna.* EASTERN MEADOWLARK. (e NA, MA, Cuba, n SA). . _____

❑ *Sturnella lilianae.* LILIAN'S MEADOWLARK. (cs US, cn Mex). . . . . . . _____

❑ *Sturnella neglecta.* WESTERN MEADOWLARK. (w NA-Mex; ◆ Haw Is). _____

❑ *Pseudoleistes guirahuro.* YELLOW-RUMPED MARSHBIRD. (se SA). . . . _____

❑ *Pseudoleistes virescens.* BROWN-AND-YELLOW MARSHBIRD. (se SA) . _____

❑ *Amblyramphus holosericeus.* SCARLET-HEADED BLACKBIRD. (se SA). _____

❑ *Hypopyrrhus pyrohypogaster.* RED-BELLIED GRACKLE. (Colom). . . . . _____

❑ *Curaeus curaeus.* AUSTRAL BLACKBIRD. (s SA). . . . . _____

❑ *Curaeus forbesi.* FORBES'S BLACKBIRD. (e Braz). . . . . _____

❑ *Gnorimopsar chopi.* CHOPI BLACKBIRD. (sc,e,se SA). . . . . _____

❑ *Oreopsar bolivianus.* BOLIVIAN BLACKBIRD. (mts Bol). . . . . _____

❑ *Lampropsar tanagrinus.* VELVET-FRONTED GRACKLE. (w,se Amaz). . . _____
    ___*L. (t.) tanagrinus.* VELVET-FRONTED GRACKLE. (w Amaz)
    ___*L. (t.) violaceus.* VIOLACEOUS GRACKLE. (sw Amaz Braz)
    ___*L. (t.) boliviensis.* BOLIVIAN GRACKLE. (n,e Bol)

❑ *Macroagelaius imthurni.* GOLDEN-TUFTED GRACKLE. (Pant nc SA). . . _____

❏ *Macroagelaius subalaris.* MOUNTAIN GRACKLE. (Andes Colom). . . . . _____

❏ *Dives atroviolacea.* CUBAN BLACKBIRD. (Cuba). . . . . _____

❏ *Dives dives.* MELODIOUS BLACKBIRD. (MA). . . . . _____

❏ *Dives warszewiczi.* SCRUB BLACKBIRD. (cw SA). . . . . _____
    ___*D. (d.) warszewiczi.* SCRUB BLACKBIRD. (sp)
    ___*D. (d.) kalinowskii.* PERUVIAN BLACKBIRD. (w Peru)

❏ *Quiscalus mexicanus.* GREAT-TAILED GRACKLE. (sw,sc US-w,n SA) . _____

❏ *Quiscalus major.* BOAT-TAILED GRACKLE. (e,se US). . . . . _____

   Quiscalus palustris. SLENDER-BILLED GRACKLE. (†c Mex). . . . . _____

❏ *Quiscalus nicaraguensis.* NICARAGUAN GRACKLE. (sw Nica, n CR). . . _____

❏ *Quiscalus quiscula.* COMMON GRACKLE. (c,e NA). . . . . _____
    ___*Q. (q.) versicolor.* BRONZED GRACKLE. (c,ne NA)
    ___*Q. (q.) quiscula.* PURPLE GRACKLE. (se US)

❏ *Quiscalus niger.* GREATER ANTILLEAN GRACKLE. (G Ant). . . . . _____

❏ *Quiscalus lugubris.* CARIB GRACKLE. (L Ant, n SA). . . . . _____

❏ *Euphagus carolinus.* RUSTY BLACKBIRD. (n NA; ◊-se US). . . . . _____

❏ *Euphagus cyanocephalus.* BREWER'S BLACKBIRD. (w,c NA; ◊-Mex) . _____

❏ *Molothrus badius.* BAY-WINGED COWBIRD. (e,sc SA). . . . . _____
    ___*M. (b.) fringillarius.* PALE COWBIRD. (e Braz)
    ___*M. (b.) badius.* BAY-WINGED COWBIRD. (sc SA)

❏ *Molothrus rufoaxillaris.* SCREAMING COWBIRD. (se SA). . . . . _____

❏ *Molothrus bonariensis.* SHINY COWBIRD. (se US, W Indies-SA). . . . . . _____

❏ *Molothrus aeneus.* BRONZED COWBIRD. (sw US, MA, cn Colom). . . . . _____
    ___*M. (a.) aeneus.* BRONZED COWBIRD. (sw US, MA)
    ___*M. (a.) armenti.* BRONZE-BROWN COWBIRD. (cn Colom)

❏ *Molothrus ater.* BROWN-HEADED COWBIRD. (NA, Mex). . . . . _____

❏ *Scaphidura oryzivora.* GIANT COWBIRD (MA, n,c,e SA). . . . . _____

❏ *Dolichonyx oryzivorus.* BOBOLINK. (n,c NA; ◊ SA). . . . . _____

TOTALS: **9702 species** in **2063 genera:** *nonpasserine*—3963 species in 895 genera;
       passerine—5739 species in 1168 genera.

Abeillia, 65
Abroscopus, 268
Aburria, 4
Acanthagenys, 186
Acanthidops, 327
Acanthisitta, 138
Acanthiza, 188
Acanthorhynchus, 186
Acanthornis, 187
Accipiter, 119-120
Aceros, 35
Acestrura, 74
Achaetops, 263
Acridotheres, 236
Acrocephalus, 263-264
Acropternis, 178
Acryllium, 12
Actenoides, 41
Actinodura, 276
Actophilornis, 106
Adelomyia, 70
Aechmophorus, 126
Aegithalos, 245
Aegithina, 213
Aegolius, 80
Aegotheles, 81-82
Aegypius, 117
Aenigmatolimnas, 101
Aepypodius, 5
Aeronautes, 62
Aethia, 115
Aethopyga, 287
Afropavo, 11
Agamia, 130
Agapornis, 54
Agelaius, 335
Agelastes, 11
Aglaeactis, 70
Aglaiocercus, 73
Agriocharis, 11
Agriornis, 150
Ailuroedus, 179
Aimophila, 310-311
Aix, 16
Ajaia, 132
Alaemon, 280
Alauda, 281-282
Alca, 115
Alcedo, 39-40
Alcippe, 276
Aleadryas, 196
Alectoris, 6
Alectroenas, 94
Alectrurus, 151
Alectura, 5
Alethe, 224-225
Alisterus, 52
Alle, 115

Alophoixus, 252-253
Alopochen, 15
Amadina, 301
Amalocichla, 189
Amandava, 298
Amaurocichla, 266
Amaurolimnas, 101
Amaurornis, 101
Amaurospiza, 330
Amazilia, 68-69
Amazona, 58-59
Amazonetta, 16
Amblycercus, 334
Amblyornis, 179
Amblyospiza, 296
Amblyramphus, 335
Ammodramus, 310
Ammomanes, 280
Ammoperdix, 6
Ampeliceps, 236
Ampelioides, 155
Ampelion, 155
Amphilais, 268
Amphispiza, 310
Amytornis, 180
Anabacerthia, 171
Anabazenops, 171
Anairetes, 145
Anaplectes, 295
Anarhynchus, 109
Anas, 16-18
Anastomus, 133
Ancistrops, 170
Andigena, 31
Androdon, 64
Andropadus, 250-251
Androphobus, 195
Anhima, 13
Anhinga, 127
Anisognathus, 144
Anodorhynchus, 55
Anomalospiza, 296
Anorrhinus, 34
Anous, 114
Anser, 14
Anseranas, 13
Anthocephala, 70
Anthochaera, 186
Anthornis, 186
Anthoscopus, 243
Anthracoceros, 34
Anthracothorax, 65
Anthreptes, 283-284
Anthus, 290-292
Antilophia, 157
Anumbius, 170
Anurolimnas, 99
Anurophasis, 8

Apalis, 256-257
Apaloderma, 36
Apalopteron, 183
Aphanotriccus, 148
Aphantochroa, 69
Aphelocephala, 189
Aphelocoma, 198
Aphrastura, 166
Aphriza, 105
Aplonis, 233-234
Aprosmictus, 52
Aptenodytes, 134
Apteryx, 1
Apus, 62-63
Aquila, 123
Ara, 55
Arachnothera, 287
Aramides, 100-101
Aramidopsis, 100
Aramus, 98
Aratinga, 55-56
Arborophila, 8-9
Arcanator, 271
Archboldia, 179
Archilochus, 73
Ardea, 129
Ardeola, 129-130
Ardeotis, 96
Arenaria, 105
Argusianus, 11
Arremon, 311
Arremonops, 311-312
Arses, 212
Artamella, 217
Artamus, 204
Arundinicola, 151
Ashbyia, 186
Asio, 81
Aspatha, 38
Asthenes, 168-169
Astrapia, 203
Asturina, 121
Atalotriccus, 146
Atelornis, 38
Athene, 80
Atlantisia, 100
Atlapetes, 312-313
Atrichornis, 179
Attagis, 103
Atthis, 74
Atticora, 246-247
Attila, 151
Augastes, 73
Aulacorhynchus, 30
Auriparus, 242
Automolus, 171-172
Aviceda, 115-116
Avocettula, 65
Aythya, 18

Babax, 275
Baeopogon, 251
Baillonius, 31
Balaeniceps, 132
Balearica, 97
Bambusicola, 9
Bangsia, 321-322
Bartramia, 105
Baryphthengus, 39
Basileuterus, 316-317
Basilornis, 237
Batara, 158
Bathmocercus, 262
Batis, 215-216
Batrachostomus, 82
Bebrornis, 264
Berlepschia, 170
Bias, 215
Biatas, 159
Biziura, 14
Bleda, 252
Blythipicus, 27
Boissonneaua, 71
Bolbopsittacus, 51
Bolborhynchus, 57
Bombycilla, 218
Bonasa, 11
Bostrychia, 131-132
Botaurus, 130-131
Brachycope, 295
Brachygalba, 32
Brachypteracias, 38
Brachypteryx, 224
Brachyramphus, 115
Bradornis, 225
Bradypterus, 262
Branta, 14-15
Brotogeris, 57-58
Bubalornis, 292
Bubo, 78
Bubulcus, 129
Buccanodon, 29
Bucco, 32-33
Bucephala, 18-19
Buceros, 34
Bucorvus, 35
Buettikoferella, 269
Bulweria, 136
Buphagus, 237
Burhinus, 107
Busarellus, 121
Butastur, 121
Buteo, 121-122
Buteogallus, 121
Buthraupis, 322
Butorides, 130

Cacatua, 50-51
Cacicus, 333
Cacomantis, 44
Cairina, 15
Calamanthus, 187
Calamonastes, 257
Calamospiza, 309
Calandrella, 281
Calcarius, 309
Calicalicus, 216
Calidris, 106
Caliechthrus, 45
Callacanthis, 305
Callaeas, 217
Callipepla, 12
Calliphlox, 73
Callocephalon, 22
Callonetta, 16
Calochaetes, 321
Calocitta, 199
Caloenas, 91
Calonectris, 136
Caloperdix, 9
Calorhamphus, 28
Calothorax, 73
Calypte, 73
Calyptocichla, 251
Calyptomena, 140
Calyptophilus, 319
Calyptorhynchus, 22
Calyptura, 155
Camarhynchus, 331
Camaroptera, 257
Campephaga, 207
Campephilus, 26
Campethera, 22
Campochaera, 206
Camptorhynchus, 18
Camptostoma, 143
Campylopterus, 64-65
Campylorhamphus, 174
Campylorhynchus, 239-240
Canirallus, 98
Capito, 30
Caprimulgus, 84-86
Capsiempis, 143
Cardellina, 315
Cardinalis, 332
Carduelis, 303-304
Cariama, 98
Caridonax, 41
Carpococcyx, 46
Carpodacus, 305
Carpodectes, 156
Carpornis, 155
Carpospiza, 289
Caryothraustes, 332
Casiornis, 151

Casmerodius, 129
Casuarius, 1
Catamblyrhynchus, 326
Catamenia, 330
Cataponera, 220
Catharacta, 111
Catharopeza, 314
Cathartes, 133
Catharus, 221
Catherpes, 240
Catoptrophorus, 105
Catreus, 10
Celeus, 25
Centrocercus, 11
Centropus, 46-47
Cephalopterus, 156
Cephalopyrus, 243
Cepphus, 115
Ceratogymna, 35
Cercibis, 131
Cercococcyx, 44
Cercomacra, 162-163
Cercomela, 233
Cercotrichas, 230
Cereopsis, 15
Cerorhinca, 115
Certhia, 239
Certhiaxis, 168
Certhidea, 331
Certhilauda, 280
Certhionyx, 181-182
Ceryle, 42
Cettia, 261-262
Ceuthmochares, 45
Ceyx, 40
Chaetocercus, 74
Chaetops, 217
Chaetoptila, 185
Chaetorhynchus, 209
Chaetornis, 269
Chaetura, 62
Chaimarrornis, 231
Chalcophaps, 89
Chalcopsitta, 22
Chalcostigma, 72
Chalybura, 69
Chamaea, 278
Chamaepetes, 4
Chamaeza, 175
Charadrius, 108-109
Charitospiza, 326
Charmosyna, 22
Chasiempis, 211
Chauna, 13
Chaunoproctus, 305
Chelictinia, 116
Chelidoptera, 33
Chenonetta, 16

Cheramoeca, 247
Chersomanes, 280
Chersophilus, 281
Chilia, 166
Chionis, 107
Chiroxiphia, 157
Chlamydera, 179
Chlamydochaera, 224
Chlamydotis, 96
Chlidonias, 114
Chloebia, 300
Chloephaga, 15
Chlorestes, 66
Chloridops, 307
Chloroceryle, 42
Chlorocharis, 261
Chlorochrysa, 323
Chlorocichla, 251
Chloropeta, 264-265
Chlorophanes, 326
Chlorophonia, 323
Chloropipo, 158
Chloropsis, 191
Chlorornis, 318
Chlorospingus, 318
Chlorostilbon, 66
Chlorothraupis, 319
Chondestes, 310
Chondrohierax, 116
Chordeiles, 83
Chrysococcyx, 44-45
Chrysocolaptes, 27
Chrysolampis, 65
Chrysolophus, 10
Chrysomma, 274
Chrysothlypis, 319
Chrysuronia, 67
Chthonicola, 187
Chunga, 98
Cichladusa, 230
Cichlherminia, 220
Cichlocolaptes, 170
Cichlopsis, 98
Cicinnurus, 202-203
Ciconia, 133
Cinclidium, 231
Cinclocerthia, 238
Cinclodes, 165-166
Cincloramphus, 268-269
Cinclosoma, 195
Cinclus, 218
Cinnycerthia, 240
Cinnyricinclus, 235
Circaetus, 118
Circus, 118-119
Ciridops, 307
Cissa, 199
Cissopis, 318

Cisticola, 254-255
Cistothorus, 240
Cittura, 40
Cladorhynchus, 108
Clamator, 44
Clangula, 18
Claravis, 90
Cleptornis, 260
Clibanornis, 170
Climacteris, 178
Clytoceyx, 40
Clytoctantes, 160
Clytolaema, 70
Clytomyias, 179
Clytorhynchus, 211
Clytospiza, 297
Cnemarchus, 149
Cnemophilus, 202
Cnemoscopus, 318
Cnemotriccus, 147
Cnipodectes, 146
Coccothraustes, 306
Coccycolius, 235
Coccyzus, 47
Cochlearius, 130
Cochoa, 231-232
Coeligena, 71
Coenocorypha, 104
Coereba, 317
Colaptes, 25
Colibri, 65
Colinus, 12
Colius, 43
Collocalia, 60-61
Colluricincla, 197
Colonia, 151
Colorhamphus, 149
Columba, 86-88
Columbina, 90
Compsothraupis, 318
Conioptilon, 156
Conirostrum, 317
Conopias, 153
Conopophaga, 176-177
Conopophila, 185
Conostoma, 277
Conothraupis, 318
Contopus, 148
Conuropsis, 56
Copsychus, 230-231
Coracias, 38
Coracina, 205-206
Coracopsis, 53
Coracornis, 196
Coragyps, 133
Corapipo, 157
Corcorax, 195
Cormobates, 178

Corvinella, 192
Corvus, 200-202
Corydon, 140
Coryphaspiza, 326
Coryphistera, 170
Coryphospingus, 326
Corythaeola, 75
Corythaixoides, 75
Corythopis, 142
Coscoroba, 14
Cosmopsarus, 235-236
Cossypha, 229-230
Cotinga, 156
Coturnicops, 99
Coturnix, 8
Coua, 46
Cracticus, 203
Cranioleuca, 168
Crateroscelis, 187
Crax, 4-5
Creagrus, 113
Creatophora, 236
Crecopsis, 100
Creurgops, 320
Crex, 100
Crinifer, 75
Criniger, 252
Crocias, 276-277
Crossleyia, 277
Crossoptilon, 10
Crotophaga, 48
Crypsirina, 200
Cryptophaps, 96
Cryptospiza, 297
Crypturellus, 2
Cuculus, 44
Culicicapa, 228
Culicivora, 145
Curaeus, 335
Cursorius, 111
Cutia, 275
Cyanerpes, 326
Cyanicterus, 321
Cyanochen, 15
Cyanocitta, 198
Cyanocompsa, 332
Cyanocorax, 198-199
Cyanolanius, 217
Cyanolimnas, 101
Cyanoliseus, 56
Cyanoloxia, 332
Cyanolyca, 198
Cyanophaia, 67
Cyanopica, 199
Cyanopsitta, 55
Cyanoptila, 227
Cyanoramphus, 53
Cyclarhis, 193

Cyclopsitta, 51
Cyclorrhynchus, 115
Cygnus, 14
Cymbilaimus, 158
Cymbirhynchus, 140
Cynanthus, 67
Cyornis, 228
Cyphorhinus, 242
Cypseloides, 60
Cypsiurus, 62
Cypsnagra, 318
Cyrtonyx, 13

Dacelo, 40
Dacnis, 325-326
Dactylortyx, 13
Damophila, 67
Daphoenositta, 195
Daption, 135
Daptrius, 124
Dasyornis, 187
Deconychura, 173
Delichon, 248
Delothraupis, 144
Deltarhynchus, 152
Dendragapus, 11
Dendrexetastes, 173
Dendrocincla, 172
Dendrocitta, 199-200
Dendrocolaptes, 173
Dendrocopos, 23-24
Dendrocygna, 13
Dendroica, 313-314
Dendronanthus, 289
Dendropicos, 22-23
Dendrortyx, 12
Deroptyus, 59
Dicaeum, 282-283
Dichrozona, 161
Dicrurus, 209-210
Didunculus, 96
Diglossa, 330-331
Diglossopis, 331
Dinemellia, 292
Dinopium, 26-27
Diomedea, 137-138
Dioptrornis, 225
Discosura, 66
Diuca, 327
Dives, 336
Dolichonyx, 336
Doliornis, 155
Dolospingus, 330
Donacobius, 239
Donacospiza, 327
Doricha, 73
Doryfera, 64
Drepanis, 307

Drepanoptila, 94
Dromaeocercus, 262
Dromaius, 1
Dromas, 110
Dromococcyx, 48
Drymocichla, 256
Drymodes, 191
Drymophila, 162
Drymornis, 173
Dryocopus, 25-26
Dryolimnas, 100
Dryoscopus, 213-214
Dryotriorchis, 118
Dubusia, 144
Ducula, 94-96
Dulus, 217
Dumetella, 237
Dumetia, 274
Dupetor, 130
Dysithamnus, 160
Dysmorodrepanis, 306

Eclectus, 52
Ectopistes, 89
Egretta, 128-129
Elaenia, 143-144
Elanoides, 116
Elanus, 116
Electron, 38-39
Eleothreptus, 86
Elminia, 210
Elseyornis, 109
Elvira, 69
Emberiza, 307-309
Emberizoides, 328
Embernagra, 328
Emblema, 299
Eminia, 257
Empidonax, 148-149
Empidonomus, 153
Empidornis, 225
Enicognathus, 57
Enicurus, 231
Enodes, 237
Ensifera, 71
Entomodestes, 98
Entomyzon, 186
Eolophus, 22
Eophona, 306
Eopsaltria, 190
Eos, 22
Ephippiorhynchus, 133
Epimachus, 202
Epthianura, 186
Eremalauda, 281
Eremiornis, 269
Eremobius, 170
Eremomela, 265

Eremophila, 282
Eremopterix, 280
Ergaticus, 315
Eriocnemis, 71-72
Erithacus, 229
Erythrocercus, 210
Erythrogonys, 109
Erythrotriorchis, 120
Erythrura, 299-300
Estrilda, 298
Eubucco, 30
Eucometis, 320
Eudocimus, 131
Eudromia, 3
Eudromias, 109
Eudynamys, 45
Eudyptes, 134
Eudyptula, 134
Eugenes, 70
Eugerygone, 189
Eugralla, 177
Eulabeornis, 102
Eulacestoma, 197
Eulampis, 65
Eulidia, 74
Eumomota, 39
Eumyias, 227
Euneornis, 331
Eunymphicus, 53
Eupetes, 195
Eupetomena, 65
Euphagus, 336
Eupherusa, 69
Euphonia, 322-323
Euplectes, 295-296
Eupodotis, 96-97
Euptilotis, 36
Eurocephalus, 192
Eurostopodus, 83
Euryceros, 217
Eurylaimus, 140
Eurynorhynchus, 106
Euryptila, 257
Eurypyga, 96
Eurystomus, 38
Euscarthmus, 145
Euschistospiza, 297
Euthlypis, 316
Eutoxeres, 64
Eutrichomyias, 210
Eutriorchis, 118

Falco, 125-126
Falculea, 217
Falcunculus, 196
Ferminia, 240
Ficedula, 226-227
Florisuga, 65

Fluvicola, 151
Formicarius, 174
Formicivora, 162
Forpus, 57
Foudia, 295
Foulehaio, 183
Francolinus, 6-7
Fraseria, 225
Fratercula, 115
Frederickena, 158
Fregata, 133-134
Fregetta, 138
Fregilupus, 236
Fringilla, 302
Fulica, 102
Fulmarus, 135
Furnarius, 166

Galbalcyrhynchus, 32
Galbula, 32
Galerida, 281
Gallicolumba, 91-92
Gallicrex, 102
Gallinago, 104
Gallinula, 102
Gallirallus, 99-100
Galloperdix, 9
Gallus, 9
Gampsonyx, 116
Gampsorhynchus, 276
Garrodia, 138
Garrulax, 269-271
Garrulus, 199
Gavia, 134
Gecinulus, 27
Geobates, 165
Geococcyx, 48
Geocolaptes, 22
Geoffroyus, 51
Geomalia, 98
Geopelia, 89
Geophaps, 89
Geopsittacus, 53
Geositta, 165
Geospiza, 331
Geothlypis, 315
Geotrygon, 91
Geranoaetus, 121
Geranospiza, 121
Geronticus, 132
Gerygone, 188-189
Glareola, 111
Glaucidium, 79-80
Glaucis, 63
Glossopsitta, 22
Glycichaera, 182
Glyphorynchus, 173
Gnorimopsar, 335

Goethalsia, 67
Goldmania, 67
Gorsachius, 130
Goura, 96
Gracula, 237
Grafisia, 234
Grallaria, 175-176
Grallaricula, 176
Grallina, 213
Graminicola, 269
Granatellus, 317
Grandala, 231
Grantiella, 186
Graueria, 265
Graydidascalus, 58
Griseotyrannus, 153
Grus, 97
Guadalcanaria, 183
Gubernatrix, 313
Gubernetes, 151
Guira, 48
Guiraca, 332
Guttera, 12
Gygis, 114
Gymnobucco, 28
Gymnocichla, 163
Gymnocrex, 101
Gymnoderus, 156
Gymnogyps, 133
Gymnomystax, 335
Gymnomyza, 185
Gymnophaps, 96
Gymnopithys, 164
Gymnorhina, 203
Gymnorhinus, 198
Gymnostinops, 333
Gypaetus, 117
Gypohierax, 117
Gypopsitta, 58
Gyps, 117

Habia, 320
Habroptila, 102
Haematoderus, 156
Haematopus, 107-108
Haematortyx, 9
Haematospiza, 306
Halcyon, 40
Haliaeetus, 117
Haliastur, 117
Halobaena, 136
Hamirostra, 116
Hapalopsittaca, 58
Hapaloptila, 33
Haplophaedia, 72
Haplospiza, 326-327
Harpactes, 37
Harpagus, 116

Harpia, 122
Harpyhaliaetus, 121
Harpyopsis, 122
Heinrichia, 224
Heleia, 261
Heliactin, 73
Heliangelus, 71
Heliobletus, 172
Heliodoxa, 70
Heliolais, 256
Heliomaster, 73
Heliopais, 98
Heliornis, 98
Heliothryx, 73
Hellmayrea, 168
Helmitheros, 314
Hemicircus, 27
Hemignathus, 307
Hemiphaga, 96
Hemiprocne, 63
Hemipus, 207
Hemispingus, 318-319
Hemitesia, 266
Hemithraupis, 319
Hemitriccus, 141-142
Hemixos, 253
Henicopernis, 116
Henicophaps, 89
Henicorhina, 242
Herpetotheres, 124
Herpsilochmus, 161-162
Hesperiphona, 306
Heteralocha, 217
Heterocercus, 158
Heteromirafra, 280
Heteromunia, 301
Heteromyias, 190
Heteronetta, 14
Heterophasia, 277
Heterospingus, 320
Heteroxolmis, 150
Hieraaetus, 123
Himantopus, 108
Himantornis, 98
Himatione, 307
Hippolais, 264
Hirundapus, 61-62
Hirundinea, 147
Hirundo, 247-248
Histrionicus, 18
Histurgops, 292
Hodgsonius, 231
Horizorhinus, 228
Humblotia, 226
Hydrobates, 138
Hydrochous, 60
Hydrophasianus, 107

Hydropsalis, 86
Hyetornis, 47
Hylacola, 188
Hylexetastes, 173
Hylia, 266
Hyliota, 268
Hylocharis, 67
Hylocitrea, 196
Hylocryptus, 172
Hyloctistes, 171
Hylomanes, 38
Hylonympha, 70
Hylopezus, 176
Hylophilus, 194
Hylophylax, 164
Hylorchilus, 240
Hymenolaimus, 16
Hymenops, 151
Hypargos, 297
Hypergerus, 257
Hypnelus, 33
Hypocnemis, 163
Hypocnemoides, 163
Hypocolius, 253
Hypocryptadius, 261
Hypoedaleus, 158
Hypogramma, 284
Hypopyrrhus, 335
Hypositta, 217
Hypothymis, 210
Hypsipetes, 253
I
bidorhyncha, 108
Ichthyophaga, 117
Icteria, 317
Icterus, 334-335
Ictinaetus, 123
Ictinia, 116
Idiopsar, 327
Ifrita, 195
Ilicura, 157
Illadopsis, 272
Incaspiza, 327
Indicator, 20
Inezia, 144
Iodopleura, 155
Iole, 253
Irania, 229
Irediparra, 107
Irena, 191
Iridophanes, 325
Iridosornis, 144
Ispidina, 40
Ithaginis, 9
Ixobrychus, 130
Ixonotus, 251
Ixos, 253

Jabiru, 133
Jabouilleia, 272
Jacamaralcyon, 32
Jacamerops, 32
Jacana, 107
Jubula, 79
Junco, 309
Jynx, 20

Kakamega, 272
Kaupifalco, 119
Kenopia, 272
Ketupa, 78
Klais, 65
Knipolegus, 150-151
Kupeornis, 276

Lacedo, 40
Lafresnaya, 70
Lagonosticta, 297-298
Lagopus, 11
Lalage, 206-207
Lampornis, 69
Lamprolaima, 69
Lamprolia, 213
Lampropsar, 335
Lamprospiza, 318
Lamprotornis, 235
Laniarius, 214
Laniisoma, 154
Lanio, 320
Laniocera, 151
Lanioturdus, 213
Lanius, 191-192
Larosterna, 114
Larus, 111-113
Laterallus, 99
Lathamus, 53
Lathrotriccus, 147-148
Latoucheornis, 307
Legatus, 153
Leiothrix, 275
Leipoa, 5
Leistes, 335
Lemuresthes, 300
Lepidocolaptes, 174
Lepidopyga, 67
Leptasthenura, 166
Leptodon, 116
Leptopoecile, 266
Leptopogon, 140-141
Leptopterus, 217
Leptoptilos, 133
Leptosittaca, 56
Leptosomus, 38
Leptotila, 90
Lerwa, 6
Lesbia, 72

Lessonia, 150
Leucippus, 68
Leucochloris, 67
Leucopeza, 315
Leucopsar, 236
Leucopternis, 121
Leucosarcia, 89
Leucosticte, 304-305
Lewinia, 100
Lichenostomus, 183
Lichmera, 182
Limicola, 106
Limnodromus, 105
Limnornis, 170
Limnothlypis, 314
Limosa, 104
Linurgus, 303
Liocichla, 271
Lioptilus, 276
Liosceles, 177
Lipaugus, 155-156
Loboparadisea, 202
Lochmias, 170
Locustella, 263
Loddigesia, 73
Lonchura, 300-301
Lophaetus, 123
Lophodytes, 19
Lophoictinia, 116
Lopholaimus, 96
Lophophorus, 9
Lophorina, 202
Lophornis, 66
Lophospingus, 327
Lophostrix, 79
Lophotibis, 132
Lophotriccus, 146
Lophozosterops, 260-261
Lophura, 9-10
Loriculus, 54
Lorius, 22
Loxia, 306
Loxigilla, 330
Loxioides, 306
Loxipasser, 330
Loxops, 307
Lullula, 281
Lurocalis, 83
Luscinia, 229
Lybius, 29
Lycocorax, 202
Lymnocryptes, 104
Lysurus, 313

Macgregoria, 202
Machaerirhynchus, 213
Machaeropterus, 158
Macheiramphus, 116

Machetornis, 151
Mackenziaena, 158
Macroagelaius, 335-336
Macrocephalon, 5
Macrodipteryx, 86
Macronectes, 135
Macronous, 274
Macronyx, 290
Macropsalis, 86
Macropygia, 88
Macrosphenus, 266
Madanga, 260
Malacocincla, 271
Malaconotus, 215
Malacopteron, 271
Malacoptila, 33
Malacorhynchus, 18
Malcorus, 256
Malia, 253
Malimbus, 295
Malurus, 179-180
Manacus, 157-158
Mandingoa, 297
Manorina, 186
Manucodia, 202
Margaroperdix, 8
Margarops, 238
Margarornis, 170
Marmaronetta, 18
Mascarinus, 53
Masius, 157
Mayrornis, 211
Mearnsia, 61
Mecocerculus, 144
Megaceryle, 42
Megacrex, 102
Megadyptes, 134
Megalaima, 27-28
Megalurulus, 269
Megalurus, 268
Megapodius, 5
Megarynchus, 153
Megastictus, 160
Megatriorchis, 121
Megaxenops, 172
Megazosterops, 261
Meiglyptes, 27
Melaenornis, 225
Melampitta, 202
Melamprosops, 307
Melanerpes, 21-22
Melanitta, 18
Melanocharis, 288
Melanochlora, 245
Melanocorypha, 281
Melanodera, 326
Melanodryas, 190
Melanopareia, 177

Melanoperdix, 8
Melanoptila, 237
Melanospiza, 331
Melanotis, 237
Melanotrochilus, 65
Meleagris, 11
Melichneutes, 20
Melidectes, 184-185
Melidora, 41
Melierax, 119
Melignomon, 20
Melilestes, 182
Meliphaga, 182-183
Melipotes, 185
Melithreptus, 183-184
Melitograis, 184
Mellisuga, 74
Melocichla, 263
Melophus, 307
Melopsittacus, 53
Melopyrrha, 330
Melospiza, 309
Melozone, 311
Menura, 178
Merganetta, 16
Mergellus, 19
Mergus, 19
Meropogon, 42
Merops, 42-43
Merulaxis, 177
Mesembrinibis, 131
Mesitornis, 103
Mesophoyx, 129
Metabolus, 211
Metallura, 72
Metopidius, 107
Metopothrix, 170
Metriopelia, 90
Micrastur, 124
Micrathene, 80
Microbates, 242
Microcerculus, 242
Microchera, 69
Microdynamis, 45
Microeca, 189
Microgoura, 92
Microhierax, 124
Microligea, 315
Micromacronus, 274
Micromonacha, 33
Micronisus, 119
Micropalama, 106
Microparra, 106
Micropsitta, 51
Micropygia, 99
Microrhopias, 162
Microstilbon, 73
Miliaria, 309

Milvago, 124
Milvus, 117
Mimizuku, 78
Mimodes, 238
Mimus, 237
Minla, 276
Mino, 236
Mionectes, 140
Mirafra, 279-280
Mitrephanes, 148
Mitrospingus, 319
Mitu, 4
Mniotilta, 314
Modulatrix, 271
Moho, 185
Mohoua, 196
Molothrus, 336
Momotus, 39
Monachella, 189
Monarcha, 211-212
Monasa, 33
Monias, 103
Monticola, 218
Montifringilla, 289
Morococcyx, 48
Morphnus, 122
Morus, 127
Motacilla, 289-290
Mulleripicus, 27
Muscicapa, 225-226
Muscicapella, 228
Muscigralla, 150
Muscipipra, 151
Muscisaxicola, 150
Musophaga, 75
Myadestes, 220-221
Mycerobas, 306
Mycteria, 133
Myiagra, 213-214
Myiarchus, 152
Myiobius, 147
Myioborus, 315-316
Myiodynastes, 153
Myiopagis, 143
Myioparus, 226
Myiophobus, 147
Myiophonus, 218-219
Myiopsitta, 57
Myiornis, 146
Myiotheretes, 149
Myiotriccus, 147
Myiozetetes, 153
Myornis, 177
Myrmeciza, 163-164
Myrmecocichla, 233
Myrmia, 74
Myrmoborus, 163
Myrmochanes, 163

Myrmorchilus, 161
Myrmornis, 164
Myrmothera, 176
Myrmotherula, 160-161
Myrtis, 74
Mystacornis, 277
Myza, 185
Myzomela, 181
Myzornis, 277

Namibornis, 230
Nandayus, 56
Nannopsittaca, 58
Napothera, 272-273
Nasica, 173
Neafrapus, 61
Necropsar, 236
Necrosyrtes, 117
Nectarinia, 284-287
Nemosia, 319
Neochelidon, 247
Neochen, 15
Neochmia, 299
Neocichla, 235
Neocossyphus, 218
Neocrex, 101
Neoctantes, 160
Neodrepanis, 140
Neolalage, 211
Neolestes, 253
Neomixis, 273
Neomorphus, 48
Neopelma, 158
Neophema, 53
Neophron, 117
Neopipo, 158
Neopsephotus, 53
Neopsittacus, 50
Neospiza, 303
Neothraupis, 318
Neotis, 96
Neoxolmis, 150
Nephelornis, 326
Nesasio, 81
Nesillas, 263
Nesocharis, 297
Nesocichla, 220
Nesoclopeus, 99
Nesoctites, 21
Nesofregetta, 138
Nesomimus, 237-238
Nesopsar, 335
Nesospingus, 318
Nesospiza, 327
Nesotriccus, 143
Nestor, 51
Netta, 18
Nettapus, 16

Newtonia, 265-266
Nicator, 252
Nigrita, 296
Nilaus, 213
Niltava, 227-228
Ninox, 80-81
Nipponia, 132
Nonnula, 33
Northiella, 52
Notharchus, 32
Nothocercus, 1-2
Nothocrax, 4
Nothoprocta, 2-3
Nothura, 3
Notiochelidon, 246
Notiomystis, 184
Nucifraga, 200
Numenius, 105
Numida, 11
Nyctanassa, 130
Nyctea, 78
Nyctibius, 82-83
Nycticorax, 130
Nyctidromus, 83
Nyctiphrynus, 84
Nyctiprogne, 83
Nyctyornis, 42
Nymphicus, 51
Nystalus, 33

Oceanites, 138
Oceanodroma, 138
Ochthoeca, 149
Ochthornis, 149
Ocreatus, 72
Oculocincta, 261
Ocyalus, 333
Ocyceros, 34
Odontophorus, 12
Odontorchilus, 240
Oedistoma, 288
Oena, 89
Oenanthe, 232-233
Ognorhynchus, 56
Oncostoma, 146
Onychognathus, 234-235
Onychorhynchus, 147
Ophrysia, 9
Opisthocomus, 48
Opisthoprora, 73
Oporornis, 315
Orchesticus, 317
Oreocharis, 288
Oreoica, 196
Oreomanes, 317
Oreomystis, 307
Oreonympha, 73
Oreophasis, 4

Oreophilais, 256
Oreopholus, 109
Oreopsar, 335
Oreopsittacus, 50
Oreornis, 183
Oreortyx, 12
Oreoscoptes, 238
Oreoscopus, 187
Oreostruthus, 299
Oreothraupis, 326
Oreotrochilus, 70
Origma, 187
Oriolia, 217
Oriolus, 204-205
Oriturus, 311
Ornithion, 143
Oroaetus, 124
Ortalis, 3
Orthogonys, 320
Orthonyx, 191
Orthorhyncus, 65
Orthotomus, 265
Ortygospiza, 299
Ortyxelos, 19
Oryzoborus, 329-330
Otidiphaps, 92
Otis, 96
Otus, 76-78
Oxylabes, 277
Oxylophus, 43-44
Oxypogon, 73
Oxyruncus, 156
Oxyura, 13-14

Pachycare, 196
Pachycephala, 196-197
Pachycephalopsis, 190
Pachycoccyx, 44
Pachyphantes, 295
Pachyptila, 136
Pachyramphus, 154
Padda, 301
Pagodroma, 135
Pagophila, 113
Palmeria, 307
Pandion, 115
Panterpe, 67
Panurus, 277
Panyptila, 62
Papasula, 127
Parabuteo, 121
Paradigalla, 202
Paradisaea, 203
Paradoxornis, 277-278
Paramythia, 288
Pardalotus, 186
Pardirallus, 101
Parmoptila, 296

Paroaria, 313
Parophasma, 276
Paroreomyza, 307
Parotia, 202
Parula, 313
Parus, 243-245
Passer, 288-289
Passerculus, 310
Passerella, 309
Passerina, 332-333
Patagona, 70
Pauxi, 4
Pavo, 11
Pedionomus, 103
Pelagodroma, 138
Pelargopsis, 40
Pelecanoides, 137
Pelecanus, 132
Pellorneum, 271
Peltohyas, 109
Peltops, 204
Penelope, 3-4
Penelopides, 34-35
Penelopina, 4
Peneothello, 190
Percnostola, 163
Perdicula, 8
Perdix, 7
Pericrocotus, 207
Periporphyrus, 332
Perisoreus, 199
Perissocephalus, 156
Pernis, 116
Petroica, 189-190
Petronia, 289
Petrophassa, 89
Peucedramus, 302
Pezopetes, 313
Pezophaps, 86
Pezoporus, 53
Phacellodomus, 169-170
Phaenicophaeus, 45-46
Phaenicophilus, 319
Phaenostictus, 165
Phaeochroa, 64
Phaeomyias, 143
Phaeoprogne, 246
Phaethon, 126
Phaethornis, 63-64
Phaetusa, 114
Phainopepla, 217
Phainoptila, 217
Phalacrocorax, 127-128
Phalaenoptilus, 83
Phalaropus, 106
Phalcoboenus, 124
Phapitreron, 92
Phaps, 89

Pharomachrus, 36
Phasianus, 10
Phedina, 247
Phegornis, 109
Phelpsia, 153
Pheucticus, 331
Phibalura, 155
Phigys, 49
Philemon, 184
Philentoma, 216
Philepitta, 140
Philesturnus, 217
Philetairus, 292
Philodice, 73
Philohydor, 153
Philomachus, 106
Philortyx, 12
Philydor, 171
Phimosus, 131
Phlegopsis, 164-165
Phleocryptes, 170
Phlogophilus, 70
Phodilus, 76
Phoebetria, 138
Phoenicircus, 154
Phoenicopterus, 131
Phoeniculus, 35-36
Phoenicurus, 231
Pholidornis, 243
Phragmacia, 256
Phrygilus, 326
Phylidonyris, 185
Phyllanthus, 276
Phyllastrephus, 251-252
Phyllolais, 265
Phyllomyias, 142
Phylloscartes, 145-146
Phylloscopus, 266-268
Phytotoma, 155
Piaya, 47
Pica, 200
Picathartes, 217
Picoides, 24
Piculus, 24-25
Picumnus, 20-21
Picus, 26
Piezorhina, 327
Pilherodius, 129
Pinarocorys, 280
Pinaroloxias, 331
Pinarornis, 233
Pinguinus, 115
Pinicola, 306
Pionites, 58
Pionopsitta, 58
Pionus, 58
Pipile, 4
Pipilo, 311

Pipra, 157
Pipraeidea, 322
Pipreola, 155
Piprites, 158
Piranga, 320-321
Pitangus, 153
Pithecophaga, 122
Pithys, 164
Pitohui, 197
Pitta, 139
Pittasoma, 175
Pitylus, 332
Pityriasis, 204
Platalea, 132
Platycercus, 52
Platycichla, 221
Platylophus, 198
Platyrinchus, 146-147
Platysmurus, 198
Platysteira, 216
Plectorhyncha, 185
Plectrophenax, 309
Plectropterus, 15
Plegadis, 131
Plocepasser, 292
Ploceus, 293-295
Pluvialis, 108
Pluvianellus, 107
Pluvianus, 110
Pnoepyga, 273
Podager, 83
Podargus, 82
Podica, 98
Podiceps, 126
Podilymbus, 126
Podoces, 200
Poecilodryas, 190
Poecilotriccus, 141
Poeoptera, 234
Poephila, 299
Pogoniulus, 28-29
Pogonocichla, 228
Poicephalus, 53-54
Polemaetus, 123
Polihierax, 124
Poliocephalus, 126
Poliolais, 265
Polioptila, 242-243
Polioxolmis, 150
Polyboroides, 119
Polyborus, 124
Polyonymus, 72
Polyplectron, 10
Polysticta, 18
Polystictus, 145
Polytelis, 52
Polytmus, 68
Pomarea, 211

Pomatorhinus, 272
Pomatostomus, 191
Pooecetes, 310
Poospiza, 327-328
Popelairia, 66
Porphyrio, 102
Porphyrolaema, 156
Porphyrospiza, 333
Porzana, 101
Premnoplex, 170
Premnornis, 170
Prinia, 255-256
Prioniturus, 51-52
Prionochilus, 282
Prionodura, 179
Prionops, 215
Priotelus, 36
Probosciger, 50
Procellaria, 136
Procelsterna, 114
Procnias, 156
Prodotiscus, 20
Progne, 246
Promerops, 282
Prosobonia, 105
Prosopeia, 52
Prosthemadera, 186
Protonotaria, 314
Prunella, 292
Psalidoprocne, 248-249
Psaltria, 246
Psaltriparus, 246
Psarisomus, 140
Psarocolius, 333
Pselliophorus, 313
Psephotus, 52-53
Pseudalaemon, 281
Pseudelaenia, 143
Pseudeos, 49
Pseudibis, 132
Pseudobias, 215
Pseudocalyptomena, 140
Pseudochelidon, 246
Pseudocolaptes, 170
Pseudocolopteryx, 145
Pseudocossyphus, 218
Pseudodacnis, 325
Pseudoleistes, 335
Pseudonestor, 307
Pseudonigrita, 292
Pseudopodoces, 200
Pseudoscops, 81
Pseudoseisura, 170
Pseudotriccus, 141
Psilopogon, 27
Psilorhamphus, 177
Psilorhinus, 199
Psittacella, 51

Psittacula, 54-55
Psittaculirostris, 51
Psittacus, 53
Psitteuteles, 49
Psittinus, 51
Psittirostra, 306
Psittrichas, 52
Psophia, 98
Psophocichla, 221
Psophodes, 195
Pteridophora, 203
Pterocles, 103
Pterodroma, 135-136
Pteroglossus, 30-31
Pteronetta, 15
Pterophanes, 71
Pteroptochos, 177
Pteruthius, 275
Ptilinopus, 93-94
Ptilocichla, 272
Ptilogonys, 217
Ptilonorhynchus, 179
Ptilopachus, 9
Ptiloprora, 184
Ptiloris, 202
Ptilorrhoa, 195
Ptilostomus, 200
Ptychoramphus, 115
Ptyrticus, 272
Pucrasia, 9
Puffinus, 136-137
Pulsatrix, 79
Purpureicephalus, 52
Pycnonotus, 249-250
Pycnoptilus, 187
Pycnopygius, 184
Pygarrhichas, 172
Pygiptila, 160
Pygoscelis, 134
Pyrenestes, 297
Pyriglena, 163
Pyrocephalus, 149
Pyroderus, 156
Pyrrhocoma, 319
Pyrrhocorax, 200
Pyrrholaemus, 187
Pyrrhomyias, 147
Pyrrhoplectes, 306
Pyrrhula, 306
Pyrrhura, 56-57
Pytilia, 297

Quelea, 295
Querula, 156
Quiscalus, 336

Rallina, 99
Rallus, 100

Ramphastos, 31-32
Ramphocaenus, 242
Ramphocelus, 321
Ramphocinclus, 238
Ramphocoris, 281
Ramphodon, 64
Ramphomicron, 72
Ramphotrigon, 152
Ramsayornis, 185
Randia, 265
Raphus, 86
Recurvirostra, 108
Regulus, 249
Reinwardtipicus, 27
Reinwardtoena, 88-89
Remiz, 243
Rhabdornis, 278
Rhagologus, 196
Rhamphomantis, 44
Rhaphidura, 61
Rhea, 2
Rhegmatorhina, 164
Rheinardia, 10
Rhinocrypta, 177
Rhinomyias, 225
Rhinopomastus, 36
Rhinoptilus, 110-111
Rhipidura, 208-209
Rhizothera, 8
Rhodacanthis, 306
Rhodinocichla, 319
Rhodonessa, 18
Rhodopechys, 305
Rhodophoneus, 215
Rhodopis, 73
Rhodospingus, 326
Rhodostethia, 113
Rhodothraupis, 332
Rhopocichla, 274
Rhopophilus, 255
Rhopornis, 163
Rhyacornis, 231
Rhynchocyclus, 146
Rhynchopsitta, 56
Rhynchortyx, 13
Rhynchostruthus, 303
Rhynchotus, 2
Rhynocchos, 98
Rhytipterna, 151
Rimator, 272
Riparia, 247
Rissa, 113
Rollandia, 126
Rollulus, 9
Roraimia, 170
Rostratula, 106
Rostrhamus, 116
Rougetius, 100

Rowettia, 327
Rukia, 260
Rupicola, 156
Rynchops, 111

Sagittarius, 124
Sakesphorus, 159
Salpinctes, 240
Salpornis, 239
Saltator, 332
Saltatricula, 326
Salvadorina, 16
Sapayoa, 140
Sapheopipo, 27
Sappho, 72
Sarcogyps, 117
Sarcops, 237
Sarcoramphus, 133
Sarkidiornis, 15
Saroglossa, 236
Sarothrura, 98
Sasia, 21
Satrapa, 151
Saurothera, 47
Saxicola, 232
Saxicoloides, 231
Sayornis, 149
Scaphidura, 336
Sceloglaux, 81
Scelorchilus, 177
Scepomycter, 262
Schetba, 217
Schiffornis, 154
Schistochlamys, 318
Schizoeaca, 166-167
Schoenicola, 269
Schoeniophylax, 167
Schoutedenapus, 61
Scissirostrum, 237
Sclateria, 163
Sclerurus, 172
Scolopax, 104
Scopus, 131
Scotocerca, 255
Scotopelia, 78
Scytalopus, 177-178
Scythrops, 45
Seicercus, 268
Seiurus, 314-315
Selasphorus, 74
Selenidera, 31
Seleucidis, 203
Semioptera, 202
Semnornis, 30
Sephanoides, 71
Sericornis, 187
Sericossypha, 318
Sericulus, 179

Serilophus, 140
Serinus, 302-303
Serpophaga, 144
Setophaga, 314
Setornis, 253
Sheppardia, 228-229
Sialia, 220
Sicalis, 328
Sigelus, 225
Silvicultrix, 149
Simoxenops, 171
Siphonorhis, 84
Sipodotus, 179
Siptornis, 170
Siptornopsis, 169
Sirystes, 152
Sitta, 238-239
Sittasomus, 173
Skutchia, 165
Smicrornis, 188
Smithornis, 140
Somateria, 18
Spartanoica, 170
Speculipastor, 235
Speirops, 258
Spelaeornis, 273
Speotyto, 80
Spermophaga, 297
Sphecotheres, 205
Spheniscus, 134
Sphenocichla, 273
Sphenoeacus, 263
Sphyrapicus, 22
Spiloptila, 256
Spilornis, 118
Spindalis, 321
Spiza, 331
Spizaetus, 123-124
Spizastur, 123
Spizella, 310
Spiziapteryx, 124
Spizixos, 249
Spizocorys, 281
Sporophila, 328-329
Sporopipes, 292
Spreo, 235
Stachyris, 273-274
Stactolaema, 28
Stagonopleura, 299
Starnoenas, 91
Steatornis, 82
Steganopus, 106
Stelgidopteryx, 247
Stellula, 74
Stenostira, 265
Stephanoaetus, 124
Stephanophorus, 322
Stephanoxis, 65

Stercorarius, 111
Sterna, 113-114
Sternoclyta, 70
Stictonetta, 14
Stigmatura, 145
Stiltia, 111
Stiphrornis, 228
Stipiturus, 180
Strepera, 205
Streptocitta, 237
Streptopelia, 88
Streptoprocne, 60
Stresemannia, 182
Strigops, 53
Strix, 79
Struthidea, 195
Struthio, 1
Sturnella, 335
Sturnus, 236
Sublegatus, 143
Suiriri, 143
Sula, 127
Surnia, 79
Surniculus, 45
Swynnertonia, 228
Sylvia, 278-279
Sylvietta, 266
Sylviorthorhynchus, 166
Sylviparus, 245
Syma, 41
Synallaxis, 167-168
Syndactyla, 171
Synthliboramphus, 115
Syrigma, 128
Syrmaticus, 10
Syrrhaptes, 103

Tachornis, 62
Tachuris, 145
Tachybaptus, 126
Tachycineta, 246
Tachyeres, 15
Tachymarptis, 62
Tachyphonus, 320
Tadorna, 15
Taeniopygia, 299
Taeniotriccus, 141
Talegalla, 5
Tangara, 323-325
Tanygnathus, 52
Tanysiptera, 41-42
Taoniscus, 3
Tapera, 48
Taphrolesbia, 73
Taphrospilus, 68
Taraba, 159
Tarsiger, 229
Tauraco, 74-75

Tchagra, 214
Telacanthura, 61
Teledromas, 177
Telespiza, 306
Telophorus, 215
Temnurus, 200
Tephrodornis, 216
Tephrozosterops, 260
Terathopius, 118
Terenura, 162
Teretistris, 315
Terpsiphone, 210-211
Tersina, 326
Tesia, 261
Tetrao, 11
Tetraogallus, 6
Tetraophasis, 6
Tetrax, 96
Thalassoica, 135
Thalassornis, 13
Thalurania, 67
Thamnistes, 160
Thamnolaea, 233
Thamnomanes, 160
Thamnophilus, 159-160
Thamnornis, 263
Thaumastura, 73
Theristicus, 131
Thescelocichla, 251
Thinocorus, 103
Thinornis, 109
Thlypopsis, 319
Thraupis, 321
Threnetes, 63
Threskiornis, 132
Thripadectes, 171
Thripophaga, 169
Thryomanes, 240
Thryorchilus, 242
Thryothorus, 240-241
Tiaris, 330
Tichodroma, 239
Tickellia, 268
Tigriornis, 130
Tigrisoma, 130
Tijuca, 155
Tilmatura, 73
Timalia, 274
Timeliopsis, 182
Tinamotis, 3
Tinamus, 1
Tityra, 154
Tmetothylacus, 290
Tockus, 33-34
Todirhamphus, 41
Todirostrum, 142
Todus, 39
Tolmomyias, 146

Topaza, 70
Torgos, 117
Torreornis, 311
Touit, 58
Toxorhamphus, 288
Toxostoma, 238
Trachyphonus, 29-30
Tragopan, 9
Tregellasia, 190
Treron, 92-93
Trichastoma, 271
Trichixos, 231
Trichocichla, 269
Trichodere, 182
Trichoglossus, 49
Tricholaema, 29
Tricholestes, 253
Trichothraupis, 320
Triclaria, 59
Trigonoceps, 117
Tringa, 105
Trochilus, 67
Trochocercus, 210
Troglodytes, 241-242
Trogon, 36-37
Trugon, 92
Tryngites, 106
Turacoena, 89
Turdoides, 274-275
Turdus, 221-224
Turnagra, 197
Turnix, 19
Turtur, 89
Tylas, 217
Tympanuchus, 11
Tyranneutes, 158
Tyrannopsis, 153
Tyrannulus, 143
Tyrannus, 152-153
Tyto, 75-76

Upucerthia, 165
Upupa, 35
Uraeginthus, 298
Uragus, 305
Uratelornis, 38
Uria, 115
Urochroa, 70
Urocissa, 199
Urocolius, 43
Urocynchramus, 307
Uroglaux, 81
Urolais, 256
Uromyias, 145
Uropelia, 90
Uropsalis, 86
Uropsila, 242
Urosphena, 261
Urosticte, 72

Urothraupis, 326
Urotriorchis, 121

Vanellus, 109-110
Vanga, 217
Veniliornis, 24
Vermivora, 313
Vestiaria, 307
Vidua, 301
Vini, 49
Vireo, 193-194
Vireolanius, 193
Viridonia, 307
Volatinia, 328
Vultur, 133

Wetmorethraupis, 322
Wilsonia, 315
Woodfordia, 261

Xanthocephalus, 335
Xanthomyza, 186
Xanthotis, 183
Xema, 113
Xenerpestes, 170
Xenicus, 138
Xenocopsychus, 230
Xenodacnis, 326
Xenoglaux, 80
Xenoligea, 317
Xenopipo, 158
Xenopirostris, 217
Xenops, 172
Xenopsaris, 154
Xenornis, 160
Xenospingus, 327
Xenospiza, 310
Xenotriccus, 148
Xiphidiopicus, 22
Xiphirhynchus, 272
Xiphocolaptes, 173
Xipholena, 156
Xiphorhynchus, 173-174
Xolmis, 149-150

Yuhina, 277

Zaratornis, 155
Zavattariornis, 200
Zebrilus, 130
Zeledonia, 317
Zenaida, 89-90
Zimmerius, 143
Zonerodius, 130
Zonotrichia, 309
Zoonavena, 61
Zoothera, 219-220
Zosterops, 258-260

Accentor, 292; Alpine, 292; Black-throated, 292; Brown, 292; Hedge, 292; Japanese, 292; Maroon-backed, 292; Mongolian, 292; Radde's, 292; Robin, 292; Rufous-breasted, 292; Rufous-streaked, 292; Siberian, 292; Yemen, 292

Adjutant, 133; Greater, 133; Lesser, 133

Akalat, 228-229; Alexander's, 228; Bocage's, 228; East Coast, 229; Equatorial, 228; Gabela, 229; Iringa, 229; Lowland, 228; Malawi, 229; Sharpe's, 228; Usambara, 229

Akekee, 307

Akepa, 307; Hawaii, 307; Maui, 307; Oahu, 307

Akialoa, 307; Greater, 307; Lesser, 307

Akiapolaau, 307

Akohekohe, 307

Albatross, 137-138; Amsterdam Island, 137; Black-browed, 137; Black-footed, 137; Buller's, 138; Chatham Islands, 137; Grey-backed, 137; Grey-headed, 137; Laysan, 137; Light-mantled, 138; Royal, 137; Short-tailed, 137; Shy, 137; Sooty, 138; Wandering, 137; Waved, 137; Yellow-nosed, 138

Alethe, 224-225; Brown-chested, 224; Cholo, 224; Fire-crested, 225; Red-throated, 224; White-chested, 224; White-tailed, 225

Alseonax, 226; Ashy, 226; Cassin's, 226; Chapin's, 226; Dusky, 226; Itombwe, 226; Little Grey, 226; Olivaceous, 226; Swamp, 226; Yellow-footed, 226

Amakihi, 307; Common, 307; Greater, 307; Kauai, 307

Amaui, 220

Andean-Tyrant, 150; Black, 150; Plumbeous, 150

Anhinga, 127

Anianiau, 307

Antbird, 161, 162-164, 165; Ash-breasted, 163; Bananal, 162; Banded, 161; Band-tailed, 163; Bare-crowned, 163; Bertoni's, 162; Bicolored, 164; Black, 163; Black-and-white, 163; Black-chinned, 163; Black-faced, 163; Black-headed, 163; Blackish, 162; Black-tailed, 163; Black-throated, 164; Buff-banded, 164; Caura, 163; Chestnut-backed, 163; Chestnut-crested, 164; Chestnut-tailed, 164; Dot-backed, 164; Dull-mantled, 164; Dusky, 162; Dusky-tailed, 162; Esmeraldas, 164; Ferruginous, 162; Ferruginous-backed, 163; Goeldi's, 164; Grey, 162; Grey-bellied, 164; Grey-headed, 164; Hairy-crested, 164; Harlequin, 164; Immaculate, 164; Jet, 163; Long-tailed, 162; Lunulated, 164; Manu, 163; Mato Grosso, 163; Ocellated, 165; Ochre-rumped, 162; Plain-backed, 164; Plumbeous, 164; Rio Branco, 163; Rio de Janeiro, 162; Rufous-tailed, 162; Rufous-throated, 164; Santarem,

164; Scale-backed, 164; Scaled, 162; Scalloped, 163; Sclater's, 162; Silvered, 163; Slate-colored, 163; Slender, 163; Sooty, 164; Spot-backed, 164; Spotted, 164; Spot-winged, 163; Squamate, 164; Striated, 162; Stripe-backed, 161; Stub-tailed, 163; Sulphur-breasted, 163; Warbling, 163; White-bellied, 163; White-bibbed, 163; White-breasted, 164; White-browed, 163; White-cheeked, 164; White-lined, 163; White-masked, 164; White-plumed, 164; White-shouldered, 164; White-throated, 164; Wing-banded, 164; Wing-spotted, 163; Yapacana, 164; Yellow-browed, 163; Yellow-tipped, 163

Anteater-Chat, 233; Northern, 233; Southern, 233

Antpecker, 296; Jameson's, 296; Red-fronted, 296; White-breasted, 296; Woodhouse's, 296

Antpipit, 142; Ringed, 142; Southern, 142

Antpitta, 175-176; Amazonian, 176; Bay, 176; Bicolored, 175; Black-crowned, 175; Brown-banded, 176; Brown-breasted, 176; Chestnut, 176; Chestnut-crowned, 175; Chestnut-naped, 175; Crescent-faced, 176; Cundimarca, 175; Elusive, 175; Flammulated, 176; Fulvous-bellied, 176; Giant, 175; Great, 175; Grey-naped, 176; Hooded, 176; Leymebamba, 176; Moustached, 175; Ochre-breasted, 176; Ochre-fronted, 176; Ochre-striped, 175; Pale-billed, 175; Peruvian, 176; Pichincha, 175; Plain-backed, 175; Puno, 175; Red-and-white, 176; Rufous, 176; Rufous-breasted, 176; Rufous-crowned, 175; Rufous-faced, 176; Russet-capped, 175; Rusty-breasted, 176; Rusty-tinged, 176; Santa Marta, 175; Scaled, 175; Scallop-breasted, 176; Scrub, 175; Slate-crowned, 176; Speckle-breasted, 176; Spectacled, 176; Spotted, 176; Stripe-headed, 175; Tachira, 175; Tawny, 176; Thrush-like, 176; Undulated, 175; Variegated, 175; White-bellied, 175; White-browed, 176; White-lored, 176; White-throated, 175; Yellow-breasted, 175

Antshrike, 158-160; Amazonian, 159; Bamboo, 158; Band-tailed, 159; Bar-bellied, 159; Bar-crested, 159; Barred, 159; Black, 159; Black-backed, 159; Black-crested, 159; Black-hooded, 159; Blackish-grey, 159; Black-throated, 158; Bluish-slate, 160; Bolivian, 159; Castelnau's, 159; Chapman's, 159; Chestnut-backed, 159; Cinereous, 160; Cocha, 159; Collared, 159; Dusky-thorated, 160; Fasciated, 158; Giant, 158; Glossy, 159; Great, 159; Grey-capped, 159; Large-tailed, 158; Lined, 159; Marcapata, 160;

Mountain, 159; Mouse-colored, 159; Pearly, 160; Peruvian, 160; Plain-winged, 159; Rufous-capped, 160; Rufous-winged, 159; Russet, 160; Saturnine, 160; Silvery-cheeked, 159; Slaty, 159; Speckled, 160; Spot-backed, 158; Spot-winged, 160; Streak-backed, 159; Tawny-bellied, 159; Tufted, 158; Undulated, 158; Uniform, 159; Upland, 159; Variable, 159; White-bearded, 159; White-shouldered, 159

Ant-Tanager, 320; Black-cheeked, 320; Crested, 320; Red-crowned, 320; Red-throated, 320; Salvin's, 320; Sooty, 320

Antthrush, 174-175; Barred, 175; Black-faced, 174; Black-headed, 174; Hoffmann's, 174; Mexican, 174; Northern Short-tailed, 175; Rufous-breasted, 174; Rufous-capped, 174; Rufous-fronted, 174; Rufous-tailed, 175; Schwartz's, 175; Short-tailed, 175; Southern Short-tailed, 175; Striated, 175; Such's, 175

Ant-Thrush, 218; Red-tailed, 218; White-tailed, 218

Antvireo, 160; Bicolored, 160; Plain, 160; Plumbeous, 160; Rufous-backed, 160; Spot-breasted, 160; Spot-crowned, 160; Streak-crowned, 160; White-spotted, 160

Antwren, 160-162; Alagoas, 162; Ash-throated, 161; Ash-winged, 162; Ashy, 161; Bahia, 161; Band-tailed, 161; Black-bellied, 162; Black-capped, 161; Black-hooded, 162; Black-throated, 161; Boucard's, 162; Brown-bellied, 161; Checker-throated, 161; Cherrie's, 160; Chestnut-saddled, 161; Chestnut-shouldered, 162; Creamy-bellied, 161; Dot-winged, 162; Dugand's, 161; Foothill, 161; Garbe's, 161; Grey, 161; Griscom's, 160; Ihering's, 161; Klages's, 160; Large-billed, 162; Leaden, 161; Long-winged, 161; Lower Amazonian, 162; Narrow-billed, 162; Ornate, 161; Pectoral, 162; Perija, 162; Plain-throated, 160; Plain-winged, 161; Pygmy, 160; Rio de Janeiro, 161; Rio Suno, 161; Roraiman, 161; Rufous-bellied, 160; Rufous-rumped, 162; Rufous-tailed, 161; Rufous-winged, 162; Rusty-backed, 162; Salvadori's, 161; Sclater's, 160; Serra, 162; Short-billed, 160; Slaty, 161; Spot-backed, 161; Spot-tailed, 161; Star-throated, 161; Stipple-throated, 161; Streak-capped, 162; Streaked, 160; Stripe-chested, 160; Todd's, 161; Unicolored, 161; Upper Amazonian, 162; White-eyed, 161; White-flanked, 161; White-fringed, 162; Yellow-breasted, 162; Yellow-rumped, 162; Yellow-throated, 160

Apalis, 256-257; Bamenda, 257; Bar-throated, 256; Black-backed, 257; Black-capped, 256; Black-collared, 256; Black-faced, 256; Black-headed, 257; Black-throated, 256; Brown-headed, 257; Brown-tailed, 257; Buff-throated, 257; Chapin's, 257; Chestnut-throated, 257; Chirinda, 257; Collared, 256; Gosling's, 257; Grey, 257; Grey-headed, 256; Kabobo, 257; Karamoja, 257; Kungwe, 257; Masked, 256; Mouse, 256; Namuli, 256; Peters's, 257; Red-faced, 257; Rudd's, 257; Sharpe's, 257; Straus's, 257; Teita, 256; White-winged, 256; Yellow-breasted, 257; Yellow-throated, 256

Apapane, 307

Apostlebird, 195

Aracari, 30-31; Azara, 31; Black-necked, 31; Brown-mandibled, 31; Chestnut-eared, 31; Collared, 31; Curl-crested, 31; Fiery-billed, 31; Green, 30; Ivory-billed, 31; Lettered, 30; Many-banded, 31; Pale-mandibled, 31; Red-necked, 30; Stripe-billed, 31

Argus, 10-11; Crested, 10; Great, 11; Ocellated, 10

Asity, 140; Schlegel's, 140; Sunbird, 140; Velvet, 140; Yellow-bellied, 140

Astrapia, 203; Arfak, 203; Huon, 203; Ribbon-tailed, 203; Splendid, 203; Stephanie's, 203

Attila, 151; Bright-rumped, 151; Cinnamon, 151; Citron-bellied, 151; Dull-capped, 151; Grey-hooded, 151; Ochraceous, 151; Rufous-tailed, 151

Auk, 115; Great, 115

Auklet, 115; Cassin's, 115; Crested, 115; Least, 115; Parakeet, 115; Rhinoceros, 115; Whiskered, 115

Avadavat, 298; Green, 298; Red, 298

Avocet, 108; American, 108; Andean, 108; Pied, 108; Red-necked, 108

Avocetbill, 73; Mountain, 73

Awlbill, 65; Fiery-tailed, 65

Babbler, 191, 271, 272, 273, 274-275, 276, 277; Abbott's, 271; Angola, 275; Arabian, 275; Arrow-marked, 275; Ashy-headed, 271; Bagobo, 271; Bare-cheeked, 275; Black-browed, 271; Blackcap, 275; Black-capped, 271; Black-chinned, 273; Black-crowned, 273; Black-lored, 275; Black-throated, 274; Brown, 275; Brown-capped, 271; Buff-breasted, 271; Buff-chested, 273; Capuchin, 276; Chestnut-capped, 274; Chestnut-crowned, 191; Chestnut-faced, 273; Chestnut-rumped, 274; Chestnut-winged, 274; Common, 274; Crescent-chested, 274; Cretschmar's, 275; Crossley's, 277; Dark-fronted, 274; Deccan, 275; Deignan's, 273; Dusky, 275; Ferruginous, 271; Flame-templed, 273; Golden, 273; Golden-crowned, 273; Grey-breasted, 271; Grey-crowned, 191; Grey-headed, 274; Grey-

throated, 274; Hall's, 191; Horsfield's, 271;
Iraq, 274; Jerdon's, 274; Jungle, 275; Large
Grey, 274; Marsh, 271; Melodius, 271;
Moustached, 271; New Guinea, 191;
Ochraceous-throated, 271; Orange-billed,
275; Puff-throated, 271; Pygmy, 273; Red-
breasted, 191; Rufous, 275; Rufous-bellied,
274; Rufous-capped, 273; Rufous-crowned,
271; Rufous-fronted, 273; Rufous-tailed,
274; Rusty-crowned, 273; Scaly, 275; Scaly-
crowned, 271; Short-tailed, 271; Slender-
billed, 274; Snowy-throated, 274; Sooty,
274; Sooty-capped, 271; Spiny, 274; Spot-
necked, 274; Spot-throated, 271; Striated,
274; Sulawesi, 271; Tawny-bellied, 274;
Temminck's, 271; Thrush, 272; Vanderbilt's,
271; White-bibbed, 274; White-breasted,
274; White-browed, 191; White-chested,
271; White-hooded, 276; White-necked,
274; White-rumped, 275; White-throated,
274; Yellow-billed, 275; Yellow-eyed, 274
Balicassiao, 210
Bamboo-Partridge, 9; Chinese, 9; Mountain, 9
Bamboo-Tyrant, 141; Brown-breasted, 141;
Drab-breasted, 141; Flammulated, 141
Bamboowren, 177; Spotted, 177
Bananaquit, 317; Bahama, 317; Common, 317
Barbet, 27-28, 29-30; Anchieta's, 28; Banded, 29;
Bearded, 29; Black-backed, 29; Black-
banded, 27; Black-billed, 29; Black-
breasted, 29; Black-browed, 28; Black-
collared, 29; Black-girdled, 30; Black-
spotted, 30; Black-throated, 29; Blue-eared,
28; Blue-throated, 28; Bornean, 28; Bristle-
nosed, 28; Brown, 28; Brown-breasted, 29;
Brown-chested, 30; Brown-headed, 27;
Brown-throated, 27; Chaplin's, 29;
Coppersmith, 28; Crested, 29; Crimson-
fronted, 28; Crimson-throated, 28;
D'Arnaud's, 30; Double-toothed, 29; Fire-
tufted, 27; Five-colored, 30; Flame-fronted,
28; Gilded, 30; Gold-whiskered, 27;
Golden-naped, 28; Golden-throated, 28;
Great, 27; Green, 28; Green-eared, 27;
Grey-throated, 28; Hainan, 28; Hairy-
breasted, 29; Lemon-throated, 30; Lineated,
27; MacClounie's, 29; Miombo, 29;
Mountain, 28; Moustached, 28; Naked-
faced, 28; Orange-fronted, 30; Pied, 29;
Prong-billed, 30; Red-and-yellow, 30; Red-
crowned, 27; Red-faced, 29; Red-fronted,
29; Red-headed, 30; Red-throated, 27; Red-
vented, 27; Scarlet-crowned, 30; Scarlet-
hooded, 30; Sladen's, 28; Sowerby's, 28;
Spot-crowned, 30; Spot-flanked, 29; Spot-
headed, 29; Taiwan, 28; Toucan, 30;
Usambiro, 30; Versicolored, 30; Vieillot's,
29; White, 29; White-bellied, 29; White-

cheeked, 27; White-eared, 28; White-
headed, 29; White-mantled, 30; White-
tailed, 29; Whyte's, 28; Woodward's, 28;
Yellow-billed, 29; Yellow-breasted, 29;
Yellow-cheeked, 29; Yellow-crowned, 28;
Yellow-fronted, 28; Yellow-spotted, 29
Barbtail, 170; Paria, 170; Roraiman, 170; Rusty-
winged, 170; Spotted, 170; White-throated,
170
Barbthroat, 63; Band-tailed, 63; Bronze-tailed,
63; Pale-tailed, 63; Sooty, 63
Bare-eye, 164-165; Argus, 164; Black-spotted,
164; Pale-faced, 165; Reddish-winged, 165
Barred-Woodcreeper, 173; Northern, 173;
Southern, 173
Barwing, 276; Formosan, 276; Hoary-throated,
276; Rusty-fronted, 276; Spectacled, 276;
Streaked, 276; Streak-throated, 276
Bateleur, 118
Batis, 215-216; Angola, 216; Black-headed, 216;
Boulton's, 215; Cape, 216; Chinspot, 216;
Fernando Po, 216; Grey-headed, 216; Ituri,
216; Malawi, 216; Pale, 216; Pririt, 216;
Pygmy, 216; Reichenow's, 216; Ruwenzori,
215; Senegal, 216; Short-tailed, 216;
Sokoke, 216; Verreaux's, 216; West African,
216; Zululand, 216
Bay-Owl, 76; Congo, 76; Oriental, 76
Baza, 115-116; African, 115; Black, 116;
Jerdon's, 116; Madagascar, 116; Pacific, 116
Bean-Goose, 14; Forest, 14; Tundra, 14
Beardless-Tyrannulet, 143; Northern, 143;
Southern, 143
Becard, 154; Barred, 154; Black-and-white, 154;
Black-capped, 154; Chestnut-crowned, 154;
Cinereous, 154; Cinnamon, 154; Crested,
154; Glossy-backed, 154; Green-backed,
154; Grey-collared, 154; Jamaican, 154;
One-colored, 154; Pink-throated, 154; Rose-
throated, 154; Slaty, 154; White-winged,
154; Yellow-cheeked, 154
Bee-eater, 42-43; Black, 42; Black-headed, 43;
Blue-bearded, 42; Blue-breasted, 42; Blue-
cheeked, 43; Blue-headed, 42; Blue-tailed,
43; Blue-throated, 43; Boehm's, 43;
Chestnut-headed, 43; Cinnamon-chested,
42; Ethiopian, 42; European, 43; Little, 42;
Little Green, 43; Madagascar, 43; Northern
Carmine, 43; Purple-bearded, 42; Rainbow,
43; Red-bearded, 42; Red-throated, 42;
Rosy, 43; Somali, 43; Southern Carmine,
43; Swallow-tailed, 42; White-fronted, 42;
White-throated, 43
Bellbird, 156, 186, 196; Bare-throated, 156;
Bearded, 156; Crested, 196; New Zealand,
186; Three-wattled, 156; White, 156
Bentbill, 146; Northern, 146; Southern, 146
Berryeater, 155; Black-headed, 155; Hooded, 155

Berrypecker, 288; Black, 288; Crested, 288; Fan-
tailed, 288; Lemon-breasted, 288; Obscure,
288; Olivaceous, 288; Spotted, 288;
Streaked, 288; Tit, 288
Besra, 120
Bird-of-paradise, 202-203; Blue, 203; Crested,
202; Emperor, 203; Goldie's, 203; Greater,
203; King, 203; King-of-Saxony, 203;
Lesser, 203; Loria's, 202; Macgregor's, 202;
Magnificent, 202; Raggiana, 203; Red, 203;
Superb, 202; Twelve-wired, 203; Wilson's,
202; Yellow-breasted, 202
Bishop, 295-296; Black, 296; Black-winged, 296;
Fire-fronted, 295; Golden-backed, 296;
Orange, 296; Red, 296; Taha, 295; Yellow,
296; Yellow-crowned, 295; Zanzibar, 296
Bittern, 130-131; African, 131; American, 130;
Australasian, 131; Black, 130; Black-
backed, 130; Cinnamon, 130; Dwarf, 130;
Eurasian, 131; Forest, 130; Great, 131;
Least, 130; Little, 130; Pinnated, 131;
Schrenck's, 130; Stripe-backed, 130; White-
crested, 130; Yellow, 130
Blackbird, 222, 335, 336; Austral, 335; Bolivian,
335; Brewer's, 336; Chestnut-capped, 335;
Chopi, 335; Cuban, 336; Eurasian, 222;
Forbes's, 335; Goodenough, 222; Grey-
winged, 222; Jamaican, 335; Melodious,
336; New Guinea, 222; Nilgiri, 222; Oriole,
335; Pale-eyed, 335; Peruvian, 336; Red-
breasted, 335; Red-winged, 335; Rusty, 336;
Saffron-cowled, 335; Scarlet-headed, 335;
Scrub, 336; Tawny-shouldered, 335;
Tricolored, 335; Unicolored, 335; Vinous-
tinted, 222; White-browed, 335; White-
collared, 222; Yellow-headed, 335; Yellow-
hooded, 335; Yellow-shouldered, 335;
Yellow-winged, 335
Black-Bishop, 296; Angola, 296; Northern, 296;
Southern, 296
Blackcap, 278
Black-Chat, 233; White-fronted, 233; White-
headed, 233
Black-Cockatoo, 50; Glossy, 50; Red-tailed, 50;
Slender-billed, 50; White-tailed, 50; Yellow-
tailed, 50; Yellow-tinted, 50
Blackeye, 261; Mountain, 261
Black-Flycatcher, 225; Northern, 225; Southern,
225; West African, 225; Yellow-eyed, 225
Black-Hawk, 121; Common, 121; Cuban, 121;
Great, 121; Mangrove, 121
Blackstart, 233
Black-Tyrant, 150, 151; Amazonian, 150; Blue-
billed, 151; Crested, 151; Hudson's, 150;
Rufous-tailed, 151; Velvety, 151; White-
winged, 151
Bleeding-heart, 91; Luzon, 91; Mindanao, 91;
Mindoro, 91; Negros, 91; Sulu, 91

Blossomcrown, 70
Bluebill, 297; Grant's, 297; Western, 297; Red-
headed, 297; Usambara, 297
Bluebird, 220; Eastern, 220; Mountain, 220;
Western, 220
Bluebonnet, 52; Common, 52; Little, 52
Blue-Flycatcher, 210, 228; African, 210;
Bornean, 228; Hainan, 228; Hill, 228;
Large-billed, 228; Malaysian, 228;
Mangrove, 228; Palawan, 228; Pale, 228;
Pygmy, 228; Rueck's, 228; Sulawesi, 228;
Tanahjampea, 228; Tickell's, 228; Timor,
228; White-bellied, 228; White-tailed, 210
Blue-Pigeon, 94; Comoro, 94; Madagascar, 94;
Mauritius, 94; Seychelles, 94
Blue-Tit, 245; African, 245; Eurasian, 245
Bluethroat, 229
Boatbill, 213; Black-breasted, 213; Yellow-
breasted, 213
Boat-billed Heron, 130; Northern, 130; Southern,
130
Bobolink, 336
Bobwhite, 12; Black-throated, 12; Crested, 12;
Northern, 12; Spot-bellied, 12
Bokikokiko, 264
Bonelli's-Warbler, 267; Eastern, 267; Western,
267
Boobook, 80; Australian, 80; Lord Howe Island,
80; Norfolk Island, 80; Northern, 80; Red,
80; Southern, 80; Spotted, 80; Sumba, 80
Booby, 127; Abbott's, 127; Blue-footed, 127;
Brown, 127; Masked, 127; Peruvian, 127;
Red-footed, 127
Boubou, 214; Bulo Burti, 214; Fuelleborn's, 214;
Gabon, 214; Mountain, 214; Slate-colored,
214; Sooty, 214; Southern, 214; Tropical,
214; Turati's, 214; Yellow-breasted, 214
Bowerbird, 179; Archbold's, 179; Fawn-breasted,
179; Fire-maned, 179; Flame, 179; Golden,
179; Golden-fronted, 179; Great, 179;
Macgregor's, 179; Regent, 179; Sanford's,
179; Satin, 179; Spotted, 179; Streaked, 179;
Uniform, 179; Vogelkop, 179; Western,
179; Yellow-breasted, 179
Bracken-Warbler, 262; Cinnamon, 262
Brambling, 302
Brant, 15; Black, 15; White-bellied, 15
Brilliant, 70; Black-throated, 70; Empress, 70;
Fawn-breasted, 70; Green-crowned, 70;
Pink-throated, 70; Rufous-webbed, 70;
Velvet-browed, 70; Violet-fronted, 70
Bristlebill, 252; Common, 252; Green-tailed,
252; Grey-headed, 252
Bristlebird, 187; Eastern, 187; Rufous, 187;
Western, 187
Bristlefront, 177; Slaty, 177; Stresemann's, 177
Bristlehead, 204; Bornean, 204

Bristle-Tyrant, 145; Antioquia, 145; Marble-faced, 145; Southern, 145; Spectacled, 145; Variegated, 145; Venezuelan, 145

Broadbill, 140; African, 140; Banded, 140; Black-and-red, 140; Black-and-yellow, 140; Dusky, 140; Grauer's, 140; Green, 140; Grey-headed, 140; Hodgson's, 140; Hose's, 140; Long-tailed, 140; Rufous-sided, 140; Silver-breasted, 140; Wattled, 140; Whitehead's, 140

Brolga, 97

Bronze-Cuckoo, 44-45; Golden, 45; Gould's, 45; Green-cheeked, 45; Horsfield's, 45; Little, 44; Pied, 45; Rufous-throated, 45; Shining, 45; White-eared, 45

Bronzewing, 89; Brush, 89; Common, 89; Flock, 89; New Britain, 89; New Guinea, 89

Brownbul, 251; Northern, 251; Terrestrial, 251

Brown-Dove, 92; Amethyst, 92; Dark-eared, 92; White-eared, 92

Brubru, 213; Angola, 213; Black-browed, 213; Northern, 213; Southern, 213

Brush-Finch, 312-313; Bay-crowned, 312; Black-headed, 312; Black-spectacled, 312; Celica, 312; Chestnut-capped, 312; Dusky-headed, 312; Fulvous-headed, 312; Green-striped, 312; Grey-striped, 313; Moustached, 312; Ochre-breasted, 312; Olive-headed, 312; Pale-headed, 312; Pale-naped, 312; Paynter's, 312; Plain-breasted, 312; Rufous-capped, 312; Rufous-eared, 312; Rufous-naped, 312; Rusty-bellied, 312; Santa Marta, 312; Simons's, 312; Slaty, 312; Stripe-headed, 313; Taczanowski's, 312; Tepui, 312; Tricolored, 312; White-cheeked, 312; White-headed, 312; White-naped, 312; White-rimmed, 312; White-winged, 312; Yellow-striped, 312; Yellow-throated, 312

Brushrunner, 170; Lark-like, 170

Brush-turkey, 5; Australian, 5; Black-billed, 5; Brown-collared, 5; Bruijn's, 5; Red-billed, 5; Wattled, 5

Brush-Warbler, 263, 264; Aldabra, 263; Anjouan, 263; Madagascar, 263; Grand Comoro, 263; Moheli, 263; Rodriguez, 264; Seychelles, 264

Budgerigar, 53

Buffalo-Weaver, 292; Northern Red-billed, 292; Red-billed, 292; Southern Red-billed, 292; White-billed, 292; White-headed, 292

Bufflehead, 19

Bulbul, 249-250, 252-253; Ashy, 253; Bearded, 252; Black, 253; Black-and-white, 249; Black-collared, 253; Black-crested, 249; Black-crested Yellow, 249; Black-fronted, 250; Black-headed, 249; Black-headed Yellow, 249; Blue-wattled, 250; Brown-breasted, 250; Brown-eared, 253; Buff-vented, 253; Cape, 250; Chestnut, 253; Comoro, 253; Cream-striped, 249; Cream-vented, 250; Dark-capped, 250; Dodson's, 250; Egyptian, 250; Finsch's, 252; Flavescent, 250; Garden, 250; Golden, 253; Green-backed, 252; Grey-bellied, 250; Grey-cheeked, 253; Grey-eyed, 253; Grey-headed, 249; Hairy-backed, 253; Himalayan, 250; Hook-billed, 253; Light-vented, 250; Madagascar, 253; Mauritius, 253; Mountain, 253; Nicobar, 253; Ochraceous, 252; Olivaceous, 253; Olive, 253; Olive-winged, 250; Orange-spotted, 250; Philippine, 253; Puff-backed, 250; Puff-throated, 252; Red-eyed, 250; Red-tailed, 252; Red-vented, 250; Red-whiskered, 250; Reunion, 253; Ruby-throated, 249; Scaly-breasted, 249; Scrub, 253; Seychelles, 253; Somali, 250; Sooty-headed, 250; Spectacled, 250; Spot-necked, 249; Straw-headed, 249; Streaked, 253; Streak-breasted, 253; Streak-eared, 250; Striated, 249; Stripe-throated, 250; Styan's, 250; Sulphur-bellied, 253; Sunda, 253; White-bearded, 252; White-browed, 250; White-eared, 250; White-headed, 253; White-spectacled, 250; White-throated, 252; White-vented, 250; Yellow, 249; Yellow-bearded, 252; Yellow-bellied, 253; Yellow-browed, 253; Yellow-eared, 250; Yellow-throated, 250; Yellow-vented, 250; Yellow-wattled, 250; Yellowish, 253; Zamboanga, 253

Bullfinch, 306; Azores, 306; Baikal, 306; Brown, 306; Eurasian, 306; Grey-bellied, 306; Grey-headed, 306; Orange, 306; Red-headed, 306; White-cheeked, 306

Bullfinch, 330; Cuban, 330; Greater Antillean, 330; Lesser Antillean, 330; Puerto Rican, 330

Bunting, 307, 308-309, 332, 333; African Golden-breasted, 308; Angola, 308; Black-faced, 308; Black-headed, 308; Blue, 332; Brown-rumped, 308; Cabanis's, 308; Cape, 308; Chestnut, 308; Chestnut-breasted, 308; Chestnut-eared, 308; Cinereous, 308; Cinnamon-breasted, 308; Cirl, 308; Corn, 309; Crested, 307; Cretzschmar's, 308; Godłewski's, 308; Grey, 309; Grey-necked, 308; House, 308; Indigo, 332; Lark, 309; Lark-like, 308; Lazuli, 332; Little, 308; McKay's, 309; Meadow, 308; Mongolian, 309; Ochre-rumped, 309; Orange-breasted, 333; Ortolan, 308; Painted, 333; Pallas's, 309; Pine, 308; Pink-tailed, 307; Red-headed, 308; Reed, 309; Rock, 308; Rose-bellied, 333; Rufous-backed, 308; Rustic, 308; Slaty, 307; Snow, 309; Socotra, 308; Somali Golden-breasted, 308; Three-streaked, 308; Tibetan, 308; Tristram's, 308; Varied, 332; Yellow, 308; Yellow-breasted, 308; Yellow-browed, 308; Yellow-throated, 308

Bushbird, 160; Black, 160; Recurve-billed, 160; Rondonia, 160

Bushchat, 232; Black, 232; Grey, 232; Jerdon's, 232; Pied, 232; White-bellied, 232; White-browed, 232; White-throated, 232

Bush-Crow, 200; Stresemann's, 200

Bush-hen, 101

Bush-Quail, 8; Jungle, 8; Manipur, 8; Painted, 8; Rock, 8

Bush-Robin, 229; Collared, 229; Golden, 229; Orange-flanked, 229; Rufous-breasted, 229; White-browed, 229

Bushshrike, 214, 215; Black-fronted, 215; Bokmakierie, 215; Doherty's, 215; Fiery-breasted, 215; Four-colored, 215; Gabela, 214; Green-breasted, 215; Grey-green, 215; Grey-headed, 215; Lagden's, 215; Luehder's, 214; Many-colored, 215; Monteiro's, 215; Olive, 215; Orange-breasted, 214; Perrin's, 215; Red-crowned, 214; Red-naped, 214; Rosy-patched, 215; Serle's, 215; Sulphur-breasted, 215; Tsavo, 215; Uluguru, 215

Bush-Tanager, 318, 326; Ashy-throated, 318; Black-backed, 326; Brown-headed, 318; Buff-breasted, 318; Common, 318; Dotted, 318; Drab-breasted, 318; Dusky, 318; Golden-bellied, 318; Grey-hooded, 318; Pirre, 318; Red-billed, 318; Sooty-capped, 318; Tacarcuna, 318; Yellow-breasted, 318; Yellow-green, 318; Yellow-throated, 318; Yellow-whiskered, 318

Bushtit, 246; Black-eared, 246; Common, 246; Lead-colored, 246

Bush-Tyrant, 149, 150; Red-rumped, 149; Rufous-bellied, 149; Rufous-webbed, 150; Santa Marta, 149; Smoky, 149; Streak-throated, 149

Bush-Warbler, 261-262; Aberrant, 262; African, 262; Brown, 262; Brownish-flanked, 261; Ceylon, 262; Chestnut-backed, 262; Chestnut-crowned, 262; Chinese, 262; Fiji, 261; Formosan, 262; Friendly, 262; Grey-sided, 262; Japanese, 261; Javan, 262; Long-billed, 262; Long-tailed, 262; Manchurian, 261; Palau, 261; Pale-footed, 261; Philippine, 261; Russet, 262; Spotted, 262; Sunda, 261; Tanimbar, 261; Timor, 262; Yellowish-bellied, 262

Bustard, 96-97; Arabian, 96; Australian, 96; Barrow's, 97; Black, 97; Black-bellied, 97; Blue, 97; Buff-crested, 96; Denham's, 96; Great, 96; Hartlaub's, 97; Heuglin's, 96; Houbara, 96; Indian, 96; Karoo, 97; Kori, 96; Little, 96; Little Brown, 97; Ludwig's,

96; Nubian, 96; Red-crested, 96; Rueppell's, 97; Savile's, 96; Senegal, 97; Stanley, 96; White-bellied, 97; White-quilled, 97

Butcherbird, 203; Black, 203; Black-backed, 203; Grey, 203; Hooded, 203; Pied, 203; Silver-backed, 203; Tagula, 203

Buttonquail, 19; Barred, 19; Black-breasted, 19; Black-rumped, 19; Buff-breasted, 19; Chestnut-backed, 19; Hottentot, 19; Lark, 19; Little, 19; Madagascar, 19; New Caledonian, 19; Painted, 19; Red-backed, 19; Red-chested, 19; Small, 19; Spotted, 19; Sumba, 19; Sunda, 19; Worcester's, 19; Yellow-legged, 19

Buzzard, 116, 119, 121, 122; Archer's, 122; Augur, 122; Black-breasted, 116; Common, 122; Grasshopper, 121; Grey-faced, 121; Jackal, 122; Japanese, 122; Lizard, 119; Long-legged, 122; Madagascar, 122; Mountain, 122; Red-necked, 122; Rufous-winged, 121; Upland, 122; White-eyed, 121

Buzzard-Eagle, 121; Black-chested, 121

Cachalote, 170; Brown, 170; Rufous, 170; White-throated, 170

Cacique, 333-324; Chapman's, 334; Ecuadorian, 333; Golden-winged, 333; Mountain, 333; Pacific, 333; Red-rumped, 333; Saffron-rumped, 333; Scarlet-rumped, 333; Selva, 333; Solitary, 333; Subtropical, 333; Yellow-billed, 334; Yellow-rumped, 333; Yellow-winged, 333

Cactus-Finch, 331; Common, 331; Large, 331

Calamanthus, 187; Rock, 187; Rufous, 187; Rusty, 187; Striated, 187

Calyptura, 155; Kinglet, 155

Camaroptera, 257; Green-backed, 257; Grey-backed, 257; Hartert's, 257; Olive-green, 257; Yellow-browed, 257

Canary, 302, 303; Black-faced, 302; Black-headed, 303; Brimstone, 303; Cape, 302; Damara, 303; Forest, 302; Island, 302; Papyrus, 302; Sao Tome, 303; White-bellied, 303; White-throated, 303; Yellow, 303; Yellow-crowned, 302; Yellow-fronted, 303

Canary-Flycatcher, 228; Citrine, 228; Grey-headed, 228

Canastero, 168-169; Austral, 169; Berlepsch's, 169; Bolivian, 169; Cactus, 169; Canyon, 168; Chestnut, 169; Cipo, 169; Cordilleran, 169; Cordoba, 169; Creamy-breasted, 169; Dusky-tailed, 169; Hudson's, 169; Junin, 169; Lesser, 168; Lillo's, 169; Line-fronted, 169; Many-striped, 169; Maquis, 168; Pale-tailed, 169; Patagonian, 169; Puno, 169; Rusty-fronted, 168; Scribble-tailed, 169; Short-billed, 168; Streak-backed, 169; Streak-throated, 169; White-tailed, 169

Canvasback, 18

Capercaillie, 11; Black-billed, 11; Western, 11

Capuchinbird, 156

Caracara, 124; Black, 124; Carunculated, 124; Chimango, 124; Crested, 124; Guadalupe, 124; Mountain, 124; Red-throated, 124; Southern, 124; Striated, 124; White-throated, 124; Yellow-headed, 124

Cardinal, 313, 332; Black-eared, 313; Crimson-fronted, 313; Long-crested, 332; Northern, 332; Red-capped, 313; Red-cowled, 313; Red-crested, 313; Vermilion, 332; Yellow, 313; Yellow-billed, 313

Carib, 65; Green-throated, 65; Purple-throated, 65

Casiornis, 151; Ash-throated, 151; Rufous, 151

Cassowary, 1; Dwarf, 1; Northern, 1; Southern, 1

Catbird, 179, 237, 276; Abyssinian, 276; Black, 237; Green, 179; Grey, 237; Spotted, 179; Tooth-billed, 179; White-eared, 179

Cattle-Egret, 129; Common, 129; Eastern, 129

Cave-Chat, 230; Angola, 230

Chachalaca, 3; Brazilian, 3; Buff-browed, 3; Chaco, 3; Chestnut-winged, 3; Colombian, 3; Grey-headed, 3; Little, 3; Plain, 3; Rufous-bellied, 3; Rufous-headed, 3; Rufous-tipped, 3; Rufous-vented, 3; Scaled, 3; Speckled, 3; West Mexican, 3; White-bellied, 3

Chaco-Finch, 326; Many-colored, 326

Chaffinch, 302

Chanting-Goshawk, 119; Dark, 119; Eastern, 119; Pale, 119

Chat, 186, 230, 232, 233, 317; Boulder, 233; Brown-tailed, 233; Buff-streaked, 232; Canary Islands, 232; Crimson, 186; Familiar, 233; Grey-throated, 317; Herero, 230; Indian, 233; Karoo, 233; Moorland, 233; Orange, 186; Red-breasted, 317; Rose-breasted, 317; Rueppell's, 233; Sicklewing, 233; Sombre, 233; Sooty, 233; Tractrac, 233; Tres Marias, 317; White-fronted, 186; Yellow, 186; Yellow-breasted, 317

Chatshrike, 213

Chat-Tanager, 319; Highland, 319; Lowland, 319

Chat-Tyrant, 149; Blackish, 149; Brown-backed, 149; Chestnut-belted, 149; Crowned, 149; D'Orbigny's, 149; Golden-browed, 149; Jelski's, 149; Piura, 149; Rufous-breasted, 149; Slaty-backed, 149; White-browed, 149; White-fronted, 149; Yellow-bellied, 149

Chatterer, 275; Fulvous, 275; Rufous, 275; Scaly, 275

Chickadee, 244; Black-capped, 244; Boreal, 244; Carolina, 244; Chestnut-backed, 244; Mountain, 244; Mexican, 244

Chiffchaff, 266; Caucasian, 266; Common, 266; Eurasian, 266; Mountain, 266; Siberian, 266

Chilia, 166; Crag, 166

Chlorophonia, 323; Blue-crowned, 323; Blue-naped, 323; Chestnut-breasted, 323; Golden-browed, 323; Yellow-collared, 323

Chough, 195, 200; Red-billed, 200; White-winged, 195; Yellow-billed, 200

Chowchilla, 191

Chuck-will's-widow, 84

Chukar, 6

Cicadabird, 206; Black-bibbed, 206; Black-shouldered, 206; Kai, 206; Pale, 206; Slender-billed, 206; Sula, 206; Sulawesi, 206; Sumba, 206

Cinclodes, 165-166; Bar-winged, 165; Blackish, 166; Cordoba, 165; Dark-bellied, 165; Grey-flanked, 165; Long-tailed, 165; Orlog's, 165; Royal, 165; Seaside, 166; Stout-billed, 165; Surf, 166; White-bellied, 166; White-winged, 166

Cisticola, 254-255; Aberdare, 255; Angola, 254; Ashy, 254; Awemba, 254; Black-lored, 254; Black-necked, 255; Black-tailed, 255; Boran, 254; Brown-backed, 254; Bubbling, 254; Carruthers's, 254; Chattering, 254; Chirping, 254; Chubb's, 254; Churring, 254; Cloud-scraping, 255; Croaking, 255; Desert, 255; Dorst's, 254; Foxy, 255; Golden-headed, 255; Grey, 254; Hunter's, 254; Island, 255; Lazy, 254; Lepe, 254; Luapula, 254; Lynes's, 254; Madagascar, 255; Mongalla, 254; Pectoral-patch, 255; Piping, 255; Rattling, 254; Red-faced, 254; Red-headed, 254; Red-pate, 254; Rock-loving, 254; Rufous, 255; Siffling, 255; Singing, 254; Socotra, 255; Stout, 254; Tabora, 255; Tana River, 254; Tink-tink, 255; Tinkling, 254; Tiny, 255; Trilling, 254; Wailing, 254; Whistling, 254; Winding, 254; Wing-snapping, 255; Zitting, 255

Citril, 302; African, 302; Corsican, 302; East African, 302; European, 302; Kenya, 302; Western, 302

Clapper-Lark, 279; Cape, 279; Damara, 279; Namaqua, 279

Cliff-Chat, 233; Abyssinian, 233; Bambara, 233; Mocking, 233; White-crowned, 233; White-winged, 233

Cochoa, 231-232; Green, 231; Javan, 231; Purple, 232; Sumatran, 232

Cockatiel, 51

Cockatoo, 50, 51; Blue-eyed, 50; Ducorps's, 51; Gang-gang, 50; Little, 50; Palm, 50; Philippine, 50; Pink, 50; Salmon-crested, 50; Sulphur-crested, 50; Tanimbar, 50; White, 50; Yellow-crested, 50

Cock-of-the-rock, 156; Andean, 156; Guianan, 156

Colasisi, 54

Coleto, 237

Collared-Dove, 88; African, 88; Eurasian, 88; Island, 88; Mourning, 88; Red, 88; White-winged, 88

Comb-Duck, 15; African, 15; American, 15

Comet, 72, 73; Bronze-tailed, 72; Grey-bellied, 73; Red-tailed, 72

Condor, 133; Andean, 133; California, 133

Conebill, 317; Bicolored, 317; Blue-backed, 317; Blue-capped, 317; Bolivian, 317; Capped, 317; Chestnut-vented, 317; Cinereous, 317; Giant, 317; Pearly-breasted, 317; Rufous-browed, 317; Tamarugo, 317; White-browed, 317; White-capped, 317; White-eared, 317

Coot, 102; American, 102; Caribbean, 102; Common, 102; Giant, 102; Hawaiian, 102; Horned, 102; Red-fronted, 102; Red-gartered, 102; Red-knobbed, 102; Slate-colored, 102; White-winged, 102

Coquette, 66; Black-crested, 66; Butterfly, 66; Dot-eared, 66; Festive, 66; Frilled, 66; Peacock, 66; Racket-tailed, 66; Rufous-crested, 66; Short-crested, 66; Spangled, 66; Tufted, 66; White-crested, 66

Cordonbleu, 298; Blue-breasted, 298; Blue-capped, 298; Red-cheeked, 298

Corella, 50; Long-billed, 50; Western, 50

Cormorant, 127-128; Bank, 127; Black-faced, 127; Brandt's, 127; Cape, 128; Crowned, 127; Double-crested, 127; Flightless, 127; Great, 128; Guanay, 128; Indian, 127; Japanese, 128; Little, 127; Little Black, 128; Little Pied, 127; Long-tailed, 127; Neotropic, 127; Pallas's, 127; Pelagic, 128; Pied, 127; Pygmy, 127; Red-faced, 128; Red-legged, 128; Socotra, 128; White-breasted, 128; White-throated, 127

Coronet, 71; Buff-tailed, 71; Chestnut-breasted, 71; Velvet-purple, 71

Cotinga, 154-155, 156; Banded, 156; Bay-vented, 155; Black-and-gold, 155; Black-faced, 156; Black-tipped, 156; Blue, 156; Buckley's, 154; Chestnut-crested, 155; Grey-winged, 155; Lovely, 156; Plum-throated, 156; Pompadour, 156; Purple-breasted, 156; Purple-throated, 156; Red-crested, 155; Shrike-like, 154; Snowy, 156; Spangled, 156; Swallow-tailed, 155; Turquoise, 156; White-cheeked, 155; White-tailed, 156; White-winged, 156; Yellow-billed, 156

Coua, 46; Blue, 46; Coquerel's, 46; Crested, 46; Giant, 46; Red-breasted, 46; Red-capped, 46; Red-fronted, 46; Running, 46; Snail-eating, 46; Verreaux's, 46

Coucal, 46-47; Bay, 47; Biak, 46; Black, 46; Black-faced, 47; Black-hooded, 46; Black-throated, 47; Blue-headed, 47; Brown, 46;

Buff-headed, 46; Burchell's, 47; Coppery-tailed, 47; Gabon, 47; Goliath, 46; Greater, 46; Greater Black, 46; Green-billed, 47; Kai, 46; Lesser, 47; Lesser Black, 46; Madagascar, 46; Neumann's, 47; Pheasant, 46; Philippine, 46; Pied, 46; Rufous, 47; Senegal, 47; Short-toed, 46; Sunda, 46; Timor, 46; Violaceous, 46; White-browed, 47

Courser, 110-111; Bronze-winged, 110; Burchell's, 111; Cream-colored, 111; Double-banded, 110; Indian, 111; Jerdon's, 111; Temminck's, 111; Three-banded, 111

Cowbird, 336; Bay-winged, 336; Bronze-brown, 336; Bronzed, 336; Brown-headed, 336; Giant, 336; Pale, 336; Screaming, 336; Shiny, 336

Crab-Hawk, 121; Rufous, 121

Crag-Martin, 247; Dusky, 247; Eurasian, 247; Pale, 247

Crake, 99, 100, 101; African, 100; Andaman, 99; Ash-throated, 101; Australian, 101; Baillon's, 101; Band-bellied, 101; Black, 101; Black-banded, 99; Black-tailed, 101; Brown, 101; Chestnut-headed, 99; Colombian, 101; Corn, 100; Dot-winged, 101; Grey-breasted, 99; Hawaiian, 101; Henderson Island, 101; Kosrae, 101; Laysan, 101; Little, 101; Ocellated, 99; Paint-billed, 101; Red-legged, 99; Red-necked, 99; Ruddy, 99; Ruddy-breasted, 101; Rufous-sided, 99; Russet-crowned, 99; Rusty-flanked, 99; Slaty-legged, 99; Spotless, 101; Spotted, 101; Striped, 101; Uniform, 101; White-browed, 101; White-throated, 99; Yellow-breasted, 101

Crane, 97; Black-necked, 97; Blue, 97; Common, 97; Demoiselle, 97; Hooded, 97; Red-crowned, 97; Sandhill, 97; Sarus, 97; Siberian, 97; Wattled, 97; White-naped, 97; Whooping, 97

Crane-Hawk, 121; Banded, 121; Blackish, 121; Grey, 121

Creeper, 239, 307; Hawaii, 307; Kauai, 307; Lanai, 307; Maui, 307; Molokai, 307; Oahu, 307; Spotted, 239

Crescent-chest, 177; Collared, 177; Elegant, 177; Maranon, 177; Olive-crowned, 177

Crested-Flycatcher, 210; African, 210; Blue-headed, 210; Dusky, 210; White-bellied, 210; White-tailed, 210

Crested-Jay, 198; Javan, 198; Malay, 198; Sumatran, 198

Crested-Tern, 113; Chinese, 113; Great, 113; Lesser, 113

Crested-Tinamou, 3; Elegant, 3; Quebracho, 3

Crimson-Finch, 299; Common, 299; Pale, 299

Crimson-wing, 297; Abyssinian, 297; Dusky, 297; Red-faced, 297; Shelley's, 297

Crocias, 276-277; Grey-crowned, 276; Spotted, 277

Crocodile-bird, 110

Crombec, 266; Ansorge's, 266; Cape, 266; Chapin's, 266; Green, 266; Lemon-bellied, 266; Northern, 266; Red-capped, 266; Red-faced, 266; Short-billed, 266; Somali, 266; White-browed, 266; Yellow-bellied, 266

Crossbill, 306; Parrot, 306; Red, 306; Scottish, 306; White-winged, 306

Crow, 200-201; American, 201; Australian, 201; Banggai, 200; Bougainville, 200; Brown-headed, 201; Cape, 201; Carrion, 201; Collared, 201; Cuban, 201; Fish, 201; Flores, 200; Grey, 201; Hawaiian, 201; Hooded, 201; House, 200; Jamaican, 201; Jungle, 201; Large-billed, 201; Little, 201; Long-billed, 200; Mariana, 200; New Caledonian, 200; New Guinea, 201; Northwestern, 201; Palm, 201; Pied, 201; Piping, 200; Sinaloa, 201; Slender-billed, 200; Tamaulipas, 201; Tanimbar, 201; Torresian, 201; White-billed, 201; White-necked, 201

Crowned-Crane, 97; Black, 97; Grey, 97

Crowned-Pigeon, 96; Southern, 96; Victoria, 96; Western, 96

Crowned-Warbler, 267; Eastern, 267; Western, 267

Cuckoo, 43-44, 45, 47, 48; African, 44; African Emerald, 45; Ash-colored, 47; Asian Emerald, 45; Banded Bay, 44; Barred Long-tailed, 44; Bay-breasted, 47; Black, 44; Black-and-white, 43; Black-bellied, 47; Black-billed, 47; Black-eared, 45; Brush, 44; Channel-billed, 45; Chestnut-bellied, 47; Chestnut-breasted, 44; Chestnut-winged, 44; Cocos, 47; Common, 44; Dark-billed, 47; Dideric, 45; Drongo, 45; Dwarf, 47; Dusky Long-tailed, 44; Fan-tailed, 44; Great Spotted, 44; Grey-bellied, 44; Grey-capped, 47; Guira, 48; Indian, 44; Klaas's, 45; Lesser, 44; Levaillant's, 44; Little, 47; Long-billed, 44; Madagascar, 44; Mangrove, 47; Moluccan, 44; Olive Long-tailed, 44; Oriental, 44; Pallid, 44; Pavonine, 48; Pearly-breasted, 47; Pheasant, 48; Pied, 43; Plaintive, 44; Red-chested, 44; Rusty-breasted, 44; Squirrel, 47; Striped, 48; Sunda, 44; Thick-billed, 44; Violet, 45; Yellow-billed, 47; Yellow-throated, 45

Cuckoo-Dove, 88-89; Andaman, 88; Bar-tailed, 88; Barred, 88; Black, 89; Black-billed, 88; Brown, 88; Crested, 89; Dusky, 88; Great, 88; Little, 88; Mackinlay's, 88; Philippine, 88; Pied, 88; Ruddy, 88; Slender-billed, 88; White-faced, 89

Cuckooshrike, 205-206, 207; Ashy, 206; Bar-bellied, 205; Black, 207; Black-bellied, 206; Black-faced, 205; Black-headed, 206; Black-winged, 206; Blackish, 206; Blue, 206; Boyer's, 205; Buru, 205; Cerulean, 205; Ghana, 207; Golden, 206; Grauer's, 206; Grey, 206; Grey-headed, 206; Ground, 205; Halmahera, 206; Himalayan, 206; Hooded, 206; Indochinese, 206; Javan, 205; Kai, 205; Large, 205; Lesser, 206; Little, 205; Mauritius, 206; McGregor's, 206; Melanesian, 205; Moluccan, 205; New Caledonian, 206; New Guinea, 206; Oriole, 207; Papuan, 205; Petit's, 207; Pied, 205; Purple-throated, 207; Pygmy, 206; Red-shouldered, 207; Reunion, 206; Slaty, 205; Solomon Islands, 206; Stout-billed, 205; Sunda, 205; Timor, 205; Wallacean, 205; White-bellied, 205; White-breasted, 206; White-rumped, 205; White-winged, 206; Yellow-eyed, 205

Curassow, 4-5; Alagoas, 4; Bare-faced, 5; Black, 5; Blue-knobbed, 4; Crestless, 4; Fasciated, 5; Great, 4; Helmeted, 4; Horned, 4; Natterer's, 5; Nocturnal, 4; Razor-billed, 4; Red-billed, 4; Salvin's, 4; Wattled, 5; Yellow-knobbed, 5

Curlew, 105; Bristle-thighed, 105; Eskimo, 105; Eurasian, 105; Far Eastern, 105; Hudsonian, 105; Long-billed, 105; Little, 105; Slender-billed, 105

Currawong, 203; Black, 203; Black-winged, 203; Brown, 203; Clinking, 203; Great-billed, 203; Grey, 203; Pied, 203

Cutia, 275

Cut-throat, 301

Dacnis, 325-326; Black-faced, 325; Black-legged, 325; Blue, 326; Scarlet-breasted, 326; Scarlet-thighed, 326; Tit-like, 326; Viridian, 326; White-bellied, 325; Yellow-bellied, 325; Yellow-tufted, 325

Dacnis-Tanager, 325; Turquoise, 325

Dapple-throat, 271

Darter, 127; African, 127; Australian, 127; Oriental, 127

Dickcissel, 331

Dipper, 218; American, 218; Brown, 218; Rufous-throated, 218; White-backed, 218; White-capped, 218; White-throated, 218

Diuca-Finch, 327; Common, 327; Lesser, 327; White-winged, 327

Diucon, 149; Fire-eyed, 149

Diving-Petrel, 137; Common, 137; Falkland, 137; Kerguelen, 137; Magellanic, 137; Peruvian, 137; South Georgia, 137

Dodo, 86

Dollarbird, 38
Donacobius, 239; Black-capped, 239
Doradito, 145; Crested, 145; Dinelli's, 145;
    Subtropical, 145; Warbling, 145
Dotterel, 109; Black-fronted, 109; Eurasian, 109;
    Inland, 109; Red-kneed, 109; Tawny-
    throated, 109
Dove, 88, 89-90, 94; Bar-shouldered, 89; Barred,
    89; Brazilian, 90; Brown-backed, 90;
    Caribbean, 90; Cloven-feathered, 94;
    Diamond, 89; Eared, 90; Emerald, 89;
    Galapagos, 90; Golden, 94; Grenada, 90;
    Grey-chested, 90; Grey-fronted, 90; Grey-
    headed, 90; Inca, 90; Laughing, 88; Lemon,
    88; Mourning, 89; Namaqua, 89; Ochre-
    bellied, 90; Orange, 94; Pacific, 90; Pallid,
    90; Peaceful, 89; Red-eyed, 88; Ring-
    necked, 88; Scaled, 90; Socorro, 89;
    Spotted, 88; Stephan's, 89; Tambourine, 89;
    Tolima, 90; Vinaceous, 88; Whistling, 94;
    White-faced, 90; White-tipped, 90; White-
    winged, 90; Zebra, 89; Zenaida, 90
Dovekie, 115
Dowitcher, 105; Asian, 105; Long-billed, 105;
    Short-billed, 105
Drongo, 209-210; Aldabra, 209; Andaman, 210;
    Ashy, 209; Black, 209; Bronzed, 209;
    Comoro, 209; Crested, 209; Crow-billed,
    209; Fork-tailed, 209; Greater Racket-tailed,
    210; Grey, 209; Hair-crested, 209; Lesser
    Racket-tailed, 209; Mayotte, 209; Principe,
    209; Pygmy, 209; Ribbon-tailed, 210;
    Sharpe's, 209; Shining, 209; Spangled, 210;
    Square-tailed, 209; Sulawesi, 210;
    Sumatran, 210; Velvet-mantled, 209;
    Wallacean, 210; White-bellied, 209
Duck, 13-14, 15, 16-17, 18; African Black, 16;
    American Black, 16; Andean, 13; Black-
    headed, 14; Blue, 16; Blue-billed, 14; Comb,
    15; Crested, 16; Eastern Spot-billed, 16;
    Falcated, 16; Freckled, 14; Harlequin, 18;
    Hartlaub's, 15; Hawaiian, 16; Indian Spot-
    billed, 16; Labrador, 18; Lake, 14; Laysan,
    16; Long-tailed, 18; Maccoa, 13; Mandarin,
    16; Maned, 16; Masked, 13; Meller's, 17;
    Mottled, 16; Muscovy, 15; Musk, 14;
    Pacific Black, 17; Philippine, 16; Pink-
    eared, 18; Pink-headed, 18; Red-billed, 18;
    Ring-necked, 18; Ruddy, 13; Spectacled, 16;
    Spot-billed, 16; Torrent, 16; Tufted, 18;
    White-backed, 13; White-headed, 13;
    White-winged, 15; Wood, 16; Yellow-
    billed, 17
Dunlin, 106

Eagle, 117, 121, 122-123, 124; Adalbert's, 123;
    Bald, 117; Black, 123; Black-and-chestnut,
    124; Bonelli's, 123; Booted, 123; Crested,
    122; Crowned, 121; Golden, 123; Greater
    Spotted, 123; Great Philippine, 122;
    Gurney's, 123; Harpy, 122; Imperial, 123;
    Lesser Spotted, 123; Little, 123; Long-
    crested, 123; Martial, 123; New Guinea,
    122; Rufous-bellied, 123; Solitary, 121;
    Steppe, 123; Tawny, 123; Verreaux's, 123;
    Wahlberg's, 123; Wedge-tailed, 123; White-
    tailed, 117
Eagle-Owl, 78; Akun, 78; Barred, 78; Cape, 78;
    Dusky, 78; Eurasian, 78; Fraser's, 78;
    Lesser, 78; Mackinder's, 78; Pharaoh, 78;
    Philippine, 78; Rock, 78; Shelley's, 78;
    Spot-bellied, 78; Spotted, 78; Usambara, 78;
    Verreaux's, 78
Eared-Nightjar, 83; Great, 83; Malaysian, 83;
    Mountain, 83; Papuan, 83; Satanic, 83;
    Spotted, 83; White-throated, 83
Eared-Pheasant, 10; Blue, 10; Brown, 10;
    Tibetan, 10; White, 10
Earthcreeper, 165, 170; Band-tailed, 170;
    Bolivian, 165; Buff-breasted, 165; Chaco,
    165; Plain-breasted, 165; Rock, 165; Scale-
    throated, 165; Straight-billed, 165; Striated,
    165; White-throated, 165
Egret, 128, 129; American, 129; Cattle, 129;
    Chinese, 129; Dimorphic, 129; Great, 129;
    Intermediate, 129; Lesser, 129; Little, 129;
    Plumed, 129; Reddish, 128; Slaty, 128;
    Snowy, 129; Yellow-billed, 129
Eider, 18; Common, 18; King, 18; Pacific, 18;
    Spectacled, 18; Steller's, 18
Elaenia, 143-144; Brownish, 144; Caribbean,
    143; Chilean, 144; Chinchorro, 143; Duida,
    144; Forest, 143; Great, 144; Greater
    Antillean, 144; Greenish, 143; Grey, 143;
    Highland, 144; Jamaican, 143; Large, 144;
    Lesser, 144; Mottle-backed, 144; Mountain,
    144; Noronha, 144; Olivaceous, 144;
    Pacific, 143; Peruvian, 144; Plain-crested,
    144; Roraiman, 144; Rufous-crowned, 144;
    Sierran, 144; Slaty, 144; Small-billed, 144;
    White-crested, 144; Yellow-bellied, 144;
    Yellow-crowned, 143
Elepaio, 211
Emerald, 66, 68, 69; Andean, 68; Bartlett's, 68;
    Blue-tailed, 66; Brace's, 66; Canivet's, 66;
    Coppery, 66; Coppery-headed, 69; Cozumel,
    66; Cuban, 66; Cuyuni, 68; Fork-tailed, 66;
    Garden, 66; Glittering-bellied, 66;
    Glittering-throated, 68; Golden-crowned,
    66; Green-tailed, 66; Hispaniolan, 66;
    Honduran, 68; Narrow-tailed, 66; Plain-
    bellied, 68; Pucheran's, 66; Puerto Rican,
    66; Red-billed, 66; Salvin's, 66; Santander,
    66; Sapphire-spangled, 68; Short-tailed, 66;
    Tachira, 68; Tepui, 68; Versicolored, 68;
    White-bellied, 68; White-chested, 68;
    White-tailed, 69

Emerald-Dove, 89; Indian, 89; Pacific, 89

Emu, 1

Emu-tail, 262, 268; Brown, 262; Grey, 268

Emuwren, 180; Mallee, 180; Rufous-crowned, 180; Southern, 180

Eremomela, 265; Black-necked, 265; Burnt-neck, 265; Green-backed, 265; Greencap, 265; Rufous-crowned, 265; Salvadori's, 265; Senegal, 265; Turner's, 265; Yellow-bellied, 265; Yellow-rumped, 265; Yellow-vented, 265

Euphonia, 322-323; Antillean, 323; Black-tailed, 323; Blue-rumped, 323; Bronze-green, 323; Chestnut-bellied, 323; Finsch's, 323; Fulvous-vented, 323; Golden-rumped, 323; Golden-sided, 323; Green-chinned, 323; Jamaican, 322; Olive-backed, 323; Orange-bellied, 323; Orange-crowned, 323; Pale-vented, 322; Plumbeous, 322; Purple-throated, 322; Rufous-bellied, 323; Scrub, 322; Spot-crowned, 323; Tawny-capped, 323; Thick-billed, 323; Trinidad, 322; Velvet-fronted, 323; Violaceous, 323; White-lored, 323; White-vented, 323; Yellow-crowned, 322; Yellow-throated, 323

Fairy, 73; Black-eared, 73; Purple-crowned, 73

Fairy-bluebird, 191; Asian, 191; Philippine, 191

Fairywren, 179-180; Black-and-white, 180; Black-backed, 180; Blue-and-white, 180; Blue-breasted, 180; Broad-billed, 179; Campbell's, 179; Emperor, 180; Lavender-flanked, 180; Lovely, 180; MacGillivray's, 180; Orange-crowned, 179; Purple-backed, 180; Purple-crowned, 180; Red-backed, 180; Red-winged, 180; Rogers's, 180; Splendid, 180; Superb, 180; Turquoise, 180; Variegated, 180; Wallace's, 179; White-shouldered, 179; White-winged, 180

Falcon, 124, 125-126; Amur, 125; Aplomado, 125; Barbary, 126; Bat, 125; Black, 125; Brown, 125; Eleonora's, 125; Grey, 125; Laggar, 125; Lanner, 125; Laughing, 124; New Zealand, 125; Orange-breasted, 126; Peregrine, 125; Prairie, 125; Pygmy, 124; Red-footed, 125; Red-necked, 125; Saker, 125; Sooty, 125; Teita, 126; White-rumped, 124

Falconet, 124; Black-thighed, 124; Collared, 124; Philippine, 124; Pied, 124; Spot-winged, 124; White-fronted, 124

Fantail, 208-209; Bismarck, 209; Black, 208; Black-and-cinnamon, 208; Blue, 208; Blue-headed, 208; Brown, 208; Brown-capped, 208; Chestnut-bellied, 208; Cinnamon-tailed, 208; Dimorphic, 208; Dusky, 208; Friendly, 208; Grey, 208; Kadavu, 208; Long-tailed, 209; Malaita, 209; Mangrove, 208; Manus, 209; Matthias, 209; Northern, 208; Palau, 209; Pied, 208; Pohnpei, 209; Rennell, 208; Rufous, 209; Rufous-backed, 209; Rufous-tailed, 208; Rusty-bellied, 209; Samoan, 208; Spot-breasted, 208; Spotted, 208; Streaked, 208; Streaky-breasted, 209; Sula, 209; Tawny-backed, 209; White-bellied, 208; White-browed, 208; White-throated, 208; White-winged, 208; Yellow-bellied, 208

Fernbird, 268; Chatham Islands, 268; New Zealand, 268

Fernwren, 187

Fieldfare, 223

Field-Tyrant, 150; Short-tailed, 150

Figbird, 205; Green, 205; Timor, 205; Wetar, 205; Yellow, 205

Fig-Parrot, 51; Coxen's, 51; Double-eyed, 51; Edwards's, 51; Large, 51; Orange-breasted, 51; Salvadori's, 51

Finch, 299, 300, 301, 302, 303, 305, 306, 313, 326-327, 328, 331; Black-crested, 327; Black-masked, 326; Black-ringed, 299; Black-tailed, 299; Black-throated, 299; Canary-winged, 326; Cassin's, 305; Chestnut-eared, 299; Cinereous, 327; Citril, 302; Coal-crested, 326; Cocos, 331; Crimson, 299; Crimson-browed, 306; Crimson-winged, 305; Desert, 305; Double-barred, 299; Gold-naped, 306; Gough, 327; Gouldian, 300; Grey-crested, 327; House, 305; Large-footed, 313; Laysan, 306; Long-tailed, 299; Mangrove, 331; Masked, 299; Mongolian, 305; Nightingale, 327; Nihoa, 306; Olive, 313; Oriole, 303; Peg-billed, 327; Pelzeln's, 328; Pileated, 326; Plum-headed, 299; Purple, 305; Red-crested, 326; Red-headed, 301; Saffron, 328; St. Lucia Black, 331; Scarlet, 306; Short-tailed, 327; Slaty, 326; Slender-billed, 327; Sooty-faced, 313; Spectacled, 305; Star, 299; Sulphur-throated, 328; Tanager, 326; Trumpeter, 305; Uniform, 327; Vegetarian, 331; Warbler, 331; Wilkins's, 327; Woodpecker, 331; Yellow-billed Blue, 333; Yellow-bridled, 326; Yellow-green, 313; Yellow-thighed, 313; Zebra, 299

Finchbill, 249; Crested, 249; Collared, 249

Finch-Tanager, 326; Crimson, 326

Finfoot, 98; African, 98; Masked, 98

Fireback, 10; Crested, 10; Crestless, 10; Malaysian, 10; Siamese, 10; Vieillot's, 10

Firecrest, 249

Firecrown, 71; Green-backed, 71; Juan Fernandez, 71

Fire-eye, 163; Fringe-backed, 163; White-backed, 163; White-shouldered, 163

Firefinch, 297-298; African, 297; Bar-breasted, 297; Black-bellied, 297; Black-faced, 298; Black-throated, 298; Brown, 297; Jameson's, 298; Mali, 297; Pale-billed, 297; Red-billed, 297; Reichenow's, 298; Vinaceous, 298

Firetail, 299; Beautiful, 299; Diamond, 299; Mountain, 299; Painted, 299; Red-browed, 299; Red-eared, 299

Firethroat, 229

Firewood-gatherer, 170

Fiscal, 192; Common, 192; Grey-backed, 192; Latakoo, 192; Long-tailed, 192; Newton's, 192; Somali, 192; Teita, 192; Uhehe, 192

Fish-Eagle, 117; African, 117; Grey-headed, 117; Lesser, 117; Madagascar, 117; Sanford's, 117; White-bellied, 117

Fishing-Owl, 78; Pel's, 78; Rufous, 78; Vermiculated, 78

Fish-Owl, 78; Blakiston's, 78; Brown, 78; Buffy, 78; Tawny, 78

Flameback, 26-27; Black-rumped, 27; Common, 27; Greater, 27; Himalayan, 26

Flamecrest, 249

Flamingo, 131; American, 131; Andean, 131; Chilean, 131; Greater, 131; Lesser, 131; Puna, 131

Flatbill, 146, 152; Dusky-tailed, 152; Eye-ringed, 146; Fulvous-breasted, 146; Large-headed, 152; Olivaceous, 146; Pacific, 146; Rufous-tailed, 152

Flicker, 25; Andean, 25; Campo, 25; Chilean, 25; Cuban, 25; Fernandina's, 25; Field, 25; Gilded, 25; Guatemalan, 25; Northern, 25; Red-shafted, 25; Yellow-shafted, 25

Florican, 97; Bengal, 97; Lesser, 97

Flowerpecker, 282-283; Ashy, 283; Bicolored, 282; Black-fronted, 283; Black-sided, 283; Blood-breasted, 283; Brown-backed, 282; Buff-bellied, 283; Buzzing, 283; Cambodian, 283; Cebu, 282; Crimson-breasted, 282; Crimson-crowned, 283; Fire-breasted, 283; Flame-breasted, 283; Flame-crowned, 282; Golden-rumped, 282; Grey-sided, 283; Louisiade, 283; Luzon, 283; Midget, 283; Mottled, 283; Olivaceous, 283; Olive-backed, 282; Olive-capped, 282; Olive-crowned, 283; Orange-bellied, 283; Palawan, 282; Pale-billed, 283; Plain, 283; Pygmy, 283; Red-banded, 283; Red-capped, 283; Red-chested, 283; Red-crowned, 282; Red-striped, 282; Scarlet-backed, 283; Scarlet-breasted, 282; Scarlet-collared, 282; Scarlet-headed, 283; Streak-breasted, 282; Striped, 282; Sulu, 283; Thick-billed, 282; Wallacean, 283; Whiskered, 282; White-throated, 282; Yellow-bellied, 282; Yellow-breasted, 282; Yellow-crowned, 282; Yellow-rumped, 282; Yellow-sided, 282; Yellow-vented, 282

Flower-piercer, 330-331; All-black, 330; Black, 330; Black-throated, 330; Bluish, 331; Chestnut-bellied, 330; Cinnamon-bellied, 330; Deep-blue, 331; Glossy, 330; Greater, 331; Grey-bellied, 331; Indigo, 331; Masked, 331; Merida, 330; Moustached, 330; Rusty, 330; Santa Marta, 330; Scaled, 331; Slaty, 330; Venezuelan, 330; Vuilleumier's, 330; White-sided, 330

Flufftail, 98; Buff-spotted, 98; Chestnut-headed, 98; Lynes's, 98; Madagascar, 98; Red-chested, 98; Slender-billed, 98; Streaky-breasted, 98; Striped, 98; White-spotted, 98; White-winged, 98

Flycatcher, 140-141, 143, 146, 147-149, 152, 153, 210, 212-213, 225-227, 228; Acadian, 148; Alder, 148; Apical, 152; Ash-throated, 152; Ashy-breasted, 226; Asian, 226; Baird's, 153; Bearded, 147; Belted, 148; Biak, 213; Black-and-rufous, 227; Black-banded, 227; Black-billed, 148; Black-capped, 149; Black-tailed, 147; Blue-and-white, 227; Blue-breasted, 228; Blue-crested, 213; Blue-fronted, 228; Blue-throated, 228; Boat-billed, 153; Boehm's, 226; Bran-colored, 147; Broad-billed, 213; Brown-breasted, 226; Brown-crested, 152; Brownish, 146; Brown-streaked, 226; Buff-breasted, 149; Buff-rumped, 147; Channel Islands, 148; Chat, 225; Chestnut, 147; Chestnut-capped, 210; Cinnamon, 147; Cinnamon-chested, 227; Cliff, 147; Cocos, 143; Collared, 226; Cordilleran, 148; Crowned Slaty, 153; Cryptic, 227; Damar, 227; Dark-capped, 152; Dark-grey, 213; Dark-sided, 226; Dohrn's, 228; Dull, 213; Dull-blue, 227; Dusky, 148; Dusky-blue, 226; Dusky-capped, 152; Dusky-chested, 153; Euler's, 147; European Pied, 226; Ferruginous, 226; Fiscal, 225; Flammulated, 152; Flavescent, 147; Fork-tailed, 153; Fuscous, 147; Galapagos, 149; Gambaga, 225; Golden-bellied, 153; Golden-crowned, 153; Great Crested, 152; Grenada, 152; Grey, 148; Grey-breasted, 148; Grey-capped, 153; Grey-crowned, 146; Grey-hooded, 140; Grey-streaked, 226; Guam, 212; Hammond's, 148; Handsome, 147; Himalayan, 226; Humblot's, 226; Inca, 141; Indigo, 227; Island, 227; Kashmir, 227; La Sagra's, 152; Large, 225; Large-billed, 152; Lawrence's, 147; Leaden, 213; Least, 148; Lemon-browed, 153; Lesser Antillean, 152; Little Grey, 225; Little Pied, 227; Little Slaty, 227; Livingstone's, 210; Lompobattang, 227; MacConnell's, 140; Malaysian, 227; Mangrove, 212; Mariqua, 225; Matinan, 228; Melanesian, 213;

Mugimaki, 226; Narcissus, 226; Nilgiri, 227; Nutting's, 152; Oceanic, 212; Ochraceous-breasted, 147; Ochre-bellied, 140; Ochre-headed, 213; Olive, 148; Olive-chested, 147; Olive-sided, 148; Olive-striped, 140; Ometepe, 152; Orange-banded, 147; Orange-crested, 147; Ornate, 147; Pacific-slope, 148; Palawan, 227; Pale, 225; Pale-chinned, 228; Pale-edged, 152; Panama, 152; Paperbark, 213; Pelzeln's, 152; Pileated, 148; Pine, 148; Piratic, 153; Pohnpei, 212; Puerto Rican, 152; Puno, 147; Red-breasted, 227; Red-throated, 227; Restless, 213; Roraiman, 147; Royal, 147; Ruddy-tailed, 147; Rufescent, 147; Rufous, 152; Rufous-breasted, 140; Rufous-browed, 227; Rufous-chested, 227; Rufous-gorgeted, 227; Rufous-tailed, 152; Rufous-throated, 227; Rusty-margined, 153; Rusty-tailed, 226; Sad, 152; Samoan, 213; Sapphire, 227; Satin, 213; Scissor-tailed, 153; Semicollared, 226; Sepia-capped, 141; Shining, 213; Short-crested, 152; Slaty-backed, 226; Slaty-blue, 227; Slaty-capped, 141; Snowy-browed, 227; Social, 153; Solitary, 153; Sooty, 226; Sooty-crowned, 152; Spotted, 225; Steel-blue, 213; Stolid, 152; Streaked, 153; Streak-necked, 140; Sulphur-bellied, 153; Sulphur-rumped, 147; Sulphury, 153; Sumba Brown, 226; Sumba, 227; Swainson's, 152; Swallow, 147; Tawny-breasted, 147; Tawny-chested, 148; Tessmann's, 226; Thomson's, 210; Three-striped, 153; Tufted, 148; Ultramarine, 227; Unadorned, 147; Ussher's, 226; Vanikoro, 213; Variegated, 153; Venezuelan, 152; Verditer, 227; Vermilion, 149; Vermilion-crowned, 153; Wajir, 225; Whiskered, 147; White-bearded, 153; White-gorgeted, 227; White-ringed, 153; White-tailed, 228; White-throated, 148; Whitely's, 152; Wied's Crested, 152; Willow, 148; Yellow, 210; Yellow-bellied, 148; Yellow-breasted, 146; Yellow-margined, 146; Yellow-olive, 146; Yellow-rumped, 226; Yellow-throated, 153; Yellowish, 148; Yucatan, 152

Flycatcher-shrike, 207; Bar-winged, 207; Black-winged, 207

Flycatcher-Thrush, 218; Finsch's, 218; Rufous, 218

Flycatcher-Warbler, 264-265; Mountain, 264; Thin-billed, 265; Yellow, 264

Flyrobin, 189; Canary, 189; Golden-bellied, 189; Kimberley, 189; Lemon-bellied, 189; Olive, 189; Yellow-legged, 189

Fody, 295; Forest, 295; Madagascar Red, 295; Mauritius, 295; Red-headed, 295; Seychelles, 295; Yellow, 295

Foliage-gleaner, 171-172; Alagoas, 171; Baer's, 171; Black-capped, 171; Brown-rumped, 172; Buff-browed, 171; Buff-fronted, 171; Buff-throated, 171; Chestnut-capped, 172; Chestnut-crowned, 172; Chestnut-winged, 171; Cinnamon-rumped, 171; Crested, 171; Dusky-winged, 171; Guttulated, 171; Henna-hooded, 172; Lineated, 171; Montane, 171; Ochre-bellied, 171; Ochre-breasted, 171; Olive-backed, 172; Ruddy, 172; Rufous-backed, 171; Rufous-necked, 171; Rufous-rumped, 171; Rufous-tailed, 171; Russet-mantled, 171; Scaly-breasted, 171; Slaty-winged, 171; Spot-breasted, 171; White-browed, 171; White-collared, 171; White-eyed, 172; White-throated, 172

Forest-Falcon, 124; Barred, 124; Buckley's, 124; Collared, 124; Lined, 124; Plumbeous, 124; Slaty-backed, 124

Forest-Flycatcher, 225; African, 225; White-browed, 225

Forest-Rail, 99; Chestnut, 99; Forbes's, 99; Mayr's, 99; White-striped, 99

Forktail, 231; Black-backed, 231; Chestnut-naped, 231; Formosan, 231; Little, 231; Slaty-backed, 231; Spotted, 231; Sunda, 231; White-crowned, 231

Francolin, 6-7; Acacia, 7; Ahanta, 7; Black, 6; Cameroon, 7; Cape, 7; Chestnut-naped, 7; Chinese, 6; Clapperton's, 7; Coqui, 6; Crested, 6; Double-spurred, 7; Elgon, 7; Erckel's, 7; Ethiopian, 7; Finsch's, 6; Forest, 6; Grey, 6; Grey-striped, 7; Grey-winged, 6; Handsome, 7; Hartlaub's, 7; Harwood's, 7; Hildebrandt's, 7; Hueglin's, 7; Jackson's, 7; Kirk's, 6; Moorland, 6; Nahan's, 7; Natal, 7; Ochre-breasted, 7; Orange River, 7; Painted, 6; Red-billed, 7; Red-winged, 6; Ring-necked, 6; Scaly, 7; Schlegel's, 6; Shelley's, 7; Swamp, 6; Swierstra's, 7; White-throated, 6

Friarbird, 184; Black-faced, 184; Brass's, 184; Cape York, 184; Dusky, 184; Grey, 184; Grey-necked, 184; Helmeted, 184; Little, 184; Melville Island, 184; Meyer's, 184; New Britain, 184; New Caledonian, 184; New Guinea, 184; New Ireland, 184; Noisy, 184; Plain, 184; Silver-crowned, 184; White-naped, 184; White-streaked, 184

Frigatebird, 133-134; Ascension, 134; Christmas Island, 134; Great, 134; Lesser, 134; Magnificent, 133

Frogmouth, 82; Blyth's, 82; Bornean, 82; Ceylon, 82; Dulit, 82; Gould's, 82; Hodgson's, 82; Indochinese, 82; Javan, 82; Large, 82; Marbled, 82; Papuan, 82; Philippine, 82; Plumed, 82; Short-tailed, 82; Sunda, 82; Tawny, 82

Fruit-Dove, 93-94; Atoll, 94; Beautiful, 93; Black-backed, 93; Black-banded, 93; Black-chinned, 93; Black-naped, 94; Blue-capped, 93; Carunculated, 94; Claret-breasted, 94; Cook Islands, 94; Coroneted, 93; Cream-bellied, 93; Crimson-crowned, 93; Dwarf, 94; Flame-breasted, 93; Geelvink, 94; Grey-green, 94; Grey-headed, 94; Henderson Island, 94; Jambu, 93; Knob-billed, 94; Makatea, 94; Many-colored, 93; Mariana, 93; Maroon-chinned, 93; Negros, 94; Orange-bellied, 94; Orange-fronted, 93; Ornate, 93; Palau, 94; Papuan, 94; Pink-headed, 93; Pink-spotted, 93; Purple-capped, 93; Rapa, 94; Red-bellied, 93; Red-eared, 93; Red-moustached, 94; Red-naped, 93; Rose-crowned, 93; Scarlet-breasted, 93; Silver-capped, 93; Superb, 93; Tanna, 93; Wallace's, 93; White-bibbed, 94; White-capped, 94; White-headed, 94; Wompoo, 93; Yellow-bibbed, 94; Yellow-breasted, 93

Fruitcrow, 156; Bare-necked, 156; Crimson, 156; Purple-throated, 156; Red-ruffed, 156

Fruiteater, 155; Band-tailed, 155; Barred, 155; Black-chested, 155; Black-headed, 155; Bluish-crowned, 155; Fiery-throated, 155; Golden-breasted, 155; Greeen-and-black, 155; Handsome, 155; Masked, 155; Orange-breasted, 155; Red-banded, 155; Scaled, 155; Scarlet-breasted, 155

Fruit-hunter, 224; Black-breasted, 224

Fulmar, 135; Northern, 135; Southern, 135

Fulvetta, 276; Brown, 276; Brown-cheeked, 276; Chinese, 276; Dusky, 276; Gold-fronted, 276; Golden-breasted, 276; Grey-cheeked, 276; Javan, 276; Ludlow's, 276; Mountain, 276; Nepal, 276; Rufous-throated, 276; Rufous-winged, 276; Rusty-capped, 276; Spectacled, 276; Streak-throated, 276; White-browed, 276; Yellow-throated, 276

Gadwall, 16; Common, 16; Coues's, 16

Galah, 50

Gallinule, 102; Allen's, 102; Azure, 102; Purple, 102; Spot-flanked, 102

Gallito, 177; Crested, 177; Sandy, 177

Gannet, 127; Australian, 127; Cape, 127; Northern, 127

Garganey, 17

Geomalia, 219

Gerygone, 188-189; Biak, 188; Black-headed, 188; Black-throated, 188; Brown, 189; Brown-breasted, 189; Buff-breasted, 189; Chatham Islands, 189; Dusky, 188; Fairy, 188; Fan-tailed, 189; Golden-bellied, 189; Green-backed, 188; Grey, 189; Large-billed, 188; Lord Howe Island, 189; Mangrove, 189; Mountain, 188; Norfolk Islands, 189; Northern, 189; Plain, 189; Rufous-sided, 189; Waigeo, 188; Western, 189; White-bellied, 188; White-throated, 188; Yellow-bellied, 188

Giant-Petrel, 135; Antarctic, 135; Hall's, 135

Gibberbird, 186

Glossy-Starling, 235; Angola, 235; Black-bellied, 235; Bronze-tailed, 235; Burchell's, 235; Copper-tailed, 235; Greater Blue-eared, 235; Iris, 235; Lesser Blue-eared, 235; Long-tailed, 235; Meves's, 235; Principe, 235; Purple, 235; Purple-headed, 235; Red-shouldered, 235; Rueppell's, 235; Sharp-tailed, 235; Southern Blue-eared, 235; Splendid, 235

Gnatcatcher, 242-243; Berlepsch's, 243; Black-capped, 242; Black-tailed, 242; Blue-grey, 242; California, 242; Creamy-bellied, 243; Cuban, 242; Guianan, 243; Maranon, 243; Masked, 243; Slate-throated, 243; Tropical, 243; White-browed, 243; White-lored, 242

Gnateater, 176-177; Ash-throated, 177; Black-bellied, 177; Black-cheeked, 177; Caatinga, 176; Chestnut-belted, 176; Chestnut-crowned, 177; Hooded, 177; Rufous, 176; Silvery-tufted, 176; Slaty, 177

Gnatwren, 242; Black-tailed, 242; Collared, 242; Long-billed, 242; Tawny-faced, 242

Go-away-bird, 75; Bare-faced, 75; Grey, 75; White-bellied, 75

Godwit, 104; Bar-tailed, 104; Black-tailed, 104; Hudsonian, 104; Marbled, 104

Goldcrest, 249

Goldeneye, 18-19; Barrow's, 19; Common, 18

Goldenface, 196

Golden-Myna, 236; Eastern, 236; Western, 236

Golden-Oriole, 204; African, 204; Eurasian, 204

Golden-Plover, 108; American, 108; Eurasian, 108; Pacific, 108

Golden-Sparrow, 289; Arabian, 289; Sudan, 289

Goldentail, 67; Blue-throated, 67

Goldenthroat, 67-68; Green-tailed, 68; Tepui, 68; White-tailed, 67

Golden-Weaver, 293; African, 293; Holub's, 293

Goldfinch, 304; American, 304; European, 304; Grey-crowned, 304; Lawrence's, 304; Lesser, 304

Gonolek, 214; Black-headed, 214; Common, 214; Crimson-breasted, 214; Papyrus, 214; Sierra Leone, 214

Goose, 13, 14-15; Andean, 15; Ashy-headed, 15; Bar-headed, 14; Barnacle, 15; Bean, 14; Blue, 14; Blue-winged, 15; Brent, 15; Cackling, 15; Canada, 15; Cape Barren, 15; Egyptian, 15; Emperor, 14; Greater White-fronted, 14; Greylag, 14; Hutchins's, 15; Kelp, 15; Lesser White-fronted, 14; Magpie, 13; Orinoco, 15; Pink-footed, 14; Red-breasted, 15; Ross's, 14; Ruddy-headed, 15;

Snow, 14; Spur-winged, 15; Swan, 14; Tule, 14; Tundra, 15; Upland, 15

Goshawk, 119, 120, 121; African, 119; American, 120; Australian, 119; Black, 120; Black-mantled, 119; Brown, 119; Chestnut-shouldered, 120; Chinese, 119; Crested, 119; Doria's, 121; Eurasian, 120; Fiji, 119; Frances's, 119; Gabar, 119; Grey, 119; Grey-bellied, 119; Grey-headed, 120; Henst's, 120; Lesser, 119; Meyer's, 120; Moluccan, 119; New Britain, 120; Northern, 120; Pied, 119; Red, 120; Red-chested, 119; Rufous-breasted, 119; Spot-tailed, 119; Sulawesi, 119; Variable, 119; White-bellied, 119

Grackle, 335-336; Boat-tailed, 336; Bolivian, 335; Bronzed, 336; Carib, 336; Common, 336; Golden-tufted, 335; Greater Antillean, 336; Great-tailed, 336; Mountain, 336; Nicaraguan, 336; Purple, 336; Red-bellied, 335; Slender-billed, 336; Velvet-fronted, 335; Violaceous, 335

Grandala, 231

Grassbird, 268, 269; Bristled, 269; Broad-tailed, 269; Buff-banded, 269; Fan-tailed, 269; Fly River, 268; Little, 268; Marsh, 268; New Caledonian, 269; Rufous-rumped, 269; Striated, 268; Tawny, 268

Grass-Finch, 328; Duida, 328; Grey-cheeked, 328; Wedge-tailed, 328

Grasshopper-Warbler, 263; Common, 263; Gray's, 263; Middendorff's, 263; Pallas's, 263; Pleske's, 263; Sakhalin, 263

Grass-Owl, 75-76; African, 75; Eastern, 76

Grassquit, 328, 330; Black-faced, 330; Blue-black, 328; Cuban, 330; Dull-colored, 330; Sooty, 330; Yellow-faced, 330; Yellow-shouldered, 330

Grass-Tyrant, 145; Sharp-tailed, 145

Grass-Warbler, 263; Cape, 263; Moustached, 263

Grasswren, 180; Black, 180; Carpentarian, 180; Dusky, 180; Eyrean, 180; Grey, 180; Rufous, 180; Striated, 180; Thick-billed, 180; Western, 180; White-throated, 180

Grebe, 126; Alaotra, 126; Atitlan, 126; Australasian, 126; Black-necked, 126; Chilean, 126; Clark's, 126; Colombian, 126; Falkland, 126; Great Crested, 126; Great, 126; Hoary-headed, 126; Hooded, 126; Horned, 126; Junin, 126; Least, 126; Little, 126; Madagascar, 126; New Zealand, 126; Pied-billed, 126; Puna, 126; Red-necked, 126; Short-winged, 126; Silvery, 126; Western, 126; White-tufted, 126

Greenbul, 250-252; Ansorge's, 251; Appert's, 252; Cabanis's, 251; Cameroon, 250; Dusky, 252; Fischer's, 251; Golden, 251; Green-throated, 251; Grey, 251; Grey-crowned, 252; Grey-headed, 252; Grey-olive, 252; Grey-throated, 251; Hall's, 251; Honeyguide, 251; Icterine, 252; Joyful, 251; Kakamega, 251; Liberian, 252; Little, 251; Long-billed, 252; Mountain, 251; Olive-headed, 251; Pale-olive, 251; Placid, 251; Plain, 251; Prigogine's, 251; Sassi's, 252; Sharpe's, 252; Shelley's, 251; Simple, 251; Slender-billed, 251; Sombre, 251; Spectacled, 252; Spotted, 251; Stripe-cheeked, 251; Swamp, 251; Tiny, 252; Usambara, 252; White-tailed, 251; White-throated, 252; Xavier's, 252; Yellow-bellied, 251; Yellow-necked, 251; Yellow-streaked, 252; Yellow-throated, 251; Yellow-whiskered, 251

Greenfinch, 303; Black-headed, 303; European, 303; Grey-capped, 303; Vietnamese, 303; Yellow-breasted, 303

Greenlet, 194; Amazon, 194; Ashy-headed, 194; Brown-headed, 194; Buff-cheeked, 194; Dusky-capped, 194; Golden-fronted, 194; Grey-chested, 194; Grey-eyed, 194; Grey-fronted, 194; Grey-headed, 194; Lemon-chested, 194; Lesser, 194; Olivaceous, 194; Red-fronted, 194; Rufous-crowned, 194; Rufous-naped, 194; Scrub, 194; Tawny-crowned, 194; Tepui, 194; Yellow-bellied, 194; Yellow-green, 194

Green-Pigeon, 92-93; African, 92; Andaman, 92; Bruce's, 92; Buru, 92; Cinnamon-headed, 92; Delalande's, 92; Flores, 92; Grey-cheeked, 92; Korthals's, 93; Large, 92; Little, 92; Madagascar, 92; Orange-breasted, 92; Pemba, 92; Philippine, 92; Pin-tailed, 92; Pink-necked, 92; Pompadour, 92; Sao Tome, 92; Sumatran, 92; Sumba, 92; Thick-billed, 92; Timor, 92; Wedge-tailed, 93; Whistling, 93; White-bellied, 93; Yellow-footed, 92; Yellow-vented, 93

Greenshank, 105; Common, 105; Nordmann's, 105

Grenadier, 298; Common, 298; Purple, 298

Grey-Hornbill, 34; Ceylon, 34; Indian, 34; Malabar, 34

Greytail, 170; Double-banded, 170; Equatorial, 170

Griffon, 117; Cape, 117; Eurasian, 117; Himalayan, 117; Rueppell's, 117

Grosbeak, 303, 305-306, 307, 331, 332; Black-and-yellow, 306; Black-backed, 331; Black-faced, 332; Black-headed, 331; Black-thighed, 331; Black-throated, 332; Blue, 332; Blue-black, 332; Bonin, 305; Chapman's, 331; Collared, 306; Crimson-collared, 332; Evening, 306; Golden-bellied, 331; Golden-winged, 303; Hooded, 306; Indigo, 332; Japanese, 306; Kona, 307; Pine,

306; Red-and-black, 332; Riobamba, 331; Rose-breasted, 331; Slate-colored, 332; Spot-winged, 306; Ultramarine, 332; White-winged, 306; Yellow, 331; Yellow-billed, 306; Yellow-green, 332; Yellow-rumped, 331; Yellow-shouldered, 332

Grosbeak-Canary, 303; Abyssinian, 303; Kenya, 303

Groundcreeper, 170; Canebrake, 170

Ground-Cuckoo, 46, 48; Banded, 48; Coral-billed, 46; Lesser, 48; Red-billed, 48; Rufous-vented, 48; Rufous-winged, 48; Scaled, 48; Sunda, 46

Ground-Dove, 90, 91-92; Bare-eyed, 90; Bare-faced, 90; Black-winged, 90; Blue, 90; Blue-eyed, 90; Bronze, 92; Caroline Islands, 91; Cinnamon, 91; Common, 90; Croaking, 90; Ecuadorian, 90; Friendly, 91; Golden-spotted, 90; Long-tailed, 90; Maroon-chested, 90; Marquesan, 92; Palau, 92; Picui, 90; Plain-breasted, 90; Polynesian, 91; Purple-winged, 90; Ruddy, 90; Santa Cruz, 91; Sulawesi, 91; Tanna, 92; Thick-billed, 92; Wetar, 92; White-bibbed, 91; White-throated, 91

Ground-Finch, 331; Large, 331; Medium, 331; Sharp-beaked, 331; Small, 331

Ground-Hornbill, 35; Abyssinian, 35; Southern, 35

Ground-Jay, 200; Iranian, 200; Mongolian, 200; Tibetan, 200; Turkestan, 200; Xinjiang, 200

Ground-Pigeon, 92; Thick-billed, 92

Ground-robin, 189; Greater, 189; Lesser, 189

Ground-Roller, 38; Long-tailed, 38; Pitta-like, 38; Rufous-headed, 38; Scaly, 38; Short-legged, 38

Ground-Sparrow, 311; Prevost's, 311; Rusty-crowned, 311; White-eared, 311

Ground-Thrush, 219-220; Abyssinian, 219; Black-eared, 219; Cameroon, 219; Crossley's, 219; Grauer's, 219; Grey, 219; Kibale, 219; Kivu, 219; Oberlaender's, 219; Orange, 219; Spotted, 220

Ground-Tyrant, 150; Black-fronted, 150; Chestnut-naped, 150; Cinereous, 150; Cinnamon-bellied, 150; Dark-faced, 150; Little, 150; Ochre-naped, 150; Paramo, 150; Plain-capped, 150; Puna, 150; Rufous-naped, 150; Spot-billed, 150; White-browed, 150; White-fronted, 150

Grouse, 11; Black, 11; Blue, 11; Caucasian, 11; Chinese, 11; Dusky, 11; Franklin's, 11; Hazel, 11; Red, 11; Ruffed, 11; Sage, 11; Sharp-tailed, 11; Siberian, 11; Sooty, 11; Spruce, 11

Guaiabero, 51

Guan, 3-4; Andean, 4; Band-tailed, 3; Baudo, 4; Bearded, 3; Black, 4; Cauca, 4; Chestnut-

bellied, 4; Crested, 4; Dusky-legged, 4; Green-backed, 4; Highland, 4; Horned, 4; Marail, 4; Red-faced, 4; Rusty-margined, 4; Sickle-winged, 4; Spix's, 4; Wattled, 4; White-browed, 4; White-crested, 4; White-winged, 4

Guillemot, 115; Black, 115; Kurile, 115; Pigeon, 115; Spectacled, 115

Guineafowl, 11-12; Black, 11; Crested, 12; Helmeted, 11; Kenya, 12; Plumed, 12; Tufted, 11; West African, 11; White-breasted, 11; Vulturine, 12

Gull, 111-113; Andean, 113; Armenian, 112; Atlantic, 112; Audouin's, 112; Band-tailed, 111; Black-billed, 113; Black-tailed, 112; Bonaparte's, 113; Brown-headed, 112; Brown-hooded, 113; California, 112; Common Black-headed, 113; Dark-backed, 112; Dolphin, 111; Franklin's, 113; Glaucous, 112; Glaucous-winged, 112; Great Black-backed, 112; Great Black-headed, 112; Grey, 112; Grey-headed, 112; Heermann's, 112; Herring, 112; Heuglin's, 112; Iceland, 112; Ivory, 113; Kamchatka, 112; Kelp, 112; King, 112; Kumlien's, 112; Laughing, 113; Lava, 113; Lesser Black-backed, 112; Little, 113; Mediterranean, 113; Mew, 112; Olrog's, 112; Pacific, 111; Red-billed, 113; Relict, 113; Ring-billed, 112; Ross's, 113; Sabine's, 113; Saunders's, 113; Silver, 112; Slaty-backed, 112; Slender-billed, 113; Sooty, 112; Swallow-tailed, 113; Thayer's, 112; Vega, 112; Western, 112; White-eyed, 112; Yellow-footed, 112; Yellow-legged, 112

Gyrfalcon, 125

Hamerkop, 131

Hanging-Parrot, 54; Black-billed, 54; Blue-crowned, 54; Ceylon, 54; Green-fronted, 54; Moluccan, 54; Orange-fronted, 54; Red-billed, 54; Sangihe, 54; Sulawesi, 54; Vernal, 54; Wallace's, 54; Yellow-throated, 54

Hardhead, 18

Harrier, 118-119; American, 118; Black, 118; Cinereous, 118; Hen, 118; Long-winged, 118; Montagu's, 119; Northern, 118; Pallid, 119; Pied, 119; Spotted, 118; Swamp, 118

Harrier-Hawk, 119; African, 119; Madagascar, 119

Hawfinch, 306

Hawk, 116, 120, 121-122; Barred, 121; Bat, 116; Bicolored, 120; Black-collared, 121; Black-faced, 121; Broad-winged, 122; Chilean, 120; Cooper's, 120; Crane, 121; Ferruginous, 122; Galapagos, 122; Grey, 121; Grey-backed, 121; Grey-lined, 121;

Gundlach's, 120; Harlan's, 122; Harris's, 121; Hawaiian, 122; Juan Fernandez, 122; Long-tailed, 121; Mantled, 121; Plain-breasted, 120; Plumbeous, 121; Puna, 122; Red-backed, 122; Red-shouldered, 121; Red-tailed, 122; Ridgway's, 122; Roadside, 121; Rough-legged, 122; Rufous-tailed, 122; Rufous-thighed, 120; Savanna, 121; Semicollared, 120; Semiplumbeous, 121; Sharp-shinned, 120; Short-tailed, 122; Slate-colored, 121; Spotted, 120; Swainson's, 122; Tiny, 120; White, 121; White-breasted, 120; White-browed, 121; White-necked, 121; White-rumped, 122; White-tailed, 122; White-throated, 122; Zone-tailed, 122

Hawk-Cuckoo, 44; Common, 44; Hodgson's, 44; Large, 44; Moustached, 44; Northern, 44; Philippine, 44; Sulawesi, 44

Hawk-Eagle, 123-124; African, 123; Ayres's, 123; Black, 123; Black-and-white, 123; Blyth's, 123; Cassin's, 123; Changeable, 123; Crested, 123; Crowned, 124; Javan, 123; Mountain, 123; Ornate, 124; Philippine, 123; Sulawesi, 123; Sunda, 123; Wallace's, 123

Hawk-Owl, 81; Andaman, 81; Bismarck, 81; Brown, 81; Christmas Island, 81; Hume's, 81; Jungle, 81; Manus, 81; Mindanao, 81; Mindoro, 81; Moluccan, 81; Ochre-bellied, 81; Papuan, 81; Philippine, 81; Russet, 81; Solomon Islands, 81; Speckled, 81; White-browed, 81

Helmetcrest, 73; Bearded, 73

Helmetshrike, 215; Angola, 215; Chestnut-bellied, 215; Chestnut-fronted, 215; Curly-crested, 215; Gabon, 215; Grey-crested, 215; Retz's, 215; Southern, 215; Straight-crested, 215; White, 215; Yellow-crested, 215

Hemispingus, 318, 319; Black-capped, 318; Black-eared, 319; Black-headed, 319; Drab, 319; Grey-capped, 319; Ochraceous, 319; Oleaginous, 319; Orange-browed, 318; Parodi's, 318; Puno, 318; Rufous-browed, 319; Slaty-backed, 319; Superciliaried, 318; Three-striped, 319; White-bellied, 318; White-browed, 318; Yellow-browed, 318

Hermit, 63-64; Boucard's, 64; Broad-tipped, 64; Bronzy, 63; Buff-bellied, 64; Cinnamon-throated, 64; Dusky-throated, 64; Great-billed, 63; Green, 63; Grey-chinned, 64; Hartert's, 63; Hook-billed, 64; Jalisco, 63; Koepcke's, 64; Little, 64; Long-tailed, 63; Margaretta's, 63; Minute, 64; Needle-billed, 64; Pale-bellied, 64; Planalto, 64; Porculla, 64; Reddish, 64; Rufous-breasted, 63; Rusty-breasted, 63, 64; Saw-billed, 64; Scale-throated, 64; Sooty-capped, 64; Sooty-throated, 64; Straight-billed, 64; Streak-throated, 64; Stripe-throated, 64; Tawny-bellied, 63; White-bearded, 64; White-browed, 64; White-whiskered, 63

Heron, 128-129, 130; Agami, 130; Black, 128; Black-headed, 129; Boat-billed, 130; Cape Verde, 129; Capped, 129; Cocoi, 129; Galapagos, 130; Goliath, 129; Great Blue, 129; Great White, 129; Great-billed, 129; Green, 130; Grey, 129; Humblot's, 129; Little Blue, 129; Mauritanian, 129; Pacific, 129; Pied, 129; Purple, 129; Rufous-bellied, 130; Squacco, 129; Striated, 130; Tricolored, 128; Whistling, 128; White-bellied, 129; White-faced, 128; Zigzag, 130

Hill-Babbler, 272; Abyssinian, 272; Ruwenzori, 272

Hill-Myna, 237; Eastern, 237; Southern, 237

Hillstar, 70; Andean, 70; Black-breasted, 70; Bolivian, 70; Ecuadorian, 70; Green-headed, 70; Stripe-bellied, 70; Wedge-tailed, 70; White-sided, 70; White-tailed, 70

Hoatzin, 48

Hobby, 125; African, 125; Australian, 125; Eurasian, 125; Oriental, 125

Honey-buzzard, 116; Barred, 116; Black, 116; European, 116; Indian, 116; Javan, 116; Long-tailed, 116; Malaysian, 116; Oriental, 116; Palawan, 116; Philippine, 116; Siberian, 116

Honeycreeper, 307, 325, 326; Golden-collared, 325; Green, 326; Laysan, 307; Purple, 326; Red-legged, 326; Shining, 326; Short-billed, 326

Honeyeater, 181-184, 185-186; Arfak, 185; Banded, 181; Bar-breasted, 185; Barred, 185; Black, 182; Black-backed, 184; Black-chested, 182; Black-chinned, 184; Black-headed, 183; Black-throated, 183; Blue-faced, 186; Bonin, 183; Bougainville, 182; Bridled, 183; Brown, 182; Brown-backed, 185; Brown-headed, 184; Buru, 182; Crescent, 185; Crow, 185; Dark-brown, 182; Eungella, 183; Forest, 182; Fuscous, 183; Giant, 185; Golden-backed, 183; Graceful, 182; Green-backed, 182; Grey, 185; Grey-fronted, 183; Grey-headed, 183; Guadalcanal, 183; Helmeted, 183; Hill-forest, 182; Indonesian, 182; Kadavu, 183; Leaden, 184; Lewin's, 182; Long-billed, 182; Macleay, 183; Mangrove, 183; Marbled, 184; Mayr's, 184; Mimic, 182; Mottle-breasted, 182; New Hebrides, 185; New Holland, 185; Obscure, 183; Olive, 182; Olive-streaked, 184; Orange-cheeked, 183; Painted, 186; Pale-eyed, 182; Pied, 182; Plain, 184; Puff-backed, 182; Purple-gaped, 183; Regent, 186; Rufous-backed, 184; Rufous-banded, 185; Rufous-sided,

184; Rufous-throated, 185; Scaly-crowned, 182; Scrub, 182; Seram, 182; Silver-eared, 182; Singing, 183; Smoky, 185; Spangled, 185; Spiny-cheeked, 186; Spotted, 183; Stevens's, 182; Streak-headed, 184; Streaky-breasted, 183; Striped, 185; Strong-billed, 184; Tagula, 182; Tawny-breasted, 183; Tawny-crowned, 185; Varied, 183; Wattled, 183; White-cheeked, 185; White-eared, 183; White-eyed, 182; White-fronted, 185; White-gaped, 183; White-lined, 182; White-naped, 183; White-plumed, 183; White-streaked, 182; White-throated, 183; White-tufted, 182; White-winged, 186; Yellow, 183; Yellow-eared, 182; Yellow-faced, 183; Yellow-gaped, 182; Yellow-plumed, 183; Yellow-spotted, 182; Yellow-throated, 183; Yellow-tinted, 183; Yellow-tufted, 183

Honeyguide, 20; Cassin's, 20; Dwarf, 20; Greater, 20; Green-backed, 20; Least, 20; Lesser, 20; Lyre-tailed, 20; Malaysian, 20; Pallid, 20; Scaly-throated, 20; Spotted, 20; Thick-billed, 20; Wahlberg's, 20; Willcocks's, 20; Yellow-footed, 20; Yellow-rumped, 20; Zenker's, 20

Hookbill, 170, 306; Chestnut-winged, 170; Lanai, 306

Hoopoe, 35; African, 35; Eurasian, 35; Madagascar, 35

Hoopoe-Lark, 280; Greater, 280; Lesser, 280

Hornbill, 33-35; African Grey, 34; African Pied, 34; Allied, 34; Assam, 34; Black, 34; Black-and-white-casqued, 35; Black-casqued, 35; Black Dwarf, 34; Blyth's, 35; Bradfield's, 34; Brown, 34; Brown-cheeked, 35; Bushy-crested, 34; Crowned, 34; Eastern Yellow-billed, 34; Great, 34; Helmeted, 34; Hemprich's, 34; Jackson's, 34; Knobbed, 35; Luzon, 34; Mindanao, 35; Mindoro, 34; Monteiro's, 34; Narcondam, 35; Palawan, 34; Pale-billed, 34; Piping, 35; Plain-pouched, 35; Red-billed Dwarf, 34; Red-billed, 34; Rhinoceros, 34; Rufous, 34; Rufous-necked, 35; Samar, 35; Silvery-cheeked, 35; Southern Yellow-billed, 34; Sulawesi, 35; Sulu, 34; Sumba, 35; Tarictic, 34; Trumpeter, 35; Von der Decken's, 34; White-crested, 33; White-crowned, 35; White-thighed, 35; Wreathed, 35; Wrinkled, 35; Writhed, 35; Writhed-billed, 35; Yellow-casqued, 35

Hornero, 166; Crested, 166; Lesser, 166; Pacific, 166; Pale-billed, 166; Pale-legged, 166; Pileated, 166; Rufous, 166; Wing-banded, 166

House-Finch, 305; Common, 305; Guadalupe, 305; McGregor's, 305

House-Martin, 248; Asian, 248; Nepal, 248; Northern, 248

House-Swallow, 247; Eastern, 247; Small, 247

House-Wren, 241; Antillean, 241; Northern, 241; Southern, 241

Huet-huet, 177; Black-throated, 177; Chestnut-throated, 177

Huia, 217

Hummingbird, 64, 65, 67, 68-70, 71, 73, 74; Admirable, 70; Allen's, 74; Amazilia, 69; Amethyst-throated, 69; Anna's, 73; Antillean Crested, 65; Azure-crowned, 68; Beautiful, 73; Bee, 74; Berylline, 68; Black-bellied, 69; Black-chinned, 73; Blue-capped, 69; Blue-chested, 68; Blue-headed, 67; Blue-tailed, 68; Blue-throated, 69; Broad-billed, 67; Broad-tailed, 74; Buff-bellied, 69; Buffy, 68; Bumblebee, 74; Calliope, 74; Cerise-throated, 74; Charming, 68; Chestnut-bellied, 69; Cinnamon, 69; Cinnamon-sided, 69; Copper-rumped, 68; Costa's, 73; Cuvier's, 64; Doubleday's, 67; Dusky, 67; Edwards's, 69; Emerald-chinned, 65; Escudo, 69; Fiery-throated, 67; Garnet-throated, 69; Giant, 70; Gilded, 67; Glow-throated, 74; Green-and-white, 68; Green-bellied, 68; Green-fronted, 69; Heliotrope-throated, 74; Indigo-capped, 68; Lucifer, 73; Luminous, 67; Magnificent, 70; Mangrove, 68; Many-spotted, 68; Mosquitia, 68; Oasis, 73; Olive-spotted, 68; Purple-chested, 68; Robert's, 64; Rose-throated, 74; Ruby-throated, 73; Ruby-topaz, 65; Rufous, 74; Rufous-cheeked, 67; Rufous-tailed, 69; Sapphire-bellied, 67; Sapphire-throated, 67; Scaly-breasted, 64; Scintillant, 74; Scissor-tailed, 70; Shining-green, 67; Snowy-bellied, 69; Snowy-breasted, 69; Sombre, 69; Sparkling-tailed, 73; Speckled, 70; Spot-throated, 68; Steely-vented, 68; Stripe-tailed, 69; Swallow-tailed, 65; Sword-billed, 71; Tooth-billed, 64; Tumbes, 68; Vervain, 74; Violet-bellied, 67; Violet-capped, 67; Violet-chested, 70; Violet-crowned, 69; Violet-headed, 65; Volcano, 74; Wedge-billed, 73; White-bellied, 68; White-eared, 67; White-tailed, 69; White-throated, 67; Wine-throated, 74; Xantus's, 67

Hwamei, 270

Hylacola, 188; Chestnut-rumped, 188; Shy, 188

Hylia, 266; Green, 266

Hyliota, 268; Southern, 268; Violet-backed, 268; Yellow-bellied, 268

Hypocolius, 253; Grey, 253

Ibis, 131-132; Andean, 131; Australian, 132; Bald, 132; Black-faced, 131; Black-headed, 132; Buff-necked, 131; Crested, 132; Giant,

132; Glossy, 131; Green, 131; Hadada, 131; Madagascar, 132; Olive, 131; Plumbeous, 131; Principe, 131; Puna, 131; Red-naped, 132; Sacred, 132; Sao Tome, 131; Scarlet, 131; Sharp-tailed, 131; Spot-breasted, 132; Straw-necked, 132; Wattled, 131; Whispering, 131; White, 131; White-faced, 131; White-shouldered, 132; White-winged, 132

Ibisbill, 108

Ibon, 261; Cinnamon, 261

Ifrit, 195

Iiwi, 307

Illadopsis, 272; Blackcap, 272; Brown, 272; Grey-chested, 272; Moloney's, 272; Mountain, 272; Pale-breasted, 272; Puvel's, 272; Rufous-winged, 272; Scaly-breasted, 272

Imperial-Pigeon, 94-96; Baker's, 95; Banded, 95; Bismarck, 95; Black, 95; Chestnut-bellied, 95; Christmas Island, 95; Cinnamon-bellied, 95; Collared, 95; Dark-backed, 95; Elegant, 95; Enggano, 95; Finsch's, 95; Green, 95; Grey, 95; Grey-headed, 94; Island, 95; Kimberley, 95; Marquesan, 95; Micronesian, 95; Mindoro, 94; Mountain, 95; New Caledonian, 95; Nutmeg, 95; Pacific, 95; Peale's, 95; Pied, 95; Pink-bellied, 94; Pink-headed, 95; Pinon, 95; Polynesian, 95; Purple-tailed, 95; Red-knobbed, 95; Shining, 95; Spice, 95; Spotted, 94; Timor, 95; Torresian, 95; White, 95; White-bellied, 94; White-eyed, 95; Yellow-tinted, 96

Inca, 71; Black, 71; Bronzy, 71; Brown, 71; Collared, 71; Gould's, 71

Inca-Finch, 327; Buff-bridled, 327; Great, 327; Grey-winged, 327; Little, 327; Rufous-backed, 327

Indigobird, 301; Baka, 301; Dusky, 301; Green, 301; Jambandu, 301; Pale-winged, 301; Purple, 301; South African, 301; Twinspot, 301; Variable, 301; Village, 301; Zaire, 301

Iora, 213; Common, 213; Great, 213; Green, 213; White-tailed, 213

Jabiru, 133

Jacamar, 32; Black-chinned, 32; Blue-necked, 32; Bluish-fronted, 32; Bronzy, 32; Brown, 32; Chestnut, 32; Coppery-chested, 32; Dusky-backed, 32; Great, 32; Green-tailed, 32; Pale-headed, 32; Paradise, 32; Purplish, 32; Rufous-and-green, 32; Rufous-tailed, 32; Three-toed, 32; White-chinned, 32; White-eared, 32; White-throated, 32; Yellow-billed, 32

Jacana, 106-107; African, 106; Bronze-winged, 107; Comb-crested, 107; Lesser, 106; Madagascar, 106; Northern, 107; Pheasant-tailed, 107; Wattled, 107

Jackdaw, 200; Daurian, 200; Eurasian, 200

Jacky-winter, 189

Jacobin, 65; Black, 65; White-necked, 65

Jaeger, 111; Long-tailed, 111; Parasitic, 111; Pomarine, 111

Jay, 198-199; Azure, 198; Azure-hooded, 198; Azure-naped, 198; Beautiful, 198; Black-capped, 199; Black-chested, 199; Black-collared, 198; Black-crowned, 199; Black-headed, 199; Black-throated, 198; Blue, 198; Brandt's, 199; Brown, 199; Bushy-crested, 198; California, 198; Cayenne, 198; Crested, 198; Curl-crested, 198; Dwarf, 198; Eurasian, 199; Florida, 198; Green, 199; Grey, 199; Himalayan, 199; Inca, 199; Iranian, 199; Japanese, 199; Lidth's, 199; Mexican, 198; Pinyon, 198; Plush-crested, 199; Purplish, 198; Purplish-backed, 198; San Blas, 198; Santa Cruz, 198; Scrub, 198; Siberian, 199; Sichuan, 199; Silvery-throated, 198; Steller's, 198; Sumichrast's, 198; Tufted, 199; Turquoise, 198; Unicolored, 198; Violaceous, 198; White-collared, 198; White-faced, 199; White-naped, 199; White-tailed, 199; White-throated, 198; Woodhouse's, 198; Yucatan, 198

Jery, 273; Common, 273; Green, 273; Stripe-throated, 273; Wedge-tailed, 273

Jewel-babbler, 195; Blue, 195; Chestnut-backed, 195; Spotted, 195

Jewelfront, 70; Gould's, 70

Junco, 309; Baird's, 309; Chiapas, 309; Dark-eyed, 309; Grey-headed, 309; Guadalupe, 309; Guatemala, 309; Mexican, 309; Oregon, 309; Pink-sided, 309; Red-backed, 309; Slate-colored, 309; Volcano, 309; White-winged, 309; Yellow-eyed, 309

Jungle-Flycatcher, 225; Brown-chested, 225; Eyebrowed, 225; Fulvous-chested, 225; Grey-chested, 225; Henna-tailed, 225; Rufous-tailed, 225; Russet-backed, 225; Slaty-backed, 225; Streaky-breasted, 225; White-browed, 225; White-throated, 225

Junglefowl, 9; Ceylon, 9; Green, 9; Grey, 9; Red, 9

Kagu, 98

Kaka, 51; New Zealand, 51; Norfolk Island, 51

Kakapo, 53

Kamao, 220

Kea, 51

Kestrel, 125; American, 125; Australian, 125; Banded, 125; Common, 125; Dickinson's, 125; Fox, 125; Greater, 125; Grey, 125; Lesser, 125; Madagascar, 125; Mauritius, 125; Seychelles, 125; Spotted, 125

Killdeer, 108

Kingbird, 152-153; Cassin's, 153; Couch's, 153; Eastern, 153; Giant, 153; Grey, 153; Loggerhead, 153; Snowy-throated, 152; Thick-billed, 153; Tropical, 153; Western, 153; White-throated, 153

Kingfisher, 39-41, 42; Amazon, 42; American Pygmy, 42; Angola, 40; Azure, 39; Banded, 40; Beach, 41; Belted, 42; Bismarck, 39; Black-backed, 40; Black-billed, 40; Black-capped, 40; Blue-and-white, 41; Blue-banded, 39; Blue-black, 41; Blue-breasted, 40; Blue-capped, 41; Blyth's, 39; Brown-hooded, 40; Brown-winged, 40; Caroline Islands, 41; Chattering, 41; Chestnut-bellied, 41; Chocolate-backed, 40; Cinnamon-banded, 41; Collared, 41; Common, 39; Crested, 42; Dwarf, 40; Flat-billed, 41; Forest, 41; Giant, 42; Green, 42; Green-and-rufous, 42; Green-backed, 41; Grey-headed, 40; Guam, 41; Half-collared, 39; Hook-billed, 41; Indigo-banded, 39; Javan, 40; Lazuli, 41; Lilac-cheeked, 40; Little, 40; Madagascar, 39; Malachite, 39; Mangaia, 41; Mangrove, 40; Marquesan, 41; Micronesian, 41; Mountain, 41; Moustached, 41; New Britain, 41; Philippine, 40; Pied, 42; Principe, 39; Red-backed, 41; Ringed, 42; Ruddy, 40; Rufous-backed, 40; Rufous-collared, 41; Rufous-lored, 41; Ryukyu, 41; Sacred, 41; Sao Tome, 39; Scaly, 41; Shining-blue, 39; Silvery, 39; Small Blue, 39; Sombre, 41; Spotted, 41; Stork-billed, 40; Striped, 40; Sulawesi, 40; Tahiti, 41; Talaud, 41; Tuamotu, 41; Ultramarine, 41; Variable, 40; White-bellied, 39; White-rumped, 41; White-throated, 40; Woodland, 40; Yellow-billed, 41

Kinglet, 249; Canary Islands, 249; Golden-crowned, 249; Ruby-crowned, 249

King-Parrot, 52; Australian, 52; Moluccan, 52; Papuan, 52

Kioea, 185

Kiskadee, 153; Great, 153; Lesser, 153

Kite, 116-117; Black, 117; Black-eared, 117; Black-shouldered, 116; Black-winged, 116; Brahminy, 117; Cape Verde, 117; Cuban, 116; Double-toothed, 116; Grey-headed, 116; Hook-billed, 116; Indonesian, 116; Letter-winged, 116; Mississippi, 116; Pearl, 116; Plumbeous, 116; Red, 117; Rufous-thighed, 116; Scissor-tailed, 116; Slender-billed, 116; Snail, 116; Square-tailed, 116; Swallow-tailed, 116; Whistling, 117; White-collared, 116; White-tailed, 116; Yellow-billed, 117

Kittiwake, 113; Black-legged, 113; Red-legged, 113

Kiwi, 1; Brown, 1; Great Spotted, 1; Little Spotted, 1

Knot, 106; Great, 106; Red, 106

Koa-Finch, 306; Greater, 306; Lesser, 306

Koel, 45; Asian, 45; Australian, 45; Black-billed, 45; Dwarf, 45; Long-tailed, 45; White-crowned, 45

Kokako, 217; North Island, 217; South Island, 217

Kookaburra, 40; Blue-winged, 40; Laughing, 40; Rufous-bellied, 40; Shovel-billed, 40; Spangled, 40

Lammergeier, 117

Lancebill, 64; Blue-fronted, 64; Green-fronted, 64

Lapwing, 109-110; Andean, 110; Australian, 110; Banded, 110; Black-headed, 110; Blacksmith, 110; Black-winged, 110; Brown-chested, 110; Cayenne, 110; Crowned, 110; Grey-headed, 110; Javanese, 110; Long-toed, 110; Masked, 110; Northern, 109; Pied, 110; Red-wattled, 110; River, 110; Senegal, 110; Sociable, 110; Southern, 110; Spot-breasted, 110; Spur-winged, 110; Wattled, 110; White-headed, 110; White-tailed, 110; Yellow-wattled, 110

Lark, 279-280, 281, 282; Abyssinian, 280; Angola, 279; Archer's, 280; Ash's, 279; Asian Short-toed, 281; Athi Short-toed, 281; Australasian, 279; Bar-tailed, 280; Bimaculated, 281; Black, 281; Blanford's, 281; Botha's, 281; Bradfield's, 280; Buckley's, 279; Calandra, 281; Cinnamon, 279; Clapper, 279; Collared, 280; Crested, 281; Degodi, 280; Desert, 280; Dune, 280; Dunn's, 281; Dupont's, 281; Dusky, 280; Erlanger's, 281; Fawn-colored, 280; Ferruginous, 280; Flappet, 279; Friedmann's, 279; Gillett's, 280; Gray's, 280; Greater Short-toed, 281; Horned, 282; Horsfield's, 279; Hume's, 281; Indian, 280; Indian Short-toed, 281; Karoo, 280; Kordofan, 279; Large-billed, 281; Latakoo, 279; Lesser Short-toed, 281; Long-billed, 280; Madagascar, 279; Malabar, 281; Masked, 281; Mongolian, 281; Monotonous, 279; Obbia, 281; Pink-billed, 281; Pink-breasted, 280; Przewalski's, 282; Razo, 282; Red-capped, 281; Red-winged, 279; Rudd's, 280; Rufous-naped, 279; Rufous-rumped, 280; Rufous Short-toed, 281; Rufous-tailed, 280; Rufous-winged, 280; Rusty, 280; Sabota, 280; Sclater's, 281; Short-clawed, 280; Short-tailed, 281; Sidamo, 280; Singing, 279; Somali, 279; Somali Long-

billed, 279; Spike-heeled, 280; Stark's, 281;
Sun, 281; Tawny, 281; Temminck's, 282;
Thekla, 281; Thick-billed, 281; Tibetan,
281; White-tailed, 279; White-winged, 281;
Williams's, 279; Wood, 281
Laughingthrush, 269-271; Ashy-headed, 269;
Bare-headed, 269; Barred, 270; Black, 269;
Black-eared, 270; Black-faced, 270; Black-
hooded, 269; Black-throated, 269; Blue-
winged, 270; Brown-capped, 270; Brown-
cheeked, 270; Chestnut-backed, 269;
Chestnut-capped, 270; Chestnut-crowned,
270; Collared, 270; Courtois's, 270; Elliot's,
270; Giant, 270; Greater Necklaced, 269;
Grey, 269; Grey-breasted, 270; Grey-eared,
270; Grey-sided, 270; Lesser Necklaced,
269; Masked, 269; Moustached, 270; Plain,
270; Red-tailed, 271; Red-winged, 271;
Rufous-breasted, 270; Rufous-chinned, 270;
Rufous-fronted, 269; Rufous-necked, 269;
Rufous-vented, 270; Rusty, 270; Scaly, 270;
Snowy-cheeked, 270; Spot-breasted, 270;
Spotted, 270; Streaked, 270; Striated, 269;
Striped, 270; Sunda, 269; Variegated, 270;
White-browed, 270; White-cheeked, 269;
White-crested, 269; White-necked, 269;
White-speckled, 270; White-throated, 269;
White-whiskered, 270; Wynaad, 270;
Yellow-throated, 270
Leafbird, 191; Blue-masked, 191; Blue-winged,
191; Golden-fronted, 191; Greater Green,
191; Jerdon's, 191; Lesser Green, 191;
Orange-bellied, 191; Philippine, 191;
Yellow-headed, 191; Yellow-throated, 191
Leaf-love, 251
Leaftosser, 172; Black-tailed, 172; Grey-throated,
172; Rufous-breasted, 172; Scaly-throated,
172; Short-billed, 172; Tawny-throated, 172
Leaf-Warbler, 267, 268; Blyth's, 267; Brooks's,
267; Ijima's, 267; Island, 268; Large-billed,
267; Lemon-throated, 268; Mountain, 268;
New Guinea, 268; Numfor, 268; Pale-
legged, 267; Philippine, 268; Plain, 267;
Sakhalin, 267; San Cristobal, 268; Sombre,
268; Sulawesi, 268; Tickell's, 267; Timor,
268; Tytler's, 267; White-tailed, 267
Leiothrix, 275; Red-billed, 275
Lemon-Dove, 88; Eastern, 88; Western, 88
Limpkin, 98
Linnet, 304; Eurasian, 304; Warsangli, 304;
Yemen, 304
Liocichla, 271; Crimson-headed, 271; Crimson-
winged, 271; Omei Shan, 271; Red-faced,
271; Steere's, 271
Lizard-Cuckoo, 47; Great, 47; Hispaniolan, 47;
Jamaican, 47; Puerto Rican, 47
Locustfinch, 299; Common, 299; Zaire, 299
Logrunner, 191; New Guinea, 191; Southern, 191

Longbill, 266, 288; Bocage's, 266; Green-
crowned, 288; Grey, 266; Grey-winged,
288; Kemp's, 266; Kretschmer's, 266;
Plumed, 288; Pulitzer's, 266; Pygmy, 288;
Yellow, 266
Longclaw, 290; Abyssinian, 290; Cape, 290;
Fuellerborn's, 290; Grimwood's, 290;
Pangani, 290; Rosy-throated, 290; Yellow-
throated, 290
Longspur, 309; Chest-collared, 309; Lapland,
309; McCown's, 309; Smith's, 315
Longtail, 256; Cricket, 256; Green, 256
Loon, 134; Arctic, 134; Black-throated, 134;
Common, 134; Green-throated, 134; Pacific,
134; Red-throated, 134; Yellow-billed, 134
Lorikeet, 49-50; Blue, 49; Blue-crowned, 49;
Blue-fronted, 50; Duchess, 50; Fairy, 50;
Goldie's, 49; Iris, 49; Josephine's, 50;
Kuhl's, 49; Little, 49; Meek's, 49; Mindanao,
49; Musk, 49; New Caledonian, 50; Olive-
headed, 49; Orange-billed, 50; Ornate, 49;
Palm, 49; Papuan, 50; Plum-faced, 50;
Pohnpei, 49; Purple-crowned, 49; Pygmy,
50; Rainbow, 49; Red-chinned, 49; Red-
collared, 49; Red-flanked, 50; Red-fronted,
50; Red-throated, 50; Scaly-breasted, 49;
Stephen's, 49; Striated, 50; Ultramarine, 49;
Varied, 49; Yellow-and-green, 49; Yellow-
billed, 50
Lory, 48-49; Black, 48; Black-capped, 49; Black-
winged, 49; Blue-eared, 49; Blue-streaked,
49; Brown, 48; Cardinal, 48; Chattering, 49;
Collared, 49; Dusky, 49; Purple-bellied, 49;
Purple-naped, 49; Rajah, 48; Red, 49; Red-
and-blue, 48; Violet-necked, 49; White-
naped, 49; Yellow-bibbed, 49; Yellow-
streaked, 48
Lovebird, 54; Black-cheeked, 54; Black-collared,
54; Black-winged, 54; Fischer's, 54; Grey-
headed, 54; Lilian's, 54; Red-headed, 54;
Rosy-faced, 54; Yellow-collared, 54
Lyrebird, 178; Albert's, 178; Superb, 178

Macaw, 55; Blue-and-yellow, 55; Blue-headed,
55; Blue-throated, 55; Blue-winged, 55;
Chestnut-fronted, 55; Cuban, 55; Glaucous,
55; Great Green, 55; Hispaniolan, 55;
Hyacinth, 55; Indigo, 55; Little Blue, 55;
Military, 55; Red-and-green, 55; Red-
bellied, 55; Red-fronted, 55; Red-
shouldered, 55; Scarlet, 55; Yellow-collared,
55
Magpie, 198, 199, 200, 203; Australasian, 203;
Azure-winged, 199; Black, 198; Black-
backed, 203; Black-billed, 200; Blue, 199;
Bornean, 199; Ceylon, 199; Formosan, 199;
Gold-billed, 199; Green, 199; New Guinea,
203; North African, 200; Short-tailed, 199;

Western, 203; White-backed, 203; White-winged, 199; Yellow-billed, 200; Yellow-breasted, 199

Magpie-Jay, 199; Black-throated, 199; White-throated, 199

Magpie-lark, 213

Magpie-Robin, 230; Madagascar, 230; Oriental, 230; Seychelles, 230

Maleo, 5

Malia, 253

Malimbe, 295; Ballmann's, 295; Black-throated, 295; Crested, 295; Gray's, 295; Ibadan, 295; Rachel's, 295; Red-bellied, 295; Red-crowned, 295; Red-headed, 295; Red-vented, 295; Yellow-legged, 295

Malkoha, 45-46; Black-bellied, 45; Blue-faced, 45; Chestnut-bellied, 45; Chestnut-breasted, 45; Green-billed, 45; Raffles's, 45; Red-billed, 45; Red-crested, 46; Red-faced, 45; Scale-feathered, 46; Sirkeer, 45; Yellow-billed, 45

Mallard, 16; Common, 16; Mexican, 16

Malleefowl, 5

Mamo, 307; Black, 307; Hawaii, 307

Manakin, 157-158; Almirante, 158; Band-tailed, 157; Black, 158; Blue-backed, 157; Blue-crowned, 157; Blue-rumped, 157; Cerulean-capped, 157; Club-winged, 158; Crimson-hooded, 157; Exquisite, 157; Fiery-capped, 158; Flame-crested, 158; Golden-collared, 158; Golden-crowned, 157; Golden-headed, 157; Golden-winged, 157; Green, 158; Greenish-bellied, 157; Helmeted, 157; Jet, 158; Lance-tailed, 157; Long-tailed, 157; Olive, 158; Opal-crowned, 157; Orange-collared, 157; Orange-crested, 158; Pin-tailed, 157; Red-capped, 157; Red-headed, 157; Round-tailed, 157; Scarlet-horned, 157; Snow-capped, 157; Striped, 158; Swallow-tailed, 157; Tepui, 157; Velvety, 157; White-bearded, 158; White-bibbed, 157; White-collared, 157; White-crowned, 157; White-fronted, 157; White-ruffed, 157; White-throated, 157; Wire-tailed, 157; Yellow-crested, 158; Yellow-headed, 158; Yungas, 157; Zeledon's, 157

Mango, 65; Antillean, 65; Black-throated, 65; Ecuadorian, 65; Green, 65; Green-breasted, 65; Green-throated, 65; Jamaican, 65; Prevost's, 65; Veraguas, 65

Mangrove-Robin, 190; Australian, 190; New Guinea, 190

Manucode, 202; Crinkle-collared, 202; Curl-crested, 202; Glossy-mantled, 202; Hunstein's, 202; Jobi, 202; Trumpet, 202

Mao, 185

Marshbird, 335; Brown-and-yellow, 335; Yellow-rumped, 335

Marsh-Harrier, 118; African, 118; Eastern, 118; Madagascar, 118; Reunion, 118; Spot-backed, 118; Spotted, 118; Western, 118

Marsh-Tit, 243; Asian, 243; Black-bibbed, 243; Eurasian, 243

Marsh-Tyrant, 151; White-headed, 151

Marsh-Wren, 240; Eastern, 240; Western, 240

Martin, 246, 247, 248; Banded, 247; Brazza's, 247; Brown-chested, 246; Caribbean, 246; Congo, 247; Cuban, 246; Fairy, 248; Galapagos, 246; Grey-breasted, 246; Mascarene, 247; Peruvian, 246; Plain, 247; Purple, 246; Rock, 247; Sand, 247; Sinaloa, 246; Southern, 246; Tree, 248

Masked-Owl, 75; Australian, 75; Bismarck, 75; Lesser, 75; Manus, 75; Minahassa, 75; New Guinea, 75; Taliabu, 75; Tasmanian, 75

Masked-Weaver, 293-294; Heuglin's, 293; Katanga, 294; Northern, 293; Ruwet's, 294; Southern, 294; Tanzania, 294; Victoria, 293; Vitelline, 293

Meadowlark, 335; Eastern, 335; Lilian's, 335; Long-tailed, 335; Pampas, 335; Peruvian, 335; Western, 335

Melampitta, 202; Greater, 202; Lesser, 202

Melidectes, 184-185; Belford's, 185; Bismarck, 184; Cinnamon-browed, 185; Huon, 185; Long-bearded, 185; Ornate, 185; San Cristobal, 185; Short-bearded, 185; Sooty, 184; Vogelkop, 185; Yellow-browed, 185

Merganser, 19; Auckland Islands, 19; Brazilian, 19; Common, 19; Hooded, 19; Red-breasted, 19; Scaly-sided, 19

Merlin, 125

Mesia, 275; Silver-eared, 275

Mesite, 103; Brown, 103; Subdesert, 103; White-breasted, 103

Metaltail, 72; Black, 72; Black-throated, 72; Brassy, 72; Colombian, 72; Coppery, 72; Ecuadorian, 72; Fire-throated, 72; Neblina, 72; Perija, 72; Reddish, 72; Scaled, 72; Tyrian, 72; Violet-throated, 72; Viridian, 72

Millerbird, 264; Laysan, 264; Nihoa, 264

Miner, 165, 186; Bell, 186; Black-eared, 186; Campo, 165; Coastal, 165; Common, 165; Creamy-rumped, 165; Dark-winged, 165; Dusky, 186; Greyish, 165; Noisy, 186; Puna, 165; Rufous-banded, 165; Short-billed, 165; Slender-billed, 165; Thick-billed, 165; Yellow-throated, 186

Minivet, 207; Ashy, 207; Brown-rumped, 207; Fiery, 207; Flame, 207; Flores, 207; Grey-chinned, 207; Little, 207; Long-tailed, 207; Rosy, 207; Ryukyu, 207; Scarlet, 207; Short-billed, 207; Small, 207; Sunda, 207; White-bellied, 207

Minla, 276; Blue-winged, 276; Chestnut-tailed, 276; Red-tailed, 276

Mistletoebird, 283

Mockingbird, 237-238; Bahama, 237; Black-eared, 237; Blue, 237; Blue-and-white, 237; Blue-grey, 237; Brown-backed, 237; Chalk-browed, 237; Charles, 237; Chilean, 237; Galapagos, 237; Hood, 238; Isabela, 237; Long-tailed, 237; Northern, 237; Patagonian, 237; St. Andrew, 237; San Cristobal, 238; Socorro, 238; Tropical, 237; White-banded, 237

Monal, 9; Chinese, 9; Himalayan, 9; Sclater's, 9

Monarch, 210, 211-212; Biak, 212; Black, 211; Black-and-white, 212; Black-backed, 212; Black-bibbed, 212; Black-chinned, 212; Black-faced, 211; Black-naped, 210; Black-tailed, 212; Black-tipped, 212; Black-winged, 211; Bougainville, 211; Buff-bellied, 211; Camiguin, 210; Celestial, 210; Chestnut-bellied, 212; Djaul, 212; Fatuhiva, 211; Flores, 212; Frill-necked, 212; Frilled, 212; Golden, 212; Hooded, 212; Iphis, 211; Island, 211; Kulambangra, 212; Loetoe, 212; Manus, 212; Marquesan, 211; Ogea, 211; Pacific, 210; Pearly, 211; Pied, 212; Rarotonga, 211; Rufous, 211; Rufous-collared, 212; Short-crested, 210; Slaty, 211; Spectacled, 212; Spot-winged, 212; Tahiti, 211; Tinian, 212; Truk, 211; Vanikoro, 211; White-breasted, 212; White-capped, 212; White-collared, 212; White-eared, 212; White-naped, 212; White-tailed, 212; White-tipped, 212; Yap, 212

Monjita, 149-150; Black-and-white, 150; Black-crowned, 149; Grey, 149; Rusty-backed, 150; Salinas, 150; White, 150; White-rumped, 150

Monklet, 33; Lanceolated, 33

Moor-Chat, 233; Congo, 233

Moorhen, 102; Common, 102; Dusky, 102; Gough, 102; Lesser, 102; Samoan, 102; San Cristobal, 102; Tristan, 102

Morepork, 80

Morningbird, 197

Morning-Thrush, 230; Spotted, 230

Mossie, 289

Motmot, 38-39; Blue-crowned, 39; Blue-diademed, 39; Blue-throated, 38; Broad-billed, 38; Highland, 39; Keel-billed, 39; Lesson's, 39; Plain-tailed, 38; Rufous, 39; Rufous-capped, 39; Russet-crowned, 39; Tawny-bellied, 39; Tody, 38; Turquoise-browed, 39

Mountain-Babbler, 276; Blackcap, 276; Chapin's, 276; Red-collared, 276; White-throated, 276

Mountain-Cacique, 333; Northern, 333; Southern, 333

Mountaineer, 73; Bearded, 73

Mountain-Finch, 304, 327; Black-headed, 304; Chestnut-breasted, 327; Cochabamba, 327; Plain, 304; Tucuman, 327

Mountain-gem, 69; Green-breasted, 69; Green-throated, 69; Grey-tailed, 69; Purple-throated, 69; Variable, 69; White-bellied, 69; White-throated, 69

Mountain-Pigeon, 96; Long-tailed, 96; Pale, 96; Papuan, 96

Mountain-Tanager, 322; Black-bellied, 322; Black-chested, 322; Black-chinned, 322; Blue-rumped, 322; Blue-shouldered, 322; Blue-winged, 322; Buff-breasted, 322; Carriker's, 322; Chestnut-bellied, 322; Golden-backed, 322; Hooded, 322; Lacrimose, 322; Masked, 322; Santa Marta, 322; Scarlet-bellied, 322

Mountain-Toucan, 31; Black-billed, 31; Grey-breasted, 31; Hooded, 31; Plate-billed, 31

Mourner, 151; Cinereous, 151; Greyish, 151; Pale-bellied, 151; Rufous, 151; Speckled, 151

Mousebird, 43; Blue-naped, 43; Red-backed, 43; Red-faced, 43; Speckled, 43; White-backed, 43; White-headed, 43

Mouse-warbler, 187; Bicolored, 187; Mountain, 187; Rusty, 187

Munia, 300; Alpine, 301; Bengalese, 300; Bismarck, 301; Black, 301; Black-and-white, 300; Black-breasted, 301; Black-faced, 300; Black-headed, 300; Black-throated, 300; Bronze, 300; Brown-backed, 300; Chestnut-breasted, 301; Dusky, 300; Five-colored, 300; Grand, 300; Grey-banded, 300; Grey-crowned, 300; Grey-headed, 300; Hooded, 300; Indian Black-headed, 300; Javan, 300; Madagascar, 300; Magpie, 300; Mottled, 300; New Hanover, 301; New Ireland, 301; Pale-headed, 300; Pictorella, 301; Red-backed, 300; Scaly-breasted, 300; Snow Mountain, 301; Southern Black-headed, 300; Streak-headed, 300; White-bellied, 300; White-capped, 300; White-headed, 300; White-rumped, 300; White-spotted, 300; Yellow-rumped, 301

Murre, 115; Common, 115; Thick-biled, 115

Murrelet, 115; Ancient, 115; Craveri's, 115; Japanese, 115; Kittlitz's, 115; Marbled, 115; Scripps's, 115; Xantus's, 115

Myna, 236-237; Apo, 237; Bali, 236; Bank, 236; Bare-eyed, 237; Ceylon, 237; Collared, 236; Common, 236; Crested, 236; Fiery-browed, 237; Finch-billed, 237; Golden, 236; Golden-crested, 236; Helmeted, 237; Hill, 237; Jungle, 236; Long-crested, 237; Pale-bellied, 236; Sulawesi, 237; White-necked, 237; White-vented, 236; Yellow-faced, 236

Myza, 185; Dark-eared, 185; White-eared, 185

Myzomela, 181; Ashy, 181; Banda, 181; Black, 181; Black-bellied, 181; Black-headed, 181; Cardinal, 181; Crimson-hooded, 181; Drab, 181; Dusky, 181; Ebony, 181; Micronesian, 181; Moluccan, 181; Mountain, 181; New Caledonian, 181; Olive-yellow, 181; Orange-breasted, 181; Red, 181; Red-bellied, 181; Red-brown, 181; Red-collared, 181; Red-headed, 181; Red-rumped, 181; Red-throated, 181; Rotuma, 181; Scarlet, 181; Scarlet-bibbed, 181; Scarlet-naped, 181; Sooty, 181; Sulawesi, 181; Sumba, 181; Wakolo, 181; White-chinned, 181; Yellow-vented, 181

Myzornis, 277; Fire-tailed, 277

Native-hen, 102; Black-tailed, 102; Tasmanian, 102

Needletail, 61-62; Brown-backed, 62; Papuan, 61; Philippine, 61; Purple, 62; Rupchand's, 61; Silver-backed, 61; White-throated, 61

Negrito, 150; Andean, 150; Patagonian, 150

Negrofinch, 296; Chestnut-breasted, 296; Grey-crowned, 296; Grey-headed, 296; Kungwe, 296; Pale-fronted, 296; Western, 296; White-breasted, 296

Nene, 14

Newtonia, 265-266; Archbold's, 265; Common, 265; Dark, 265; Red-tailed, 266

Nicator, 252; Eastern, 252; Yellow-spotted, 252; Yellow-throated, 252

Nighthawk, 83; Antillean, 83; Band-tailed, 83; Chestnut-banded, 83; Common, 83; Least, 83; Lesser, 83; Nacunda, 83; Rufous-bellied, 83; Sand-colored, 83; Short-tailed, 83

Night-Heron, 130; Black-crowned, 130; Japanese, 130; Malayan, 130; Rufous, 130; White-backed, 130; White-eared, 130; Yellow-crowned, 130

Nightingale, 229; Common, 229; Thrush, 229

Nightingale-Thrush, 221; Black-backed, 221; Black-billed, 221; Black-headed, 221; Grey-headed, 221; Olive, 221; Orange-billed, 221; Ruddy-capped, 221; Russet, 221; Slaty-backed, 221; Spotted, 221

Nightingale-Wren, 242; Northern, 242; Scaly, 242; Southern, 242

Nightjar, 84-86; Abyssinian, 85; Band-winged, 84; Bates's, 85; Black-shouldered, 85; Blackish, 84; Bonaparte's, 85; Brown, 84; Buff-collared, 84; Cayenne, 84; Collared, 85; Cuban, 84; Donaldson-Smith's, 85; Dusky, 84; Egyptian, 85; Eurasian, 84; Fiery-necked, 85; Franklin's, 85; Freckled, 85; Golden, 85; Greater Antillean, 84; Grey, 84; Hispaniolan, 84; Indian, 85; Itombwe, 85; Jerdon's, 85; Ladder-tailed, 86; Large-tailed, 85; Little, 84; Long-tailed, 85; Long-trained, 86; Ludovic's, 85; Lyre-tailed, 86; Madagascar, 85; Moco, 85; Montane, 85; Nubian, 85; Pennant-winged, 86; Philippine, 85; Plain, 85; Puerto Rican, 84; Pygmy, 84; Red-necked, 84; Roraiman, 84; Ruddy, 84; Rufous, 84; Rufous-cheeked, 85; Ruwenzori, 85; St. Lucia, 84; Salvadori's, 85; Savanna, 85; Scissor-tailed, 86; Scrub, 84; Sickle-winged, 86; Silky-tailed, 84; Slender-tailed, 85; Sombre, 84; South African, 85; Spot-tailed, 84; Square-tailed, 86; Standard-winged, 86; Star-spotted, 85; Sulawesi, 85; Swallow-tailed, 86; Swamp, 85; Sykes's, 85; Tawny-collared, 84; Usambara, 85; Vaurie's, 85; White-tailed, 84; White-winged, 84; Yucatan, 84

Niltava, 227-228; Large, 227; Small, 227; Fujian, 227; Rufous-bellied, 227; Rufous-vented, 227; Vivid, 228

Noddy, 114; Black, 114; Blue, 114; Blue-grey, 114; Brown, 114; Grey, 114; Lesser, 114

Nothura, 3; Chaco, 3; Darwin's, 3; Lesser, 3; Spotted, 3; White-bellied, 3

Nukupuu, 307

Nunlet, 33; Black, 33; Black-fronted, 33; Brown, 33; Chestnut-headed, 33; Costa Rican, 33; Fulvous-chinned, 33; Grey-cheeked, 33; Pale-winged, 33; Rufous-capped, 33; Rusty-breasted, 33; White-faced, 33; White-fronted, 33; Yellow-billed, 33

Nutcracker, 200; Clark's, 200; Eurasian, 200; Indian, 200; Spotted, 200

Nuthatch, 238-239; Beautiful, 239; Blue, 239; Brown-headed, 238; Chestnut-bellied, 238; Chestnut-vented, 238; Corsican, 238; Eurasian, 238; Giant, 239; Kabylie, 238; Kashmir, 238; Krueper's, 239; Oriental, 238; Pygmy, 238; Red-breasted, 239; Snowy-browed, 239; Southern, 238; Sulphur-billed, 239; Velvet-fronted, 239; White-breasted, 239; White-browed, 238; White-cheeked, 239; White-tailed, 238; Wood, 238; Yellow-billed, 239; Yunnan, 239

Oilbird, 82

Oliveback, 297; Fernando Po, 297; Grey-headed, 297; White-collared, 297

Olive-Greenbul, 252; Baumann's, 252; Cameroon, 252; Toro, 252

Olive-Pigeon, 86; African, 86; Cameroon, 86; Comoro, 86; Sao Tome, 86

Olomao, 220

Omao, 220

Oo, 185; Bishop's, 185; Hawaii, 185; Kauai, 185; Oahu, 185

Openbill, 133; African, 133; Asian, 133

Orangequit, 331

Origma, 187

Oriole, 204, 205, 334-335; African Black-headed, 205; Altamira, 334; Audubon's, 334; Baltimore, 334; Bar-winged, 335; Black, 205; Black-and-crimson, 205; Black-backed, 334; Black-cowled, 334; Black-eared, 204; Black-hooded, 205; Black-naped, 204; Black-tailed, 205; Black-vented, 334; Black-winged, 205; Brown, 204; Bullock's, 334; Campo, 334; Dark-headed, 205; Dark-throated, 204; Dusky-brown, 204; Epaulet, 334; Greater Antillean, 334; Green, 204; Green-headed, 204; Grey-collared, 204; Hooded, 334; Isabela, 204; Jamaican, 334; Maroon, 205; Martinique, 334; Montserrat, 334; Moriche, 334; Northern, 334; Ochre, 334; Olive-backed, 204; Olive-brown, 204; Orange, 334; Orange-backed, 334; Orange-crowned, 334; Orchard, 334; Philippine, 204; St. Lucia, 334; Sao Tome, 204; Scarlet-headed, 334; Scott's, 335; Silver, 205; Slender-billed, 204; Spot-breasted, 334; Streak-backed, 334; Tres Marias, 334; Western Black-headed, 205; White-edged, 334; White-lored, 204; Yellow, 334; Yellow-backed, 334; Yellow-shouldered, 334; Yellow-tailed, 334
Oropendola, 333; Amazonian, 333; Band-tailed, 333; Baudo, 333; Black, 333; Black-billed, 333; Casqued, 333; Chestnut-headed, 333; Crested, 333; Dusky-green, 333; Green, 333; Monteuma, 333; Olive, 333; Para, 333; Russet-backed, 333
Osprey, 115
Ostrich, 1; African, 1; Somali, 1
Ou, 306
Ouzel, 222; Ring, 222
Ovenbird, 314
Owl, 75, 76, 78, 79, 80, 81; Abyssinian, 81; Ashy-faced, 75; Band-bellied, 79; Bare-legged, 78; Barking, 80; Barn, 75; Barred, 79; Black-and-white, 79; Black-banded, 79; Boreal, 80; Buff-fronted, 80; Burrowing, 80; Crested, 79; Elf, 80; Fearful, 81; Flammulated, 76; Fulvous, 79; Great Grey, 79; Great Horned, 78; Hume's, 79; Jamaican, 81; Laughing, 81; Little, 80; Long-eared, 81; Madagascar, 81; Madagascar Red, 75; Maned, 79; Marsh, 81; Mottled, 79; Northern Hawk, 79; Northern Saw-whet, 80; Palau, 78; Powerful, 80; Rufous, 80; Rufous-banded, 79; Rufous-legged, 79; Rusty-barred, 79; Saw-whet, 80; Short-eared, 81; Snowy, 78; Spectacled, 79; Spotted, 79; Striped, 81; Stygian, 81; Sulawesi, 75; Tawny, 79; Tawny-browed, 79; Unspotted Saw-whet, 80; Ural, 79
Owlet, 79, 80; African Barred, 80; Albertine, 80; Asian Barred, 80; Chestnut, 80; Chestnut-backed, 80; Collared, 79; Forest, 80; Javan, 80; Jungle, 80; Long-whiskered, 80; Ngami, 80; Pearl-spotted, 79; Red-chested, 80; Scheffler's, 80; Sjostedt's, 80; Spotted, 80
Owlet-Nightjar, 81-82; Archbold's, 82; Australian, 81; Barred, 81; Feline, 81; Long-whiskered, 81; Mountain, 82; New Caledonian, 81; Wallace's, 82
Oxpecker, 237; Red-billed, 237; Yellow-billed, 237
Oxylabes, 277; White-throated, 277; Yellow-browed, 277
Oystercatcher, 107-108; African, 107; American, 107; Black, 107; Blackish, 108; Canary Islands, 107; Chatham Islands, 108; Eurasian, 107; Magellanic, 108; Pied, 107; Sooty, 108; South Island, 107; Variable, 108

Painted-Bunting, 333; Eastern, 333; Western, 333
Painted-snipe, 106; American, 106; Greater, 106
Palila, 306
Palmchat, 217
Palmcreeper, 170; Point-tailed, 170
Palm-Swift, 62; African, 62; Antillean, 62; Asian, 62; Fork-tailed, 62; Madagascar, 62
Palm-Tanager, 319; Black-crowned, 319; Grey-crowned, 319
Palm-Thrush, 230; Collared, 230; Rufous-tailed, 230
Pampa-Finch, 328; Great, 328; Olive, 328; Pale-throated, 328; Red-billed, 328
Paradigalla, 202; Long-tailed, 202; Short-tailed, 202
Paradise-crow, 202
Paradise-Flycatcher, 210-211; African, 211; Annobon, 210; Asian, 211; Bannerman's, 210; Bates's, 210; Bedford's, 210; Black-headed, 210; Blue, 211; Cerulean, 210; Grey-headed, 211; Japanese, 211; Luzon, 211; Madagascar, 211; Mascarene, 211; Rufous, 211; Rufous-vented, 210; Sao Tome, 211; Seychelles, 211; Talaud, 211
Paradise-Kingfisher, 41-42; Biak, 42; Black-headed, 42; Brown-headed, 42; Buff-breasted, 42; Common, 42; Kofiau, 42; Little, 41; Numfor, 42; Red-breasted, 42
Paradise-Whydah, 301; Broad-tailed, 301; Eastern, 301; Long-tailed, 301; Northern, 301; Togo, 301
Parakeet, 53, 54-58; Alexandrine, 54; Andean, 57; Antipodes, 53; Astral, 57; Aztec, 56; Barred, 57; Berlepsch's, 57; Black-capped, 57; Black-fronted, 53; Blaze-winged, 56; Blossom-headed, 55; Blue-crowned, 55; Blue-margined, 57; Blue-throated, 56; Brown-breasted, 57; Brown-throated, 56; Burrowing, 56; Caatinga, 56; Canary-winged, 57; Carolina, 56; Chapman's, 56;

Cobalt-winged, 57; Cordilleran, 55; Crimson-bellied, 56; Crimson-fronted, 56; Cuban, 56; Derbyan, 55; Dusky-headed, 56; El Oro, 57; Fiery-shouldered, 57; Golden, 55; Golden-capped, 56; Golden-plumed, 56; Golden-winged, 57; Green, 55; Green-cheeked, 56; Grey-cheeked, 57; Grey-headed, 54; Grey-hooded, 57; Hispaniolan, 56; Horned, 53; Intermediate, 54; Jamaican, 56; Jandaya, 56; Layard's, 55; Long-tailed, 55; Lord Howe Island, 53; Magdalena, 57; Malabar, 55; Maroon-bellied, 56; Maroon-tailed, 57; Mauritius, 54; Mitred, 56; Monk, 57; Mountain, 57; Nanday, 56; New Caledonian, 53; Newton's, 54; Nicobar, 55; Norfolk Island, 53; Olive-throated, 56; Orange-chinned, 57; Orange-fronted, 56; Ouvea, 53; Pacific, 55; Painted, 56; Peach-fronted, 56; Pearly, 56; Plain, 57; Plum-headed, 55; Raiatea, 53; Red-breasted, 55; Red-eared, 57; Red-fronted, 53; Red-masked, 56; Red-throated, 55; Rose-headed, 57; Rose-ringed, 54; Rufous-fronted, 57; Santa Marta, 56; Scarlet-fronted, 55; Seychelles, 54; Slaty-headed, 54; Slender-billed, 57; Socorro, 55; Sulphur-winged, 57; Sun, 56; Tui, 58; Veraguas, 56; White-eared, 56; White-eyed, 56; White-necked, 57; Yellow-chevroned, 57; Yellow-fronted, 53

Pardalote, 186; Black-headed, 186; Forty-spotted, 186; Northern, 186; Red-browed, 186; Red-tipped, 186; Spotted, 186; Straited, 186; Yellow-rumped, 186; Yellow-tipped, 186

Pardusco, 326

Parotia, 202; Carola's, 202; Eastern, 202; Lawes's, 202; Wahnes's, 202; Western, 202

Parrot, 51, 52-54, 56, 58-59; Alexandra's, 52; Black, 53; Black-billed, 59; Black-headed, 58; Black-lored, 52; Black-winged, 58; Blue-backed, 52; Blue-bellied, 59; Blue-cheeked, 59; Blue-collared, 51; Blue-fronted, 59; Blue-headed, 58; Blue-naped, 52; Blue-rumped, 51; Blue-winged, 53; Bourke's, 53; Bronze-winged, 58; Brown-headed, 54; Brown-hooded, 58; Brown-necked, 53; Caica, 58; Cape, 53; Cuban, 58; Diademed, 59; Dusky, 58; Eclectus, 52; Elegant, 53; Festive, 59; Golden-shouldered, 53; Great-billed, 52; Grey, 53; Ground, 53; Hispaniolan, 59; Hooded, 52; Imperial, 59; Indigo-winged, 58; Kawall's, 59; Lilac-crowned, 59; Maroon-fronted, 56; Mascarene, 53; Mealy, 59; Meyer's, 53; Mulga, 52; Niam-niam, 53; Night, 53; Olive-shouldered, 52; Orange-bellied, 53; Orange-cheeked, 58; Orange-winged, 59; Paradise, 53; Pesquet's, 52; Pileated, 58; Plum-crowned, 58; Puerto Rican, 59; Red-

bellied, 54; Red-billed, 58; Red-browed, 59; Red-capped, 52; Red-cheeked, 51; Red-crowned, 59; Red-faced, 58; Red-fan, 59; Red-fronted, 53; Red-lored, 59; Red-necked, 59; Red-rumped, 52; Red-spectacled, 59; Red-tailed, 59; Red-winged, 52; Regent, 52; Rock, 53; Rose-faced, 58; Rueppell's, 54; Rusty-faced, 58; Saffron-headed, 58; St. Lucia, 59; St. Vincent, 59; Salvin's, 59; Scaly-headed, 58; Scaly-naped, 59; Scarlet-chested, 53; Senegal, 53; Short-tailed, 58; Singing, 51; Speckle-faced, 58; Superb, 52; Swift, 53; Thick-billed, 56; Tucuman, 59; Turquoise, 53; Vasa, 53; Vinaceous, 59; Vulturine, 58; White-bellied, 58; White-capped, 58; White-crowned, 59; White-fronted, 59; Yellow-billed, 59; Yellow-crowned, 59; Yellow-eared, 56; Yellow-faced, 59; Yellow-fronted, 54; Yellow-headed, 59; Yellow-lored, 59; Yellow-naped, 59; Yellow-shouldered, 59

Parrotbill, 277-278, 307; Ashy-eared, 278; Ashy-throated, 278; Bearded, 277; Black-breasted, 277; Black-browed, 278; Black-throated, 278; Blyth's, 278; Brown, 277; Brown-winged, 278; Fulvous, 278; Golden, 278; Great, 277; Grey-headed, 277; Grey-hooded, 278; Maui, 307; Reed, 278; Rufous-headed, 278; Rusty-throated, 278; Short-tailed, 278; Spectacled, 277; Spot-breasted, 277; Three-toed, 277; Vinous-throated, 278

Parrotfinch, 299-300; Blue-faced, 299; Fiji, 299; Green-faced, 299; Papuan, 299; Pin-tailed, 299; Pink-billed, 300; Red-eared, 299; Red-headed, 299; Red-throated, 299; Royal, 300; Tawny-breasted, 299; Tricolored, 299

Parrotlet, 57, 58; Amazonian, 58; Blue-fronted, 58; Blue-winged, 57; Brown-backed, 58; Dusky-billed, 57; Golden-tailed, 58; Green-rumped, 57; Lilac-tailed, 58; Mexican, 57; Pacific, 57; Red-fronted, 58; Sapphire-rumped, 58; Scarlet-shouldered, 58; Spectacled, 57; Spot-winged, 58; Tepui, 58; Yellow-faced, 57

Partridge, 6, 7-9; Annam, 9; Arabian, 6; Bar-backed, 8; Barbary, 6; Black, 8; Buff-throated, 6; Campbell's, 8; Chestnut-bellied, 8; Chestnut-breasted, 8; Chestnut-headed, 9; Chestnut-necklaced, 9; Chestnut-throated, 6; Crested, 9; Crimson-headed, 9; Daurian, 7; Ferruginous, 9; Formosan, 8; Grey, 7; Grey-breasted, 8; Hainan, 9; Hill, 8; Kinabalu, 8; Long-billed, 8; Madagascar, 8; Orange-necked, 8; Philby's, 6; Red-billed, 9; Red-breasted, 8; Red-legged, 6; Rock, 6; Rufous-throated, 8; Rusty-necklaced, 6; Sand, 6; Scaly-breasted, 9; See-see, 6; Sichuan, 8; Snow, 6; Stone, 9; Tibetan, 7; White-cheeked, 8; White-necklaced, 8

Parula, 313; Northern, 313; Socorro, 313; Tropical, 313

Pauraque, 83

Peacock-Pheasant, 10; Bornean, 10; Bronze-tailed, 10; Germain's, 10; Grey, 10; Malayan, 10; Mountain, 10; Palawan, 10

Peafowl, 11; Congo, 11; Green, 11; Indian, 11

Pelican, 132; American White, 132; Australian, 132; Brown, 132; Dalmatian, 132; Great White, 132; Peruvian, 132; Pink-backed, 132; Spot-billed, 132

Peltops, 204; Lowland, 204; Mountain, 204

Penduline-Tit, 243; African, 243; Black-headed, 243; Buff-bellied, 243; Chinese, 243; Eurasian, 243; Forest, 243; Mouse-colored, 243; Sennar, 243; Southern, 243; White-crowned, 243; White-throated, 243; Yellow, 243; Zambesi, 243

Penguin, 134; Adelie, 134; Chinstrap, 134; Emperor, 134; Erect-crested, 134; Fiordland, 134; Galapagos, 134; Gentoo, 134; Humboldt, 134; Jackass, 134; King, 134; Little, 134; Macaroni, 134; Magellanic, 134; Moseley's, 134; Rockhopper, 134; Royal, 134; Snares, 134; White-flippered, 134; Yellow-eyed, 134

Peppershrike, 193; Black-billed, 193; Chaco, 193; Ochre-crowned, 193; Rufous-browed, 193; Yellow-backed, 193

Petrel, 135-136; Antarctic, 135; Atlantic, 136; Barau's, 135; Beck's, 135; Bermuda, 136; Black, 136; Black-capped, 136; Black-winged, 135; Blue, 136; Bonin, 135; Bulwer's, 136; Cape Verde, 136; Cape, 135; Chatham Islands, 135; Collared, 135; Cook's, 135; Defilippe's, 135; Fiji, 135; Galapagos, 135; Gould's, 135; Great-winged, 136; Grey, 136; Hawaiian, 135; Herald, 135; Jamaican, 136; Jouanin's, 136; Juan Fernandez, 135; Kerguelen, 135; Kermadec, 135; Madeira, 136; Magenta, 136; Mascarene, 135; Mottled, 135; Murphy's, 135; Phoenix, 135; Providence, 136; Pycroft's, 135; Snow, 135; Soft-plumaged, 136; Stejneger's, 135; Tahiti, 135; Trindade, 135; Westland, 136; White-chinned, 136; White-headed, 136; White-necked, 135

Petronia, 289; Bush, 289; Chestnut-shouldered, 289; Yellow-spotted, 289; Yellow-throated, 289; Little Purple-banded, 287; Tsavo Purple-banded, 287

Pewee, 148; Blackish, 148; Dark, 148; Greater, 148; Greater Antillean, 148; Lesser Antillean, 148; Ochraceous, 148; Short-legged, 148; Smoke-colored, 148; Tropical, 148; White-throated, 148

Phainopepla, 217

Phalarope, 106; Red, 106; Red-necked, 106; Wilson's, 106

Pheasant, 9-10; Blood, 9; Bulwer's, 10; Cheer, 10; Common, 10; Copper, 10; Edwards's, 10; Elliot's, 10; Golden, 10; Green, 10; Horsfield's, 9; Hume's, 10; Imperial, 9; Kalij, 9; Koklass, 9; Lady Amherst's, 10; Lineated, 9; Mikado, 10; Reeves's, 10; Ring-necked, 10; Salvadori's, 10; Silver, 9; Sumatran, 10; Swinhoe's, 10; Vietnamese, 10

Philentoma, 216; Maroon-breasted, 216; Rufous-winged, 216

Phoebe, 149; Black, 149; Eastern, 149; Say's, 149; White-winged, 149

Piapiac, 200

Piculet, 20-21; African, 21; Antillean, 21; Bar-breasted, 20; Chestnut, 21; Eduadorian, 20; Fine-barred, 21; Golden-fronted, 20; Golden-spangled, 20; Greyish, 21; Guianan, 20; Guttate, 21; Lafresnaye's, 20; Mottled, 21; Ocellated, 21; Ochraceous, 21; Ochre-collared, 21; Olivaceous, 21; Orinoco, 20; Para, 20; Pilcomayo, 21; Plain-breasted, 21; Rufous, 21; Rufous-breasted, 21; Rusty-necked, 20; Scaled, 20; Speckle-chested, 20; Speckled, 20; Spotted, 20; Tawny, 21; Varzea, 21; White-barred, 21; White-bellied, 20; White-browed, 21; White-wedged, 21

Pied-Babbler, 275; Hinde's, 275; Northern, 275; Sharpe's, 275; Southern, 275

Pied-Hornbill, 34; Malabar, 34; Malaysian, 34; Northern, 34; Oriental, 34

Piedtail, 70; Ecuadorian, 70; Peruvian, 70

Pigeon, 86, 87, 88, 89, 91, 92, 96; Afep, 86; Band-tailed, 87; Bare-eyed, 87; Berlepsch's, 87; Bolle's, 86; Chilean, 87; Choiseul, 92; Crested, 89; Dusky, 87; Eastern Bronze-naped, 88; Hill, 86; Laurel, 86; Metallic, 87; New Zealand, 96; Nicobar, 91; Norfolk Island, 96; Pale-backed, 86; Pale-capped, 87; Pale-vented, 87; Partridge, 89; Passenger, 89; Peruvian, 87; Pheasant, 92; Picazuro, 87; Pink, 88; Plain, 87; Plumbeous, 87; Purple-tinted, 87; Red-billed, 87; Red-plumed, 89; Ring-tailed, 87; Rock, 86; Ruddy, 87; Ryukyu, 87; Sao Tome Bronze-naped, 88; Scaled, 87; Scaly-naped, 87; Short-billed, 87; Snow, 86; Somali, 86; Sombre, 96; Speckled, 86; Spinifex, 89; Spot-winged, 87; Squatter, 89; Stock, 86; Tooth-billed, 96; Topknot, 96; Trocaz, 86; Western Bronze-naped, 87; White-collared, 86; White-crowned, 87; White-headed, 87; White-naped, 87; White-necked, 87; Wonga, 89; Yellow-legged, 87

Piha, 155-156; Cinnamon-vented, 156; Dusky, 155; Grey-tailed, 155; Olivaceous, 155;

Rose-collared, 156; Rufous, 156; Scimitar-winged, 155; Screaming, 156

Pilotbird, 187

Pintail, 17; Crozet, 17; Eaton's, 17; Galapagos, 17; Kerguelen, 17; Niceforo's, 17; Northern, 17; South Georgia, 17; White-cheeked, 17; Yellow-billed, 17

Piopio, 197; North Island, 197; South Island, 197

Piping-Guan, 4; Black-fronted, 4; Blue-throated, 4; Gray's, 4; Natterer's, 4; Red-throated, 4; Stripe-crowned, 4; Trinidad, 4; White-headed, 4

Pipipi, 196

Pipit, 290-292; African, 290; Alpine, 292; American, 291; Australasian, 290; Bannerman's, 291; Berthelot's, 291; Blyth's, 291; Buffy, 291; Bush, 291; Cameroon, 290; Chaco, 292; Correndera, 291; Golden, 290; Goodson's, 291; Hellmayr's, 291; Jackson's, 291; Long-billed, 291; Long-legged, 291; Malindi, 291; Meadow, 291; Menzbier's, 291; Moco, 291; Mountain, 290; New Zealand, 290; Nilgiri, 291; Ochre-breasted, 292; Olive-backed, 291; Paddyfield, 290; Paramo, 291; Pechora, 291; Plain-backed, 291; Red-throated, 291; Richard's, 290; Rock, 291; Rosy, 291; Sharpe's, 290; Short-billed, 291; Short-tailed, 291; Sokoke, 291; South Georgia, 291; Sprague's, 291; Striped, 290; Tawny, 291; Tree, 291; Upland, 291; Water, 291; Woodland, 291; Yellow-breasted, 290; Yellow-tufted, 290; Yellowish, 292

Piprites, 158; Black-capped, 158; Grey-headed, 158; Wing-barred, 158

Pitohui, 197; Black, 197; Crested, 197; Hooded, 197; Rusty, 197; Variable, 197; White-bellied, 197

Pitta, 139; African, 139; Azure-breasted, 139; Banded, 139; Bar-bellied, 139; Black-crowned, 139; Black-faced, 139; Black-headed, 139; Blue, 139; Blue-banded, 139; Blue-headed, 139; Blue-naped, 139; Blue-rumped, 139; Blue-winged, 139; Eared, 139; Elegant, 139; Fairy, 139; Garnet, 139; Giant, 139; Green-breasted, 139; Gurney's, 139; Hooded, 139; Indian, 139; Ivory-breasted, 139; Mangrove, 139; Noisy, 139; Rainbow, 139; Red-bellied, 139; Rusty-naped, 139; Schneider's, 139; Sula, 139; Superb, 139; Two-striped, 139; Whiskered, 139

Plains-wanderer, 103

Plantain-eater, 75; Eastern Grey, 75; Western Grey, 75

Plantcutter, 155; Peruvian, 155; Rufous-tailed, 155; White-tipped, 155

Ploughbill, 197; Wattled, 197

Plover, 107, 108-109, 110; Caspian, 109; Chestnut-banded, 109; Collared, 109; Common Ringed, 108; Crab, 110; Double-banded, 109; Forbes's, 109; Greater Sand, 109; Grey, 108; Hooded, 109; Javan, 109; Kentish, 109; Kittlitz's, 109; Little Ringed, 108; Long-billed, 108; Madagascar, 108; Magellanic, 107; Malaysian, 109; Mongolian, 109; Mountain, 109; Oriental, 109; Peruvian, 109; Piping, 109; Puna, 109; Red-breasted, 108; Red-capped, 109; Rufous-chested, 109; St. Helena, 109; Semipalmated, 108; Shore, 109; Snowy, 109; Three-banded, 109; Tibetan, 109; Two-banded, 109; White-fronted, 109; Wilson's, 108

Plovercrest, 65; Black-breasted, 65; Violet-crested, 65

Plumeleteer, 69; Black-vented, 69; Blue-bellied, 69; Bronze-tailed, 69; Ecuadorian, 69; White-vented, 69

Plushcap, 326

Plushcrown, 170; Orange-fronted, 170

Pochard, 18; Baer's, 18; Common, 18; Ferruginous, 18; Madagascar, 18; Red-crested, 18; Rosy-billed, 18; Southern, 18

Pond-Heron, 129-130; Chinese, 129; Indian, 129; Javan, 130; Madagascar, 130

Poo-uli, 307

Poorwill, 83-84; Common, 83; Eared, 84; Jamaican, 84; Least, 84; Ocellated, 84; Yucatan, 84

Potoo, 82-83; Andean, 83; Common, 83; Great, 82; Grey, 83; Hispaniolan, 83; Large-tailed, 82; Long-tailed, 82; Paraguayan, 83; Rufous, 83; White-winged, 83

Prairie-chicken, 11; Greater, 11; Lesser, 11

Pratincole, 111; Australian, 111; Black-winged, 111; Collared, 111; Grey, 111; Madagascar, 111; Oriental, 111; Rock, 111; Rufous-collared, 111; Small, 111; White-collared, 111

Prickletail, 170; Spectacled, 170

Prinia, 255-256; Ashy, 256; Banded, 256; Bar-winged, 256; Black-chested, 256; Black-faced, 256; Brown, 255; Drakensburg, 256; Graceful, 255; Grey-breasted, 255; Grey-crowned, 255; Hill, 255; Jungle, 255; Karoo, 256; Long-tailed, 255; Pale, 256; Plain, 256; River, 256; Rufescent, 255; Rufous-fronted, 255; Rufous-vented, 255; Sao Tome, 256; Sierra Leone, 256; Striated, 255; Swamp, 255; Tawny-flanked, 256; White-chinned, 256; Yellow-bellied, 256

Prion, 136; Antarctic, 136; Broad-billed, 136; Fairy, 136; Fulmar, 136; MacGillivray's, 136; Medium-billed, 136; Slender-billed, 136

Ptarmigan, 11; Rock, 11; White-tailed, 11; Willow, 11

Puaiohi, 220

Puffback, 213-214; Black-backed, 214; Large-billed, 214; Northern, 213; Pink-footed, 214; Pringle's, 213; Red-eyed, 214; Zanzibar, 214

Puffbird, 32-33; Barred, 33; Black-breasted, 32; Black-streaked, 33; Brown-banded, 32; Buff-bellied, 32; Chestnut-capped, 32; Collared, 33; Crescent-chested, 33; Moustached, 33; Pied, 32; Rufous-necked, 33; Russet-throated, 33; Semicollared, 33; Sooty-capped, 33; Spot-backed, 33; Spotted, 32; Striolated, 33; Two-banded, 33; White-chested, 33; White-eared, 33; White-necked, 32; White-whiskered, 33

Puffin, 115; Atlantic, 115; Horned, 115; Tufted, 115

Puffleg, 71-72; Black-breasted, 71; Black-thighed, 72; Blue-capped, 72; Colorful, 72; Coppery-bellied, 72; Emerald-bellied, 72; Glowing, 71; Golden-breasted, 72; Greenish, 72; Hoary, 72; Sapphire-vented, 71; Turquoise-throated, 71

Purpletuft, 155; Buff-throated, 155; Dusky, 155; White-browed, 155

Pygmy-goose, 16; African, 16; Cotton, 16; Green, 16

Pygmy-Kingfisher, 40; African, 40; Madagascar, 40

Pygmy-Owl, 79-80; Amazonian, 79; Andean, 79; Austral, 80; Cuban, 80; Eurasian, 79; Ferruginous, 80; Hardy's, 79; Least, 79; Mountain, 79; Northern, 79; Peruvian, 80; Yungas, 79

Pygmy-Parrot, 51; Buff-faced, 51; Finsch's, 51; Geelvink, 51; Meek's, 51; Red-breasted, 51; Yellow-capped, 51

Pygmy-Tyrant, 141, 145, 146; Black-capped, 146; Bronze-olive, 141; Double-banded, 146; Eared, 146; Golden-scaled, 146; Hazel-fronted, 141; Helmeted, 146; Long-crested, 146; Pale-eyed, 146; Rufous-headed, 141; Rufous-sided, 145; Scale-crested, 146; Short-tailed, 146; Tawny-crowned, 145; White-bellied, 146

Pyrrhuloxia, 332

Pytilia, 297; Green-winged, 297; Lineated, 297; Orange-winged, 297; Red-faced, 297; Red-winged, 297

Quail, 8, 9, 12, 13; African, 8; Banded, 12; Blue, 8; Blue-breasted, 8; Brown, 8; California, 12; Common, 8; Elegant, 12; Eurasian, 8; Gambel's, 12; Harlequin, 8; Himalayan, 9; Japanese, 8; Montezuma, 13; Mountain, 12; New Zealand, 8; Ocellated, 13; Rain, 8; Salle's, 13; Scaled, 12; Singing, 13; Snow Mountain, 8; Stubble, 8; Swamp, 8; Tawny-faced, 13

Quail-Dove, 91; Blue-headed, 91; Bourcier's, 91; Bridled, 91; Buff-fronted, 91; Crested, 91; Dark, 91; Grey-headed, 91; Key West, 91; Lined, 91; Martinique, 91; Olive-backed, 91; Pink-faced, 91; Purple-crowned, 91; Purplish-backed, 91; Ruddy, 91; Rufous-breasted, 91; Russet-crowned, 91; Sapphire, 91; Violaceous, 91; White-faced, 91; White-throated, 91

Quailfinch, 299; African, 299; Ethiopian, 299; Red-billed, 299

Quail-thrush, 195; Chestnut, 195; Chestnut-breasted, 195; Cinnamon, 195; Nullarbor, 195; Painted, 195; Spotted, 195; Western, 195

Quelea, 295; Cardinal, 295; Red-billed, 295; Red-headed, 295

Quetzal, 36; Crested, 36; Golden-headed, 36; Pavonine, 36; Resplendent, 36; White-tipped, 36

Racket-tail, 72; Booted, 72

Racquet-tail, 51-52; Blue-crowned, 51; Blue-headed, 51; Blue-winged, 51; Buru, 52; Golden-mantled, 51; Green, 51; Mindanao, 51; Montane, 51; Yellow-breasted, 51

Rail, 98-100, 101-102; Auckland Islands, 100; Austral, 100; Bald-faced, 101; Bar-winged, 99; Bare-eyed, 101; Barred, 99; Black, 99; Blackish, 101; Bogota, 100; Brown-banded, 100; Buff-banded, 99; Chatham Islands, 100; Chestnut, 102; Clapper, 100; Dieffenbach's, 100; Galapagos, 99; Gilbert, 99; Grey-throated, 98; Guam, 100; Highland, 100; Inaccessible Island, 100; Invisible, 102; Kaffir, 100; King, 100; Kioloides, 98; Lewin's, 100; Lord Howe Island, 99; Madagascar, 100; New Britain, 99; New Caledonian, 99; New Guinea Flightless, 102; Nkulengu, 98; Okinawa, 99; Peruvian, 100; Plain-flanked, 100; Plumbeous, 101; Red-and-white, 99; Rouget's, 100; Roviana, 99; Rufous-faced, 99; Sakalava, 101; Sharpe's, 100; Slaty-breasted, 100; Snoring, 100; Speckled, 99; Spotted, 101; Swinhoe's, 99; Tahiti, 100; Virginia, 100; Wake Island, 100; Water, 100; Western, 100; White-throated, 100; Woodford's, 99; Yellow, 99; Zapata, 101

Rail-babbler, 195; Malaysian, 195

Raven, 201-202; Australian, 201; Brown-necked, 201; Chihuahuan, 201; Common, 201; Dwarf, 201; Fan-tailed, 201; Forest, 201; Little, 201; Relict, 201; Thick-billed, 202; White-necked, 202

Rayadito, 166; Mas Afuera, 166; Thorn-tailed, 166

Razorbill, 115

Recurvebill, 171; Bolivian, 171; Peruvian, 171

Red-Cotinga, 154; Black-necked, 154; Guianan, 154

Redhead, 18

Redpoll, 304; Common, 304; Hoary, 304; Hornemann's, 304; Lesser, 304

Redshank, 105; Common, 105; Spotted, 105

Redstart, 231, 314, 315-316; Ala Shan, 231; American, 314; Andean, 316; Black, 231; Blue-capped, 231; Blue-fronted, 231; Brown-capped, 315; Collared, 316; Common, 231; Daurian, 231; Golden-fronted, 316; Hodgson's, 231; Moussier's, 231; Painted, 315; Rufous-backed, 231; Rufous-crowned, 316; Saffron-breasted, 316; Slate-throated, 315; Spectacled, 316; Tepui, 315; White-bellied, 231; White-faced, 316; White-fronted, 316; White-throated, 231; White-winged, 231; Yellow-bellied, 315; Yellow-crowned, 316; Yellow-faced, 315

Redthroat, 187

Redwing, 223

Reed-Bunting, 309; Dark, 309; Northern, 309; Pale, 309

Reed-Finch, 327; Long-tailed, 327

Reedhaunter, 170; Curve-billed, 170; Straight-billed, 170

Reed-Warbler, 263-264; African, 263; Australian, 264; Basra, 264; Black-browed, 263; Blyth's, 263; Caroline Islands, 264; Clamorous, 264; Cook Islands, 264; Eurasian, 263; Great, 263; Heinroth's, 264; Henderson Island, 264; Large-billed, 264; Manchurian, 263; Marquesan, 264; Nauru, 264; Nightingale, 264; Oriental, 263; Pitcairn, 264; Rimatara, 264; Rufescent, 263; South African, 263; Streaked, 263; Tahiti, 264; Tuamotu, 264

Reef-Egret, 129; Arabian, 129; Pacific, 129; West African, 129; Western, 129

Rhabdornis, 278; Long-billed, 278; Stripe-breasted, 278; Stripe-sided, 278

Rhea, 1; Darwin's, 1; Greater, 1; Lesser, 1; Puna, 1

Riflebird, 202; Eastern, 202; Magnificent, 202; Paradise, 202; Victoria's, 202

Rifleman, 138

Ringneck, 52; Cloncurry, 52; Mallee, 52; Port Lincoln, 52

River-Martin, 246; African, 246; White-eyed, 246

River-Tyrant, 151; Amazon, 151; Orinoco, 151

Roadrunner, 48; Greater, 48; Lesser, 48

Robin, 189-190, 224, 228, 229, 231; Alpine, 189; American, 224; Ashy, 190; Black-backed, 231; Black-chinned, 190; Black-sided, 190; Black-throated, 190; Black-throated Blue, 229; Blue-fronted, 231; Blue-grey, 190; Brown-backed, 231; Buff-sided, 190; Chatham Islands, 190; Dusky, 190; European, 229; Flame, 190; Forest, 228; Garnet, 189; Green-backed, 190; Grey-breasted, 190; Grey-headed, 190; Hooded, 190; Indian, 231; Indian Blue, 229; Japanese, 229; Mangrove, 190; New Zealand, 190; Northern Pale-yellow, 190; Olive-yellow, 190; Pale-yellow, 190; Pink, 190; Red-capped, 190; Rose, 190; Rufous-collared, 224; Rufous-headed, 229; Rufous-tailed, 229; Ryukyu, 229; San Lucas, 224; Scarlet, 189; Siberian Blue, 229; Smoky, 190; Snow Mountain, 189; Southern Pale-yellow, 190; Sunda, 231; Swynnerton's, 228; Torrent, 189; White-breasted, 190; White-browed, 190; White-eyed, 190; White-faced, 190; White-rumped, 190; White-starred, 228; White-tailed, 231; White-throated, 229; White-winged, 190; Yellow, 190; Yellow-bellied, 190

Robin-Chat, 229-230; Archer's, 229; Blue-shouldered, 229; Cape, 229; Chorister, 230; Grey-winged, 229; MacClounie's, 229; Malawi, 229; Mbulu, 229; Mountain, 229; Mozambique, 229; Olive-flanked, 229; Red-capped, 230; Rueppell's, 230; Snowy-crowned, 230; White-bellied, 229; White-browed, 230; White-crowned, 230; White-headed, 230; White-throated, 229

Rockfinch, 289; Pale, 289

Rockfowl, 217; Grey-necked, 217; White-necked, 217

Rock-jumper, 217, 263; Damara, 263; Orange-breasted, 217; Rufous, 217

Rock-Martin, 247; African, 247; Red-throated, 247

Rock-Nuthatch, 239; Eastern, 239; Western, 239

Rock-Pigeon, 89; Chestnut-quilled, 89; White-quilled, 89

Rock-Thrush, 218; Benson's, 218; Blue, 218; Blue-capped, 218; Cape, 218; Chestnut-bellied, 218; Forest, 218; Little, 218; Littoral, 218; Miombo, 218; Red-bellied, 218; Rufous-tailed, 218; Sentinel, 218; Short-toed, 218; Transvaal, 218; White-throated, 218

Roller, 38; Abyssinian, 38; Blue-bellied, 38; Blue-breasted, 38; Blue-throated, 38; Broad-billed, 38; Burmese, 38; Cuckoo, 38; European, 38; Indian, 38; Lilac-breasted, 38; Northern, 38; Purple, 38; Purple-winged, 38; Racket-tailed, 38; Rufous-crowned, 38; Southern, 38; Weigall's, 38

Rook, 201

Rosefinch, 305; Beautiful, 305; Blyth's, 305;
    Common, 305; Crimson, 305; Dark-
    breasted, 305; Dark-rumped, 305; Great,
    305; Long-tailed, 305; Pale, 305; Pallas's,
    305; Pink-browed, 305; Pink-rumped, 305;
    Pinkish-backed, 305; Red-fronted, 305; Red-
    mantled, 305; Sharpe's, 305; Spot-winged,
    305; Streaked, 305; Three-banded, 305;
    Tibetan, 305; Vinaceous, 305; White-
    browed, 305

Rosella, 52; Crimson, 52; Eastern, 52; Green, 52;
    Northern, 52; Pale-headed, 52; Western, 52;
    Yellow, 52

Rosy-Finch, 304-305; Asian, 304; Black, 305;
    Brown-capped, 305; Grey-crowned, 304

Royal-Flycatcher, 147; Amazonian, 147;
    Northern, 147; Swainson's, 147; Western,
    147

Ruby, 70; Brazilian, 70

Rubythroat, 229; Siberian, 229; White-tailed, 229

Ruff, 106

Rufous-Sparrow, 288, 289; Kenya, 288;
    Kordofan, 288; Shelley's, 288; Southern,
    289

Rushbird, 170; Wren-like, 170

Rush-Tyrant, 145; Many-colored, 145

Sabrewing, 64-65; Buff-breasted, 65; Curve-
    winged, 64; Grey-breasted, 65; Lazuline, 65;
    Long-tailed, 65; Napo, 65; Rufous, 65;
    Rufous-breasted, 65; Santa Marta, 65;
    Violet, 65; Wedge-tailed, 64; White-tailed,
    65

Saddleback, 217

Saltator, 332; Black-cowled, 332; Black-headed,
    332; Black-throated, 332; Black-winged,
    332; Buff-throated, 332; Golden-billed, 332;
    Green-winged, 332; Greyish, 332; Lesser
    Antillean, 332; Masked, 332; Middle
    American, 332; Orinocan, 332; Rufous-
    bellied, 332; Streaked, 332; Thick-billed,
    332

Sanderling, 106

Sandgrouse, 103; Black-bellied, 103; Black-
    faced, 103; Burchell's, 103; Chestnut-
    bellied, 103; Close-barred, 103; Crowned,
    103; Double-banded, 103; Four-banded,
    103; Lichtenstein's, 103; Madagascar, 103;
    Namaqua, 103; Painted, 103; Pallas's, 103;
    Pin-tailed, 103; Spotted, 103; Tibetan, 103;
    Yellow-throated, 103

Sand-Martin, 247; Common, 247; Eastern, 247

Sandpiper, 105, 106; Baird's, 106; Broad-billed,
    106; Buff-breasted, 106; Common, 105;
    Curlew, 106; Green, 105; Least, 106; Marsh,
    105; Pectoral, 106; Purple, 106; Rock, 106;
    Semipalmated, 106; Sharp-tailed, 106;

Solitary, 105; Spoonbill, 106; Spotted, 105;
    Stilt, 106; Tahitian, 105; Terek, 105;
    Tuamotu, 105; Upland, 105; Western, 106;
    White-rumped, 106; Wood, 105

Sandpiper-Plover, 109; Diademed, 109

Sapayoa, 140; Broad-billed, 140

Sapphire, 66, 67; Blue-chinned, 66; Blue-headed,
    67; Flame-rumped, 67; Golden-tailed, 67;
    Rufous-throated, 67; White-chinned, 67

Sapphirewing, 71; Great, 71

Sapsucker, 22; Yellow-bellied, 22; Red-breasted,
    22; Red-naped, 22; Williamson's, 22

Sawwing, 248-249; Black, 249; Blanford's, 249;
    Blue, 249; Brown, 249; Eastern, 249;
    Ethiopian, 249; Fanti, 249; Mangbettu, 249;
    Mountain, 248; Petit's, 249; Shari, 249;
    Square-tailed, 248; White-headed, 248

Scaup, 18; Greater, 18; Lesser, 18; New Zealand,
    18

Schiffornis, 154; Brown, 154; Greater, 154;
    Greenish, 154; Thrush-like, 154

Scimitar-Babbler, 272; Chestnut-backed, 272;
    Coral-billed, 272; Indian, 272; Large, 272;
    Red-billed, 272; Rusty-cheeked, 272; Short-
    tailed, 272; Slender-billed, 272; Spot-
    breasted, 272; Streak-breasted, 272; White-
    browed, 272

Scimitar-bill, 36; Abyssinian, 36; Black, 36;
    Common, 36

Scops-Owl, 76-77; African, 76; Andaman, 76;
    Anjouan, 77; Bornean, 76; Collared, 77;
    Common, 76; Comoro, 77; Elegant, 76;
    Enggano, 76; Eurasian, 76; Everett's, 77;
    Flores, 76; Formosan, 76; Indian, 77;
    Japanese, 77; Javan, 76; Luzon, 76;
    Madagascar, 77; Malagasy, 77; Mantanani,
    76; Mentawai, 77; Mindanao, 76; Mindoro,
    76; Moluccan, 76; Mountain, 76; Negros,
    77; Oriental, 76; Palawan, 77; Pallid, 76;
    Papuan, 76; Pemba, 77; Philippine, 77;
    Rajah, 77; Reddish, 76; Sandy, 76; Sao
    Tome, 76; Seychelles, 76; Simeulue, 76;
    Sokoke, 76; Sulawesi, 76; Sulu, 76;
    Vandewater's, 76; Wallace's, 77; White-
    faced, 77; White-fronted, 76

Scoter, 18; American, 18; Asiatic, 18; Black, 18;
    Surf, 18; Velvet, 18; White-winged, 18

Screamer, 13; Horned, 13; Northern, 13;
    Southern, 13

Screech-Owl, 77-78; Austral, 77; Balsas, 77;
    Bare-shanked, 77; Black-capped, 78;
    Cinnamon, 77; Cloud-forest, 77; Coastal,
    77; Colombian, 77; Eastern, 77; Hoy's, 78;
    Koepcke's, 77; Long-tufted, 78; Oaxaca, 77;
    Pacific, 77; Puerto Rican, 78; Rufescent, 77;
    Santa Barbara, 77; Tawny-bellied, 77;
    Tropical, 77; Variable, 78; Vermiculated,
    78; Vinaceous, 77; West Peruvian, 77;

Western, 77; Whiskered, 77; White-throated, 78

Scrub-bird, 179; Noisy, 179; Rufous, 179

Scrub-Flycatcher, 143; Amazonian, 143; Northern, 143; Smooth, 143; Southern, 143

Scrubfowl, 5; Dusky, 5; Mariana, 5; Melanesian, 5; Micronesian, 5; Moluccan, 5; New Guinea, 5; Niaufoou, 5; Nicobar, 5; Orange-footed, 5; Palau, 5; Sula, 5; Tabon, 5; Tanimbar, 5; Vanuatu, 5

Scrub-Robin, 191, 230; African, 230; Bearded, 230; Black, 230; Brown, 230; Brown-backed, 230; Eastern Bearded, 230; Forest, 230; Greyish, 230; Kalahari, 230; Karoo, 230; Miombo, 230; Northern, 191; Red-backed, 230; Rufous-tailed, 230; Southern, 191; White-browed, 230; White-winged, 230; Zanzibar Bearded, 230

Scrubtit, 187

Scrub-Warbler, 255, 262; African, 262; Bamboo, 262; Cameroon, 262; Fernando Po, 262; Grauer's, 262; Ja River, 262; Knysna, 262; Ruwenzori, 262; Streaked, 255; Victorin's, 262; White-winged, 262

Scrubwren, 187; Atherton, 187; Beccari's, 187; Brown, 187; Buff-breasted, 187; Buff-faced, 187; Grey-green, 187; Large, 187; Large-billed, 187; Pale-billed, 187; Papuan, 187; Perplexing, 187; Spotted, 187; Vogelkop, 187; White-browed, 187; Yellow-throated, 187

Scythebill, 174; Black-billed, 174; Brown-billed, 174; Curve-billed, 174; Greater, 174; Red-billed, 174

Sea-Eagle, 117; Pallas's, 117; Steller's, 117

Seaside-Sparrow, 310; Cape Sable, 310; Common, 310; Dusky, 310

Secretarybird, 124

Seedcracker, 297; Black-bellied, 297; Crimson, 297; Large-billed, 297; Lesser, 297; Rothschild's, 297; Urungu, 297

Seedeater, 302, 303, 328-329, 330; Abyssinian Yellow-rumped, 302; Band-tailed, 330; Black, 328; Black-and-tawny, 329; Black-and-white, 329; Black-backed, 329; Black-bellied, 329; Black-eared, 303; Blackish-blue, 330; Blue, 330; Brown-rumped, 303; Buffy-fronted, 328; Capped, 329; Chestnut, 329; Chestnut-bellied, 329; Chestnut-throated, 329; Cinnamon-rumped, 329; Dark-throated, 329; Double-collared, 329; Drab, 329; Dubois's, 329; Grey, 328; Grey-and-chestnut, 329; Grey-backed, 329; Hooded, 329; Kenya Yellow-rumped, 302; Kipengere, 303; Lemon-breasted, 302; Lesson's, 329; Lined, 329; Marsh, 329; Narosky's, 329; Paramo, 330; Parrot-billed, 329; Plain-colored, 330; Plumbeous, 328;

Principe, 303; Reichard's, 303; Ruddy-breasted, 329; Rusty-collared, 329; Santa Marta, 330; Sao Paulo, 329; Slate-blue, 330; Slate-colored, 328; Southern Yellow-rumped, 302; Streaky, 303; Streaky-headed, 303; Tawny-bellied, 329; Temminck's, 328; Thick-billed, 303; Tumaco, 329; Variable, 328; West African, 303; White-bellied, 329; White-collared, 329; White-naped, 330; White-rumped, 302; White-throated, 329; White-winged, 303; Wing-barred, 328; Yellow-bellied, 329; Yellow-browed, 303; Yellow-throated, 302

Seed-Finch, 329-330; Black-billed, 329; Chestnut-bellied, 330; Great-billed, 329; Large-billed, 329; Lesser, 330; Nicaraguan, 329; Thick-billed, 330

Seedsnipe, 103; Grey-breasted, 103; Least, 103; Rufous-bellied, 103; White-bellied, 103

Seriema, 98; Black-legged, 98; Red-legged, 98

Serin, 302, 303; Ankober, 303; European, 302; Fire-fronted, 302; Indonesian, 303; Mindanao, 303; Mountain, 303; Olive-rumped, 302; Syrian, 302; Tibetan, 302; Yemen, 303

Serpent-Eagle, 118; Andaman, 118; Congo, 118; Crested, 118; Madagascar, 118; Mentawai, 118; Mountain, 118; Natuna, 118; Nias, 118; Nicobar, 118; Philippine, 118; Ryukyu, 118; Simeulue, 118; Small, 118; Sulawesi, 118

Shag, 128; Antarctic, 128; Auckland Islands, 128; Blue, 128; Bounty Islands, 128; Bronze, 128; Campbell Island, 128; Chatham Islands, 128; European, 128; Imperial, 128; Kerguelen, 128; Pitt Island, 128; Rock, 128; Rough-faced, 128; South Georgia, 128; Spotted, 128

Shama, 230-231; Black, 231; Rufous-tailed, 231; White-browed, 230; White-crowned, 230; White-rumped, 230; White-vented, 231

Sharpbill, 156

Sheartail, 73; Mexican, 73; Peruvian, 73; Slender, 73

Shearwater, 136-137; Audubon's, 137; Balearic, 137; Bannerman's, 137; Black-vented, 137; Buller's, 136; Cape Verde, 136; Christmas Island, 137; Cory's, 136; Flesh-footed, 136; Fluttering, 137; Great, 136; Heinroth's, 137; Hutton's, 137; Levantine, 137; Little, 137; Manx, 137; Mediterranean, 137; Newell's, 137; Persian, 137; Pink-footed, 136; Short-tailed, 136; Sooty, 136; Streaked, 136; Townsend's, 137; Wedge-tailed, 136

Sheathbill, 107; Black-faced, 107; Snowy, 107

Shelduck, 15; Australian, 15; Common, 15; Crested, 15; Paradise, 15; Radjah, 15; Ruddy, 15; South African, 15

Shikra, 119; Northern, 119; Southern, 119

Shining-Parrot, 52; Crimson, 52; Masked, 52; Red, 52

Shoebill, 132

Short-toed Lark, 281; Asian, 281; Athi, 281; Greater, 281; Indian, 281; Lesser, 281; Rufous, 281

Shortwing, 224; Caroline's, 224; Gould's, 224; Great, 224; Indigo-blue, 224; Lesser, 224; Rusty-bellied, 224; White-bellied, 224; White-browed, 224

Shoveler, 17; Australian, 17; Cape, 17; Northern, 17; Red, 17

Shrike, 191-192; Bay-backed, 192; Black-headed, 192; Brown, 192; Bull-headed, 191; Burmese, 192; Chinese Grey, 192; Emin's, 192; Great Grey, 192; Grey-backed, 192; Isabelline, 191; Japanese, 192; Lesser Grey, 192; Loggerhead, 192; Long-tailed, 192; Mackinnon's, 192; Magpie, 192; Masked, 192; Mountain, 192; Northern, 192; Philippine, 192; Red-backed, 191; Rufous-backed, 192; Rufous-tailed, 191; Saharan, 192; Southern Grey, 192; Souza's, 192; Tiger, 191; White-crowned, 192; White-rumped, 192; Woodchat, 192; Yellow-billed, 192

Shrike-Babbler, 275; Black-eared, 275; Black-headed, 275; Chestnut-fronted, 275; Green, 275; White-browed, 275

Shrikebill, 211; Black-throated, 211; Fiji, 211; Rennell, 211; Southern, 211

Shrike-flycatcher, 215; African, 215; Black-and-white, 215; Ward's, 215

Shrike-Tanager, 320; Black-throated, 320; Fulvous, 320; White-throated, 320; White-winged, 320

Shrike-thrush, 197; Bower's, 197; Brown, 197; Grey, 197; Little, 197; Rufous, 197; Sandstone, 197; Sooty, 197; Western, 197

Shrike-tit, 196; Crested, 196; Eastern, 196; Northern, 196; Western, 196

Shrike-Tyrant, 150; Black-billed, 150; Great, 150; Grey-bellied, 150; Lesser, 150; White-tailed, 150

Shrike-Vireo, 193; Chestnut-sided, 193; Green, 193; Slaty-capped, 193; Yellow-browed, 193

Sibia, 277; Beautiful, 277; Black-capped, 277; Black-eared, 277; Black-headed, 277; Grey, 277; Long-tailed, 277; Rufous, 277; Rufous-backed, 277; White-eared, 277; White-spectacled, 277

Sicklebill, 64, 202; Black, 202; Black-billed, 202; Brown, 202; Buff-tailed, 64; Pale-billed, 202; White-tipped, 64

Sierra-Finch, 326; Ash-breasted, 326; Band-tailed, 326; Black-hooded, 326; Carbonated, 326; Grey-hooded, 326; Mourning, 326;

Patagonian, 326; Peruvian, 326; Plumbeous, 326; Red-backed, 326; White-throated, 326

Silktail, 213

Silky-flycatcher, 217; Black-and-yellow, 217; Grey, 217; Long-tailed, 217

Silverbill, 300; African, 300; Grey-headed, 300; White-throated, 300

Silverbird, 225

Silvereye, 260; Grey-backed, 260; Grey-breasted, 260; Western, 260

Sirystes, 152; Sibilant, 152; White-rumped, 152

Siskin, 302, 303, 304; Abyssinian, 302; Andean, 304; Antillean, 304; Black, 304; Black-capped, 304; Black-chinned, 304; Black-headed, 304; Cape, 303; Drakensberg, 303; Eurasian, 304; Hooded, 304; Olivaceous, 304; Pine, 304; Red, 304; Saffron, 304; Thick-billed, 304; Yellow-bellied, 304; Yellow-faced, 304; Yellow-rumped, 304

Sittella, 195; Black, 195; Black-capped, 195; Orange-winged, 195; Papuan, 195; Striated, 195; Varied, 195; White-headed, 195; White-winged, 195

Skimmer, 111; African, 111; Black, 111; Indian, 111

Skua, 111; Brown, 111; Chilean, 111; Great, 111; South Polar, 111; Southern, 111

Skylark, 281; Eurasian, 281; Japanese, 281; Oriental, 281

Slaty-Antshrike, 159; Eastern, 159; Western, 159

Slaty-Flycatcher, 225; Abyssinian, 225; Angola, 225; White-eyed, 225

Slaty-Thrush, 223; Andean, 223; Eastern, 223

Smew, 19

Snake-Eagle, 118; Banded, 118; Beaudouin's, 118; Black-chested, 118; Brown, 118; Fasciated, 118; Short-toed, 118

Snipe, 104; African, 104; Andean, 104; Chatham Islands, 104; Common, 104; Fuegian, 104; Giant, 104; Great, 104; Imperial, 104; Jack, 104; Latham's, 104; Madagascar, 104; Magellanic, 104; Noble, 104; Paraguayan, 104; Pintail, 104; Puna, 104; Solitary, 104; South American, 104; Subantarctic, 104; Swinhoe's, 104; Wilson's, 104; Wood, 104

Snow-Petrel, 135; Greater, 135; Lesser, 135

Snowcap, 69

Snowcock, 6; Altai, 6; Caspian, 6; Caucasian, 6; Himalayan, 6; Tibetan, 6

Snowfinch, 289; Afghan, 289; Black-winged, 289; Plain-backed, 289; Rufous-necked, 289; Small, 289; White-rumped, 289; White-winged, 289

Social-Weaver, 292; Black-capped, 292; Grey-headed, 292

Softtail, 169; Orinoco, 169; Plain, 169; Russet-mantled, 169; Striated, 169

Solitaire, 86, 220-221; Andean, 221; Black, 221; Black-faced, 221; Brown-backed, 220; Cuban, 220; Guyanan, 221; Reunion, 86; Rodriguez, 86; Rufous-brown, 221; Rufous-throated, 220; St. Vincent, 220; Slate-colored, 221; Townsend's, 220; Varied, 221; White-eared, 221

Sombre-Greenbul, 251; Frick's, 251; Southern, 251; Zanzibar, 251

Songlark, 268-269; Brown, 268; Rufous, 269

Sooty-Owl, 75; Greater, 75; Lesser, 75

Sora, 101

Spadebill, 146-147; Cinnamon-crested, 146; Golden-crowned, 146; Russet-winged, 147; Stub-tailed, 146; White-crested, 147; White-throated, 146; Yellow-crested, 146; Yellow-throated, 147

Sparrow, 288, 289, 301, 309, 310-312; American Tree, 310; Bachman's, 311; Baird's, 310; Belding's, 310; Bell's, 310; Black-capped, 311; Black-chested, 310; Black-chinned, 310; Black-striped, 311; Black-throated, 310; Botteri's, 311; Brewer's, 310; Bridled, 310; Cape, 289; Cassin's, 311; Chestnut, 289; Chipping, 310; Cinnamon-tailed, 310; Clay-colored, 310; Dead Sea, 288; Desert, 289; Eurasian Tree, 289; Field, 310; Five-striped, 310; Fox, 309; Golden-crowned, 309; Golden-winged, 311; Grasshopper, 310; Grassland, 310; Green-backed, 311; Grey-headed, 289; Harris's, 309; Henslow's, 310; House, 288; Iago, 288; Indian, 288; Ipswich, 310; Java, 301; Large-billed, 310; Lark, 310; Le Conte's, 310; Lincoln's, 309; Oaxaca, 311; Olive, 311; Orange-billed, 311; Pacific, 311; Parrot-billed, 289; Pectoral, 311; Peten, 311; Plain-backed, 288; Rock, 289; Rufous-collared, 309; Rufous-crowned, 311; Rufous-winged, 311; Russet, 288; Rusty, 311; Saffron-billed, 311; Sage, 310; Savannah, 310; Saxaul, 288; Seaside, 310; Sharp-tailed, 310; Sierra Madre, 310; Sind, 288; Slaty-backed, 311; Socotra, 288; Somali, 288; Song, 309; Spanish, 288; Stripe-capped, 310; Stripe-headed, 310; Striped, 311; Swahili, 289; Swainson's, 289; Swamp, 309; Timberline, 310; Timor, 301; Tocuyo, 311; Tumbes, 311; Vesper, 310; White-crowned, 309; White-throated, 309; Worthen's, 310; Yellow-browed, 310; Yellow-shouldered, 311; Zapata, 311

Sparrowhawk, 119-120; Chestnut-flanked, 119; Collared, 120; Eurasian, 120; Imitator, 120; Japanese, 120; Levant, 119; Little, 120; Madagascar, 120; New Britain, 120; Nicobar, 119; Ovampo, 120; Red-thighed, 120; Rufous-chested, 120; Rufous-necked, 120; Slaty-mantled, 119; Small, 120; Vinous-breasted, 120

Sparrow-Lark, 280; Ashy-crowned, 280; Black-crowned, 280; Black-eared, 280; Chestnut-backed, 280; Chestnut-headed, 280; Fischer's, 280; Grey-backed, 280

Sparrow-Weaver, 292; Chestnut-backed, 292; Chestnut-crowned, 292; Donaldson-Smith's, 292; White-browed, 292

Spatuletail, 73; Marvelous, 73

Speirops, 258; Black-capped, 258; Cameroon, 258; Fernando Po, 258; Principe, 258

Spiderhunter, 287; Bornean, 287; Grey-breasted, 287; Little, 287; Long-billed, 287; Naked-faced, 287; Spectacled, 287; Streaked, 287; Thick-billed, 287; Whitehead's, 287; Yellow-eared, 287

Spinebill, 186; Eastern, 186; Western, 186

Spinetail, 61, 167-168, 169; Apurimac, 167; Ash-browed, 168; Azara's, 167; Baron's, 168; Bat-like, 61; Black, 61; Black-throated, 167; Blackish-headed, 167; Brown-tailed, 167; Buff-browed, 167; Cabanis's, 167; Cassin's, 61; Chestnut-throated, 167; Chicli, 167; Chinchipe, 168; Chotoy, 167; Cinereous-breasted, 167; Coiba, 168; Creamy-crested, 168; Crested, 168; Dark-breasted, 167; Dusky, 167; Elegant, 167; Fraser's, 168; Great, 169; Grey-bellied, 167; Grey-headed, 168; Hoary-throated, 168; Light-crowned, 168; Line-cheeked, 168; MacConnell's, 167; Malagasy, 61; Maranon, 167; Marcapata, 168; Mottled, 61; Necklaced, 168; Ochre-cheeked, 168; Olive, 168; Pale-breasted, 167; Pallid, 168; Pinto's, 167; Plain-crowned, 167; Red-and-white, 168; Red-faced, 168; Red-shouldered, 167; Ruddy, 167; Rufous, 167; Rufous-breasted, 168; Rufous-capped, 167; Russet-bellied, 167; Rusty-backed, 168; Rusty-headed, 167; Sabine's, 61; Sao Tome, 61; Scaled, 168; Silver-rumped, 61; Silvery-throated, 167; Slaty, 167; Sooty-fronted, 167; Speckled, 168; Streak-capped, 168; Stripe-breasted, 168; Stripe-crowned, 168; Sulphur-bearded, 168; Tepui, 168; White-bellied, 167; White-browed, 168; White-lored, 167; White-rumped, 61; White-whiskered, 168; Yellow-chinned, 168

Spinifex-bird, 269

Spoonbill, 132; African, 132; Black-faced, 132; Eurasian, 132; Roseate, 132; Royal, 132; Yellow-billed, 132

Spotted-Owl, 79; California, 79; Mountain, 79

Spot-throat, 271

Spurfowl, 7, 9; Bare-throated, 7; Ceylon, 9; Cranch's, 7; Grey-breasted, 7; Painted, 9; Red, 9; Red-necked, 7; Swainson's, 7; Yellow-necked, 7

Squatter-Pigeon, 89; Northern, 89; Southern, 89
Standardwing, 202
Starfrontlet, 71; Blue-throated, 71; Buff-winged, 71; Dusky, 71; Golden, 71; Golden-bellied, 71; Rainbow, 71; Violet-throated, 71; White-tailed, 71
Starling, 233-236; Abbott's, 235; African Pied, 235; Ashy, 236; Asian Glossy, 234; Asian Pied, 236; Atoll, 234; Babbling, 235; Black-collared, 236; Black-winged, 236; Bornean, 234; Brahminy, 236; Bristle-crowned, 235; Brown-winged, 234; Chestnut-bellied, 235; Chestnut-cheeked, 236; Chestnut-tailed, 236; Chestnut-winged, 234; Common, 236; Fischer's, 235; Golden-breasted, 235; Hildebrandt's, 235; Kenrick's, 234; Kosrae, 234; Long-tailed, 234; Loyalty Islands, 234; Madagascar, 236; Magpie, 235; Metallic, 234; Micronesian, 234; Moluccan, 234; Mountain, 233; Mysterious, 234; Narrow-tailed, 234; Norfolk, 234; Pale-winged, 234; Pohnpei, 233; Polynesian, 234; Purple-backed, 236; Rarotonga, 234; Red-billed, 236; Red-winged, 234; Rennell, 234; Reunion, 236; Rodriguez, 236; Rosy, 236; Rusty-winged, 233; Samoan, 234; San Cristobal, 234; Sharpe's, 235; Shelley's, 235; Short-tailed, 234; Singing, 234; Slender-billed, 235; Socotra, 234; Somali, 234; Spot-winged, 236; Spotless, 236; Striated, 234; Stuhlmann's, 234; Superb, 235; Tanimbar, 234; Tristram's, 234; Vinous-breasted, 236; Violet-backed, 235; Waller's, 234; Wattled, 236; White-billed, 235; White-cheeked, 236; White-collared, 234; White-crowned, 235; White-eyed, 234; White-faced, 236; White-headed, 236; White-shouldered, 236; Yellow-eyed, 234
Starthroat, 73; Blue-tufted, 73; Long-billed, 73; Plain-capped, 73; Stripe-breasted, 73
Steamerduck, 15; Chubut, 15; Falkland, 15; Flightless, 15; Flying, 15
Steppe-Buzzard, 122; Eastern, 122; Western, 122
Steppe-Eagle, 123; Eastern, 123; Western, 123
Stilt, 108; Banded, 108; Black, 108; Black-necked, 108; Black-winged, 108; Ceylon, 108; Hawaiian, 108; White-backed, 108; White-headed, 108
Stint, 106; Little, 106; Long-toed, 106; Rufous-necked, 106; Temminck's, 106
Stitchbird, 184
Stonechat, 232; Common, 232; Ethiopian, 232; Reunion, 232; Siberian, 232; White-tailed, 232
Stork, 133; Abdim's, 133; Black, 133; Black-necked, 133; Green-necked, 133; Maguari, 133; Marabou, 133; Milky, 133; Oriental, 133; Painted, 133; Saddle-billed, 133;

Storm's, 133; White, 133; Wood, 133; Woolly-necked, 133; Yellow-billed, 133
Storm-Petrel, 138; Ashy, 138; Band-rumped, 138; Black, 138; Black-bellied, 138; European, 138; Fork-tailed, 138; Grey-backed, 138; Guadalupe, 138; Leach's, 138; Least, 138; Markham's, 138; Matsudaira's, 138; Polynesian, 138; Ringed, 138; Socorro, 138; Swinhoe's, 138; Tristram's, 138; Wedge-rumped, 138; White-bellied, 138; White-faced, 138; White-vented, 138; Wilson's, 138
Straightbill, 182; Olive, 182; Tawny, 182
Streamcreeper, 170; Sharp-tailed, 170
Streamertail, 67; Black-billed, 67; Red-billed, 67
Striped-Babbler, 273-274; Luzon, 273; Panay, 273; Negros, 274; Palawan, 274
Striped-Swallow, 248; Greater, 248; Lesser, 248
Stubtail, 261; Asian, 261; Bornean, 261; Timor, 261
Sugarbird, 282; Cape, 282; Gurney's, 282
Suiriri, 143; Campo, 143; Chaco, 143
Sunangel, 71; Amethyst-throated, 71; Gorgeted, 71; Little, 71; Longuemare's, 71; Merida, 71; Orange-throated, 71; Purple-throated, 71; Royal, 71; Tourmaline, 71
Sunbeam, 70; Black-hooded, 70; Purple-backed, 70; Shining, 70; White-tufted, 70
Sunbird, 283-287; Amani, 284; Amethyst, 285; Anchieta's, 284; Anjouan, 285; Apo, 287; Apricot-breasted, 285; Banded, 284; Bannerman's, 284; Bates's, 284; Beautiful, 287; Black, 285; Black-bellied, 287; Black-breasted, 285; Black-throated, 287; Blue-headed, 284; Blue-throated Brown, 284; Bocage's, 286; Bronze, 286; Brown-throated, 284; Buff-throated, 285; Cameroon, 284; Carmelite, 285; Collared, 284; Congo, 286; Copper, 286; Copper-throated, 285; Crimson, 287; Crimson-backed, 285; Dusky, 286; Eastern Double-collared, 286; Elegant, 287; Fire-tailed, 287; Flame-breasted, 285; Flaming, 287; Fork-tailed, 287; Gadow's, 286; Golden-winged, 286; Gould's, 287; Greater Double-collared, 286; Green, 284; Green-headed, 284; Green-tailed, 287; Green-throated, 285; Grey-chinned, 284; Grey-headed, 283; Grey-hooded, 287; Grey-throated, 284; Henke's, 285; Humblot's, 285; Hunter's, 285; Javan, 287; Johanna's, 287; Kenya, 283; Kenya Violet-backed, 284; Little Green, 284; Little Purple-banded, 287; Long-billed Green, 287; Long-billed, 286; Lovely, 287; Loveridge's, 286; Malachite, 286; Mariqua, 286; Mayotte, 285; Metallic-winged, 287; Mindanao, 285; Miombo Double-collared, 286; Montane Double-collared, 286;

Moreau's, 286; Mouse-brown, 284; Mouse-colored, 284; Neergaard's, 286; Newton's, 284; Nile Valley, 284; Northern Double-collared, 286; Olive, 284; Olive-backed, 285; Olive-bellied, 286; Orange-bellied, 285; Orange-breasted, 284; Orange-tufted, 285; Oustalet's, 285; Palestine, 285; Pemba, 287; Pinto's Double-collared, 286; Plain, 284; Plain-backed, 283; Plain-throated, 284; Prigogine's Double-collared, 286; Principe, 284; Purple, 285; Purple-banded, 287; Purple-breasted, 286; Purple-naped, 284; Purple-rumped, 285; Purple-throated, 285; Pygmy, 284; Red-chested, 286; Red-throated, 284; Red-tufted, 286; Regal, 286; Reichenbach's, 284; Rockefeller's, 286; Ruby-cheeked, 284; Rufous-winged, 286; Sao Tome, 284; Scarlet, 287; Scarlet-chested, 285; Scarlet-tufted, 283; Seychelles, 285; Shelley's, 286; Shining, 286; Socotra, 285; Souimanga, 285; Southern Double-collared, 286; Splendid, 287; Stuhlmann's Double-collared, 286; Superb, 287; Swahili, 286; Tacazze, 286; Tiny, 286; Tsavo Purple-banded, 287; Uluguru Violet-backed, 284; Ursula's, 285; Van Hasselt's, 285; Variable, 285; Violet-breasted, 287; Violet-tailed, 284; Western Violet-backed, 284; White-bellied, 285; White-breasted, 285; White-flanked, 287; Yellow-bellied, 285; Yellow-breasted, 285; Yellow-chinned, 284; Zambian, 285

Sunbittern, 96
Sungem, 73; Horned, 73
Sungrebe, 98
Surfbird, 105
Swallow, 246-248; Andean, 248; Angola, 247; Bahama, 246; Barn, 247; Black-and-rufous, 248; Black-capped, 246; Black-collared, 247; Black-vented, 248; Blue, 248; Blue-and-white, 246; Brown-bellied, 246; Cave, 248; Ceylon, 248; Chestnut-collared, 248; Chilean, 246; Cinnamon-throated, 248; Cliff, 248; Ecuadorian, 248; Ethiopian, 247; Eurasian, 247; Forest, 248; Golden, 246; Grey-rumped, 247; Hill, 247; Lesser Striated, 248; Mangrove, 246; Mosque, 248; Northern Rough-winged, 247; Pacific, 247; Pale-footed, 246; Patagonian, 246; Pearl-breasted, 248; Pied-winged, 248; Preuss's, 248; Red Sea, 248; Red-chested, 247; Red-rumped, 248; Red-throated, 248; Ridgway's Rough-winged, 247; Rufous-chested, 248; South African, 248; Southern Rough-winged, 247; Streak-throated, 248; Striated, 248; Tawny-headed, 247; Tree, 246; Violet-green, 246; Welcome, 247; West African, 248; West Peruvian, 246; White-backed,

247; White-banded, 246; White-rumped, 246; White-tailed, 248; White-thighed, 247; White-throated, 247; White-throated Blue, 247; White-winged, 246; Wire-tailed, 247
Swallow-wing, 33
Swamphen, 102; African, 102; Eastern, 102; Indian, 102; Lord Howe Island, 102; Philippine, 102; Purple, 102; Western, 102
Swamp-Warbler, 264; Cape Verde, 264; Greater, 264; Lesser, 264; Madagascar, 264
Swan, 14; Bewick's, 14; Black, 14; Black-necked, 14; Coscoroba, 14; Mute, 14; Trumpeter, 14; Tundra, 14; Whistling, 14; Whooper, 14
Swift, 60, 61, 62-63; African, 62; Alexander's, 62; Alpine, 62; Andean, 62; Ash-rumped, 62; Ashy-tailed, 62; Band-rumped, 62; Bates's, 63; Biscutate, 60; Black, 60; Bradfield's, 63; Chapman's, 62; Chestnut-collared, 60; Chimney, 62; Common, 62; Dark-rumped, 63; Dusky-backed, 62; Fernando Po, 62; Forbes-Watson's, 63; Fork-tailed, 63; Great Dusky, 60; Great Swallow-tailed, 62; Grey-rumped, 62; Horus, 63; House, 63; Lesser Antillean, 62; Lesser Swallow-tailed, 62; Little, 63; Loanda, 63; Madagascar, 63; Mottled, 62; Nyanza, 62; Pale-rumped, 62; Pallid, 62; Plain, 62; Pygmy, 62; Rothschild's, 60; Scarce, 61; Schouteden's, 61; Short-tailed, 62; Sooty, 60; Spot-fronted, 60; Tepui, 60; Vaux's, 62; Waterfall, 60; White-chested, 60; White-chinned, 60; White-collared, 60; White-fronted, 60; White-naped, 60; White-rumped, 63; White-throated, 62; White-tipped, 62; Yucatan, 62
Swiftlet, 60-61; Atiu, 61; Australian, 60; Bare-legged, 61; Black-nest, 61; Brown-rumped, 61; Caroline Islands, 61; Cave, 60; Chinese, 60; Edible-nest, 61; German's, 61; Glossy, 60; Grey, 61; Grey-rumped, 60; Himalayan, 60; Indian, 60; Indochinese, 60; Mariana, 61; Marquesan, 61; Mascarene, 60; Mayr's, 61; Micronesian, 61; Moluccan, 60; Mossy-nest, 61; Mountain, 60; Palau, 61; Palawan, 61; Papuan, 61; Philippine, 60; Pygmy, 60; Seychelles, 60; Tahiti, 61; Thunberg's, 61; Uniform, 61; Volcano, 60; White-bellied, 60; White-rumped, 60; Whitehead's, 60
Sylph, 73; Blue-throated, 73; Green-tailed, 73; Long-tailed, 73; Venezuelan, 73; Violet-tailed, 73

Tachuri, 145; Bearded, 145; Grey-backed, 145
Tailorbird, 265; African, 265; Ashy, 265; Black-headed, 265; Common, 265; Dark-necked, 265; Grey-backed, 265; Long-billed, 265; Mountain, 265; Olive-backed, 265;

Philippine, 265; Rufous-fronted, 265; Rufous-headed, 265; Rufous-tailed, 265; White-eared, 265; Yellow-breasted, 265

Takahe, 102

Tanager, 317-318, 319-322, 323-325, 326; Aragua, 321; Azure-rumped, 323; Azure-shouldered, 321; Bay-and-blue, 324; Bay-and-green, 324; Bay-headed, 324; Bay-headed, 324; Beautiful, 324; Beryl-spangled, 325; Black-and-gold, 321; Black-and-white, 318; Black-and-yellow, 319; Black-backed, 324; Black-capped, 325; Black-cheeked, 325; Black-faced, 318; Black-goggled, 320; Black-headed, 325; Blue-and-black, 325; Blue-and-gold, 321; Blue-and-yellow, 321; Blue-backed, 321; Blue-bellied, 322; Blue-browed, 325; Blue-capped, 321; Blue-grey, 321; Blue-necked, 325; Blue-whiskered, 324; Brassy-breasted, 324; Brazilian, 321; Brown, 317; Brown-flanked, 319; Buff-bellied, 319; Buff-naped, 325; Burnished-buff, 324; Chat, 319; Cherry-throated, 319; Chestnut-backed, 324; Chestnut-headed, 319; Cinnamon, 318; Cone-billed, 318; Crimson-backed, 321; Crimson-collared, 321; Darwin's, 321; Diademed, 322; Dotted, 324; Dusky-faced, 319; Emerald, 324; Fawn-breasted, 322; Flame-colored, 320; Flame-crested, 320; Flame-faced, 324; Flame-rumped, 321; Fulvous-crested, 320; Fulvous-headed, 319; Gilt-edged, 324; Glaucous, 321; Glistening-green, 323; Gold-ringed, 322; Golden, 324; Golden-chested, 321; Golden-chevroned, 321; Golden-collared, 322; Golden-crowned, 322; Golden-eared, 324; Golden-hooded, 325; Golden-naped, 325; Grass-green, 318; Green-and-gold, 324; Green-capped, 325; Green-headed, 324; Green-naped, 325; Grey-and-gold, 324; Grey-crested, 320; Grey-headed, 320; Guira, 319; Hepatic, 320; Hispaniolan, 321; Hooded, 319; Huallaga, 321; Jamaican, 321; Lemon-spectacled, 319; Lesser Antillean, 324; Magpie, 318; Masked Crimson, 321; Masked, 325; Metallic-green, 325; Moss-backed, 322; Multicolored, 323; Napo, 320; Natterer's, 320; Ochre, 324; Ochre-breasted, 319; Olive, 319; Olive-backed, 319; Olive-green, 320; Opal-crowned, 325; Opal-rumped, 325; Orange-eared, 323; Orange-headed, 319; Orange-naped, 325; Orange-throated, 322; Palm, 321; Paradise, 324; Perija, 324; Plain-colored, 323; Puerto Rican, 318; Purplish-mantled, 322; Red, 320; Red-billed Pied, 318; Red-headed, 321; Red-hooded, 321; Red-necked, 324; Red-shouldered, 320; Rose-throated, 321; Ruby-crowned, 320;

Rufous-cheeked, 325; Rufous-chested, 319; Rufous-crested, 320; Rufous-headed, 319; Rufous-throated, 324; Rufous-winged, 324; Rust-and-yellow, 319; Saffron-crowned, 324; Sayaca, 321; Scarlet, 321; Scarlet-and-white, 319; Scarlet-browed, 320; Scarlet-rumped, 321; Scarlet-throated, 318; Sclater's, 324; Scrub, 324; Seven-colored, 324; Silver-backed, 325; Silver-beaked, 321; Silver-throated, 324; Silvery-breasted, 325; Sira, 325; Slaty, 320; Spangle-cheeked, 325; Speckled, 324; Spotted, 324; Straw-backed, 325; Stripe-headed, 321; Sulphur-rumped, 320; Summer, 320; Swallow, 326; Tambillo, 325; Tamiapampa, 325; Tawny-crested, 320; Tooth-billed, 320; Turquoise, 323; Vermilion, 321; Western, 321; White-banded, 318; White-bellied, 323; White-capped, 318; White-lined, 320; White-rumped, 318; White-shouldered, 320; White-winged, 321; Whitely's, 325; Yellow-backed, 319; Yellow-bellied, 324; Yellow-crested, 320; Yellow-faced, 324; Yellow-lored, 319; Yellow-rumped, 321; Yellow-scarfed, 322; Yellow-throated, 322; Yellow-winged, 321

Tapaculo, 177-178; Andean, 178; Ash-colored, 177; Blackish, 177; Brasilia, 178; Brown-rumped, 178; Chestnut-sided, 178; Chiriqui, 178; Chucao, 177; Dusky, 178; Large-footed, 177; Magellanic, 178; Mouse-colored, 178; Narino, 177; Northern White-crowned, 177; Ocellated, 178; Ochre-flanked, 177; Rufous-vented, 177; Rusty-belted, 177; Santa Marta, 177; Sharp-billed, 178; Silvery-fronted, 178; Southern White-crowned, 177; Tacarcuna, 177; Unicolored, 177; Venezuelan, 178; White-breasted, 178; White-browed, 178; White-throated, 177

Tattler, 105; Grey-tailed, 105; Wandering, 105

Tawny-Eagle, 123; African, 123; Asian, 123

Tchagra, 214; Anchieta's, 214; Black-crowned, 214; Brown-crowned, 214; Marsh, 214; Moroccan, 214; Southern, 214; Souza's, 214; Three-streaked, 214

Teal, 16, 17-18; Andaman, 17; Andean, 17; Baikal, 17; Bernier's, 17; Blue-winged, 17; Brazilian, 16; Brown, 17; Cape, 16; Chestnut, 17; Cinnamon, 17; Common, 17; Flightless, 17; Green-winged, 17; Grey, 17; Hottentot, 18; Marbled, 18; Puna, 17; Ringed, 16; Salvadori's, 16; Silver, 17; Speckled, 17; Sunda, 17; Yellow-billed, 17

Tern, 113-114; Aleutian, 114; Antarctic, 114; Arctic, 114; Black, 114; Black-bellied, 114; Black-fronted, 114; Black-naped, 113; Bridled, 114; Caspian, 113; Cayenne, 113; Common, 114; Damara, 114; Elegant, 113;

Fairy, 114; Forster's, 114; Grey-backed, 114; Gull-billed, 113; Inca, 114; Kerguelen, 114; Large-billed, 114; Least, 114; Little, 114; Peruvian, 114; River, 113; Roseate, 113; Royal, 113; Sandwich, 113; Saunders's, 114; Snowy-crowned, 114; Sooty, 114; South American, 114; Whiskered, 114; White-cheeked, 114; White-fronted, 113; White-winged, 114; Yellow-billed, 114

Tesia, 261; Chestnut-headed, 261; Grey-bellied, 261; Javan, 261; Russet-capped, 261; Slaty-bellied, 261

Teydefinch, 302

Thicketbird, 269; Bismarck, 269; Bougainville, 269; Guadalcanal, 269; Long-legged, 269; New Hebrides, 269; Rusty, 269

Thicket-Fantail, 208; Black, 208; Karimui, 208; Sooty, 208; White-bellied, 208

Thick-knee, 107; Beach, 107; Bush, 107; Double-striped, 107; Eurasian, 107; Great, 107; Peruvian, 107; Senegal, 107; Spotted, 107; Water, 107

Thistletail, 166-167; Black-throated, 167; Eye-ringed, 166; Itatiaia, 167; Mouse-colored, 166; Ochre-browed, 166; Perija, 166; Puna, 167; Vilcabamba, 166; White-chinned, 166

Thornbill, 72, 188; Black-backed, 72; Blue-mantled, 72; Broad-tailed, 188; Bronze-tailed, 72; Brown, 188; Buff-rumped, 188; Chestnut-rumped, 188; Inland, 188; Mountain, 188; Olivaceous, 72; Papuan, 188; Purple-backed, 72; Rainbow-bearded, 72; Rufous-capped, 72; Slaty-backed, 188; Slender-billed, 188; Striated, 188; Tanami, 188; Tasmanian, 188; Varied, 188; Western, 188; Whitlock's, 188; Yellow, 188; Yellow-rumped, 188

Thornbird, 169-170; Chestnut-backed, 170; Freckle-breasted, 169; Greater, 169; Little, 169; Northern, 169; Orange-eyed, 170; Peruvian, 169; Red-eyed, 170; Rufous-fronted, 169; Spot-breasted, 169; Streak-fronted, 169

Thorntail, 66; Black-bellied, 66; Coppery, 66; Green, 66; Wire-crested, 66

Thrasher, 238; Bendire's, 238; Brown, 238; California, 238; Cozumel, 238; Crissal, 238; Curve-billed, 238; Grey, 238; Le Conte's, 238; Long-billed, 238; Ocellated, 238; Pearly-eyed, 238; Sage, 238; Scaly-breasted, 238; White-breasted, 238

Thrush, 219, 220, 221-224; Abyssinian, 222; African, 221; Amami, 220; American Mountain, 223; Anjouan, 222; Ashy, 219; Austral, 223; Australian Olive-tailed, 220; Aztec, 219; Bare-eyed, 222; Bicknell's, 221; Black, 223; Black-billed, 223; Black-breasted, 222; Black-hooded, 223; Black-

throated, 222; Bonin, 220; Brown-headed, 222; Buru, 219; Cameroon Mountain, 221; Cape, 222; Cauca, 223; Chestnut, 222; Chestnut-backed, 219; Chestnut-bellied, 223; Chestnut-capped, 219; Chiguanco, 223; Chinese, 223; Clay-colored, 224; Cocoa, 224; Comoro, 222; Creamy-bellied, 223; Dagua, 224; Dark, 223; Dark-sided, 220; Dark-throated, 222; Dusky, 223; Eastern Red-legged, 223; Ecuadorian, 224; Enggano, 219; Ethiopian, 221; Everett's, 219; Eyebrowed, 222; Fawn-breasted, 220; Fernando Po, 221; Forest, 220; Giant, 223; Glossy-black, 223; Grand Cayman, 223; Grand Comoro, 222; Grayson's, 224; Great, 223; Grey-backed, 222; Grey-cheeked, 221; Grey-flanked, 224; Grey-sided, 222; Groundscraper, 221; Hauxwell's, 224; Hermit, 221; Horsfield's, 220; Island, 222; Izu, 222; Japanese, 222; Kurrichane, 222; La Selle, 224; Lawrence's, 223; Lesser Antillean, 224; Long-billed, 220; Long-tailed, 220; Maranon, 223; Mistle, 223; Moheli, 222; Moluccan, 219; Naumann's, 223; New Britain, 220; Oldean's, 222; Olivaceous, 222; Olive, 222; Olive-backed, 221; Olive-tailed, 220; Orange-banded, 219; Orange-headed, 219; Pale, 222; Pale-breasted, 223; Pale-eyed, 221; Pale-vented, 223; Papuan Olive-tailed, 220; Paraguayan, 224; Pied, 219; Plain-backed, 220; Plumbeous-backed, 223; Red-backed, 219; Red-legged, 223; Red-throated, 222; Roehl's, 222; Rufous-backed, 224; Rufous-bellied, 223; Rufous-flanked, 224; Russet-backed, 221; Russet-tailed, 220; San Cristobal, 220; Scaly, 220; Seram, 219; Siberian, 219; Slaty-backed, 219; Somali, 222; Song, 223; Sooty, 223; Spot-winged, 220; Sulawesi, 220; Sunda, 220; Swainson's, 221; Swynnerton's, 222; Teita, 222; Tickell's, 222; Tristan, 220; Unicolored, 224; Varied, 219; Western Red-legged, 223; White-backed, 222; White-chinned, 223; White-eyed, 224; White-necked, 224; White-throated, 224; Wood, 221; Yellow-eyed, 224; Yellow-legged, 221; Yemen, 222

Thrush-Tanager, 319; Rosy, 319

Tiger-Heron, 130; Banded, 130; Bare-throated, 130; Fasciated, 130; Lineated, 130; Rufescent, 130; Salmon's, 130

Tiger-Parrot, 51; Brehm's, 51; Madarasz's, 51; Modest, 51; Painted, 51

Tinamou, 1-3; Andean, 2; Barred, 2; Bartlett's, 2; Berlepsch's, 2; Black, 1; Black-capped, 2; Brazilian, 2; Brown, 2; Brushland, 2; Chilean, 3; Cinereous, 2; Choco, 2; Colombian, 2; Curve-billed, 3; Dwarf, 3; .

Garlepp's, 2; Great, 1; Grey, 1; Grey-legged, 2; Highland, 1; Hooded, 2; Kalinowski's, 2; Little, 2; Magdalena, 2; Ornate, 2; Pale-browed, 2; Patagonian, 3; Puna, 3; Red-legged, 2; Red-winged, 2; Rusty, 2; Santa Marta, 2; Slaty-breasted, 2; Small-billed, 2; Solitary, 1; Taczanowski's, 2; Tataupa, 2; Tawny-breasted, 2; Tepui, 2; Thicket, 2; Traylor's, 2; Undulated, 2; Variegated, 2; White-throated, 1; Yellow-legged, 2

Tinkerbird, 28-29; Golden-rumped, 29; Green, 28; Lemon-rumped, 29; Moustached, 28; Red-fronted, 29; Red-rumped, 29; Speckled, 28; Western, 28; Yellow-fronted, 29; Yellow-rumped, 29; Yellow-throated, 29

Tit, 243, 244-245, 246; Alpine, 245; Ashy, 244; Azure, 245; Black, 244; Black-browed, 245; Black-crested, 244; Black-headed, 245; Black-lored, 245; Black-throated, 245; Blue, 245; Carp's, 244; Chinese, 245; Cinereous, 245; Cinnamon-breasted, 244; Coal, 244; Crested, 244; Dark-grey, 244; Dusky, 244; Elegant, 244; European, 245; Fire-capped, 243; Great, 245; Green-backed, 245; Grey, 244; Grey-crested, 244; Hyrcanian, 243; Japanese, 245; Long-tailed, 245; Marsh, 243; Miombo, 244; Palawan, 244; Pygmy, 246; Red-throated, 244; Rufous-bellied, 244; Rufous-vented, 244; Rusty-breasted, 244; Siberian, 244; Sikkim, 244; Somali, 244; Sombre, 243; Songar, 243; Stripe-breasted, 244; Sultan, 245; Turkestan, 245; Varied, 245; White-backed, 244; White-bellied, 244; White-browed, 244; White-cheeked, 245; White-fronted, 245; White-naped, 245; White-necklaced, 245; White-shouldered, 244; White-throated, 245; White-winged, 244; Willow, 243; Yellow, 245; Yellow-bellied, 244; Yellow-breasted, 245; Yellow-browed, 245; Yellow-cheeked, 245

Tit-Babbler, 274; Brown, 274; Fluffy-backed, 274; Grey-cheeked, 274; Grey-faced, 274; Miniature, 274; Striped, 274

Tit-Flycatcher, 226; Grey, 226; Grey-throated, 226

Tit-hylia, 243

Titmouse, 245; Black-crested, 245; Bridled, 245; Plain, 245; Ridgway's, 245; Tufted, 245

Tit-Spinetail, 166; Andean, 166; Araucaria, 166; Brown-capped, 166; Plain-mantled, 166; Rusty-crowned, 166; Streak-crowned, 166; Streaked, 166; Striolated, 166; Tawny, 166; Tufted, 166; White-browed, 166

Tit-Tyrant, 145; Agile, 145; Ash-breasted, 145; Juan Fernandez, 145; Maranon, 145; Pied-crested, 145; Tufted, 145; Unstreaked, 145; Yellow-billed, 145

Tit-Warbler, 266; Crested, 266; White-browed, 266

Tityra, 154; Black-crowned, 154; Black-tailed, 154; Masked, 154

Tody, 39; Broad-billed, 39; Cuban, 39; Jamaican, 39; Narrow-billed, 39; Puerto Rican, 39

Tody-Flycatcher, 142; Black-backed, 142; Black-headed, 142; Buff-cheeked, 142; Common, 142; Golden-winged, 142; Maracaibo, 142; Ochre-faced, 142; Painted, 142; Ruddy, 142; Rusty-fronted, 142; Slate-headed, 142; Smoky-fronted, 142; Spotted, 142; Yellow-browed, 142; Yellow-lored, 142

Tody-Tyrant, 141-142; Active, 141; Black-and-white, 141; Black-throated, 141; Boat-billed, 141; Buff-breasted, 141; Buff-throated, 141; Cinnamon-breasted, 141; Duida, 141; Dwarf, 141; Eye-ringed, 141; Fork-tailed, 142; Hangnest, 141; Johannes's, 141; Kaempfer's, 141; Magdalena, 141; Pearly-vented, 141; Pelzeln's, 141; Rufous-crowned, 141; Snethlage's, 141; Stripe-necked, 141; Tricolored, 141; White-bellied, 141; White-cheeked, 141; White-eyed, 141; Yungas, 141; Zimmer's, 141

Tomtit, 190

Topaz, 70; Crimson, 70; Fiery, 70

Torrent-Duck, 16; Chilean, 16; Colombian, 16; Peruvian, 16

Torrent-lark, 213

Toucan, 31-32; Ariel, 31; Black-mandibled, 31; Channel-billed, 31; Chestnut-mandibled, 31; Choco, 31; Citron-throated, 31; Cuvier's, 31; Keel-billed, 31; Red-billed, 31; Red-breasted, 31; Toco, 32; Yellow-ridged, 31

Toucanet, 30, 31; Blue-banded, 30; Blue-throated, 30; Chestnut-tipped, 30; Crimson-rumped, 30; Emerald, 30; Golden-collared, 31; Gould's, 31; Groove-billed, 30; Guianan, 31; Langdorff's, 31; Saffron, 31; Spot-billed, 31; Tawny-tufted, 31; Yellow-billed, 30; Yellow-browed, 30; Yellow-eared, 31

Towhee, 311; Abert's, 311; California, 311; Canyon, 311; Collared, 311; Eastern, 311; Green-tailed, 311; Olive-backed, 311; Rufous-sided, 311; Socorro, 311; Spotted, 311; White-throated, 311

Tragopan, 9; Blyth's, 9; Cabot's, 9; Satyr, 9; Temminck's, 9; Western, 9

Trainbearer, 72; Black-tailed, 72; Green-tailed, 72

Treecreeper, 178; Allied, 178; Black, 178; Black-tailed, 178; Brown, 178; Little, 178; Papuan, 178; Red-browed, 178; Rufous, 178; White-browed, 178; White-throated, 178

Tree-Creeper, 239; American, 239; Bar-tailed, 239; Brown-throated, 239; Eurasian, 239; Rusty-flanked, 239; Short-toed, 239

Tree-Finch, 331; Large, 331; Medium, 331; Small, 331

Treehunter, 170, 171, 172; Black-billed, 171; Buff-throated, 171; Flammulated, 171; Pale-browed, 170; Sharp-billed, 172; Streak-breasted, 171; Streak-capped, 171; Striped, 171; Uniform, 171

Treepie, 199-200; Andaman, 200; Bornean, 200; Collared, 200; Grey, 199; Hooded, 200; Racket-tailed, 200; Ratchet-tailed, 200; Rufous, 199; Sumatran, 200; Sunda, 200; White-bellied, 200

Treerunner, 170, 172; Beautiful, 170; Fulvous-dotted, 170; Pearled, 170; Ruddy, 170; White-throated, 172

Treeswift, 63; Crested, 63; Grey-rumped, 63; Moustached, 63; Whiskered, 63

Trembler, 238; Brown, 238; Grey, 238

Triller, 206-207; Black-and-white, 206; Black-browed, 207; Long-tailed, 207; Mussau, 207; Pied, 206; Polynesian, 207; Rufous-bellied, 207; Samoan, 207; Varied, 207; White-browed, 207; White-rumped, 207; White-shouldered, 207; White-winged, 207

Trogon, 36-37; Amazonian, 37; Baird's, 36; Bar-tailed, 36; Bare-cheeked, 36; Black-headed, 37; Black-tailed, 36; Black-throated, 37; Blue-crowned, 37; Blue-tailed, 37; Brazilian, 37; Chapman's, 36; Cinnamon-rumped, 37; Citreoline, 37; Collared, 37; Coppery-tailed, 37; Cuban, 36; Diard's, 37; Eared, 36; Elegant, 37; Gartered, 37; Highland, 37; Hispaniolan, 36; Jalapa, 37; Large-tailed, 36; Lattice-tailed, 36; Malabar, 37; Masked, 37; Mountain, 37; Narina, 36; Orange-bellied, 37; Orange-breasted, 37; Philippine, 37; Red-headed, 37; Red-naped, 37; Scarlet-rumped, 37; Slaty-tailed, 36; Surucua, 37; Violaceous, 37; Ward's, 37; Whitehead's, 37; White-eyed, 36; White-tailed, 37

Tropicbird, 126; Red-billed, 126; Red-tailed, 126; White-tailed, 126

Troupial, 334

Trumpeter, 98; Dark-winged, 98; Grey-winged, 98; Pale-winged, 98

Tuftedcheek, 170; Buffy, 170; Pacific, 170; Streaked, 170

Tui, 186

Turaco, 74-75; Bannerman's, 74; Black-billed, 74; Fischer's, 74; Great Blue, 75; Guinea, 74; Hartlaub's, 75; Knysna, 74; Livingstone's, 74; Purple-crested, 75; Red-crested, 74; Ross's, 75; Ruspoli's, 75; Ruwenzori, 75; Schalow's, 74; Violet, 75; White-cheeked, 75; White-crested, 75; Yellow-billed, 74

Turca, 177; Moustached, 177

Turkey, 11; Ocellated, 11; Wild, 11

Turnstone, 105; Black, 105; Ruddy, 105

Turtle-Dove, 88; Adamawa, 88; Dusky, 88; European, 88; Madagascar, 88; Oriental, 88

Twinspot, 297; Brown, 297; Dusky, 297; Dybowski's, 297; Green-backed, 297; Peters's, 297; Pink-throated, 297

Twite, 304

Tyrannulet, 142-143, 144-146; Alagoas, 146; Ashy-headed, 142; Bay-ringed, 146; Black-capped, 142; Black-fronted, 145; Bolivian, 143; Brown-capped, 143; Buff-banded, 144; Chapman's, 145; Ecuadorian, 145; Golden-faced, 143; Greenish, 142; Grey-and-white, 143; Grey-capped, 142; Guianan, 143; Minas Gerais, 145; Mistletoe, 143; Mottle-cheeked, 146; Mouse-colored, 143; Narrow-billed, 146; Olive-green, 146; Oustalet's, 145; Pale-tipped, 145; Paltry, 143; Peruvian, 143; Plain, 144; Planalto, 142; Plumbeous-crowned, 142; Red-billed, 143; Reiser's, 142; River, 144; Rough-legged, 142; Rufous-browed, 146; Rufous-lored, 145; Rufous-winged, 144; Sao Paulo, 145; Sclater's, 142; Serra do Mar, 145; Slender-billed, 144; Slender-footed, 143; Sooty, 144; Sooty-headed, 142; Sulphur-bellied, 144; Tawny-rumped, 142; Torrent, 144; Tumbes, 143; Urich's, 142; Venezuelan, 143; White-banded, 144; White-bellied, 144; White-crested, 144; White-fronted, 142; White-lored, 143; White-tailed, 144; White-throated, 144; Yellow, 143; Yellow-bellied, 143; Yellow-crowned, 143; Yellow-green, 146; Zeledon's, 142

Tyrant, 141, 149, 150, 151; Andean, 150; Black-chested, 141; Cattle, 151; Chocolate-vented, 150; Cinereous, 150; Cock-tailed, 151; Long-tailed, 151; Patagonian, 149; Riverside, 151; Rufous-tailed, 151; Shear-tailed Grey, 151; Spectacled, 151; Strange-tailed, 151; Streamer-tailed, 151; Tumbes, 149; Yellow-browed, 151

Tyrant-Manakin, 158; Cinnamon, 158; Dwarf, 158; Pale-bellied, 158; Saffron-crested, 158; Sulphur-bellied, 158; Tiny, 158; Wied's, 158

Ula-ai-hawane, 307

Umbrellabird, 156; Amazonian, 156; Bare-necked, 156; Long-wattled, 156

Vanga, 216-217; Bernier's, 217; Blue, 217; Chabert's, 217; Helmet, 217; Hook-billed, 217; Lafresnaye's, 217; Nuthatch, 217; Pollen's, 217; Red-tailed, 216; Rufous, 217; Sickle-billed, 217; Tylas, 217; Van Dam's, 217; White-headed, 217

Veery, 221

Velvetbreast, 70; Mountain, 70
Verdin, 242
Violet-ear, 65; Brown, 65; Green, 65; Mountain, 65; Sparkling, 65; White-vented, 65
Vireo, 193-194; Bell's, 193; Black-capped, 193; Black-whiskered, 194; Blue Mountain, 193; Blue-headed, 193; Brown-capped, 194; Cassin's, 193; Chivi, 194; Cozumel, 193; Cuban, 193; Dwarf, 193; Flat-billed, 193; Golden, 193; Grey, 193; Hutton's, 193; Jamaican, 193; Mangrove, 193; Mayan, 193; Noronha, 194; Old Providence, 193; Philadelphia, 194; Plumbeous, 193; Puerto Rican, 193; Red-eyed, 194; St. Andrew, 193; Slaty, 193; Thick-billed, 193; Veracruz, 193; White-eyed, 193; Yellow-green, 194; Yellow-throated, 194; Yellow-winged, 193; Yucatan, 194
Visorbearer, 73; Hooded, 73; Hyacinth, 73
Vulture, 117, 133; Black, 133; Cinereous, 117; Egyptian, 117; Greater Yellow-headed, 133; Hooded, 117; Indian, 117; King, 133; Lappet-faced, 117; Lesser Yellow-headed, 133; Long-billed, 117; Palm-nut, 117; Red-headed, 117; Turkey, 133; White-backed, 117; White-headed, 117; White-rumped, 117

Wagtail, 289-290; African Pied, 290; Angola, 290; Ashy-headed, 290; Black-backed, 289; Black-headed, 290; Blue-headed, 290; British Pied, 289; Cape, 290; Citrine, 290; Forest, 289; Green-headed, 290; Grey, 290; Grey-headed, 290; Japanese, 289; Madagascar, 290; Masked, 289; Moroccan, 289; Mountain, 290; Wells's, 290; White, 289; White-browed, 289; White-chinned, 290; White-headed, 290; Yellow, 290; Yellow-headed, 290; Yellowish-crowned, 290
Wagtail-Tyrant, 145; Greater, 145; Lesser, 145
Waldrapp, 132
Wallcreeper, 239
Warbler, 187, 255, 256, 257, 261, 262, 263, 264, 265, 266, 267, 268, 278-279, 302, 313-314, 315, 316-317; Adelaide's, 314; Aquatic, 263; Arctic, 267; Arrowhead, 314; Ashy-throated, 267; Audubon's, 314; Bachman's, 313; Banded, 278; Barred, 278; Bay-breasted, 314; Bay-crowned, 316; Black-and-white, 314; Black-capped Rufous, 262; Black-cheeked, 317; Black-crested, 316; Black-eared, 315; Black-faced Rufous, 262; Black-faced, 268; Black-fronted, 316; Black-throated Blue, 314; Black-throated Green, 314; Black-throated Grey, 314; Blackburnian, 314; Blackpoll, 314; Blue-winged, 313; Blunt-winged, 263; Bonelli's, 267; Booted, 264; Briar, 256; Bright-green, 267; Broad-billed, 268; Brown, 278; Buff-barred, 267; Buff-bellied, 265; Buff-browed, 267; Buff-rumped, 317; Buff-throated, 267; Cabanis's, 316; Canada, 315; Cape May, 314; Cerulean, 314; Cetti's, 262; Chestnut-capped, 316; Chestnut-crowned, 268; Chestnut-sided, 313; Citrine, 316; Colima, 313; Connecticut, 315; Crescent-chested, 313; Cyprus, 279; Dartford, 279; Desert, 278; Dusky, 267; Elfin-woods, 314; Eurasian River, 263; Evergreen Forest, 262; Fairy, 265; Fan-tailed, 316; Flame-throated, 313; Flavescent, 317; Garden, 278; Golden, 313; Golden-bellied, 316; Golden-browed, 317; Golden-cheeked, 314; Golden-crowned, 316; Golden-spectacled, 268; Golden-winged, 313; Grace's, 314; Grauer's, 265; Green-tailed Ground, 315; Greenish, 267; Grey-and-gold, 316; Grey-capped, 257; Grey-cheeked, 268; Grey-headed, 316; Grey-hooded, 268; Grey-throated, 316; Hermit, 316; Hooded, 315; Icterine, 264; Inornate, 267; Kentucky, 315; Kirtland's, 314; Kopje, 257; Lanceolated, 263; Layard's, 278; Lemon-rumped, 267; Lucy's, 313; MacGillivray's, 315; Magnolia, 314; Mangrove, 313; Marmora's, 279; Marsh, 263; Melnertzhagen's, 279; Melodious, 264; Menetries's, 279; Mourning, 315; Moustached, 263; Mrs. Moreau's, 262; Myrtle, 314; Namaqua, 256; Nashville, 313; Neotropical River, 317; Neumann's, 266; Olivaceous, 264; Olive, 302; Olive-capped, 314; Olive-tree, 264; Orange-crowned, 313; Oriente, 315; Oriole, 257; Orphean, 278; Paddyfield, 263; Pale-legged, 316; Pale-rumped, 267; Palm, 314; Pine, 314; Pink-headed, 315; Pirre, 317; Plumbeous, 314; Prairie, 314; Prothonotary, 314; Radde's, 267; Rand's, 265; Red Sea, 278; Red, 315; Red-faced, 315; Red-winged Grey, 256; Red-winged, 256; Richardson's, 316; Roraima, 316; Rueppell's, 279; Rufous-capped, 316; Rufous-eared, 256; Rufous-faced, 268; Rufous-vented, 278; Russet-crowned, 316; Salvin's, 316; Santa Marta, 316; Sardinian, 279; Savi's, 263; Sedge, 263; Semper's, 315; Shade, 261; Sikang, 267; Smoky, 267; Speckled, 187; Spectacled, 279; Stripe-crowned, 316; Subalpine, 279; Sulphur-bellied, 267; Sulphur-breasted, 267; Sunda, 268; Swainson's, 314; Sykes's, 264; Tennessee, 313; Thamnornis, 263; Thick-billed, 264; Three-banded, 316; Three-striped, 317; Townsend's, 314; Tristram's, 279; Two-banded, 316; Two-barred, 267; Upcher's, 264; Virginia's, 313; Vitelline, 314; Whistling, 314; White-bellied, 316;

White-browed Chinese, 255; White-browed, 317; White-lored, 316; White-spectacled, 268; White-striped, 317; White-tailed, 265; White-winged, 317; Willow, 266; Wilson's, 315; Wood, 267; Worm-eating, 314; Yellow, 313; Yellow-bellied, 268; Yellow-breasted, 268; Yellow-browed, 267; Yellow-headed, 315; Yellow-rumped, 314; Yellow-streaked, 267; Yellow-throated, 314; Yellow-vented, 267; Yemen, 278

Warbling-Finch, 327-328; Bay-chested, 327; Black-and-chestnut, 327; Black-and-rufous, 327; Black-capped, 328; Bolivian, 327; Buff-throated, 327; Cinereous, 328; Cinnamon, 327; Collared, 327; Grey-throated, 327; Plain-tailed, 327; Red-rumped, 327; Ringed, 328; Rufous-breasted, 327; Rufous-sided, 327; Rusty-browed, 327

Warbling-Vireo, 194; Eastern, 194; Western, 194

Water-Redstart, 231; Luzon, 231; Plumbeous, 231; White-capped, 231

Water-Tyrant, 149, 151; Black-backed, 151; Drab, 149; Masked, 151; Pied, 151

Watercock, 102

Waterhen, 101; Isabelline, 101; Rufous-tailed, 101; White-breasted, 101

Waterthrush, 314-315; Louisiana, 315; Northern, 314

Wattlebird, 186; Brush, 186; Little, 186; Red, 186; Yellow, 186

Wattle-eye, 216; Banded, 216; Black-necked, 216; Black-throated, 216; Brown-throated, 216; Chestnut, 216; Jameson's, 216; Kungwe, 216; Red-cheeked, 216; White-fronted, 216; White-spotted, 216; Yellow-bellied, 216

Waxbill, 298; Abyssinian, 298; Anambra, 298; Arabian, 298; Black-cheeked, 298; Black-crowned, 298; Black-faced, 298; Black-headed, 298; Black-rumped, 298; Black-tailed, 298; Bocage's, 298; Cinderella, 298; Common, 298; Crimson-rumped, 298; Fawn-breasted, 298; Kandt's, 298; Lavender, 298; Orange-cheeked, 298; Red-rumped, 298; Swee, 298; Yellow-bellied, 298; Zebra, 298

Waxwing, 218; Bohemian, 218; Cedar, 218; Japanese, 218

Weaver, 292-293, 294-295, 296; Asian Golden, 294; Baglafecht, 293; Bannerman's, 293; Bar-winged, 295; Bates's, 293; Baya, 294; Bertrand's, 293; Black-backed, 294; Black-billed, 293; Black-breasted, 294; Black-chinned, 293; Black-headed, 294; Black-necked, 293; Bob-tailed, 295; Bocage's, 293; Brown-capped, 295; Cape, 293; Chestnut, 294; Chestnut-and-black, 294; Cinnamon, 294; Clarke's, 294; Compact, 295; Dark-

backed, 294; Emin's, 293; Forest, 294; Fox's, 294; Giant, 294; Golden-backed, 294; Golden-naped, 294; Golden Palm, 293; Grey-backed, 294; Grosbeak, 296; Kilombero, 293; Layard's, 294; Lesser Masked, 293; Little, 293; Loango, 293; Maxwell's Black, 294; Mottled, 294; Nelicourvi, 294; Northern Brown-throated, 293; Olive-headed, 295; Orange, 293; Parasitic, 296; Preuss's, 295; Principe Golden, 293; Red-headed, 295; Red-winged, 295; Reichenow's, 293; Rueppell's, 293; Rufous-tailed, 292; Sakalava, 294; Salvadori's, 294; Sao Tome, 295; Scaly, 292; Slender-billed, 293; Sociable, 292; Southern Brown-throated, 293; Speckle-fronted, 292; Spectacled, 293; Speke's, 294; Spot-backed, 294; Spot-headed, 294; Strange, 293; Streaked, 294; Stuhlmann's, 293; Swainson's, 293; Taveta Golden, 293; Usambara, 295; Vieillot's Black, 294; Village, 294; West African, 293; Weyns's, 294; Yellow, 294; Yellow-capped, 295; Yellow-collared, 294; Yellow-mantled, 294

Wedgebill, 195; Chiming, 195; Chirruping, 195

Weebill, 187; Brown, 187; Yellow, 187

Weka, 99

Wheatear, 232-233; Afghan, 233; Arabian, 232; Black, 232; Black-eared, 232; Black-throated, 232; Botta's, 233; Capped, 233; Cyprus, 232; Desert, 233; Finsch's, 232; Heuglin's, 233; Hooded, 232; Hume's, 232; Isabelline, 233; Mountain, 232; Mourning, 232; Northern, 232; Pied, 232; Red-rumped, 232; Rufous-tailed, 233; Schalow's, 232; Somali, 232; Variable, 232; White-tailed, 232

Whimbrel, 105

Whinchat, 232

Whipbird, 195; Eastern, 195; Northern, 195; Papuan, 195; Western, 195

Whip-poor-will, 84; Eastern, 84; Stephens's, 84

Whistler, 196-197; Balim, 196; Bare-throated, 197; Black-headed, 197; Black-tailed, 197; Bornean, 196; Brown, 196; Brown-backed, 196; Drab, 197; Fawn-breasted, 196; Gilbert's, 196; Golden, 196; Golden-backed, 197; Green-backed, 196; Grey-headed, 196; Hooded, 197; Island, 196; Lorentz's, 197; Mangrove, 196; Maroon-backed, 196; Mottled, 196; New Caledonian, 197; Norfolk Island, 196; Olive, 196; Olive-flanked, 196; Palawan, 196; Red-lored, 196; Regent, 197; Robust, 197; Rufous, 197; Rufous-naped, 196; Rusty, 196; Samoan, 197; Sclater's, 197; Sulphur-bellied, 196; Tongan, 197; Vogelkop, 196; Wallacean, 197; White-bellied, 197; White-breasted, 197; White-vented, 196; Yellow-bellied, 196

Whistling-Duck, 13; Black-bellied, 13; Fulvous, 13; Lesser, 13; Plumed, 13; Spotted, 13; Wandering, 13; West Indian, 13; White-faced, 13

Whistling-Thrush, 218-219; Blue, 219; Brown-winged, 219; Ceylon, 218; Formosan, 219; Large, 219; Malabar, 219; Malayan, 219; Shiny, 219; Sunda, 219

White-eye, 258-261; Abyssinian, 258; African Yellow, 258; Alor, 259; Ambon Yellow, 259; Annobon, 258; Arfak Black-fronted, 259; Ashy-bellied, 259; Australian Yellow, 259; Banded, 260; Bare-eyed, 261; Biak, 259; Bicolored, 260; Black-capped, 259; Black-crowned, 259; Black-fronted, 259; Black-headed, 259; Black-masked, 261; Bridled, 259; Broad-ringed, 258; Buru Yellow, 259; Cape, 258; Capped, 259; Caroline Islands, 259; Ceylon, 258; Chestnut-flanked, 258; Chestnut-sided, 258; Christmas Island, 259; Comoro, 258; Creamy-throated, 259; Crested, 261; Crookshank's, 259; Dusky, 260; Enggano, 258; Everett's, 259; Ganongga, 260; Giant, 261; Golden, 260; Golden-bellied, 259; Golden-green, 259; Green, 258; Green-backed, 260; Grey-brown, 260; Grey-hooded, 261; Grey-throated, 260; Hermit, 260; Heuglin's, 258; Japanese, 258; Javan Grey-throated, 260; Javan, 259; Kenya, 258; Kikuyu, 258; Kirk's, 258; Kosrae, 260; Large Lifou, 260; Layard's, 260; Lemon-bellied, 259; Lemon-throated, 259; Long-billed, 260; Lord Howe Island, 260; Louisiade, 260; Lowland, 258; Madagascar, 258; Malagasy, 258; Malaita, 260; Mascarene Grey, 258; Mauritius Olive, 258; Mayotte, 258; Mountain, 259; New Guinea, 259; Oriental, 258; Pale, 258; Pale-bellied, 259; Papuan Black-fronted, 259; Pearl-bellied, 259; Pemba, 258; Plain, 259; Principe, 258; Pygmy, 261; Rennell, 260; Reunion Olive, 258; Robust, 260; Rota, 259; Rufous-throated, 260; Saipan, 259; Samoan, 260; Sanford's, 261; Santa Cruz, 260; Seychelles Grey, 258; Seychelles Yellow, 258; Slender-billed, 260; Small Black-fronted, 259; Small Lifou, 260; Solomon Islands, 260; Splendid, 260; Spot-breasted, 261; Streaky-headed, 261; Teita, 258; Thick-billed, 261; Truk, 260; White-bellied, 259; White-breasted, 258; White-chested, 260; White-throated, 259; Yap Olive, 260; Yellow-browed, 261; Yellow-fronted, 260; Yellow-spectacled, 259; Yellow-throated, 260

Whiteface, 189; Banded, 189; Chestnut-breasted, 189; Southern, 189

Whitehead, 196

White-Tern, 114; Atlantic, 114; Common, 114; Little, 114

Whitethroat, 278; Greater, 278; Lesser, 278; Small, 278; Hume's, 278

Whitetip, 72; Purple-bibbed, 72; Rufous-vented, 72

Whydah, 301; Pin-tailed, 301; Queen, 301; Steel-blue, 301; Straw-tailed, 301

Widowbird, 296; Black, 296; Buff-shouldered, 296; Cinnamon-shouldered, 296; Fan-tailed, 296; Jackson's, 296; Long-tailed, 296; Marsh, 296; Red-collared, 296; Red-naped, 296; White-shouldered, 296; White-winged, 296; Yellow-mantled, 296; Yellow-shouldered, 296

Wigeon, 16; American, 16; Chiloe, 16; Eurasian, 16

Willet, 105

Willie-wagtail, 208

Wiretail, 166; Des Murs's, 166

Wire-tailed Swallow, 247; African, 247; Asian, 247

Woodcock, 104; Amami, 104; American, 104; Eurasian, 104; Moluccan, 104; Rufous, 104; Sulawesi, 104

Woodcreeper, 172-174; Bar-bellied, 173; Barred, 173; Berlepsch's, 174; Black-banded, 173; Black-striped, 174; Blue-eyed, 172; Buff-throated, 174; Chestnut-rumped, 174; Cinnamon-throated, 173; Cocoa, 174; Cross-barred, 173; D'Orbigny's, 172; Dusky-billed, 174; Ecuadorian, 173; Elegant, 174; Great Rufous, 173; Hellmayr's, 173; Hoffmanns's, 173; Ihering's, 173; Ivory-billed, 174; Lesser, 174; Line-throated, 172; Lineated, 174; Long-billed, 173; Long-tailed, 173; Montane, 174; Moustached, 173; Narrow-billed, 174; Ocellated, 173; Olivaceous, 173; Olive-backed, 174; Ornate, 174; Pale-billed, 173; Plain-brown, 172; Planalto, 173; Red-billed, 173; Ruddy, 172; Rusty-breasted, 173; Scaled, 174; Scimitar-billed, 173; Snethlage's, 173; Spix's, 173; Spot-crowned, 174; Spot-throated, 173; Spotted, 174; Straight-billed, 173; Streak-headed, 174; Streak-throated, 173; Striped, 173; Strong-billed, 173; Tawny-winged, 172; Thrush-like, 172; Tyrannine, 172; Uniform, 173; Vila Nova, 173; Wedge-billed, 173; White-chinned, 172; White-striped, 174; White-throated, 173; Zimmer's, 173

Wood-Dove, 89; Black-billed, 89; Blue-headed, 89; Blue-spotted, 89; Emerald-spotted, 89

Woodhaunter, 171; Striped, 171

Woodhoopoe, 35-36; Black-billed, 36; Forest, 36; Grant's, 36; Green, 35; Violet, 36; White-headed, 36

Wood-Owl, 79; African, 79; Brown, 79; Mottled, 79; Sichuan, 79; Spotted, 79

Wood-Partridge, 12; Buffy-crowned, 12; Bearded, 12; Long-tailed, 12

Wood-Pewee, 148; Eastern, 148; Western, 148

Wood-Pigeon, 86, 87; Andaman, 87; Ashy, 87; Bonin, 87; Ceylon, 87; Common, 86; Japanese, 87; Nilgiri, 87; Silvery, 87; Speckled, 86

Wood-Quail, 12; Black-breasted, 12; Black-eared, 12; Black-fronted, 12; Chestnut, 12; Dark-backed, 12; Gorgeted, 12; Marbled, 12; Rufous-breasted, 12; Rufous-fronted, 12; Spotted, 12; Spot-winged, 12; Starred, 12; Stripe-faced, 12; Tacarcuna, 12; Venezuelan, 12; Ani, 48; Greater, 48; Grooved-billed, 48; Smooth-billed, 48

Wood-Rail, 100-101; Brown, 100; Giant, 100; Grey-necked, 100; Little, 100; Red-winged, 101; Rufous-necked, 100; Slaty-breasted, 100

Wood-Wren, 242; Bar-winged, 242; Grey-breasted, 242; White-breasted, 242

Woodland-Warbler, 266; Redfaced, 266; Laura's, 266; Yellow-throated, 266; Black-capped, 266; Uganda, 266; Brown, 266; Babax, 275; Chinese, 275; Giant, 275; Tibetan, 275

Woodnymph, 67; Blue-crowned, 67; Colombian, 67; Emerald-bellied, 67; Fork-tailed, 67; Green-crowned, 67; Long-tailed, 67; Mexican, 67; Violet-capped, 67

Woodpecker, 21-26, 27; Abyssinian, 22; Acorn, 21; Andaman, 26; Arabian, 23; Arizona, 24; Ashy, 27; Bamboo, 27; Banded, 26; Bar-bellied, 24; Bay, 27; Bearded, 23; Beautiful, 21; Bennett's, 22; Black, 26; Black-and-buff, 27; Black-backed, 24; Black-bodied, 25; Black-cheeked, 21; Black-headed, 26; Black-necked, 25; Blond-crested, 25; Blood-colored, 24; Bronze-winged, 25; Brown-backed, 23; Brown-capped, 23; Brown-eared, 22; Brown-fronted, 23; Buff-necked, 27; Buff-rumped, 27; Buff-spotted, 22; Cardinal, 22; Cayman, 22; Checker-throated, 26; Checkered, 24; Chestnut, 25; Chestnut-colored, 25; Chestnut-crested, 25; Choco, 24; Cinnamon, 25; Cream-backed, 26; Cream-colored, 25; Crimson-bellied, 26; Crimson-breasted, 23; Crimson-crested, 26; Crimson-mantled, 25; Crimson-winged, 26; Cuban Green, 22; Cuban Ivory-billed, 26; Darjeeling, 23; Dot-fronted, 24; Downy, 24; Elliot's, 23; Eurasian Green, 26; Fine-banded, 22; Fine-spotted, 22; Fire-bellied, 23; Fulvous-breasted, 23; Gabon, 23; Gila, 22; Golden-breasted, 25; Golden-cheeked, 22; Golden-collared, 24; Golden-crowned, 23; Golden-fronted, 22; Golden-green, 24;

Golden-naped, 21; Golden-olive, 25; Golden-tailed, 22; Great Slaty, 27; Great Spotted, 23; Green-backed, 22; Green-barred, 25; Grey, 23; Grey-and-buff, 27; Grey-breasted, 22; Grey-capped, 23; Grey-crowned, 24; Grey-faced, 26; Grey-headed, 23; Ground, 22; Guadeloupe, 21; Guayaquil, 26; Hairy, 24; Heart-spotted, 27; Helmeted, 25; Himalayan, 24; Hispaniolan, 21; Hoffmann's, 22; Iberian, 26; Imperial, 26; Ivory-billed, 26; Jamaican, 21; Japanese, 26; Johnston's, 23; Knysna, 22; Laced, 26; Ladder-backed, 24; Lesser Spotted, 23; Levaillant's, 26; Lewis's, 21; Lilford's, 23; Lineated, 25; Lita, 24; Little, 24; Little Green, 22; Little Grey, 22; Little Spotted, 22; Magellanic, 26; Maroon, 27; Melancholy, 23; Middle Spotted, 23; Mombasa, 22; Northern Ivory-billed, 26; Nubian, 22; Nuttall's, 24; Okinawa, 27; Olive, 23; Olive-backed, 26; Orange-backed, 27; Pale-billed, 26; Pale-crested, 25; Pale-headed, 27; Philippine, 23; Pileated, 25; Powerful, 26; Puerto Rican, 21; Pygmy, 23; Ramsay's, 23; Red-bellied, 22; Red-cockaded, 24; Red-collared, 26; Red-crowned, 22; Red-headed, 21; Red-necked, 26; Red-rumped, 24; Red-stained, 24; Reichenow's, 22; Ringed, 25; Robust, 26; Rufous, 25; Rufous-bellied, 23; Rufous-headed, 25; Rufous-winged, 24; Russet-crested, 25; Scaly-bellied, 26; Scaly-breasted, 25; Scarlet-backed, 24; Sind, 24; Smoky-brown, 24; Sooty, 27; Speckle-breasted, 22; Splendid, 26; Spot-breasted, 25; Stierling's, 23; Streak-breasted, 26; Streak-throated, 26; Strickland's, 24; Stripe-breasted, 23; Stripe-cheeked, 24; Striped, 24; Sulawesi, 23; Sunda, 23; Syrian, 23; Three-toed, 24; Tullberg's, 22; Tweeddale's, 27; Waved, 25; West Indian, 22; White, 21; White-backed, 23; White-bellied, 26; White-fronted, 21; White-headed, 24; White-naped, 27; White-spotted, 24; White-throated, 24; White-winged, 23; Yellow-browed, 24; Yellow-crowned, 23; Yellow-eared, 24; Yellow-fronted, 21; Yellow-throated, 24; Yellow-tufted, 21; Yellow-vented, 24; Yucatan, 22

Woodshrike, 216; Common, 216; Large, 216

Woodstar, 73, 74; Amethyst, 73; Bahama, 73; Chilean, 74; Esmeraldas, 74; Gorgeted, 74; Little, 74; Magenta-throated, 73; Purple-collared, 74; Purple-throated, 73; Rufous-shafted, 74; Santa Marta, 74; Short-tailed, 74; Slender-tailed, 73; White-bellied, 74

Woodswallow, 204; Ashy, 204; Bismarck, 204; Black-faced, 204; Dusky, 204; Fiji, 204;

Great, 204; Ivory-backed, 204; Little, 204; Masked, 204; White-breasted, 204; White-browed, 204; White-vented, 204

Wren, 138, 239-242; Apolinar's, 240; Band-backed, 240; Banded, 241; Bay, 241; Bewick's, 240; Bicolored, 240; Black-bellied, 240; Black-capped, 241; Black-crowned, 240; Black-throated, 240; Boucard's, 239; Brown-throated, 241; Buff-breasted, 241; Bush, 138; Cactus, 239; Canebrake, 241; Canyon, 240; Carolina, 241; Chestnut-breasted, 242; Clarion, 242; Coraya, 241; Cozumel, 241; Dusky-tailed, 241; Fasciated, 240; Fawn-breasted, 241; Flutist, 242; Giant, 239; Grass, 240; Grey, 241; Grey-barred, 240; Grey-mantled, 240; Happy, 241; House, 241; Inca, 241; Long-billed, 241; Marsh, 240; Merida, 240; Mountain, 242; Moustached, 241; Musician, 242; Nava's, 240; Niceforo's, 241; Northern, 241; Ochraceous, 242; Organ, 242; Plain, 241; Plain-breasted, 240; Plain-tailed, 240; Riverside, 241; Rock, 240; Rufous, 240; Rufous-and-white, 241; Rufous-backed, 240; Rufous-breasted, 241; Rufous-browed, 242; Rufous-naped, 240; Santa Marta, 242; Sclater's, 240; Sedge, 240; Sepia-brown, 240; Sinaloa, 241; Slender-billed, 240; Socorro, 240; Song, 242; Sooty-headed, 240; South Island, 138; Speckle-breasted, 241; Spot-breasted, 241; Spot-chested, 240; Spotted, 239; Stephens Island, 138; Stripe-backed, 240; Stripe-breasted, 241; Stripe-throated, 241; Sumichrast's, 240; Superciliated, 241; Tepui, 242; Thrush-like, 240; Timberline, 242; Tooth-billed, 240; Whiskered, 241; Whistling, 242; White-bellied, 242; White-browed, 241; White-headed, 240; Wing-banded, 242; Winter, 241; Yucatan, 239; Zapata, 240

Wren-Babbler, 272-273; Bar-winged, 273; Black-throated, 272; Bornean, 272; Eyebrowed, 273; Falcated, 272; Large, 272; Limestone, 273; Long-billed, 272; Long-tailed, 273; Marbled, 272; Mountain, 273; Nepal, 273; Pygmy, 273; Rabor's, 273; Rufous-throated, 273; Rusty-breasted, 272; Rusty-throated, 273; Scaly-breasted, 273; Sorsogon, 273; Spotted, 273; Streaked, 273; Striated, 272; Striped, 272; Sumatran, 272; Tawny-breasted, 273; Wedge-billed, 273; White-throated, 272

Wren-Spinetail, 170; Bay-capped, 170

Wrenthrush, 317

Wrentit, 278

Wren-Warbler, 257; Barred, 257; Grey, 257; Stierling's, 257; Western, 257; Zambia, 257

Wrybill, 109

Wryneck, 20; Eurasian, 20; Rufous-necked, 20

Xenops, 172; Great, 172; Plain, 172; Rufous-tailed, 172; Slender-billed, 172; Streaked, 172

Xenopsaris, 154; White-naped, 154

Yellowbill, 45

Yellow-Finch, 328; Bright-rumped, 328; Citron-headed, 328; Grassland, 328; Greater, 328; Greenish, 328; Misto, 328; Montane, 328; Northern, 328; Orange-fronted, 328; Patagonian, 328; Puna, 328; Raimondi's, 328; Siberian, 290; Stripe-tailed, 328

Yellowhammer, 307

Yellowhead, 196

Yellowlegs, 105; Greater, 105; Lesser, 105

Yellownape, 26; Lesser, 26; Greater, 26

Yellow-Robin, 190; Eastern, 190; Northern, 190

Yellowthroat, 315; Altamira, 315; Bahama, 315; Belding's, 315; Black-lored, 315; Black-polled, 315; Chapala, 315; Chiriqui, 315; Common, 315; Grey-crowned, 315; Hooded, 315; Masked, 315; Olive-crowned, 315

Yellow-Wagtail, 290; Alaska, 290; Siberian, 290

Yuhina, 277; Black-chinned, 277; Burmese, 277; Chestnut-crested, 277; Collared, 277; Formosan, 277; Rufous-vented, 277; Striated, 277; Stripe-throated, 277; Whiskered, 277; White-bellied, 277; White-browed, 277; White-collared, 277; White-naped, 277